BABYLON
WITH GHOST

Children, Computers, Career in the Eighties

WAYNE SLINGLUFF

outskirts
press

TABLE OF CONTENTS

PREFACE

FOREWORD

MEMOIR WRITING IS egotism distilled. Brave attempts to embellish minor variations on lifetime themes everyone has already experienced first-hand. Pathetic extensions by bored crones conjuring mists from once-upon-a-time-when-I-was-important. Irrelevance doubly true where tales are of normal people in normal times. Imagined comforts of documenting family heritage spurs effort, but in harsh truth, my descendants ought to be too busy with their own adventures and problems to read such tedious pretentiousness.

Selfish acts at least furnish individual joy. If fortunate enough to age into seventies, our memories dim. I have increasing difficulty recalling details of family life forty-odd years ago. Fears of fading entirely are slightly assuaged by temporarily stabilizing distant scattered threads onto ink and paper. I accept myself as solitary audience. That is not an excuse to skimp effort. As both author and reader, I refuse to bore myself.

By, for, about me, no exaggeration required, hardly cause to invent. Some slight literary embellishment, a few mistaken dates. Perhaps too much philosophic interpretation layered from this "wiser" old self. While I have time, energy, desire, and mind—why not?

I do believe I owe a warning or apology to the reader. Some themes repeat too much, stated in slightly different ways, in slightly different situations. I can only say in defense that in fact identical themes were recurring for us during those years, so I might defend it as a kind of truthful interweaving. Also, I have not a kept a thesaurus handy, so common words are overused. Plain tales, plainly told. A good writer (which I am not) would have written in a more interesting manner. A good editor (which I am not) would have forced the author to make revisions. I am happy with the result, even recognizing its sizable flaws.

INTRODUCTION

USUALLY RIGHT AFTER winter holidays, our local library assumes seasonal affective disorder has set in among its retiree patrons. Libraries treasure such seniors, for—if properly coddled—they consistently support annual budgets. To ward off suspected depression, slightly competitive classes are initiated encouraging people to write memoirs—"preserving history"—usually directed at grandchildren, since any sane person knows their own children rarely care about common pasts until it is too late. It keeps us off the streets and quiet at almost no cost.

I've never taken advantage of those offers, being a hermit by nature and preference. Consequently, I've missed whatever tips might have developed sparkling style. Just three ways to approach this task. Notable people like General Grant or Benjamin Franklin relate famous narratives with insight. Professional writers like Twain or Proust invent exaggerations or smother tales with style as delicate fish is enveloped in sauce. Memoirs from most of us common clay are candied tales of olden days, prettily arranged, leavened with self-conscious humor, soggy with gratuitous commentary .

I ain't Homer. No simultaneous actions in different places nor diverting flashbacks. But even a dense guy like me knows "we did this, then we did that, then we did the next thing…" is deadly. I won't attempt poetry. One decade in a book is long enough. Even so, to maintain my own interest there are differing voices—"Wayne and Joan," "Me", "Ghost. "

I guess I should explain Ghost.

Sanity maintains that Ghost is a literary convention to express doubts and multiple viewpoints. I've always had multiple threads of thought chattering away inside. One of them can hijack my consciousness temporarily. Why not present that as a garishly gowned and strident Greek chorus? Or chorus personification?

I could embroider a tad and claim that these voices have become louder and more persistent over time, possibly from increased medications. Maybe Ghost is more real to me than I dare reveal. So far, at least, I don't make people save space for him at the dinner table.

Ghost himself says you can blame Walt Disney. Subjecting an impressionable young boy to a film that showed conscience as a talking cricket with an umbrella. What do you expect from mental abuse like that? Anyway, he says, a ghost is more appropriate for mental personification than some insect or moldy ancient actors. Ghost tends to melodramatic extravagance, complete with setting, costume, props. Oddly, he remains always the same and always completely different. Just like you and me.

1978—NERVOUS CALM

INDEPENDENCE

ANOTHER CAREFULLY AIMED shot disintegrated a chunk of amorphous life form. Wayne sprawled on the living room floor, oblivious to his dirty jeans caked with rainbow acrylic paint smears, his stained blue tee shirt. Stifling heat engulfed this apartment in spite of open windows futilely inviting breezes of city fumes and noise. He silently cursed as the "creature" on the tiny black and white screen began to divide again and froze everything. There just <u>had</u> to be some way to speed up that routine ....

A loud klaxon broke the spell—no, he realized as he came out of his trance, it was their phone. Strange, hardly anyone called unexpectedly. He forced his numbed limbs into the first movement in an hour or so—jeez it was that late already? Ringing continued from behind the large fish tank, although the zebras and swords apparently heard nothing. He finally lifted the heavy receiver off its immense rotary dial base.

A voice, who? "Oh, hi Cheryl," as recognition dawned. "What? Wait a minute ...." From the back kitchen window, deafening thunder as another Red Line subway blasted out of its tunnel, temporarily overwhelming nearly continuous ambulance wails from Mass General Hospital. "No, she's not here right now .... Shopping down on Charles Street, I think. Maybe an hour? I can have her call back?" He didn't much like talking on phones in any case, and this was nearly a stranger. Somewhere up here—ah empty back of envelope from cluttered mail pile—"Can I take a message?"

Cheryl was Joan's best friend. From way-back childhood Long Island, where she remained. Five years after geographic separation, they gossiped like next-door neighbors, sometimes hours at a time. Wayne usually tried to finish any such conversation after a few minutes, not that he kept in touch with anyone. A flaw in his character drove anyone not seen in person for a while out of mind, out of memory.

"What's that? Oh, yeah, the Fourth of July," make a note. "Sure, it's wonderful up here. Yeah, we do plan to watch the fireworks on the esplanade and hear the concert—you're coming up? No, don't bother with details, Joan can work it out with you later. Yep, I'll tell her as soon as she gets back. Right, she'll be calling you. Look forward to it …"

Looking around with imagined wifely eyes, he glumly realized there would be a solid week of chores. The rug was filled with dust which also coated every other surface. Windows were streaked. Fish tanks greenish and cloudy. Piles of clutter, magazines, books, papers, oh my. And that was just what he could see from this counter separating the living room from the kitchen area. He groaned, right, clean the fridge, scrub the sink, scour the stove, damn pots and pans and dishes to carefully rewash and dry by hand. A vision of bathroom tasks rivaling those by Hercules cleaning the Augean stables. And other rooms …

Well, probably time to save and turn off the bulky iron-encased computer with its massive nine inch TV perched on top. That would be the first thing that had to get tucked out of the way somewhere.

Two firm knocks. I'm halfway there, ready to flip the lock, when I realize where I am. Perfect recreation of that fifth floor railroad apartment walk-up on Phillips Street. So, I know who is there before I open the door to the stairwell.

Ghost grins vacantly and wanders in, bushy long hair obviously self-trimmed barely reaching shoulders stretching the thin material of a cheap dark blue pocket tee shirt. Old jeans worn colorlessly smooth at the knees, white socks drooped around ankles, old sneakers have eons-ago seen better days. Surprisingly, for once he sports wire rim glasses. Before this I hadn't realized how closely he always resembles me back in my early thirties.

"Hey there, Wayne, got something cold in the fridge?"

"Beer. As usual," I answer, in resignation. There's no escaping Ghost. "What brings you around this lovely summer morning? By the way," I add, "nice touches on the scenery. Exactly how I remember it?"

"Well, why not? Look at the raw material I have to use. Anyway, you had five years to burn it in, almost no changes in all that time, easy enough. You guys never were very adventurous on arrangements once you settled. Everything frozen in place for years and years."

"I suppose," I agree absently.

"Just like your lives, really," he continues. "That's what makes this year so fraught."

"Fraught?" I sputter. "Nobody ever talks like that, Ghost. Not even you."

"Fraught," he pops open the can of Schlitz and gulps. Grimaces. "Crap! You always had lousy taste. But anyway, your comfortable little lives are about to be shaken and shattered, you already feel the tremors."

"The cheap stuff works just as well. But to answer your implication, we hardly knew what was going to happen."

"You're post-editing already. Look here," he sweeps his arm, "romantic haze on everything, even the dirt and cockroaches."

"It was nice enough for us."

"Listen to yourself. The reason for this visit, as Dickens might warn, is that I'm going to try to keep you honest."

"I am honest."

"To a point, maybe. You think you always tell the truth?"

"Sure, mostly."

"But do you really know the truth?" he probes.

"This!" I hit the wall with my fist "Is truth. Solid reality." I remember where I am, a little confusion here, "in the real world anyway. You know what I mean."

"Standard argument, hurt your hand, pinch yourself, truth. Maybe in the moment. But can anyone remember truth."

Trick question. "Um, that's a bit more complicated."

"Right. You still haven't figured out your particular memory truths from college, or Vista, or California, have you?"

"I don't care anymore." I state firmly.

"But here you are, writing what you purport to be truth. Admit it, it's all just fantasy, something your decaying neurons try to pick out of vanishing RNA."

"Nothing is decaying all that much yet, you bastard," I yell.

"You wouldn't know anyway. It's apparent to me."

"Well, in any case, it's truly what I remember now. I don't care about cosmic aspects of the question."

"You should, you know." He flips the empty into the sink, and heads back to the hallway. I can't help thinking that I was pretty trim back then, all five and a half feet. He scampers down the winding flights, calling back "Sorry, gotta run, game starts in half an hour."

Once upon a time, two castaways met in Boston. Each had survived a personal shipwreck of hopes and dreams—minor disasters more apparent to them than to outside observers. After a few years working together as teachers at a day-care facility, almost by accident, they became friends, then lovers, then married. By the time this story begins, in spite of miniscule incomes, Wayne and Joan had carved out a comfortable urban life. Their rent-controlled Beacon Hill apartment was sunny, clean, and large, their work and lifestyle required no car. Downtown, parks, shopping were steps away.

They were becoming restless and bored.

This story will become less a fairy tale than description of pilgrimage. Poor and slightly confused wanderers set out to find true happiness and meaning, lurch through roadside adventures, and eventually arrive somewhere. Along the way—encounters, observations, tests, and meditations.

As this year dawned, Wayne had pushed himself into a new career. Joan was leaving years of professional security, seniority and good will. Her employer, Roberts Day School had always struggled on the brink of insolvency. She had loved teaching, but her rewards were little more than a pleasant smile and additional work. Five years of stability while they enjoyed dreams and hopes, but few financial rewards and only more of the same looming forever.

Their nest provided every comfort. Decorated, lovingly, mostly with furniture built from scratch or rescued from the street, and with accumulated treasures of a decade. "Railroad" layout ran from street to back courtyard with three bedrooms and a large open living area including kitchen.

Sunny front bedroom had become a den, furnished with desk, floor to ceiling wooden bookshelves, and lately a two by two foot computer resembling an enclosed typewriter. Living area displayed a few art books, was packed with flowers along the windows, a hard pew couch for visitors, a wicker rocker and beanbag chair for them. A shakily constructed wooden counter separated the kitchen area and provided a stand for the phone, and storage space. Old but serviceable kitchen with antique gas stove, back window on the courtyard ailanthus tree. Hook around the corner past the bathroom to their bedroom, dark, bed on simple metal frame, usually cluttered, with a large tank of breeding guppies as nightlight. Wayne had claimed the back bedroom as painting studio. It was filled with jars and tubes of pigment, stretchers, canvases, bright spotlights, shelves for brushes and paints and various media, none of which, fortunately, smelled. Years of output were rolled and lying against side walls.

Their tiny refuge opened on the world. Rationally, they knew they were living like royalty, well fed, entertained, happy, even hopeful and dreaming of better times.

And yet—well, somehow, all this was not really theirs, and always felt like a temporary stopover.

"You know, Wayne, this place is a mess." Joan surveyed her domain like some ancient queen. In her own mind, at least, she was royalty. As always her hair and appearance were just so, her clothes neatly arranged, her movements supple but stately. In fact, Wayne realized with a mild shock, about the only thing most people would see in common between the two of them was their heights.

"Well, yeah, but we have a week to get ready," he protested, already well aware of what was coming.

Joan had finished constructing her internal outline as she paced from room to room, scanning each with a holographic eagle eye, comparing what was with what should be. Like all her family, she held an exact idea of how the world should present itself. Mostly, the world was lacking.

Finally organized, she began listing necessary improvements aloud in no particular order. Most were possible, some were difficult, a few mere wishes. By now, Wayne had pen and paper in hand, beginning to translate her commands into shorthand notes. The telepathy of permanent couples helped him edit dismay and despair into definite chores.

"This kitchen is terrible. We have to scrub down all those stained pots. Oh, shit, look at these plates and glasses, why don't you just dry them like I tell you? We'll have to do a clothes wash. Can't you clean those books off the floor by the computer? We need to vacuum. We need to wash the kitchen floor. The windows are filthy. Did you see the bathroom? Your studio? Oh, no, just look at that fish tank…." Stream of consciousness visions of future presentability, what she assumed would be noticed and judged by every guest who arrived.

Wayne resignedly didn't argue, quietly continued his list, mentally translated each "we" to "you." When she finally ran down, he added. "Ok, Ok, most of this won't take all that long. I'll wash and vacuum this afternoon, start fish tanks tomorrow, dishes and pans tonight, and the rest is pretty quick. It's not as bad as you say," Joan just snorted, "You need to clean up some of your own clutter." There were various papers and school materials lying about from her endless evening school projects, "What will we need for food? What should do with her. When did she say she was coming, and for how long?"

"She wasn't quite sure. I think she gets here Saturday afternoon, and is leaving after the Fourth, probably Wednesday afternoon, maybe Thursday."

"That's a long time. Quite a few days to fill in."

"Not hard, she and I can talk anywhere to fill the time." Wayne could have said something snarky, but kept his peace. "Maybe one day at the market, the Aquarium. Copley and around the Public Gardens. I don't think there will be much trouble keeping her busy."

"What does she eat? Is she vegetarian or macrobiotic or anything weird?" Wayne had become used to all his peers heading off into various fanatic spiritual and digestive byways. He assumed Joan's were no different.

"I don't think so. She didn't say anything when I talked to her. But you know how she changes all the time. We are not," Joan added firmly, "going to serve any of your fried stuff. What a mess."

"But my sweet and sour pork is great…"

"No." There would be no argument there. Besides, it really was too hot to cook. "Salads, vegetables, maybe some cold cuts. Besides, we can just get some stuff from the stores. And sometimes she just brings her own."

"What's she going to do while we're working?"

"That's probably only Monday. I'll just take her in with me, then she can walk around Cambridge if she wants to. We'll figure it out. She's a grown woman, after all?"

"All right, so the first thing is to make sure we have the cleaning supplies we need." Wayne needed a short walk to clear his head, line up his activities, and not least firm his resolve.

It was going to be a busy and noisy few days ….

An author is the very definition of a god—omniscient, omnipotent, capricious. Yet surely you, the reader, are something more—for you can terminate that god and its universe by simply turning away. So introduction of authorial voice to reader is performed with some trepidation. Should it be sly, wise, humorous, nasty, cynical, detached? I've no clear idea—by the way, hello there—so it can be worked out as we go. For now, perhaps, philosophical will do.

We had hesitantly asked ourselves, how were we doing? Eternal human uncertainty, varied by tense—how will we do, how did we do? Compared to what? Compared to who? Regardless of our always equivocal reply, the follow-up what should we do next?

As our lives had settled, we floated in contentment. Day care kindergarten rewarded immediately with the joy of very young children developing and thriving . Our work was proudly socially useful, although perhaps we took too much credit for happy results. Joan believed she continued to advance her lifetime career. I needed temporary income until I could sell my paintings. After almost five years in this situation, we awakened uneasy.

We suddenly realized that parents were aging rapidly. Their previously subtle chorus about us moving closer and raising a family had taken on a degree of urgency. Joan heard biological clocks echoing ominously, and noticed friends on better career ladders. Passing thirty, I abandoned art dreams. Computers consumed all my hours. Ten years had been devoted to sacrifice to the gods of art—they had not responded. I learned rites at fresh altars of technology . As far as family or place—well, whatever Joan wanted was now fine with me. I had no particular roots in Boston.

Time to move on. In 1978 we leaped emotionally from everything we had built to something—we didn't really know what. We hardly realized exactly how turbulent the next decade would be.

Brutally cold wind cuts off as the subway roars into elevated Charles Street station. I just have time enough to slip two quarters into the turnstile and follow Ghost through the open doors. Heading for Cambridge, I notice. No room to sit—well, that's pretty normal.

As we pull out, Ghost slides over, clinging to the rail overhead. "Seems just like it was, doesn't it?"

"Yeah, just as I remember. Could be yesterday." I crouch down a bit to catch the open view up the river.

"Right." Ghost has his plan. "What color are the seats?"

"What?" I realize I don't know.

"Are there advertisements overhead?"

Embarrassing. What seemed a clear and perfect memory has been revealed as fog. "Fine, I can't remember perfectly. We knew this already."

Ghost hovers vaporously "And it calls everything else into question. For example, did this particular Fourth of July really happen?"

"Well, stuff like this occurred on the Fourth of July in Boston one year or another. Maybe I'm merging and fudging ..."

"And inventing ...."

"... things a little bit. I can't really tell...."

"See, You mean you're lying. Cheryl might or might not have come up that year, you certainly don't know what exact conversations you and Joan had and ...."

"Oh, stuff it, Ghost. It's a distilled episode of true events. We had conversations like that all the time. Cheryl did visit one Fourth. Things happened like this. Besides," I add smugly, "there's really no way to prove me wrong. What are you going to do, materialize and go around interviewing everybody?"

"You could at least do some research on the internet, pull out old books and photographs. "

"Not that kind of book."

"You're just too lazy."

"Well, that too, I suppose."

"I can't believe how easy it is for you writers to get away with pure fiction when you claim to be delivering truth," he mutters.

"In my writing, describing detailed edges matters less than basic feelings and outlines."

"Oh sure," he exits as we squeal to a stop at Kendal Square, "you can justify anything in the name of whatever you want."

Tuesday would be tough. Public school teacher Cheryl had summers off. Wayne and Joan fought to get a day. When they had announced they were to be married back in '75, Mrs. Dalrymple was thrilled and delighted. With obvious difficulty, but respecting their long trip to the Island for the weekend ceremony, she finally magnanimously allowed them to both be absent the following Monday while they returned on the train. Their honeymoon still resided in the future.

Neither even considered calling in sick after a holiday. In tiny enterprises, everyone knows your business, so no lie, however white, could hold for long. Anyway, truth was so congenitally part of their nature that it formed a foundation for their bond.

Weekends would be tough. Normal chores piled relentlessly and here came an unexpected load. Clean, plan, prepare. Minor but annoying details, like where Cheryl would park. Open parking spaces on Beacon Hill rare as unicorns—they were clueless since neither had owned a car for years. So locate a parking lot, check cost, and let Cheryl know how to find it when she arrived, an aggravating task before cell phones or internet.

Sanity began with lists. Lists of things to be cleaned, lists of things to be purchased, lists of things that could be done together, lists of what to have for meals. Fortunately, the holiday was near enough a weekend that vegetables and whatever else bought at the market Saturday would remain reasonably fresh and unspoiled—guests could be extraordinarily picky about food. Immediately—major cleaning—scraping fish tanks clear of accumulated green algae, change filters to clarify water. Books put away neatly, scattered papers tucked out of sight. All surfaces wiped, hoping to keep cockroaches more or less at bay, at least when lights were on. Finish one chore, cross it off, sigh as requirements were added.

By now they were used to this fire-drill. People knew they lived in the heart of Boston. Wayne and Joan were able to conduct interesting walking tours of almost everything worth seeing. Parents came up a few times a year. Brothers and sisters and long lost friends could pop in almost any time. No constant stream of visitors, but never far from hosting somebody.

Moderately affluent, quite happy, but guilty of not reaching "full potential." Tendrils of uncertainty had begun to creep into our self-justifications. Joan and I could have happily remained doing what we were doing forever. Forever? We had adequate food, clothing, and shelter, fun and entertainment. We immersed ourselves in pulsing city vitality as we pursued internal visions of social responsibility. Day to day was mostly wonderful.

But. Incomes were stagnant and pitiful. Options were vanishing, leaving late-night worries of where we might be ten years hence.

Finally surfacing from deeper inner drives, we realized that our true long-term goal was to raise a family. Knowing ourselves, we were not surprised that this just built into our personalities, but were staggered at how quickly and forcefully it emerged to overturn assumptions. At one stroke, it eliminated augmenting existential issues. A family would please parents. Now was critical—time was running late. Everything changed overnight, as a revised attitude completely upset our familiar world.

From that core decision, secondary massive shock waves. Neither thought we could raise a child on Beacon Hill. Not enough money. Not enough time. No support structure.

So we must move. Grandparents would be happier, and available to help. Joan was adamantly a stay-at-home girl, even after being away from "home" for years—we were Long Island bound. My own parents were surrounded by my siblings—one granddaughter already. Joan wasn't about to pioneer the howling wilderness of suburban Philadelphia.

Dominoes implacably fell into place, dragging us along. There would be pregnancy, new jobs, whole new careers, new geography, new lives. Turmoil gained momentum as we frantically yet stoically tried to enjoy our last days of relative freedom, looking forward with some fear to the certain great unknown.

Midday resting on a park bench at the Public Gardens near the ducklings statues, watching lazy swan boats as tourists snap pictures. Tired, but my early Saturday morning free time is drawing to a close, and I have to head back up Charles in a minute to help Joan with common chores. I suppose I'll be spending a chunk of this fine afternoon at the laundromat up the street.

Ghost materializes out of a bush, tourist to the core with camera around his neck and loud shirt. Uninvited, he plops down beside me. "Are you confirming any of these 'memories' with your wife, or just winging it and depending on your own fragile and fallible neurons?"

"Hey, Ghost, they're your neurons too!" I retort. "I check a few things with her, unobtrusively, but I'm the one doing the writing. I need a certain amount of poetic license."

"What, even in a supposedly non-fiction work."

"I think especially in a non-fiction work. The memories I have of a time and place may be more real and relevant to my life than any actual even magical recording would ever be. After all, nothing but me can capture or express my thoughts, moods, or experience."

"So your claimed non-fiction is fiction?"

"No, not that. I do think what I write is true, just a little edited."

"You don't even have any photos, do you?"

"Oh, I'm sure we have a few. We had a camera, after all, and took pictures with people when they came to visit. I was always taking slide shots of my paintings when I finished them, in the futile hope of submitting them to galleries."

"But no real artifacts."

"Drop it Ghost. I remember what I remember. You're not going to find anyone or anything to contradict me, and I'm going to claim that makes it fundamentally true."

Sultry heat lingered through late sunset. Salad and sandwich dinner with beer and wine complete, Joan, Cheryl and Wayne felt warmth radiating from red brick sidewalks on Philips and Charles Street. Surging throngs carrying coolers and dragging small children flowed into a molten stream at the base of the subway exit and footbridge over Storrow Drive to the Esplanade. Eventually, with a certain amount of pushing and shoving, but mostly just adrift in Brownian crowd movement, they found a space with decent views of the Hatch Shell. A fun prelude, a forgettable mixed set, were followed by what everyone had been waiting for—the inspired raucous performance of "Stars and Stripes Forever," then booming canon mixing with pealing nearby church bells closing the traditional 1812 Overture. Huge applause. Expectation building.

Ignoring thoughts of rats, they settled on rock embankments covered with underbrush along the river, conversing happily until fireworks burst overhead accompanied by cheers. Extensive show climaxed with a tremendous finale. Near quiet returned. Exhausted families began to trudge back to cars and trains, almost regretfully, contemplating another marker of another year gone. Joan, Cheryl and Wayne decided this evening was too lovely to return inside, so instead of going with the flow back towards their sweltering hot apartment, they strolled in the opposite direction into a cooling breeze, talking about nothing in general, absorbed in the nighttime views of lights across the river and illuminated skyscrapers off near Copley. Completely mellow and relaxed.

Suddenly, a young man—another lurking behind—emerged from shadows and interrupted their reverie with quiet menace. "Don't worry, we won't hurt you, just give us your wallets and don't say nothin'."

Sensibly, each knew enough not to provoke desperate people with stupid heroic acts. In fact, Wayne had almost no money on him. But he had been mugged in Cambridge a few years ago—losing his desperately needed payday cash, license, and other identification.

He got angry, as hours of beer surged into bravado. So he started to scream and yell. There were, after all, many people around and (somewhere) police. Clearly taken aback, the muggers stood their ground for a minute, as his aggravated shouts grew louder and others noticed the commotion. The confrontation basically won, should have been over. But filled with adrenaline, Wayne took a step forward. Instantly he faced a knife.

At that point, sanity took over on all sides. All hope of an unnoticed robbery was gone. Wayne was pulled back by Joan and Cheryl, clearly aghast at the turn of events. Folks were heading purposely towards the commotion. With mutters and final menacing echoes, the intruders ran into shadows up river, fading into darkness as rapidly as they had appeared. Wayne's stressed throat prevented him from speaking, Cheryl and Joan assured everyone that things were ok.

Stupid moments can happen to anyone anywhere, no matter how sane they consider themselves. Often anybody can wish they'd resisted some dangerous impulse, which only seemed irresistible. From then on, Wayne became more careful in reaction to stressful situations.

Cheryl remained forever convinced of his basic inner craziness. Joan, of course, already knew.

Science, pseudoscience, raw capitalism, and celebration of extremes constitute what meditative core there is to contemporary culture. Science works at fringes, "extending" research. Pseudoscience, such as sociology and economics, examines trends and breaking points. Capitalist myth provides a bloody Darwinian vision of struggle and survival. Extremes of poverty, pain, gain, or anger thrill jaded audiences. The statistical middle is ignored, folded into some great grey glop, unimportant. Most people exist there. I have lived there. You expect a dull story.

A normal life may not accomplish anything recognized as enduring cultural achievement. A normal life may not encounter immense obstacles. But—a normal life is normal. Perhaps people should avoid focus on freakish outliers. No matter what, I remain the center of my universe. Maybe that is why religion—focused on each individual relation to being—still retains power.

Joan and I gloried in considering ourselves normal. Our lives, not mercilessly driven by overtly intellectual nor hidden drives, had adequate portions of comedy, tragedy, experience, ambition, success, and failure. Naturally we looked up to role models—although always with perspective, constantly near at hand. Parents, friends, acquaintances were our comparisons, not Napoleon.

Those provided enough incentive and pressure. We gradually recognized our distorted perceptions of what others endure. Each human life is infinitely complex, when related to others, its narrative is often honed and heightened to provide interest. Any wasted old bum on the street can tell tales of grace and beauty; any serene old sage can describe moments of horror and despair. All lives are filled with massively important incidents and themes which are intensely interesting to the individual experiencing them. All the truth, all the time? Hardly

But this year, Joan and I felt adrift in our calm raft, while the seas of importance seethed around us. No matter where we looked, we seemed to have failed mightily.

Professionally, it was obvious I was not going to become a professional artist. Perhaps I could find a good alternate career, but that was uncertain. Joan couldn't find a path into public school. We began to worry that we were wasting time enjoying life.

Our parents had struggled against long odds, performed heroically, wrested success from a harsh universe, and were enjoying the fruits of their long labors. Siblings prospered. Old friends were better off. Even newer friends were engineers, or teachers, or artists actually making a living off their creativity. Only we remained orphans from fortune.

Later we discovered that others had their own troubles, some worse than ours. Our parents faced health problems, financial difficulties, concerns about their descendants. Siblings and friends had just as many worries, heartbreaks, and problems to come as we did, and sometimes, I am sure, envied us our "simple and uncomplicated" lives. In the end it all evened out.

We seethed in the cauldron of the great middle of everything, which is exactly what life is. Miraculous continuous profusion everyday, rather than momentous peaks and valleys of unique cosmic novelty.

Away from North Church mall, the North end was shabby bricks, potholed streets, and rusty warehouses along decaying wharves. Local politicians had managed to provide a park on the water, with lovely views of Piranesian corroded gigantic expressways and bridges carrying I95 onward to Maine.

Ghost raises his voice over traffic din. "So you say truth changes as you learn more over time? That's clearly wrong—not knowing truth simply reveals your own ignorance."

"Well, Ghost, I'm not going to fight with you on such a beautiful day, but I am not so sure the truth as you describe it at any given moment exists at all. Truth is a very slippery concept."

"Oh, come on," says an exasperated Ghost, "of course there is truth. You exist, the sky exists, one plus one is two."

I feel like splitting hairs. "No," I reply stubbornly, "I do not count mere facts and logical conjectures as truth. Truth, to me, is the whole ball of wax, what I think about meaning and the universe and everything else at one time."

"Right," snorts Ghost. "And the answer is always 42."

"If you paid attention," I instruct, "that was because the correct question was not asked. I think truth is actually about both the question and the answer. I'm not sure truth is as objectively real as you say. For one thing, it depends what I am concerned with."

"What? Nonsense ...."

"No, no, I mean—well look at our thoughts about how we were doing compared to everyone else. That was a form of question and answer and some of what was involved could only be sorted out by whatever came about in the unknowable future. Other times, truth was about whether I was or could be an artist or was doing right by universal morality. The filters of consciousness changed, the questions were different. And truth, as an answer, always remains provisional."

"A good philosophy for an amoral person, I suppose."

"I admit it all gets tangled with cultural relativism." I add with malice, "And that is the truth."

For one unanticipated reason or another, Joan and Wayne both managed the next day off. Putting on their tourist caps, they artfully guided Cheryl through previously selected spots as if spontaneously wandering. She had seen parts previously during with what had become the "standard tour" for first-time visitors: the new and sparkling Quincy Market on the rapidly reviving waterfront, Public Gardens and Common, various historic markers. Late afternoon they sat and chatted on a bench overlooking the river (keeping a wary eye for anyone suspicious.) Sailboats were out in force near the crowded boathouse. Trash covered lawns where mobs had gathered.

As they loosened and relaxed, they admitted worry, in one way or another, about the present and the future. They weren't getting any younger. The world was not becoming any kinder.

Their youthful idealistic heart-felt visions had become traps, preventing their concentration on mundane facts of aging, mortality, and common sense hard grit. Getting into their thirties magically transformed outlooks from fine fantasy into harsh prediction that they were not destined for importance and fortune. In fact, they would have to scrabble hard to be well regarded even by immediate friends and family.

Sun shone bright, food was good, summer stretched lovely. Cheryl would be gone early evening, leaving only memories. But, of course, memories are all that are ever left of any day at all.

Louisburg Square, center of expensive old homes, high iron fence around inviting flower-filled private park. Nowhere to sit, but we enjoy strolling as if bystanders in some period movie.

"I still say none of it is true," Ghost sullenly continues. "You're making a lot of this up out of a tissue of memories."

"Well, that's what humans have," I answer. "I trust my memories to be more true to my reality than anything else."

"Especially if you ignore contemporary photographs, videos, notebooks, or whatever from that era," snaps Ghost.

"There aren't any."

"Yeah, yeah, you say. You aren't trying very hard. I don't agree anyway. Unsupported memories at this distance are attenuated manipulated dreams."

"Harsh, aren't you. This is my life. This is what I remember. I think it's true."

"You might as well be writing some cheap novel with chocolate vampires and moons exploding in the skies. Don't pretend otherwise. A lie is a lie. "

"These are not lies. They at least try to represent the truth of my existence in that time …."

"Bah. Any novelist would say the same thing. 'Fiction is more real than fact,' they blubber. Feeling and motivations …."

"But they invent it all," I protest.

"I'm beginning to think, so do you," concludes Ghost triumphantly. "I rest my case."

We exit uphill towards the looming Statehouse dome.

Soon enough the future began to murder what had been.

Wayne was up at dawn, dressing quietly, snatching breakfast. He unlocked his bicycle in the basement, opened the back door into the courtyard under the subway, and headed off across the pepper pot bridge. Joan would follow shortly, taking the train up to Central Square and walking the four or five blocks to Roberts Day School.

Their grind was back. Daily necessities of earning a living, dreaming happiness, surviving another day and another week. Everything was in flux, they anxiously awaited the new, but mostly the same old suspension continued indefinitely hour after hour, day after day.

WAGES WAGER

WAYNE BROODED IN his nifty little office. Desk, comfortable chair, books, phone, even a window with a river view over recently demolished rubble of a nineteenth century casket manufacturing company. No demonstrations scheduled today, little to do. He was reading yet another programming book, having already taken it upon himself to weed the front flower boxes to make the new home of Kurzweil Computers a bit more presentable to the usual parade of curious industrial groups.

His title had advanced to "building manager and head industrial reading machine demonstrator." He had two bosses—Aaron the executive vice president, and Dennis, his supervisor. He was in a dynamically mushrooming technological company, in on the ground floor, appreciated and promoted. Everything was working out perfectly. He was making more money than he ever had in his life. Apparently the sky was the limit.

He was profoundly unhappy.

The cause of his malaise was that he was not doing what he wanted nor what he liked. The reading machine had been fun at first, but now was rote and mechanical. His only experiences with code remained at home. No possibility of breaking into the technical gang here, all recent MIT geniuses who wrestled with esoteric concepts, languages, and electronics.

His worth was proximity. Nobody else could make it so easily and quickly from home to this site if alarms went off at any odd hour. Management was grateful to hand the task down to the lowest person they trusted. There was a solid future here, but it was the wrong one.

Intense fog suspending dancing black and white dots resolves into a padded featureless boardroom, fake paneling, gigantic cheap laminated wooden table in its center. Brown faux leather chairs face a large beige paper pad sitting on an easel at one end. Ghost stands dressed in a grey business suit with white collar shirt and striped grey and black tie. He straightens when he sees me and grimaces. "So, you sold out after all, I see," he remarks.

"Aren't you getting a little carried away here?" I ask sardonically, leaning back. "Surely all we need for these conversations is a straight back chair or two with a naked lightbulb overhead."

"My, my, how melodramatic. You like to demean my existence—Jiminy Cricket, indeed! I myself consider myself more as an omnipotent emissary from other conceptual worlds—like Dickens' Christmas Carol figures. I shall compose our virtual realities as I wish. I find such exercise quite refreshing. Deal with it."

"It's disquieting," I mumble.

"Meant to be, meant to be. To this particular point, now: here you are, absolutely sold out to the establishment."

"Temporary, and necessary. I had to start somewhere."

"Ah, but the first step puts you on that slippery slope to conformity."

"I guess. Our lifestyle had become a little boring, maybe a tiny bit desperate. We'd reached some internal limit where we started to worry about the future.."

"Next thing, you'll be voting Republican…."

"I doubt it."

"But look—just another grey man in another grey office doing another grey job. Exactly what you always feared most. Anonymous and lost in multitudes of clerks."

"For a while, anyway."

"Maybe, maybe, we shall see…." He turns to his pad and uncaps a magic marker.

As Wayne became more experienced in day care and advanced to better positions, he had decided to become a real public school teacher. That required certification. Boston State, in the heart of the city, offered evening courses, so for a couple of years he his bike or the subway out past Fenway after work. His grades being excellent, he finally presented his transcript to the appropriate office, expecting an easy glide to the necessary documentation.

Wrong. A few more courses, which he expected. A full year of unpaid full-time volunteering as a trainee at some public school, which he did not. He had no car, and certainly no money to take such time off. Besides, he was getting a little tired of children anyway. That plan vanished. He searched for a realistic alternative, and finally decided to concentrate on computers.

Once more, he ignored all the rational approaches which might have gotten him somewhere, and fashioned his own idiosyncratic pathway. He bought dense textbooks from the MIT student store, religiously consumed each issue of Byte magazine, and programmed games on his little OSI home computer. Amazingly, he began to realize that this stuff was easy and fun. Using computers would not be his problem. The biggest hurdle would be sneaking into a computer job which required no particular formal experience or certification.

He had by then taken one course at Northeastern. The technical schools were apparently running a decade behind the industry, and the teachers were magnificent illustrations of "those that can't." Advertised openings matching his minimal qualifications were for key-entry operators who typed well. The catch-22 was the first year of employment, without which he could not get the first year of employment. He finally resolved to leap into whatever low-level job might come up, especially if it was a reasonable distance from their apartment.

To guide him, he had only ads in the Sunday paper. No business contacts to give him an appropriate lead or reference. His resume was a mess—he finally slashed it to two pages after realizing his life story would interest nobody. Eventually, a possibility came up right across the river in Kendal Square. Interesting name—Kurzweil Computer.

"You understand this is just an operator job," said Aaron, who had introduced himself as the vice president of this small new company in a very old red brick building. "You will not actually be doing programming."

"Well, I feel I need to get into the environment," replied Wayne honestly. He was dressed uncomfortably in suit and tie and tried to resist squirming in the stiff hard chair in front of the scruffy desk. Even the windows in the dusty office were streaked with dirt.

"And it really doesn't pay much, especially for someone with a college degree. Frankly, I am not sure you cannot find something better." He was probably worried that a new employee would bolt after a month or so of real keying work.

Wayne didn't want to admit that the salary offered looked princely compared to what he was currently making in day care. "Everyone needs to start somewhere," he shrugged. He wanted to appear earnest, not desperate. He had read a book on interview technique somewhere, and used that to glide into "So what, exactly, does Kurzweil do?"

"Well, we're pretty new, you know. But Dr. Kurzweil has invented a reading machine for the blind—you put a book down on it and a computer decodes each letter and word into binary, then reads out loud in a computer voice. An incredible device. Though we continually improve it, it is already quite famous in the blind community, to which we are committed. But we are also trying to break into a commercial area which is scanning books and records of all types into electronic records. We think there is tremendous potential there which fits our mission exactly."

"And what would I be doing, then," asked Wayne.

"Oh, it would mostly involve training the machine—it needs to be recalibrated to the actual font used in each book." Wayne had never heard of fonts before, but he tried to look as if he understood. "You would be assisting our demonstrator and probably typing passages that could not be recognized. This might eventually involve computer operations like nightly backup, but that would depend on you and how things go."

"I understand. It sounds like a good beginning. Do you use IBM here."

"No," laughed Aaron. "We started with Digital Equipment but we ended up with a much better deal from Data General, so we have their latest and fastest mini computers." DG made smaller "engineering-oriented" machines, much like DEC, and very different from the business computers of the big-iron companies.

"In Fortran?" asked Wayne, since he thought he might study up at home.

"I'm not really sure of the technical details, but I think some is in Fortran. Most of it, of course for speed reasons, almost all our proprietary software, is in assembly code, which only the geniuses in the other lab building understand. We only hire the best out of MIT, you understand, mostly classmates of Ray. Like me," he said kind of sheepishly.

"But you're not a programmer...." began Wayne.

"No, but someone needs to take care of the business side. I have an MBA to take care of finances and such. I see you majored in economics."

"Yes, but that's a long ways in the past."

"And now you do day care. That's important, I think, for the demonstration side of the job. You obviously have to like and get along with all kinds of people."

Wayne wasn't quite sure about that—one of the assumed attractions of programming was solitude—but he wasn't about to argue at an interview.

This went on to pleasantries for an hour or so, then wrapped up with a job offer.

"That's all we can afford right now. If you're interested, when could you start?"

"Well, I need to give my school a two week notice. That's it, I'm ready right after that."

"Ok, Wayne. I'll call your references and if everything checks out we'll see you then. I look forward to having you on board."

"Thank you very much sir," said Wayne, shaking hands. He danced onto the cobblestones and jauntily began walking the bridge home before he collapsed in nervous reaction. Well, step one of the quest complete. Hopefully that necessary first year underway. Computers reading out loud, he marveled. Like living in a science fiction novel.

Turning thirty had been shocking—never expecting to live that long, I'd hardly planned what should happen next. Yet circumstance reshuffled possibility as dramatically as new scenes in a play. Wild youthful memories, true or false, would never recur. Body and mind yearned for "normality." The key question was not if, but how, to discover and follow a solid pathway to a future that included supporting a family as Joan and I thought proper. With being a teacher—something that had only partially excited me anyway—off the table, I was freed to investigate a multitude of options.

We had cultivated independence and isolation. Some was from being in Boston, but most emanated from our predilection for internal motivation and introversion. We weren't hermits, enjoyed society, but didn't yearn for pools of exotic new friends or public recognition. Given half a chance I preferred to take a walk or curl up with a book, while Joan liked her school-related art projects and window shopping in stores. None of that was going to propel us into networks from which tendrils of employment would beckon.

I had only fantasies of what lucrative jobs entailed. I didn't quite understand why anyone was paid for anything except grunt work, of which I had done quite a bit. I didn't fear mindless labor, but it wasn't much of a career.

Accenting our naivety, neither liked debt or risk. We were unwilling to sacrifice certainty for possibility. Changing careers is a big risk. Anxiety pervaded everything I investigated. Surveys of the labor market quickly demonstrated that options were limited.

Way too late, for example, to become a doctor or lawyer, even if I had the desire—which I didn't—even if I could arrange the finances—which I couldn't. Likewise scientific research or academic pursuits. Business always beckoned, at the mail room level. I was resigned to heading that way. One gleaming ray of hope was the sudden appearance of computer programming.

No experience or qualifications there, of course. But demands in that exploding industry were so fluid that apparently anyone could fake their way in. The real trick was doing well thereafter. And that turned out to be pure happy luck.

Ghost is wearing the same old suit, and the same slicked haircut, but he has turned everything black and white, with the walls replaced by amorphous foggy grey, and a huge colorless wooden desk behind which he floats. "Ah, so sold out to the demons of Hell after all, did we?" he cackles.

"Almost," I admit. "That's what I was willing to accept, and I braced myself for the torments of the damned. No more fun, just hours, days, years of nit-picking numbers, droning meetings, endless phone calls, and mountains of paperwork, forever and ever."

"Desperate times, desperate measures." He sits back, folding his hands, tight dark grin.

"Oh, worse that desperate. But financial despair is a hard driver, and I wasn't getting any younger, and there was no way I could do day care at the level I was for much longer. Too much energy, too little long term prospects."

"But what about the great artist?"

"I'm afraid he had died a while ago. Some of the spirit kept going with inertia, but that dream became impossible. Especially considering our plans."

"So here you are, fully ready to take on the worst nightmares of your early youth."

"Yep. But there was that hope for a professional computer career. I seemed to be smart enough. It was the one light in all the darkness that kept me smiling no matter what."

"An exit from Hell?" he muses.

"An exit, anyway."

I'm getting tired of this same old trite fog rolling in at the end of each of his scenarios.

Wayne immediately foundered on complicated basic stuff, barely grasping arcane technical requirements expected. Fortunately the enterprise was understaffed, which provided many opportunities to take on any relatively low-level job nobody else had time for. He sweated through a crash course on backups, reboots, restarts, updates, tapes, scratch disks, and—yes—crashes. Big bonus was acquiring never-taught-at-school jargon of computer back rooms.

Sadly, all code was remote and off limits—he never saw any nor even found where it was stored. The interface console was devoted to starting and controlling the reading application, with a few startup and shut down operations. In that sense, his career was going nowhere. An operator—such as he was starting to call himself—was a minor step up from a data entry clerk. On the other hand, every day was more documented experience in the industry. Like everyone else he could massage and magnify his resume and polish his next interview. Not that he was in in hurry—this was a necessary grounding for where he wanted to go. The application itself was fascinating.

Just as important was accepting the ins and outs of daily American business practice. Who did what when, dress codes, making contacts in other departments, playing the games at meetings and company events. A few weeks in, he participated in a softball game at the annual picnic. And he was originally shocked to be answering the phone as giants of global industry—such as IBM and AT&T—would call asking about information or wanting to set up appointments.

But the grand takeaway for the next thirty years career was honing an ability to plan, execute, and finesse demonstrations. That skill would always be a bit of gold in his pocket. He found ways to slide a nervous potential client into a comfort zone with strange technology, quickly establish some kind of shared relationship, build trust that he was telling the truth. It always <u>was</u> the truth—just not the whole truth or nothing but the truth. This required a certain amount of creativity as demonstrations often got stuck or blew up completely. At such times even humbly admitting that this was a disaster but "they will be working full time on this particular issue to get it resolved immediately," would come across as naked admission of limits, and somehow serve to (usually) save the day.

Anyway, I was in the door. Astoundingly, industry positions were even more wide open than advertisements indicated. Not only were computers mysterious and associated with math, but long term prospects seemed risky and there was a fog as to how to really make money below the "top tier" business giants like IBM and Burroughs, or maybe the Department of Defense. Someone had not long ago said that the world needed maybe ten or so computers to do everything forever. With a limited future, few non-technical people were interested, once you got beyond clerks and secretaries.

Besides, most startups saw little need for business people. Who wanted accountants when your product required genius programmers and designers? Before you worry about the balance sheet, you need the stuff to sell. The common wisdom was that accounting could sort itself out as income grew. As for everything else—physical plant, human resources, whatever—that could just take care of itself somehow using bits and pieces of whatever was lying around.

Consequently, there were immense opportunities for anyone willing to take on additional responsibilities. A telephone receptionist could soon find herself as office manager or even some higher position—eventually, in almost no time, becoming a top-level manager of something or other. Of course, money did not often come with the titles, but the titles were given away as freely as the chores. For every firm that made it big, multitudes faded away, failed utterly, or were bought out with riches for the owners and life on the street for everyone else. But in those days, nobody worried much, because opportunities were exploding all around, and any individual's future looked bright indeed.

Ghost has upgraded to a designer outfit, and the background fog has been congealed into an oily, vaguely paneled look. The furniture is sleek real leather. But everything remains completely and utterly shades of gray, in a totally hushed environment. "All of the world spread before you," he accuses, "and you remained unhappy?"

"I wanted to be a programmer," I state stubbornly.

"But here you were, at the fulcrum. Why you could have been almost anything."

"Well, maybe. Maybe not. I always found that I expanded my job immensely no matter what I was doing—I always took on additional stuff and enjoyed it. But I never desired my boss's job. So although I quickly became treasured and irreplaceable in whatever I was doing, my very competence doing my job froze me where I was. I might get raises, but never promotions."

"Surely that was your fault."

"Oh yes, it was personality. I hated confrontation and being aggressive. I never went after a promotion. I really liked having my own little empire which I controlled completely."

"But you could have found more lucrative empires. You had the chances, like here."

"But I wanted to do what I liked doing." I repeat. "I'm stubborn that way. You spend as much time at work as I had to and I damn well want to have some fun at it. Life is too short."

"So you never did nearly as well as you could have," he accuses. "Cheating your family."

"All speculation. We can never know. For who I am and what I wanted, I did pretty damn well. I'm happy enough with the results."

"Possibly," Ghost adds darkly, "you're the only one who is."

"OK, Laura," said Wayne, "this is how we train the machine." He placed the open demonstration book face-down on a previously selected page and switched the screen menu to training mode.

In the background, Dennis was persuading the big guns, painting overall concepts and insisting the Kurzweil reader, having already revolutionized access for the blind community, could now aggressively court business people just like them who had compelling needs to digitize paper documents.

This new demonstration room here was larger and nicer than the old one, but still resembled a mad scientist's attic, possibly on purpose. Technical papers scattered everywhere, a few disks piled in a corner, the dominating presence of the DG cabinet—larger than a refrigerator—lights blinking furiously—on the back wall, the operations screen, keyboard, and scanner facing the opposite wall.

The canned part of these demonstrations almost always went well. It should, they practiced constantly. This "randomly chosen" book had been carefully prescreened as were the very pages on which to train and the demonstration chapter he was about to present. Often they would cheat a little by calling up a previous training file and simply adding to it.

"You see," Wayne explained, "the way characters are formed on any document tends to vary a little bit, whether created by a typewriter or even published. You know, detectives can actually tell which typewriter created a given page, just by examining the letters closely. This machine can do a pretty good job on identifying letters all on its own, but we fine-tune it with those it might have trouble with in a particular case." Which was, if not a falsehood, at least a good stretch of truth. The machine in an untrained state was maybe 50% reliable, which more or less meant a slow typist could transcribe the whole thing faster than it could be scanned and corrected.

As training began, the scanner came to life, bright lights shining up like a science fiction movie. The rubes were impressed. Cables and wires began their purposely exposed movements, letters and words began to appear on the screen. A pause would occur wherever something was questionable, and Wayne would type in the correct choice, for the computer to remember later. This page, he knew, had only a few problems which was comforting to those watching the deliberately slow but adequately rapid few minutes.

"Ok, I think this is trained well enough for now. Do you have any questions yet?"

"Does it always take this long for every document," asked one of the suits in back.

Dennis replied, casually, "No, we deliberately pick a fairly hard piece. And of course, if you have documents from the same source, you don't need any training at all."

"You can save each training session to a file like this," Wayne showed Laura the selection, "and then call it back whenever you want to." He proceeded to do that as well. Denis smiled benignly, the clients looked almost convinced.

'Now for the fun part." Wayne opened the book to chapter two—this was the cleanest one in the book—and carefully flattened the first page on the scanner. "Here we go." He pushed a button and sat back dramatically.

Whirring and cruising along, the cables slithering hypnotically, the lights on the computer blinking furiously, the entire contraption suddenly began to show rows of perfectly identified words in glowing green letters on the screen. As the first page ended, Wayne moved to the second, pressed a button, and sat with arms folded. Ten pages or so later, they decided to wrap it up.

"So, as you see, it is a pretty simple operation once it's all set up." Exactly how true that was he didn't want to get into. "We have scanned at—" and here he brought up another page on the screen with output information, "a little over 60 words a minute, with only ten errors in the whole run."

"A good typist can do that easily," noted a man in back.

"Well, of course," replied Dennis smoothly. "But we are not trying to replace good typists. Anyone—even a clod like Wayne here—" everyone laughed (although actually Wayne could do over 100 wpm if necessary)—"can do this. And it can go on day and night, without break, all you need is someone to keep changing the pages."

Dollar sign glimmers appeared in eyes. This could be a cash machine, everyone suddenly realized.

"It goes into IBM readable code?"

"Actually," said Wayne, "technically it goes into ASCII, which is the native coding for Data General computers. If you need to get it into the EBCDIC that IBM uses, there is a simple program to run for conversion."

"Well, that's the demonstration," continued Dennis. We can leave Laura with Wayne if you want her to ask any particular technical questions. We can go tour the facilities, meet some of the people who would handle your account, answer business questions. If you want, you can send in or bring some of your own materials in the future."

And that was that. Laura had no idea of what might be important to ask. Wayne had comforting pat answers to just about anything. As long as they didn't pull papers out of their pocket and demand an on the spot perusal of their own material, the demonstration was home free.

A successful demonstration was almost like a religious conversion. It is hard to recreate the naivety with which most people approached computers back then. They had heard wonderful tales, of course, as well as horror stories, but nobody had any experience with them at all. Few executives even had encountered a pocket calculator. There were no screens anywhere except for broadcast television. Close encounters with computing equipment were unknown except to total dweebs. Big corporations locked their machines and staff away in sealed environments, alien from the rest of the business.

So people would come in not sure what to expect, but pretty certain it would be sealed and mysterious and hardly something they'd be excited about. Then the magic happened—lights blinked, motors whirred, words appeared across a screen. And they were spellbound and believed almost anything. Every glitch was a passing phenomenon, every problem would be ironed out once the coders got into action on it.

For years, my colleagues and I sold business applications on the constantly changing bleeding edge. We didn't believe we were really lying, at least not too much. We honestly imagined that all problems were minor and could be addressed with a little effort by the guys (almost all guys) in the back room. It didn't matter if it was a text reader, or an accounting application, or an automated custom inventory system. We were the solution, and all problems could be resolved.

We had to be nimble. Gloss over issues, have glib explanations handy, admit (temporary) defeat just often enough to remain credible. And it worked. Clients bought the products and were trapped for the long term. Often enough, things worked pretty well. But it turned out no solution was miraculous, problems remained, and some things were clearly failures. But it was a fun pitch, selling the big show, watching people become excited about what you truly thought you could deliver, although it might take more time and money than they anticipated.

Ghost has changed into black robes, and sits at a high bench overlooking the still comfortable chairs. "So, what circle of hell should you be placed in," he murmurs to himself.

"Hey, I didn't do anything wrong. "

"Sounds like simple fraud to me."

"No, no, the fine print was always honest. Believe me, those early firms might skimp on administration, but they had good lawyers from the get go. You got exactly what was promised."

"But the promises in the fine print never matched what you said would happen in the demonstration," he accuses.

"Not exactly maybe. But we really almost always thought it would, eventually. You know, we were duped somewhat too."

"Mitigating? How do you figure that?"

"Oh, we didn't do any of the down and dirty code, you know. We just used what the programmers sent us, and believed what they said when we made requests, and trusted the promises of their managers. It's a constant salesperson dilemma. Sometimes your own organization is giving you the runaround."

"Perhaps...."

"And, believe me, the clients were no dummies, no matter how much they might think they loved the product. They had their own lawyers and their own fine print, and often enough extracted their own pound of flesh. It was just a question of who ended up donating it."

"Ok," he banged his gavel dubiously. "Recess for another decade." Exit in a swirl of dark cloth.

Eventually, I trekked countless hidden paths through tangled woods in computer programming careers. The ecology kept mutating.

Even back then, sclerosis had seized parts of the industry. IBM and its ilk were modeled on standard industrial revolution labor. Skilled workers were hired and placed on a permanent career track for life. Programmers came from particular certified schools, were carefully graded and advanced in tidy progressions through a known sequence. It was assumed that such people were company people for life. An IBMer had real cachet.

The IBM programmers laughed at technical toy mini-computers used by DEC or DG programmers primarily for engineering-related programs. These were considered far lesser beasts than the behemoths that ran accounting and payroll and other vast operations. DEC and DG programmers didn't care, and found that their industry war far less set in its ways, although any given company might not have a lot of upward opportunity. The normal path was to get in to any company that used the hardware as, say, a programmer with a programming certificate of some type, and then advance through degrees from junior to senior level. Along the way, you would pick up the skills of a designer or client interface specialist, but most of the time to get to the next level on those tracks required that you change jobs. The new employer would already see you as a designer, all they cared about was experience, and in that capacity you might take on architectural or management duties. And so it went, up and down the line. Even some key entry people and operators, with sufficient luck, pluck, and brains could bypass the initial certification alto- gether, although they were always slightly handicapped compared to those with a more formal start.

By the time I began, there was already background gossip concerning practical business uses for personal computers. The DEC and DG guys, naturally, thought of those as complete wastes of time, fine for recreation, but not particularly useful. Nevertheless, places like Kurzweil were already bleeding talent to some tiny startups in that niche—like Visicalc across town that had come up with an electronic spreadsheet which was starting to make waves in the accounting community. Personal computers were cheaper by the week, and more capable by the month, and stunning in what was beginning to be available on them. Getting into any job in personal computers was basically as easy as wanting to do so. The problem was finding a way to make money, or at least stable money over time.

Ghost stands in front of a raised dais, grey sheets all around, tables spread with yellowing certificates and a few gold and red trophies. Mist curls up from the floor. "Congratulations," he beams, "you were finally making everyone proud and at least trying to live up to your presumed potential."

"Yeah, yeah, I know. My parents were ecstatic, even though they didn't have a clue what computers might do. I could finally talk business jargon with Dad. It was a culmination of a makeover that they firmly believed began with my meeting Joan, who had reformed me."

"Do you dispute that?"

"No not really. But it felt more complicated. Anyway, yeah, they were happy, she was happy, her parents were happy. Everybody was happy but me."

"But you were happier than you had been in day care."

"Well, yeah, at least at the end. I was pretty sure this would go somewhere good. It was just boring and confusing some of the time, and hard to figure out what steps to take next. And a little overwhelming."

"But you always liked that," he responds.

"I know. But I didn't have a chance to create anything. That's what I really missed."

Wayne sat in his tiny office, door open, as cold rain pounded down outside. His bike ride home was going to be miserable. Meanwhile, another boring day. No demonstrations, nothing scheduled until next week. Reading and studying, projects on hold—details for the next corporate contracts were being developed upstairs. No new code to test out, to see if known bugs had been removed or new ones created (he seemed to have a knack for finding those, and that was fun, even if it made the programmers furious.)

He was leafing through the DG operations manual relating to the latest NOVA beast due to come in next week. Not that he would have much to do with it directly—someone would just put up the menus he was supposed to use and lock him into them. Without hands-on, instructions remained a confusing mishmash.

His current recognition, outside of his actual job, was in being able to write and type up various documentation. Everybody hated documentation, but it was always required. Core products, of course, had professional documenters. But little stuff that operations people needed—like common errors or what to do in the night stream—were good to have around, even as a checklist. It was easy to forget something and mess up. So everyone was grateful if he made up some typed short manual of steps, and it helped him feel he was doing something. And subconsciously he knew it made it just a bit harder to lay him off if the time came.

He knew his real ace was being on call so Aaron or someone else did not have to drive in from the suburbs if the alarm went off. They would probably pay him just for that—to show up in the middle of the night or on the weekend—because somebody authorized had to turn it off and sign paperwork with security company or police. Although stormy cold nights were terrors, days were uneventful. It was almost impossible for him to be fired, no matter what.

It should have made him happy and secure. But he heard clocks ticking, and he was restless, and he had already started to look around to see what else might be available.

PIVOT

WAYNE HAD WASHED up in Boston in 1972, after a three year whirlwind of post-college excitements in mid-America and West Coast. He had arrived broken and penniless, taking odd jobs, certain of the early doom of all romantically failed artists. Ah, how they would wail when he was gone; how the pretty girls would sigh as they viewed his now-famous work on the walls of a museum! Escaping that self-imposed trap with difficulty, after reaching a rocky bottom of despair and hopeless ambition, he had begun to rebuild a more modestly defined destiny. Girls seemed not to notice.

Like a beachcomber suddenly trapped by slowly rising tide, he blinked one morning and everything had changed. Here was Joan. Many of Wayne's friends gave her full credit, but he secretly understood that such a miracle only happened because he had cleaned up his own act, abandoned his pretentious inner shell, and reevaluated. What would accomplish even the minimal needs of a happy existence? Socially rusty almost to the point of illness, he began to take part in group activities, found a steady job. Like a fairytale, the rest unfolded in a few frantic years. Now life majestically rolled on slowly and happily.

Joan arrived from similar, if less hopelessly grandiose, broken dreams and frustrated ambitions. She had always sought no more than to be an art or elementary school teacher, for which she had spent her whole life preparing.

Yet she graduated into the teeth of a looming recession when for years Long Island offered nothing but throw-away temporary positions. Frustrated, she accepted her older brother's offer of a place to stay, and visited Boston. She loved the city so much that she remained, even though job opportunities were if anything more dismal than back home.

Two lost waifs, coming together in sheer surprise. The stuff of a romantic movie, except that they never noticed they were particularly attracted to one another. For each it seemed just proximity and comfort—someone to listen to, talk with, and depend on. A companionable exotic pet. Love crept up, always under logical control, one step sliding into another until one day, in amazement, they realized that the coupling seemed to be permanent. That had no immediate impact on their finances or careers, but it gave them an anchor in a troubled world.

Misty blue hills roll on the horizon, carefully tended fields checkerboard between split rail fence and occasional oak tree-breaks. Ghost rises from waist-high grain alongside the dusty dirt road. Rustic overalls hitched up, stalk of wheat dangling from his mouth. "Strange stuff, feller," he drawls. "You both hailed from suburban backgrounds. Why become city folk?"

"Yeah, pretty strange, considering that back then cities were something to escape from. The middle class was fleeing to bright new developments far away. Actually, I guess that's the only reason we could afford to live there."

"So you guys just running away from home?"

"No, don't think so. Neither of us sought wild bright city lights trying to make it big. But once we were there, well it was just—fun."

"Leaving them what raised you alone and forgotten."

"Neither of us could find anything nearer home!" I snap. "I liked freedom, Joan fled impossibility. Boston was engaging and exciting and something neither of us had experienced before."

"Lost little lambs, wandering helplessly." He insinuates lack of nerve. "Squatting in despair."

"No, I don't think so. We always felt temporary, even as we settled in. Nomads enjoying a pasture, well aware that destiny would eventually pull us back. We were just in no particular rush to pick up tents and move on."

"Nice pastures around here," he remarks, with a wide arm wave.

"Wrong crops," I grin. "We wanted to grow little people, not corn."

I glance at a nearby orange butterfly, and by the time I look back he is gone.

Wayne and Joan, like countless young people before them, found urban life a breath of fresh air. Infinite freedom—everyone else was busy and had little time for you. Anonymity when a little ashamed of being a failure is a welcome thing. The attraction of the city was leaving wreckage behind, or at least sweeping it under the rug.

Wayne had been unexpectedly attracted to cities since he graduated high school. He had never liked cars. Walking streets in Hartford and later Kansas City, Berkeley and Cambridge was liberating. He loved the Boston subway, on which for a quarter he could reach out for miles, to oceans, to the zoo, to huge parks, to wonderful other sites. For a pittance they could ride trains to small New England towns, on the seacoast like Marblehead or drenched in history like Concord. And, once he had his bicycle shipped up, he could quickly get anywhere, anytime, even—surprisingly—in the depth of winter.

The thing was—well novels always presented the metropolis as a field of dreams, full of immense hopes and driving ambitions. That surely was true for some. But for Wayne and Joan it was also a field of distractions, forgetfulness, immediate pleasures. They had both been arrow-straight through childhood into college, and almost for the first time they could sit back and breathe and enjoy without guilt. They enjoyed the experience.

Strolling sidewalks was entertaining—they never knew what might pop up. Formally there were attractions, galleries, new shows, old famous tourist sights. Watching people along the Charles River esplanade could pass hours. Wayne sketched to his heart's content with nobody bothering him. Any momentary desire—to dine out, to start breeding guppies, to engage the art scene, to pursue cooking—could be fulfilled and more than fulfilled in a few eventful weekends. Life was a never ending carnival of wonders. Once they paid rent and food, it was almost all free for the taking.

Not quite proto-yuppies because they were professionals only in their secret hearts. They more resembled those people who spent entire forgotten lives in tiny little rooms filled with books in Greenwich Village. By discarding acquisitive impulses, they became engaged with the world.

There remained one worm in the apple. This was not the ultimate goal of their lives. They had no illusions about becoming important in Boston, or anywhere else. They wanted to eventually establish themselves as a respectable family, with children, just as their parents and grandparents before them. But, like Saint Augustine concerning chastity, not quite yet.

Colorfully dressed young people passed by constantly, well bundled against the grey cold breeze sprinkled with raindrops. As usual, crowds filled Harvard Square this March Saturday late afternoon. Wayne and Joan sat in a warm booth, enjoying falafels at a tiny middle-eastern restaurant.

Wayne had recently discovered that all his work for getting a teaching certificate was for naught. Following a visit from her mother, Joan had become desperately homesick. Meditative silences stretched into the tangy aromas.

"I think we should maybe go back to Long Island," ventured Joan wistfully. "Maybe I could find a job now."

"I don't know where we would live. It looks like it would be easier to get into programming around here, the papers are full of want ads. You know I've been sending out resumes."

"But none of them have panned out, right?"

"Well, no. Just about everywhere wants some kind of experience. But I'm sure if I keep mailing from the ads every Sunday—I mean I think I must have sent thirty just this week—something will turn up. Once I get my first job and my feet in the door—well, with a career started <u>then</u> it makes sense to go back."

"And children? I'm not getting any younger you know."

"Children, sure. But we probably can never earn enough to bring them up properly in a city—we'd both be working and we're not making nearly the money to afford a school and what not. Besides, kids like to run around a yard."

"We have to get out of here sometime."

"I agree. We'll miss it. How about giving it just a couple more years. If I can't get a job, less."

"That's your plan. How about instead I try to get pregnant, and whenever that happens we move back to the Island?"

Well, there it was. Naked decisions forced. Wayne gulped and thought about it and realized there was really no choice. He could no longer imagine life without Joan. And Joan could no longer enjoy life away from her close relatives.

"OK."

"OK?" she looked up, shocked, having expected a stronger argument.

"Yeah, OK. You're right. It's not getting any earlier. We'll just have to do whatever is necessary. I'll keep trying to get a job and we can try to have a baby."

That cheered the scene up a good deal, and they finished the lunch in an almost festive mood.

As they stepped out into the bracing air, it began to sink in that suddenly they were in goodbye mode. From here on, every experience was going to eventually go away. No more Harvard Square, no more subway, no more bicycling to teach small children. No quick visits to museums and aquariums. Each of them, for their own reasons, were a little saddened underneath the excitement of facing some future completely new and different.

We are affected by deep and unconscious motivations, which we modify only with a great deal of work, and sometimes with very little reason. The most important set includes what we expect from life, what we hope for, what will truly make us feel worthwhile and happy. If we are fortunate, we discover those keys in time to use them.

Joan and I enjoyed the city but it couldn't satisfy our souls. It was like eating candy all the time. There were constant distractions, and joys and marvels, and we could easily lose ourselves in the bustle of activities. We experienced things that would have been impossible elsewhere. But, late at night, we often felt our true mission was being ignored, and we both experienced growing dissatisfaction with the circus of the streets.

Usually we could access some project—cooking odd Chinese meals with fresh ingredients from Haymarket, maintaining tanks of tropical fish from the well-stocked store on the corner of Charles Street, or even becoming fully immersed in our jobs. I would sometimes turn to the comforts of creating paintings or writing or designing computer games. But we always knew it would have to end.

By 1978 we were ready to say farewell to it all. To our naïve youth, to our unhurried life, to our lack of obligations and ongoing growth. We were suddenly over thirty. Our parents were aging before our eyes. The world was not becoming more generous. The city remained a wonderful and charming place, but increasingly we understood we had to leave.

Loud persistent moos are the main clue, as rows of chest-high early corn come into focus on the other side of the gravelly road. Weightless Ghost perches on a decrepit fence rail, leaves rustling behind him in a warm breeze. "Ah, back to the land, eh?" He tips a wide-brimmed straw hat.

"Over the top," I comment, "even for you. If you call suburbs 'the land.' Yeah, back to the land. In your current idiom, 'from whence we came.'"

"Per Lincoln, calling suburbs the land don't make them so," he observes. "Suburbs are sterile and lifeless and tacky. Neither flesh nor fowl."

"You know, when we grew up it was a lot more like land. Outposts of small family plots in rural landscapes like this. Farms everywhere nearby. Heck, Joan and I both had operating dairy farms—with your cows—within easy bicycling distance."

"Hard to believe these days. Sure ain't that way no more."

"Your attempts at being a bumpkin are quite annoying, you know." Ghost shrugs. "But you're right, it's all become asphalt and strip malls and automobiles and smog. Every horror of city life with none of the conveniences. But for a while for a kid in the fifties it was growing home vegetables, exploring endless woods, watching farm crops ripen."

"Sounds like you fellas really should be heading upcountry."

"Nice to visit," I shudder involuntarily, "not for us day after day. Honestly, even when we got back in 1980, there were still lots of farms and undeveloped areas. Nothing like that now, of course."

"The world changes," he says sagely, gazing over the horizon.

"True enough. Now it seems that anyone who can is streaming into the city. And staying there."

But as wind rises and clouds cover scorching sun, Ghost has dissolved into shimmering hot air.

The seventies contained their own vicious little recession, a bout of what was called, eventually, "stagflation" where the economy was stagnant but prices kept going up. That followed general malaise and social anger over Vietnam, when many "establishment" social and political priorities were challenged. It was a period when those with good jobs cruised on their gravy boat while many drowning alongside were unable to climb on board.

Neither Wayne nor Joan had ever been deep social activists totally rejecting American culture. They had for one reason or another never mainstreamed into the traditional good life. What they had was hardly grim, but their current path exposed no shining future. For the moment, even the worst jobs usually provided health care of some kind, food was always available, and stabilized rents were abundant. More astoundingly, from the standpoint of later bitter class antagonism, the wealthy felt a certain sympathy for the poor.

In the countryside, countless communes explored alternate lifestyles that might survive the expected imminent collapse of capitalism. In cities, unions and political machines required votes from poorer elements of society to retain residual power. It was hardly a kind and gentle time, but it was not Spenserian bloody ruthless either. Many fine social experiments remained underway, such as the Boston Phoenix "alternate press."

Wayne and Joan wandered on the edges. Wayne had been active in a public dance group, both were touched by attempted unionization of day care workers, and in Cambridge and Boston student radicalism was impossible to miss. Always young and naïve and expecting that they knew what the world was all about and what it had to do. As war faded, women's issues, racial equality, and the morality of poverty were incessant topics.

Wayne's career move was uncertain. Joan, growing older, realized doors to success closed firmly and rapidly. For five years they accepted that as inevitable and made the best of their situation. No complaints, that had been a satisfying chunk of life. Over and done. Deciding was easy, not so learning to walk the walk.

Our faith rested in the Church of Universal American Betterment. Heretics might challenge the universal optimistic assumption that our world would always get better, but we remained congregants of our childhood cult. We had better lives than our parents, as they had better lives than theirs, and our (eventual) children would no doubt have much better than ours. It was simply a matter of defining "better." On that issue there were severe disagreements, bordering on violence.

My internal dynamic was the hope that eventually my art would sell. Admittedly, this was bounded by the romantic certainty that I would die young and unnoticed. I never imagined myself at forty or fifty, which meant that fourth decade arrived as an unexpected shock. Our financial and personal future loomed real and frightening. Joan had assumed that if she waited long enough things would eventually work out. That wasn't happening either—no public school jobs were available. She began to wonder if that was truly the career she wanted. For the first time, she also began to examine alternate futures.

Our lives together had worn down some of the hard edges of rebellion and determination, so we were less antagonistic or traumatized by ongoing hints from our parents. We began to understand the wisdom of how they had lived, and actively tried to understand how they had done all they had. That was, inevitably, intimidating, since they had endured so much more than we had, and had so much more to show for it. On the other hand, we did not yet have the perspective to understand that at our age, they had been almost as desperate as we ourselves.

Our most important realization, however, was that the world did not care at all. We were not trying to impress civilization, we were not trying to become immortally known, we were not even lynchpins in creating a better society. Our true self judgment was what we wanted, but that more and more lined up identically with our parents desires. We did not have to make the universe happy, we did have to please ourselves and each other. We wanted to stand proud when we saw our families for visits or holidays. I guess it was maturity.

Longer vistas, flat crops to the horizon, no fences in sight. A horse saunters up the endlessly straight road between the cornfields. Ghost is attired into old stained clothes, his face aged into deep seams and weathered skin. "Yep," he muses, "you young 'uns sure got it wrong for a hell of a while…."

"Too far," I protest. "Drop the pretend dialect. We've got the point."

"Jest answer the question, sonny."

"What question?"

"Did ya regret yer years of futility?"

"No," I correct him firmly. "I don't think so. We did exactly what was proper for people our age, completely and effectively and happily."

"But ya missed that there boat you was talkin' 'bout."

"Maybe the gravy boats had arrived for many of those we knew," I respond, "with family and money and careers. A lot of those ships foundered later, in a string of divorces and lost lives and regrets. Once we got ours together, we cruised along pretty steadily for a long time."

"Pollyanna," he scoffs.

"Nope. I always took to heart that bible quote about gaining the world and losing your soul. I never wanted to lose my soul just to make money."

"Your loss," he points out. "And your family's too, of course."

"I disagree."

"Your wife might not."

"Depends on the day. We all have some regrets sometimes. But all in all, no, ours worked out fine, old man. As you well know. And drop this scenario, it's creepy and stupid."

"Matches the topic." He turns the horse off the dust and into the field, vanishing as quickly as he came.

Streaming with sunlight onto the living room rug, warmth on cool early spring Sunday morning. Wayne stretched on the floor, red magic marker in hand, circling want ads in the Boston Globe help wanted section. Many pages, but without a car or experience, with only a vague idea of exactly what he was looking for, by the time he was done there were only twenty-odd offers worth pursuing.

Dutifully, he sat at his desk in the den and copied each onto a three by five card, for his records, then addressed a business envelope and inserted his latest, much slimmed down resume. At least he finally understood that no hiring manager wanted to read a five or ten page autobiographical essay. Just the facts, just the time date and places of what he had been paid for. Stamps on the whole bundle, out the door and down to the corner mailbox, another early chore done.

He and Joan were going to walk up the river and visit the Science museum later. Neither of them thought it spectacular. Some of the exhibits were interesting, and it was warm and a big open space. Hopefully no groups of kids today. A nice well-bundled walk along the old unimproved banks of the Charles below the pepperpot bridge, then maybe take the green line up to government center later.

First he had to go down and pick up the laundry, dry by now at the laundromat up the street. He snuck chores in where he could, a two-for-one accomplishment. He folded shirts and underwear at the stand-up tables, stuffed pillowcases for the short haul back and exertions up four flights of stairs. Anyway, Joan appreciated the effort.

"Are you ready to go yet," he called back towards the bathroom.

"Just a few minutes," floated the reply. Always a few minutes turning, somehow, into many minutes. He had the rest of the paper to read. The day was young. His hopes and dreams were safely entrusted to the mail delivery system. He felt ready for whatever the week might bring.

October puffed a whiff of affluence. Regular job supplied a paycheck that overcame bills. One afternoon after work, Wayne strolled down the river a few blocks to Lechmere, a huge electronics store. He was astounded to be allowed to open their first credit card, using which he purchased a gigantic—18 inch!—color television. It seemed a bigger dent in the budget to pay for the taxi required to bring it home. The console weighed a ton, so getting it up the stairs was a daunting challenge. It worked poorly with indoor rabbit-ears until he pirate-spliced it into an existing cable descending past the kitchen window from an antenna on the roof. Miraculously, it picked up all the regular channels. .

A step towards TV-standard-American normal. Wayne didn't trust that everyone lived as shown in sitcoms, but certainly the homes that he and Joan had grown up in were a bit out of their reach. Well, to be brutally honest, completely and unimaginably out of reach. He had no idea how they would deal with a future with children, presumably in some expensive suburb. He hoped this new job would lead to something better, but it all looked a lot more hopelessly molasses slow than he had expected—again as expected from movies and books.

He had a range of cheap suits, mostly from discounts at Filene's basement with Joan's help, since he had no taste in apparel. Thank heaven for those on-going markdowns of fifty or sixty or more off. His spending money was now mostly going into work-related materials rather than art books and tropical fish. Priorities were gradually taking their due. His home computer was a money sink—more memory, of course, but also seemingly infinite books and magazines.

Wayne's big saving was art supplies. That had been his one real extravagance. Acrylic paint was never cheap, nor canvas, even though he could reuse frames. But he had no time anymore, what with trying programming in his spare hours, and even less energy.

Living with hope, however premature, was a heck of a lot better than living in despair. Rising income and better prospects always brought hope. Beyond that, there was a measure of self-satisfaction and respect from others now that he had changed fields. Computers still had a more magical cachet than taking care of little kids, no matter what the balance of genuine benefit to society.

"Finally," Ghost observes, waving his pitchfork toward the hayloft in an old wooden barn, "you were well and truly trapped by the great American Establishment."

"We went through this already in your other overblown production. I never really thought of it that way."

"The reason I keep bringing it up is precisely because you <u>did</u> very much and always think of it that way. Color television, suits for god's sake. You abandoned thoughts of rebellion, you decided to take the straight and narrow, you dropped your idealistic futures. Your youth had been wasted. And you had completely sold out. What would you call it?"

"I don't call it anything. It was just an adjustment to circumstance. I never went around yelling 'capitalist pig' slogans anyway. Most labels about people's lives are infantile."

"Easy for you to say from your high and mighty perch now. Back then—sellout!"

"Everybody changes as they grow. We should. If we don't we are missing a great deal of the wonders of experience. I always believed that, I believe that still. Different times and different circumstances are just a spur to understand and perform more widely."

"Sellout!"

"You seem to have lost that farmer guise. Why don't you paint yourself some signs and go march on the street corner somewhere …."

He stalks out, heading for the stinking pig pens. Nice effects, randomly effective questions.

Wayne knew, sometimes facing the facts, that he was giving up most of what he had thought was important. He could not become an artist, he would not be living in the city, he was not about to make some kind of important mark in anything, and he would have to give up almost all his time now to what others thought he should be doing. Looked at that way it was frightening. But from the other direction, it was kind of liberating. Something new and different with, in a magical way, a complete loss of guilt and responsibility. Reborn benediction.

The broken dreams of his twenties were oddly a cenotaph as if he <u>had</u> died at thirty as he had always anticipated. But instead it was those dreams that were interred. He himself rose like a phoenix from ashes, with new hope. Although nothing tangibly financial had come from a decade pursuing art and life, he realized that he would not regret that time. No amount of money or fame could have equaled the personal growth, the deepening of sensibility, the centering into the world, the necessary ripening in his personality that came from all those "lost" years. He was grateful that he had the opportunity to do things he could otherwise never have done.

So, although worried about what would be next, he abandoned regrets or urges to return to that ancient world. He had immigrated into the land of expected normal, and he would do what was necessary to adjust. It might take a while, but he was learning the folklore already. He was confident that success was just a matter of time.

"You were just one lucky dude, I think," says Ghost, spitting a tobacco cud onto a patch of grass.

"Dude? Anachronism, Ghost. But that's true. If I had not met Joan— well who knows? But I suspect my life would have been far worse. I always considered myself lucky, no matter what."

"Lucky and lazy and poor. "

"Not so poor. We always had a nice place to stay, always had good food to eat, believed in each other. What else does one really need in life?"

"Hope."

"Oh, I was always stuffed full of hope. It's just that most of it was hopelessly unrealistic. But hope was always available. I thrived on its fantasies."

Big changes take time. Once in a while they linger more in the mind than in reality. Wayne and Joan had revised plans dramatically. But urban life continued around them, good and bad, day by day, slow as public transit. The same apartment, the same chores, the same rituals. Only the daytime work efforts, and a few ongoing activities like sending out resumes, indicated anything was different.

So they walked the same streets, enjoyed the same restaurants, shopped and enjoyed the sights, and continued to feel part of the city. There was still a lot to do, a lot of fun to be had, changes everywhere, excitement popping up unexpectedly, entertainment for free. Once in a while, if they thought much, they regretted it would be going away. But most of the time—well something happening in a year or so no matter how seemingly definite seemed almost infinitely far away.

What they did not do, now, was try to put down new anchors. While they didn't break off old friendships or associations, they didn't try hard to settle into anything permanent or binding. The apartment had always been lease by lease, they had no intention of leaving it. They still didn't want a car until the last minute. They still balanced exactly on money in and expenses out.

Wayne stopped frequenting the galleries, and most of the art events. He immersed himself in reading and studying for computers, when hired he spent as much time as possible at work and in front of the machines. At home, he continued to program and read and design code. No more forays for cheap art books, no more rides up the Charles to the Utrecht store up by Boston University. Joan even started to look at alternatives to education, going over the want ads when Wayne was done with them. It was the conceptual completion of the dead ends, and that meant dropping some old comfortable habits.

But in the meantime—well Boston was coming alive, changing in front of their eyes, exciting and young and hopeful. And they were still there, fully enjoying it, now on extended vacation rather than beginning residence. Most of the time, a wonderful state of mind.

Roots

FRANTIC MASSIVE ACTIVITY—WAYNE'S parents due Friday afternoon. Clear shelves, dust, wash, vacuum. Sparkling clean was out of the question, but at least spray to drive the most aggressive cockroaches out of sight, stuff whatever could be jammed into closets. Even his painting studio should look presentable. Unfortunately, stowing everything to make the apartment look good also made it almost unlivable. At least Mom and Dad would be staying in the Holiday Inn down the hill. Most visitors were content to sleep on a floor mattress. Furniture was sparse, mostly rescued from the street or built college-dorm style from pine planks.

This scramble was actually modest. Things were relatively neat and clean—Wayne's latest enthusiasm called for books and papers but not much mess. Move the computer from the floor to the desk. Cooking had settled into quotidian simplicity so the kitchen was fine. Besides, these people had seen it all several times, and seen it worse. This would be a tourist ramble, with just short rests in their home. Maybe a dinner, but Mom and Dad liked to dine out and were willing to pay.

They were driving up by car, parking right under the hotel. Somebody had to be around in the afternoon for the call after they checked in. Wayne had arranged to leave early, not much of a problem. That evening, they could eat on Charles Street somewhere and get reacquainted. Nothing exciting, after all they stayed in touch by phone every week.

Nevertheless, Wayne was nervous. He reviewed comparisons and justifications and years of guilty feelings about not measuring up. Mom and Dad didn't mention it—Joan was the jackpot prize, they thought, and now trusted the story to turn out fine. But in his own skull, the same dark thoughts would creep out and run around, coating every encounter with the grime of time lost and opportunities missed.

Crunch of crushed stone behind me, I turn as Ghost walks by with a platter of raw steaks. As the scene comes into focus, I recognize where I grew up, here on the patio where we were part of so many barbeques. "Good times," he begins. "Solidly American times. At least you finally began to recognize how nice such a life could be."

"This section is still set in the city," I note. "I for one had no desires to return to patios and barbeques."

"Can't escape your roots," says Ghost, pontificating like some second-rate college professor. "You will be what you were."

"That's hardly an American tradition."

"Well, at least all your life is part of your makeup. You want what you remember."

"What a load of crap," I answer. "By that reasoning I spent as much time in cities than I did on this patio—probably more. I should be completely trapped in my new patterns. Life's a lot more complex than that."

"So why such trepidation during this visit?" Ghost finally puts down the tray and pops a beer.

"Well, I admit we were carrying the—excuse me, Ghost—ghosts of our parents' dreams with us all the time, always trying to measure up to what we imagined we thought they thought we should be doing."

"Confusing as hell, I would think."

"No, not that so much. Conflicting with what we had actually done, quite forcibly. We still could not, for example, afford to take them out to dinner where they took us."

"Filled with guilt, right?"

"Oh, a fair amount deep down. We hid it with false bravado and fancy rationalizations. "

"They fell for that?"

"I don't think so. But like I said, they were happy we finally seemed on the right track. They had faith things would work out for us. After all, their early world had been considerably worse, filled with depression and war."

"Yes, there was always that," Ghost reflects.

"They felt we had time, now that we had come to our senses."

"And you agreed?"

"Joan and I were not nearly so sure."

Wayne and Joan had quickly (and forcefully) discovered how difficult it is to satisfy all the demands of several strong families. Naively, they figured that limiting their own autonomy and acquiescing to important needs of their partner would be all that was required. There was more. Expectations of getting "home" (which home?) for the holidays and other special events, or of entertaining relatives who arrived to chat pleasantly (and just incidentally get free room, board, and tours of Boston) were enervating. Fortunately, they still had no idea how much of a tangled burden would be added to the mix with the arrival of their own offspring. For the moment, there was enough to consider.

First was the matter of who got what when. Christmas was the big prize—which family would see them for a few days when all the relatives gathered with momentous inertia. Thanksgiving was a poor second, and very little favored by Wayne who hated the massive travel delays and had early on cut that from his schedule. How about Easter, or at least the spring, the Fourth of July, or at least the summer vacation (what vacation, they asked each other.) Over years, they had worked out a delicate combination tap dance and ballet pleasing everyone a little, nobody too much.

One thing was certain, nobody was going to visit them in the winter. So generally, late spring through early fall was their own busy season, when they sometimes felt they were running a board and breakfast inn on the side. It's not that they didn't enjoy the visits—they loved taking people around and fortunately they both also enjoyed everybody in the families immensely.

But keeping things interesting on the fifth or sixth visit—especially with age beginning to affect some people—was becoming challenging. Somehow, they managed to find a lot to do, and easy ways to get around, even if they personally never used really easy mechanisms of transport like taxi cabs.

The thing was, of course, it was not merely the actual visit that disturbed their already tight routines. There were the preparations—what food to have handy, what plans to make, what contingencies to prepare if the weather didn't cooperate. Always the heavy fix up and cleaning, making themselves and the place presentable. All that normally took at least a week before people arrived, in a constant crescendo of anxiety. Keyed up at the arrival and first moments, until everything settled down into a nice rhythm. Staying on guard to not say or do anything hurtful or stupid, either to visitors or to make each other mad. Then, finally, simply being tired for a week afterward from the release of tension, while, nevertheless, they had to fully resume their normal hectic lives.

But they dealt with it, and were basically happy that they had the chance, and all in all life went on—interrupted—with only minor fluctuations and generally in the right direction.

Around six, reddening sun still high late summer, not too hot, they gathered in front of the Union Oyster House at Haymarket square. This would be expensive—Joan and Wayne never ate at such places—and touristy—but it was probably exactly what Dad would love.

They went in and were seated in an extremely dark wooden booth. Mom was thrilled, to her the darker the ambience the more high-class the restaurant. Joan, who loved bright lights, was less captivated. Dad goggled at the massive choices of oysters on the menu. They had drinks, talked trivia, ordered various seafood extravaganzas.

"So, I hear you are thinking of starting a family," began Mom, leaving unsaid the implied "finally."

"Yes, it seems about time," replied Joan.

"Will you be staying here, do you think?" asked Dad.

"No, probably not," answered Wayne. "We don't think we will have enough money to take care of a child properly in the city. And Joan really wants to be living near her parents. They don't have any grandchildren at all yet."

"How is work coming along?"

"Well, I'm learning an awful lot at the new job, and putting together a lot of experience on the resume. But it's not exactly what I want to do, so I assume I would be changing soon even if we didn't move."

"Are there computer jobs in New York?"

"I haven't looked much, but as far as I can tell there are computer jobs almost anywhere if you have a little experience. We'll just have to see."

"Well, good for you," said Mom. "We've been a little worried. You've been married a while now."

"We've been busy. We really didn't think much about it until recently. Anyway, here we are…"

They broke to eat as the food was served, all delicious. As always on such visits, Dad picked up the check and Wayne refused to be embarrassed. That was just the way of the world—older people had money, younger people did not. Unthinking acceptance of what was.

"We'll be expecting you to visit, of course," said Mom. "Although that should be easier for you and us if you live nearer New York. This is a pretty long trip."

"Although we do love visiting here, very interesting town," added Dad.

"We have a ways to go yet. We don't want to move until the last minute," noted Wayne, "because I think I have a better chance for more career growth here initially than I would down there."

"Are you planning to live in the city, Joan?" asked Mom.

"No, no, out on the Island," she answered. "New York is just too big and frantic. I want to be near the water and back where I might be able to teach in the schools some day. And be able to use my parents as resources, of course."

"Good idea, I know Anita was always grateful that we could help babysit Traci."

"Besides, it will make them very happy. And honestly, I am beginning to get tired of all the crowds and noise."

"But it won't be next week," stressed Wayne.

"But near future, good plans, good idea," finished Dad. "This has been an excelled dinner," he looked at the bill, "although at these prices it should be." They all laughed. "Thanks for bringing us here."

They headed out into the mild evening, for a quick tour of the newly refurbished Long Wharf beyond the horrid overhead expressway.

By then, conversations were far less fraught than once upon a time. For a few years, every visit home was anguish, since pursuing art on the fringes of alternate lifestyle was completely foreign to solid middle class values. With Joan, all that had mellowed out. Now that I was entering the world of business, intergeneration conversations became increasingly normal and interesting.

But there could still be a great deal of misunderstanding, since Joan and I would always compare, in our own hearts, how we were doing compared to how we thought they thought we should be doing. And always coming up short, of course. Instinctively too, we would compare the high points of other lives we knew to our own average—if someone had a good job they were doing better than we were, for example, even if it later turned out that the rest of their life was a miserable slog. People always tend to present themselves in the best light (unless, as they grow older and more beat up, they are just asking for sympathy.)

Both Joan and I always did accept responsibility for our choices and our situation. We never fell into the trap of feeling victims of circumstance. Instinctively and from upbringing we were quite aware that circumstance is simply the environment you must utilize and find your best path as you can. We were never able to blame the culture nor other people for our failings. That ended up being an important strength over the years, an attitude that made life far more endurable. Being in control—even if that may be a somewhat illusory control—seemed preferable to being helpless pawns.

Anyway, no doubt as we grew older our own hopes and fears and happinesses and desires did merge more with those of our families. We began, once again, to get pleasure from what pleased them. Our rebellious years had been accomplished, and like the prodigal son we were ready to return, once we found the secret doors in society that would let us do so. Selling out, possibly, or becoming mature. Just different sides of the same coin, I always thought.

Vague blurry bluish objects in a barely visible room. Quiet feeling of comfort. "Ah, the young folks gain perspective," Ghost puffs complacently on a pipe, filling the air with noxious sweet smoke, just as my father once did. He slowly swivels his brown easy chair to face me.

"Nostalgia?" I ask, more annoyed than confused.

"No. Expectations." Ghost knocks some ashes into a nearby tray. "Disappointments."

"Hey, this section is about finally meeting expectations," I protest.

"Finally is the word. After wasting all those years and opportunities," he gestures at me with the wet stem.

"Oh, I don't know. I would never trade my childhood no matter how successful I might have become if I had. Even now, I do not regret my young adulthood ."

"Ah, your inner Edith Piaf," he warbles mockingly.

"Life is too short to spend it all following some stupid career or job. Especially when you are at your peak and young. What a waste that would have been." Perhaps I am a bit too defensive.

"Rationalization. You're just making blind excuses."

"I don't think so. I've seen real warts on too many other lives. Everyone has challenges and problems, no matter how immaculate their presentation to the outside. Success is part of life, at least internal success. External recognition of success is pretty minor compared to existence itself."

"Well, you're still a fool, then," Ghost declares with a force that sends ashes flying.

"Maybe so. Lack of envy makes me happy. Say what you will, I have always managed to be relatively happy."

"Ah, but the question is, did you make others happy?"

"That's a fair question, and a fair answer is yes, mostly, I think so."

"Egotistic bastard."

"Possibly yes. But a laughing egotistic bastard."

"Could have been better."

"Could have been much worse."

Smoke billows, thickens, fades away with all the rest.

We were listening now, for the first time since we were small tots, and trying to learn from the stories we could drag out. For some reason, older folks never wanted to talk much about the war or the great depression or, for that matter, their childhoods. That would have interested us, but they were far more concentrated (and healthy because of it) in the present, and where they were now, and where we were going. We wanted to learn the secrets and tricks of their success, but they were certain there weren't any secrets or tricks at all—you worked hard and smart and everything worked out. That was their basic life narrative, as they saw it. Luck came along, and they took advantage of it, but luck only came along because they had tried really hard to be ready for it.

But even so, they were already caught in their own social whiplash of confusing change. The steady and stolid world they imagined would last forever after the war had begun to fray and dissolve at the corners. There was Wayne's rejection of a normal life, for example. Joan's older brothers had not produced the expected families. Wayne's sister had been properly married, and then (with cause) quickly divorced and raising a daughter on her own. Some of the tales of friends and offspring had become hair-raising. There was comfort, to be sure, in the staid old mass media, where violence was properly directed at savages, and mention of sex was rare except as laughable double entendre. Yet there were multicultural intrusions in surprising places, a sexual revolution that their children seemed to be close to experimenting with, a chasm on the (ended) Vietnam War that was unbridgeable and simply avoided in polite circles.

Nowhere was change more evident than in the world of employment. Many baby boomers were settling into "straight" jobs. But there were an awful lot of leftovers, "doing their own thing," scratching out a living. Expectations were failing. The treasured American work narrative was transforming.

Boomers had expected that, if they could stomach it, they could eventually find jobs as their parents had—solid, decently paying, available as long as you were willing to work. A life in one company, with raises and merited promotions, was a promise. After thirty or forty years of hard labor, livable retirement with a pension and perhaps a gold watch in parting. Good companies would survive and grow rich—and most American companies for the last twenty years had been such good companies. The biggest were the safest. A corporate life, no matter how stale the job, was a comfortable and secure perch from which to pursue the American dream.

It's easy for old people to wax nostalgic, often about things as they never were, but I know I believed that myth fervently. What I found over the next thirty years bore little or no relation to that vision. Big companies failed, and ruthlessly exploited most workers, discarding them like used husks when necessary. The biggest companies could be sold off and broken up and employees thrown on the street unexpectedly and overnight. Competition from overseas caused bankruptcies, or withheld growth and riches except to a determined and selfish few. What foreign imports did not destroy, automation did. What took its place was a cauldron of menial worse jobs with no future prospects. Most wealthy people—as in the great depression—were entertainers or con artists.

Full-time jobs were once assumed to be forty hours on-site with full benefits. Perhaps you were expected to work a little or even a lot more (especially if you were trying to climb a corporate ladder) but even the most stressed people found moments of absolute release and free time. "Normal benefits" was an expression often heard when being hired, usually by the person who was hiring you, (without going through "human resources," endless forms, standardized exams, and drug tests.) You would work out or you wouldn't, but if you were employed any job had certain expectations.

None of that is true any more. And in that respect, the social contract, which my parents believed in firmly and which was inherited by me and many of my generation, has been broken irremediably. We are holding together, it seems to an old guy, simply by inertia, and if I let myself do so I can become depressed by what I think will be the likely futures.

"So, poor thing, you think you're the only people ever caught in a generational conflict?" sneers Ghost, puffing out another white ring, lidded eyes half asleep.

"Never imagined such a thing. In fact, I believe that normal people were human. It's an elder plot."

"What!" Ghost glances up startled.

"Sure. Old folks go around always babbling about how 'We got it right and you don't have a clue.' Comforts their anxiety as they lose control."

"But, after all, they did shape your world as it is …"

"No, they lived their world as it was."

"Improved the world!" Ghost emanates enraged elderness.

"I'll grant they made it better, at least some of them, at least some of the time."

"You're incorrigible," he squawks.

"What are you so high and mighty about, now, Ghost. You don't have a dog in this hunt."

"Somebody has to defend the honorable dead," he mutters, with another long drag.

"Oh, I do that all the time. I don't say they were wrong. Just that they weren't necessarily right. They did live their own lives mostly well. I believe in the whole role model thing."

"Then what are you yapping about?"

"Well, by the time the next generation rolls along, social requirements are unrecognizable, their specific advice is useless, and a lot of times their general advice is way off the mark."

"But you are now an old person, yourself," Ghost points out slyly.

"Yeah," I sigh, "and I find my confusion about helping my grown children is only exceeded by my helplessness in figuring out how to do so."

It's impossible, after all these years, to know precisely what we did exactly when. Bright moments flash in memory, instants or afternoons etched clearly but disconnected with such artificialities as calendar dates. I'm not about any specifics, including this weekend.

One time we took my folks on one of our favorite trips to Gloucester. Out to corroded B&M North Station, rattling ancient diesel cars with smoky engines in their middle, a bit less than an hour up the coast. Walked with Mom through the neglected weedy graveyard nearby, then along winding picturesque streets, remarkably resembling those in Hopper paintings, until we reached the famous fisherman statue on the harbor. The rest of that perfect image dissolves into fog—where we ate, what we did, I'm not sure.

There must be overlays. We would visit Joan's parents at their summer cabin near Lake George where I recall riding the Minnehaha stern-wheeler with them one afternoon, beer in hand. But was this before or after the children came along? All activities, upstate and on the Jersey shore and everywhere except Boston itself are like that.

And, naturally, the conversations are even less easily placed. A sharp technicolor bit will come out of nowhere like some movie trailer, triggered by a random taste or smell or dying neuron, and we will say "oh yes!" But sadly, it all blends and vanishes into the past, leaving a vast jumble of our days together. On the other hand, I never had a desire to be Proust, excavating my past like some careful withered archeologist. The present is too much present.

I suppose that is why people take pictures—old photographs can rekindle some of these experiences. It would have been useful had I kept a careful diary of the times. But we were young, and such thoughts never entered our minds. We didn't plan to look back, we could easily remember yesterday, life was rushing along. So there are few if any artifacts to anchor with certainty.

Vast mounds of picture albums are as tedious as old racks of vacation slides we were once forced to endure. It is pleasant enough to dreamily recall what you can, to concentrate on people and places and wrap them in a golden haze. But life still streams along, and fortunately every day continues to engage me completely. I have little enough time to finish today, remember yesterday, and plan tomorrow. Perhaps occasionally refreshing whatever we can in our faulty wetware storage systems is the best solution after all.

I contrast ages. As I began writing I am sixty seven. In 1978, I was just thirty one, Dad was sixty one—always a shocking thought. I still consider sixty one fondly as part of my youth. We dragged them up and down hills, along the Freedom Trail, down to the waterfront, walking the Esplanade, hanging out in the Public Garden. Little rest, we were heedless of age, stayed on the go for days. I'm sure they left exhausted.

We talked incessantly, particularly Joan and Mom who hit it off well. Dad and I had a few intense conversations, particularly stories about work or the world, but the women never stopped and we were generally content to listen and take pleasure from their chatter. But blessedly there was little of the sharpness of earlier years. Life had begun to move in common directions and newly focused goals had a great deal in common. This was a particularly happy time, often leading to a letdown as soon as they left. Visit complete, we could no longer dwell in the imaginary circus land of the future, and had to face the grueling realities of normal day to day.

Ghost looks sharp in his striped suit and tie, martini in hand. He sips casually, swivels the bar stool to face me, pint of Guinness on the counter. In the background, I hear train departures being announced. "Pretty brave front for a couple of people with no money at all."

"Well, it's true our finances were tight—never really hopeless, we always paid our bills and ate and stayed warm and had income. But our hearts were pure."

"Ha. Surely you expected a lot more in a reasonable amount of time."

"Frankly, I didn't know what to expect. Nobody really talked about money, and even the ads were pretty coy about salaries. Heck, I never did know what Dad made. I just knew we would need more than we had."

"So you expected what—double, triple the pay?"

"Like I said, I had no idea of amounts. It was clear we would need a car at some point, and we would be living on Long Island where apartments might be more or less. Children would cost us more, of course. We didn't think of dollars but of future necessities. That was the measurement. Our own house, for example, seemed out of the question in the near future."

"Pretty poorly prepared, then," he laughs.

"Oh, naïve as hell. Other people made money, we knew, but nobody told us how much. Big hush hush in America at the time—your salary was as secret or more secret than your sex life."

"Odd taboo."

"Very. I never really understood it until I realized that other people measured success by comparative income."

"But not you."

"No, I was stupid or innocent, but I never cared. I just wanted a happy life."

"Boring."

"Not to me."

Distant echoes claim the 7:12 to Ronkonkoma is about to pull out. I would have some time to relax, if this scene just holds together a bit longer.

Children are not purchased as a kit with reference manual. Some are brought up perfectly and turn into antisocial destructive monsters. Some are raised in terrifying squalid conditions and become saints. Most just grow up, with influence but not control from their immediate families. We are privileged to experience multiple viewpoints—being a child, being a parent, observing the efforts of those around us.

I did not worship my father or mother. I admired them a great deal. I never wanted to do more than they did, or somehow meet whatever career expectations they had for me. Joan was much the same, although her brothers were in awe of their father's accomplishments. Eventually, as most people do, we reached easy accommodation. This year was one of the big turning points in that change of attitude. Consequently, there was still some tension. We were happy to see parents arrive, and happy to see them leave.

A lot of it emanates from internal outlook of life. I had a happy childhood, relatively exciting and interesting years as a young adult. I just wanted life to go on more or less the same way, no need for more. Like one of those provincial Tuscan peasants in movies. I knew people who instead aimed for every day to be better than the last, as constant test to excel, to outperform, to race and to claw towards a wonderful future, the present as merely a tool for what would be. Joan's parents—like many immigrants—were forced into that outlook. They did not come from happy Tuscan peasant backgrounds—rather miserable impoverished peasants. I believed life was basically good, they knew how terrible it could become.

We make too much of logic. We can bask in the accomplishments of ancestors, or hinge redemption on the triumphs of children. What I find, however, is that everybody and everything is far more subtle and complicated than literature and political analysis would suggest. People are unpredictable, but often constant, driven by strange motivations, or unconscious of motivation at all. Society is, in modern jargon, more like the Heisenberg quantum universe than the placid Newtonian one. Little makes sense, contradictions abound, and at any particular level predictions are impossible. Raising children is the prime example.

Ghost faces me on the crushed white stone patio alongside of my boyhood house as twilight falls. We lean back, listening to distant traffic, inhaling air fragrant with green, waving at mosquitoes beginning to whine about. Lightning bugs wink in dark corners of the lawn. "Very profound, very mushy, hardly accurate," he comments.

"I suppose you mean children. I agree it hardly matches the common viewpoint around here. I think sometimes I was born into the wrong country."

"Oh, c'mon, you're as American as apple pie. You'd probably be miserable as an expatriate. You like everything here."

"I know, I know, but I never wanted more. I just wanted things to stay the same."

"Ain't no country anywhere, ain't never been, where that's true," chuckles Ghost. "Life changes. The cavemen had to deal with glaciers arriving and receding, herds thick and thin. And they grew up and became old—just like you, only even faster."

"Well, the Tuscan peasant myth sounds good."

"A lot of myths sound great—look at Horatio Alger."

"Guess you're right, Ghost."

"I'm definitely right. You're just a romantic in a hard ass era. Your decision, really."

"Well, anyway, I don't care. Worked for me."

"Selfish bastard, aren't we?" Darkness falls before I reply.

Nine at night, they'd said goodbye and were back at the apartment. Wayne sat quietly with a glass of wine, unopened Sunday paper nearby. Joan busied herself with lesson plans for the next day.

So it was back to normal, whatever normal might be. As everything changed, as even their hopes were in revised, normal became an illusion anyway. Normal now was constant learning at work, constant turmoil at home, constant goodbyes to old familiar places. Normal was another day, another brick in the wall, and yet a straining to leave. Confusing and a bit enervating.

Anyway, normal from the standpoint that it was them and nobody else. No one to please for a while, except of course the bosses. Nobody to compare to, except their own self image. That, at least, was a comfortable and familiar exercise, even if disquieting on some particularly dark nights.

"Do you need help with anything?" he called.

"No, I just have to get my clothes ready. I hope I didn't gain any weight."

"Sure was a lot of rich food," he agreed. "But I think they had fun."

"I hope so. Mom and I get along really well, she's quite remarkable."

"We noticed that you talked a lot ..."

"You seemed more relaxed this time."

"Oh, it's all good. Dad totally approves of my career track now. Takes the edge off. I did enjoy some of his stories."

"Maybe we should have done this a long time ago."

"I don't know. Water under the bridge. We just go on from here."

1979 DELAYED TRANSITION

Ancient Boston

WAYNE AROSE EXTRA early this October Saturday morning, with much to do. Joan remained catching up on sleep as he showered and dressed, grabbed a quick breakfast, and paced down Charles Street toward the Common. Shops were just opening, crowds and traffic sparse. Stores along the way continued to mutate and upscale—already the used bookstore he had once frequented had been replaced by some trendy boutique. Old brick sidewalks still dimpled beneath his feet, and in spite of modern "renewal" he vividly imagined colonial settlers anxious for news from across the ocean.

Being joined to history was important, he thought, as he continued across the Common. Most trees were brilliantly turned by now, many already past peak, leaves crunching underfoot on the pathways. As always, he admired the gold dome of the Capitol to his left, and spent a moment reading the plaques on the civil war memorial. People who had died for their beliefs—or maybe others' beliefs trumpeted from church pulpits. He reflected how everyone ends coerced into the turmoil and persuasions of the day. The fresh social wounds of the Vietnam War had hardly healed. But it was always well to remember that war was only one of many social issues that people just like him had endured.

Deep thoughts, although continually inevitable on his strolls, were not his goal today. He wanted to see what might be in the book section in Filene's basement. He had a little extra pocket change, and if it was not exactly burning a hole in his pocket, it was at least keeping it warm. Filene's basement at that time was a wonder—forgotten items perpetually automatically marked down from the vast department store upstairs, until two subterranean caverns were stuffed with discoveries literally selling for pennies on the dollar. He and Joan bought most of their clothing there, elbowing through crowds of middle-aged women looking for—well—anything.

He didn't need more art books, he reminded himself. He should be saving up for another trip to the MIT bookstore to get some computer texts. Theory of computing and techniques of design were still sadly lacking in his programming toolkit. But who could resist what he had once found—a giant complete Abrams book on Hopper, for example, for a few bucks simply because a couple of pages in the middle were printed upside down. He still dabbled enough in art to enjoy leafing through pictures whenever he became discouraged in life.

He turned onto Washington, perpetually being upgraded from shabby to overlaid shabby, and went downstairs. The books were on the upper section, off to the right, and he was soon happily engaged for twenty minutes or so. But there wasn't anything that really caught his eye, so it would be a light trip back. There was still a lot to do this day.

The return trip down Cambridge was uneventful. He ignored gigantic barren government plaza with its hideous concrete fortress city hall—deserted, much of it roped off. Corrupt contractors had neglected to account for salt and corrosion, and almost from the day the expanse opened over the slums that once lay below, it had buckled and split, as if the spirits of ancient Foley Square tenements were seeking escape from their bulldozed graves. Past the lovely Otis building, and the library branch and on to Mass General, where he turned and was home before eleven.

Ghost leans back in the sticky brownish leather booth, beer mug half drained. No windows in the dim light of this neighborhood bar. "By then, you were beginning to appreciate days off on weekends, weren't you?"

"Really. My daycare job had spoiled me a little bit. Heck, early or late shifts would let me get things done while other people were busy working. And of course, at Kurzweil I had no commute. This latest one—yeah, it was a treat to have a weekend arrive."

"But you always had a hangover."

"No, not really. I know, I know, I was drinking a little too much."

"A little?" he comments sarcastically.

"Yeah, really just a little most of the time. Friday and Saturday, especially."

"But still too much on Friday." Ghost is relentless.

"Well, maybe I had a moderate hangover. But I didn't drink all that much the night before, and in any case Saturday was my real problem day, if I wasn't careful. My worst times in Boston were long before this."

"I'm amazed it didn't affect you more."

"Well, I was still relatively young, and I exercised a lot, and it was just what everyone else was doing."

"Always a good excuse," he wants to make that cutting, but can't make it stick.

"Yes, it was," I end, with satisfaction.

Saturdays were chore days. Do wash at the coin laundromat up the street, pay whatever bills had come due, straighten the apartment, clean the fish tanks, water the plants. Of course, Wayne and Joan attempted to offload to weeknights, but lately weeknights followed extremely tiring days, and they often had energy for little more than eating and preparing for next morning.

Every weekend, like clockwork, they food-shopped for the coming week, and unscrambled whatever unavoidable odds and ends had piled up. Saturday was rigidly scheduled, and exhausting. They frequently collapsed by evening, although they tried to manage a walk out to the Charles River.

Often, dinner came from an odd little place built into the vast blackened granite wall of the old prison under the subway tracks at Charles Circle. This presented a portal into infinity. A miniscule lonely window-sized serving counter punched through stone blocks was surrounded by signs advertising grinders, fried chicken, and just about any kind of greasy food imaginable from any culture on the planet. After taking an order, the silent clerk would disappear into dark depths for a few minutes and reappear with satisfying and inexpensive fare. They might felt guilty, but it was delicious and filling and they could take it to the river for a picnic, or home, or eat it right there on wooden tables under flickering fluorescent lights while enjoying an occasional deafening roar of a train going overhead. At least that would drown grinding gears and incessant honking of belching traffic rushing and merging around the traffic lanes. Fumes added to the flavor.

Sundays were a puzzle. They both wanted to sleep as late as possible, but also insert some entertaining highlight to their week. Maybe a bike excursion, a train ride, a visit to some familiar or unfamiliar spot like a museum or town. It helped them stick together in what had otherwise become a centrifugal world. In a weird twist, going somewhere on Sunday was equivalent of attending church—appreciating God and family in their own peculiar manner, blessed with secular benediction and grace.

Groceries finally unpacked, remnants of dinner cleaned up, darkness fallen. Wayne was reading with a glass of wine nearby in the living room, trying to decipher yet another incomprehensible computer manual. Joan finally got off the phone with Cheryl.

"So, Joan, what should we do tomorrow afternoon, do you think?"

"What's the weather?"

"I think they said not too cold, clouds but no rain. Typical early fall. The leaves are nice, maybe we should go out to Marblehead or Gloucester."

"I don't know. To get there we'd have to get up early for the train and I don't want to get up that early. Isn't there something closer?"

"Well, it's too cold for a trip to the harbor islands—besides, there's no color from the water anyway. I guess we could bicycle to the arboretum."

"Look, Wayne, I'm just too tired to do all that much. Something really, really, simple. I don't feel like a grand adventure."

"Oh all right. Let me think a minute. Is there anywhere you can think of?" That pretty much left a walk to the North End, or the Common and Public Garden, or maybe a ride to the Fens. Well, they could always head back to Cambridge and watch the crowds in Harvard Square. Or even just stroll up the esplanade…

Joan interrupted his musing, "Wayne, why don't we just go to the

Aquarium? We haven't been there for a while, and I can look at Quincy market to see what they have. It's not really too early to start looking for Christmas—you know how hard it is to find something for your mom."

That was actually a great idea. They had memberships to the aquarium and visited it a lot in the winter, when two hours in warm moist air while hypnotized by big fish and turtles circling the huge tank could seem like a mini tropical vacation. And the market was always changing these days, still new and sparkling and with the energy of all recently completed architectural conceptions.

"Great. I like that. Good idea."

As part of the planned transition of those years, we were making evaluations of what we really needed and what we wanted and how we could get what was necessary and desirable. A life in the New York suburbs hopefully with family would be an awful lot different than in Boston. It would require unthinkable investments—a car, for example. A change in shopping patterns. No more giant art books, no spending time at the aquarium or trips to historic seasides.

Life in any major city has certain spending patterns. Most income gets tied up in rent, much of the rest in food and necessities. But after that, life is nearly free. You can walk for anything, you can join an aquarium or museum for a small sum and get in for free for a year, there are always people doing something for nothing—spectacles in parks, fairs. The town itself assures that gardens are tended and flowers are usually blooming wherever possible. Life, once you have paid the rent, can be extravagant on a pittance.

We knew routines would adjust. We didn't know how much, but even the minor changes in our patterns were already affecting our complacent joys. Fish tanks, for example, would have to go—so no more shopping for guppies and swordfish and zebras—maybe emptying them when they got really dirty next time. The painting had already stopped—no more cycling to the Utrecht store for more supplies. Commuting costs were eating into daily cash flow, and there was a need for new clothes to dress better now that I was not a day-care worker.

No matter how much we tried to save, we could not make headway. That was the core equation, of being in the city where we were, because we could not cut back on rent, and rent was where most of the money had always been going. So we avoided extravagance, and for the first time started to feel as if we were almost poor, but additional nickels and dimes we deposited didn't grow our small bank account. Besides, hefty inflation was outpacing the interest rate, and what we put away and saved was worth a lot less next year in terms of spending power.

Noisy crowd, Ghost wanders back from the men's room as I nurse my beer. He grins crookedly, "Ah, capitalism. You have to work to live. A terrible system, a waste of human potential."

"What, you've been taking Marxism 101?" I chuckle. "Everybody works, Ghost. You know that. Farmers have to grow crops, kings have ceremonial or war duties, rich people turn summersaults to stay rich. Very few escape the wheel, and they usually do not escape to a happy place."

"But like a lot of people, you sometimes thought you were the one singled out for victimhood, right?"

"Nah, never a victim except of my own device. Everyone had to work somehow, and I still believed capitalism was working fairly well."

"I notice your use of the past tense," he remarks.

"Well, I'm not so sure in the modern world what work means. The 'real' work our parents and grandparents would recognize has vanished, and what I thought was necessary is almost gone too. Automation, robotics, globalism. Good jobs for a very select few. And yet the standard of living higher than ever. I'm confused."

"I don't think the world has changed as much as you think," Ghost states, pulling on his leather coat.

"Perhaps it has changed even more." We head out the door to the bright lights of Charles Circle.

Wayne and Joan discovered that an extended transition could be harder than an abrupt one. Their timing was hostage to pregnancy, which was taking longer than expected. What had seemed a fixed time limit stretched on

BABYLON WITH GHOST

and on and on. In the meantime Wayne furthered his career in programming by staying right where he was and growing into the job. Circumstances were temporary and subject to sudden reevaluation, but they had to accept actual immobility. That could create an uncomfortable dissonance as months passed.

Letting employers know they were planning to move down the coast was out of the question. If not actually fired, work life would become miserable. Maybe, somewhere in their minds, they also hoped for a miracle of some sort—they had no idea what—which would mean they could stay as they were and yet go where they wanted. It was an impossible vision, because completely contradictory, but it hovered tantalizingly in the back of their minds.

Doing almost anything long-term was becoming tiresome. Fixing up the apartment, local involvement, even ties to friends that would soon be all but inaccessible just seemed too much trouble on top of everything else. Yet they missed the dreams, the friends, the hopes of a better day, even if all a better day contained was another angelfish or new chair or crisp book, or shiny bauble from Quincy market. They hardly had energy to visit all the places they had been "one last time," especially being aware that any given trip might not be the last time at all. It was a padded and comfortable purgatory, awaiting the trumpet call which they were sure would sound momentarily.

Even simple things like eating were affected, now that Joan was paying attention to myths and legends of what to consume when trying to become pregnant. They both knew that when a child was on the way, her diet would be much more restricted. Wayne understood that once at her parent's house there would be no more homemade deep fried onion rings—in fact most of the food would just have to be accepted as provided. He had no idea if he would be able to drink wine as he liked—so did that mean he should gurgle as much down as possible now in a pre-Lenten orgy, or should he begin to adapt to the inevitable by cutting back. Dumb simple questions, but since they were raised constantly, they created a grinding friction affecting daily happiness.

Friends, of course, were aware of what was up, but what that really meant for young adults was that they would soon be moving out of each other's orbit. Before social media internet, that was almost the equivalent of planning to take a Conestoga wagon to Oregon and promising to write sometime from the new land.

Everything became short term. Maddeningly, the short term stretched on and on …

We were both deeply family oriented. Our underlying psychologies assumed that the real purpose of being alive was to raise children, no matter how irrational or selfish we might intellectually realize such a purpose might be. We were wired to believe that a family would make us happier than anything else we might do. We were level-headed enough to know that time was now marching on rapidly, and although the concept of a biological clock was not yet in vogue, we heard the cosmic ticking.

Part of it, of course, was to please our parents with grandchildren. They never put overt and heavy pressure on us, but the implications were always in the air. Joan's parents had no grandchildren so far, and mine only one. Both our tight little families, in different ways, judged ultimate success if not by quantity of descendants, at least by providing well for a sufficient number. Until we fulfilled our part of the bargain for which they had worked so hard, we felt quite guilty.

Driven by biological imperatives, we were ready to go. We had achieved what we had dreamed of ten years previously. But the train kept getting delayed.

Ghost sips from his glass stein as the afternoon grows later and the patron mix evolves, "Time to grow up, right?"

"Well, I guess you could put it that way …"

"And I will. You could have saved a lot of time by dealing with all this earlier."

"You're right," I sip also, "But also wrong."

"How can I be both?"

"We could have done so earlier. And yet, we look back, and almost everyone we know who did so earlier ended up doing so too soon for them—and they ended up divorced or otherwise unhappy. Not that there was anything wrong with their courses in life, but the point is they also were going encounter upheavals as significant as ours, just in a different rhythm. But, you know,

Ghost, I think it was really good to get all that out of our systems right in the beginning."

"Art crap?"

"Everything—fame, fortune, art, fun, urban life. Our twenties was the time to do that, and we took full advantage of them."

"But if you'd gone the straight and narrow path you would have made a lot more money …."

"For sure, but there would have been regrets. I treasure those years in Boston, in their own way, although I could never go back."

"You were lucky it all worked out," muttered Ghost.

"Maybe so, maybe so. But sometimes it is good to realize there is more time in your life than the anxious prophets of doom are shouting constantly."

Wayne returned to their apartment before lunch, Joan finally up and about. Both had agendas and chores to coordinate.

"I'll buy some of those great steaks," remarked Joan.

"Ok, I'll pick up some fish, I guess. Is there anything special you want?"

"No, whatever you come up with."

"We have anything planned tonight?"

"I'll see how I feel."

"Ok, later." Strapping on his backpack, he whisked down five flights of stairs to the basement, unchained bike from supporting pole next to burner, wheeled out wooden back door through cement courtyard with its solitary ailanthus tree, under corroded Red Line ironwork overpass, until he could finally start up Cambridge Street towards the center of town.

Bicycling to Haymarket was a quick ride, trivial when his pack was empty. It was a true pleasure in the summer when it was sunny and warm. But in the winter or when antediluvian autumn rains hit it could be a real pain, sometimes even forcing an expedition on foot. Fortunately today was cool, calm, and beautiful, only requiring a light jacket. He quickly curved at the Otis house before Government Plaza and was soon locking chain to lamp post.

Haymarket huddled behind an odd cluster of decaying buildings anchored by the ancient Union Oyster House. This was about the only traditional historic activity that had remained vibrant through urban renewal, abandonment of Quincy Market, and rot of wharf docks over the last fifty years. Somehow, the North End had held its own in spite of the travesty of the Green Monster, an elevated expressway plopped down by suburban government architect bureaucrats who never noticed what their wonderful roads might destroy. One tradition of the North End was manning pushcart stalls at the vegetable market. A surprising equivalent joy of suburbanites was to drive in to that market for food on weekends.

There were usually about two rows of fruit and vegetable wheeled stands, lining tight in the back of the row of restaurants and buildings. Maybe a hundred vendors, each selling loose tomatoes, lettuce, oranges, whatever, with a few fish mongers thrown in. Wayne had the idea they did it more for fun and petty cash and out of habit than necessity—nobody would really want to stand here in all kinds of weather and fickle crowds for the kind of return they were likely to get.

Underneath the buildings on the inside aisle, small meat, cheese and specialty shops resided in basements a flight of concrete steps down. Hawkers stood outside of each entrance, all but grabbing people as they passed by, as if they were selling forbidden drugs or fencing stolen wares. "Meat? You want some nice chops?" "Fresh chickens, only local!" "C'mon down, you won't believe what we've got today...." Wayne ignored them, that was mostly Joan's job, she was more particular about it than he was. Most of the time he went to the same exact store and bought the same exact boneless pork chops for his Chinese wok cooking.

Usually he took two full passes to gauge the current range of prices and merchandise selection. If he began too early, prices were pretty high, but quality of offerings was equivalent. Late in the afternoon, odds and ends were practically being given away, and the trick was to not buy too much to stuff into the backpack. The place was closed every other day, so by four or five o'clock, especially in bad weather, he could get a bag of cod for a dollar or so, more tomatoes or onions than he could use for some spare change. He and Joan always felt they never ate so well as they did in those years.

And it was, he admitted, really fun, especially if you were there every week and knew the ropes. The vendors were humorous, trying to pass time with pleasantry, knowing some of the same faces. The shoppers (in those days before the full explosion of tourist tackiness at Quincy) were also used to certain people, and trusted some more than others. Everyone was having a good time, most of the afternoon, and he happily passed an hour or so being entertained as he shopped for bargains, and figured out what he could do with unusual items over the next week.

He might or might not run into Joan, bustling along on her own to find steaks and other items assigned to her. Depending on the various states of their bags, they would wheel home either alone or together, Wayne wobbling a little under the shaky weight of the week's purchases in his backpack. If walking, this was by far the most difficult part of the whole afternoon, topped off by climbing those four flights yet again.

Even for an impecunious couple, there were countless possibilities, varying by season, incredibly rich and complex. Nearby were the aquarium, the science museum, the library, downtown shopping, Charles Street, Beacon Hill, the esplanade along the river, the Common and Public Garden. Not much further were all the tourist attractions like Paul Revere house, North Church, and hidden byways and rundown ancient industrial structures (which Wayne particularly loved.) It was never hard to spend a day walking, and views were always different.

If they got tired of that they could head to Copley Square and window shop Newberry Street, or go back to their old haunts in Central and Harvard Squares over in Cambridge. The Peabody and Fogg at Harvard were special treats. Short subway or bike rides would take them to the Fine Arts museum or the Gardiner Palace.

When the weather was nice they could cycle out the river, sometimes as far as Mount Auburn cemetery. If particularly bored, they could go to Quincy town at the end of the subway line, or cycle to Concord via Lexington, tracing the British march of 1775. On hot summer days, Joan could catch the Blue Line subway to the waterfront beach at Revere. In the spring and fall, Wayne could cycle out the Mystic River to barren parklands upstream. Once in a while they could go to a free concert, or an almost free ticket to a baseball afternoon at Fenway Park. Life seemed rich, and full, and distractions infinite and always changing.

Their longest regular trips were north of the city, to Gloucester, Rockport,

Salem and Marblehead. The Boston and Maine out of North station would run its old grimy and smoke laden WWII-era self-propelled diesel cars for reduced rates on the weekends, and an hour or so would bring them to different worlds. Wayne's particular favorite was Dogtown, an abandoned desolate and deserted wilderness stretch on the Ipswich peninsula, although he was once startled by a huge rat snake sunning itself on the trail and scaring him half to death as it reared up and slithered into the woods.

"Ah, nostalgia," remarks Ghost sardonically, coming back to the sticky wooden table with yet another glass of beer. "Always ready to cast its ideal golden glow over the troubled past."

"Too cynical an attitude, Ghost," I kept nursing my original. "Our stay in Boston was perfect and wonderful. In fact, in terms of day to day life, it was a completely fulfilling. It was always the future that bothered us, and that nagging sense that we were missing the boat."

"Trapped in the land of lotus eaters," adds Ghost.

"Exactly. It was magical, but the rest of the world seemed to be aging away from us. We felt we were staying the same and making the most of all our time, but even our close friends and acquaintances were having children, our siblings were advancing their careers, and our parents were getting no younger. And of course, the money worries …."

"So Peter Pan will have to leave Neverland…."

"We'd already decided to do that. This particular year was even stranger than the notion. Time remained kind of frozen, and yet it continued to speed by too fast, and yet nothing was happening fast enough. An odd ambience."

Every stage of life can be exactly what it should be, although what "should" might be changes all the time. To be young, free, and adequately (if not extravagantly) supplied with resources often takes first or second place in our memories (vying with childhood itself) as the best time of all. Some people cling to its charms for the rest of their lives, seeking to preserve the magic.

Awareness of time passing ruins that enchantment. As our twenties receded from view, "should" became radically redefined. Forsake the charming

BABYLON WITH GHOST

hedonism in which we were immersed. Climb onto the rocky shores of nasty (but maybe well-paying) employment and regimented (but meaningful) family values. Ah well. Gains require sacrifices, and neither of us wanted to reach old age without having tried to become parents.

There are those who push philosophies for all, who have a one-size-fits-everybody scheme of the meaning of the world and the purpose of their lives. Some are religious, some merely extend what they know is working for them. I always thought it the height of folly for a middle-aged person to attempt to force a child into a middle-aged outlook. I feel equivalent disdain for old folks who chant the value of motionless meditation to hormone-rich young adolescents, or young idiots who think old people should dance, work, and do more for the common good. There are stages to life, and the most useful philosophical track is to adapt to them. "When I was a child, I thought as a child...." And that is completely proper.

We must discover the proper time to adapt. Old warriors eventually leave heavy fighting to younger bodies; family patriarchs cannot flee mistakes as easily as adolescents. We assume responsibilities, we lose responsibilities, we find capabilities mutating or vanishing. Fortunate are those in a culture—like ours right now—who have the freedom of choice in such matters, and are not merely forced into anguish and forgotten death. This is one of the true tests of the worth of a civilization—what does it do with its citizens of all ages, not just the young and healthy who do OK in any kind of situation. A society that does not find place for all does not deserve to continue.

"You, of course, avoided conflicts back then by drinking too much," slurs Ghost, just a little flushed with a startling pinkish haze all over his somewhat wavering translucency.

"Well, yes, probably too much. Definitely too much. It was a kind of reconciliation tool where I wouldn't have to consider big issues and local pains for a while."

"A pretty bad sin, I would say."

"It's true. Too often in my life I resorted to alcohol as a combination sedative and therapy. I do not hide it. I found it useful."

"But you often took it too far," he accuses.

"That will remain a problem until some cure is found. I'm not quite sure if it is actually alcohol, or if it is having an addictive personality."

"Oh, come on," says Ghost, "you were never close to addiction to anything else, not even cigarettes. You never took even mild drugs more than once, and damn few of them for the times. But, God, were you a lush."

"No, Ghost, never a lush. A sometime drunk, a borderline functional alcoholic, ok. But I had rules and pride and I held to them, mostly. In Boston, I would hold off as long as possible each week, striving for Friday night, even if I slipped sometimes, but I knew I had to get up the next day, which tempered it all. And on Sunday I never drank at all, no matter how painful."

"But too much."

"I already agreed. I just thought it was better to stick with something legal and tested by countless generations."

"And you were ready to reform when you reached Long Island?"

"That was frightening, and remained to be seen."

In a glare of incandescent multicolored sparkles, Ghost slides to the floor and melts through the cracks.

The aquarium was warm and humid as always, although extremely crowded on this weekend. They had strolled back through the reinvigorated Quincy Market, a new and unusual showplace, looking at little items for Christmas and enjoying the emanations of happy people all around. Recession gripped the economy, but this little area was an island of consumer refuge. It had deep history preserved and mixed in, they had even stopped over at Faneuil Hall to wander through the colonial past. Joan bought a little figure for his Mom, and a scarf for hers. They kept trying to believe it was the thought that counts, not the actual amount spent.

As late afternoon shadows covered the bricks and cobblestones, they had chatted their way back to Philips Street, anticipating a few hours of doing nothing at all. Phone calls would be made, "yes, yes, everything's all right, how are you?" and Wayne would sink into the Sunday Boston Globe with its incomprehensible politics and excited sports and upbeat local urban renewals. Staying busy was the best way to only drink water, and today it had not been hard at all.

Tomorrow would be early, and difficult, and the week would fly by until next Saturday when exhaustion would once again greet the morning. But in the meantime, this had been a short respite of what had been in confusing projections of what would be.

Tomorrow would be early, and difficult, and the week would fly by until next Saturday when exhaustion would once again greet the morning. But in the meantime, this had been a short respite of what had been in confusing projections of what would be.

NIGHT CALL

INSISTENT TELEPHONE RINGS from the kitchen startled him in darkness. He stumbled out of bed and tried to get there before it woke Joan. They would keep this up until he answered. Why did it always have to be three o'clock in the morning?

"Yes, yes, I understand. I'll be there in about ten minutes."

A glance out the window indicated the hard April rain had not let up. Old clothes then—nobody would see him anyway. Throw on anything at all, rinse with mouthwash, grab the poncho. Down the stairs, unchain the bike, out the back door, onto slick streets. Lonely shadows and streetlight reflections might have been Paris, not that he much cared as the full force of the wind almost knocked him over, his plastic wrapping streamed out behind.

What did burglars think they could possibly steal, anyway, he wondered. You break in—it's not a commercial establishment, no cash. Everything has to be hooked up to something else to work, and if you did magically get the whole hardware setup, what possible price could an engineering mini-computer bring on the black market? Could there even be such a thing, complete with rogue James Bond technicians to keep equipment running? Did they have to steal every operating system update too?

The real treasure, were there any, would be the programming. He was sure no clumsy burglars smashing windows at midnight would be trying to suck out source code or carry away removable disks. No, it was probably just a dog or bird or something—even more likely the rain itself—creating a short circuit and setting off the alarms.

He wheeled along Commercial Street and pulled up in front of the low brick building. A police car sat with lights flashing, occupants secure from the wet. He knocked on the side window. He had keys, of course, so they stood in the lobby while he entered the codes, verified with Aaron on the phone that everything was clear, signed the necessary paperwork, reset the security system, locked up, and bid goodbye to the cops. The rain didn't notice. Soaked clear through now, he mounted and cycled back as carefully as he could, slipping on the roadway, keeping an eye out for late traffic, probably someone tipsy who would not notice him in spite of a dimly lit bike flashlight strapped to his leg.

Not much of the computer life he had imagined, he thought ruefully. Maybe he could grab a few more hours of sleep, with a good excuse for being late.

Gigantic, sunlit corner office, sleek modern furniture, immense picture windows overlooking a stone and tiled European cityscape. Ghost lounges back on a burgundy leather sofa, cappuccino in hand, dressed in among other garish oddities an unbuttoned yellow vest and bright crimson cloth beret. Scattered about are tripods, cameras, movie posters, memorabilia, apparently more as props than useful objects. "Ah, Monsieur Wayne," his voice fruity, "I have here the script, finally. A few questions. Edits perhaps."

"You've got to be kidding," I can't help smiling in amazement. "You finally have it all, I see."

"You do something, you do something right," he sings with a fake Italian accent. "This big long project, it may need a little pizazz, some prosciutto bubbles, no?"

"No," I state firmly. "No bubbles. Just what happened."

"Ah, but what happened, it was so much, it needs a theme."

"No."

"Ah," he ignores me completely, "and here I think I have it. Your attraction to older, successful men."

"What?" I holler. "Some kind of secret—even from me—sex compulsion?"

"Hardly that," he continues. "I mean simply that you always tried to find someone brash and successful so you could ride along with them. You never seemed to want to be the one leading."

"Ah, well, that, well. It's probably true," I admit. "I thought my best role was supporting people who knew what they were doing commercially. I had little talent for making money on my own."

"Not a mentor, then."

"Did Michelangelo consider the Pope a mentor? Of course not. I wanted a totally different, supportive sphere."

"But well paid."

"Paid well enough, anyway, most of the time. "

"A strange strategy."

"A strategy that worked, at least for me."

"OK. I can see that," he looks at me through squared fingers. "You're hardly leading man hero material anyway."

"Hey, I thought it was <u>my</u> documentary."

"Maybe, maybe. I, on the other hand, have creative control of how it is told…."

Things might have been set, had Wayne accepted a different outlook. Kurzweil was a fun and growing young company, cutting edge technology, on the right side of socially responsible, and an almost certain fast track to becoming a large and wealthy corporation. He liked all the people he met and was growing technically by leaps and bounds. Aaron had taken a fancy to him.

So he sat, like a caged bird, in a nice little office looking out on the road, and tried to find things to do. Without much of a raise he was now a building manager, and starting to be involved in ordering things and doing what needed to be done. It was a nice, solid, collegiate career opportunity, with plenty of room for growth either here or elsewhere if he did it well. There was absolutely no reason he could not do it well.

And he was unhappy. He wanted to leave. Desperately. He was finally finding a way to break out.

BABYLON WITH GHOST

But why? Because. This simply wasn't what he wanted to do. He had no joy in managing an office, dreaming of a bigger office, hanging out with more important people. Programming had become a kind of art disease to him, he wanted to program. He couldn't do that here. He was willing to drop it all for a chance to write real code for a living.

It was a mad and stupid move, now that the ducks of financial security could finally line up. But—well there was happiness to consider too. So he made his decision.

The vast thickly-carpeted corner office, naturally, had a grand piano in the center. Ray Kurzweil was an authentic Renaissance-type genius, a preternaturally gifted piano artist, an MIT graduate whiz on complex new forms of programming, and a financially astute entrepreneur. He was also a large man, dominating the room as he motioned Wayne to come in and sit down.

"Wayne, Aaron has told me good things about you. He thinks we should make an effort to retain you, that you are going to a big help to this company. And, you know, we have big plans."

"Yes, sir," replied Wayne. "I admire everything here very much and have been extremely grateful for the opportunities you've offered. But..."

"Yes?" asked Mr. Kurzweil, impatiently. No doubt he was doing this as a favor to Aaron, who was also one of his old college buddies as well as being financial vice president.

"The truth is, sir, I want to be a programmer. I don't see that happening here."

"Do you have any formal background, any courses?"

"No, sir, none at all. Just some work on a home computer and what I've been doing here."

"Unfortunately, all of our computer work is very advanced, and all of our technical employees near the top of their class. "

"I understand that, sir. That's why I'm looking for somewhere I would fit."

"Well, if that's your choice, then..." said Mr. Kurzweil, dismissing this small interruption in an extremely crowded schedule.

It was a really stupid move. Later on, Wayne would occasionally daydream that he might have been like one of those secretaries at Microsoft, offered stock instead of salary, become a multimillionaire in a decade. But, of course, he wasn't offered stock. This company wasn't Microsoft. And he pretty well knew that even if he had been in that position at Microsoft, he probably would also have walked away to find what he thought he really wanted.

"Thank you, sir," he said, edging toward the door.

No reply, as a phone call had to be answered while he let himself out into the second floor hallway.

I never knew if I had minor attention disorder or some other fashionable malady, but I was easily bored in most people-related jobs. I didn't like small talk, I liked doing things with my hands, I loved designing things with my mind, and conversation going nowhere quickly bored me. That made me a terrible fit for many positions. However, because I was always jumping around finding something to do, I tended to pick up all the loose jobs that were available.

So, most of the time, I could find something that would pay, and fairly soon I would be securely fitted into whatever new roles had come along. But that did not mean I liked it. I would look up and find myself encrusted with trivial, boring, dead end work. Stuff that the company was willing to pay for, and that provided a kind of status, but nothing I was proud of in my own dreams.

And I really detested being bored. By myself, I could easily be entertained walking or reading or cooking or painting or writing. But having to wait for a meeting or a phone call, sitting through a long lecture, filling out useless identical paperwork—well, that was a horrible to way to spend a third of your life, half of your waking hours.

Like any golden cage, there was always risk in opening the door and flying away. And I also detested too much risk. So the pressure had to become pretty great—or the opportunities too massive to ignore—before I would take a chance.

And here, in a pleasant little office with everything going well, the pressure from my internal hopes and daily passions had reached a point of explosion.

"So, what do you think the opening shot should be here? The most important first statement," asks Ghost stalking around the thickly carpeted space.

"Well, I guess realization of my place in life. You know,"

"What, exactly?"

"Well, some kids dream of being a pro football quarterback, others want to be Einstein or a famous political figure. But as you get older, you realize that you cannot possibly be one of those, for various deficiencies. You're not a genius, or don't have the athletic build, or have a personality that doesn't fit the requirements."

"In the abstract, anyway,"

"No even in reality. Mr. Kurzweil, for example, was a real live example of what I might have wanted to be, had I been something else. But I recognized fully I was not that."

"Pretty convoluted to try to put into cinema."

"I know, I know. That's why the quarterback thing works for most people."

"But you could have been something, perhaps, more than you were."

"There's always that, I suppose. America runs on striving to be the most you can be. I simply twisted what the most I could be away from making money or seeking fame."

"Sounds like a recipe for settling for something less than your potential."

"Yep. Some sure saw it that way."

"Not you?"

"On a few dark occasions, maybe. Mostly not."

"Well, I'll get script design on it. But no promises. Pretty abstract and boring."

"So go with the night ride."

"We might have to."

Wayne had found something he enjoyed doing, something that it looked like companies were willing to pay for decently. More importantly, he could apprentice at his age, and without certification. And most important, all aspects enchanted him—which made it all the more surprising that apparently few people wanted to get into the field. Or in any case, few people could actually do it.

At that point, it was hardly a question of finding the most perfect way forward. But, on the other hand, he was still not quite desperate enough— given this alternative opportunity—to follow anything no matter where it might lead. He suspected management would not be the best long term bet for either his fortune or his psyche.

One thing, however, was immediately apparent. He had arrived at the party old and late. The young lions in the programming den were fresh out of school, and jabbered jargon-laced gibberish and had immature temper tantrums. The most well-prepared—out of the best technical schools—were in fact some kind of geniuses, floating alone in the clouds of esoterica only they could understand. That was the reality of working for big computer organizations, anyway, or in coding pits of engineering technology. He realized early on that he was not about to break into any of that at his age and with his background, no matter how good he became.

On the other hand, the business world needed legions of lower level, less well prepared semi-geniuses. That was obvious from the ads in the papers. They were hiring, apparently, if you could tell a terminal screen from a keyboard. Furthermore, he had the advantage of a degree in economics, and could at least describe what a budget and balance sheet was, and even the experience in teaching seemed to be a plus. So it seemed it would just be a matter of trying out a few places until he found a better fit.

Cold analytical consideration of the most lucrative career never entered the picture. In that, he had not changed from the hopeless artist he had always thought he might be.

Modern industrial society trumpets its corrosive myth that "anybody can be anything." Wrong. Individuals have unique restrictions. They are limited by intelligence, physique, personality, and uncontrollable situations. A poor little flower girl only becomes a duchess in comforting fairy tales. Capitalism encourages any religion where promises are only fulfilled after death precisely so it can ignore poor flower girls.

The second most corrosive myth is that any of these "defects" can be overcome with desire and hard work. No matter how many weights someone lifts or how much one studies, genetics limit ultimate possibilities. A dwarf cannot play professional basketball. No matter how much education is fed into a mind, a person with low IQ cannot perform abstract mathematical analysis. And, I believe, trying to change a personality is just as impossible, though more mysterious. A personality that enjoys solitude must suppress natural gifts to appear an extrovert, usually retaining inner scars and rarely succeeding in the new external role.

I was mesmerized by the Greek philosophic goal of the good life. Use consciousness to best advantage for current and future appreciation and enjoyment of our universe. Without betraying that goal, try to find adequate security and control over my surroundings. Once those were accomplished— and only then—could I reach out to affect others.

I also believed that if I lost sight of those goals, no matter how much I accomplished, everything would degrade into useless junk. In the words of my childhood bible lessons, I would have "Lost my soul."

"Excellent!" exclaims Ghost. "I see it now! Brash young genius artist smashed by the world begins triumphant makeover ..."

"Well, that's fine if this is entirely fiction," I point out sourly. "It manages to avoid the fact that I was hardly brash, no longer young, recognized that I was not a genius, and had come to the conclusion that being an artist was an inner perception regardless of what the world thought of your artifacts. Before we get to the triumphant makeover you might as well throw in a gunfight, car chase, gratuitous sex, and space aliens."

"Ah," Ghost pauses and looks out on the tiled roofs, "ahh, this is, after all, being designed with a pseudo-European surrealist sensibility. I suppose we could stretch a little and fit in..."

"I'm kidding!" I yell. "Absolutely not! No. I won't have it!"

"It would be a lot more fun for everyone, you know."

"It would not be true."

"True. True. What is true, in our strange and unknowable world?"

"Sorry, I never got that European."

"Rewrite again," he pushes a button on his phone and waves me out of the room.

One reason Wayne felt he could make it as a programmer was because of his progress in The Game of Life. That takes a bit of explanation.

The home computer he had purchased came with BASIC language pre-loaded as part of the operating system—mostly it was the whole operating system. BASIC read all instructions line by line from beginning to end as soon as you typed RUN and hit enter, no compilation waits, no checks. There were books with all kinds of simple games you could write and save to an audio tape recorder (then reload if you wanted them later.) Some of these were pure text "Do you want to turn (R)ight or ((L)eft," for example, where an R or L key could send you to one of the next instructions.

But the fun games used graphics (black and white only, back in the dark ages.) For example, Pong—a game like tennis with a bouncing ball and brackets on each side of the terminal—could be played in BASIC using instructions that would "POKE" a given character to a matrixed pixel on the display. So it was simple to design (or copy) code from a book to compute the next square and tell the machine to POKE a round shape to location 128,50. These were thrilling for a while.

A more complicated situation was the "Game of Life" where an amoeboid entity would grow or shrink depending on the location of cells. It was a fascinating imitation of survival. Wayne thought it made a wonderful core for a game he wanted to code himself.

He lost himself in this every spare moment for a while. The idea was that while the amoeba grew, you could direct a spaceship around the screen and shoot certain cells to kill them. If you were clever, you could eventually make the life form vanish. If you were not, it would eventually engulf your ship and that was the end of it. A lot of things had to be worked out, without printouts of course, and tested, and he learned an immense amount about design and code and testing. So, that was the start, and it was a good one, and he was very proud when it worked perfectly.

But—well, there was a problem. It was slower than shit. The problem was in the time it took to calculate the next "organism" as it grew larger. The glacial pace of each iteration made it a very boring activity indeed.

So he ordered the coding for "assembly code" modules that could be incorporated. That was a whole new ball game. For one thing, that code had to be precompiled before it was run. For another, the instructions were incredibly simplistic and intricate. A lot of obstacles in data storage had to be considered. But—when he was done—the game finally ran beautifully.

Most importantly, in the accomplishment of that self-determined task, he considered that he had become a real programmer. He understood what they were talking about at work concerning compilation. He had at least a clue about the complexities of dealing with graphics. His esoteric jargon level had jumped into fluent foreign language. He had to read the magazines, feel like he was one of the guys, and by the end, all by himself, he felt somehow part of a community of technical professionals. All he needed was a job to confirm that.

Besides, he had learned over those dark and frustrating months, often alone late at night as the snow fell outside, that he had the temperament to deal with this. He understood now why a lot of people could not. For him, it was one vast game system. A game to come up with an idea, a game to design a computer program to implement it, a game to overcome the challenges of code and bugs. To someone else—well, it was awful once they got past the initial idea.

An advertised job for a computer professional was perfect except for one little detail. It was in Wellesley. That was not far if you had an automobile, but on public transport it was a long and sometimes desperate ride, especially going against the normal rush hours of people streaming into the center city in the morning and back out at night.

As darkness fell, he waited at the Wellesley Green Line trolley stop. The intermittent bus had dropped him here a half hour or more ago. He could only hope it would be more regular during rush hours, because just getting out to the small office in the middle of the town had taken almost two hours this morning.

It was a wonderful opportunity, even if the place looked like an old detective noir movie set. A small room held a brand new Radio Shack TRS computer, complete with disk drive and printer. It had not taken long for him to understand what they were doing and become excited. Fortunately, his various skills—especially non-computer ones—seemed a perfect fit. And the code was in BASIC, so he was pretty much home free.

The two owners had been running a consulting business for jewelry stores, with seminars on how to increase profits for small business owners. The key to their success was that these seminars were held in various attractive places such as San Francisco or Miami or Boston at the perfect times of year for each location. Because the seminar was entirely business-related, most of the expenses involved could be written off, so the net result was a tax-free vacation for the participants and their (employee) wives. Sure, there was a real product, and real advice, but a lot of people skipped out early and didn't much care. Anyway, through advertising and good will Jewelco had a very good reputation in that community.

One of the biggest issues of the time was the skyrocketing price of gold. Each day, it would climb to some stratospheric new high. And each day, jewelers were presented with a new headache—how to price their inventory in light of the change. They needed to know what to pay, what to charge, and even just what to declare for insurance purposes. With thousands of individual works, each containing a lot or a little gold, in various carat types, this was almost impossible.

Enter the small business computer. All they would have to do would be to enter each piece of jewelry as they acquired it (or sold it) with the appropriate amount and type of gold content for each. Then sit back each day, enter the latest price of gold, and presto! a completely revalued inventory in a few minutes. No more getting cheated because somebody walked out with an old piece purchased for a markup based on its original value.

The system was completely designed and mostly coded by the third man in the triumvirate—a computer consultant with a business background. All Wayne had to do, initially, was to turn on the machine, make corrections the consultant would provide, and help write the user documentation. Later, perhaps, he could actually help with coding the printouts and other various side applications that might become necessary.

He sat waiting for the trolley, excited and wishing and hoping that this would happen. The pay was better than he had currently, the opportunity was immense, and he would be doing exactly what he wanted. They seemed to like him, he saw rainbows ahead. If the stupid trolley would just show up, he could collapse and wait impatiently for the phone call confirmation he hoped would come soon.

"How about this," asks Ghost, waving the latest script book triumphantly. "Nobody understands the secret you, until you blossom."

"Fine, except I had no secret me."

"But you were good at declaring yourself something that nobody else would expect."

"Like what," I am a little curious.

"Well, like being an artist. Who ever said you would be an artist? Nobody. You just up and declared one day that you were working at being an artist."

"But everybody does that."

"No, everybody does not. Everybody else lets what they actually do define them. You are what you get paid to work at, you know."

"That's ridiculous. It is not what other people I know do."

"Oh yeah? How come the first thing you learn about anyone is what they do for a living? What they make money at."

"Just a social convention."

"You rejected social convention. An artist for years after it was clear you were not and would not be any such thing. Now sitting on the floor with some silly game and deciding you are a programmer."

"I was, in fact, a programmer."

"Nobody paying you."

"It's coming.."

"As your Mom used to say in April, so's Christmas."

Wayne overstated his qualifications, but how different could it be than what he had learned already? As it turned out, he knew just about nothing. He had never had to work with a disk operating system—and TRSDOS presented an immense learning environment, not least because it often did not work as the manual claimed. More importantly, he had never used a database. For him, storage and retrieval of data had simply been SAVE or LOAD the entire contents of program memory. Not so here.

He quickly had to try to come up to speed on the concepts of primary and secondary keys, field types, screen presentation and input. There were whole books to review on database design and usage. The problems of entry, retrieval, change, and deletion were a lot more complicated than he could have imagined. Backup became a paranoid process. Even though much of this had been partially done for him, he was drowning.

The most useful parts of the day, for the first month, became the long two hour commutes, where he had nothing to do but read and reread the manuals until they started to make sense and even the vocabulary became second nature. He somehow made it through the dangerous first weeks, when he would sit in despair trying to figure out what to do next, or how to recover from something he didn't understand.

Fortunately, the whole field was so much in infancy that even the consultant wasn't sure what was what. He had trained on "real" big systems, he wasn't quite sure what this toy computer could do. The theory of database design had not yet come to include reorganization, or security, or auditing. Wayne gradually realized that even the professionals were only a few steps ahead of him here, frantically trying to figure out the new rules themselves as they went along.

Of course the clients, his bosses, like the naïve everywhere had bought into the dream, not the harsh reality. The plans were clean and the vision clear. Inventory, computer, automatic. What was the problem?

The problem, as always, was the details and execution and above all the oversell. But at first, Wayne was much more like his bosses than like those who were familiar with the actual product.

"Finally," smiles Ghost, "something that I can use and will fit with how I dream this should be."

"Uh oh," I worry about what might be coming.

"We can shoot the Green Line sequence as a series of hallucinatory disorientations—rainbows and heightened colors. Perhaps intercut with hand held black and white shots from the commuter bus to add disorientation. Once in a while I can slap some jargon in big red letters, a kind of subliminal thread."

"But, well, I was completely logical and rational all the time."

"But you do claim you were confused."

"Yes, but rationally confused, if you know what I mean."

"Of course I know what you mean. Surrealism. That's exactly how we can present this. A poor logical Alice lost in surreal new technological jungles."

"I never, ever, felt like that. Just stupid."

"Well, that's Alice, isn't it?"

"I can't argue any more. It seems silly."

"Maybe so. But it will come across as true."

In the end, Wayne realized he was in way over his head. But, by the time he caught on, he understood that so was everyone else. He ended up covering the consultant, the consultant ended up covering him. His bosses came to trust him more and more as he found elegant ways to simply explain complex problems. His training with children helped a lot, there.

The original design wouldn't work. There were innumerable modifications, patches, workarounds, unconsidered realities. The vision itself required expansion—because every jeweler they brought it to wanted more than a simple gold evaluation system. Shouldn't they be able to note various prices— say the original purchase cost, the current insured evaluation, the planned retail price? Shouldn't the screen be able to do simple percentage calculations. Wasn't there some way to make the tedious entry of many similar pieces easier by keeping some of the data on the screen. And—well, let's not even think about the reporting requirements.

The computer system itself often failed. It would reboot for no reason, or for the very good reasons that the power blinked or the dust-filled room was sweltering. The floppy diskettes would become scratched and unusable, or unreadable simply because they were badly manufactured. The operating system and database might freeze or do strange things, necessitating calls to Radio Shack where most supporting technicians knew less than he did. The only really reliable information came from monthly magazines, out of date before they were printed.

But things moved along, and in a fairly short time Wayne was confident, the system could give a remarkable demonstration, and everyone was happy. Now the fun of sales could begin.

READY, SET, ... READY

WAYNE SLUMPED ON a bench looking over the Charles, watching the sailboats on a lazy August morning, heat due later. He reflected that this whole year had the ambience of the end of summer vacation he remembered as a child. Nothing was rushing, but nevertheless everything was ending in slow motion. Decisions had been made, leaving was inevitable, activities like resting here would become as distant memories as bike rides in the Berkeley hills years ago.

He was conscious that this was a time of "lasts." Any given trip to Gloucester or Lexington, even to nearby places like the Peabody museum, might be the last time he got there in his life. Or might not. But the plain truth was there was little time to plan grand tours. Weekdays were ferocious, nights were recovery and study, and weekends were taken up with chores. Neither Joan nor he had any residual energy to explore. Anywhere they might go they had gone to already, and they had little desire to find anything new.

Overall mood was a little sad, premature nostalgia. In movies people get teary-eyed over the last time they will be leaning on a favorite lamppost. But he accepted leaving places, forever more or less, even if he did not do it all that often. Soon this would be just another place, and another set of marvels would replace these.

He concentrated on trying to freeze these scenes, these thoughts, in his memory. But that was futile as well. He always did do a pretty good job of noticing and saving where he was. Still, time was moving on, and if anything the real last would be this period in his life, living more or less free, without children or major responsibility. The genuine farewells here were to an entire way of life.

I jump as a monstrously loud deep horn sounds overhead. Beyond this narrowly-planked wooden deck is nothing but brilliant azure ocean. I turn, startled by Ghost who stands at attention in a snappy blue blazer with embroidered cap. "Welcome," he calls, a bit too stridently, "welcome to the farewell cruise."

"You are a great fan of the dramatic."

"Ah, but it fits, does it not. Long, slow, always the same but due to end any time. Eat, drink, be merry for tomorrow—who knows?"

"Try to sort out your metaphors, at least, for Pete's sake. Are we on a boat or about to enter the gladiator's ring?"

"No, no, just a nice long vacation trip. Lots of time to see the sea. Many waves. Ah, who knows when you will look on their like again."

I stare for a few minutes. "But they're all the same," I note.

"No, each wave, actually, like everything else in this world, is guaranteed unique. Different number of molecules, untold differences in quark composition."

Patiently, I repeat, "they look the same to me."

"That's your problem," he offers a spyglass. "Your perceptions not finely enough tuned. But here is just like Boston, no? Days looking the same, never exactly the same, things to remember?"

"No," I insist. "It doesn't feel that way at all.'

"But it is, but it was, but whatever." He gestures around. "The time goes by, the days go on, you still need to eat and shit."

"Now ….'

"You will see. Ah, I must go." He strides off, leaving me alone on the deck with the wind and cries of always hungry sea gulls.

Most of the day trips were out of the question already. By the time they were done what they needed to do each Saturday, they were simply exhausted. Sunday morning they both wanted to sleep late and relax a bit. Ambition to do what had been normal for so many years was just lacking.

The closest things, like taking a harbor cruise, were still possible, but Sunday trips were a lot more crowded than the weekday ones they had been spoiled on before, and on a nice day George's Island was packed. Bicycling through Mystic to the strange open rocky forest parks was just too far, same with trying to get to Concord or Lexington. Mt. Auburn Cemetery became psychologically inaccessible, even though the bike trip was smooth and flat. Each of the outer strange trips they were used to taking, once in a while, became definite final visits if they could get up the energy to attempt them.

Day trips had once served a purpose in their life, a way to go beyond all the daily hustle, pleasant although inner Boston and Cambridge were. It was one of the reasons they had both liked Boston so much—you could escape relatively easily into suburbs or even countryside, by train by trolley by bike. Now, well, now a day trip was a day. A day they never seemed to find.

This would probably be their last ride on the B&M, Wayne thought as they headed to Rockport on the dirty, smoky cars. The strange diesel motors overhead in the middle of each passenger car droned and fumed, houses trackside quickly thinned, familiar stops crawled by as the lone conductor this weekend collected tickets from the sparse outbound crowd.

"We won't be doing this much anymore," he began.

"I don't know. This whole thing is taking longer than I thought," Joan replied pensively.

That was a reference to becoming pregnant. They had both thought it pretty simple—Joan would stop taking birth control pills and bang—things would move right along. But first there was a problem restarting the menstrual cycle, time at the clinic, medicine. Then nothing. Then testing sperm and some issues with slow swimmers. Net result—nothing was happening as they had imagined. Any time, possibly. Or, they began to worry, never.

"Well, at least I've had time to get a little more established here," he always emphasized the bright side.

"But I want to go home with Mom now."

"We will, we will. It's just easier if I have more experience. Otherwise, who knows what job I can get down in New York." Secretly Wayne was terrified of the whole project—not the child so much as New York City, place and work. He knew he didn't have many strong actual credentials at this point, and he was also worried about legendary traffic. He hadn't driven in years, still didn't have a car. And any son-in-law thinks long and hard about moving in with the in-laws.

"You may think so, but she's not getting any younger. She misses me. She wants grandchildren."

"Well, we are trying."

"We've been trying. Maybe we should just move down there first."

"Ok, I see the point. How about we go end of next year no matter what. That should give me a year to polish my resume and skills—heck maybe we'll be doing well enough by then that I can get a great job down there."

"Ok, I guess," she agreed reluctantly. "As long as you agree to the firm date."

"I do. I hope it all works out."

"Stop worrying," she said, for once. "It will all be fine."

Concentrating days resembled the end of vacation. Mixed with sadness at leaving current circumstances was excitement about fresh challenges. A tense uncertainty fermented into a stimulating tonic. We had accomplished all we wished as young urban adults.

What we had learned in the fifties were simplified fairy tales, with moral overtones. Horatio Alger was a piker compared to what was expected of "the best and the brightest" generation growing up in the most advanced, most scientific, most wonderful, most perfect society in the world. Mutations in society and science and everything else have, indeed, exceeded expectations. Whether good or not is still an open question.

Meanwhile, simplicity was also a casualty of progress. Biology, physics, all the sciences have undergone revolutions acknowledging the complexity underlying "simple" truths that we took for granted a long time ago. Societies and politics are not minor problems to be solved with technocratic laws of economics or control or slogans or even individual good works. Most especially, which philosophy should guide our actions is only valid for given situations and moments of existence.

Hedonism has always been a happy possibility for youth. Another is to fulfil a quest—being "purpose-driven." The very old often relax into pleasant contemplation, middle-aged folks bloat with hubris and certainty. All of those are correct, sometimes. A purpose-driven ancient crone is usually a cackling narcissistic monster. A supremely fit young adult wallowing in passive contemplation is a lazy lout.

We were metamorphosing to the next stage. It was not that we were finally getting better. It is not that we had given up what we believed in. The time had come to accept that we would now be in our thirties, and make the best of that decade, as we both felt we had of our twenties.

We're standing on a nice shuffleboard court, while old geezers amble around to look over the sea, a few of them striding off briskly and grim. "Isn't this appropriate?" gushes Ghost. "Shuffleboard is just like life itself, always the same and always different."

"The human mind is a wonderful thing," I reply ironically, "but also prone to idiotic comparisons, observations, and conclusions. This, I think, is one of the worst I have come across in some time."

"But don't you see how perfect it is?"

"No. Even if you could convince me, I don't think it would be much of a pattern for the future. "

"But. Even you have said life can be like a game ..."

"Maybe so, I don't remember that. But one difference between games and life is that games have rules, and some way to enforce them. There is also a clear goal defined as a win."

"Not life?" he asks.

"Not life. I'm not really sure there is any goal, other than to be alive.

Certainly no rules. Definitely no way to tell if you are winning or not at any given moment."

"Well, I thought it was handy and cute."

"Cute maybe. Meaningful, not. This is a lot like all the junk I see on the various media lately. Maybe you should try your hand on the internet—they don't care."

"Maybe I have already."

A chilly dense fog rolls in and quickly clears folks off the deck.

An unexpected and welcome outcome of their plans, Wayne discovered, was that family gatherings were less tense. Apparently, having grandchildren had been the elephant in the room. Now the elephant was fully visible, everyone was happy to be able to talk about it and to wander freely without bumping into it by accident and making someone angry or upset.

Joan and Wayne had always accepted, deep down, that the real purpose of everything was to raise a family. They just believed in taking their time. Maybe they took a bit too much time, he thought, but on the other hand there were so many other things to try out first. But, always, they had known that somehow they wanted to end up with a couple of normal kids, living whatever a normal life was. That was a goal far more intense than success, money, status, or even personal fulfillment.

But—well, they had both thought there was almost infinite time. Their twenties had rushed by, at least in retrospect, and suddenly they were getting old and had to think serious thoughts. Serious. Well, as serious as they could. But firm decisions had opened floodgates of parental gratitude. All stories now were about what they would be doing next, and all tone was optimistic and pleasant.

So when they visited either set of parents, carnival. Now they were joining the familiar club. They were treated as full equals, little to prove. Mature and taking on the world, for better or worse, just as their ancestors had done. Wayne found that change of attitude pleasant, interesting, and, just a tad, irritating. As if instead of doing all the wonderful things they knew they had been doing, they had simply been delaying the inevitable in a wasted interlude. Compared to tensions of years past, that was a trivial annoyance.

Deciding to have children, within a defined time frame, changes every-thing. Raising the child changes even more. Knowing one should be coming is almost a trauma. Nothing prepares you completely for the experience, but we both knew the habits we cherished would be scrambled.

As with many major decisions, however, a good deal of what must hap-pen remains tantalizingly in the future. No matter how inevitable tomorrow, today must be dealt with—and often today looks an awful lot like the day before and the days before that. We were still in Boston, still using the same markets, still riding the same subway. It was supposed to all go away, but the plain fact was that it had not gone away.

That curious feeling of transition, when you are between worlds, putting down no new roots but reluctant to pull out old ones. After a while, even the novelty of "this may be the last time that…" wore off. The shiny promise of new life dawning tarnishing into environments lingering.

"So there!" exclaims Ghost in triumph. "It was just like this cruise. Stuck in place, but going somewhere, and having left somewhere else."

"OK, I'll give you that much. What's with these metaphors anyway?"

"Like you," he says, "I am easily bored. Why not pursue my little plea-sures. The sea, is it not beautiful? A cruise can be a wonderful, relaxing thing."

"A cruise," I note, "is only relaxing if you feel you are safe and know where you are going. We were not quite so sure of that."

"Well, all metaphors have slight imperfections,"

"All metaphors are evasions of reality, which is always more complex."

"Ah, ah, look at the time! You must go get dressed for the evening meal.…"

"What?"

"Yes, yes, just like you had to keep eating and going to work every day. This ship, she sails on somewhere and you with it, but you still have your times to fill and duties to perform."

"You'd be a lot more fun," I tell him, "if you just relaxed and didn't try so hard for theatrical effects."

"Just wait until I end the perfect weather and begin the hurricane," he promises, moving away before I can recover my wits.

When they transferred to new jobs, neither of them had accumulated vacation. One week at best, begging a day here or there. Wayne had no human resources bureaucracy to deal with, and Joan's company was relatively paternalistic.

They had no time for long visits. For years now, Christmas season holiday trips to each parents' house were simply extended (or not) weekends. Travel, hi, how are you, bye, travel home and wiped out. Perhaps a few days for a summer stop as well.

Desperate efforts kept peace, but were enervating. Late Friday, they would rush out from work and travel two to five hours on public transportation, usually an ancient train, to Huntington via New York City, or to Gwynedd Valley via Philadelphia. Rarely they scraped up airplane tickets for a shuttle flight. Then it was back on Sunday, leaving no later than noon. A torturous and boring and interminable duty fulfilled which turned holidays into dreaded events.

Huntington was a lovely place. A block down the road was a harbor with a swimming beach. The neighborhood was crowded with neat houses already evoking an earlier epoch of American culture. A mile or so away was a little village. There was always a lot of food.

Gwynedd Valley was a lovely place. Nearby were open fields—until recently farms—where houses were built on extended and ample lots. Within easy driving distance were historic and beautiful reminders of America's past. Wayne and Joan could walk a mile or so and be in open horse country, Wayne recalling many runs he had done here over a decade gone. And there was always food.

Wayne and Joan both knew they could never afford to live like that.

For each of them, there were moments of déjà vu and crystalline remembrances of times past, overlaid with a patina of instant nostalgia. All seemed eternally the same—only they had changed. But that, too, was illusion, for everything else had changed as well. From psychological necessity, in their own minds they clung to a hope of stability elsewhere, since their own world

BABYLON WITH GHOST

seemed in turmoil. These were anchors and roots. Anchors and roots should not move.

Leisure activities fell by the wayside. No matter how much time was freed up, it all disappeared into the maw of new activities. For Wayne there were vampire commutes, sucking three or more hours out of each weekday. Then the necessity to learn lots of new stuff, even when at home, for both new careers. Finally, and most unexpected, were the medical necessities of testing and follow up to see what was going on with delayed pregnancy. Visits to clinics, conversations at home, more exotic reading.

Their world constricted. It was a pleasant but tiny place—Beacon Hill, the Charles River, the Common, Haymarket and Faneuil Hall. Extended fringes of that kingdom might still include Harvard Square and Washington Street with Filene's and the Arts Museum. But inevitably, they found themselves too tired to often take advantage of anything beyond easy walking distance.

I'm stretched out on a brightly striped canvas lounge chair, Ghost offering me a clear plastic glass of fruity red stuff. "Here," he says, "try one of these. You deserve it, poor thing."

I struggle to sit up, "But I don't want …"

"Sure you do," he insists. "Take a sip, relax. You're having a hard year. All these upsets, all this uncertainty. I know how you must feel."

"But I don't have time to just sit here."

"All the time in the world," he replies. "These dreams don't count in moments."

"Well, all right—not bad, what is it?"

"Black cherry soda and vodka—what, you think I'm a bartender?"

"Better than I would have thought."

"Well, fortunately, you have no palate anyway."

"Anyway, I was sitting all the time, it seemed. Sitting at work in front of the computer, sitting on the bus, sitting on the trolley, sitting as I read documentation. Compared to working in day care—even compared to working at Kurzweil—it seemed all I did was sit. I need to get up and walk a bit."

"Rest, rest."

"Too much of that," I argue. "In addition to sitting and sitting, it seemed nothing was moving along. I was ready for it to move along, I yearned for it to move along, but nothing happened, day after day after day. Just sitting."

"Welcome to the bourgeois lifestyle," he laughs, drifting off to serve one of the other passengers.

Wayne soon felt like he was living in some kind of infinitely long, endlessly extended farewell concert tour. Every day, every month, every place he would walk by thinking "all this will go away and I will never do it again." The Red Line, the Charles River, Harvard Square, the Long Wharf—so many things to bid goodbye. And yet, every day, every month, every season he would find himself going by the same places, thinking the same thoughts, over and over.

On most farewell tours, the old songs are repeated ad nauseum, and few new tunes are written, none are produced. They didn't have energy to attempt anything new, no projects for life or apartment, no dreams of finding more hidden treasures of experience. And once they had said goodbye to hard to reach places—like Rockport—they had little desire to make the trip again.

Consequently, they continued to find their empire collapsing inward. The farthest reaches had been reviewed, and besides they were often tired. They kept up a happy appearance, but both wondered when would this long enervating expectation finally burst into bloom.

Deep night, brilliant stars overhead, Ghost puffing his pipe, me relaxing on some soft deck chair with a glass of wine in hand, warm, and content and just a bit tipsy.

"Sounds to me," observes Ghost, "that you were getting old pretty fast."

"I have to admit that I had felt a change. Sounds silly, doesn't it? I was only thirty two."

"Well, that was older than you had ever been."

"And a completely new psychological decade. I did feel I had left youth."

"You certainly took your time, reaching maturity," he notes.

"Oh, I never reached maturity," I insist. "Besides, I'm not particularly excited by what this culture calls maturity. No, not maturity. Just a different stage than when I was younger."

"I see. You're one of those people who still thinks they're middle-aged at seventy five."

"Possibly. Doesn't hurt anyone."

"But you were tired. And stuck. And acquiring numerous obligations."

"Yeah, that's true.'

"Getting old, I say," Ghost knocks some ashes out, and we both sit watching the night go by.

Sunday night again, already. Nothing to drink again, early start tomorrow, again, the alarm set for five forty five. Looked to be a cold and frosty day. Still time to review some of the operating system, a few bugs to deal with already.

Wayne was sure this would be a good week. He was finally getting a handle on some of the esoteric parts of the operating system. Of course, almost every week he had gone in expecting it would be a good week, and almost every week he had been unpleasantly surprised. The advantages of being an optimist, never expecting the past to repeat. Anyway, he had survived so far, which he could only hope would be a prediction for the future.

The changes necessary for sales were beginning to stack up. Jim and Dick were getting touchy. Bob was less cooperative with them—but more friends with Wayne, because he could pass off some of the blame and just generally complain about poorly communicated requirements. That would not change for the next three decades.

But it was still fun, still a challenge, still something more to look forward to than to dread. Joan was finishing up her stuff, he started to clean his books and pack the backpack for tomorrow.

LATE EXPECTATIONS

FRIDAY NIGHT, WAYNE sat with a glass of wine in the back studio, surrounded by paintings, canvas, paints, brushes, sketchpads. His incomplete final piece hung on the wall in front of him. He hadn't worked on it this week. It wasn't developing the way he wanted anyway, inspiration drained away.

This "career" was finished. Heights had passed a couple of years ago, after which he ruefully accepted that professional fine art was a dead end career for him. He missed the intense internal fires, momentary passions for work and hobbies were poor substitutes for a self-directed drive to excellence.

This dark introspective night, he could not be consoled by dreams of future normality. His art had not been about success, or money, or even recognition. Art was binding of artist and universe, regardless if any other audience ever noticed. He was glad he had created so much for so long. Tangible results like this canvas could travel with him the rest of his life.

But—his art didn't pay the bills. Didn't put bread on the table. He had thought the compromise of teaching day care was brilliant—enough to live on, a socially acceptable day job, something that he actually liked doing and was good at—but their expenses kept growing, and now projected lives required much more cash.

So he sat, quietly remembering, not quite drunk, not completely sober, contemplative as one of those ancient sages gazing at the moon while they consumed plum wine as depicted in Chinese ink scrolls. He gazed at what he had been and what he had wanted to do. The moon through the streaky glass was interrupted a late subway crashing out of its tunnel. Time to leave the pavilion.

I'm standing on a rock, surrounded by white cliffs and boulders, squinting in harsh sunlight. Squinting, in fact, at a radiantly reflective white robe in front of me. Ah, Ghost and his tricks.

"And this is?" I gesture around me.

"What, you don't recognize it?"

"Never been any such place. Limestone desert? Looks a little like some of southern France, I guess. Nope."

"Welcome to Delphi."

"The oracle?"

"None other."

"And to what," I ask wearily, "do I owe this odd pleasure, if it is to be such?"

"Now, now, weren't you just saying how you wanted to figure out your future course?"

"No, not exactly."

"Sure you were. Giving up your artist dreams, looking for a more lucrative occupation."

"All right. And for that I need an oracle?"

"Better than logic, kid. The logical counselors are almost always wrong. "

I point to the sign carved in rock, in English no less, <u>Know Yourself</u>. "That could be taken sarcastically, you realize."

"Haven't a clue what you mean."

"Well, as in please give me some water—get it yourself."

Ghost turns majestically and strides carefully down the path, sandals sliding on pebbles. "Sorry, have to make it in time for the sacrifice. See you later."

Wayne had early planned to become bourgeois, since his middle-class family seemed wonderful. He had never fixated on a career, but expected to be somewhere in science, or business or perhaps law. A wretched transition after high school had thrown him into being an artist by default, although he retained enough sanity to be able to earn his living in any way possible. He had come into teaching through a back door. As he explored the byways of corporate life, he resignedly noticed he was back where he started.

Joan had been the one with burning straight-arrow plans, following a standard process to a known goal. But that too had turned to ashes. Times were tough. Fate is cruel to some, and although cousins and friends and others much less dedicated than she eventually did get the position she craved, doors never opened and Joan would go through her career as an outsider, never allowed to do that which she yearned for and excelled at.

As a result, they were both skeptical about any long range advice and projections. Wayne because he knew how wrong things could go, Joan because she had hit so many walls. They saw everyone else begin to succeed, but they had hunkered down perhaps a bit too much in their various disappointments.

By necessity, they tended to be very conservative with money and dreams. Milk each day and week and year for all it was worth, enjoy what is freely available, but don't count on raises or good jobs or promotions. Such had never showed up in the past, in spite of rosy promises. Their leap of faith to Long Island was one of the most daring things they had tried—against psychological profiles—in a long time.

Wayne and Joan luxuriated in visiting the still-shiny-new aquarium during bleak winter afternoons. The balmy moist air invoked tropical relaxation. Slow-moving giants in the gigantic central salt-water tank, even brilliant exhibits of curious fish in tanks along the walls were comical and calming. Concrete walls and the structure's acoustics somehow kept the tone quiet, in spite of occasional yells of gangs of children. They had been members for years, and could dash in for an hour or two all the time without having to spend a nickel.

"Well, guess we won't have this much longer," commented Wayne, looking around with pre-nostalgic regret.

"We can always come back to visit, I suppose," replied Joan.

"Easy to say. I don't know, people and places just seem to fade away into my past. I can't imagine trying to go back to—say—high school for any reason."

"Not even to see what happened to your girlfriend?"

"Especially not to find out what happened to her. All gone. How about Danny? Will he be around?"

"No, I think he moved somewhere."

They had each had the adolescent affliction which believed that first love was going to be love forever. They had each run soon enough into adolescent reality. In a way, it was good to have become cynical about the whole phenomenon relatively early.

"It's funny, you know," said Joan. "I was really in love with him like I never was with you. I mean, you were a good friend, you grew on me, but it wasn't that kind of love. Did you ever feel that way about me?"

"No, not exactly. I think the thing was I never again gave up the rest of me to center on you. I kept my own life, my own ideas. So did you. That's probably why we argue so much."

"We don't argue all that much."

"Yes we do …"

Well, that could go on for a while.

"But at least we managed to find a good partner for life. That's what matters," noted Joan.

"And the sex. Not making love was pretty frustrating for me for a long time."

"Well, you get enough now, at least when the thermometer says so." That was the prescription. If Joan was anywhere near ovulation, copulation was required every day, without fail, no matter what. It could, surprisingly, become a tedious chore.

"I hope that all works soon," replied Wayne honestly. "I had no idea it was going to be such a complicated thing."

They turned to the tank where a scuba diver began to feed various tidbits to large fish, ignoring the huge sharks constantly swimming by. Spectators clustered about, with morbid anticipation of something exciting happening.

By now, we had grown so comfortable with each other that we hardly noticed how odd that fact was. Not that we had different backgrounds, not even that we managed to keep our own private ambitions and spaces without too much friction. But simply at how differently our family life and expectations had turned out from what we had imagined a short decade ago.

We had each been through romantic passion turning to ashes and despair, and had no desire to relive that trauma ever again. On the other hand, we had begun to realize the importance of someone who is absolutely with you no matter what, and with whom you can argue honestly. Somebody you can trust all the time. Support in bad times, a necessary bucket of cold water when dreams were running out of control. Especially as everything began to change.

The world, of course, was exactly the same, as it often is. But a change in outlook moves us into another dimension, a different planet, as surely as any warp drive or alternate universe machine. What we notice, what is important, what we ignore change so completely that a rock in our hand is suddenly no longer a rock. Nothing is as it was, and yet everything to an outside observer is exactly the same.

But we had grown up on the same movies, the same books, the same expectations. Others we knew had found immediate gratification in soul mates, were married long ago, had children growing furiously. But—well, not for us. Anyway, some of those ideal couplings were rumored to be less wonderful than they seemed, which turned out to be true in a later round of divorces and breakups. The books and myths in those days hardly touched on break- ups and divorces, it was all find prince or princess charming and things will be happy ever after.

What was certain already, to both of us, was that plans rarely turned out as designed. That was why we tended to be so cautious about change—we knew what we had, we knew the risk, and we were happy enough not to care- lessly give it up for a couple of magic beans. But—well sometimes it turned out there was little choice. The world might not change much, but our per- ceptions of it clearly did.

Ghost is back, waving an olive branch (stupidly with olives still on it)

chanting some gibberish, gazing sightlessly into the painfully clear blue sky. "Ahh, ahhh, ahhhh, fortune beckons, ahhhhh."

"Give it up," I tell him. "There's nobody else around to impress, and I sure don't give a damn. You're just plain silly."

"Don't you want the advice of the oracle?" he asks, sweeping both arms dramatically as an olive falls on his head.

"No, thank you. Aren't you the fella that foretold a mighty empire would fall without bothering to note which empire he was referring to?"

"Um, yes.'

"And lately, I hear, scientists have ascribed most of these visions and pronouncements to hallucinogenic vapors coming from the cave."

"Mysterious are the ways of the gods," he intones.

"Right. Mysterious are my ways as well. If you promise to go away soon, I'll listen to your pronouncement. Fair enough?"

Ghost spins five times and staggers to one side, slips on pebbles, and falls onto his tree branch. He sits up slowly, hands scraped and slightly bloody. "I'm all right," he begins.

'Naturally, Ghost, you're a ghost."

"Ahhhhh," he moans again, "Lives will change for the better."

"I don't suppose you could specify exactly for whose better, or how changed?"

"No. Ahhhhh, happiness will abound"

"Same question."

"No. Ahhhhh, children bring fortune."

"Good or bad? Never mind, I've heard enough. Go take care of yourself. I guess they haven't invented band aids around here yet. "

He stumbles down the path, weaving slightly, the chant rising in volume as he vanishes around a huge jagged boulder.

Wayne remained stubbornly anti-capitalist. He treated money as a convenient tool, not a goal. He adjusted expenses to what he had, he adjusted income to what he absolutely needed. Money was never a yardstick of success, even in jobs for which he was getting paid. A severe handicap, not to mention social blindness, in a culture which worshiped wealth.

He was disappointed with annual raises (common in that era), as at Kurzweil. He could also be unhappy with his initial salary, as at Jewelco. But he did not possess the aggressive nature to bargain at such times. He mistakenly thought his work spoke for itself. It did not, of course, or at least not much, so other more aggressive, self-centered, confident associates usually won more valuable prizes.

Wayne did set an absolute internal floor on wage and conditions—and would walk rather than fight if they were not met. That unnerved several employers through the years, who just did not understand his mechanics. On the other hand, quite often times he was fairly treated and paid quite in line with the market. A few more dollars or switching jobs frequently might have generated more unhappiness than they delivered.

My real work challenge was rarely money, but rather environment. Having a career much in demand, I had the luxury of being able to leave if my environment became toxic. I figured I was spending a third of my life actively in a job, and more than that if you counted just getting to and from the office or thinking about problems or dealing with issues during off hours. I swore not to let employment waste the experience of my life.

Like a knight of the round table, I counted each day as a quest out of the gates of Camelot to adventure in search of the holy grail of ultimate security and stability. A day became a series of trials to be met, complete with fair damsels in distress when their terminals froze, or angry dragons bellowing from the front office to be dealt with by pulling out the thorns of software bugs and soothed with the balm of honeyed jargon and promises (only rarely slain by stranding them and their broken systems). Then I would ride back, having made the world at least for the moment a better place. And, more importantly, having had a rousing time doing it.

Of course, it was impossible to constantly sustain such a fantasy, but surprisingly, that general mood was far more often true than false. I can honestly say I hardly ever got bored—I always found something else to work on in hopes of making things better. Most of what I touched was improved—I was never good at simply talking my way out of real problems.

Like a technological Don Quixote, I became an expert at shaping my world to exactly resemble what I expected, and happily living in that fantasy. Each day became a set of minor triumphs over great odds. Each path became a way to a bright and wonderful future. For the times, it was a pleasant and useful way to get through some situations that could be decidedly boring and ugly to anyone with a different outlook.

Infinite stars burn clearly in the crystal black sky. Down the hillside echo shouts and laughter around a large bonfire shooting occasional spark fountains over the surrounding rocks. Ghost and I are sitting apart in the chilling air, sipping watery sour wine from bowls. "Seems you've found a decent gig here," I mutter. "Does this go on all the time?"

"Nah, the boys are just letting off a little steam. We can celebrate the end of one of our main festivals, filled with demanding tourists and anxiety. Predicting the future is not easy, you know."

"Oh, so you claim to predict the future now?" I ask. "I sure could have used you back when I was going through such confusion."

"I disagree," Ghost dips more of the noxious liquid from a pottery krater. "You don't want to know what is going to happen. Besides, it all worked out fine, didn't it?"

"But you make a living doing predictions," I protest. "Are you so cynical?"

"Look," says Ghost, "it's a business. At least for those of us who need to keep it running. Basically, it's simple. If the client is rich and powerful, you tell them what they want to hear, as ambiguously as possible. If they win, we get lots of expensive gifts down the road. If they lose, we never hear from them again. Unless ..." his voice trailed off morosely.

"Unless?" I encouraged.

"Unless they lose and somehow survive and come back full of fire and brimstone," he shuddered. "That's why we try to keep things ambiguous. Of course it was a lot easier in the old days."

"How so?"

"Oh, before writing, nobody remembered exactly what we said anyway. Those were the days."

"Even now, then, I cannot use you to tell me what is going to happen."

"Of course I can tell you what is going to happen," he retorts. "You will live out your ordained days and die. That's the easy part, but no mention of how long. 'The gods assure that you will be remembered appropriately forever.' That's the part that can't be checked by the relevant party. But more important, it indicates that if you remain famous for a while, your relatives will bring us gifts. If you drop out of memory instantly, even if other potential clients know what we said, that 'appropriately' lets us off the hook because, well, you deserve whatever you got."

"Neat," I exclaim.

"It pays the bills." Ghost takes another deep draught of wine.

"Wait up," called Joan, as Wayne hurried along the empty road. "I want to look at that lavender shrub over there."

They were surrounded by flowering trees and bushes and borders this warm May Sunday afternoon. It had been a pleasant ride on the bicycle paths along the Charles, on the West Bank to BU, then across to the bridge and up past the Harvard rowing area all the way out here to Mt. Auburn cemetery. Mt. Auburn, apparently, had world-wide fame as one of the first planned garden "resting places", and was filled with more vegetation than gravestones and elegant monuments. Their bikes were chained back by the main gate as they strolled around the manicured grounds.

Wayne loved cemeteries, particularly old historic ones. This one, of course, was a scant one hundred years, not like the ancient burying grounds nearer the center of the towns. They had their own charms, and more famous names. He reflected that the known famous names are almost always from when a land is nearly depopulated. Perhaps they merely stood out more from a sparse crowd, or maybe living in wide open society made people capable of greater achievements. But the illustrious names commemorated here were forgotten, compared to, say, that of Paul Revere or John Hancock.

His Mom had passed this on to him. He wasn't sure what she most enjoyed about walking among gravestones, but for him it was a kind of Buddhist humbling. You are nothing, all vanity is illusion, the world wraps infinite continuation. The rich and famous had been laying themselves here (figuratively, anyway, since the actual work was normally performed by the survivors) for quite a while. Their splendid statues and well-crafted epitaphs on imposing monuments were designed to reach out and recall greatness. Yet, truly, the only real remnant was the splendid landscaping, which attracted students and others in droves especially in spring.

You read the signs, calculated dates, and thought about lives, some painfully young, some amazingly old, and realized that it didn't take thousands of years and a bare desert to become Ozymandias. A few decades would do to be completely forgotten and irrelevant for even the most mighty and powerful. A year or so for everyone else. None of the young typically wanted to think about that—well hardly any of the old did either. Mortality could be a touchy subject, unless one believed that this world was a mere prelude, a tryout for the big time in heaven. If so, whatever remained behind didn't matter much anyway.

Cultural immortality was a fraud commonly accepted. A pleasing myth. "Heroes will be remembered forever." Until they are not. But they had their stones and their engraved stories and their statues.

These were the lucky and successful exceptions. Most people, if buried properly at all, ended up in small plots recycled every century or so, unless by some fickle whim of fate they became tourist attractions. In most graveyards, the plots were recycled every few decades—a hundred years at most—space being at a premium. No survivors visited by then to leave flowers. Nobody walked by to remember. Most places are full of the relatively recently dead, in spite of the constant advertisements of perpetual rest and care.

"What is this?" asked Joan.

Wayne walked over, trying to identify the plant. That had been one of his hobbies these last few years, learning the names of trees and major flowering plants. "Probably some kind of magnolia," he hazarded.

"Beautiful."

"Very nice," he agreed.

They wandered on, engrossed in the quiet beauty of the day, thinking not at all of death and only of the new blooming life around them, and enjoying the frequent lovers sitting or holding hands on the winding pathways. Life, they thought, is for us right now always.

Necessity versus integrity is always a problem at crucial points in life.

For example, should I remain true to my dreams or adjust to what seems to be a reality that destroys them. All of that, of course, complicated by the fact that we have many dreams, and many of them are conflicting. Which take priority?

You want to be happy? Make money. But the time and effort to make money might leave you unhappy. And how can you be relatively sure that anything you do—no matter how much it conflicts with what you would rather do—actually will bring forth the changes you desire?

For example, if you want to be an artist, you can create work for years, living on a shoestring, getting nowhere. Many artists do. Then a lot of them grow up, get a different career, and do just fine. But some do badly. And a few, who stick it out, succeed as artists. There is no easy path.

I had wanted to be an artist, mostly so that I could do what I wanted. But I also wanted the security of a family, and a relatively comfortable lifestyle. When one began to preclude the other—well, in spite of the conventions of novels it was hardly a blinding flash. Just a gradual awareness of change over days and months and even years. And what happens then, often, is that by the time you consciously make serious decisions, you have already made them deeper down. Otherwise, change rarely works.

Some original elements of personality remain, no matter what the outer manifestations. I was, for better or worse, a relatively contented person with almost no envy. Perhaps I had a few degrees too much empathy—no matter what lives I saw in others, I tended to see problems as well as wonders. I was never willing to trade places. I suppose that is an asset spiritually, but it tended to manifest as a serious lack of aggressive ambition. Knowing all the possibilities also tended to make me more risk-adverse than I should have been, in a society that placed a premium on risk. To me, a bird in the hand was worth all the others in the bush.

But the years went by, and I realized gradually that I was hardly exceptional, I was not going to do anything spectacular, and my art was slipping rather than nearing a goal. Giving up dreams is easier if they have become tarnished. Sure, much of that is simply rationalized sour grapes, but mostly I just ignored what had been and moved on into what was now.

Not too far from the main assemblage of buildings, Ghost stands in front of an amphitheater carved out of a limestone hill. About twenty young men are gradually walking away, just as I materialize on the stone front bench. "What, you missed the lecture?" demands Ghost.

"I thought you fellows strolled about in olive groves. This looks more nineteenth century."

"I get some leeway," Ghost waves. "You want to walk, we can walk, ok?" Suddenly everything was replaced by crumbly ground with large fruited trees. "There, better?"

"For what?"

"Ah, well, the class, you see, was in probability. Important for predictions. Critical for your life."

"Yes, I know, hardly need it," I turned to walk back.

"But," he noted, "highly ambiguous for an individual. Any given person can beat a statistic. Well, almost, some are easy."

"Like what?" I ask, curious.

"Oh, you know, the young idiots who come along and ask something like if they get covered with feathers and drink a magic potion will they be able to fly. We don't like them much, of course, because they tend not to give gifts unless we provide positive reinforcement, and in this case there is just no way to do it. So we try for a lot of pre-oracular screening."

"Ah, like a game show?"

"Exactly. That helps a lot. But sometimes there is someone too important to ignore, with something too slippery to decide easily, even though the odds go in one direction or another."

"For example?"

"Oh, the other day, a rich ruler of a minor city asked if he killed his rival would his throne be secure. We get a lot of that kind of junk."

"The answer is...."

"The answers <u>are:</u>" he held up his fingers one by one, "(1) The gods rarely reward what they abhor. (2) Bold actions meet the reward they deserve. (3) A secure leader is assured. (4) Strong enemies confound the best ruler. You get the idea."

"Impressive and meaningless."

"I try to get the kids to come up with ten for each problem. Then we can tune to what we think the client wants to hear. That's half of it, more than half. The rest is just making sure it is presented with the right wrapping."

"So you could never actually help me."

"You used your own probabilities. A future in computers was probably, but not certainly, better than one in the arts or teaching. Might change next week. Depends a bit on things beyond your control. But you can't just sit around like a log."

"Thank you, Mr. Platitudes."

"Always glad to help," Ghost walks off and fades away.

Wayne was becoming aware of what he would later call the quantum nature of his own life. At the time, he referred to it as the contradiction of chunky and smooth. The central issue was did you try to see your existence as one seamless whole, or as a series of discrete situations and events.

Specifically, for example, thinking as an artist, he had always felt he was an artist, and everything around him played into that. Whether he was sketching or painting, walking or thinking, doing something else entirely, he was still always the artist inside, trying to integrate all his experiences into something that would somehow later be expressed appropriately. He never left that framework.

By the same token, he was who he had always been. Perhaps a little older, arguably a little wiser, somewhat changed when he was a child or a teenager, and yet with a smooth and clear transitional pathway into the past, so he could say "I am as I was." All the deep thoughts and instincts and feelings did not vary much.

And yet, there were other things that were chunky, meaning they were turned off and on as necessary. When he was at work, he was just at work, focused on computers or teaching or whatever was necessary to be paid. He could leave that all behind, turn it off, close the door to the room, and not think about it until the next day when he left at night. He did not walk around all weekend trying to see how his wanderings, what he thought, and random enjoyments would make him a better programmer.

Along the same lines, there was no disputing that at thirty he was a far different person than he had been at twenty or ten. He could not go back to being one of those folks. The situation and personality were as closed to him as revisiting the eras of Napoleon or the Roman Empire. The past, even an hour ago, is completely unreachable.

So, as he went forward, what was the answer? Would what he was doing, what he would become, be chunky or smooth? And eventually he realized that like the nature of light, it was in all contradiction both at the same time.

Ghost sits beside a spring, under a tree, scribbling on a wax tablet. He looks up as I wander over. "Just let me finish this, ah yes, ok."

"What's that all about?" I wonder.

"Trying to formulate the rules for reevaluation," he said. "It should make my name in the profession."

"Rules of reevaluation?"

"Oh, you know, showing how something like 'a mighty empire will fall' is true no matter what happens."

"You mean figuring out the lie."

"Not the lie. Never the lie. Telling the appropriate story, with supporting moral."

"I call it a lie."

"No, a narrative is just an alternate way of stringing together the same set of facts. You do it all the time, I heard you refer to sour grapes a while ago. That's narrative rearrangement. 'Oh, it all worked out for the best' requires that you put together the story of why that is true. We all do it."

"But oracles have to be smoother because they are professionals?"

"Exactly. Exactly. It's a knack. But I think I can help my students here."

"So no matter what happens, we end up using it to our own ends and determine what it means in our own way."

"Most of the time. Of course, some things are just beyond any reinterpretation. But for most things, there are all kinds of ways to weave them into why stuff is just as it should be."

"And," I laugh, "no matter what, you guys want to take the credit."

"Well, we're entertainers and healers too. We want to keep them coming back for more...."

He had eventually wandered into his den under bookshelves crammed with thoughts and pictures of ages. His computer sat cold next to him, manuals for the new machine piled alongside it. The desk had a few more work-related binders, but he had finished those a while ago. He looked up at the light overhead, surrounded by a tin can cut into various abstract shapes, and took another sip of cheap port from a heavy hand-blown goblet he had acquired at a craft festival years ago in Berkeley. What next?

Usually, by now, he would be painting. But the plain fact was that this new commute in the morning was killing his endurance. He had no energy to go try to figure out what to do on the current canvas. Worse, his mind was so filled with the necessary new learning that he also realized that if he did get back into the studio and pick up a brush, he could not slip into the necessary concentration and focus. He could never paint with half a mind. It was total, or nothing. And right now, nothing was pretty much what was there.

This, then, was the end of the artistic road. Not a romantic death, leaving his treasures to an uncaring world, a final flare in an imagined novel of the self. No, a slack ebbing of the tide of creativity. Well, maybe not creativity, he was creative enough at work, at the new patterns of code. An ebbing of the certainty of the wonder of art. That too, required too much energy and uninterrupted emotion.

So it was sit, and let the thoughts run loose, and remember, and even worry a bit about next week. Another sip or two and he knew what he really needed, and worse what he really wanted, was to go to bed. No more real late nights, challenging the universe with promethean fantasies. Just get some sleep and enjoy the weekend to come.

The new future and present enveloped him, and changed his ways to match. Well, he would make the most of it, and see what happened. He struggled to his feet and began the nighttime routines.

1980 BRAVE NEW WORLDS

Treasure Hunt

Wayne was dressed suitably in dark ill-fitting suit, a nerd out of place among the casual crowd. He had spent most of the morning on his back on the thinly-carpeted hotel floor, hooking up and testing cables for the TRS-80 microcomputer on the table above him. Meanwhile Dick and Dave had been laying out their brochures and stacking the course binders, chatting with the attendees. Here he was in San Francisco, but there had been no time at all to sightsee.

The last few weeks had been nightmarish, as bugs crawled from the programs and crashed the system. He'd been on the phone to Microsoft for hours, to Radio Shack support for hours more, and finally everything seemed to work, at least during their carefully rehearsed demo. That was his job, to prove to potential clients that promises in the seminar were real.

Dave had come up with this business many years before. Small jewelers were rich stable small mom-and-pop shops, often handed down within the family for generations. Many were in desperate need of education on sales, accounting, and organizational skills. His company had originally done seminars simply to show how each small store could double or more profits with a few simple changes. It was a brilliant idea, and worked well for everyone.

The biggest hook was the location of the seminars. Dave would schedule them in wonderful tourist destinations at the best times of year. Then he would keep the sessions short, just enough to convince the IRS that this was indeed a legitimate business training event, which meant that the cost of room and board (and his fees) were completely deductible. Since many of these small shops were family affairs, a wife and husband would almost always attend together, often accompanied by the younger generation who worked at the place.

Dave's latest brainstorm had involved two completely different trends. One was computerization. Jewelers had little real need for computers—they mostly knew their inventory intimately, and pricing was a dark art handed down from parents to children. They knew their clientele and were convinced advertising would not bring many more sales. But—and this was the key— they could no longer keep track of the true valuation of the gold content of their wares. That was the second key—the price of gold was fluctuating and rising incredibly, day by day, almost hour by hour. How could they know what to charge, or even what to pay for new merchandise?

Voila—put the gold content of each piece into a database, simply enter the new price of gold each morning, and let the computer magically do the work.

Ah, if it were only so simple. But Wayne didn't know that yet. He was having enough trouble with balky cables, scratched floppy disks, and a jammed printer. Nevertheless, Dick and Dave knew that just having a working computer put them at a terrific psychological advantage over competitors. And they themselves were sure it would work out fine.

Late that afternoon, Dick approached and asked Wayne "Could you do me a favor? See, I have this girl here who comes to see me and expects ...." The indication was something of a sexual nature, "but I've gotten another hot bite and I wondered if you could sort of take care of the first ..." Wayne, more or less newly married and always shy, declined. Instead he went down to Fisherman's Wharf and drank wine as the sun sank over the bridge and into the fog.

I find myself in a long bare ballroom, no windows, a little stuffy, with card tables and more exotic displays spread out like some old scholastic science fair. Earnest young salesmen or nicely dressed young women aggressively man each booth, seeking to literally grab browsers as they go by to give them a pitch, handing out materials and various mnemonic goodies like key chains. Ghost and I can't quite make out the wording, but that hardly matters. "Well, what about it?" I ask.

Ghost answers, "The land of small commercial dreams, isn't it. Everyone here thinks of how they can do better, maybe even hit the big time and get rich. The huge players are elsewhere, these are the folks with hopes great and small. Including you, I might mention, who got to do both sides."

"No fair," I say, "that's jumping ahead. But you're right. But with no internet to talk to each other, how else can anyone exchange information reliably with their peers."

"Oh, these were great things," Ghost admits. "Fully necessary at the time. And fun too."

"Well," I add, "as I recall they were a lot more fun to think about than to attend. Mostly that ended up being a boring drag."

"But that was for you, really. You were never much of a communicator. Fish out of water when all you were supposed to do was network and make contacts."

"I did miss the boat. What could I do? I didn't even get the point."

"Nope."

"Typical geeky nerd, huddling with software alone in a corner while around him a brilliant social scene whirls."

"Sorry?"

"Nah, not really." I try to be honest. "That was never me, still isn't, and I'd rather be true to myself than trying to play a movie role I wouldn't be able to do anyway."

"Defeatist, in the hall of dreams."

"That was another problem …"

As it turned out, Wayne's first real job in the computer industry was typical of his entire career. He was always implementing the frontiers of the new, exploiting capabilities for commercial use. It fit him well, because computers were logical and he could learn almost anything and apply it nearly instantaneously, not as a chore but as a game. In a rapidly changing field, that was a great advantage for a programmer.

But, unfortunately, like all gifts it had a double edge. It reinforced his tendency to do everything on his own, simply because he could and was better at it. Instead of figuring out ways to hire people to develop ideas and sell possibilities to customers, he ended up always being the connecting link, getting the ideas of others to work for the needs of still others. It was a fun place, mostly, although very challenging, but it was not what needed to be done to amass fame and fortune.

What he rapidly did learn at the bleeding edge of commerce was that there was an almost infinite gap between clean application conception and actual real world implementation. There was always a need or a desire for "just this little something more." There too, his skill handicapped him, for since anything seemed fairly easy he was always willing to modify to customized needs. Of course, this tended to make customers happy, but was not a way to generate a mass market package that could be resold for ongoing profit.

Sometimes he would try to think like the boss, but that bored him. People were too unpredictable, too complicated, almost too unknowable. Sometimes they cared less about how well you did than how much they liked you. They'd occasionally rather talk about their family than how elegant this particular solution to a problem would be. At such times, he felt bored and lost. As soon as he could, he would escape back into his clean digital logic world, as well-ordered in its own way as any mathematical fantasyland.

The first real account ended up being a large jewelry store in Courtyard Square in Springfield, Illinois. A large wooden balcony wrapped around a floor filled with showcases. Lots of aged wood and glass, a fittingly antique plush facing the square across from Lincoln's old law office, which Wayne visited at lunch. The computer setup was going to be upstairs, the operator/manager a bright young woman very happy to be advancing into technology. Real problems were soon apparent as they began to enter inventory.

Wayne had carefully walked her through the startup procedure, inserting the large floppy disk, and picking the first menu item (there were only five options.) Operating system, like programming language, was burned into ROM memory at the factory and could not be changed. The whole application was pulled into memory from one disk, data loaded and saved on another, manually swapped with prompts at the appropriate time. He took the list the owner had given them to demonstrate the simple core of the system.

There was one program option to add new items, one to change them, one to delete them, one to save or load another disk, one to enter price of gold and recalculate values, one to reprint price tags, and a final one to print out a list. That was it. Expensive as hell, hardware, software, and time. Nobody even thought about end of life or upgrades, it was expected to be something like a desk calculator or telephone. Fixes and changes to the software were ignored—what could go wrong? All it was, really, was a big saved listing.

So he took the first item and said, "OK, which of these is the key of the item?"

"Do you mean the tag number?"

"Yes, I guess so, it has to be unique to the piece."

"Oh, well I guess it's this one, "JB 1546"

"No, it has to be a number."

"But we don't use just number. The characters mean something. How are we going to put this in?"

That took up a morning long distance call back East to Dave, who had a long chat with the owner, who had a chat with Susan, who came back less eager to continue. This work was all being added on to her normal duties since everyone assumed it was quick, easy, and trivial. Retagging the entire collection of multiple thousands of items was not a happy thought, although they had quickly decided to work with only the most valuable.

"Fine, so we enter the item, '99 1546" and press this big return key." The next field showed up.

"Now we add the description—what is that?"

"Probably just a 'ring.' But how can I put that one," she pointed to an entry further down the list, describing a complex broach with multiple jewels, "into this tiny space you have?"

"Well, yes, I guess you'll have to abbreviate."

"Then we won't know which it is from the new price tag," she noted. "We have to put in a much larger description or nobody will be able to negotiate."

Another set of calls.

Within a short time another issue had showed up. They didn't really know how much of an item's value was related to the gold content and how much to workmanship, age, and gemstones. They only had codes for certain gems and not others. And why no valuations on the diamonds which fluctuated in value almost as much as gold? And on and on, while Wayne tried to explain the limits of 75K of disk storage for everything.

Finally, when everything was going nicely, the computer burped and everything crashed. Another hour finding the (electrical) problem, rebooting, recovering what could be recovering, and more of the same, for three sweaty days (no air conditioning in the old Midwest.) Wayne began to realize what a nightmare distant support was going to be, but this wasn't IBM and nobody could afford to keep him on site. Mutually suspicious, but with hope of better times and promises, he and Susan finally said goodbye, although they would unfortunately come to know each other much better by phone over the next month.

In the beginning—and this truly was the beginning of computers for almost all small businesses—everyone was willing to put up with a lot of problems. The whole field was so new that the entrepreneurs selling systems compromised with the programmers who didn't know better than to compromise with balky operating systems and languages. The clients were thrilled by stories in trade magazines of wonders to come and couldn't wait to get bragging rights and were willing to put up with a lot of anguish to say they were on the road to the future with an edge in competitiveness.

Dave for example really did know the jewelry business hands down and had been advising on inventory for years. He was simply putting into practice what his seminars had taught. Wayne had to cut corners a bit to fit everything required, but they were both pleased enough and the system generated lots of interest at the conference. A jewelry store downstairs in Wellesley had volunteered for test status in exchange for a free system (extremely common in the eighties) and everything had been working well enough there, although Wayne was always available for fixes and changes. But...

The big but was that every small business back then had its own peculiar methods of doing things, its own way of handling accounts receivable, its own coding and handling of merchandise. And because everything was human or paper, it was all easily and infinitely changeable—you just told Susan or someone to do this instead of that and everything went on. But computer software, at the time, was forever. You truly got what you paid for, and that was it. It was worse than trying to customize your car after you bought it, and any changes were often impossible.

So our trial store only put in pure gold items, with karat type and gram weight, standard in the industry. But, reasonably, many other stores wanted to include partial gold items, encrusted or reworked. No can do. The problem of unique item code was typical—in a jewelry store a hidden marker might be the actual location or case—item #23 in case AC was totally different from item #23 somewhere else. That had to be mapped. Multiply that problem by hundreds, and we soon realized that there was no typical small business jewelry store. In fact, I was to find out there was not truly average small business anywhere I later worked.

But the glittering promise and the excitement of the new overcame almost all obstacles, and people once burned kept coming back. And, to be honest, even the terrible old systems usually worked quite well enough at their core purposes to adequately give a real return on investment. It was just a lot more aggravating than anyone had supposed.

Ghost gestures at the long line of tables and booths, fading into distance as instrumental music plays softly. "Some day, no doubt, these will be yours as you head for fame and fortune in the exciting and profitable computer industry. At least so you thought."

"Surprisingly no to both questions," I respond. "I only did a couple of booths in my life, both abject failures and really my heart wasn't in it. Honestly, I did not much think about it. I believed in the mousetrap paradigm."

"What?"

"You know, build a better mousetrap and the world will beat a path to your door."

"Oh, that garbage," he grunts. "Doesn't happen much, if at all."

"So I eventually found out," I admit ruefully. "Overselling a possible better mouse trap works far better. But I did end up building what I considered better mousetraps for most of my career."

"A failure, then."

"No, because I didn't really truly want to be devoted to that. I called it the brass ring, a lottery ticket that might come in but probably never would. I was very concerned at the time, and later, about stability and security and a job I could have fun at. I wasn't about to take tremendous risks and make myself do things I really hated."

"Like standing at booths telling lies," commented Ghost.

"Got that right in one."

These days, you can go from one company to another hardly noticing a difference in operational methods, Computers do much the same things with the same interfaces everywhere. Standardization, from crude beginnings in the early industrial revolution, has now reached into management, accounting, sales, and just about everything else, which means it is itself on the verge of being automated completely.

As late as the 1980's, that was not true. Each small firm had its quirks, each large firm its unique pride, and each computer a different interface. Especially in the milieu in which I worked, medium-sized business firms computerizing for the first time, those differences were overwhelming and difficult to convince owners to give up. It was all very well to tell them they were getting the best, "world-class" software, used by countless thousands of companies just like theirs. Deep in their hearts, they believed their firm was not just like any other. And operations proved it.

A lot ran on intuition and skill. A good senior accountant could smell something wrong immediately, a decent sales manager could depend on his gut to determine what was going right or wrong. From the lowest clerk to the CEO or president, each level had their own way of flagging problems, knowing what to ignore, ways to separate important problems from trivial daily chaff. And none of that intuition and skill could be embedded in "standard world-class packages." My job was largely to jump through hoops to make the impossible somehow workable.

Every accounting department, for example, knew they had to watch payables and receivables closely, delaying their own payments as much as possible, dunning clients who had overdue bills. But there were layers and layers, often built up over generations, sometimes updated only with gossip. Who was an excellent account but always paid late, but paid in full. Who could be danced on to gain another month before giving them payment because, perhaps, there was special leverage and connection between owners' families. Who was a pet project of one of the corporate bigwigs, not to be upset no matter what because the future was extremely promising. These were standard operating procedure, all dealt with by paper use of special folders, color coding, alternate filing, whatever. Critically reported separately from the standard run of the mill other accounts, which were often far less important to the upper levels of management.

But—bang—that package put everything on the same level. Aging out by months, flags on overdue bills, all on endless green bar, all mixed up, the big with the small, the important with the to-be-ignored. Even "exception reports" of the most overdue, or the biggest, or whatever, were totally confusing in completeness with no understanding.

The first time those fat reports actually landed on the desks of the top brass, as opposed to their usual summaries, the shit hit the fan. Mr. Vice President screamed for the department head, the department head explained, Mr. Vice President understood immediately that the department head knew what he or she was talking about. Time to get the computer guys on the carpet.

Computer manufacturers sold those wonderful packages, but they sold them to the top management who often had little clue what was actually going into making the operational sausage. The clerks and lower managers tried to complain all through the training process, to little avail. I had increasingly queasy feelings, but there were extreme limits to what I could reasonably do, given our cost considerations. And then, inevitably, came the showdown my company, and not the computer company, who had washed their hands of the affair once the ink had dried on their lawyer-prepared iron-clad contracts promising very little except that the machines would light up when turned on.

Then the problem was simple. The packages were, in fact, pretty awful for real life operations. They could do double entry bookkeeping just fine, never made a mistake adding (well, at least if you didn't count the problems of rounding errors and overflows), and chugged away at sums and fancy ratios all night long. But they didn't know how to make sausage, and instead delivered garbage with everything ground up together and virtually useless. So badly out of tune that many firms ended up constructing parallel systems, which simply doubled work for staff and made everyone even more surly. So could we salvage the situation or would we be thrown out, possibly sued for breach of promise, and how close could we come to getting paid somewhat reasonably for the hours I would have to put in? Oh, those were exciting times.

And every account, every single one, was completely different, even in identical industries. Each one knew it was better, each one knew it was right, each one knew that everybody else was stupid or crazy. They could all see the obvious advantages, but none could accept the problems. That is where I lived, sometimes thrived, but tap-danced many a time.

From 1977 on, the computer revolution has been one long science fiction novel. People only dreamed of instant communications and graphics. I remember once in 1975 going to a party at MIT, where crowds in the common room were mesmerized by a black and white TV hooked by wires to some massive hidden machine displaying a slow game of pong being played by the students. Such mundane reality didn't prevent extravagant predictions and science fiction dreams, of course.

All kinds of personal computers became available in the late seventies: Altair, Commodore, and my own Ohio Scientific. But these were expensive hobby curiosities, limited by storage on audio tape. The first real commercial splash was the Radio Shack TRS-80, with a true Disk Operating System accessing "floppy" magnetic disks that could be inserted into a slot in the front. It carried most of that OS in chip memory, like its BASIC programming language, and neither could be updated nor changed without buying an updated computer. It was expensive, but infinitely less than mini computers like DEC or Data General. Crucially for business, it could load, display, add, change, delete, and save data on multiple disks. It could use the same to load programmed applications. And with the data, it could perform simple arithmetic or sort alphameric characters fairly quickly. It was the equivalent of Ford's model T, a mass market phenomenon for small business.

But nobody knew best practices. New programmers jumped in all the

BABYLON WITH GHOST

time—with no testing methodology, crude flowcharting and design, and an inability to spot bugs in a program that was never compiled—thus liable to crash whenever an unexpected error occurred (which was, unfortunately, quite often.) Not to mention hardware issues and the fact that adequate power was rarely available—my installations were usually in hot dusty unventilated walk-in closets running off an extension cord from an outlet somewhere out in the hallway. When something went wrong there was a round robin pointing at Radio Shack, Microsoft (who supplied the operating system and BASIC), the company selling the application, the programmer, the computer operator, conditions of operation. More than once an exasperated voice at the other end of the phone would cry "Why would anyone ever do that?"

Changes were constant and ferocious, expectations were sky-high, competition was always promising the moon, and the reality was always much less than the promises. There was no common understanding of how machines worked—static was ok, operators thought, but were scared to death that a wrong keystroke would cause a fire. "Why can't it just," was the standard refrain of the owners. All in all, nobody was very happy, but everyone thought it would eventually work. Just like the Model T.

Nighttime, filled with flashing lights, laughter, scents of food, and loud sales pitches. Summertime state fair carnival, booths and cotton candy and fried corndogs on a stick. Barkers promising delights, dressed in striped suits and straw hats. Ghost standing beaming at the crowds.

"Aw, c'mon," I complain, "it wasn't that bad."

"Oh no? You don't see yourself right there in that stall, demonstrating inventory software, promising happiness and joy to anyone who tried it out?"

"Well, no, not exactly."

"And, of course," he continues relentlessly, "when they get it home it breaks right away and never works."

"Not on purpose," I state, "I thought it would work."

"But it didn't very often, right?"

"Well eventually ..."

"Oh, eventually something would come of it or you'd get thrown out. But hardly ever what they expected."

"It's just that the first cut is a little primitive …."

"More like the first cut is stealing candy from babies."

"No. We all believed. Early adapters and technology evangelicals rarely get the first pass right. Better to wait, really, until things have matured."

"So why didn't you wait?"

"Because by then the most aggressive competition has stolen the account! Besides, for all of us it was a lot of fun."

"And a lot of pain. And more than a few companies died in the process. Me, I see a different metaphor."

"I don't know if I want to hear this," I say slowly. Fireworks are going off over the midway.

"I see you as boat craftsmen selling rowboats to cross the Atlantic. They float, but the guy who buys one never gets to the other side, and sometimes dies trying. And then you sell a newer, better rowboat to the next sucker that comes along."

"Early adapters didn't care. And they did get one big competitive advantage, in spite of the pain."

"I can't imagine what."

"They were prepared to take advantage of the next things that came along, and when that happened they actually did become stronger than other firms and they did very well indeed."

"Oh, I'll leave you with your little rationalizations. Would you like a slice of pizza?"

It turned into a long and eventful summer, professionally and otherwise. Wayne finally passed his driving test, got a new license, and purchased a five year old Dodge Dart he found in the suburbs after researching Consumer Reports. With Joan pregnant, it was only a matter of time before she could no longer climb the stairs to the Charles Street station and make it to her office job, but she dutifully kept at it as long as possible, though she swelled considerably, in order to be able to take advantage of the generous pregnancy leave. The jewelry programs settled down to routine maintenance and support for existing clients, another installation in downtown Pittsburgh, no great rush of new buyers.

In the middle of all this, during the entire month of September Wayne was trapped in an antiquated Boston jury system that insisted he spend every day sitting in a non-air-conditioned courthouse, even though he only ended up serving on one case. He read technical books, pored over pages of code printouts, and before and after each session walked home to call the office in those days before portable or cell phones. Once in a while on the weekend he would drive out to Wellesley to clean or fix something or other, but mostly that remained on track.

What was increasingly hard to face was fear of what was coming. Joan was due in December, and it was clear she must soon leave. The apartment contents would finally have to be broken down and somehow shipped south. There would be a need for a new job, but there was no way to do anything yet since he could not get to interviews, and all he could do would be to try to read more openly, trying to find more information on areas he know acknowledged as deficiencies such as database design and screen interfaces. But the future looked pretty frightening, not so bad in the long term maybe, but insoluble in the short run.

I found myself in a completely new career position. For the first time, my resume and experience were real and counted toward the next job, moreover in a field where demand was high. I wasn't sure what I might do in New York, but I was sure I could find something that would pay at least what I was making.

Amazingly, I had turned into a unicorn. Anyone who had a college degree , could touch-type rapidly, and was not afraid of a keyboard was rare enough. Also being able to translate most code into human and speak the increasing technical jargon with confidence was even more unusual. And enjoying the puzzles of programming and the intellectual excitement (and frustration) of constant change was almost unheard of.

This was a time of wonders. I had taken to programming and design like a duck to water. I enjoyed the challenges and loved working for long spells by myself, doggedly making the machine do what I wanted. Yet I was still social enough to be able to talk easily to owners and users and anyone else. That all turned out to be a rare combination, which I had become aware of as I read the massive want ads with more targeted comprehension.

Oh, I was still on the outside, far removed from the top tier. The genius graduates of MIT, Stanford, and Carnegie Mellon more than filled the available spots in the giants of the computer industry—IBM, DEC, Data General, Sperry-Rand, and so forth. Big Iron remained completely locked. So there would be no huge salaries and bonuses and cushy retirement pensions.

But here was something I loved doing, with no real limit, a constant learning environment. Almost like art, in that I could create something out of thin air and my mind. Unlike art in that many companies were willing to spend real money for my kind of skills. I was, consequently, unsure what I might find after the move to Long Island, but not too concerned that something would show up once I got the lay of the land.

All I really had to learn was to puff up my experience and resume. I never took well to actual lies, but in an industry where almost nobody knew anything it was easy enough to exaggerate previous accomplishments and current skills. The flip side of that, of course, was that lies were quickly exposed if I was truly incompetent, but that was mitigated by my happily being an extremely fast learner and willing to spend all my spare time in whatever new things I needed to know.

As late fall approached, the hammer began to drop.

Surprisingly, I'm dressed in button down shirt, tie, and dark sport shirt with dress shoes. Before I can fully realize anything, the crowd behind me shoves me through the fire doors into a large room resembling a standard-issue school gymnasium, filled with cheap fold down tables covered by paper tablecloths. At each station, glossy folders are being handed out by extremely young, presentable, glassy-eyed men and women. Here and there, a few of the crowd industriously fill out multi-page stapled forms. I spy Ghost lurking in a corner, under the huge banner reading "Hilton Mid-Island Computer Jobs Fair."

"This is completely anachronistic, you know," I inform him. "There was nothing like this for maybe another decade or more."

"Oh, I suppose," he replies smugly, "but it nicely encapsulates the whole idea of early hiring in this field, doesn't it? I mean, you were never far from most of the issues raised here, even if you were just answering a newspaper ad or going on an early interview."

"Well, maybe," I admitted. "The hiring was a little dubious for a lot of reasons."

He began to tick off fingers, "Nobody knew exactly what they wanted to hire nor for what. All the applicants were lying in one way or another, either on purpose or not. There were no exact fits of qualifications with needs. There were no relevant exams or certifications available. Salary offers varied insanely. Many of the programmers were entering this market for the first time, self-taught. Networks of professionals did not exist. Formats for resumes often read like (illiterate) experimental literature. Companies either wanted to keep the good employees or get rid of the bad ones and would consequently shade any recommendations. Past performance, as they say, was not a reliable indicator of the future in a rapidly changing industry. And...." He looked down and realized he had run out of fingers, so I finished for him.

"Even worse, the actual worth of a programmer was asymptotic. A bad programmer could ruin everything, a mediocre programmer could grind application development to a halt, an average programmer would fold uselessly when the chips were down. A great programmer was worth his (let's be honest, almost no women back then, and all those in management or sales) weight in gold, not only for what he did but because he could increase department productivity by three to five times, prevent disasters, perform miracles when necessary, and salvage sinking projects."

"And ..."

"And the worst was there was no way to predict, since it was such a new mass market. Great programmers could burst like novae out of the basement or garage, self-taught fanatics, with no track record at all. Top programmers with expansive resumes, again like novae, might suddenly burn out and turn into dregs, or worse give it up entirely to go play the flute somewhere. Like dealing with high-strung artists."

"Companies weren't ready for it."

"Right. And, at the time few companies had human resource departments so an awful lot of the hiring decisions were made by a manager or vice president directly, seat-of-the-pants and hope. It's amazing anything ever worked."

This was the first time Wayne ever had to do something with which he became increasingly familiar over the years—handing off his project in preparation for moving on. In this case, he knew before his employers, and had a lot of time to outline and sketch in the details during the month of jury duty. He alone knew the timeline, and simply folded it all under the broad umbrella of "documentation."

There were no published guidelines nor best practices available for how to accomplish this. Like everything else, he learned as he went along. It was a given that as he developed he carefully outlined and fleshed in the broad outlines of the application in normal English, so clients and his bosses could understand clearly what could (and could not be) done. It was always critical to provide clear and robust user documentation, written as close to the bone as possible (now press this key, now do that, now notice that, etc.) The final act was always a kind of novelistic pseudocode developed from the routines themselves, so another programmer could presumably step in and continue support without needing more instruction.

This was a professional and correct thing to do. Furthermore, it was absolutely necessary if Wayne was ever to move on to what he enjoyed most, which was developing new stuff from scratch. There was nothing more disrupting than to be yanked out of the reverie of what might be in order to deal with some clogged toilet of a forgotten old program. So he became somewhat of a fanatical about it, as time went by. Surprisingly, in doing so, he actually did clean everything up enough that the documentation was often hardly used.

Perhaps this was where his former education and especially typing skills came most into play. The translation of computer jargon to peoplespeak, the voluminous exposition of what took a few characters of codeline, was something he ended up being able to do better than many of his peers. Furthermore, it was a facility that easily impressed all of his future employers, whatever their job and position in the company. Surprisingly, it was the one thing he just could not seem to teach new trainees.

Much of the fall was spent scribbling on yellow pads, transcribing to computer text, reworking in spare time when traveling to work and back. A pile of documents grew. It kept him focused at a time when focus was sorely needed.

Almost informal, a conference room with padded chairs and about fifteen people in various comfortable business attire, all facing me, piles of paper everywhere. Ghost opposite obviously running the committee.

"OK, Mr. Slingluff, we are ready to commence your termination interview."

"Gotcha Ghost. Fine, I get the picture, you can drop the dramatics."

"It seemed correct. You did this often enough."

"Hardly ever a termination interview, however," I protest. "I never had overstayed my welcome—well except a couple of times when I was part of a huge group layoff—and left on good terms with everyone. Usually they were begging me to stay in touch and be available to help for a while."

"But you did go through a few of these, evaluating your performance and whatnot."

"Nope, not at the end. This all happened in yearly reviews, if at all. At the end it was mostly all sweetness and light because, regardless of the conditions, everyone felt they needed me. It was a nice occasional feeling of power."

"Which you exercised quite often."

"No, not at all. My colleagues all were far jumpier. I usually stayed too long for my own good, because almost anywhere I went I ended up creating a comfortable niche for myself. I mean, most of my stays were at least five years, more like ten. That was quite abnormal in a business where the inside information was to jump every few years or so."

"But this time you left them in the lurch."

"This time, I had no real choice. Choosing between family and work was always family. It's how I was built."

"I suppose you think that an admirable trait, even though it may have held back your career considerably."

"Yep. And no, I don't think it did, particularly. Back then, loyalty still counted for something.

Wayne had time to reflect on his career as he drove out of Boston in a late November rainstorm. He felt he had finally gone through his apprenticeship and was ready to move on to journeyman status. Dreams of future possibilities danced in his head, although he remained a little intimidated by the possible new job down on Wall Street. That still rubbed his "movement" sensibilities wrong, the ultimate sell-out. But, as most people eventually discover, he had to eat. And it was at least something.

As it turned out, these two first computer jobs had been a wonderful introduction—almost a paid two year internship or graduate course—into the exact path he would be following from now on. The intersection of smaller business and increasingly capable low-end computers was going to be his métier. It was a rich and almost unexplored vein of capitalism, with no end in sight, but with constant surprises and even mine-collapse disasters (that fortunately he had no idea about yet.)

His economics and college background worked to let him easily work with various nabobs of moderate sized companies. His time in Vista, Berkeley, and teaching let him instruct and help users with little condescension and a lot of sympathy, which was sometimes in short supply in his industry. His native capabilities let him work out the most complicated algorithms easily and quickly chart machine courses for verbal desires—if possible, of course. He loved design and code, he enjoyed writing up the various documents, and change kept everything fresh. Finally, it was a very nice artisan feeling, always creating new art, perhaps not a masterwork, but something tangible and useful and deeply satisfying.

Rain and wind increased, and he focused on the road, leaving other thoughts and worries for the future.

ALL ABOARD!

WHEN NOT FRANTICALLY busy, Wayne found himself wandering familiar haunts in a depressed and maudlin mood. So much of his created life had centered here, so much of what he had been trying to build was being left forever. This was the problem, he knew, of concentrating on the present and paying little attention to the future. He always cared much more about where he actually was than where he might be going. Others had mighty goals, he simply wanted to make the most of each day. And now, all the careful edifices he had constructed to enrich each moment would be cast aside. Only his memories would remain.

He could not get excited about what was to come. He was leaving a place he loved for somewhere he was pretty sure he would hate. Soon there would be no sidewalks to stroll on, no cute little shops to visit, no sites drenched in history to contemplate, no bustle of crowds and plentiful artists on the streets and in cafes. No exciting demonstrations, no undercurrents of rebellion, no massive renewals such as Quincy market. No hope of lightning striking.

No, where they were headed looked a lot like what he had run away from long ago. Driving a car to go anywhere, long unpleasant commutes to work, malls and box stores and everything bland vanilla and standardized. Grey people in grey lives, thinking and speaking only of real estate and employment and competing with similarly dull neighbors. No rebellion, no grand themes, unusual people (whether racial or ethnic or cultural) as rare as bald eagles. The only question was whether it would be purgatory or Hell itself.

He had worked so hard, he thought, to build this independent life. And he and Joan had done so, a proud little outpost in a strange place which they fit perfectly. And that was over now. Not only was it all being given up forever, but where he was going would not accommodate any of what he now considered important. They would have only grudging space from her parents, all his books and art materials packed away and unavailable. He would be tolerated rather than respected, as a slightly suspect appendage of the return of the prodigal daughter and prized grandchild-to-be. His freedom was to be eliminated as surely as that of any slave; commuting, at work, shopping, at home, none of his time and desires would be his own.

Wayne slogged on down Cambridge Street in Cambridge itself, almost tearfully feeling the uneven brick sidewalks around the thick plane tree trunks as he wandered on toward Harvard Yard. He knew he would never be back, and each place he went now with all its attached associations was probably the final time he would encounter what had meant so much to them this decade.

Choking dust billows thickly, merciless sun beats down on endless stiff grass to the horizons, my throat is parched and I know I would itch if I were not caked with dirt and sweat, ragged clothing even more filthy than my exposed skin. I squint forward and make out Ghost cantering toward our mule-drawn cart on a great brown horse, big hat covering a grizzled tanned face. I wave as he draws near.

"Ho! Failed pioneer!" he calls out.

It's then I notice the long line of Conestoga wagons nearby, heading in the opposite direction. "Failed?" I ask.

"Why sure. California turned out to be too far, the Rockies too high, the great American desert too dry, and your wife too fragile. Back home for you, with less than you started out with, a failure there, a failure in your imagined future, a pretty sorry failure today, if I may say so."

"Seems a harsh judgement," I begin.

"Harsh life," he cuts me off. "Much too harsh for you. 'The cowards never started and the weak died on the road ...'" he begins to quote.

"But we started ..."

"And they don't bother mentioning everyone who had to ditch their possessions and hopes and come back because they were just unable to cope."

"Family is important..." I tried to insert.

"The promised land is that way," he points behind us, "and you ain't headin' there, pardner."

That was a bit too much, even for one of his scenarios. I began to laugh, which got him annoyed, and pretty soon he had managed to scare up some thunder in the distance as we trudged along.

They had early on decided that their current city situation was nowhere fit to raise a child. Time dragged on, and eventually, in spite of extra nighttime acrobatics, it almost seemed an indefinite postponement, as Wayne surged forward on his new career. Besides, like everyone else he knew that pregnancy lasted nine months, which he unconsciously rounded to year. In a year he could be ready for anything, so he relaxed and concentrated on what he was doing.

It wasn't until April that they suspected, and not until May confirmed, and suddenly time was short. Joan would have to get home in October, Wayne following soon after for the December due date. That left only summer and a few odd months to prepare. Suddenly there was no time at all, and every farewell and casual encounter might be the last. There were lots of things to do, and yet the daily requirements never let up. A frantic time ensued.

Not that the actual move would take all that much effort. A concentrated week of packing books and art, taking down bookshelves, throwing out most furniture, cleaning would have them ready to leave. More than enough time to get ready there. The psychological housekeeping was a lot harder.

A metaphorical raven perched on his shoulder as he went through the summer. "Nevermore!" it cawed as he browsed the dark dusty and always discounted caverns of Filene's basement, or the ancient scrubbed and fragrant hall of Quincy Market. "Nevermore!" as he picked out vegetables and fish at Haymarket, walked up Cambridge street past the Otis house, relaxed on the Esplanade, browsed Utrecht Art Supplies over by the Fens, walked at dawn through the Public Gardens to the Green line trolley. "Nevermore! Nevermore!" at Harvard Square and Central Square and almost everywhere he turned, each step he took, each happiness he grabbed, each memory that any scene recalled. Intellectually, he knew that the future might work out quite well, but emotionally that old bird just kept jeering.

He'd moved before, of course, Leaving Philadelphia, or Hartford, or Kansas City, or Berkeley had been just as final. This was the first place where he had spent almost a decade, put down roots, established friends and routines and plans, had imagined a future. It was not just the move that was so affecting, he eventually realized, but the complete discontinuity. Joan was ecstatically happy, but except for her there would be no support for him.

Fortunately, Wayne remained too busy to become morose very often. He had never been one to make lists (and the term bucket list had not yet been invented) so his conscious last time visits to various once-important places were pretty limited. As always, he had a gift for letting the past be the past, cleanly distinguished from here-and-now. When he knew somewhere was gone forever, it was gone, no regrets, few thoughts, once the cerebral ceremonies were completed.

Consequently, instead of departure angst becoming greater and more overwhelming, it became condensed and narrow, a shrinking sphere of what was immediately around him. Cambridge faded off to the far horizon, as did all thought of trips to the countryside they had biked through. Soon enough, all he was concerned with were a few streets around Beacon Hill and Charles Circle. Friends and acquaintances faded to ghostly corners as he said final goodbyes. By the last months, it was all mechanical, almost robotic, as he performed the last rites in Boston and prepared to go.

As that circle closed, nothing new was opening. The future was worse than foggy, it was a blank wall rushing at him. That, more than anything else, kept him awake at night.

Sweltering Saturday morning in early September, the open windows providing no relief, sweat from just moving around the apartment. Wayne had taken care of some necessary chores, Joan was finally getting up, out of the

BABYLON WITH GHOST

bathroom. Her pregnancy was becoming more than noticeable, she seemed to be carrying large. They kept reminding each other that in just over another month she could take maternity leave at Bradford—it would be the only income they would have at the end of the year, and with their meagre savings at least they would not be complete paupers before Wayne started his new job.

"How are you feeling?" Wayne asked solicitously, as she walked carefully into the kitchen.

"More tired than ever. This is so hard. I can't believe it's so hot already."

"So I guess you don't want to do much today?"

"Like what? I sure can't ride the bike…"

"No, I'll take care of the shopping later."

"Well, to tell the truth, I kinda want to go to Stop and Shop for the air conditioning. And to get out of this place. I just can't carry anything."

"Sure, I'll go with you whenever you want. I'll do Haymarket around it. Maybe we should just hang out on the Esplanade later, or eat somewhere cool."

"I don't know, I only seem to want normal food, anything strange makes me feel like throwing up."

"I'd rather not drive anywhere …." They finally had a car, which Wayne hated driving to work although he went in reverse rush hour directions. Anywhere they usually visited the parking was impossible, and neither of them had enough energy to contemplate going very far. Besides, on return, parking was absolutely horrendous.

"It's only for another few months, Joan. Just try to hang on," Wayne tried to be consoling.

"Easy for you to say," she snorted. "You don't have to waddle down flights of stairs each morning, then climb up two to that packed red line and onto steaming Washington street."

"At least you have air-conditioning all day," he pointed out.

"That's the only thing that really keeps me going," she admitted. "Maybe the Esplanade would be nice this evening. After dinner."

"What do you want me to get?"

And so it went, almost every weekend for a couple of months, little varied. For Joan, at least, it was all an exercise in tedium. Wayne felt increasingly tethered, unable to roam freely about as they had always done, constantly nearby and always conscious of returning. For both of them, by now, whatever might loom on Long Island would be a relief.

You can never redo the past. No matter how you live, you age and change day by day as the world changes around you. The saddest realization in life is discovering that you have not used ephemeral opportunities to their fullest extent. That is what seems terrible about children deprived of their childhoods, either by being thrust into responsibility too soon or by having goals too firmly established by elders. Childhood should be innocence and play and unthinking unworried happiness, for there will never be another time like it in our lives (although we sometimes vicariously reclaim it by proxy in our own children.)

Similarly, there is only one adolescence, which has angst and troubles and expanding awareness, first love, and the only true certainty we ever possess in life. When we are older we become confused and frustrated by an environment that seems to follow no rules, but—ah—when we are in the first flush of youth every problem has an answer, and all dilemmas are crystal clear, and we are always the only ones who know. Adolescence varies in length and degree and then opens into young adulthood.

There remain disputes about exactly what anyone should try to do as a young adult. The old fogy conservatives in society encourage sacrifice, a good job, saving for the future, building a solid foundation for coming prosperity. Younger peers counsel a wild fling, constant parties, travel, partners, no binding ties, and as much unencumbered excitement as possible. Most of us, like me, hew to some sort of middle course, although skewed toward pleasure rather than sacrifice. What I have noticed is that those most buttoned-down in their twenties often become the most chaotically unhinged in their middle age.

However one passes through these stages, there are natural beginnings, middles, and ends. A child is glad to end childhood and grow up, we are all eventually grateful to escape adolescence sane and alive (if indeed we do so.) Finishing up young adulthood is no different. Joan and I were proud of what we accomplished—we felt we had both done a lot of what we needed to do, proved what we wanted to prove. We had done everything we desired deeply and often. And—yes—it was time to move on.

So for all my sadness, there was satisfaction that we were starting a family, acceptance of a new career which forswore all the previous dreams of art immortality, slipping back into "normal" society after years fighting against it. Even following the bitter pill of accepting the advice and aid of our parents as we transitioned to a new life. When we looked back, not very often because we rapidly became too busy, we realized that the old Boston life had begun to grow stale and stagnant, and we were absolutely right to leave when we did and move into the next stage of our lives together.

Dusty light filters through a tiny window into the drab wooden room. Two huge chests dominate the floor, both open and partially packed with clothing and odds and ends. Inching closer, I see blue below me, it finally resolves into San Francisco Bay, packed with sailing ships along the wharves, and anchored close offshore.

"Argh, matey," comes a growl from a dark corner, as Ghost rises from a chair. Dressed disreputably, smoking a pipe, the very image of an imagined seaman of the era. "So it's back to the begrimed smoky East ye be goin', tail between yer legs, beat up and down and out. With yer poor little wifey, and prospects as poor as yer wallet."

"Jeez Ghost, no need to get melodramatic about it."

"Melodramatic, is it? Others out here gettin' richer than Midas ev'ry day, gold, land, commerce jest lying around t' make fortunes. All slipped by yer little fingers, past yer convoluted brain. Tickets set and shippin' on t' New York, takin' back the few things worth takin' and a mess that ain't."

"We're fine. We're doing what we want. We accomplished what we wanted. We're rational and can make our parents happy."

"Oh, aye, they're all fer the grandchild and aseein' the daughter. You, not hardly, jest dragged in like flotsam."

"I'll get a job, things should work out."

"Piss poor track record, though. Nary a one iv yer pitchurs sold, scarce a certificate to teach, scant year or so playin' with 'lectronic toys. Fool failure, runnin' back down and out, beggin' for help."

"At least stop mixing in anachronistic idioms," I yell. "Worked for others, even from places like this. I mean, uh, look at Ulysses Grant..."

"Ah, so now ye're a man o' destiny, is't? Expectin' a war t' turn yer suggy fortunes?"

"No, but something could come of programming. There's opportunity there."

"Been opportunity all around, ten years a'wastin' Ain't never come yours, though."

"I've got a brain, I've got ideas, I've developed plans ..."

"As always, me lad," he admitted with a coughing laugh, "As always. Niver close to bein' right, though, as I recall."

"Well, yeah, that could be a complication ...."

I never mastered lying, which was unfortunate because it is not only a pathway to better outcomes, but often a necessary social lubricant. I was too lazy to juggle multiple stories with different people. Besides, I had a physiology which quickly betrayed any attempt at shading the truth—enough of an affliction that merely keeping quiet in the face of unrealistic promises was difficult. If I was sure of facts, it was the facts I would live by, hell or high water. I regarded myself as immaculately honest.

I would never tell you the moon is made of green cheese, or that we could harvest some if you would just put some money into my model rocket. I had enough trouble getting through the Santa Claus years with my children. More practically, I could not promise my clients the full-blown, insanely overstated paradises being trumpeted by golden-tongued salesmen. This often hurt me, because naturally the folks being sold to assumed I was lying as much as everyone else, and tended, at least at first, to discount what I was saying.

Defending what I thought was truth, unfortunately, did not mean I was right. It took time to learn that. My logical lawyerly mind can fully believe in and convince myself of any side of an argument in which facts or conclusions are not cut and dried. I might not be able to sell rockets to the moon, but in the proper mood I could convince myself and others that our rocket company might do great things. In a later reconsideration, I would realize it was all doomed to failure. Neither perception was wholly true—not much is. Instead I swayed pathetically in the middle. Eventually, my best option was to remain as quiet as possible.

At that time in my life, I was consistently wrong about the world and myself. I consumed vast volumes of information, digested it, constructed

BABYLON WITH GHOST

exquisite summary outlines, declaimed well on any subject, and was comically or tragically ignorant concerning what actually happened. I still run into debaters of that type, annoyingly sure of themselves until they change their minds. I possessed every intellectual facility except common sense.

What I needed—and our move concentrated the process—was to slog in the mud of reality, not worry about visionary confections, and focus on day-to-day tasks. Computer coding reinforced that attitude nicely because it was very much one thing after another, tightly coupled, and if you ignored any of the immediate in-between steps, you could forget about getting your program to work. Vision almost always turned out to be the least of my problems.

On the other hand, I never grew out of truthfully telling myself and others that the next grand design was going to work magnificently. Sometimes, it even did.

Cardboard boxes filled the den. Many were stuffed with books, some were empty awaiting more packing. Obviously, none of the wood shelves could be dismantled until cleared. Wayne paused, sweating, and tried not to think how hard this was all going to be to truck down to Long Island.

A few boxes were also out in the kitchen, where Joan was going through an agonizing choice of what old chipped dishware to save and what to toss out. Both of them were not particularly hoarders, but they were not people who bought things recklessly, either. A lot of this stuff, however battered, had been with them a long time and was loaded with memories. A dish, a platter, a pot were much more to them than what they appeared to others. How the Spagnolos would look at crates of this junk clogging their garage was another thing entirely.

Take the fish tanks. They had been really fond of fish, raising guppies, watching angelfish and Siamese fighting fish flicker and die. But of course there would be no place for fish, so the tanks had to be emptied and cleaned, the survivors offered to the pet store on Charles, the gravel bagged, the underwater doo-dads scrubbed and cushioned, the air pumps carefully coiled, the sides scraped clean of algae. But … they knew there would never again be time nor opportunity. Nevertheless, they couldn't bring themselves to part with all of it. Likewise the plants.

The liquor store, also on Charles, supplied all the cardboard boxes they could possibly want. They were only slightly worried about cockroaches—their apartment had more than enough already, so what came in would hardly add to the collection. The main thing was to keep each box at some ideal weight—neither too heavy to lug down four flights of stairs, nor too light so that too many boxes would have to be carried. And of course there was the constant need for newspapers for cushioning, and the more difficult than it seemed problem of labeling the boxes with markers so they had some idea both of what was inside and also how soon they might want it.

The numerous plants were a special problem, old friends, and yet most of them had to go. Few would survive a trip, almost none could be grown in the new house. So plants remained until the very end, gentle reminders of the lovely nest this once had been as it gradually returned to the cold, clean, and empty apartment they had moved into years ago.

Rundown old wooden cabin, cleared fields ending in deep forest, mountains poking up in the distance. We rumble down the dirt lane in an old cart, as Joan's father steps out on the porch, musket in hand. He regards me with a jaundiced eye, suppressed anger at his daughter having chosen someone so useless, mitigated slightly by the fact that his daughter had chosen anyone at all. He comes down the steps and extends a hesitant hand, "Welcome to our old homestead," he says. "Isn't much, compared to your grand city, but we like it. You can probably have part of the back forty over that hill—stony as hell but with hard work you should be able to raise something. Hard work …" he mutters, turning away.

"Stop right there!" I yell at the sky. All turns quiet as heavy fog rolls in and Ghost materializes in overalls. "I've had just about enough of this stupid one-sided bunch of scenarios you keep rolling out. You're playing on one side—my fears—and ignoring everything else."

"But, " begins Ghost.

"Shut up! Joan is not returning sad and forlorn but triumphant. She's found a husband, brings back a family, moves along her desired destiny. She's aglow with happiness, and generally I'm happy for her. Her parents may be a little worried, but bottom line is they're ecstatic too. First grandchild and all."

"But you.."

"Yeah, me! I'm not some poor dopey drug addict running back to Mommy. I've had jobs, I have a job lined up. This isn't _my_ roots, after all. It may be the suburbs, but they are strange suburbs, as strange as any city I ever moved to. It's a tremendously exciting and hopeful thing, a wonderful change in my life, and for all the regrets most of the time I know we are doing not only the right thing for us, but a good and fine thing for me as well. So get off the prodigal son high horse and stop these idiotic scenarios."

"Poor, drinking, unable to get your own place ..."

"All temporary. All to be resolved. Any problems are only as they are in any transition. We are sure this will work out, neither of us plan to lounge around forever in the old house. You have the context all wrong, and this time I won't put up with it."

Sullen and with a clap of thunder, Ghost strides away.

Wayne stood next to his beige Dart on Philips Street, looking up at the fifth floor window, bereft of flower boxes, for the last time. Apartment keys remained inside on the kitchen counter. Every last item, leftovers, final necessities had been pulled out and jammed into the car. He could hardly see out the back, and had only the left side mirror to tell what was happening behind. Appropriately here at three o'clock, a light drizzle was falling from grey skies.

A decent headache reminded him of his personal farewells to all the old streets and local parks the night before. He didn't know what would happen in the family house in Long Island, there was no use thinking about it, so he had spent all his time remembering what they had done, where he had been, trying to believe it had all been important and the next stage could somehow build on what he had learned. It was cool enough for a jacket, but unseasonably warm for mid-November.

Well, time to go. He had a ferry appointment in New London at five, then a quick trip down the back roads of the North Fork to the LIE, on to Huntington. He was leaving now to avoid traffic, and also because he had wanted to be sure he had time to get everything without rushing. Should be in the new world by dark.

As he passed Route 128 on the expressway out, the rain turned heavy.

Traffic jams caused him to worry he might miss the boat. As they cleared, he concentrated on trying to drive when he had trouble seeing behind. He was glad he'd get off soon. By the time he got to New London his shoulders ached, he was cramped, but here he was and the worst was over.... But why was the parking lot so empty?

He ran through the gusting downpour to the small overheated ancient waiting room next to the even more decrepit train station. What? His ride was cancelled? No more until tomorrow, maybe? He couldn't believe a north-easter like this could halt a huge ferry, but—well it had. Back then, the "ferry" was actually a converted landing craft from World War II, seaworthy enough when the weather was fair, but in danger whenever the waves got strong.

Crap. He hadn't bothered to call ahead, and of course there was no internet nor GPS. He had no map of New York. Before cell phones, he wasted more time standing in line to call Joan on a public phone and get directions down 95 to the Throgs Neck, and back out to Huntington. By the time he left, it was getting dark under the forbidding skies.

Wayne always remembered that dark slog down as a nightmare. Glaring lights in the wet, huge trucks, heavy traffic, unexpected snarls, potholes, all the terror of not knowing what was behind him or if he could safely change lanes. Already physically exhausted from the unaccustomed long ride, he had to more than double the distance. At least there were no decisions to make through Bridgeport, then the mess into the Bronx, more horrible jams, more lights, finally the bridge.

Somehow he made it over and found routes barely remembered, ending up on Northern Boulevard. That route was less traveled at least, but dark and slick as the torrents continued. Miles crawled by, but finally after midnight he pulled in the driveway, all but ready to collapse, and gratefully accepted a beer before he fell into bed.

Cool early November, barely evening, apartment stark and forlorn, piled with stuff like some nineteenth century warehouse. Even the lights glared, now that they had removed all the shades. It was time to get the bulk of their belongings to Long Island, more importantly time to get Joan to Long Island and the comforts of her parent's house. A big rented Ryder truck sat just outside, by some miracle a spot had opened up on the street a scant hour ago and Wayne had promptly moved there, legal through the morning. He never recalled that spot being open before, but he would accept any help as it came along.

Joan had been supervising for a while as he lugged boxes down the four rounded flights and out the door. Books and bric-a-brac, treasures they could just not leave behind. Art materials. His legs were holding up, but he was sore already, and it seemed he had hardly made a dent in the mountains. As he drank a beer, sweating mildly, the downstairs doorbell rang. Ah, they were here. Joan buzzed them in.

Joanne and Jonas were ten-year-old friends from Vista, who had some-how ended up living in Cambridge across the river. Wayne had kept in touch with them as much as he ever did with anyone, they had offered to help, which was gratefully accepted. Quick greetings and then the worst of the move—the big stuff that took several people: couch, a few long bundles of pine boards, a couple of old chairs, rugs, rolled paintings. With some diffi-culty, they navigated the corners and got everything into the capacious cargo area.

After that it was just a matter of ant-like carry, box after box, load after load, carefully positioning at first, then more and more just stuffing it where they could as the load got higher and higher. By eleven, it was all but done, everyone was exhausted, Joanne had long ago joined Joan sitting in the kitch-en talking. Final farewells, promises to keep in touch, and then—emptiness. Mattress on floor in empty bedroom. Exhaustion provided comfort enough.

The next day they were up early with nervous energy, Wayne loaded in clothing and toiletries and some food, and they were on their way. No prob-lems, no traffic, the ferry accommodated them well, and going down the back road from Greenport was rural and simple, if a little scary for Wayne being unaccustomed to the size of the vehicle. They stopped at a gas station, and as the truck pulled out they heard a bang as it knocked off a sign overhead, but they just kept going.

No incidents to Huntington, fortunately, Joan knew the way well, and they pulled into the driveway, greetings all around, until her father gazed in dismay at all the garbage to be stored in his garage. No putting the car away this winter… The next day Wayne managed to unload everything, taking his time, and get the truck dropped off. An evening of rest, then onto the train at the LIRR Huntington station, to NYC, and out the old New Haven line to Boston. He had a few weeks to himself, to finalize his job and odds and ends such as mail, cleaning, and so forth. Lots of time to think, as late fall scenery crawled by.

Dark and gloomy room, sunlight casting visible beams onto the walls and cases filled with strange pictures and objects. There appear to be about three glassed-in displays, nobody here, a graveyard hush over everything. I recognize the template immediately. Every small town the world over seems to have its own dusty quaint museum, stuffed with artifacts from times past. Most of those items are of too little importance to have been scooped up into larger institutions. They simply provide a link to the past, a handle on nostalgia.

Coughing from a desk near the barely visible door reveals Ghost sitting quietly, dressed in an ancient corduroy jacket with leather patches on the elbows. He's even wearing thin-frame steel glasses, precariously set half-way down his nose. "What do you think, eh?" he asks.

"Interesting, I guess. What's it got to do with me?"

"Ah, have you looked in your garage or basement lately?" he chortles.

"Oh, yeah, I get it. We do have a little detritus hanging around."

"A little? Don't make me laugh. Why Joan still has lesson papers from the day care center. You have things never unpacked, overlayered with decades of similar accretion. If it all magically vanished overnight I doubt either of you would notice."

"Afraid you're right on that. We find it hard to let go."

"Hoarders …"

"No, I don't think so. I think this museum is appropriate. All that old stuff is a kind a talisman, a guardian of our memories. We remember the pictures, the time we bought a vase or book or some stupid pretty decoration. And all the times we looked at or moved or cleaned or whatever with that from then on. It's hard to throw away our past."

"So your house fills and overflows."

"Not that either, for we rarely buy anything new except food and clothing and electronics. I did eventually get rid of all the old computers and televisions and such."

"Hard, wasn't it."

"Hard to make the decision, not much to it once I had done so. Anyway, we like our basement and garage museum. Maybe we should charge for a tour."

"Hah! Good luck! You're the first visitor I've had here in weeks.

As usual, Wayne arrived alone, and mostly remained alone. Although he tended to break old attachments when he moved on, he rarely made new ones quickly. Those he did were temporary, usually conditioned by environment such as friends at work. It was his nature.

Some would claim that was a fault to be corrected, and at times Wayne also felt it so. But no matter how hard he tried, he could not remember people well, could not recognize them when he ran into them except from environmental clues. He tried all the books and shortcuts, trying to attach names to mnemonics. Although that worked well enough to remember a name once he was clued in, it did nothing to help him pick out a face in a crowd. He might know that Jack owned a large boat, or that a given large boat belonged to Jack, but he could often not determine who was Jack at a cocktail party. Eventually, he just accepted it as some deeper psychological or physical issue that he had no time to deal with, and just had to handle as well as he could.

As always, that made him very dependent on family and work employees, because they were always sorted by environment, and usually provided enough clues to determine who was who. He was not going to run into his wife or father-in-law at work, he was not likely to find his boss or business colleague at a family gathering. With the set of possible people thus restricted, he could often match other clues such as weight and height and age to likely identity. But it was always difficult, and tended to make him happier to hang out in the corners, talking to the same folks all the time.

Anyway, it was who he was. It hardly mattered. He enjoyed being alone, thinking quietly to himself, having a world to explore inside his head and fed by his own perceptions. He had always felt he might have made a good monk. He needed human companionship once in a while, but not the way others seemed to. They also had their own peculiarities and faults, he know, so he eventually just decided to cultivate his own. Fortunately, his situation and career were such that this was not a big problem.

Obviously a frontier town, crude wooden buildings mixed with more elegant New England types, the only thing missing was a mournful harmonica. Yet where was the dust? This seemed an overly green place, trees beyond the fields, some areas just stumps in rolling ground. Ah, of course, Ohio.

"Hey, there, stranger!" Ghost calls a greeting across the muddy road. "You stayin' here or moving through on West."

"No good, Ghost. I'm not moving to a frontier at all. I've come back to civilization."

"For you, son, everywhere is a frontier. No matter where you go you are doomed to be the stranger."

"Be that as it may, I'm not alone here. There's Joan and her vast family and old friends."

"That's fine for Joan. You remain apart."

"But still, more support than I ever had when moving from where I grew up or from city to city. No, hardly a stranger."

"Always. It's your nature and you can't deny it. Half the time you seek isolation. Frankly, I have no idea how you managed to hold on to a family."

"Joan is a patient woman."

"Joan is, as the saying goes, a saint," replies Ghost.

"Well, yeah."

"Her parents and brothers, perhaps, less so."

"Yeah, that too."

Sure enough, Ghost pulls out his harmonica and begins a soulful dirge.

Helluva year, thought Wayne to himself, chugging another bottle of beer in the quasi-privacy of the front bedroom. It wasn't so much getting the beer in, it was trying to dispose of the empties that had become difficult. He and Joan shared two small bedrooms with a bathroom in-between here on one side of the house, fortunately separated from the rest of the single-floor common space in the rest of the house by a door. One big helluva year.

He was hiding out again, at least for a few minutes. Bleak December rain fell unrelentingly outside, cold and miserable, chilling even this area. Yet another group of well-wishers was visiting, talking of babies and old times and, inevitably for this area it seemed, real estate. He endured as long as he could, then slipped in here for another break, then back out to try to be sociable and make Joan comfortable.

A year ago, he reflected, they were sitting fat and happy and almost content. Joan was doing more than well at her downtown insurance job. He was embarked on his first real programming employment and proving more than up to the task. They were making more money than they ever had while married, and if they knew it might end whenever a child showed up, that seemed increasingly something off in the indefinite future. A year ago Boston was their home and their universe and their foreseeable future.

He couldn't pretend it had been all sweetness and light, but it was familiar and mostly comfortable. And suddenly—well, he hadn't had such a shock since the end of college, and back then he had known exactly when the shock would occur for years. This was unexpected. For him, this was almost blink blink blink impossibly new, a wild animal captured and caged.

Nobody was giving him too much of a hard time yet, here in the middle of his month-long sabbatical. Explicitly, Joan's parents were as cautious with him as he was with them. After all, they knew this would be his only vacation—the city job was all lined up, he was all set, after the new year things would take off and normalize. They could handle his moods and idiosyncrasies and even beer-drinking for that long. He finished the last gulp and prepared himself to go back into the living room.

Helluva year. He wondered what the next Christmas would be like, what this year would unfold, and what would hold together and what might fall apart. Sometimes his world seemed as fragile as tissue paper, simply hanging together from inertia. Merry Christmas to all ....

STRANGER IN PARADISE

WAYNE WAS SOON lectured concerning this best of all possible places to live. Huntington was on the fringe of the once-fabulous Gold Coast, home of Gatsby fictional millionaires and century-old sprawling estates, now either broken up, torn down, or beatified into underfunded public parks. He was surprised at how closely it matched much of where he had grown up—also covered with the detritus of decaying self-proclaimed aristocracy. On most of Long Island suburbanization had metastasized, a few once-extensive farms were disappearing under bulldozers. The harbor provided a pleasant echo of summers on the Jersey shore. The relatively self-contained and modest brick town echoed those of Pennsylvania. There were the same commuter train connections to a vast city. All in all, from what he was learning as a first impression that December, it was much like what he had fled over a decade ago.

Rain and cold and unfamiliarity assured that much of what he first experienced was glimpsed from the back seat of a car, as he was chauffeured through special places and shown areas of interest. Often this was on the way to something or other having to do with parties and relatives. Shopping was surprisingly confined to a few supermarkets only a mile or so away. Of course a requisite mall loomed a bit further off, a novel marvel of that age, in which everyone congregated as at a newly built cathedral.

160

His own perambulation brought him along the lovely waterfront, opened to a public road, that ran from the bottom of the hill where they lived to head of harbor where the town had been founded in 1650 or so (again as in Pennsylvania.) Nathan Hale had been captured nearby. So landscape and history and nature—he could do worse. Of course, their home here was temporary, but he figured he might as well take advantage of it for the next short year or so. Besides, he had always believed in the necessity of pulling as much as possible out of anywhere he might be, especially by walking and looking and thinking.

He hiked to escape and to be alone and to settle his thoughts. Sometimes weather would be too dismal, or too many tasks piled up, but when he could get away he tried to center himself under open sky as much as possible.

I had realized Joan's family was different than mine from the time I first met her. Instead of never mentioning, nor much thinking of, parents and siblings, Joan constantly referred to her father and mother and chatted often on the phone to her brothers. That trait was only emphasized by brief visits to her parents' house over the years, such as during the wedding, when all kinds of close and distant relatives came out of woodwork and from surrounding lands to engulf her. So I knew I was heading into a familial maelstrom of some type. To be honest, from a distance at least, I found it refreshing and hoped it might be something we could emulate with our own children.

What I didn't quite anticipate was the intrusive omnipresence. Oh, I had casually realized that we would all be in the same house, sharing dishes, and living with each other, yet I had somehow thought it would be like my other roommate experiences at college or communal living in Berkeley. We would share meals and chores and go our own way, doing our own things. That turned out not to be the case.

All actions were surveyed and implicitly or explicitly judged. Although they tried to give me leeway and the benefit of the doubt as new to the system, it was quickly apparent that in all things there was the right way and the wrong way to do things. The right was always their way. Argument was futile—they were older and knew better and—whose house was it anyway? So I had to adapt and become acquiescent to such demands very quickly, without overt resentment, going along to keep things smooth, even if it involved, sometimes, shading the truth a bit.

Joan's brothers and relatives, like her parents, were also full of advice on career and real estate and what must be done next and, of course, the proper way to do it. Each was absolutely certain of being correct, which did not seem to mean that they necessarily agreed with each other. But the way of communicating here was to be firm and sure of oneself. It reminded me uncomfortably of my father, and I did my best to float along, putting on a face of knowing what I was doing even though I was pretty insecure deep down.

For better or worse, I quickly realized that the family was always there, even when Joan and I were separated from them, because we would have to return to sleep. Our actions, our plans, our very thoughts were conditioned by having to once again return and agree. After all, and always, whose house was it?

Thank you.

Nothing fancy, almost an elementary school classroom, primitive desks, a long table in front, white board available behind the teacher, dressed casually. I look around and find mostly people in their late twenties and early thirties, all looking quite serious. The professor, if such it is, turns around and naturally transmutes into Ghost.

"Welcome," he booms stentoriously, "to Sociology 203, Family Relationships. My name is Doctor ...."

"Ghost," I interrupt. "Just great. Doctor Ghost. What next."

"Well," he answers, "you could certainly have used this class to adjust to your new home. Naturally, you must also purchase and follow my expensive textbook."

"I think I ended up coping very nicely, thank you."

"Not according to other witnesses. "

"According to me. That counts for something. Mostly I survived and didn't commit any unpardonable mistakes. It's about all you could expect in the circumstances."

"Oh, perhaps, perhaps. But you certainly could have put everyone more on your side. You brought down a fair amount of credit just for marrying into the family, you know."

"Sure, but I still had to find my own way. And not step on too many toes doing it. Everyone was telling both of us what to do next."

"They had their own experiences to draw on."

"Which were not ours. That's the trouble with generations. What one goes through is never really applicable to the next, exactly. Generalities, I'll give you. Specifics, no. And circumstances ...."

"Still defensive, I see."

"Realist."

"Well, one old adage you did learn totally."

"And that was?"

"He who pays the piper calls the tune ..."

Getting rid of the empties was becoming a problem. Wayne found it not so hard to slip in a six pack to their private area, but eventually the bottles would become too much even for the large trash bag or paper shopping bags he had there. Trying to get them out of the house was embarrassing, since someone was always in the kitchen, watching and commenting. Well, at least he could clean up here.

Joan came in and, seeing what he was doing, said "Dad told me 'your husband has a problem.' You are drinking a lot, you know."

"Not all that much," said Wayne defensively. "Just beer, just in the evenings. Besides, this is the only vacation I'm likely to get for a long time."

"Oh, I guess," she sighed. "But it seems like a lot."

Wayne privately thought it was a lot less than in Boston. Nothing but beer, never to full intoxication, just trying to maintain a social buzz in the late afternoon or evening. But the Spagnolos were not like his parents, who had cocktails every evening, with Dad enjoying beer most weekends. Here a glass of wine at the table was only for an occasional celebration, maybe twice a month. Perhaps too jealously, he tried to maintain his own developed lifestyle.

"How are you feeling today," he asked, hoping to change the subject.

"Heavy, very heavy. I don't know how often I can go through this." She claimed to have gained 40 pounds, and that was an awful lot for her slight frame. "I hope you'll be able to drive me to the hospital."

"No problem. I've gotten you to the checkups ok so far, right?"

"Well, yes. But you know this could happen any time."

"And I'll be ready. But you don't think it will be today, and the doctor says it will be over a week, and in the meantime I just wait and pass the time. I hope we're all cleared up by the time I start work."

"Not half as much as me," she sighed. "If this baby's late I may kill it. I want to get back to normal."

Wayne doubted either of them would be "back to normal" anytime soon. He defiantly opened another beer and took a gulp.

It was a cute tiny town, Wayne had to admit, which organically sprouted from passes through some surprisingly steep and high sand bluffs rising from its harbor towards inland plains. Unconsciously he had expected an island to be smaller. He assumed Huntington would resemble all the honky-tonk towns he had known on the Jersey shore barrier beaches.

But this geography was complex and huge. Locally it had the usual variety of stores and shops, hardware, clothing, food, drugstores, jewelry and places to eat, most dating back a decade or before. It also encompassed much history, dating to its founding in 1653, with preserved buildings from that era and many old structures since. Even oddities from the turn of the century, an Odd Fellows Hall, for example, and a decaying theater.

Most surprisingly, and happily, it had more than one wonderful bookstore, including a few that sold used books. Oscar's was his favorite, with its endless basement of unsorted and barely priced treasures. That was a place he could disappear into and enjoy for a while, just like some in Boston. In fact, he gradually came to feel it was not much inferior, for his purposes, to Cambridge. But then, he always did adjust fairly easily, and had relatively modest demands. He carried his world on the inside, barely affected by his surroundings anyway.

Joan's knowledge of the area was surprisingly meagre. She had grown up here since the age of four, but her experiences were largely limited to the immediate harbor shores below her house and the surrounding woodlands, now subdivided into homes. She stuck to known routes into favorite parts of town—the church, the high school. She knew how to get to one mall, but beyond that she had hardly ventured more than five miles from her home. She had not visited many parks, or museums, or much of anything else. Finding the obstetrician in Hauppauge had proved a challenge that Wayne had to solve with the aid of maps and her father's directions.

Wayne would have been more critical, but it occurred to him that much the same could be said of his own knowledge of the places where he grew up. After all, most of those years were spent well before he could drive, and after that a few years of being mobile were likewise restricted by schedule and necessity. Anyway, there was enough friction already, and he hesitated to tease or criticize anything for fear a joke might escalate into an explosion.

Expecting something completely different, as I had experienced in all my other relocations, it came as something of a shock to find how closely Huntington resembled my roots in the Delaware Valley suburbs. Almost the same age, sharing a lot of the same history. At home we had Valley Forge, here there was "Halesite" where Nathan Hale supposedly was captured by the British before being hung as a spy in New York. In the Historic Cemetery, filled with eroding tombstones, plaques described the "outrage" when many of them had been used for a gun platform to control the harbor during that war. And historic senses and pride ran deep.

The homes too were familiar, as were the new cookie-cutter housing developments filling rapidly disappearing estates and farms. Long Island seemed more advanced in the process than Philadelphia, but some of that was because I was not witness to the same phenomena and I remembered that area as it had been two decades before. In short, if you put Huntington and Ambler side by side, or switched them, hardly anyone would much notice.

So my shock was not because of adapting to new settings or homes or parks or hills or ambience. The shock was being returned to childhood in a place that was different only in place names and the presence of a bit more open water. From my perspective, I might as well have moved to Pennsylvania.

I was not much of a social observer, but a few differences were striking. Long Island was more New York raw, more immigrant driven, much more ethnic and far less old settled German. I had expected to find no ethnic communities, but they were in profusion, the blacks in their circumscribed enclaves, Italians, Jews, Poles and old time WASP wealth and baymen poverty.

The main difference which came up in conversation was the constant drive for more. Everyone talked about their next house and their next job and the next opportunities they wanted to be part of. New York aggressiveness filled their blood and their dreams. Nobody lived where they had grown up, and those who did rarely wanted to remain. It was on to the next, improve what you have, keep moving up and out. The point of life was to have more and more. Fully American, to be sure, but I had come from a settled enclave where the great dream was to hold on to what was wonderful and have a happy and contented life. Eventually, that became the biggest hurdle for me to overcome—it was really hard for me to spend hours listening to folks cud-chewing over property prices.

"Ah, Mr. Slingluff, so nice that you could come. Please sit over there. Sorry your wife could not make it, perhaps next time, yes?" Ghost is white on white in a white room with a white window looking out at white clouds in the sky. Only his dark goatee and glasses add contrast. I chuckle darkly.

"Yes, next time no doubt. And the time after that. You certainly want there to be a next time, at least once a week for a few years, hopefully forever. At a good price per hour, I'm sure."

"So cynical," he sighs.

"And what, exactly are we to discuss today, Doctor. I assume you would like to be a doctor in this scenario."

"And so irreverent besides. We need to discuss your goals, of course, and how they interface with other people and society."

"My goals. I see. My goals," I state proudly, "are quite my own. There, are we done?"

"What, no outside references at all?"

"Well, let's see, Doctor," I try to sound as sarcastic as possible. "No, not really. I would like to please my parents, of course, but not to the extent of giving up my own visions. College disabused me of caring much about what the culture expects. I learned in France how fragile the imagined wonders of historic fame and cultural achievement could be. California taught me to suspect most of the hot flash enthusiasms of my peers. So, not much left really. Except Joan, of course."

"Ah, now we are getting somewhere. Joan, at least, matters to you, what she thinks."

"Well, of course. You are a dense person, are you not?" He sits back calmly, writing notes. I continue "Joan does help keep me grounded and holds me from getting too extreme in myself. I trust her judgement implicitly, and when she gets too angry or upset I know it is time to reconsider myself. Sure, I want that."

"But here, in this place, even that frays, no?"

"Only at first. Then we figured out that as a unit we were still separate from her beginnings too. We're lucky that way, I guess, we both kind of think the same."

"But she reveres her family..."

"I love mine too, you know. We just don't let them make us do things we don't want to. Like most healthy people, I think. Don't suppose you get too many of those in here, though."

"You are too cruel," he murmurs.

"Can I please go now."

"Your loss," he says. "See you next week?"

"Not a chance, Doctor. Have a good life."

"And this," said Joan happily, "is Uncle Xjglekg and here is aunt Dlklkggg. They're the parents of cousin Svilll over there and her husband Bltlegx." This happened not once, not twice, but seemingly in an unending round of new faces and names he would never remember. Wayne smiled and nodded and was led from one cluster to another.

The whole month seemed to be one big social gathering. Older people who were not working, including neighbors, came by all month to see Joan and congratulate her parents. People Wayne's age stopped in to visit and invite them out, Joan declining most because she was feeling weighed down. Weekends were fiestas—sometimes he imagined he had been magically transported to an Italian village. The atmosphere was accented with Christmas decorations and special holiday foods being prepared in grand old traditions.

He had no experience with all this. Although he had known relatives when he was young, his was not a far-flung close-knit family, and contacts had grown more tenuous as he grew up. And there were never as many in as thick a web as all this. It seemed Joan had grown up communally in a tight-knit group with all her cousins, friends, and playmates of her older brothers. Her parents had brothers and sisters in profusion, and most of them lived in the city or on Long Island, and they were always seeing each other in person to compare notes. There was no letup.

He had no clues here. All the new people were in the same rooms, they all looked more or less the same, he had no handle on knowing them. So he tried to pick up an idea of who each was as he ran into them again from the conversation, and not look like a complete dope. Mostly, he failed, but he stayed as pleasant as possible.

He guessed that a lot of this would drop off after the birth and the excitement of returning home like a long-lost orphan had worn off. He was wrong.

Perhaps the most difficult short-term adjustment was the overwhelming closeness of Joan's family. I had been left alone for a long time, and Joan and I retained our separate spaces and spheres, pretty much leaving each other to go our own ways when we so desired. I was not used to people always on top of me, always asking things, always suggesting things, always finding something which I should do differently.

It wasn't nasty or grating. Nobody was being mean. It was just their style. But it seemed to include everything from how I dressed to how I combed my hair, how I cut my hair, how I held my knife, what I planned to do. Everything I said was dissected as if I were a politician running for office, and then more or less discounted to nothing while someone else suggested a better course of action or thought.

That was how a tight family was, I guess, them against the world. Her father, after all, was a true immigrant from Italy and had been alone except for relatives when he arrived at Ellis Island at the age of nine. Her Mom had been born in Brooklyn, to immigrant parents who mostly spoke Italian and lived in one of the ethnic enclaves common at the time. All resources were within established webs described by blood and marriage. Before The Godfather, but on a more benign scale it was much the same thing.

Sometimes I felt like running away and screaming, especially that first month when there were no other distractions. Once I was working, my whole day was spent elsewhere, and I was too notably tired at night to pay much attention even if criticism were offered. But at first, with nothing to do, and just having come down, and with the future up in the air, it was all I could do to remain civil and as composed as possible. Even so, I often escaped into the outer cold or the inner sanctum of our rooms, which fortunately were respected as such.

I knew it had been part of the bargain when we got married. I even liked everybody. Her Mom and Dad were fine people that I could learn a lot from, and I had expected to have to listen to them. What I had not expected much were her brothers and cousins and aunts and uncles and second cousins. All, as it were, taking me aside as in <u>The Graduate</u> to whisper the magic word "plastics"—although here the magic word was always "real estate."

Well, somehow the month went on and somehow I made it through reasonably well. There was always the coming baby to redirect the conversation if things got too sticky. After all, that was the prime cause of our being here, of my being here, and the central mission of the immediate future. Real estate or not.

"Breathe deeply, in, out, slower, in, out, in out. Imagine a beach, sand under your shoulders, warm sun shining on your closed eyes, waves gentle in the distance, in, out, in, out …." Only the rhythmic sounds of several people lying on mats, relaxing. I peek out and see Ghost next to me in a dim vaguely pastel green room.

"In, out," he chants, as everyone tries to follow. "In, out …"

"Uh, Ghost, hate to interrupt but …"

"Hush. In, out…"

"Is this the whole thing, then? Just lying, breathing."

"Empty your mind. Deeper now. Deep in, deep out."

"OK, OK. I get it. I just have to accept the situation and stay calm."

"Center on your navel. Feel fresh air down from mouth through lungs spreading outward reaching into head, fingers, toes, and then out carrying away all worries. In, out …"

"Sorry I have things to do."

"Life is just being. Being is in your core. In, out..."

"Yes, but ..."

Much of December felt as if he was just barely hanging on to sanity. He tried to make it through each day, thinking as little of the past or possible future as possible, reading technical texts, taking short walks in the increasing wet and cold. At times, Wayne almost hovered out of body, a neutral observer of a life that was someone else's.

He felt deprived, in a way, that his art dreams were now dead and gone. But not too deprived, because the plain truth was that he had given those up quite a while ago, and the drive necessary to proceed with them had been channeled into computers for some time. He resented not being able to complete his current project with the jewelry software. But not too resentful, because he recognized that it was a dead end in a minor key, going almost nowhere, and the only folks who were going to make any money were Jim and the consultants. He missed Boston and all the excitement of the city. But he also felt he had done everything and experienced everything and had truthfully become a little bored by it all.

The past, then, was just a memory mine, and probably best left undeveloped for a while. He was not some doddering old wreck recounting the good old days. The future was where everything would be exciting and different. Unfortunately, any clear vision of the future tended to end suddenly at the first image of commuting in before six in the morning to a fearful and crowded urban jungle where he would probably be overwhelmed. No, best not to think about that too much either.

So that left the present. And the present was pretty scary, with all the people, and all the bother, and all the advice, and all the adjustments, and all the lack of privacy. His thoughts and habits were supposed to change, his activities were supposed to change, his routines would have to change, where was he? As someone who always prized solitude the complete lack of it most of the time was perhaps the greatest hardship, in his mind, that he endured.

And, his rational self kept saying, that isn't so bad, is it? You're safe and warm and eating well and have a big support group and Joan and a nice future with children. How many people his age in the world would envy him and happily change places if possible. His rational intuition remained eternally sunny and optimistic, and most of the time it could harness his deeper and more chaotic hormones.

Nothing to be proud of, but I ended up hiding my fears and insecurities with a show of exaggerated confidence and boasting about where I was going. That was fairly easy, because whenever I mentioned computers people were impressed, and when I started to talk programming their eyes glazed over as if I were discussing the mathematical principles of the universe. Nobody understood anything, so with a little bit of jargon and a lot of bluster I could easily sound like an expert.

I needed that for myself as much as for anyone else. Keeping up appearances had become important in my own mind. Sure, I was a loyal and dutiful husband who had followed his wife's desire to return to her roots, no matter the consequences. That gained points. And yes, I had given up my youthful illusions to find real full time work in normal commerce. More points. And for the most part I was civil and compliant to all the pressures and currents swirling around me. So many points. So few sunk in during the dark and cold evenings and worries about what would happen in January if they all proved an illusion.

But I eventually realized that even all these illusions were tangibly real, in some sense. My insecurity could magnify problems. One thing I never had throughout my life was a decent sense of proportion—problems appeared too big or too small and only when I actually tackled them did I find out what they really were. My imagination could be my greatest friend and worst enemy at the same time, my mercurial mind could slip various imaginations into the projector at lightning speed. A month of inactivity letting it run wild was not good.

Inexorably, Christmas, the due date, and end of year ground closer. Inner tensions became more and more tightly strung. Some days I felt I would melt, some days explode, but each morning was a nice reset and I had the gift of starting each dawn as a new person.

Dark musty paneled office, books everywhere, big desk covered with papers. I knock and am gestured in by someone with his back to me, talking on
the phone. Obviously, I am not one of his star students, and this consultation
is a necessary formality of his job description. Finally, he hangs up and swivels around, ancient sports jacket neatly pressed, tie slightly askew. "Ah, Mr.
Slingluff, finally here to discuss your thesis, are you?"

Before my brain can kick in, I automatically reply, "Yes, Professor. " Then
I get ahold of myself and chuckle, "Got me there Ghost, I admit."

He forces a smoky laugh around his pipe. "So, you are planning a paper
on what, exactly?"

"Basically the need to worry about what you can control in your environment and how to ignore all the entertaining junk you cannot and will not
affect no matter what you do."

"Fairly pessimistic, that, I think. And limiting. You could be anything."

"No, I couldn't. But more importantly, to strive to become something
that does not come easily—to dedicate your entire being to a goal—is corrosive to your soul."

"My, my. And all I thought you needed was a paper."

"Anyway, I only speak for myself. I am trying to formulate exactly what
has been important to me—my immediate family, my own life outlook, my
appreciation of days, my triumph in the areas of work and home that I could
impact meaningfully. They are all distinguished by being circumscribed."

"Gloomy and selfish, young man."

"Young man no longer, Ghost," I tell him. "Less selfish than the dreams
of the mighty."

"High horse, too."

"Ah, we need to take the world we actually encounter and deal with it."

"Individually oriented Stoicism, eh? Needs work. See you next week." I
know I've been dismissed. And, I admit, probably rightly so.

Pop, pop, pop, pop. Just through the magic passage of time, bubbles and

BABYLON WITH GHOST

pressures dropped off suddenly at the end of December. Gregory was born and diverted all the family attention. Christmas came and went with almost all the relatives. New Year's marked the start of his upcoming job, which nobody could question because nobody (and hardly he himself) understood what he was going to be doing.

There was something to be said for simple survival, Wayne thought. Sometimes you are on top of the world and accomplish miracles, but sometimes it is enough just to make it out of a time when you cannot. Low expectations, perhaps, but always with the hope of a brighter tomorrow.

Special Delivery

LAUGH-FILLED CONVERSATION DRIFTED in from the living room, voices loud from the necessity of overcoming hearing loss among most of the participants. Joan rested in frequent pain on the bed, all but ignored, as the holiday celebrations continued. Wayne was at her side some of the time, as much from being shut out of relatives' ongoing pet themes as from sympathy for his wife. Otherwise her mom would take shifts with one of the aunts, or she would rest alone, waiting.

This was the true division, Wayne thought, the boundary of the old life and whatever came next. They had made the move, everything was unpacked or stored in the garage, tucked around her brother's boat trailer. Boston was an irrelevant memory, frantic days of travel and planning had slipped into infrequent dreams, the new job and new family hovered about to begin. Imminent. Probably appropriate for the Christmas season, he reflected. It was only the 20th, so he didn't think the child would arrive on Christmas day, but close enough for a parallel. Holidays were the reason for the party around a small artificial tree, Christmas lights here and there, special dinner cooking, drinks. Wayne hadn't had many of those, he was being good, worried about what might be required next. Besides, it was not really a time or company in which to relax, he still concerned about first impressions and getting along.

They'd started with a quick early morning examination at her doctor's. He was part of their relocated and unfamiliar health care plan out in Hauppauge. Just hours ago, they'd been assured there was no need to worry, it would be a day or two yet. 'Quick trips' anywhere on Long Island tended to take a half hour or more one way, shocking after everything being a few steps away in the city. Everything was carefully orchestrated. A special birthing room with all the latest "hippie" comforts had been reserved at St. John's hospital, several practice drives had given Wayne a good idea of how long it would take to get there.

Joan moaned again, he went in. "It hurts," she said.

Sympathetically, he tried to comfort her. "It can't be long now, but you know he said it won't be today. I guess all you can try do is relax. Can I get you some cookies or something?|"

She just moaned again, bringing in Mom and Aunts. Wayne wandered back out. Women exchanged obstetrical tales and tips. Dad was heading over for with more real estate advice, Wayne braced himself.

There was a lot of commotion in the bedroom, Joan rushed into the bathroom next door, aided by the other women. A short cry and then a yell. "Bloody show!" she cried accusingly to Wayne. "We need to get to the hospital <u>now</u>!" He jumped for the phone.

No mistaking a clinical medical room of the time, all harsh lighting and sterility. Ghost stands majestically in white gown. "All women's work, right?" he asks.

"Not hardly," I replied. "We were fully modern expectant parents. I was involved…"

"But when push comes to shove, Joan had to do the work."

"Well, of course, but…."

"No buts here, keep things in perspective. Men do tend to take too much credit."

"Doctors too," I insert. "Babies have been arriving for eons without any such help, you know."

Ghost is unabashed. "You think if you are sympathetic, drive to the hospital, hang around for the birth, and later change a diaper or two you are just like mothers. But anyone who has been through it knows it's not really like that. The women must, in fact, do the main and hard labor of carrying to term, delivery one way or another, initial nursing and bonding. Inevitably, almost, they get stuck with all the non-cute moments of the tiny infant. You don't see many Renaissance paintings of "Joseph and infant Jesus."

"Ok, Ghost, no real argument, but I think I tried harder. My father wasn't in the delivery room, you know."

"For the times, though, he did as much as any other father. Maybe more."

"Well, anyway, we thought I was engaged. Joan thought I was trying hard. That's what really matters."

"Not to her at that moment, of course."

"If you put it that way ....."

Changing careers, moving to a completely new location, cutting them-selves off from almost everything they had developed in the early adulthood was hard, but expected. What was not was the odyssey they encountered after they decided it was time to have a child to force the issue.

The sexual revolution, of course, had centered around the birth control pill. Battles still raged on its availability and morality, although not much among those women of child bearing age. Abortion was still a fight, but "Our Bodies, Our Selves" was the female rallying cry. And the center of woman's rights as understood in the sixties and seventies had pretty much boiled down to "let us do what we want without getting pregnant."

The naïve, like Wayne, naturally assumed that without some form of birth control, things went mechanically and automatically and almost with-out effort, a lot like eating a meal when you get hungry. Joan knew better, but was swayed by the prevailing sentiments and the experiences of her friends who had children to think it was a simple decision. Wayne even had been aware of some problems his mother had, but boys didn't normally discuss such things in family back then. So it came as a shock when Joan stopped taking her pills, months went by, and nothing happened.

At first, it was literally nothing, as menstruation did not resume on sched-ule. Finally they became worried, and sought out help. Fortunately, their new HMO and other health plans did cover family planning and what passed for fertility boosts. Clinics in Cambridge gave Joan medication to resume menstruation. After her periods restarted but nothing continued to happen, Wayne was startled to find he all but "failed" a sperm test. Time kept running along.

Joan began to religiously consult thermometers and calendars. Wayne tried to be available whenever the conditions were right. For the first and only time in their lives, sex turned into a chore, something that had to be done whether they felt like it or not. They read literature, talked to people, gossiped, and superstitiously tried various foods and positions. Finally, after almost two years had passed, success.

In the meantime, Joan had taken the new job at an office downtown. Each day, through an excessively hot and humid summer, she had to climb the high stairs to Charles street station to take the smashingly crowded Red Line a few stops to Bradford Trust. Then back again, of course. She became more and more trapped in the oven-like apartment, with only fan for relief, prisoner of four flights of narrow stairs to get out or back in. Unsurprisingly, she was tired and cranky all the time. And, on top of that, there was packing and cleaning and more packing to do. And keeping Wayne under control, more and more nervous as the actual moving date approached.

There were the constant daily exercises, which in the spirit of the times, they shared and did together, Wayne primarily acting as a "coach." Lamaze classes were offered and faithfully attended right across Cambridge Street in Mass General. Almost everything, except from those who had actually undergone childbirth, was presented a bit too rosily. The wonderful experience, when you talked to those who had endured it, was wonderful only in retrospect.

By October, Joan was all but immobilized, and Wayne did everything that could be done to expedite the change. They rented a big truck and drove it down in early November, leaving Joan on Long Island when Wayne took the train back. A few weeks later, with odds and ends cleaned up, he drove their car down and joined her, ready to start the new job in early January.

They spent some of that late fall doing the paperwork and aggravation of finding new doctors, switching the necessary forms, locating equivalent hospitals that accepted their insurance. The one in Smithtown had what they knew they wanted from conversations and reading—a special "birthing room," almost a clubhouse for the new nuclear family. They were shown a lovely, sunlit, spacious, clean room, with soft couches and cushions, all the latest in non-harsh hospital care.

Finally, it was a trip every week, then even more often, to the seemingly distant clinic where their obstetrician practiced. Unlike others in Boston, he was relatively old-school and non-nonsense conservative, young Asian Indian when they had so far only encountered young, hip, and white professionals. But, hey, millions, billions did this all the time. So they waded on through.

"Are you ready yet?" Joan asked, as she exited the bathroom.

Wayne looked up from his latest manual on the confounded operating system and replied, "Sure, whenever you are."

"You have the cushions and books?"

"Right here, in the bag like always." He got up off the floor and switched off the Red Sox game. "Just let me use the bathroom a minute."

"You're worse than I am," she complained, which was surprisingly true. He used the bathroom at a rate, it seemed, of ten to one compared to her, even now that she was going more frequently. So what, he thought.

They locked the door and he followed her down the stairs, which she held onto carefully. Pregnancy, he realized for the first time, is a kind of physical handicap once it gets really going. At least it seemed to be so here. She wasn't huge, compared to some of the other women in the class, but she was uncomfortably large compared to how thin she once had been.

Finally, they were out on Philips Street, and strolling down its narrow red brick sidewalk toward Cambridge Street. It was a lovely early evening, with the sun still shining high overhead, but not too hot although the pavement and walls around them were radiating the remnants of the day. Newly planted trees from the latest civic initiative seemed to be thriving.

"How are you doing, really, with work and all?" he asked, more to be polite than expecting an answer. With all the extra weight, she was easily winded and continually tired. Conversations had migrated indoors where Joan was more comfortable.

"It's not bad, once I get to work. Getting there and back is a real pain."

"You're lucky you don't have to go through what I'm doing," he retorted half-heartedly.

"Oh, you would say that. Here, we can cross now." Getting across Charles circle was a terrific adventure when you couldn't simply climb up and over like everyone else. Unwilling and almost unable to use the overpass they relied on chancy lights to permit their crossing to the other side, a deceptively short distance away. The trouble was the Cambridge/Charles exit circle funneled almost all the downtown traffic off of Storrow Drive, and no one expected to encounter pedestrians. Fortunately, the congestion was not too bad right now.

"Well, another few hours of breath in, breath out, push, push, push," he joked. There didn't seem that much to it.

"Everybody says we needed to take the class," she answered. "I sometimes think it's all going to be pretty useless too. I mean, it's gotta be different when you're actually in pain. And our parents never did any such thing.

"But they did use anesthesia," he pointed out.

"I don't think my Mom did," she answered. "Anyway, I don't want to do that. It's supposed to be bad for everything."

"Well, bad for everything except getting it over with. If it were me …"

"But it isn't! OK, here we are, now you be good and pay attention and do what they say."

"Yes, Joan, I always do, don't I?"

"Mostly, so far," her voice held reservations.

"Oh, relax."

The appropriate side doors on the dead end alley entrance were unlocked, they took the elevator up to the third floor and found maybe twenty other couples awaiting the instructor.

Joan went over to chat, while Wayne just relaxed and reviewed materials.

We wanted to be an informed young couple, part of a new wave of parents who were engaged in their child from the moment of conception. We were willing to challenge prevailing wisdom on the best methods of childbirth and prenatal care and postnatal environment. In that, we were helped by our old friends Joanne and Jonas whom I had met back in Kansas City Vista days. Jonas had actively trained to be a midwife, and had a wealth of advice and materials which often contradicted the standard literature.

It was part of a new movement, not entirely resisted by the medical profession many of whom were only too happy to see such involvement. Pregnancy, after all, is an odd kind of medical "condition." It is certainly not a disease that needs treatment and curing, there is nothing more fundamental in all of life's destiny than reproduction. Yet there is no denying that it is a dangerous and painful procedure.

So we could be torn on what to do. There were none of the current obsessions with caesarian sections, of course, but the big debate was on whether to just put the woman under general anesthesia and wake up presto! when it was all over, or endure as best as possible the pain of delivery. It was easy enough for a man to say "tough it out, the right way is full consciousness," but it was his partner who had to go through it.

And the fact was, no matter how the Lamaze nurses and midwives romanticized it all, there was pain involved. No amount of breathing and concentration and support could overcome that basic fact. Human requirements for big brains have almost overtaken the pelvic ability to fit heads through. Besides which the civilized world had finally hit on the point where death in childbirth was not accepted as a natural (and too frequent) possibility, and death or deformity of a child was not written off as the will of God. In that sense, of course, they were treating a medical anomaly.

All of which meant that there was a little uncertainty around the whole thing. Sexuality was in the open now, but children of boomers were just starting to become frequent. In some ways, the accepted medical technology and advice of the times was by today's standards woefully outdated. On the other hand, humans had been having children for hundreds of thousands of years without doctors, and still did so in most places in the world.

Same cheerless facility, but a smaller beige office to the side, walls covered with happyish posters, glistening sterility all around on various mysterious instruments. Ghost stares at me icily. "You were one of those faddish hippy-types, eh?"

"No, not at all. We were current and up to date."

"Same thing," he grunts, as much as an immaterial being can grunt satisfactorily. "I find there may be very little difference between fads and being inadequately informed. Common sense gets a little too much credit in a medical setting."

"I admit that the notion of truth tends to slide around over time, and make old positions somewhat silly. A few stupid people refuse to change their opinion no matter what."

Ghost thinks I mean him. He stretches his rubber gloves menacingly. "You guys always claim you are maintaining integrity in the face of opinions, all self-righteous. But there are well-founded medical standards that ought to be followed."

"We weren't planning to use a field or barn," I laugh. "But sometimes attitudes change with reason."

"Fine if you're testing granola mixes," he lectures. "Not so fine when childbirth is involved."

"Ghost, we took all the evidence we could find, decided who and what we would trust, made our decisions, and were flexible enough to change our minds in the face of massive evidence to the contrary. Besides, the medical community and doctors themselves seemed to have opinions all over the place."

"How much Lamaze is still out there," he wonders, wandering towards the door.

"OK, Mom, talk to you next week. Say hello to everyone," Wayne hung up the phone as Joan walked into the kitchen area from the back bedroom.

"Temperature's up," she announced, "I've marked it on the chart. So we have to be sure to try hard this time."

Wayne almost groaned. It was amazing, that something like sex could become work. He certainly wouldn't have believed it possible a few years ago. Now it would be over a week of making love at least once a day, every day, no excuses. No being too tired, no eating too much to indigestion, no drinking too much, nothing should prevent the evening activities.

"Ah, today's what, Sunday? So, I guess until next Wednesday or so, at least...."

"I'll keep checking," she said, "coming over and grabbing his arm. I'm sure we can do it this time, the doctor says I'm getting more and more regular."

"Yeah," Wayne replied glumly, "but my sperm count is still an issue."

"They told you to wait on that for a while, it's still borderline."

"How long, I wonder. We can't stay in suspense like this forever."

"Stop being such a baby. It's not like this is all that hard. I thought you loved me …" she added coyly.

"Cut it out," he exclaimed in irritation. "I know, I know, it's just …."

There was something so mechanical about it all. Something almost unnatural. He hadn't read enough to know how many royalty had endured the same issues, with a lot more psychological aggravations, long ago. In their own case, they wanted children, but not quite so desperately immediately as to guarantee the kingdom would continue.

Anyway, the rest of the day was lined up, noon already. A few hours strolling around, a while reading the paper, a nice stir fry for dinner (but not too spicy, not too greasy, needed to keep the stomach calm). Then early bed for the long commute tomorrow, in the freezing weather that fortunately did not promise snowfall. Trains and busses were horrible in any kind of precipitation.

As bedtime approached, they both got ready, with both anticipation and resignation. At this point, there would normally be some sort of steamy sex scene, but that is not to be here. Everything worked.

To be honest, although Wayne and Joan truly loved each other, and sex was a big component of that, they had both ended up being kind of matter of fact about it all. Whereas others were madly in lust, they had treated it all more as a recurring hunger, coming on almost predictably, satisfied when necessary, an important part of their lives together, but hardly the main glue that kept them as a couple. It was one reason they got along well, he thought.

As unprepared as we seemed to be for conception, we were far more so for actual parenthood. Naively, we believed that many years of working in day care had given us special insight into child rearing. We had, after all, read countless literature, attended numerous workshops, lived and breathed difficult and easy development, had hands-on experience with multiple types of children in various environments. What else could possibly be required?

A lot, as it turned out. There is a real difference, we were to find, between teaching as a profession and children as a constant responsibility. I would not be paid for moments with my offspring, and I would not be given time off to recover later. No, I would be working most days at something completely different and when I finally came home would immediately be designated for active duty with whatever problems were occurring today.

Joan could not hand off the class to an aide as she went outside for a cigarette break or decided to help in the kitchen for a few minutes preparing the midday snack. It would be her and the often screaming, always needy baby. Even with her mother's help, it was to become overwhelming.

Both of us would endure the normal parental grind of late night feedings and changings, rocking the wailer to sleep, being kept awake when we knew we would have to get up early the next day.

Blissfully, we were initially unaware of all that. All the concentration was on starting and growing the in-utero life, almost like a hidden houseplant, until it popped into the world and everything would, we assumed, become normal again.

We were, moreover, filled with the counterculture ideas of natural and right upbringing, a softer Dr. Spock. I believed I could take on all the roles fathers were supposed to do without aggravation or complaint. Joan knew she would somehow correctly raise perfect little family members. We both had a lot to learn. The hard way.

"In all this," Ghost puts down the questionnaire I just filled out, "You seem almost surprised by babies. What the heck did you think sex was for?"

"Oh, pleasure a little, I guess. Bonding mostly. It was our way of building and enforcing complete trust."

"Gooey rationalization. Even you must have remembered basic biology and Darwin."

"Maybe, but we seemed something different than that."

"Sex. Stupid Boomers. I get them all the time. Free love until—surprise!"

"Not true at all," I protest. "Nowadays the internet and culture keeps it front and center obsessively all the time. Pornography, I think, is one of those fads that will eventually just die away. It has become more like our work to have a baby. Back then, it was more liberating, a social protest."

"Idiots!"

"Not like today," I tell him. "Lately, I think claim they want sex just because they think they are supposed to or are missing something rather than out of any real pleasure."

"And you, by contrast, were pure and wholesome innocents in the Garden of Eden."

"Sure. When I was a kid any dirty pictures, let alone a stag film, was insanely salacious. You couldn't find them, and you felt incredibly transgressive when you did. No matter what you watch now, there's probably more guilt involved in eating a donut. We made it wholesome."

"Next, you'll be selling me a bridge in the city." He indicates the interview is over.

"Would you be interested?"

As Joan got dressed and ready to go, Wayne put the necessary gear in the car. He awaited the call back from the doctor's office, just confirmation of where to go and what to do. The early afternoon light was beginning to fade already. Finally, the phone rang.

"Mr. Slingluff?"

"Doctor Singe? Hello, yes the water just broke."

"What, I hardly believe it. Wait a second, I need to check…. Ah, you cannot go to St. John's."

"What? Why? We had all the plans …."

"Yes, I am aware of that situation. Unfortunately, you see, they are all filled today, you need to go to the backup which is Smithtown General."

"How do I find that? Is it far?"

"No, you will find it just down the road from the other. Here is the address…."

Joan was moaning in pain as they loaded her into the backseat of the old Dart, Wayne said goodbye and headed out the driveway, directions in hand. Just east on the Northern State to 347, then look to the left. He had never been there in his life. It shared nothing with the route they had been testing to the other hospital. Nothing to do about it, in those days before GPS and cell phones but to concentrate and be ready to ask for help if he needed it.

From the sounds of it, taking his time and being careful would be a mistake.

They made it out the local roads without problem from traffic or baby, but half an hour later as they whizzed down the all but empty parkway Joan plaintively asked, "Can you hurry a little more, please." Then she started to pant rapidly. Wayne pushed the gas a bit more, but it was all unfamiliar.

Ah, the end of the parkway, lights, the fork left to 347. Too long. Joan breathing heavily, repressing wails.

"Hurry up, hurry up. I don't know how long I can wait …. More breathing."

"Don't push, don't push, we're almost there," he called back more in hope than confidence.

The final intersection came into view at the top of the hill. To the left, Smithtown General shone like the promised land. There was a guard rail, a left turn lane, a dedicated signal. More moans, more insistent this time. "Almost there, just a minute, just waiting for the light …." even his voice was strained.

The light took forever, then, just as it turned ….

A fire truck blazing lights came up over the hill. It stalled the left signal, held the intersection. Brightly decorated, colored lights all over, was that a tree on top? Yes, a tree, with balls. Santa Claus waving at everyone as sirens wailed and a procession of official vehicles followed. The light changed back. The heavy traffic resumed. Another cycle of forced waiting. Heavy panting. "Don't push!"

Finally, they could make the left, cross into the parking lot, find the entrance, then get someone to help Joan up the ramp. She was hustled into a room while he tried to clean up the formalities at the desk, since they had short notice from the doctor and nothing was prepared. For a while, the nurses weren't even sure he should be allowed into the room.

No pillows. No comforting furniture. No Lamaze posters and helpful birth coaches. A no-nonsense sterile hospital room in a no-nonsense sterile hospital, equipment which at first glance seemed more appropriate for treating knife wounds and broken bones. Joan was at least made adequately comfortable on the bed, the doctor arrived and expressed shock, then managed to argue successfully that Wayne was allowed to be present at the birth. Wayne helped as taught with the breathing, keeping the rhythm with Joan, but it obviously hurt a hell of a lot. Finally, pop, and it was all congratulations and happiness and winding down.

A boy. Wayne was neutral on the matter of gender, sonograms were a bit too new so it was a surprise to them, Joan claimed she only wanted a healthy child. But she had secretly wished for a girl, and convinced herself from various tales that it would be one. No big deal, but in the immediate depression following the effort, she wondered if she could possibly go through this whole thing—pregnancy and delivery—again. Anyway, healthy, male, Gregory Lyle.

As it turned out, they were treated well for the next day or so. They had a steak dinner, probably because of the holiday. Parents came and visited and gushed. Joan got to the hard work of recovery. But it had been a bit more of an adventure than they had expected.

Conventional American puritan culture subconsciously pretended that sex without offspring as a goal was simply sinful. The sexual revolution had kind of addressed that, although many women and men still saw it as mostly waiting for the right time, the right place, the right partner. Certainly planning was more desirable than haphazard accident, and abstinence struck the modern logical scientific minds as medieval stupid when not necessary. It often seems to be forgotten that most women were not interested in using the pill so they could continuously engage in orgies—not that a few didn't—but to control their lives. And serious men understood that underlying point as well.

But planning pregnancy could become almost as psychologically fraught as accepting the consequences of sex before prevention. When and where and who, exactly, were right, and how could you ever tell?

Children have always implied more than just themselves. For some, they signify the onset of true adulthood and meaning, approbation from the appropriate tribe and family, a sense of doing the necessary duty to everything. A few think they will change life for the better, correct mistakes, bring order out of chaos, and magically clear the ills of a failing or wayward life. Others worry that a wonderful lifestyle will be irremediably lost with a burden that lasts forever, sucks away resources of time and money, and brings the completely unpredictable into a comfortable existence. And all mixtures and stages, often unknown to even those thinking hardest about them. Like life, a complicated issue, with no real answers and only outcomes.

Ghost comes out of the delivery room, beaming. "It's a boy! Healthy! Congratulations, you're a father."

"Oh! Great!" Postpartum depression strikes new mothers, but new fathers can have their sudden moments of doubt. His tone must have indicated the uncertainty.

"Surely you are joyful! This is wonderful!"

"I know the lecture, thank you. Yes, yes, I'm very content and happy …"

"What did you expect? Or was this some kind of nasty duty you weren't sure about?"

"Maybe leaning towards duty towards family," I admit. "I knew we were giving up a lot, but a lot of that lot we were bored with. We knew that our lives would become much more strange and complicated. To be honest, there seemed little alternative?"

"You felt trapped?" The room shifts just a bit and the gown is gone.

"Nah, at that point just another challenge and hurdle. At some point you just do what you have to do. It was important to all our parents, very important to Joan, and pretty exciting to me to think of being a father."

"Sweetness and light?"

"By no means. We had seen enough. But if you never take chances, where are you, really?"

The last week and first half year required adjustment to screams at all times of night, and anxiety waiting for bowel movements. With his primary job complete, Wayne took the opportunity to join in the festivities a little too completely, trying to drown out the worry about the train, the subway, New York, the new job, and everything else.

But what was done was done. He admitted that tension had dropped a notch, everyone appeared well and healthy, and finally hope dawned that everything would work out. He took some long walks, just for the restful quiet, in cold and still air. So far, very little was being requested of him, as family swarmed the newborn.

Finally the tail end of a long, eventful year, an infinitely long year, thematically centered around the most important moment of their lives so far. Wayne had signaled his full acceptance of absorption into the standard culture, he was already living a suburban lifestyle, even though it was borrowed. Talk already turned to what they would do for their new family next. Even his parents were coming up to visit soon, to bless his return to what they considered normality.

Well, he reflected, as a stray flake drifted down through the trees, it could be a lot worse. He was afraid the next few months might even prove that depressing notion.

"So," asks Ghost softly, "was it all a good thing?"

"Very good. Totally right. Nothing I could have done would have been any better or more fulfilling. Of course, I tease Joan sometimes about pretend might have beens. But no, no regrets at all."

"Don't you wish you started sooner?"

"Again, not really. Maybe I just accept what happened as what should have happened too easily, but any other time earlier would have left us somehow incomplete and unfulfilled with our other desires."

"Your more selfish desires…."

"As you will. Different, anyway. But a family at this exact time was the exact right choice for us."

"Right time, right place, right partner?"

"Exactly. Although it was sometimes tough to be sure for a year or two."

New Year's day had come and gone and although it was officially 1981, it still felt like a coda to all that had happened. Wayne set the alarm clock for an obscenely early hour the next day, unsure how long it might take to get downtown, and whatever else might be involved. He probably wouldn't sleep much anyway, but at least for now Gregory was quiet. He had lots of other things to worry about.

1981 RELENTLESS ANXIETY

WORKIN' ON THE RAILROAD

WAYNE HAD LEFT the skyscraper at almost exactly five, as usual. He dashed up Wall Street on this relatively balmy April evening, waited a while for a jammed uptown 3, bought two cans of beer at Penn Station, one consumed immediately, one for the train. He was able to shoehorn himself onto the 5:45, an earlier train than normal, but as usual it would be standing room only all the way to at least Hicksville. He settled in leaning against the wall for the hour-long ride.

Sometime after Jamaica, they crawled even slower than usual. A stuffy ten minute pause, jerky advances, another dead stop. Nobody said anything, nobody knew anything, nobody could—no cell phones, broken intercoms. Finally word came via conductors working their way collecting tickets that there was a broken rail after Syosset and everyone would have to get off.

There was always a crisis on the LIRR, but this particular one was caused by a peculiarity of the Gold Coast Era of the early 1900's. Back then, the extremely wealthy had decided to divide up the North Shore as if it were feudal France, buying vast acreage for estates and plopping faux-Renaissance mansions on it. One of them, Otto Kahn, had gained title to a big chunk of land outside Cold Spring Harbor, built Oheka castle on a bluff overlooking the distant sound, and lorded it over everyone. When the railroad tried to expand from one track to two, he fought tooth and nail, and had enough political influence to make sure that for this one short stretch below his grounds only one working track disturbed his fantasy. So when a single rail broke, with no alternate, all transport to and from the city stopped dead.

When they finally pulled in, it was already close to eight, and the scene in the parking lot was a madhouse nightmare. Wayne had no idea how these things worked. There had been mention of busses, but someone was loudly complaining about standing out in the cold for an hour already. Where was Syosset, anyway?

The line for pay phones was immense and practically immobile. There seemed to be thousands of hapless commuters milling about in the harsh parking lot lighting. Well, he knew where the next stop, Cold Spring Harbor was and that didn't seem too far to walk. He'd call Joan from there.

As I stand on the cement platform surveying masses around, below, beyond, Ghost pushes his way over, shoving people out of the way, waving a microphone in one hand, a notebook prominently sticking out of one jacket pocket. "Sir! Sir! Can you tell me about how this is affecting you?!"

"Junior Jimmy Olson, are you today?" I ask.

"Please, sir, I just need a quote or two. When did you suspect there would be trouble?"

"When I woke up this morning. There's always trouble on this damn railroad. On the rare days there isn't there's something wrong with the subway."

"So you do not approve of the way things are run?"

"Couldn't be worse, as far as I can tell. Old crowded cars, slow service, late service, expensive service. It's all bad, all the time."

"Why don't you just not take it, then?"

"Like them," I gesture at the crowd, "the money is in the city. Working out here you not only make half the salary, you also get almost no chance at promotion to the really good jobs. No choice."

"You could drive."

"That's even worse, almost twice the time sometimes. "

"But why not live in the city?"

"Wife," I shrug. "Family out here."

"One more question," Ghost pauses. "What are you going to do now? How will this affect your evening plans?"

"Not sure how I get home from here, to be honest. As far as the other— well by the time I get home after waking up before dawn to get in we never have any plans at all. Grab dinner, have a drink, watch some TV, and go to bed. Maybe tonight I'll just skip dinner."

"Thank you sir," he strides off to find more aggravated quotes and anger. Not hard to locate, this evening.

It had dawned a normal morning. As usual, the alarm went off at six, and Wayne got up, took a shower, drank a cup of coffee, made half a peanut butter sandwich which he packed in his briefcase. He tried to be quiet, baby and Joan asleep, Joan's parents as well. Out the door by six thirty or so to catch the seven ten to Manhattan. It took a while to get to the station, and he had to park over a quarter mile away down the overcrowded parking lot. Not a bad morning brisk walk, even in the cold of winter, unless of course there was snow.

Huntington was the origination point for this train, so it often pulled out on time and he always got a seat, by preference on the window. Then it stuttered its way fitfully, gradually overflowing, filled with cigarette smoke haze and occasional snoring and the rustle of morning papers. Wayne had tried to read, but it gave him a headache in the lurching and jerking, so he pensively stared at the scenery crawling by and tried not to worry too much whether they were on time or not.

With luck, they would arrive at Penn by eight thirty, and he could dash through the turnstiles dropping in a token and be ready on the platform for the next downtown express. Which would often take forever, as a mob built up, heads peering out over the tracks to see if there were lights coming down the long tunnel. This was a total communication blackout, nothing but rumors. The main question here, when a packed train pulled in, was whether to try to squeeze in or take a chance for the next one, which was often (but not always) right behind this one, but with hardly anyone on board. But sometimes a half hour passed with nothing at all, or—even worse—constant arrivals on the inaccessible local track. A game he did not like much.

Mood was never improved by the actual subway ride. The cars came either unheated or overheated, jammed to capacity, covered with painted graffiti on the walls, scratched graffiti on the windows, dirt everywhere, and don't even think about the germs. The world-war-two-era cars threw everyone around if they were not clinging tightly to the greasy, sticky poles. With nothing at all to do, men mostly in business suits stared straight ahead grimly, trying to preorganize their days. Mixed in randomly were the bums and trash of the city, drunk or angry, sleeping or scowling or mumbling, usually stinking, and able to strike fear into anyone unfamiliar with metropolitan normality.

Eventually there was a mad dash out of Wall Street Station, pushing and shoving to rush up the stairs, and then, for Wayne, a three-block walk down to the Citibank tower at the east end. He was usually there well before nine, not that anyone checked, and there were no time clocks to punch in. Most of the time he was deeply into code translation before any supervisors showed up, which got him a reputation as a hard-working and dedicated employee. Nobody ever checked what he was writing.

What he hated most in all this was what he always hated most about any long morning commute. He ended up feeling like he had put in a full day's work by the time he started his job, just getting there. Worse, he sometimes had the impression he had wasted the whole day already, and could only trudge on through the remaining hours getting braced for the equally harrowing journey home.

Dutifully, over the winter, Wayne had visited Joan's brother Philip in his cramped little office around the corner, part of a large corporate empire where he had become important. Equally because of familial nagging, Wayne had headed over to yet another big bank tower where one of Joan's cousins was the manager of a large data processing department.

That data center was fully operational, filled with whirling tape drives and blinking lights just like a futuristic Hollywood movie. It took up an entire floor. Wayne was ushered into a glassed-in area off in one corner. "You must be Wayne," a harried-looking man in rumpled suit came out from behind a desk.

"Hi, you must be Joan's cousin Steve," replied Wayne, a bit intimidated.

BABYLON WITH GHOST

"So, do you like my empire?" A few people hanging around laughed. Steve held a cigarette, the air was thick with smoke. The room was hot and humid, everyone perspiring, not least Steve, who looked like he hadn't slept in a while. "I live here," he stated, "didn't get home at all last night." Everyone laughed again, as if at some inside joke.

"It's very impressive," replied Wayne, not sure what to say. "Do you do a lot of the programming here?"

"Oh, not programming," Steve gestured. "Here, come over to my desk, sit down, how's everyone at home?" They spent a few minutes catching up, Wayne not actually knowing all that much, and neither all that interested but knowing they would later be interrogated.

"What do you do, then, Steve."

"I do the important stuff," he lit another cigarette and leaned back. "I keep people doing what they're supposed to. You wouldn't believe how many things keep going wrong, how crazy it can get. Sometimes it's just one disaster after another, sometimes I don't sleep for days. You're lucky it's calm this afternoon, last week was insane."

"Sure looks like a lot," Wayne agreed. "And you understand it all?"

"Nah, nobody understands it all, not oven the guys that write it," more sniggers from the crowd down the room a ways. "But I know what is supposed to come out of it. When that's wrong I try to catch it before the bosses do, or recover when I don't. Mostly nerve-wracking. But if you like excitement and life in the big time, kind of fun. Pay's good, at least."

Wayne didn't think it looked like fun at all. If this was what he was aiming for, he wanted to bail right away. And the programmers here didn't look any better off. No, this wasn't at all where he wanted to be in a few years.

After a little more small talk, declining a dinner invitation after work, he politely left with an escort to the street and returned to his own calm space. A lot to think about.

Business New York in the eighties—including its transportation networks—seemed to take pride in being the dark nasty boiler room of the nation's economy. The attitude was "we get the important work done down here, who gives a damn how it looks." The more grime, the more little irritations ignored, the more a sense of just keeping things going amidst chaos, the more pride in what was being accomplished.

As mentioned, the trains were ancient and falling apart, the subways dangerous and filthy, the streets stained dark, the older buildings crumbling, the new ones boring functional glass and steel with no personality at all. Businesspeople dressed alike in dark suits, walked as brisk automatons from place to place, rarely smiled during daylight hours. They just wanted to make necessary salaries so they could escape to have fun elsewhere. Get through the day, get through the week, there wasn't it all worth it?

I began not to think so. People on the train were not happy, were in fact mostly profoundly irritated. People on the subway were miserable. People at work—well the ones with no power just did what they were told, as the powerless always do. But only the really upper level folks, occasionally glimpsed, seemed to have any brighter visions, even if those were simply of exploitation of bad situations.

Maybe it was nicer in the summer. I never really found out, back then. One grim winter and spring were more than enough for me. But by the time of the Long Island accident I had fully determined I had to leave and get somewhere out on the Island as soon as possible. I surely never wanted to become like Steve, and he could keep his job as long as he wanted.

"Did you notice anything different about the ride today, sir?" Ghost is back, having gone through the crowds for a while. Apparently everyone is just as angry as they look. No pitchforks and shovels evident but pencils and pens are no doubt invoking sizzling letters to the editor. "You seem less upset than some of the rest," he prods.

"What can you do? This type of thing happens so often it's more normal than not. Anyway, I don't plan to be riding it for long, so I can kind of treat it like an adventure."

"Did you notice anything different this afternoon?"

"Nah. Same old stuff, no seat, leaning against a wall trying not to fall. The older guys doing this for years all dozing off—probably getting more sleep than they do at home. Younger crowd of course all had beers ready. For some of them it had clearly been party time since lunch. But all of that was pretty typical for an evening commute."

"No unusual stops, no announcements, no premonitions?"

"Nope. Of course, I'm pretty much a zombie like anybody else by the time I get to the station. I check if the train is on time on the boards, try to find if they changed the regular track number, run if I need to. Doubt I'd notice an elephant or tiger walking through the crowd."

"Surely you're more aware than that…"

"After work? No way. I'm either thinking about what I was doing, or what I will do, or totally tired and just hoping I can get home for dinner. The stuff around me is a like a dream."

"This doesn't resemble a dream," Ghost points at the crowd.

"A bad dream." I walk off into the darkness.

Never having spent any significant time in Manhattan, Wayne was forced to admit it contained interesting aspects, even in winter slush and cold. He enjoyed studying ornate facades of the more historic buildings in the financial district, gazing high overhead until struck by another equally self-absorbed pedestrian. He was amused at the mix of shops on side streets, in that ancient era still selling the same wares in the same ways as in the twenties or thirties. Little restaurants tucked away, pavements torn up, surfaces slathered with a patina of decaying time like dark varnish on an old master painting. During lunch break on more adventurous days, he would walk up the street to Trinity Church, stroll across the plaza of the World Trade Center, or gaze at the Statue of Liberty from Battery Park.

The crowds themselves were fascinating. Herds of similarly dressed, inwardly gazing people not so much dashing about as mechanically and efficiently transporting unconnected brains from point A to point B in bodily taxicabs. Every one of them either under immense pressure from their bosses and trying to escape their lowly position, or powerful bosses under internal immense pressure dreaming of vacation and escape to country mansions.

Oh, there were dreamers. In his own group, there was talk of the New York Teleport—which made him giggle when he first heard it, because teleportation was a standard SF gimmick—which would be a communications center. The South Street Seaport was trying to recreate the Quincy Market in Boston, although momentarily devoid of tourists. But mostly any urban renewal in the city looked lonely and forlorn, a blade of grass here or there on a plain doomed by approaching lava.

The counterpoint to frantic hope and activity was omnipresent decay. Cities were documented to be dying, anyone who could escaped to the suburbs. Maybe parts of them could be kept safe enough to visit, maybe not. In a hundred years they would all be gone, maybe in a decade they would be complete ruins. You went there at your own peril, risking your life because the hazard pay was higher than in safer spots. That was not the message of doom from some lone placard-wielding fanatic, but the common zeitgeist of all but the most deluded, of the media. Scarcely a visionary few could penetrate mental fads of the moment to glimpse an alternate vibrant reality underneath.

Many days, I would just walk down to the decaying old tall ships at the still being constructed Seaport, since it was only a few blocks away. The central area was mostly new shiny bars, where all the well-dressed business people (very few women) went to drink away an hour or so each lunch. Beer and liquor flowed freely, not so much wine. The noise and laughter would rise and overwhelm any stray thoughts.

Now that it's too late, I understand that rituals like that were important parts of working there. The fancy word these days is networking and making contacts. Although only salesmen back then were so nakedly ambitious as to push themselves onto strangers, the same social rituals were important to advancement as has ever been the case. Who do you know? What can you do for me? What can I do for you to have you obligated to me.

Not that they didn't enjoy it. Human nature can only be kept bottled up under pressure, and relaxing that pressure often resulted in good outcomes. The strict seriousness of downtown business, the grind of critical schedules, the demands of do-it-yesterday, could be relaxed for an hour at lunch, and for hours after work, and possibly well into the evening. Sometimes, maybe even often, that behavior resulted in a better position or advancement in a career.

Me—I've never been able to participate well. I hated talking with people on my time most of the time. I would go to the bars and have a beer or two, then spend the rest of the time walking around thinking great thoughts, or enjoying wonderful sights, or dreaming of what I might do to do something else. It profited my mind, but did nothing for my own professional standing.

Sometimes I thought it a fault. Sometimes I considered it a gift. Sometimes I even tried to change it. But eventually I accepted that such was simply my own unique way, and directed myself as best I could. I found other adaptations to exist well in the world anyway.

"You seem confused," observed Ghost sympathetically, taking out a notepad.

"Well, it is all unexpected and I have to figure out what to do next."

"You probably should wait for a bus or just call Joan to pick you up."

"The lines to the pay phones are huge," I point out. "And I don't see any busses arriving in the immediate future—the lines over there are even worse."

"Unless you sprout wings you don't have much of a choice here," Ghost looks around at the darkness beyond the city center."

"I don't know, I just don't know. Let me think a minute."

"Not good in emergencies, eh?"

"Actually, in real emergencies for some reason I usually do fine," I reply. "There's only one clear path, and I can just focus and do it and drop everything else. It's in these confusing happenings that are not on the regular schedule, but hardly emergencies either, that I seem to do badly."

"Too many choices?"

"Probably has more to do with the crowds. I hate being part of a mob or a herd. I like my autonomy."

"But you enjoy walking around the city, which is really jammed, or even riding the train, which can be worse."

"Well, yeah, but there I'm an outside observer, not really part of it."

"So you panic when forced into a group."

"Pretty much nail on the head, that, I think."

Maybe it was the beer, or just being tired, but it took a lot longer than it should have for Wayne to realize that trying to walk along the tracks to the next station was a really stupid idea. The cool night was a lot colder than it had seemed when he first got out of the overheated train. Walking on ballast and railroad ties in office shoes was torture and pretty dangerous in the complete dark, once he was away from the bright lights of the station.

A little over a mile down the tracks, he spied actinic glares flashing and saw dark shapes grouping in shadows. Obviously a work crew. It gave him excuse to turn around and head back to Syosset, however long it might take to get to wherever he might go.

By the time he got back, maybe wasting a little over an hour in all, everything had sorted out a great deal. Trains did keep arriving, but the major rush had passed. Busses were picking people up regularly, although hardly enough to dent the crowd. He finally got a moment at a public phone, and called Joan to pick him up.

In those days, with no cell-phone to guide each other, in an unfamiliar place, in the dark, her getting to Syosset train station was the least of their problems. He finally found her near the crossing, as she cruised slowly circling the lot. Then it was back to his car in Huntington, home for dried-out dinner, and an exhausted sleep once he calmed down a little.

He felt as if he had survived a heroic ordeal, but of course he had never been in danger, had hardly been inconvenienced. It was a commentary on how he was getting himself worked up over the city commute that he felt it was such a big deal. Everyone else just took it in stride, another delay just like encountered every other day on one system or another. Another price to pay for having a good job. Wayne knew he could not afford to pay that price much longer.

An underlying element in this year, flames fanned by experiences, was a deeply felt set of insecurities. The bedrock, fortunately, was not affected. Relations with Joan and Gregory were central and untouched, his faith in having a computer career vindicated at every turn. But over that strong foundation, the rest of his daily structure seemed to be no more than sticks and twigs, a badly built mud hut which he tried to promote externally as the beginning of a mansion. But he always knew that it remained, for all his protestations, a mud hut.

First he was poor and his family was poor in a rich area. He was living in

BABYLON WITH GHOST

a relative's house, not paying rent, because he was not making enough money to survive here on his own. Sure, it was nice to keep saying it was temporary, that the consultant job was a step up, that things would soon be better. But that was contradicted—only to his eyes—every day he went to work. The job was as close to a dead end as anyone could possibly get in the computer field. There was no possibility of advancement, and no growth into a better position with more opportunity. It was a temporary refuge in a storm, but he had to keep saying how well it was going, and wave his paychecks to prove it.

That led to the second problem, because he was no longer sure how much he knew or how well he could apply it. He was not designing or coding, he was not working on any real machines, he was not actually following his career. Was everything he had done so far irrelevant? Did it get so hard after this that he would no longer have the opportunities he had discovered in Boston? Would he be stuck in something like this forever? Inferiority was mostly caused by knowing he was randomly self-taught, and had gradually become aware of how great the gaps in his educational background really were. What could he do next, and how could he escape the trap he was in?

The third problem was support. He kept putting on a brave front, but he really didn't know anybody here. Nor was he finding it easy to do so. Sure, Joan kept producing relatives, but they were living their own lives and communication about life and work was almost impossible, not least because they were all successful and well on their way to greater heights. He had no local contacts, and hardly met anyone downtown, buried deeply in his code pages as he had to be. He was realizing finally how thin his human support had become in the world in general, and his career in particular.

And, finally, he was worried about himself. He was definitely drinking too much, even if nobody except his father-in-law seemed to notice or care. He wasn't much worse than everyone else he knew in the city, but it was worse than he wanted to be. He didn't like mindless hours on the train, and he was unable to come up with any way to use them well. He didn't like his narrowing outlooks and his decreasing horizons. There was no time to appreciate the world, and he felt himself sinking into a dark quagmire which would envelop him in conformist darkness.

Most of the time, this all condensed into simply feeling like a fraud. He was always worried that someone might break one of his various brave covers and discover that underneath it all he was hollow and afraid and had no idea what he was going to do next. That only increased his defenses, which then pushed away even more people and situations that might have helped.

"Surely," insists Ghost, pushing a microphone in my face once again as I wait for Joan, "Surely there was something about this period of time you liked."

"Well," I admit, "I suppose it was an adventure."

"What, getting on the train and riding to work? Millions of people do the same thing all the time. How could that possibly be …"

"Perhaps so," I continue, "surely so. But I hadn't done it before. I haven't done it since. And, in the brief time I was doing it I was mostly completely lost, hassled, and upset."

"But you saw so many new things, experienced exciting moments …"

"It was all new, but all kind of terrorizing. I think I developed a minor understanding of what immigrants went through arriving here—living with family, not knowing anyone in the culture, strange customs, weird expectations, and mostly doing what I was told."

"Oh, come on. You knew the language …"

"So did a lot of immigrants," I point out. "Anyway, looking back I did have an exciting time. It was an odd sensation passing Jamaica and heading into the heart of American Capitalism on the way to Wall Street. Never somewhere I had expected to be. It was even stranger to be one of the grey men in suits flowing in and out of buildings at carefully appointed hours. Even on my walks, gawking at the sights, I felt more like a lost tourist than a native."

"So you did have some positive memories."

"Like I said," I finish as I catch sight of our car, "it was an adventure. And the hallmark of a real adventure is that you are miserable when in the middle of it, but love to look back and even talk about it later."

Amazingly, I discovered what con men always knew—it is very easy to warp appearances far beyond what is supported by reality. The fact that I had a paid computer-related job somewhere on Wall Street automatically made me at least on the verge of being a successful young professional. If I didn't stagger around being bellicose and falling into things I was handling my drinking appropriately. If I came home each night, paid for food, and was nice to my wife and child I was successfully heading a family. It was easy to focus on one aspect or another of what was actually happening, and make every exaggeration seem true. An existence centered on making mountains out of molehills, as it were.

Like a con man's patter, there had to be a nugget of truth in anything I declared or did. A straight lie was easily caught. But it was so easy to let things be assumed, to protest in the right direction, to call up telling details. That was especially easy in the current instance, because nobody except Joan really knew me well, and the long-term patterns were not obvious.

Honestly, most of the horrible comparisons were in my own mind. By conventional rational standards I was doing just as well as people thought, miles ahead of where I had been three years before, moving in exactly the right direction, with a sturdy fulcrum, poised for bigger things. Only my own inner demons kept insisting I was falling behind, not doing as I should, wasting precious moments, and wallowing in failure.

Most of the time I could silence the demons. Most of the time I could tap dance the required approval tango. Most of the time life was even what it appeared to be. Even when crises occurred, I had a momentum that seemed to be pushing in the right direction. I simply had to learn to accept the speed of the rhythm.

"Now sir," Ghost was frantically following me as I began to walk away, "What do you think they should do to prevent further instances like this?"

"They can't prevent instances like this," I growl over my shoulder, "they've let the situation deteriorate way too far."

"Well, then, what should they do better when problems like this occur?"

"That's well beyond my control. But I know what I will do."

"What is that, sir," Ghost demands in exasperation.

"I will find a way to stop riding the train every day. This is madness. I don't care how rewarding it is."

"But you can never find anything equivalent on the Island."

"So I am told. But it's like that old biblical proverb."

"Which one is that," Ghost realizes I am finally getting out of the parking lot as I open the door.

"The one that goes what profits it a man to gain the world and lose his own soul."

"Oh, meaning ...."

"My soul is critically related to my time. I will not be out here again."

Next day dawned crisply cool, and brilliant. All problems on the tracks had been resolved overnight, there were rumors this would finally force the LIRR to double the track line affected. Wayne felt more clearheaded than normal—he'd eaten late and slept a solid sleep of exhaustion. He stared out the windows as precious minutes passed by, and made strong resolutions.

This had been the final straw. Time to seriously look at the Island, push hard, beef up the resume and start sending it out to anything half promising in the want ad lottery. He was never, as originally planned, going to make it a whole year at this job, nor even get deeply into the summer. He wasn't about to quit, but all his extra energy, in the city and at home, would now be devoted to getting out.

Lightly greening trees were scattered among the brown branches, here and there was a yellow patch of early forsythia. They sped by quickly, as if the train were trying to make up for last night. There was a certain joy in the ride, looking out and admiring nature and the works of man. Fun once in a while. No fun after daily rides for months. He knew every dilapidated shed along the way, in all conditions of light and weather.

His trouble had always been that he was easily satisfied. He had honed appreciation of his world into an art form. What he had spread before him was immense, what need for more? He had never wanted a bigger house, a faster car, a more beautiful wife. He had never cared that his stupid neighbor made more than brilliant himself. He carefully cultivated enjoyment—he firmly believed that reasonably accepting your place and appreciating all it offered was the clue to eternal happiness. In short, it took dynamite to get him moving beyond where he was most of the time.

The dynamite in this case had now been applied. He was ready, willing, and anxious to move on. There would be no turning back. And, hopefully, no more broken rails in the night.

RUDELY BOUNCED

WAYNE PAUSED OUTSIDE monolithic still-under-construction Citibank building, and took a deep breath of frosty air off the East River. A slow, stuffy, hesitant train ride had culminated in the usual mash of people crowding onto the graffiti-covered ancient subway cars of the 3 line. Getting off at Wall Street and the short brisk walk down here had helped clear his head of the usual hangover. He hefted his briefcase and strode past the guards to the elevator bank, as if he knew what he was doing.

The tenth floor was still being constructed, but areas had been hacked out of the dust and rubble for desks and tables. He uncloaked at his usual spot, and opened the thick binder of computer printout which was his current task. It was simple enough, at least for anyone with a certain amount of knowledge. He needed to translate DEC computer code into human language, or at least into something that convinced the people paying for the project that they had the human language documentation required by law. So it was read a few lines of goto's, ifs, variable sets, and whatnot and come out with something like "Store the customer name into the appropriate fields in the customer record."

Everyone knew it was a stupid regulation, put there by bureaucracy. Anyone who could read code could immediately see what was happening by looking at the actual source. Anyone who could not read code would never find a problem or bug by reading the "normal English" translation. But, hey, if they wanted to pay him to do this he could do it all day.

It was relatively highly paid, because anyone who actually could read code decently rapidly evolved into the still more high-paying job of writing it. And very few people could jump into reading code—it took a fair amount of hard study at least in general computer languages to be able to do so. So he sat, and translated, and his supervisors were quite pleased.

He'd been here a month, and liked it well enough except for the commute. Nobody hassled him, as long as he churned out a certain number of pages a day. The view over the river to Brooklyn was breathtaking. Working in a skyscraper in New York was almost a dream.

Beyond that, there were the lunches, when everyone went to the newly developed South Street Seaport area a few blocks away and had—at the least—a few beers. Lunches could be extended indefinitely, he found. One of the reasons he was well regarded was that he arrived early (well before nine, because he left well before dawn) and only used an hour of lunch. And, limiting his beer intake, he came back able to do more work, unlike several of his colleagues.

No, the real party usually started on the train ride home, everyone with a few cans purchased at Penn Station or on the platform itself, trying to detox not so much from the grind of the day as from the commute itself. Wayne happily, or at least resignedly, joined them as the train lurched its way back to Huntington.

"Cut" yells Ghost, jumping up from his director's chair. He's wearing a red leather beret, and has a big megaphone in his right hand. "Look, doesn't anybody get this?"

We all look at him with incomprehension. He grimaces as he strides into the set. "It's not complicated, guys. That speeding cab just misses you and you, squeals around the corner, turns into the alley where we hear a crash. You jump onto the back of that pickup, while you pull the driver out and get in the cab. Meanwhile, you guys"—he points to some uniformed police—"are running around the block and slip on that oil slick. Got it?"

"But we just did all that," I protest.

"I need some exaggeration," he says. "I need some pizazz. Think Keystone Kops here—you do know who the Keystone Kops were, right?"

We all shake our heads no. He sighs. "Ok, ok, what I want—what I want—ah what's the use. Remember, this is a kind of serious spoof. An action comedy. I want a touch of ironic lightness in the midst of serious stunts. You guys"—he points again at the police—"I want some major flailing as you slip and fall. Even cartwheels. We want the audience to gasp and laugh at the same time."

"We're tired and sore. You've had us doing this complicated scene all day. Can't we just take a break?"

"Time for break when you get it right, stupid."

"How many more scenes are we going to do, anyway, before this is all over?" I could use a few moments to reflect and recover.

"Oh, guy," he says, "from here on it is never, never over. The scenery may change, but you'll be doing this the rest of your life."

"But ..."

"Places," he yells, getting back in his chair. "Camera—action!"

Here in the front room, about three in the afternoon, pretty dark outside already this New Year's eve. Wayne sat looking at the snow falling, another bottle of beer freshly opened, quietly away from the conversations out in the kitchen. A moment of calm, tomorrow off, what a year.

Well, perhaps a little more than a strict calendar year. But it had surely been a whirlwind, an epic adventure to match the Wizard of Oz.

First leaving his increasingly interesting and promising job in Wellesley, then moving down here, then Wayne being bored. A three month stint in the city, well paid but eroding all his future skills since he never touched a computer, and a nightmare to get to. A lucky break to a huge European firm here on the Island, only twenty minutes away—a month after starting there, praised by everyone for making sense of the arcane code in an obscure typesetting computer—the company laid almost everyone off, preparatory to going out of business. Grandma's nearly fatal heart trouble, Gregory screaming, living with the in-laws. A couple of summer months unemployed, sitting on the patio, not knowing what to do next. A lucky break at Webcor, which turned out to be way over his head. He felt like he'd been hanging on by his fingernails, but had just scrambled over the clifftop and could catch his breath.

No, not quite the Wizard of Oz. After all, in spite of her many adventures, Dorothy had only landed once. He had been picked up by the whirlwinds over and over, and set down each time in a strange and uncharted territory. Would the rest of his time here continue that way? No wonder he knew he was drinking too much.

He took another gulp. He still had to reread some of the technical manuals, tonight or tomorrow. He still had to finish some outlines of plans for promised research and projects. At least now he felt like a real programmer again, even if he had a lot of administration with it. Programming was the candy for all the other junk he had to do.

Joan was calling in the other room. Probably another one of her innumerable relatives had arrived to wish happy new year. Sighing, he finished the beer, threw the empty in the paper bag next to the window, and went out with a carved-on happy face.

Wayne sat all shiny and spiffed, polished shoes, best suit, silent in the interview room. Joe was finance vice president of Webcor, which had just acquired a new computer system. Rick was more casually dressed, as consultants often were. His company had provided the software and was insisting that Joe hire an operator to take care of the daily operations. Wayne, at this point, had no objections to being a mere operator, at least it would put his fingers back on a keyboard and then—who knew?

"So, Wayne, I see from your resume," began Joe, "that you have worked with mini-computers in Boston and business systems in Wellesley. But you left your last two jobs rather abruptly. Can you explain that?"

This was the easy question. "Sure. We moved down here to be near my wife's parents since we were having our first child. My city job only involved documenting code printouts, which was not what I want to do. I obtained a programming job here on the Island which I did well at, but the company laid off most of the staff a month or so later. I'd rather get another job out here, so I've been taking time looking for my next position." He tried to imply he was interviewing them as much as they were him.

"But how much experience have you actually had on disk operating systems? You list being a trainer and manager at Kurzweil with the minicomputer, but your actual programming and operations were just on that Radio Shack microcomputer," Rick grimaced as if "microcomputer" were some kind of disease.

"I also did operations at Kurzweil," Wayne pointed out, although he had actually only done a couple of backup tapes and once in a while changed the disk pack. "And all disk operating systems, even those on microcomputers, are somewhat alike." Rick could stay unhappy, after all the hardware he was supporting was called *Microdata*.

Joe continued, "It's interesting to me that you had an economics degree and then did teaching for years but jumped into this career."

"Teaching was not paying off for me, because there was a lot of trouble getting into the public schools up there. When the smaller computers came out, I found I really enjoyed them and had a knack for working with them. And the jobs were more open."

"But only in BASIC," inserted Rick.

"Well, I wrote extensive game routines in 6502 assembly language," Wayne could throw jargon just as well, "and, after all, I understand your Pick operating system is also using BASIC."

"Besides," said Joe, pointedly, "I thought we agreed he would not be doing much programming." Rick sat sullen, caught in his own previous sales pitch.

Wayne stated, "But in the long run I do want to program and code ..."

Joe mused aloud, "Webcor is growing rapidly, and we plan to expand the IT department with it. As soon as you get things under control, you certainly can try to develop some new reports using the supposedly simple query language. Then we'll see what happens. Your primary job will be just to keep things going as directed by Rick. But in a few years—well you have the background to be a manager."

"Would I be able to write some programs on my own?"

Rick looked aghast, but Joe beat him to it, "We can just see how that works out."

After a half hour or so, Wayne left feeling satisfied. Joe was obviously happy at finally finding a candidate more well-rounded than the usual nerd. Rick was worried Wayne might be a little too big for his britches, but didn't have final hiring authority. And Wayne saw real possibilities, if they would just give him a chance.

This time period presented me with multiple sets of possibilities, in all directions and of all types. None of them particularly high level, of course. But after a few months I had been exposed to huge corporations, small departments in big companies, tiny departments in small companies, the rules of consulting, the ways of business, and increasingly dealing with all types of people. It was almost an internship in business and technical culture.

To some extent I merely felt bounced around by the waves of fate. The only really conscious move I made against inertia was to apply to the job on the Island to escape the one in Manhattan. Everything else just happened, with no logic, nor rhyme, nor reason. My fate seemed in the hands of fate, but I also became fully aware that I could shape it far more than I had thought.

Home life and goals were much the same. Multiple paths to the future flipped through multiple realities as I met people in the family who were doing completely different things than I had ever considered. With the complete break with our pasts, we provided fertile ground for all the seeds suddenly floating by in attitudes and suggestions.

Not that any of it was easy. This was also a period like what became known as boot camps—intense, difficult, confusing, and demanding. I had to completely suppress my ego, because at this point all I had done before was irrelevant and not worth a dime in the new milieu. Perhaps I would complain to myself during commutes or in stolen moments walking somewhere, but there were no sympathetic listeners beyond that. I suppose it was good for me—well, I know it was good for me—but that was by no means an easy period.

I did keep my center. I never felt worthless, and I refused to apologize for "wasting" ten years in art, teaching, and experiencing life. I liked what I had done, I liked what we had done, and I never regretted the intense moments of my young adulthood. As I have grown older, the conviction that what I did was the right path for me—maybe not monetarily but certainly spiritually—has only grown. When it became time to adjust to the "real world," the life I had lived as an artist remained a small warm jewel deep inside, to be inspected and treasured during any bleak moments I might encounter.

Ghost lounges behind a utilitarian desk, somewhat rumpled in a dark suit with bright tie. I'm surprised at his slicked down hair. Manuscripts lie tossed all around, some even on the floor. The walls are filled with signed pictures of presumably famous people. As in any detective novel, I discover from the writing on the glass-paneled door—tnegA—that he is playing agent. I guess that's why he is speaking to me so earnestly.

"Listen, this one is right up your alley. I promise. Not like all the other disasters ...."

"But I'm confused. This whole thing about buildings and languages and cultures ...."

"Listen to me," he explains, "it's brilliant. A metaphor, ok. Just like all the jobs you had, every time you enter a new building—that is a different job—you have a different culture. The culture is the operating system, you know, Data General, Radio Shack, DEC, and so forth."

"Ah, I see," I reply. "And the rooms are the various languages I need to learn to communicate with the machines."

"Right, right. The running gag ..."

"What?"

"Well, they plan to make it into a comedy, you know."

"Didn't read like a comedy." The whole script had seemed incomprehensibly grim when I glanced through it."

"Trust me, the running gag is that you are the naïve innocent and you're always walking into the next building, the next culture, the next language thinking you know it all when you don't know anything at all."

"Oh, I see, I think."

"And then," he chuckles, "you get thrown out and have to start all over again."

"Funny for you, maybe."

"Sure thing, little waif." He turns to answer the phone and waves me out. "I'll be in contact."

Until very recently, Wayne had been spared the real pains of commuting, but now he was thrown into a mix of some of the worst conditions anywhere. It was still a time when people tried to get to work by nine, and tried to leave shortly after five. Still a time when work was more or less centralized in a few downtown or suburban clusters, and when everyone was expected to be in one of those clusters to get anything done. And still a time when most people wanted to live as far away from work as possible.

The result was a rush-hour nightmare. Wayne had traveled over an hour to Wellesley for his last job in Boston, which seemed long after his 15-minute bicycle commutes in Boston (which seemed long after his 5-minute walking commute in Cambridge.) But he had not experienced the insanity of getting up before six to try to get a parking space reasonably close to the train station, nor over an hour riding into Penn Station (and much longer if there were problems), not to mention a nervous wait for the 3 train and its relatively quick (but possibly much longer) rumble to Wall Street. He often felt he had already worked a full day by the time he arrived at his destination.

After he left the commute to the city, things got much better, because both of his next jobs were relatively close half-hour—sometimes less—rides, with back roads available, and crosswise to the normal rush hour. It still seemed long, sealed away waiting for a light to change, but he soon became more reconciled to getting somewhere in a car and was able to accept the travel as a quiet meditation time, requiring minimal thought and exertion.

His main trouble, then and later, was that morning was his good time. He woke up refreshed and full of energy, ready to plunge into whatever was necessary, mind clear. Every cell screamed to be active. Being locked into a long train ride doing nothing but staring out the window was torture. Reading was almost impossible. Long term commuters had slipped into a pattern of accepting this as an extension of sleep, and often snored the whole way. He just fidgeted. The ride home was far easier, he had done things and had more to think about and was quite ready to waste time doing nothing more.

I'd never realized what a sheltered life I led, even after I left home, went through college, and the first ten years of work. Dad never brought his work home, and I had no idea what he did with his days, and never understood exactly how his company fit into the scheme of things. I had centered on school, thinking that must be what the "real world" was like, and by so concentrating did well at it. But I never looked beyond, to my later misfortune. After that, most of my jobs were simple "do this" affairs, having little to do with twentieth century business, and I never had concerned myself with their economic foundations. That started to change a little with the first computer jobs, but it was a slow awareness dimly evolving.

But the first years on Long Island were a real education. I had never seen so many types of enterprise—big corporation, small companies, consultants, and activities of every shape and size. Suddenly I was learning all kinds of things about accounting and sales and management . But more importantly, I discovered that capitalism was a rich ecosystem of all kinds of unsuspected activities. Even the environments within a given company were complex. Departments had their own cultures, just as the business had its own suppliers and clients and goals and internal structure.

In some ways, although I had at first minimal participation in all that, observing the ways of the people in these situations was more fun than coding. Fortunately, I was a quick learner, and was able to be humble enough when away from my computer that I got along well with almost everyone almost all the time. It was a big reason that I was able to survive and do ok, regardless of my lack of background.

Some kid is leading me toward a bland white trailer, set a little apart from a group of others. As I go up the steps I can make out "Scriptwriter" scribbled on duct tape near the middle of the door. I am ushered into a shabby little room filled with cigarette smoke and lingering scents of stale beer. Well, maybe not so stale—Ghost is behind the desk in sweatshirt with a mug of ale in hand.

"I hear you're bad-mouthing the script," he snarls, as the door is shut behind me.

I might as well take a seat, "Yeah, just that that isn't really the way it happened."

"So what does that have to do with anything? You know anything about writing a story?"

"Well, I read a lot …"

"Beginning, middle, end. You get that?"

"Of course, but …"

"All our stuff is just like Shakespeare," he scowls as I snort a laugh. "No, really. Meet the characters and get interested in some of them. Bring in complications. Play the complications into an impossible difficulty. Resolve the difficulty. Wrap everything up and leave the audience feeling it knows what happened. QED."

"Hamlet?" I ask.

"Hey, that's a tragedy. We don't do tragedies. Won't sell. But, since you ask, sure—you leave definitely sure you know what happened."

"All I know is this isn't exactly me. I have more …"

"Look, it's a story."

"Don't you want it to be true."

"Oh," he grins grimly, "we all love true, as long as it fits into the standard plot line. A frisson of realism adds some kick to the stupidity. But you …" he pause expectantly.

"Yes, me?"

"You just act the goddamn script as written."

I'm ushered out. The show goes on.

As usual, Wayne had arrived at Mergenthaler a half hour early. The drive over was pleasant in cool early summer, passing one of the last working farms in this part of the island. Once again, he marveled at his sparkling new gigantic modern office building, all glass and stainless, with its bold front to the landscaped grounds. He was soon at his usual spot, in front of the pre-typesetting computer that had so baffled everyone else, and settled in to continue his task of deciphering the cryptic instruction manual.

This had been a great month. A huge European firm knew how to treat its employees well, and he had been given orientations and tours. He was most impressed by the huge new linotype machine which was used to set the press runs for newspapers and magazines. Large and intricate, like an old time steam engine, with mysterious knobs and gauges all over. It was given pride of place in the large sunlit lobby.

His task had turned out to be one that all the other programmers found thankless. A new machine was supposed to interface to word processors and allow immediate controllable typesetting. But it had to be programmed, and the programming language was obscure and unique, a blend of Fortran and some one-off assembly language, full of arcane rules, nooks, and crannies. His immediate supervisor had marveled at the progress he was making at getting it working.

After a while, he became aware of an unusual hush in the usually busy office complex. A parade of employees seemed to stream by, as if in some ritual ceremony at a cathedral. Eventually, one of his colleagues said that a big layoff was in progress, and each employee led away never came back. In fact, each had been escorted out the door by security personnel.

Well, Wayne felt he was safe enough. He was a programmer, doing something important, just recently added to the payroll, and one of the little fish who would hardly make a difference on the bottom line. So he turned back to his immediate task and concentrated as the world around him faded. The tap on his shoulder came as a real shock.

Sure enough, he was led into a small room, with a grim young man across a desk, handing him a packet of departure. "Just sign this," he indicated a paper, "and you will be dismissed with two full months pay and you can apply for the recommendation of your supervisor. Understand this is a company-wide reduction, and not your fault." The various circumlocutions for staff layoffs had not yet been invented, but the fact was just as painful.

"But I just got here. I'm doing well ..." Panic welled up, as he considered this might mean he'd have to go back to some city job. If he could find it. He had no idea how to begin to find anything out here in the suburbs—he had been scanning the paper and this was about the only one he had ever had a chance to get. And how would he make it through the hiring process downtown—all kinds of empty commutes at odd hours and finding his way around the subway. It wasn't fair.

Some of his confusion and anger must have shown. Besides, the spiel was canned, this guy after all had been facing worse all morning, with many more to go. "Look, we think we are being extremely fair here. You work one month, you are getting pay for three. Nobody else is getting any better deal. Please sign now."

Wayne signed and was escorted out after a quick (escorted) trip to his desk to retrieve his sports jacket and briefcase—which was thoroughly searched. Once in his car, he contemplated the rest of the day, the rest of his life, and how he was going to face the family. And what he had to do and where he would start. Eventually it was some bitter consolation that a few months later century-old Mergenthaler ceased operations entirely and was no more, a victim of rapid computerization elsewhere that had made all of its magnificent machines obsolete nearly overnight.

I took my layoff badly for a while, frantically searching want ads, going to headhunting firms, but, as expected, nothing that fit my desires and abilities showed up. I was not quite experienced enough for real programming jobs, and overqualified for operational ones. The only things available were obviously lousy badly-paying positions at grungy small firms in Brooklyn and Queens. I decided to hold out and wait for something better.

After all, it was summer, and I did have that two months of pay. After the events of the last six months there was little resistance in convincing myself a vacation was in order. So I took walks, familiarized myself with the area, and hung out in the back yard drinking beer and reading, sometimes even studying technical manuals.

Each Sunday I dutifully checked the want ads in three papers, a task which consumed two to three hours, circling in red pencil those that might be promising. Each Monday I mailed off ten or twenty resumes to prospective openings. Discouragingly, there was no response.

My lackadaisical attitude towards it all drove my father-in-law up the wall. He couldn't understand why I didn't just get something, anything, somewhere. Sell fruit off a pushcart if necessary. Nobody my age should be willing to enjoy the afternoons as I did. This was only slightly mollified by the fact that both Joan and her brother Robert were teachers, and a long summer recess was hardly unknown to the family. But, of course, they could go back to work in the fall.

Me? Well, I was sure something would turn up when hiring resumed in September, but I had learned enough by then to know that very few people were brought on anywhere when all the existing employees and management were just cruising and taking their own vacation time with families.

Dark room, relaxing with a glass of wine amidst a few other people, watching Ghost doing something or other to a long string in the corner. Eventually, I realize he is snipping out sequences of film and letting it fall on the floor. I examine one strip out of curiosity.

"Hey," I exclaim, "you can't cut this."

"I just did," Ghost has no sympathy.

"But this is one of the best bits. It's exciting, it's well done, look at how beautifully I performed ..."

"Sorry, it just doesn't fit. We can only use some of this you know."

"But ..."

"There's an awful of material. Ten years is a very long time, some movies are based on a single day. What am I supposed to do?"

"You can at least save the good parts!" I retort.

"Most of this is, frankly, boring. Nobody cares. I'm trying to salvage this, lord knows, but it's all pretty iffy."

"I thought it was pretty good, myself."

"Surprise, surprise," Ghost says mockingly. "Just about all the actors think that about anything they do."

Naturally, Wayne felt the best place to find the job for which he searched were the want ads of the larger more reputable papers. He carefully pored over appropriate want ad sections of the New York Times and Newsday, mostly on Sunday. At least once a week, he seemed quite busy and involved in his job search, often sending resumes, but most of the time it was sadly true that he was doing nothing at all except playing on his little computer with some code of his own.

Hardly anyone else had a clue as to his profession, nor its unique characteristics. What came to be called IT (Information Technology) was already fragmenting and mutating rapidly. There were various tiers of experience for programmers, managers, and hints of what were to become designers, coders, architects and so on. Multiple platforms from at least ten manufacturers each used their own programming languages, each unrelated to one another, and experience in one did not qualify you for a job in another. Worse, the operating systems of all these computers—and various different computers from the same manufacturer—were completely incomprehensible to anyone who had not studied that particular model. And, finally, computers were being used for greatly varied roles—business, scientific, defense, government—but all the jobs were kind of lumped together.

So the first great fact was that those who put out the ads were usually ignorant of the true requirements. They looked at what they had, or listened to the consultants or salesmen (who often knew little more) and hopefully looked for a person with an exact match to their needs: "3 years experience working with IBM 360, COBOL with systems operations, in a large corporate commercial environment." Unsurprisingly, few met the rigid criteria, which were often out of date by the time of hiring, since even knowing last year's COBOL might not help with the next iteration on that platform.

The second great fact was that any really good programmer (to center of that mass of job descriptions) could rapidly adapt to anything at all. No matter what the salesmen proclaimed, the logic of one file-based disk operating system was very like another. The mechanics of one FORTRAN-type coding structure was much like another. And the final interface layers exposed to programmers and users tended to be smoothed into acceptable regularity anyway. So anyone who was any good in one system could become rapidly proficient in another—often in less than a month—if just given a chance. But nobody had a clue how to determine who was a good programmer.

So Wayne hopefully waited for the autumn. Meanwhile, his clueless mother-in-law scanned the local Penny Saver, with its little ads for house painters and baby sitters and gardeners. Sure enough, she found a cheap little ad from a local company for a "Computer operator/manager for small growing company using Microdata computer system. BASIC experience required. Good growth potential. Call ..." that was it, a few dinky lines and nothing but a phone number. After some nagging and failure to explain how stupid this was—Wayne reluctantly called and set up an interview at Webcor—they didn't even want to bother with a resume first. It wasn't that long a drive, and by then he was glad to just get out of the house.

But, as it turned out, his mother-in-law was absolutely correct, and had in the most unlikely way possible pinned down exactly the job he needed and was capable of doing.

Snow is swirling under streetlamps as we exit beneath a lurid marquee. Ghost strides beside me in a long dark wool overcoat, incongruous Australian-themed hat, and muted maroon scarf carefully flung around his neck. He needs to make an impression, and begins by imperiously dismissing a query from a woman in a small crowd that has followed, "You can read it all in the Times tomorrow. I'm paid to write the reviews, not to give speeches. Good night." He turns to me, "ready for a drink?"

"So what did you think?" I inquire anxiously.

"Oh, let's see. A few good moments, a few boring stretches, some interesting scenes. A bit too long—I was glad when it was over. And I doubt I'll see it again." He continues to march down the slippery sidewalk.

"That's it?" I'm aghast. "They pay you for that?"

"I flesh it out with examples and adjectives," he huffs. "After a couple of scotches I'll come up with a few zingers to make people chuckle."

"So you didn't like it."

"It's a movie, like all the others. Not really bad, but then nobody's narrative really is, if examined correctly. This was—well, just another. Unique in its own way. Typical of all nevertheless. Ah good," he takes out a notebook, " I think I can use that."

Wayne had taken his picturesque backroad shortcut past Oheka castle and down the winding woods of Round Swamp Road, arriving as usual before eight. His basic tasks only took half the day and were almost foolproof—verify and log last night's tape backup, start and print a few canned reports depending on the day of the week, possibly separating the multiple copies from the carbon paper between. Be ready to answer the frequent users' questions about fields. That was it.

Meanwhile, he read ferociously, trying to absorb the expansions of "Business BASIC" and the odd file configurations of the PICK operating system. But those were peripheral to what the company really wanted him to concentrate on, which were impromptu reports they had been told could be easily generated by the "ENGLISH" query language.

Those who had designed that utility had only a vague idea of what "English" meant to business executives. Anyone who needed the report was going to ask "How'd the sales guys do last week?" or "Did those sales bums make the quotas I set last month?" The "easy-to-use" query wanted something along the lines of "Sort the salesman file by gross sales in descending order showing both details and subtotals of gross orders and gross invoices total everything break on salesman." What?

Wayne found himself in an enviable position. The system, of course, had been oversold. He had the simple query language down cold in less than a week. But he couldn't do anything about missing fields or files—all he could do was pass on bad news. "There's no way to flag the special import salesmen," the consultants would woefully agree "Why would anyone want that? Nobody else does it?" The computer salesman, hopeful of a new machine delivery in the not too distant future to this prize account was pulling his hair out. Litigation was in the air. But nothing was Wayne's fault.

He began to develop ideas and plans, especially when Joe D was brought on board, a bright MBA his own age with big ideas who could grasp the benefits of custom coded extensions to the basic package.

FRAGMENTS OF FRACTURES

GREGORY GURGLED HAPPILY in his baby seat carrier next to Wayne, sitting in the car on a bright but brisk spring afternoon in the parking lot of St. Francis hospital. Everything happening at once, and now this. How many shocks, he wondered, would he have to get through?

There had been quite enough already, but this latest one seemed to top all. Mrs. Spagnolo was the pillar of the entire family, the one who centered everyone's holidays and daily activities. Indefatigable, always with advice, cooking, making sure things got done as she felt they should. For all the problems that might have arisen with a mother in law, especially when they were living together, she had done more than her part to be generous and understanding. Well, of course she was really happy to have her daughter back, and ecstatic about the first grandchild.

But suddenly there were heart pains, a heart attack, then a spell in Huntington Hospital, as things got worse and worse and became desperate. Joan's brother Phillip had stepped in, not accepting what any doctors said, not accepting anything at all, marching everyone to the "best heart hospital in the country." Somehow he forced doors open, pulling everyone there by sheer force of will.

Losing Sue would be a calamity for everyone. Joan was guilty enough already for having stayed away so long. Things were barely holding together as it was. Well, maybe the conference going on inside would help clear up possibilities. What had it been, over an hour already? He'd find out soon enough.

Gregory stirred a little and Wayne made sure everything was tight around him, and played with the tiny trusting hands.

Buffet table open at last, line forming quickly. People standing around in glorified work clothes, drinks in hand, watching the sun go down. Soft Christmas music barely audible over the noise of multiple conversations, constantly reforming, laughter sometimes nervous. I recognize Ghost in a corner, and we get to talking about old times.

"You've come up a ways in the world," He notes.

"Yeah, I guess it's better than the old days," I agree.

"Do you remember that first year down here?"

"Never forget it. I'll tell you, Ghost, that was the scariest part of one of the scariest years I ever went through. The first six months were sheer chaos. I never knew if I was coming or going, but I knew damn well I was slipping fast."

"Too much drinking."

"That too, but not mostly that. It was just everything. Here we thought we were over the hump, clear view to the promised land, and we found we were just at the bottom of the hill, wrapped in fog."

"That first job was killing you…."

"That job was dead-end, boring, and not at all what I wanted, sure. But there was the commute, the graffiti on the subways, the constant rail delays, the issues with our car, the six o'clock winter mornings to do a two hour commute in, and sometimes longer back. No peace at home, no peace in our "private" rooms, no space for me, let alone for us."

"Her parents must have been overbearing."

"No, they were doing really well to welcome us and accept us as we were. They always saw everything as a temporary situation, which we had trouble believing for a while. Perspective can make a really big difference in attitude."

We pick up some more greasy food from the roving waiters.

The first five months of 1981 went by in a horrible blur. Life was bedlam. For Joan, it was the usual maternal every-hour duties, worries about early development and everything that might go wrong, paying attention to all the advice she was getting, or learning to push back and ignore some of it. And

all in the pressure cooker of her old home, with her parents, and no escape.

Wayne would get up shortly after 5 to catch the 6 am train to the city. Back in Huntington by 7:30, home by eight. The evening began, as soon as he changed. Dinner was done and cold of course, and in those days the only way to reheat was in the oven (which dried things out) or on the stovetop (which burned them.) By nine he was tired and ready to sit back and collapse. Nine was his time to take over some of the duties with Gregory and give Joan a break. Usually he was dead in bed before eleven, hoping he would not be woken up by cries in the night, with the alarm set and nothing but dread in his heart.

His first Island job was far merrier. Leave home after seven, a pleasant June drive before traffic, along back roads with lingering farm stands, dew sparkling on fields not yet turned into subdivisions. Out of work by five sharp, home by six, and each morning a hopeful and exciting challenge to face. Until, of course, it all went crash.

Finally, the current position, a few more hours, some extra days, a bit more stress. But at least something he could fit well. It appeared by the end of the year that a good rhythm had been established, especially since the heart emergency had mostly passed, and Gregory was growing quickly and healthy.

Saturday evening in October, Joan and Wayne had slipped away in the old car with Gregory to shop at the mall. The full list of baby needs was just becoming evident, with diapers and formula and toys and stroller and stuff popping out of the woodwork every few minutes. One thing they had never ever considered was the cost of it all. Mostly, they were happy to find some time to themselves.

"How's the new job," asked Joan.

"Actually, it's really good. I think it will have a lot of what I want to do." This latest employment was relatively local and actually involved not only programming but a good deal more of business involvement. A "responsible" position, if not with pay to match. But not having to buy commuter tickets each month added a lot to the budget.

"Are you feeling better now. You seem to be drinking less. I hope you can keep it up."

"Yeah, I think a lot of that was just the train. You have no idea how bad that commute was. And then not knowing what I would do at all for those couple of months later."

"You're lucky Mom found that ad in the paper." The newspaper want ads were still the main way you found work, although even then the real way to find work was to know somebody who knew somebody.

"You're right. I don't know how I missed it. And how are you doing?"

"Oh, I'm ok. I love being home. Dad and I are looking around for a house, you know."

"Do you think we can possibly afford it."

"Well, he has that real estate license, and he says we can, if we find the right price. But…"

"But what, Joan."

"Well, there aren't really any close by. They all cost a fortune."

"But Long Island is pretty big isn't it? There have to be other neighborhoods." He hadn't had a chance to drive around much, but he had looked at maps.

"Yeah, but you have to be really careful to get in a good neighborhood. And I don't want to get too far away from support."

"Oh, I guess that makes sense. Well, we'll see what happens. Where do you want to go first?"

They turned into the mall, happy finally for an equivalent to a date night out.

Looking back, I'm glad we waited until we were thirty to have a child. Everybody's life and circumstance is different, but I don't think I could have handled all the pressures without exploding if they had been loaded on me when I was in my volatile twenties. I had to work out a lot of things before I was ready to put up with so many restrictive responsibilities. Joan, perhaps could have done so more easily, but without the years of seasoning by herself following her own way she would never have been such a strong and determined and proud woman. All in all, waiting for a while was a valuable few years for both of us, in spite of obvious drawbacks.

All dreams were changing, of course, aligning with those accepted by our parents and society in general. Old prides melted as we remolded into standard middle-class suburban parents with cookie cutter jobs and homes and needs and aspirations. In return, we were showered with grateful recognition from family members, and wealth and security from employers. It was almost as if we were new immigrants to a welcoming land, where if we simply followed rules and worked hard all would come to us in time. That was the catch, of course, "all in time." There was now, there was future, and getting from one to the other could be frustrating. But mostly we recognized we were on our way, and accepted tradeoffs as necessary.

Sometimes it hurt. I had given up art dreams, but at least replaced them with exciting tasks coding and creating computer applications. Joan not only realized that for the next few years she had no hope of trying to get back into full time teaching, but also how cruelly circumstances were beginning to weigh on her chances of becoming a permanent public school teacher. In dark nights, or when surrounded by raucous familial crowds, they both sometimes wistfully remembered free times in Boston when the day was theirs to do with as they wished. Such a short time ago, such a far country.

Sitting in a corner, watching colleagues discuss their problems, remembering other parties at other times.

"Anyway, Ghost, fairly soon we were able to let our old dreams slip away," I remark.

"Kicking and screaming , no doubt." He inspects some bit of cheese on a cracker.

"Oh, yeah, sometimes I had to stomp on the box to get it shut and locked. Giving up everything is really hard."

"Well, Joan's father did that when he left Sicily."

"Sure. And when I think about it, my Mother did to, leaving her city roots to live in the forsaken outer 'burbs."

"Did you then get a better appreciation of your parents from all of this?"

"Only later. At the time it was all just action and reaction. More like an amoeba in a test tube than a reasoning human being. I had trouble even telling myself what to do, let alone handling conflicts with anyone else."

"I'm surprised you didn't withdraw more."

"Well, there was always the train ride to get sanity, then the long car commutes. Believe it or not, I came to look forward to them. Back then, of course, I would be out of contact with the world for hours at a time."

"Like you are now."

"Yep. But now, at least, it's by choice."

Wayne was spending this lunchtime walking around the warehouse-studded block near work, peering at flowering weeds in vacant lots, trying to let thousands of new bits of information settle into comfortable positions in his inner patterns of knowledge. Webcor was challenging and unique, a genuine path towards a preferred future, but nearly overwhelming. He was immersed in computer details, worried about necessary reactions, but happily engaged in something so huge.

What a crazy year, he thought. At least it's working out now. The sun beat down on the bright afternoon, as the wind pushed early fallen leaves around the streets. He hadn't really expected to find such industrial settings on bucolic Long Island, but he hadn't expected almost anything.

Even home life was settling down a lot, now that he had more time and less travel. He could get up at a more civilized six thirty and leave by seven, he was almost always home by six thirty or seven at night, and when he worked late it was usually only for one night. Almost a picnic, in spite of the occasional Saturday mornings. That gave him time to help Joan, play with Gregory, do some chores, and be more relaxed in general and friendly in particular. Besides, he admitted, babies were a lot more fun as they got a little older.

He had rarely had to adjust his inner compass so quickly. Give up completely all the counterculture mantras acquired over ten years among peers, change clothing and appearance and thinking and watch carefully what he said among the republicanized managers so alike in outlook to his father. He was even more amazed at how thoroughly plastic his beliefs could be, how he could actually believe some of the exact opposite of what he had defended a year ago. If he had time for deeper meditation, he might have considered if that was a moral failing. Not having any such time, he was grateful for ability to camouflage and survive in novel surroundings.

He tried to remain polite to everyone except sometimes Joan, which was a fault. She had as much going on as he did. After all, she was putting up with him, and this year he had been no particular prize.

It had been an initial shock, and then more shocks, and then worse. This calm afternoon was miraculous, looked at from the perspective of the last eight months, which he had at times thought were the final moments of the final year.

But here he was. Wasn't Amerika great?

There is a common saying about night being darkest right before dawn. My spiraling year might illustrate that. A difficult move, a horrible city job, a wrenching layoff, all played against a deteriorating home environment. Until it magically all turned around and started to become good.

But that is hindsight, time, and perspective. There are no guarantees that troubles fade, or that worse things cannot continue to happen forever until you die. Dawn analogies always assume there is some inevitable cosmic cycle, no matter what you do, things will become better because the sun will rise as it always does, on schedule regardless of what we may think at any given time.

Our lives are not days of cycles, there is very little inevitable about them. Good and bad crisis can arrive at any moment from anywhere, some beyond our control, some our direct fault. And there is no guarantee a bottom will be there to bounce off of. The only final bottom is death, but you can fall a long way before that hits. Or, you can be on top of the world and it might show up anyway. Lives are complicated, dawns and nights are not.

One thing is certain, which is that although you cannot change the rising of the sun, you can certainly change your own next moments. Perhaps for better, perhaps for worse. Sometimes it is even best to sit idly by and do nothing—but even that is an action. Inevitably, you realize that to get away from where you are to where you want to be you will have to get up and push on.

So I had really dark times, and when I tried to make them better it sometimes meant that I had actually made them worse, and when I tried to fix that things got even more bleak. But generally if you try enough options, one or two will turn out pretty good, and you can try to build on them. Eventually you may triumph. (Then, of course, you run the equal curse of developing hubris.)

So, no darkest day before the dawn for me. The awful thing is, you never know when the darkest point is being reached.

We head over to the crowded drinks table to pick up another bottle of beer apiece. Everyone is being pretty careful, of course, because the managers are around and the top brass might still show up. Lacking anything more interesting, we're still reminiscing about those early days on the Island.

"So you became a moral chameleon," challenges Ghost.

"At least outwardly, I guess. We had to eat, after all. I had responsibilities."

"So if a job had opened up at the death camp, you would have naturally taken it."

"I worry about that. I don't know. I feel like a moral person, but I am never sure how severely moral I am. I am not even sure how much I admire people who are rigidly idealistic."

"But they are the compasses of the culture…."

"There aren't any valid compasses of a culture. You can only be moral in your own life, doing what you think is right as much as possible, at peace with your own conception of good."

"Solipsistic and dangerous path, if you ask me."

"I agree. Just haven't found anything better. But you also have to adapt on the outside."

"That leaves you as inconstant as the wind. Doesn't that bother you?"

"Other things bother me more. Old politicians who refuse to change their minds when circumstances change, smug wealth that marinates in self-righteousness, slithering con-artists who hop on any bandwagon to sell products …."

"You're pretty smug yourself," remarks Ghost.

"I'd prefer to call it self-esteem," I answer.

"Well, yes, you would."

Late January, Wayne's parents drove up to visit. Mostly, of course, to see the new addition to the family, more gushing over a baby that looked just about like any other baby in the world. The crowded house became a little more crowded, even though they were staying at a motel. The dense conversations continued with Wayne on good behavior.

Actually, it was all pretty painless, he realized, compared to the tense visits in Boston. From their standpoint, he had finally seen the light. They considered Joan a miracle-worker, for taking their worthless and lost son and recasting him into something respectable. Even now, to the point of having a family, dressing correctly, getting a real job, and becoming as much a true blue American as any of their friends' sons. Friends' children, no matter what the era, always seem to be doing better than yours, mostly because you are fully aware of only your own's hidden warts.

For the first time in years he could converse politely and intelligently with his father. No airy talk of Art and Culture, no bitter arguments about politics and society. Business, he noticed, was more like a shared team fan base, where you could swap stories about games and events and scores, seeming to be in agreement while actually thinking of different moments entirely. He could genuinely enjoy these exchanges, and his father was grateful that he could finally communicate a bit with the wayward son.

One thing that helped was that the bloom was still on the rose with the job in the city. The commute was hard but still not grinding, the city was still exciting to be in during the day, the job itself was going well and not yet boring. He could honestly claim to be doing very well, making more money than he ever had before, in a career that at least promised eventual recognition.

So a weekend far more relaxing and enjoyable than he had in some time passed quickly, and then they were on their way, he set the alarm, and life began its long haul.

Sometime after that, I began to feel trapped. Mostly, there were no options. I had to do this, I had to do that, I had to think about this right now, and so forth. All external commands. All absolute. Wear the suit, catch the train, buy the diapers, rock the baby. No choice, no alternative.

Being trapped, unless you are stuck in a cell in prison or a hospital bed, is pretty much in your head. It's always possible to do something else, to break away. Unfortunately, most of what is available when you do feel trapped appears pretty awful and would probably lead to something worse than where you are. So you hang on, cursing the lesser of two evils, hoping maybe something better will show up.

Sane people eventually figure out ways to use even the nastiest routines and requirements as something they can accept, perhaps even enjoy. Lots of the commuters I rode with did not waste time boiling inside at time wasted doing nothing—as I was doing—but caught up on sleep or reading or meditation. When you are relatively young, however, you always want to do what you want to do when you want to do it. And when the world does not let you, you get angry at its bullying.

Fortunately, I never considered the really exotic escapes. I had no desire to be roaming any continent alone again, I had nothing particularly wonderful in Berkeley or Boston to run back to, I had done enough adventurous things to last me for a while. I loved Joan and the baby and didn't want to ditch them no matter how annoying I might think they could sometimes be. Life was quite wonderful where I was, everywhere but in my overheated rational thinking.

So my choice was to grin and bear it. Take advantage of seeing the sights in New York. Spend time thinking about life and meaning on the train rides. Find joy in family crises and their resolution. Avoid as many confrontations as possible with anyone, for I was in no position of strength. It worked quite well.

Corporate parties often begin to clot after a while. Requisite primate tribal greetings and groomings progressively up the dominant ladder had been taken care of early, careful peer to peer conversations during dinner had played out, ceremonial rites complete with plumage were over. Finally a few groups of those who have some real attractions on commonalities go their own way into corners and hallways, often in hushed tones. Many of those less involved in any hierarchy have left already.

Desserts have replaced the carving tables, candy and ice cream and cake for those who dare, cordials for those who dare more. Appearances still matter.

Ghost and I finish off a final beer. We look around, tired but impressed at the immensity of the occasion, before he asks "So I take it you really were trapped, but you refused to admit being trapped?"

"Well, that's true of everyone, all the time, isn't it? You don't wake up and discover you have been made king of the world. You're usually pretty close to what you were yesterday."

"But that's just continuity," protests Ghost. "Without continuity you have endless moments like this year of yours. Terrifying."

"I suppose you're right."

"You'd be lucky to last five years, all that adrenaline and tension."

"OK, call it continuity if you want."

"I insist," Ghost starts to look for his coat. We check through an open door to see if snow is still falling.

"Me, I insist we are all trapped, all the time. Well, maybe not you."

"Ah," replies Ghost, "you have no idea."

By the fall a kind of détente had fallen all around the household. They were all exhausted by the various crises of jobs, medical, money. The adrenaline had surged and left. In the calm after the storm, everyone was content to let any sleeping dogs lie.

Wayne reflected how provisional and temporary the world really is. He had expected some major changes, to what he did, to where he lived to how he passed the days. But he had expected the changes, whatever they were, to stabilize quickly. By contrast it had been up and down, multiple jobs with multiple problems and multiple endings, and the heart operation out of no-where, and a kaleidoscope of needs and problems, never the same one day after another as the infant grew and Joan became more hassled.

Balancing that was the equivalent understanding that whatever he was doing was always more temporary than he had thought. These living arrangements, for example, might soon be different. His job seemed to shift unrecognizably from one week to another. The gift of the lack of stability was the certainty of mobility.

Sometimes that was extremely hard to embrace, especially something like Joan's mom's heart operation, but the future always had to be accepted and dealt with. That took so much energy, through most of this year, that all the old subconscious certainties and beliefs were broken wide open, which left the possibility of renewed growth in the coming years.

Crowd thinning, we start to put on our jackets.

"Hope rekindled, finally," notes Ghost.

"Not so finally, I guess. I mean, it was an amazing twelve months. If nothing else it taught us how wide the possibilities were and how flexible we must again become."

"So you had been sheltered?"

"Looking back, yeah, we were pretty sheltered up in Boston. We'd built a nice little shell of happiness, but a good deal of it ended up keeping most of the world at some distance. We were pretty comfortable with that."

"Are you claiming this changed everything? A turning point in your psychologies?"

"No, no. We were always building shells of one kind or another. That's who we were deep down, like oysters. I don't think you swap out the genes and memes all that easily after you are grown up."

"Then all this ruckus made no difference …"

"Probably less than it seemed at the time. But, boy, what a ride."

The car turned over painfully before starting in the frosty air. Wayne headed out into the dark morning after scraping the heavy frost off the windshield. His mind was wrapped around thoughts of what needed to be done at work, once he checked the overnights and recovered from whatever disasters may have occurred. The last evening, with Gregory screaming and Joan annoyed at him for being too tired to help much had faded with the usual good night's sleep.

He fell into the drive along quasi-back roads, through congested Cold Spring Harbor, which fortunately even when backed up gave him some reflective moments staring across the harbor at the laboratory buildings marching up the hills on the far side between the trees. Then a quick shot past the train station, and a twisty short cut past the castle, soon to be at Sunnyside Drive in an incongruously industrial part of this bucolic scenery.

This was truly his time, quiet and alone, able to relax doing very little as he did what he had to. Sure there were plans, and hopes, and problems to deal with, but not this second, not in this car, not during this short half hour. He took a deep breath and was grateful for the life which had arrived.

CONTEMPLATIVE THANKSGIVING

BITTER NORTH WIND was sweeping across whitecaps on the harbor as Wayne, well bundled, rested in grateful solitude on the Beachcroft dock this Thanksgiving morning. He had temporarily escaped the cacophony of preparations up at the house to walk here for at least a few minutes of quiet contemplation. He was surprisingly content and increasingly grateful for the surprises the world had offered him this year. Most of what had happened was beyond imagination.

These last few months, late summer through autumn, had seen vast improvements in just about everything. A comfortable truce had been tacitly declared on all sides at home, especially now that their residence together truly seemed to be more temporary. Gregory was growing and much less noisy at night, letting everyone sleep a little. Joan had regained her sense of being on the Island and no longer felt a stranger in her own neighborhood. And not insignificantly, Wayne felt he was making rapid strides at work, both in politics and understanding business, and in the actual tasks of the obscure computer system on which he was working. The near future looked very promising.

It was hardly time for congratulations, of course. A long way on all fronts remained. But there were more than glimmers of goals now, real possibilities were at hand, and perhaps they would happen almost at the same breakneck speed as he had adapted to. Claiming he enjoyed life on the edge would be exaggerating, but at least he could mostly handle it.

Not riding the train—well having glimpsed the mouth of Hell he was glad he had managed to at least avoid that fate. Long Island was beginning to look much more attractive, now that he had time to see it. Even the multitudinous relatives were starting to sort themselves out. He no longer had to be so on guard and cautious always meeting someone new. The family was comfortable.

Finally, a vast difference from life over the last decade, the world fully approved of what he was doing. His parents, her parents, Joan herself, even his internal voices all applauded that he had finally embraced the American dream and moved into the mainstream. It was a nice change from always feeling he had to defend himself. OK, so he'd lost some of the grand visionary dreams—but those had become pretty faded and tattered by the end anyway. He was busily finding replacements in his new career.

So much to be thankful for. A new life. Finally everything would settle down and if it just held a little longer—the sky would be the limit.

Insistent, loud, well-spaced knocks at the door of the house on Inlet Place. Nobody else seems to be around, so I open it cautiously to find Ghost standing outside in a long trench coat, holding a stuffed brown briefcase. He flashes ID from his wallet and pushes inside, setting up at the dining room table, scowling, without a word or apology. "Social Welfare checkup," he announces officiously.

"I've never been on welfare," I protest.

"Close enough," he sneers. "Now, we have some standard questions you need to answer."

"Or what?" I don't see why I need to put up with his whims.

"Or I'll come up with an even worse scenario."

Knowing how inventive Ghost can be, I decide maybe it is better to play along. "All right, go ahead. Make it quick."

"OK. Supporting your family ok? Food, shelter, clothing, everything in place. I need to look."

I escort him to the two rooms on the side of the house, examine the closets for clothing, check the crib, rummage through the toys. The kitchen is well stocked, the house clean. "But none of this is yours, is it? You don't pay rent or anything."

"We're saving for a house. I pay plenty," I say under my breath, "just not in money."

"OK, OK, holding a job? Can I see the paychecks, please?" He takes a close look. "Better than I expected, I must admit. Still, you haven't had this job very long."

"Long enough, and doing well. Are we done yet?"

"Let's see. Oh, yeah, how is the alcoholism? "

No use bluffing this. "I'm still drinking. Beer mostly, almost exclusively. Mostly on weekends. Much better than it was. Much better."

"Well, I'm afraid I can't find anything wrong, for now anyway." He seems disappointed.

"Of course not."

"I'll be back," he puts on his coat and heads back out to his white Cadillac. "We need to make sure you stay on the right path."

"Don't hurry," I shut the door firmly before he is out of sight.

Now that he had a better schedule, Wayne found himself helping with Gregory a little more. Holding him and just watching, of course, but some bottle feeding and diaper changing thrown in. Babysitting if nothing else while Joan escaped somewhere with her mom. He had no aversion to this and rather enjoyed it, doing something important while by any reasonable standards doing nothing at all.

Other than that, this was a fool's paradise, at least to an impartial observer. His dinners were cooked for him, he didn't have to clean (just keep things relatively picked up.) He could collapse and claim he had just had a bad day, and it was accepted. He didn't have to fix the roof or even worry about where the money would come from to fix the roof. If the car had problems he could count on a ride. And there was always spending change in his pocket, with few fears of needing to spend very much.

Not riding the train made as big a difference as he had thought. Instead of getting up early and leaving well before seven, he could get up after seven and take his time and still arrive before 8:30 at work. Instead of getting home after seven, he was frequently back by 5:30. And if he had to stay late or go in early, it was a trivial adjustment, and no worry about when the next train would leave or how the subways ran outside of rush hour. Plus he could carry tons of work and books to and fro as necessary. When he had lived in the commune, or even with Joan in Boston, it had appeared that all those people destroying the planet with cars instead of using public transportation were selfish idiots. Now he found himself one of the idiots. And, worse, could defend being so.

On the weekends his main chores were to help shop for necessary items, give Joan a break, and particularly be available for gatherings, parties, and home discussions. It was often not the favorite thing he might do, but since even with all that he had ample time to take a short walk or help around the yard he considered it a small price to pay.

What would the next year bring, he wondered, as he left the harbor and started home to help set the table and do whatever else was necessary to welcome the clan for the holidays.

"Wayne, come here a minute," called Joan from across the hall. "I want to see how you look."

Wayne gulped down the rest of the bottle of beer, carefully placed the empty in the rapidly filling paper bag on the floor, and dutifully went over to be inspected.

"You're not going to drink too much, are you?" Joan demanded. "You smell like a brewery."

"No, no. Just relaxing a little, that's all." By any standards he was not drinking too much today. His background was that holidays were for celebration, which meant alcohol. His own father certainly enjoyed them that way. Wayne didn't see anything wrong if he stuck to plain old cheap beer.

"Well, Dad told me again the other day that 'Your husband has a problem.' You better watch yourself."

The problem continued to be the empties. He could get the six packs into the house easily enough, and he was an adult, and nobody really cared nor counted. But the empties just kept piling up into bags and he had to take them out into the trash at some point and they clanked and clinked a guilty din. But if he stuck to beer, as he had been doing for months, he thought he was in a much better place than before. Besides, there were often days and stretches of days on end when he had nothing at all. He felt righteously on the right track.

"No, no, I'm fine," he insisted. "All I want is a little buzz to ease social tensions." Robert was arriving any minute, Philip might stop by, there were constant phone calls, and there was never any certainty about who might drop in or possibly if they would be forced to head out to a different house party.

"Well, I don't want you staggering around or bumping into things or falling down," Joan went on.

"I haven't done that for a long time," he mumbled. "Not since the new job, anyway."

"Well, just watch yourself," she insisted. "Here, straighten that collar."

The main trouble with this period of maturation was that I had to leave so much of what I had thought was my essential core behind. Every genera-tion has its own dragons to slay, of course, and its own ideals to pursue. We were no different. But we found ourselves sliding anyway.

For example, I had been involved with lots of people who wanted to change the standard "bad" ways of doing things, such as sexual role models. The wife was no longer supposed to be subordinate to the man, and both were supposed to equally help bring up a child, cook, and so on. The ideal was equal sharing of all chores, and both of us fully believed in all the pro-paganda. But in reality, here we were, and I was going to work every day and coming home beat up and tired. Joan was staying at home taking care of the baby and beat up and tired. I didn't do my share, at least nowhere near equal share, in baby chores. Even when I was around, I needed a little time and space to recover from the nastiness at work, not to mention reading and writ-ing the frequent homework as I tried to get up to speed on the computer. So there we were, doing things we had never done.

It was a similar story with all the "isms" that we and many of our friends had confidently sworn we would never fall into: racism, capitalism, consumerism. We were driving cars, inhabiting the suburbs, buying lots of stuff from big impersonal stores, eating whatever happened to be convenient. It had been a drift, but a really fast drift, and it was almost painful to look back a couple of years and realize how we had changed. Because somewhere, deep down, we still respected our old outlooks.

The future had become now. Now had so many demands, such requirements taking all our energy, that worries about tomorrow or the day after just fell away. There was no time, there was no energy, and if we made it to bed having simply accomplished all we thought we should be doing (and that was rarely the case) we believed we had done more than enough. Racism and sexism and all the rest would just have to take care of themselves. We had diapers to change and clothes to wash and shopping to do.

Knock, knock. Who's there? Ghost. Ghost who? Ghost again. "All right, what are you doing back again?" This time it's early morning , I'm dressed in bathrobe and slippers, with a cup of coffee. "I answered all your questions last time."

"Advanced experimental session," he shows me some kind of badge, and pushes on in, plopping down in the couch opposite my easy chair as he pulls more papers out of his briefcase, which he then uses as a desk.

"Is this the last of it?" I inquire suspiciously.

"Perhaps, perhaps. I swear I'm a slave to the vagaries of the bureaucracy at the office. OK. Let's get started so we can get it over."

I take another sip of the dark black brew.

"Now the problem is—don't take this personally—but we had you down as pretty much a total loser. Your starting a family at this late date has caused considerable concern."

"Damn personally if you ask me!" I choke. "I'm sure there are zillions of other families far worse off than ours."

"By some measures, yes. But not by the applicable ones in your case."

"And what might those be?" I demand.

"The very ones you have devised in your mind to match the families of your ancestors, especially your parents and now Joan's parents as well. Here you are lagging considerably."

"But doing well and moving fast. I know where we are going."

"Anyway, I have some metrics that …"

"Just get out," I blink and he starts to dissolve. "The only relevant judges for these relevant metrics of yours are me and Joan and the people close in our family. You can take your advanced experimental session and …"

But Ghost was already faded completely like a bad dream, leaving disturbing echoes in what had been my peaceful solitude.

Webcor was moving right along, and he was riding with it. He had smoothed out all the normal daily routines, and knew what he was doing. He could recover easily from minor problems. Everyone was as happy as they could be with the computer—not that they didn't always want improvements. And he was beginning to venture into deeper technical waters, as he finally started to digest the various manuals and begin to cautiously play around, especially with the innocuous query facility.

The company was having a good year. There seemed to be tremendous pent-up demand for phones that went well beyond the styling of the three or four traditionally offered by the phone company. The recent ruling that people could buy their own and legally put it on their home lines had coupled with the usual need for some kind of novelty at Christmas. Orders will still coming in even though the holiday was nearly here, they couldn't ship fast enough, the warehouse frantically waited for new pallets from overseas.

Accounting had never had to handle this kind of volume. Finally, they were appreciating the printed reports, and the relative ease with which an order could be shipped and invoiced. Tracking accounts, determining how salesmen were doing, figuring what to order next (in the long pipeline to the Far East) would have been impossible to accomplish manually with the sheer quantities now involved.

Since everyone knew how well things were going, the attitude at work was almost deliriously joyful. This was the beginning of great things. Webcor was very nearly the first player in this market, and with the contacts it was making it might very well become a giant in the field. Extra hours, extra load, a few hassles meant nothing. The future was assured and everybody, including Wayne, was giving it more than their all. A classic American business success story in the making.

Finally, I felt I was not over my head, not just catching up, not faking my way through rough patches. I was getting an excellent intuitive feel for this quite weird operating system, and a more balanced view of the needs of a distribution business in general. I could converse easily with management, users, external consultants, and the hardware manufacturers. In fact, I found one of my talents turned out to be translation of one jargon to another, often using analogies and metaphors which were easily accepted.

Most of the time, the daily work was not too onerous. It was really a five hour job, even on busy days, and a lot of that job still involved mindless activity—unjamming the printer, decollating the carbon paper from long multipart reports, changing and labeling the latest tape backups, applying software fixes, and not least annotating and logging everything. I began my ongoing and endless journey into providing documentation that was useful to me and could be used by others when I was not around.

I was getting pride in where I was. I was wise enough to realize that I was by no means indispensable, but I also strived to make myself well worth my salary, and the best and least painless choice available. That required treading carefully—I would not make promises I knew I could not keep, as consultants often did. I did not minimize the complexity of some issues, nor did I overcomplicate those that were relatively easy. I tried to develop bonds of trust, and would often do favors for certain departments and users so that I would have some credit in the bank if I had problems later on.

My worst fault was underestimating time, and taking documentation at face value. I would read of some possibility, and confidently predict I could use it somehow, only to find that there were hidden problems, some insoluble. And as became true forever, everything took longer than it had any reason to. Mr. Murphy made sure that everything happened at the worst possible time.

The worst possible time was always month end, which became impossibly nasty at year end. I had to wait for the formal declaration to "close" the accounting month. Until then, with the package we had bought, we could not do invoicing or shipping on the computer. Paper documents would pile up for days on end, and have to be entered in a rush as soon as the digital books were closed, all the figures sat in their proper accumulation buckets, and the paper reports were in the hands of those who needed them. Then with a huge rush, it would take days to catch up. Delays for whatever reason did not make me popular.

Most of that was because the computer was already beginning to run out of space and especially time. The company had just outgrown it, almost before it was broken in. Month-end calculations could take a good chunk of the night. If something went wrong—and it often did for some obscure reason or other—I would walk in, see the backup had not started, track down the failure, and slink into Joe's office to explain the failure, before going back and starting over. Never pleasant.

The car was warming up as I scraped ice of the windshield when I heard a cough. Ghost was standing behind me, nearly apologetic in the frosty air. "What now?" I growl. "I'm in a hurry. Can't be late for work."

"Sorry, just this one mandatory entry."

"Yeah?"

"Do you plan to abandon your family? They need to know."

I let the "they" pass without comment. "Jeez, of course not. Never did. Where did you ever get that impression."

"Well, there are notes by an informant …."

"When, for God's sake."

He squinted at the tiny writing, "Oh, around 1972 …"

"Right. Well, since I've met Joan I never wanted to abandon anything. Maybe hang out with a few beers once in a while, but that's it."

"You're sure. You have a kid now …"

"Look, I spent a few years magnificently alone and lonely. No way I'm going back to that."

"Well, if you'll just sign here," he held out the pad. I took off my glove and scribbled.

As I finished clearing and opened the door he eyed me suspiciously, "But you do have a car now …"

"Oh, yeah," I said, getting in, "this piece of junk would maybe get me all the way to Ohio before dying for good." I slam the door and carefully back out.

It was just like having a new set of dress-up clothes, or new shoes, thought Wayne. The new home and work life had started out with pain, blisters, and feeling self-conscious. But after a while, either the apparel became broken in or he became used to them and they were as easy to wear as anything else. Now it was finally all slipping into the range of comfortable.

He had relatively quickly cast off his old cultural outlooks. Driving a car, for instance, no longer felt like taking a dagger to the heart of the environment. Buying pampers and other goods at big box stores failed to rouse proper indignation. And the worst image of all—being just another consumer in the suburbs—no longer conjured existential dread as he lay awake at night. All these were taken for granted as necessary—either genuine changes in his philosophy or simply camouflage to get by with the other barbarians surrounding him.

More comfortably, everyone else had shaken off a lot of preconceptions concerning him. He and Joan no longer spent long conversations explaining why they were waiting to have children. He no longer rationalized getting ready for a better job in a prosperous career—he was there, nobody questioned his position nor his path. The route ahead was straight and narrow—better job, better car, house, more children.

There were some parts of Long Island life he never would get used to. Tales of the old days didn't even interest him when they were about his own life, let alone that of strangers. The constant patter about real estate as secular religion left him bored to tears, but it was the inevitable destination of almost any conversation with anyone. Art, social revolution, all the various elements he had been used to as background for so many years, simply vanished.

Given the turmoil of the last few years, Wayne was grateful for the respite. He had hardly ever been one to beat himself up too much anyway, and he was glad to no longer be the target of anyone else's good intentions. He might never get quite used to wearing a suit and tie, might curse many days at the commuting traffic, might feel all his time had been sucked into a grey American commercial fog, but, on the other hand, he was safe, warm, with hope, and nobody was giving him a hard time. What more could he possibly ask for?

I had hated to give up everything. Discussing art, when an opportunity presented itself (usually with Joan's brother Robert), was still fun. Taking a solitary walk outside might become restricted—maybe simply around the block during lunch—but it was still a refreshing reset to my thoughts. We still had everything we had ever owned packed tightly in the garage, for future reference if desired.

Long Island had its compensations. It was a beautiful place, even with all the building going on everywhere. The harbor was down the street, even as its wetlands vanished into huge houses. There were beaches and parks everywhere. The weather was generally not so severe as that of Boston. If I ever got the time, big old New York City with all its history and museums was a manageable hour away by train. Even Huntington had its compensations.

But mostly, it was nice to have a back yard again, our own bedroom. Quiet time could be achieved on the drive to and from work. Going shopping at ToysRUs, if restricted, could be transformed into an adventure to match that of Filene's basement.

So there I was, going native. The main thing was not to feel that the previous years had been wasted. I loved the fact that we had seemingly done so much more than many of the people we met. I was glad we had settled down into what our parents considered normality, and I was grateful that things I thought would be interminably irritating had become softly woven into the pattern of our lives. Mostly, I began to tell myself this was just another stage on a long journey, neither a beginning nor end, but just a wayside inn to whatever the future might hold.

As I leave work and cross the parking lot to the car, Ghost bustles up wearing an ill-fitting blue suit that looks like it has been coated with butter, battered briefcase in hand, waving yet another paper. "Wait! Wait!" he calls.

I'm in a rush to get home. "Thought we settled one last thing a while ago. I'm in a hurry, and I'm tired of all this harassment."

"Very important, very important. Forgot this ... what about life insurance?"

"Life insurance?" I laugh. "Never had life insurance in my life."

"Precisely," he notes seriously, as my coworkers vehicles stream away around us. "But now you have a real family, a child, responsibilities."

"OK," I concede, "I'll think about it. Now just go away."

"But the rest of the future," he persists. "The rest of the future. Your house, your second house, your other children, their college, your retirement …"

"Listen, Ghost," I answer seriously. "Most of our future at the moment consists of me holding this job until the end of the week and stretching the resulting paycheck to meet Gregory's consistently growing expensive list of necessities from the store. We'll worry about anything more than that when it arrives."

"No! No!" he gestures with the paper. "You need to start now, invest at 10 percent, get started on these expenses. You know everyone else has a head start…."

"Maybe a few people do," I admit. "Maybe a lot don't. Maybe a lot of the ones most ready will die along the way."

"Which is why you need life insurance."

"I said I'd look into it. The other, right now, is just smoke and mirrors. All we need is right now is firmer feet on the ground. Go sell these worrisome illusions to the eskimos."

He looked very puzzled. That gave me a chance to escape. Selling refrigerators to eskimos was a current joke. What Joan and I need wasn't future insurance, it was more guarantees about the present.

Older people gaze back through distorting lenses to determine transformative milestones of their lives and occasionally wonder what might have been if only. They often discover some of the greatest changes emerged subtly. Certainly our move to Huntington, the birth of Gregory, and my commitment to a solid job in a regular company were by any standards a huge dividing point in our lives.

Unlike many such markers, these were obvious at the time. We knew were going through life-current rapids that approached waterfalls. All we could do, some of the time, was to survive the day and the days and hope that calm lovely water lay somewhere ahead. And, at the time, we had no certainty that such would ever be the case.

Yet I always think of this as a tribute to the American dream. In point of fact, once we decided to change our goals and do things in certain ways, just like poor immigrants or restless entrepreneurs, we could make almost anything of our family that we wanted. There was still enough opportunity lying around back then, at least for those with education and talent in certain directions, that anyone willing to give themselves to it and work hard could succeed moderately well. I fear, very much, that is no longer the case.

Yet even in those years, limits were set by the boundaries of one's visions and dreams and commitments to other things. What were we willing to do, what would we sacrifice, in order to achieve how much? And at that point both Joan and I set possibly narrowed limits to what we considered necessities for happiness. I wanted to be near the family and not travel. She wanted to live close to her parents. We both wanted moments with our children, to simply enjoy the wondrous experiences the world could offer.

I sit on the pier in the harbor, looking at pleasure boats going in and out of the limit, as a jet ski veers over and docks below me. Ghost gets out in a bright red tee shirt with a Boston baseball cap. "There you are," he says with satisfaction as ascends the aluminum gangplank.

"Leave me alone and go away. My time!" I yell.

"You are not making enough salary for me to leave alone."

I've had it up to my neck by now. "Ghost," I shove him in the chest, "you have way too much obsession with money."

"But money is everything..."

"This whole society has way too much obsession with money. Money is a useful tool, period. Having lots of hammers is a lot less important than having one. I just need enough."

"Regulations require that ..."

"No, there are no regulations and you know it. And precious few good guidelines. The best parents are often poor, the worst often rich. Wealthy folk can be miserable, those near poverty level happy. And don't even start on what is required to be a good artist."

"But ..."

"No but. Yeah, you need a level. No, you don't need much more. Go away!"

"Don't you like being relatively well off," he whines plaintively.

"I love it," I admit. "But not enough to need to be better off at the expense of everything I treasure."

"Ok, this time, maybe," he begins to remount.

"OK, this time, forever," I say as he roars back into the channel.

Almost twelve, the house as usual comfortably cool. Greg in bed asleep, Joan Mom and Dad milling around, barely awake, Wayne in a cheerful beery haze. Guy Lombardo sonorously wafts from the television, as cameras focus on the ball ready to drop in Times Square. No work tomorrow, no issues tonight, all good with the world.

Joan comes over. "Almost happy new year," she smiles.

"Almost happy new year to you," he replies.

What a year. On top of last year. He didn't think he could take many more of these, near cardiac arrest, nearly up, nearly down, always around. Including people nearly lost—Mom was taking it easy of course, but she was a hard personality to keep quiet. She was certainly looking a lot better. Wayne prayed that would hold for a long while.

After the ball drop there would be phone calls everywhere, to his parents, to her brothers, and who know what incoming. Almost the calm before the storm. A storm like this was ok, he decided, compared to the real storms he just felt they had been through.

Announcer comes on and a countdown begins. The ball is ready to start dropping as the last seconds of the old year tick away.

Some year ends, he thought, pass without notice. Others, like this one, seem like those clichéd final instants in novels where your entire life flashes in front of your eyes. In these ten or fifteen seconds, the last year certainly flashed before his eyes, filled with adventures he hardly wanted. In parallel, his entire presumed future flashed before him—tidy house, tidy yard, steady work, growing family. "Yes sir, no ma'am," polite without measure forever and ever until he finally faded away like everyone else.

1982 LEAVES AND ROOTS

Manager In Spite of Himself

Joe D's office was small and sparse, in spite of his impressive credentials. He was a young man, just about Wayne's age, already with an MBA and hefty experience in accounting. They enjoyed speaking to each other, primarily about business and what the computer might do for the company. Joe would come up with ideas, Wayne would try to figure out ways to implement them. When they had time from other duties, half hour meetings like this were interesting, pleasant, and often exciting. The company fully approved, since Joe D was Wayne's immediate boss anyway, although without much of a computer background.

"So, you really think we could get these sales reports out more often, say weekly?"

"I can certainly schedule it on the overnight run, we have lots of power there. But of course, all the data will have to be in, so we need some way to control it if there is a problem."

"Right. We wouldn't want Victor to get excited about some automatic report if the data is totally wrong. He'd never trust us again. Hell, he doesn't really trust the computer reports now."

"That's the problem all right," said Wayne. "I guess I'll need to put in some kind of switch that tells whether to run the things or not."

"Of course, he and Joe P will get just as mad if they start to expect reports and they don't arrive …."

"Joe! Wayne! Get over here!" came a yell from Joe P's office. Joe P was Joe D's boss, and hence in Wayne's chain of command. Being called in for an impromptu meeting was rarely a good thing—eagle eyes had spotted a problem in the numbers somewhere. Uh, oh, Frank the head of accounting was sitting in there already. Notepads ready, they entered the larger windowless office.

Ghost is dressed soberly, grey hairs neatly glued in place, jowls prominent and exuding an air of superior confidence. We are sitting at a conference table, but various other participants are frozen in place. He has a slender expensively turned leather brief case, and a few carefully arranged papers in front.

"And you are?" I ask, unable to quite decide what is going on.

Ghost looks up in annoyance, "I think it should be obvious that I am your outside consultant, come here to tell you how to put things right. What a mess…."

"Yeah, you guys always say that. You work for Marvelous Associates?" A few of those folks were also sitting at the table, I see, with my bosses and a couple of heavyweight executives.

"No, I'm consulting on the role of the consultants at Victor's request. We met on the golf course the other day, and after talking a while I think I can help here."

"Doing it as a favor for free, eh?"

Ghost casts a derisive look. "You always get only what you pay for. Now, let's begin here, with what you actually do. There's hardly any indication of computer programming here, you know."

"I'm nominally the manager and operator. Marvelous Inc. still handles all the real code. I just pull dinky little reports from the data using the report generator. The regular input and all is still controlled by the consultants. For a hefty fee, of course."

"Yeah, it's not bad. You should think about your own next move—take a clue from all our Mercedes outside."

"I never did think too clearly when changing jobs," I admit. "For now my main task is simply operations. Periodic tape backups, organization, making sure reports got printed and distributed. If anything goes wrong, even operations like having to restore, we have to call Marvelous. It's in the contract."

"So you are a manager ...."

"Not even. Almost the lowest of the low. A computer operator is only a step above key entry. But the options are wide open."

"And those are, for example, creating query reports?"

"Right. They would never pay consultants to do that, and in fact one of the reasons they selected this system is that it is supposed to have an excellent query language (trademark name is, believe it or not, 'English') which would let the firm do their own reports. The brass bought into it. Not true, of course, but I picked it up fast. The real programming tricks are in automatic scheduling. I've cracked that, and things have started to calm down."

"You're spinning your wheels ..."

"No, no. I really am learning the business—any business—and reports and departments and the little necessary nuts and bolts I never knew about before. It's fascinating, really."

Webcor was a proud old name from the fifties, and many people had memories of high-quality, moderately-priced sound equipment built by that firm—even I had owned a reel-to-reel Webcor tape recorder in my youth. But this company had nothing to do with any of that—entrepreneur Victor had simply purchased the name from defunct creditors to achieve instant market recognition.

This incarnation of Webcor was an importer of goods from the Far East, mostly Japan. It had begun with cheap watches and similar consumer items. But it quickly seized an opportunity to be US representative for inexpensive telephones of all types. Personally-owned telephones were still a novelty, since until recently laws prevented their use with monopolistic Ma Bell. Excitement ran high over designs, colors, and features the old phone company had never dreamed of.

Victor was a hard-driving president who developed distant contacts in Tokyo and Hong Kong with long trips filled with entertainment he enjoyed. For a while, he was outside the US as much as home. That led to a profitable trade in electronic equipment. He had less interest in sales, but since it was in a hot market, that almost took care of itself as one chain department store after another came on board.

As a result, this sleepy little knick-knack wholesaler had suddenly found itself growing explosively. Among other adjustments, that led to a need for a big (but not too expensive) computer to handle it all. Management had been convinced to buy an off-brand Microdata machine running the Pick operating system, which fortunately (for Wayne) was based on "Business Basic" (along with its trademarked "Reality" operating system.) So although Wayne knew very little—nothing really—about such large and intricate operating systems, he did know enough Basic to convince everyone he could do the job.

Besides, those with any qualifications were few and he was cheap. Consultants had done the usual sales of "this general package for import wholesalers will fit you exactly with just a few modifications here and there," lying through their teeth as all salesmen in the trade were prone to do. Well, to be fair, many of those salesmen had no idea what they were really selling anyway. It was always the programmers and their architects who would try to implement requirements later who ended up facing the impossible.

Wayne was over his head from day one, and made a few tragically stupid mistakes in the first few months as he tried to learn, digest, and apply the information in the thick copious technical manuals. Imagined enhancements often turned out like bad science experiments. His first attempt at true programming had resulted in wiping existing code from the machine, which the aggrieved consultants came in to reload and repair, not without stern lectures to everyone. He was more careful after that.

Wayne and Joe D settled into the hot seats. Frank sat smugly off to one side, sheaf of papers near at hand. Wayne thought of him as an ancient wizened Mesopotamian, half religious about the clay cuneiform tablets he guarded, jealous of the papyrus that seemed to be replacing them. But he was a friend of Victor's from way back, and the perfect image of what the accounting professors at college had been trying to mold Wayne into all those years ago. He truly had the "gimlet eyes" of those in paperback novels, glinting whenever he found a mistake in the massive rows of numbers he pored through each day and night.

BABYLON WITH GHOST

Joe P was not nearly so old, with maybe a decade on Joe D, presiding from behind his important-looking desk piled with reports and notes. Probably of all the new people at Webcor as it began to take off, he was the most operationally important, keeping everything running as smoothly as possible, matching sales and receivables and shipping and even mundane functions like equipment and building upkeep. A big shot who usually didn't act like one, but his bite could hurt when he needed it to.

Joe P began, "I've been looking at the preliminary sales reports you've been giving me, Joe, and the numbers are a little off." Joe D turned to Wayne and said "Is that possible?"

Possible? Of course it was possible. He had used the query language for the report, the other figures came from the consultant's secret coded pathways. He could have missed something important, but "how big is the discrepancy?" he asked. He had learned really, really fast not to get defensive and say stupid things like "that's impossible." When a user said something happened, Wayne discovered, they had usually found exactly what they reported. They might do it gleefully, like Frank, but no malice would cause them to make things up out of thin air. So obviously the numbers did not match.

"Forty three cents, on the day's gross, right here," Frank pointed out triumphantly.

That was a new one. "Forty three cents? Out of what total?"

"Five thousand, two hundred eighty seven and forty six. Significant."

"But ..." Concepts of significant varied. It sure didn't seem like much to him.

Seeing his incredulousness, Frank added, "you know, we double check everything, several people," implying the computer did not. "Being a penny off no matter what the sum indicates a sloppiness that might be covering major errors."

"But ..."

Joe D stepped in quickly. "Ok, Frank, we'll see what we did wrong." This one was unwinnable. "Wayne, why don't you try to find an explanation?" That was a clue to leave and do something useful to overcome the shame they had apparently been put through.

Wayne buried himself in printouts and data, ran some test queries, narrowed down total by total until .... Ah, here it was. A few hours later, another impromptu meeting.

"Ok, what did you miss?" asked Joe P.

"Well," said Wayne nervously, "It's the way things were adding up and rounding. You see...."

Every bite counted in those early days, memory was expensive, and the results were supposed to be so whizz bang that tiny problems could be ignored. It turned out that the way subtotals were kept in "English" rounded each result into the grand total, and if there were a lot of subtotals there was a lot of rounding. On the other hand, the final result on Frank's report was in Basic, and used one accumulator with no rounding at all. Not easy to explain in those ancient days, nor easy to tell them that they could not have the report in the form they wanted using the Query function and still have it match the coded results.

After a lot of quasi-anger and difficulty, the issues were accepted for the moment and Wayne was assigned to talk to the consultants and see if there was any way around it. He thought he had done an excellent job in finding everything out, until Joe P said as they were leaving, "OK, try not to surprise me like that again...."

I arrived in the industry just as computer usage began to explode in moderate and small business use. Of course large computers from IBM and Burroughs had been used for a long time in giant corporations, and scientific computers like DEC and Data General were used in defense and scientific explorations such as at Kurzweil. All of those had immense resources thrown about and expensive boxes which required an immediate hierarchy of system architects, application architects, designers, programmers, coders, data-entry and lowly operators. But suddenly every small firm could afford new and modest machines, some of them quite radical, often scaling up from the smaller home computers, rather than down from the huge ones.

So for a brief while, as various winners (Microsoft) and losers (Microdata) fought it out over the lower end of the business market, there was a tremendous shortage of anyone who could become at all computer-knowledgeable in a practical way. Many high-level people I met later started as operators or even data-entry personnel, teaching themselves, gradually move up like workers once did in the traditional mailroom, going on to be system designers or

IT directors. It was a heady and confusing and wonderful time.

Being in such ferment was wonderful. A good professional was in high demand, and could dream of easily moving from job to job without problem. In practice that was a good deal more difficult, because of how widely the machines varied from one manufacturer to another, and the lack of standard languages and coding. A person could certainly do as much as they were willing to learn and able to comprehend. And to some extent most computer people were able to get away with things not available to anyone else on staff—hence the frequent expression that the doors to the computer room were only opened "to throw red meat to the guys."

I found myself oddly well-equipped for the times, even though a little too old to take full advantage. I was smart and learned easily and loved to make these machines do what I wanted and I was able to envisage a whole project quite easily and break it down into manageable parts. My strange varied background let me try to understand and get along with all the various demands of the users, my education let me earn the trust of upper level managers. And I was always excited by the next thing to come along.

On the other hand, I was not aggressive enough in my own demands. I dedicated myself to each task when engaged, and avoided all mention of it when off duty. I did not like hanging out with folks with no agenda, dropped people easily when they were no longer in my immediate circle, could not network, and usually underestimated my value and leverage. All in all, things ended up balancing well, but it took time, some of it rough.

After the rest had filed out of the conference room, Ghost turned to me. "So, young man, what do you see as your eventual place here? A department head?"

"I don't think so. I always wanted to be an artisan, not a manager. "

"Not much financial future in that, you know."

"Yeah, I guess I will end up doing some kind of management, even if the only person I manage is myself in my computer hat. But I don't want to do it all day, build an empire, all that."

"Still dreaming of Renaissance art, weren't you," interrupts Ghost, dropping the façade and the props around us.

"Actually, I eventually came to that outlook. But mostly in the beginning I thought of myself as more one of the early steam engineers, back when the industrial revolution was just started."

"They never got rich, of course."

"Neither did I. It was never the guys who improved and kept the trains or steamboats running who got wealthy, although they could be well paid and respected. It was always the Goulds and Fisks and Vanderbilts. What I did realize in time, thankfully, was that although management could pay well, it was even more of an incoherent, risky rat race than being a technical wizard."

"You have to fit into what you fit."

"Yeah, I'm not really flexible enough to do anything else."

Wayne soon had explored and categorized cardinal rules of development in an organization:

- Users are always happy when they first get a product, although annoyed that it took so long and cost so much.
- The magic wears off quickly and what they were thrilled with on day one becomes their minimum requirement from now on.
- There are always "just a few little things to make this perfect." These few little things, no matter how complicated and bizarre, are never, ever enough to make anything perfect.
- Just when any application nearly reaches the nirvana of acceptance, constant use, and stability—everything changes.

Since he had been uninitiated in those mysteries, dangerous situations grew when hubris whispered he had become invincible. He loved the joy of tweaking "a few little things," which although superficial brought plaudits from users. He gloried in making people happy. He was really good at understanding problems and fixing them, which led folks to expect even more. But precisely because he was so good, everyone undervalued what he seemingly effortlessly accomplished.

Prototypes are wonderful things, the salesman's dream. They seem to show unlimited promise and the immense possibilities of the product. Eyes light up, contracts are signed, money exchanges hands, designers and developers buckle down to work. And it all falls apart.

At least that was the rule in the first days of those wild systems. "Best practices" for these particular segments of industry had yet to be invented. It was easy to claim ten impossible things before breakfast, because the buyers had never seen a computer before except in the movies. It was easy for the client to expect ten miracles by dinner because they didn't know anything about the constraints of binary systems and limitations of power and time.

What really aggravated the changeover from manual to automated, however, were the misunderstood peculiarities of the manual ways of doing things. Most companies read a few textbooks and decided what was required of a "standard distributor package," using a "plain vanilla accounts receivable." Why not? You track things owed to you and things owed to others and voila—all done. Besides, it was all there in standard bookkeeping already ... you were just replacing the summing of numbers.

But ... ah the "buts". Certain accounts had to be flagged for Victor's eyes only. Certain orders had to be marked in yellow as teasers from the salesmen landing a big account—under the minimum amount for this sale only on the promise of immense future returns. You didn't care if some of the biggest clients went over 30 days because you knew they would always be good eventually. And there were more ways to slice and dice the general ledger buckets to keep various details in than anyone in an ivory tower academic environment had ever heard of.

In those early times, most programmers and consultants were more than happy to oblige almost anything—it seemed easy enough and nobody had any idea of how interconnected systems had to be to function well. Clients were unable to conceive of standardizing the ways that had always worked. If they had a special pink folder for Aunt Flo's special treatment, they wanted that immortalized in code so the business didn't come to a screeching halt. Build it or else we will get someone who will, they dictated.

And, even worse, some things had to be hidden from some people. This was before much awareness of security—printed listings with accounts receivable information and client addresses would be mindlessly tossed into the trash every month. But some sales were not to be shown to certain salesmen, some inventory was reserved away from the warehouse people, you never knew what special handling might be required. And all the possibilities and nasty interactions had to be handled on the fly, usually with a vice president showing his stuff by bellowing how awful it all was.

Ghost is gathering up his papers to put in the briefcase when he turns to me. "I'm going to give you some free advice," he straightens up and looks severely stuffed.

"Don't you always," I reply.

"Ok, but you know what I mean," he says, reverting to form. "I just want to you examine how blind to reality you have always been in regards to work."

"And what are these pearls of wisdom, oh grand poobah?" I ask.

"Please note that you ended up managing, anyway," laughs Ghost, "just like you ended up taking care of buildings back in Boston."

"All jobs that pay anything," I reply, "ended up requiring artisanship but also a good deal of sales and a certain amount of managing others. It's just a question of degree, and what you consider your proper métier."

"Oh, aren't we the high and lofty one this morning," he sniggers.

"It's true though. Even when doing pure computer work, I was always having to sell a design or idea or need for a change, or why a change did not have to happen. Even when finally coding and implementing, I needed folks to test and feedback. In most of my career, I had to do some of it all to do anything at all."

"Maybe you did. But you probably could have put a higher premium on your own mix." He heads out the door.

Around eight, cheerful and ready to try some new programming today, agenda full, Wayne unlocked the computer room, turned on the lights, and stepped inside. With a sinking feeling, he noticed the terminal had information on it, a glance at the tape reel showed it was still threaded—which usually meant it had never finished the backup. Shit, and nearly end of month, too. He hung up his coat, took a glance at the problem, and found a cup of coffee before sitting down to investigate. There was going to be hell to pay when anyone else got in.

By the end of the year, the core elements of computerization had begun to match the requirements almost exactly. The trouble was, those requirements were for the old, relatively sedate, Webcor. Over the last six months this had become a bursting, much more complex company. New reports and special processing were being tacked on all the time. Salesmen wanted key information daily, accounting wanted its stuff to tie out the previous day, special management analysis were happening on certain days. And then, when all was finished and quiet, the data had to be fully backed up in case of problems, and the computer rebooted to reset and clean pointers and storage.

Yet processing power was very limited, storage was limited. One piece of data performed multiple chores. You couldn't run heavy processes while users were trying to access the terminals, because they would be frozen out in the relatively primitive time slicing available. An operator could wait fifteen minutes for a screen to update while an intensive data operation was being run. He had learned all that the hard way.

The only solution was to do it all at night. Which mean the "night stream" became more complex and more critical, doing reports, ending with backup and reboot. When that failed, for some reason, users might not get on until ten o'clock or later. And the users were very angry if this was end of month and zillions of orders had to be entered and accounts updated. The managers went ballistic. Wayne took another cup of dark bitter black and a few deep breaths.

First—well the hard part. Let them know. He went down the hallway and told Joe D, who took him in to see Joe P. They resignedly told him to find the problem and get back when it was on its way to being resolved, or if there were choices to be made.

OK, where—ah, the report program. What the hell? Oh—a stupid zero in a field that should never contain zeros, divide by zero, crash out. His error handling routine neglected to reset the flag that would have let everything continue, so here he sat. OK—near the end, fortunately. Quick kludge up a recovery copy, start after the failure had occurred, start it going. Estimate— hour and a half. That's it, just wait and monitor. And this one, unfortunately, was entirely his fault.

"Joe, divide by zero error, and then a failure of the night stream. I've got it going now, we should be back by 9:30 or so. I'll put in more checks to be sure it doesn't happen again." Joe looked up from his coffee and papers.

"But didn't we check it all. I mean we ran the tests."

"We didn't have this particular error in any of them. Just what had been in during a few sample runs in the last couple of weeks."

"And you couldn't make allowance for this?" Well, of course if he were a seasoned genius he certainly could anticipate everything. He wasn't. In hindsight the error handling that should have been invoked was obvious. He was always trying to retroactively apply anything like this that crawled out of the woodwork, which complicated everything a lot and might introduce new errors. "Bulletproofing," they called it. And on this machine, unfortunately, the generic error routines could not be overridden at various levels, so unhandled raw errors crashed right back into the operating system.

"I guess I should have," it was no use arguing with your manager. "I'll be sure this kind of thing doesn't happen again." But another kind of thing would. The other problem of course, was that his code was not compiled, merely interpreted, and any error would go undetected until the routine was invoked. You could only edit one thing at a time, and no copying except to make a new program, which had its own dangers. So if he slipped on the keystroke, misspelled a command, nothing would be noticed until—bang—that line caused its own error. Always on a tightrope. But the users were blissfully unaware of the dark underbelly of the beast.

"All right," said Joe with resignation. I'll try to handle everyone in the office. You go let the users know."

That was almost as unpleasant as the managers. The users never liked the computer and were almost always gleeful when it went wrong. Except that they were also truly pissed off that it would put them behind schedule.

In the early eighties, small business computer usage was a confused miasma of systems meeting each other and adjusting. Not only were the ultimate clients completely new to the experience, the use of such machines in any business was novel to everyone who was working there, from managers through inventory personnel. Computer companies were not quite sure how to make money marketing smaller machines to corporations with limited budgets and no tolerance for overruns. Consultants and in-house programmers had rarely had the deep academic training that was common in big iron or defense systems. The people implementing the systems—from salesmen to programmers to operators to even data-entry people—were a ragtag group of impromptu misfits, escaping other employment into the hot new (possibly) high-paying industry.

All sides and personnel experienced nasty shocks. Hardware did not perform up to specifications, systems software was deficient and badly documented, programming languages had few rigorous standards and many gigantic gaps in capability. Most business management had never used a typewriter, salesmen were used to scraps of paper or at best triplicate carbon forms to get orders, accounting used nothing more complicated than phones and (usually mechanical) adding machines.

The requirements—ah, the requirements. Somehow, the standard, vanilla, packages managed to miss a few critical pieces. There were future expected sales to be tracked but not entered as orders, orders to be entered but not shipped, invoices to be held, merchandise returned, orders canceled, accounts put on hold, or mostly on hold. Some big accounts always aged badly but good for their money due eventually, some were watched closely lest they slip from thirty to sixty days, some could be ignored because they were gone and in litigation. Forget even talking about inventory, especially inventory in a faddish industry like importing the latest electronics—what was last year's box of old phones now worth, and how did the computer handle writedowns and damage, if at all. Nothing was simple, even before you hit the peculiarities of each firm. And, of course, in a free capitalist system it was precisely the peculiarities of each firm which were the lifeblood of its success, so they could hardly be ignored.

Nobody—not the management, not the consultants, not the users, not the programmers, not the hardware suppliers, and certainly not the articles in magazines that all of them read—had the faintest idea how much real systems would actually cost and how much time and sweat and heartbreak would be involved in even getting an adequate operation running smoothly. Hardly any of the firms involved had the deep pockets necessary to deal with it all rationally.

Like the California gold rush, really. Everybody knew it would pay off, somehow, the savings were there. Nobody quite anticipated that whole departments would eventually be gutted of staff—and often computerization led to increased employees for a while because everything had to be done twice, and the machines had to be kept running. But there were great dreams of savings to be realized <u>tomorrow</u>. Today—ah <u>today</u> was going to cost you more—a lot more—than you expected.

The room is tiny, with no windows, a small desk behind which Ghost sits ramrod straight, as he motions me to sit in the hard folding chair in front of him. I guess this is the dreaded one-on-one follow up with the big consultant who will fix everything.

"Victor has asked me to make a survey and report, to try to come up with what is wrong around here."

"Maybe nothing really is wrong," I begin defiantly.

"Well, if not, I need to find that out as well," he opens his folder and folds his hands. "First, of course, we need to get to the bottom of the various lies everyone is feeding management."

"But I'm not lying at all," I protest.

"By your account," Ghost has a malicious tone, "everybody is lying to everybody."

"I wouldn't call it lying, exactly."

"Oh, you wouldn't? Then what?"

"More like explorers on a strange continent. We all have visions of what we think we might encounter, but most of them turn out to be wrong."

"So just stupid, then?"

"Of course not. Very intelligent visions based on the best available knowledge at the time. But not, as it turned out, very accurate in detail. And one other thing…"

"What was that?"

"The landscape kept changing on us all the time. Completely."

"I'm not convinced," says Ghost, "but I will note it in my report. Pretty incompetent explorers, at any rate. We're done here. I'll see you in the computer room in a few minutes …"

"So, that's it, Joe." Wayne had turned in his written report and was going over it later that afternoon. "I've added the continuation override error routine to all the evening processing and tested it as well as I can, I tried to document the flags, and I've even added a report which will keep track of exactly where we are as the overnight continues, with a timestamp. I've tested everything as well as I can on the live system today, but we will just have to watch it carefully for a while.

"Will this prevent all the other problems with tapes and printed reports?"

"No, there's really nothing I can do about tape errors that cause the back-up to fail. If the printer jams or runs out of paper all we can do is restart in the morning."

"How about if someone were here during most of that."

"Oh, c'mon, Joe, I'm here late and in early most days as it is. Even Saturdays when it's month end. You know that."

"Joe P and I have been thinking about hiring you a backup assistant, to take care of the mechanical operator stuff and be able to handle minor problems with you over the phone."

"Oh. That might really be good. Someone to stay at night at least until most of the stuff is done."

"Or even early in the morning to be sure you know of any problems right away, and maybe get a start on fixing them for the day."

This was not entirely unexpected. They had been toying with trying to train up somebody already in one of the departments, but the plain fact was that everyone was running flat out at their current jobs. "That would be great."

"Ok," said Joe D. "Why don't you come up with the requirements and we'll write up an ad for the paper and see who we can get."

More extraneous work, leading to more extraneous management duties. Ah well, maybe it would leave more time for him to do the coding he like to do. "Ok, give me a couple of hours and I'll have something."

Surprisingly, Wayne never really considered that they might also be trying to make him a less critical single point of failure in the corporate operations.

Ghost is ushered in to the glassed in, windowless computer room, filled with reels of tape, manuals, stacks of program printouts, binders of manual operations, and naturally the refrigerator-sized computer itself, complete with massive printer alongside. Joe P surveys the room proudly, completely unaware of the underlying mission, and says, "This is the operation room itself. Wayne, please show him around what we are doing here." He closes the door and leaves with a lot more confidence than I am feeling.

"All right," Ghost almost sniffs in disdain. "Explain what your toy hardware and infantile software are trying to accomplish here."

"Give it up, Ghost," I reply angrily. "This thing is running flat out and doing a hell of a job, all things considered."

"Maybe all things considered," agrees Ghost. "Or at least what was considered when this equipment was purchased. Still toys. When will you be getting something real?"

"We're working on that," I tell him. "Joe D and I have been putting together some thoughts on potential next vendors."

"Big boss man, are you? Instant expert? Who says you'll have a say?"

"In this field, at this time, Ghost, almost anyone willing to walk in the door and work for what we offer is an expert. Even if they had almost no experience on computers at all, except maybe a little key entry. But a lot of those folks were really smart and hardworking because they wanted the career. We could train them."

"Like Mark Twain's steamboat pilot cubs on the Mississippi." I'm surprised at the analogy, but it rings true.

"Exactly. And this profession is one of the last where that is still true. Every other career else is already clogging up with cronyism and guild certifications and barriers to entry. But if you're breathing and willing to work hard you'll get a shot in IT. If you have the will and brains, you can succeed well."

"Enjoy it while it lasts," Ghost mumbles sarcastically.

"Yeah, I think you're right. Those days will soon be as far gone as the big paddlewheels on the big muddy."

"Progress."

"So we are told."

"Bye, Kathy, see you tomorrow.'

"Bye Wayne."

The new system was working magnificently. Kathy was smart and attentive and easily slipped into keeping everything going almost no matter what. And on the few occasions when an awful "what" arose, she could call him. No matter how bad that might be, he had all night to get stuff straightened out without an effect on the business.

The only problem now was that, as the timestamped overnight report increasingly indicated, they were running out of processing power and time. If the backup didn't finish until four or five in the morning, which was the case some days, there wasn't a hell of a lot of recovery hours available before people started piling on around eight each morning. Solutions to this problem would be pretty expensive.

OLD HEARTS

WAYNE SAT QUIETLY on the hot back patio this Labor Day afternoon, listening to the activity inside the house. He looked up into huge hickories overshadowing one room, which recalled the first of two cardiac near-tragedies. Over a year past, he vividly remember trees with just a hint of foliage, bushes with just a touch of flowers to come, which bordered the crowded parking lot as he sat with Gregory fussing in the car seat next to him. Joan and her immediate family had been in deep consultation in the brick buildings off to the side. St. Francis was renowned for heart surgery, and Joan's Mom was in desperate shape.

Wayne had kept the car running to stay warm, and periodically tried using a bottle or just playing fingers with his infant son. No problem really, Gregory was mostly sleeping, and happy enough if he was awake. He was, after all, very tiny, only a few months old, and about the worst thing that would happen here would be a bowel movement, wrapped up as he was.

Wayne had hardly known what to make of it all, in what seemed an era far gone already. His work life had become crazy, his commute had become crazier, his home life almost intolerable, and now this. Just when he thought he might be able to escape some of the madness, shock out of the blue. So he had taken that day off, and sat and waited and prayed a little.

At least, he admitted selfishly, events had taken some of the focus off of him. There were more immediate concerns by everybody around than worrying what the son-in-law was doing with his career. He had accepted the tradeoff, but wasn't really happy with it because Joan was so devastated.

Well, all he could do—like all of them, actually—was to watch and wait and see what happened and then deal with whatever. And it had worked out, after all, and even the next.

Here in meditative happiness, more than a year later, even with things going much better, the shock of nearby mortality continued to dampen their exuberance on such rare reflective days.

A small white office, medical charts on the walls, old equipment all over, I'm sitting on a bed in a hospital gown as Ghost opens the wooden door and strolls in. He's dressed in a white smock and has a clipboard with papers in his hand. He regards me gravely. "Well, Mr. Slingluff, you seem to have a very severe case of temporal obfuscation."

I get over my surprise and play along. "But doctor, I've never felt better."

"Perhaps, but your scores indicate rampant displacement and misdirected narrative."

"Could you put that in layman's terms?"

"Ah, surely. Simply, you are confusing years and mixing several together. Surely you realize that this event happened a year before you have it located, here."

"Of course. But it feeds naturally into my narrative. Sometimes, I think, an author needs to take liberty with a few things to pull together a theme."

"Hmm." He made another note. "So now you have illusions of being an author."

"I can be an author if I want," I insist stubbornly.

"Oh, surely. You can be Napoleon if you want. Doesn't make it true, of course."

"All I want to do is group the theme of mortality. The year is almost irrelevant. Everything happened in that general period."

"But it's not just here. You are often a bit off."

"I see you're playing doctor," I say coldly, "but you seem to have carried over more than a few of your legal pretensions. Pot calling the kettle black, I think."

He stalks out and turns off the lights.

So, backing up a bit ...

Wayne had woken up around five thirty as usual, to catch the six thirty out of Huntington. If the train ran smoothly, which it often did not, he was in the city before eight. If the subways ran smoothly, which they often did not, he could be at work high in the Citibank offices at the end of Wall Street sometime around eight thirty.

Taking the packed train back around six, standing most of the time all the way to Syosset, only two stops from his, at least two hours door to door, often longer. So he arrived around eight, starving and the worse for wear and almost ready to go to sleep. During that entire long day, he had been completely out of contact with home. He had no phone at work, and of course nobody had phones on the train.

So the bedlam that met him that spring evening had been totally unexpected. Mom had collapsed, the ambulance had taken her to Huntington Hospital, she was resting quietly after what was determined to have been a heart attack. Everyone was shocked—she was a fully active woman in her early seventies. Joan's brothers were informed and visits had been scheduled.

As the next few days dragged by, visits were frequent. Her ancient semi-private room was dingy and depressing. Long story short, she seemed to be deteriorating rapidly. Physicians dolefully indicated the family could expect the worst. Frustration blended with a degree of acceptance.

Except for Joan's older brother Philip, a lawyer with corporate background, now in real estate, successful financially, New York nasty. He accepted nothing. He immediately investigated everywhere, located top notch facilities and doctors, forced consultation and transfer, and pushed everyone to actively do something. No frustration or acceptance tolerated. At their conference, the medical team expressed grave reservations, but were willing to operate—as long as everyone understood it remained a risky procedure with no better alternative. At worst, she would die sooner. At best, they would fix her up as well as possible, maybe for years. The die was cast.

That 1981 operation had to happen immediately, fortunately succeeding beyond expectation. Mom was as strong as everyone thought. Although hospital stays were extended in those days—particularly because surgeons still sawed open the rib cage to operate and went through a lot of blood—she was home relatively soon, sitting and playing once more with the baby.

Anita's call came almost exactly a year later. Wayne's sister said Dad had woken up unable to get out of bed, and the hospital had taken one look at him after he arrived by ambulance and almost refused to let him go home before the operation. He had not yet had a heart attack, but one was imminent—he needed immediate surgery, and only Anita's professional status as a registered nurse allowed him to rest comfortably at home for the few days before he was operated on.

"You need to come down right away. We just don't know how long he will live." Anita dealt with life and death all the time, she could sound pretty fatalistic and cold when in nurse mode.

"Uh, ok," said Wayne. It had been another long day at Webcor, he was planning on bed in a few hours, but—no but. "I'll pack and be on my way in a few minutes. I should get there sometime after one."

"We'll leave the door open. Probably be up. Drive safely."

"Ok."

The trip down was a confusing nightmare, but he made it. Everyone was ready for bed or asleep, he fell into the pull-out couch in the living room and was asleep immediately.

The next days were a long nostalgic visit. Wayne was not yet at the point where he tried to drag out secret details of Dad's life. They shared work stories, and sports, and Wayne's new position, and general information. They talked a little about the new family. Anita was more optimistic in person, although she said risks were still high.

A week later what started as a triple bypass turned into a quintuple bypass when surgery went well. Same opened ribcage, same long painful recovery. Eventually Wayne and Joan and Gregory went down to visit over a weekend, and things once again became normal. But never the same.

Clocks measure standard intervals, but time is never standard. In our universes, minutes can pass slowly or be gone before we realize they have arrived. Joan and I had lived in Boston in a kind of timeless happy trance. We thought about the future in a vague way, and about the past as not that far gone, but the present just extended endlessly in all directions. Years went by in Never Never Land.

Once we became aware of the imponderable tick tock of years, when the desire for children became greater, when we realized we needed to start taking career growth seriously, time had become more intrusive and insistent. Changes were happening, months were not like others, and some things indeed went by too quickly. And in spite of that, changing jobs and homes and having a child and doing entirely new things, the world was still in most ways the comfortable one we had always inhabited, and unconsciously assumed we always would.

The double near tragedy broke the spell. Suddenly mortality was on the table. Years would not unroll forever and ever into constantly brighter futures. Parts of our being would now inevitably be ripped away, sooner or later, and what we had taken for granted would be vanished forever. Perhaps we were too sheltered and late coming to this realization, but it was all the more shattering for happening so late, and in the middle of so many other almost traumatic events.

People are always transformed when absolutely confronted with their own death. But for the young it can be almost romantic—the misunderstood artist who will be recognized when he is gone, the misunderstood maid whose virtue will be recognized as she is placed beneath the quiet maple, the eternal hero celebrated for all time—all kinds of fantasies, all kinds of improbable rationalizations. Most of our lives we just ignore personal possibilities as much as possible. But that is simply coming to terms with our own end—a difficult but restricted problem.

Much harder is the death of others. Parents we are close to are a special case, because they have always been as present as the sun and moon. The very structure of the cosmos shifts when they have gone away. Often we do not even realize it will be so until it is too late.

So, in a way, these near tragedies were fortunate in awakening us early. Suddenly, each moment counted more than it once had, each experience became a little more precious, each annoyance a bit more petty and to be avoided. We handled it as everyone must, and went on, but humbled and aware of a new and more somber outlook on the world that would come to be too soon.

"Wait, wait, wait," instructs Doctor Ghost, making frantic little marks on his pad. "Bad case of calendrical confusion, and terminal human condition denial. I hope we can find someone to help."

"Now wait a second," I yell.

"Much more common than most people think," he stares intently at the ceiling for a moment. "There are, I think, a few promising new treatments.'

"First, that was back then, and somewhere or someplace this is now. You're more confused than I am."

He glances at me, startled, then mumbles something about "Patient symptomatic transference," as he takes more notes.

"It's just a story of what happened …" I continue as he holds up his hand warningly "in a way that makes some sense. NOT strict chronological order."

"But life happens, you must understand, in strict chronological order."

"Maybe our outer states," I insist, "but never in our memories."

"Oh, well, if you want to leave science and venture into fantasy."

"Life is a but a dream," I intone.

"Well, your life here seems to be one of the peculiarly mixed up nightmares."

"All true, all real."

"More or less. And not," he states strongly, "and not exactly as told."

Wayne and Joan found they were juggling multiple universes, all based on expectations and evaluations. How were they doing? What should they be doing? How was everybody else doing? It was a complicated internal dance of possibilities that careened dizzyingly from one moment to another. They had never encountered this aspect of the human condition so frighteningly.

What distressed them was a distortion of the very concept of time. Not instant nor hourly clock time, nor even seasonal time, but the onrush of human time—the certain knowledge that they were changing and their world would never be the same year after year. A child hardly notices this nor cares, every day seems eternal. Even as young adults, cycles had been fixed, work and play, holidays, a long rhythm of predictable possibilities, which they could dip into anytime they wanted.

But then it was farewell to familiar places—well, ok, they'd done that before. Then Gregory, who definitely was not on a cyclical pattern of growth. Especially for the first born, every developmental milestone is documented and discussed and regarded as fervently as any colossal event in the rise of civilization itself. Work and its associated requirements mutated monthly. But the final nail was the near death of parents. Their outlooks on the world finally focused on limits.

Metaphors speak confusingly and often misleadingly. The straw that broke the camel's back, for example. There was no single straw here, no breaking of any back, but an inexorable, grinding, cruel and difficult dawning of perspective of limits becoming solid, insurmountable obstacles to certain formerly open pathways. Their lives were becoming constricted.

The tradeoff was that their existence was also richer. Deep engagement with children, relations, careers, even housing and cars and whatever made daily life a little harder, but also more rewarding and more brilliant. "Ah," Wayne thought, one morning as he headed off to work, "so this is maturity. Glad I put it off so long. Glad I finally found it." Then it was on to deal with the new reality.

I had early on decided there were two main approaches to life. One, call it the classic American, was that if you took care of your money and job everything else would work out eventually. The other, call it European, was take care of yourself and eventually money and everything else will work out. Neither was, of course, either totally right or wrong. And there were other approaches hardly considered—taking care of the spiritual or political, for example, to the exclusion of all the rest, or ignoring the future entirely and simply enjoying the gifts of the present.

But of the two main approaches I felt comfortable with, I was far more attracted to putting myself in order. I recognized my unruly urges, my often stupid and vain drives, my wanton laziness, my impossible fantasies, each coming to the forefront at one time or another, each clamoring for equal attention. If I could not piece them into a reasonable order, find my own way, and in the current terminology "center," I was pretty sure none of the rest would matter. I did not want to end up a neurotic wreck with a lot of money—which I felt I had been in danger of once a long time ago.

On the other hand, it was increasingly clear I did not want to end up impoverished and powerless, which is what would happen if I did not put together a career and money. But the good thing was that by now such re-adjustments deep internally were pretty easy and natural. It was not nerve wracking to switch from trying to be a great artist to trying to be a well paid programmer, now that I had developed all the tools.

I think pretty much the same was true of Joan. So while we might have been seen as late bloomers holding on to adolescence for too long, we tended to feel that we had worked out the vicious kinks that so often recently seemed to be intruding on the lives of other people we knew. We had done what we wanted to do, now we were prepared to do something else for a while. As simple and liberating as that, no matter what the pains and aggravations.

As part of that, we also became much more attuned to the local events and perceptions we could actually control. Less concern for the whole wide world and culture, less preoccupation with our own selfish immediacies, but much more attention and care and effort put into the things that actually surrounded us. Our parents were aging, we were aging, Gregory was growing, careers were changing. Finally, we thought we could handle all that one way or another.

Sitting in a chair at the ophthalmologist, Ghost shining an intense beam in one eye. "And the chart, too," he mutters.

"What's going on," I struggle to get up.

"Stay still, stay still, we're almost done. I just need to figure out your medications...."

"For what," I ask. I've always worn glasses, but what does that have to do with Ghost now.

He starts reading from a checklist. "Well, there are a significant number of problems here. First, you suffer from future myopia. Your projection vision is obscured by several inward directed cataracts. I fear that you may eventually go completely purpose-blind unless we are able to shrink your ego somewhat ."

"Boy, you sure are into jargon lately."

"Well, in little words even you can understand this is what I have found. You are unable to adjust your ideas to long term and short term goals as easily as most people—well maybe not many I have actually run into, but normal according to the books. Others have no trouble refocusing from, for example, the eternity of heaven or social remembrance back to what should be done in the next minute or day. They clearly perceive everything in between as well. You see the moment well enough, but you seem to be very fuzzy at distant time scales. Ah, ah," he held up a hand to keep me from interrupting. "Even in the near term, you miss some important tasks such as building people networks—you think talking with people about nothing in particular is wasting time. And, finally, I have yet to find any driving purpose in you beyond having a good and happy life. According to the literature, that is dangerous and never enough."

"You talk the talk," I answer. "But I don't trust your background, or your references, or your credentials. Where are they, by the way," I ask, scanning the blank walls just to annoy him.

"You never did trust anyone's, did you? That may be the root of your problems …"

"So, oh wise one, what do you prescribe?"

"Ah, actually, I would have prescribed exactly what you found—a spouse you trusted completely, and some loosening up to listen to what the people closest to you were actually doing and saying."

"No pills or lenses?"

"Not at this time. Pity, of course, that you didn't come in earlier. Say, when you were around fifteen…."

Wayne had never driven much on Long Island, outside of the standard route to work and pretty much just local roads around Huntington. His knowledge of this geography was still very vague. Getting to Philadelphia in the dead of night after a hard day's work and some bottles of beer wasn't going to be a cakewalk. He continued down 25A towards what he had been assured was the left hand turn to go to the expressway. No lights on the roads, except oncoming vehicles. Eventually, he found the left turn. Whew, tough five minutes, only three hours left… But he knew he had to go home to visit Dad before the operation.

In the confusion of Hicksville, he missed the turn to the Expressway and found himself on the Parkway, which seemed to be heading to New York and at least turned out to have no trucks. He happily went on along this multiple lane road, figuring the worst was behind him. What a strange turn of events.

He was glad, at least, that he had turned a corner in relationships with his father, and his family in general. Like the prodigal son, he was no longer lost in the wilderness, ignoring all their pleas. He had become fully reconciled, thanks to Joan, and Gregory, and his newfound career. Going back to Philadelphia was no longer a fearsome chore. Going home finally meant back to where his own family lived. If the worst happened now, he was grateful that he had resolved all this tension ahead of time. It was a lesson well worth learning—not to think there will always be another time to work things out.

The parkway crossed a few random expressways, all labeled as going to various airports. He wasn't going to any airports, so he kept straight towards New York City. More lanes widened out, embankments grew high, the lights alongside showed he was in a fully urban place. He was as frightened of New York City at night by now as anyone who read the papers in those troubled times. But all he could do was keep going. Surely there would be signs soon.

A major split in the road indicated he could either curve northward towards Manhattan, or go straight toward—ah, again—the airport and "Flatbush." Well, straight seemed good. Suddenly the road changed dramatically. The "Interboro Parkway" was a badly paved, densely dark, insanely curved interminable road. He couldn't even find a place to turn around, and surely did not want to get out in the middle of what he was sure were slums. He supposed surrounding lights were dark because of crime and poverty (actually the now-renamed Jackie Robinson Parkway goes through several gigantic, unpopulated cemeteries.) His imagination ran wild.

And then, as his fears reached a fever pitch. It just dead ended. On an urban avenue, to his troubled eyes a decayed and haunted scene of drunks, auto repair shops, and one open gas station. He had to stop, and ask where he was and where to go. In spite of his wild appearance, the attendant was courteous and helpful, giving clear directions to Pennsylvania Avenue and the Belt parkway. Wayne climbed back in the car and started off down block after block of lights, urban streets, all the frightening moments shoved into suburban folklore about the uncharted depths of Brooklyn and Queens.

But, soon enough, he was in fact on the Belt, and from them on it was a straight, long, dark, lonely ride, filled with memories and prayers, but no fears of encountering cannibals. Eventually, when he digested this all fully, it turned into just another very good lesson in how most of the time most people in most places are just fine. We carry the problems in our minds.

When we were young, even today, our cultural myth is overwhelmingly that you are responsible for what happens to you. Sometimes it veers off into extreme fantasies such as "attractors," but for the most part we accept responsibility. The only escape, for some, is to decide to be a victim, which means some areas are not your fault—but they are certainly somebody else's. We really truly believe that humans control destiny.

In some areas that is unquestionably true. What you eat, what you do, how you spend your time, is very much under our control. What your choices are at any given time may be less so. But it is not hard to look back and think about turning points, "If I had just done this or not done that, then things would have happened differently." We use that to form a life narrative, heroic or pathetic or whatever.

But the fact is we mostly do not control anything at all. We will die. We must eat. We have certain physical attributes. And the death of your parents, or other people close to you, usually are completely out of your control. When young, we handle this by thinking it could not happen, really. After all, the sun has always come up, our mother and father or whoever have always been there. This continues, of course, throughout our lives, with different roles and people. Until they are gone.

And in none of that, usually, is there any possible place where we could point and say, "If only that, then they would still be here." Inevitability is a frightening thing. Often too hard for us, in this culture, to accept at all.

BABYLON WITH GHOST

I have tried hard to avoid guilt about the past, especially about the past beyond my control. If I live today well, that is the limit of my current control. Deal with today, plan for tomorrow, the past is just a story. That's really hard, if not impossible, when that story includes people you love deeply.

"Zho, you haff come to ze fear of ze death, hmmm? " The odd voice penetrates the wool of a trance and I blurrily focus on some oddly dressed character sitting by the side of this—what, a kind of couch? What is this. I pull myself together as quickly as possible.

"Oh, jeez, drop that awful accent."

Ghost sulks. "Well, I'm somewhat limited by your own characteristics, it's not my fault."

"Yeah?" I ask, "then how did you ever grow that beard. I could never get something like that if I didn't shave my entire life."

Sheepishly, he takes off the fake white hair, then defiantly snaps it back on with the elastic over his ears. "But the fact remains, here you are finally face to face with the real possibility of death. Are you not terribly frightened?"

"No, no really, that was never one of my phobias. "

"Strange."

"Hardly so. By the time I was ten I was sure we would all die and all we did would be dust and futility when the big bombs fell. I think that stayed with me, even through the game of pretending I would die by thirty. I just was always aware that any day might be the last, and that once I was gone everything I did would soon be gone and forgotten too."

"Pretty awful life outlook."

"Not so. I appreciated each day and each moment. And I always tried to keep affairs in order because, well I never knew what might happen. So very few long drawn out plans hinging on fixing things up sometime."

"Limiting, as far as having great visions."

"Somewhat. But liberating in day to day life."

"Weren't you ever deeply afraid of the nothingness of death."

"Hardly ever. I always seemed to me just another version of the nothingness of going to sleep."

"But what about what comes after, not knowing what dreams may come?"

"Doctor, doctor. I am sure I cannot know the real deep nature of the universe. Humans are incapable. And I surely do not believe anyone who tells me they know, somehow."

"I think you need therapy."

"I think I'm the one who is sane."

"They all say that," mutters Ghost.

Another year end. He and Joan and sleepy Gregory were watching the ball coming down on TV, ancient ballroom music playing in the background as wealthy people danced. Snacks were scattered around, not too many. He'd had some beer, but was on good behavior. Anyway, no pressure, no work tomorrow. This was a good time.

What a year. What a strange combination of events. Here they were, in their own warm little house, their own little nuclear family. Here he was, working as a department manager of a fantastically growing company. His career seemed to be taking off. Here the extended family remained intact with all grandparents. Health, if not completely restored and taken for granted, at least stabilized for an indefinite period.

Previous "first nights" in Boston seemed centuries away. Heck, even the thought of going out into the cold was tiring. He was glad to just have some time to relax, although he had been at work earlier, not really out all that early. The traffic coming back, at least, had been very light. And he had a lot of technical reading for the next few days. But still—late morning. This was a wonderful time.

For once he was aware of the reality and myth of America in all its promise. Work hard, get a few breaks, be determined, and sometimes everything will work out. When it does work out, at least for a while, the results can be spectacular. Get along with friends, make relatives proud, enjoy those closest to you. He still had trouble believing the insane trajectory they had been following.

Not that they took anything for granted. He and Joan had been through too many ups and downs, particularly downs, to blindly assume the future would always be better, or even as good. They kept a tight hold on their emotions and wallets regarding the future.

But tonight? Ah, tonight was all but perfect.

Back in the bright little examination room, Ghost smiling broadly with his chart. "Congratulations," he booms, "you seem to be well cured, hale and hearty, healthy as a horse!"

"Oh, come on. Lots of problems yet to come. Lots of problems under the hood."

"Oh, yes, of course you should watch your diet. Get more exercise. Take a few vitamins. Blah, blah, blah. But this is all incidental. The big stuff is out of the way."

"I'm not sure I believe you," I respond. "I still have issues and …"

"Look, don't go all hypochondriac," he states flatly. "You are really fine. Just keep clearing things up as they come up and you are well on your way to …"

"What, perfection? Immortality? Fame and fortune?"

"No, of course not. On the way to being able to make it through a productive and happy life. Isn't that what you say you want?"

"Well, yes, but."

"Stop sulking, man! Get out into the sunshine! Stop by the receptionist on the way out to schedule your next appointment in—oh, I guess ten years or so."

Wayne had to admit, as he walked around the block with Joan and Gregory, well dressed against the moderate cold to look at Christmas lights in the rapidly darkening twilight, that he was one of the most fortunate people on the planet. From despair ten years ago he had been reborn and reset into a life seemingly without bounds, and a path that was clear and hopeful. A religious thankfulness washed over him.

Even the events of the last year or two, some nearly catastrophic, had only firmed his new feeling of well-being. After all, this time, everything had turned out all right. Turned out for the better, in many cases. It was the first time he had really experienced that fully in decades. Meeting Joan had been intense and wonderful and a turning point, but even then there were a lot of nasty issues and hard decisions avoided. Now—well, they were on the right road at least, and just in time to avoid permanent regrets if those they loved could not have shared it with them.

Fortune had smiled. That road was turning out to be pretty well paved, nearly straight, well lit and—perhaps more than that—scenic and picturesque. He had always thought a suburban tacky American life would be pretty dull, like in all the novels, filled with cotton fluff instead of interesting thoughts. But for him, that was nothing at all true. It was just a different set of sharp experiences, his mind could work as well as ever on dreams and cosmic visions—they were just tinged a little differently. And, finally, populated with more than just inner illusions.

They turned another corner and happily noted the—yes—tacky overwhelming profusion of lights and glowing Santa and reindeer statues gracing another of the boxy look-alike development homes.

Gaining Traction

Wayne soon realized that in spite of his imposing title of "Data Processing Manager," he was little more than a glorified computer operator. Imposing titles with no extra pay have been cheap rewards since at least the days of the early Roman Empire. His job was to do all the grunt work—mounting tapes, helping users, printing and distributing reports. He had nobody to manage since the department consisted of himself. He was simply there to keep things running, and to work with the consultants who provided the code.

But in those primitive days before computer security mattered very much, that gave him a great deal of potential power, and certainly a framework for learning as much as he wanted. He had full system owner privileges, after all, to apply the fixes as they came in. He was the person present at all the training sessions, and the one employees turned to when there were problems. Dealing with colleagues in all departments gave him a commanding perspective on their difficulties with golden promises from software salespeople, or media-driven cybernetic fantasies of executives.

Pretty soon he was developing manuals for users and creating operational checklists so he wouldn't forget to do anything on each appropriate day of the week, accounting period, or phase of the moon. Gradually his bosses came to trust his input when dealing with the outside vendors, and he began to sit in, mostly quietly, as problems were discussed (sometimes heatedly) or new enhancements ordered. So there was a sense of progression almost immediately.

And of course there was the machine itself. It took a while to get into some of the weirder concepts, but the ideal had been that "any user can write reports," and as it turned out he became that "anyone"—the hands that developed what the managers conceived they needed. The query language was brazenly trademarked as "ENGLISH" and he was soon an "ENGLISH" expert, churning out reports on demand. From there it was a short step to learning how to make them run automatically at night, which required coding. Then other internal computer cleanup at night and ... well there was no end.

Manuals, manuals, manuals. He was reading every night at home, he was often lost in hopeless jargon, he experimented a little, in quiet moments in the computer room. Nobody had any idea what was going on—whether he was developing a report or investigating code—who could tell? It was the first time he had ever had such freedom at a job. And as long as things ran smoothly, nobody cared at all.

Ghost slumps in the dark bar, nursing a martini, the worse for a few before I showed up. "Ah," he slurs, "how the mighty have fallen. Hail the conquering artist, who would never be another grey man!"

"Oh shut up. You're drunk anyway."

"And why not," he waves around. "You gave up on everything you believed in, so really you just wasted ten years doing nothing."

"Wasted only from the standpoint of the capitalist pig establishment," I laugh.

"But you are now in the pens yourself."

"Oh, my sensibility is intact. But I started to enjoy the challenges of computers and how they related to business and people. It was almost an art form in itself."

"Rashonalishashun," he mumbles.

"Maybe. But at least I could now make enough money to attain the basic next stage of life I wanted."

"You never caught up, you know," he points accusingly. "Always behind, you could have made a hell of a lot more with an earlier start."

"We've talked of losing souls before," I reply, "my twenties were critical to forming and keeping my soul. I treasure those moments. But it that doesn't mean I couldn't move on. "

"Oh, multiple careers? Bullshit propaganda."

"Contrary to the proverb," I say, getting ready to leave, "life is long. Art may or may not be short, but a business career is pretty much like a may-fly—it changes all the time and is never the same year to year. There was room enough for me finally, and I found it fun to take advantage of the opportunity."

In the early days of business computerization, especially among the mid-sized firms, there were less clearly marked divisions of labor and certainly far less certification than came to exist later. Wayne was nominally a manager, actually an operator, but with absolutely free rein to grow into other roles. Over time, almost unconsciously, he was able to migrate through them as the environment changed.

He was unusual in that he always thought of himself as a programmer, since he had self-trained from the beginning on his home computer. Being self-educated was at the time actually a great advantage, first because it brought you into the market far more current than the ancient classes taught by hide-bound professors, and second because it prepared you for constant self-improvement as the market and hardware and software changed radically and instantly for years and decades.

At Webcor from his perspective, there was only the computer department and everyone else—most notably accounting and sales. The entire 'computer department' consisted of one executive (who controlled software vendor, hardware vendor and internal support team), the consultants (themselves divided into salesman, designer, and programmers) , and the internal support team (Wayne). His job was to keep things running as the manager expected, and as the hardware and software salesmen had promised. That was the organizational map at the time, but it fuzzed very quickly.

Even at Webcor, Wayne found himself wearing multiple hats immediately. Hardware troubleshooter, training coordinator, software patcher, and eventually even a designer and coder and tester of things like an automated night stream. All of that was amorphously clumped onto his original title, but through it all he continued to think of himself as mostly a programmer.

Later in his career, everything would explode into specialization, training, rigid roles, and certified barriers. Designers would rarely dirty their hands with coding, coders would never see users, system analysts floated in intellectual clouds telling designers what to do, and over it all the godlike CIO began to interface with the expectations of the bill payers. Meanwhile hardware and software divorced, and multiple odd evolutions of function occurred in each until, in a way, the whole industry became one huge tower of babel, threatening to fall apart because of different jargon and concepts.

The old hands, like Wayne, navigated through those channels almost in amusement, and tended to want to keep their hands in everything—hardware, software, coding, concepts, execution, use. Although almost impossible for complex systems, it turned out to be an interesting niche for what Wayne came to call "Boutique Applications." Very much like his early experiences with the night stream at Webcor.

Wayne stood outside Joe P's door, as an inner circle conversation wrapped up. He had already gone over the issue with Joe D, explained reasonably well, but now they had to face the heat and try to educate managerial minds that had a difficult time with new systems. Joe P motioned them in, they took seats on one side, opposite the head of accounts receivable and the director of accounting.

"Now," began Joe P, "Jacob, why don't you explain the problem as you see it to begin with."

"Well," said Jacob, an older man who was neatly dressed and in fact often did wear eyeshades as he tallied columns, "the receivables are off by 55 cents again. The totals in the aging columns just do not add up to the total in the totals column. This seems to happen all the time."

"I have found the discrepancy in several important accounts," added Rose, primly. "We have too much work to do to keep going through stuff that we were told would make things easier. " She glared at Wayne. The addition of data entry to her undermanned staff had not been appreciated, especially considering all the bugs, crashes, and problems—none Wayne's fault—that had plagued the last few months of introductory computerization.

"And what have you found, Joe?" asked Joe P.

"Wayne has tracked it to a problem in the rounding subtotals," answered Joe D stolidly.

"And what exactly does that mean? Wayne?"

"A computer carries totals in various defined ways, some with more decimal places than others. The totaling in the query software uses one type for the grand total, and another for the subtotal. The problem is that it occasionally has to round some of the divisions into two decimal places. After all, it was only 55 cents in columns of thousands of dollars."

"But, you must understand," said Jacob, a partisan from the old school of double entry bookkeeping, "being a penny off anywhere may indicate a serious problem—perhaps it is a million dollars under one place, a million and one penny over another. It calls into question the whole process."

Wayne, who understood how computers calculated, could do nothing but sputter. Fortunately Joe D stepped in.

"So, Wayne, if the query were changed to use different totals in the aging columns, it should agree, correct?"

"Well, yes, but that would mean changing the software." He still worried about changing the canned software himself. Once he did that, he owned it, and was responsible for all the mistakes that he could otherwise shove off onto the developers, who had, after all, created the problem originally. "Maybe you could get Miraculous to fix it?"

That was a forlorn hope, he knew. The relationship with their vendors was rocky and getting rockier, with code promises unfulfilled and fees withheld and everything an inch from ending up in courts. This could only have one outcome.

"Wayne, why don't you write up the problem formally and go over it with Joe D and get back to me. Then I can figure out what to do with it. Wayne and Joe, you're sure this doesn't affect the core integrity of the accounts?" They both nodded. "Ok, we'll follow up Friday morning."

"Went well," said Joe, "start writing."

"Ok," said Wayne glumly. Most of this would have to be composed in longhand at home and transcribed somehow in stolen time over the next days. "I'll get back to you as soon as I can."

When we look back, we always tend to organize events and put a patina of control on them, making us feel better about the choices we made and the presumably good paths we took. But sometimes life is just honestly chaos, where you grab the best chances available, do your job, and try to hang on to the best outcomes while fending off the worst.

Saying I wanted to be a professional programmer was an interesting goal to hang on to, and did give my career track some guidance and my own self-training some relevance. But most of the time I was simply dealing with what came up with very little control over the general direction. I might be nominally an operator, but actually a sales demonstrator, or paid as a manager but really an operator, or far exceeding whatever the original job requirements were. I was always growing and taking on more responsibility wherever I was, which served me well. On the other hand, I was always growing by myself and in my own isolated bubble rather than by forming strong teams, at least on a peer level, which did not.

Usually, I was recognized as being a superior asset, and in fact after a few years irreplaceable from my original job title. I mean, obviously anyone can be replaced and I always knew that, but after a while I could not be replaced by, say, any other "data processing manager," the next holder of the position would need support for all the various roles I took part in. That was not particularly unique, I knew a lot of people especially in the computer industry who did exactly the same thing.

The biggest danger, in general, was that of somehow working yourself into a position you hated. I knew stone-cold excellent programmers who would fail as they founded a consulting firm—which required not good coding but unending salesmanship and often ruthless confrontation with eventual clients. When I ventured too far away from my core competencies—which were based on my personal interactions with computers—I got in trouble.

At most jobs, I just grew in place. I was rarely promoted into an existing position, but a new position would be created to somehow encompass all the general tasks I had taken on. Often I was fairly treated in terms of salary, almost always in terms of respect, and although I might have made a little (or a lot) more by being an aggressive money-hungry bastard, that was hardly worth it to me. I've always had a fairly odd view of what I expected out of employment.

Ghost looks much better today, even though he has a beer in front of him. The bar has quieted down also, so I slide in opposite him at one of the booths. The window looks out on—some kind of digital display.

"Always pushing the envelope, you think?" asks Ghost.

"Almost always working on the bleeding edge. Science fiction."

"Should have served you well," he says.

"You would think. But too far ahead is not profitable. I was incredibly early into microcomputers, games, minicomputers, microcomputers, Unix, Windows, networks, the internet—but always a little too early, never with a handle on the biggest mass application."

"So you never made it big."

"Nope. I always had dreams and hopes. A few major projects on my own, like educational software or visual displays of ratios, but nothing worked out."

"Why was that."

"No team. I never learned. It was always as an artist—everything on my own. That was the fun part. I didn't want debt capitalization, partners, employees, salesmen, any of the necessities. A world of business fantasy."

"You're lucky you made a living."

"Always thought so. And really, really, lucky at enjoying what I did do so much, and having people generally pay me decently to do it."

"But no brass ring."

"No winning lottery ticket."

"Financially," says Ghost, finishing his mug.

"Right, financially. Everything else—I mean, what else could I possibly wish?"

Ascii consoles, the type used by Microdata and all the computers Wayne had been familiar with, were nothing more than monochrome television sets with a keyboard. They connected directly to the main computer with the equivalent of old telephone wires—one wire from each console to the central machine. Typically there were banks of maybe eight connections, getting more required a big hardware upgrade and expense. Stringing wires was very easy, since this was a company that, after all, sold telephones and had electricians capable of working it. It was not unusual for wires to fail, and Wayne quickly become proficient at trying to keep the tangle labeled well in the computer room, where the mess came in from each room with consoles. Of course, at this point, none of the executives would be caught dead using a keyboard, so there were only a few offices with equipment.

The result of all this cutting-edge elegance was a green or amber and black computer screen with a blinking cursor, which could only be accessed by typing into the current field. Training data entry people, some of whom were far more used to hand calculators than typewriters, was difficult, and unfamiliar terms like "cursor," "escape," and "return" did not help. Mostly the final output was to printed paper, screens were just too cumbersome, and again the executives and their lackeys were much happier curled up with a green-bar printout (so called because each alternate line of the paper was dyed green.)

Printing was slow, tedious, and very loud. Often reports would bang out all day long. Some were distributed to several users. This required the special threading of carbon paper printout paper, up to four copies. Practically, that meant that each time such was required—say for the month-end reports—the printout would take several hours or overnight, and then Wayne would spend a large part of the day running it through a "decollator" which would split out each copy and pile interleaved carbon papers separately. Inevitably his hands would turn black from ink, and unclogging the frequent jams. Sometimes it was just easier to tediously separate everything by hand. Naturally, in those days before anyone thought of information security, everything was simply taken home as needed, or popped into the dumpsters out back as is, no shredding. So the company's accounts receivable and sales records—clear and in multiple copies—were available to anyone who looked. And yet, as far as was known, nothing like the fearsome "data breaches" of today occurred.

New operating system fixes, updates, and consultant changes and patches would be loaded into the computer using large nine track magnetic reels, no matter how tiny the fix. Backups started out as safe copies of everything but quickly evolved from time pressure into periodically scheduled partial saves of operating system, applications code, and (nightly) data. Since crashes were not infrequent, restoring from old tapes was unfortunately required, and dicey. Users would howl, especially if under pressure to clear up month-end.

Everyone was naïve, only salesmen were absolutely sure, and all they were sure of was themselves. We would read the various trade magazines and hear the wonderful things happening, go to shows and exhibits demonstrating wonders available, read horror stories in newspapers, and naturally pore over documentation still thickly provided in heavy vinyl binders. And yet, nobody really knew, and really could not find out.

A lot of the pressure from above came from whispers and insinuations which executives heard in mixing with their colleagues at golf courses or charity parties. Someone, it was rumored, was doing this, or doing that, and would leave everyone else in the dust. Slick presentations would arrive periodically, with slick presenters, each relatively certain that what they were pitching had at least a kernel of truth. They didn't really know, the people who knew were kept in the back rooms lest they let some scrap of fatalistic irony (which was common in back rooms) slip out to spoil the sunny daydreams.

The back room had its own problems with reality. There was always a faster processor, a better configuration, a hidden trick of code, a finer language, a miraculous operating system upgrade. They read all the manuals, half believed them, and in that were totally wrong. Because all the statistics, all the proofs, all the benchmarks were always somehow hardly relevant to what they actually had to do. You'd get a fancy new expensive processor and—well, suddenly it was slower and required an awful lot of adaptation. "Doing more," the salesmen would claim.

Most of the actual users—the people below the level where printouts were interpreted into digestible results by executive assistants—hated every minute of the changeover. They never saw less work—it was always more, always harder, always throwing a monkey wrench into their already tight schedules. What little computerization did accomplish was often just to menialize their jobs, take away all the fun and skill, and make every day drudgery and dread. That was not helped by the fact that just as they finally adjusted to one thing or another, some completely new tweak with full retraining would come down the pike from computer central.

As far as systems experts—well most of them still lived in the ivory towers of academia or large corporations, completely ignorant of the smaller shops. "Best practices"—some as simple as having a paper and pen check off list—were invented and reinvented tirelessly. Eventually, some of them became standard operating procedure, but none were obvious in the beginning. Besides, back in the day, many of the resources necessary to follow best practices were simply not available.

But at the heart of the animosity, between all parties, was simply that everyone assumed computers would give something for nothing, or at least something for very little. You buy the hardware, it runs forever. You buy or lease the software and you get the same wonderful "standard packages" used by world class big corporations. Farewell to your expensive, cranky, multitudes, hello to a few new people here or there, pressing a button to accomplish what formerly took a full department weeks to do, if at all. Strangely, at some level, everybody believed it. The analysts really thought that a few standard packages would handle all the normal business functions. The designers and coders really thought that once an application was completed, it would run without intervention for decades. The back room people really thought that with "just one more push," all the problems would clear up and they would be able to sit back and watch. The executives just thought of it as candy magic, and if it didn't work the way it was supposed to, someone was to blame—beginning a round of kicking the dog that usually only ended at the lowest operator or data entry clerk. A whole world of CYA ("cover your ass") was stolen from the jargon of the Vietnam War to make sure that no matter what happened, you could not be pointed at as being to blame.

And the salesmen? Honestly they were aggressive, and deceitful, and willfully ignorant, but they were also plainly romantics, who believed fervently that the golden age of machine technology was dawning, and they were conducting the gravy train of the future. In spite of aggravation and anger and even legal disputes, somehow there remained very little cynicism until you got to the very bottom of the pile, with the data entry clerks and lowest level consultants forced to constantly fix "bugs." A better day, perfect operations, must certainly arrive any time soon. Like Santa Claus.

"So," asks Ghost, belly to the bar with a pint of Guinness, "what was the worst long-term tendency you encountered?"

"I don't know about worst, but from the beginning a difficult incurable problem was what later became known as 'creeping featurism.'"

"Sounds like some kind of skin disease."

"Oh, it was, only worse. Every moment there was pressure to just tack on a smidgen here or there, just twist some routine to work a tiny bit differently. After all, you were almost complete, it looked pretty good, just this insignificant little modification would make it perfect."

"Doesn't sound awful."

"Ah, but the cycle never let up. Even the smallest change—say adding another figure to a report—would take more effort and testing and processing time than estimated. And some of the changes looked like nothing to a user but required massive coding revisions and intense computer usage."

"Like what?" Ghost asks curiously.

"The classic example was to give running percentages on a report, along the lines of Salesman One brought in 6000 this month which was what percent of total sales. Users would point out that you had all the figures right there on paper, all you had to do was divide and print."

"I don't get it."

"Oh, say there were four guys in the department—A,B,C,D. A simple monthly run took a few minutes and spat out figures showing their individual sales at 2000, 5000, 3000, and 8000 dollars respectively for a grand total of 18000. You'd think you were done. But users didn't care about that 2000 bucks for salesman A, they wanted to know that it was x percent of the 18000, right on the salesman's row."

"Sounds reasonable,"

"Oh, yeah, except that most early report generators just accumulated figures as they went along, they had no way to discover that the total would be 18000 until the first run finished. So, in effect, you had to run the report twice, doubling the processing time, and setting up some kind of dummy structure to hold the results while you went along. "

"Ah, twice as long."

"Twice as long, exponentially harder. And that was a simple one. Then they wanted to compare his performance to his quota. But there was no field for salesman quota, so that had to be added somewhere, with maintenance screens to update the figures. Soon they wanted breakouts by product type, which often didn't have an indicator anywhere or was linked in an obscure file that the report generator couldn't access. Some of the sales requests became fiendish."

"So I suppose you just explain the problem and ...." begins Ghost, taking another gulp.

"Ah, but in any company the sales department guys are the princes and have the immediate ear of the president or CEO or board or whatever. When they thought they needed something, they would scream. They were used to getting what they wanted, as long as they delivered results."

"But you were surely clever enough to figure it out eventually."

"Oh, yeah, and intrigued by the puzzle."

"And everyone would be happy...."

"Sure, for about three seconds until the next 'can't you just' came along."

Wayne sat in the computer room around 8 am, cup of coffee in hand. Once again he read the modification. This was his first attempt at putting something in that would run automatically each night. He had carefully read all the manuals, he had gone over the logic and code over and over. He had finally typed it in. The final thing he needed to do—the step he had not taken before—was to link this into the operations so that it would trigger at 9 pm tonight. Very proud, very excited, he was finally doing what he wanted to be doing.

He hit the enter key happily. And watched in dismay as the display froze solid. Quickly racing to the other departments in the almost deserted building, he determined that every terminal was deactivated as well. He gulped a bit of coffee, began to worry a lot, turned off and began rebooting the central unit, and headed off to Joe D to begin to explain the mess. Oh, and immediately put in a call on the hot line to the consultants.

He had learned early on that you didn't just report problems to upper management. There were two requirements, essential to survival. One was to not hide anything—it was much easier to be honest about the mess and to let them know at once so they weren't blindsided. The second was to always have a few possible courses of action (relabeled "solutions") at least sketched out for them to consider. So it was off to try to first recover from the problem and, second, absolutely assure that it could never happen again.

This was bad, of course. In no time the AR and AP departments would be screaming bloody murder. At least he had waited until end of month closing was behind them. Everybody was exhausted and caught up on work, and a few hours or half a day (which is what he was afraid it might be at this point) lost could be kind of glossed over. Possibly forgiven, since he had told Joe D what he was going to do and why. No use sneaking, there were too many potential problems.

How in hell this had happened, however, mystified him. How could one keystroke bring down the entire operation? He had modified data and code before, minor stuff directed by the consultants over the phone. What was different now? He and Joe had a short and urgent meeting, and while he went back to monitor reboot progress and begin documentation procedures and write-ups, Joe went on his way to forestall damage higher up.

Fortunately, the consultants called back within half an hour and arrived an hour after that. By then the place was in turmoil. How much was lost? How much could be recovered? What was going on? How had this happened? The machine was back up and accessible from the console, but none of the user terminals were responding to anything. That was a long, roasting, two miserable hours. Wayne sat, unable to defend himself at all, listening to rants and complaints dredged up about every problem that had occurred over the last half year. He tried to let it wash over him—old stuff, very little his fault, after all—but it was uncomfortable nonetheless. And he could do nothing but take full blame for this fiasco.

Eventually Zeke and the rest of the well-dressed tribe in their Mercedes arrived, and bustled about. While tapes whirred and the machine gradually came back to life Wayne was told in no uncertain terms to stick to being an operator and leave coding experiments to their godly selves. He took it, resentfully, under advisement. He did manage with careful obsequious questioning eventually determine exactly what he had done wrong, which was an incredibly big win.

He went home late, very late, completely wrung out. It was only Wednesday, but he grabbed a glass of wine immediately with dinner, as he recounted his very bad horrible day to Joan. Of course, not being technical, she understood nothing except the key point that at least he still had a job.

The reason for all the resentment were the accumulating little things that were really big things. The first was just how much additional work computerization had been for everyone. The second was that nothing delivered the completely bright and shiny promises of the salespeople. New anxieties had been added to closing monthly books. Many things had gone wrong. The benefits were not fully apparent.

But the grinding underlying problem was that a lot of it just didn't work right, because it didn't really fit. This was a typical generic accounting and sales package, with a few modifications to supposedly tailor it specifically to Webcor. But somehow key issues had been missed.

No designers expected new inventory items to be added or modified every day—but in this business that was a way of life. You couldn't make an order without the item existing in the proper files—but sometimes the salesmen were selling product which would not exist until months in the future based on promised deliveries by the supplier in the orient that the president himself had just booked. It was not good when the head salesman (the president's son) was unable to book a multi-thousand dollar order six months ahead because the president didn't bother to fill out the paperwork to add the necessary inventory item so the order could be input. Sometimes each 'identical' inventory item was just a little different—everything kept changing under the plastic—and you needed to make note of it somehow, but not on the order, where the customer wasn't supposed to know the difference. What did they care if transistor x had been substituted for transistor y in the Cordless Wonder Web5AX? But the back room had to know. Where was the byte to record that secret information, which had simply been scribbled on the original order back in the good old days?

The consultants kept back-peddling and adjusting and tweaking and claiming the original specifications had been wrong. The accounting clerks had learned how to play the game and blamed every issue they had and whatever deadline they missed on the problems with the computer system. The sales staff had a new whipping boy to curse, and another reason to whine about how the company wouldn't support them to meet quotas. Even the president, drumming up outside support, could claim that all the failures in meeting any targets were the result of temporary disruption as the business modernized and worked the issues out of what would make them a leading edge automated wonder.

But it all had to end up somewhere. I was it. If I did nothing and cried "consultant" all the time, the heat got harder and the yells got louder on all sides. If I took care of it, pressures reduced but left open the possibility (occasionally probability) that something would occur that could not be blamed on the outside support. In some ways I could not win. In some ways, I was as happy as I had ever been.

Ghost jerks up from his contemplation of a bloody mary in the dark light. "What, happy? Doesn't sound much like it," he grumbles.

"But it was a constant adventure," I reply. "Something different every day. Not bored at all."

"Sounds more like terrified," he says.

"Nah, there was too much general repetition. If nothing had happened, it would have been boring. But I liked the excitement. And I loved the learning and the possibilities."

"You're just weird," he waves his hand around his head.

"No, really, in some ways it was perfect," I insist. The original job was impossible—almost all of them were back then—but everybody really kind of knew that. We were just all learning as we went along."

"I'm surprised they didn't just ditch the whole thing and go back ..." mutters Ghost.

"Well, actually that was impossible. With the growth in volume they would have had to increase the accounting departments immensely, and that would have destroyed the profits. We were keen on profits—since it wasn't a public company whatever value built up would go to the original owners. Besides, they were already contemplating an IPO. No computerization, no stock listing. "

"So they found themselves riding the tiger ..."

"Sometimes I thought they just wanted to watch me ride the tiger. If I was devoured, they hoped to learn enough that the next guy might succeed."

Wayne sat back in his chair, with his ever-present mug of black coffee, surrounded by printouts and pads of paper with proposed designs and out- lines of projects. Everything was humming nicely, although the day before New Year's usually was. Most of the people were on vacation, the rest just tidying up, nobody expected much to happen anyway. He was preparing for the triple witching of end of year, end of month, and cleanup and cleanout and full backups of everything. Next week of course.

But for the moment, he could bask in satisfaction. In the last few months things had begun to resolve nicely. He could churn out standard "English" reports in an instant, if they were appropriate. With a little more work, he could give them something more complex. The end of night was humming along nicely, the only worrying thing that it was running longer and longer, and if anything went wrong it took an equivalent amount of time to recover. His coding had advanced nicely, and he felt at one with the hardware, op- erating system, and even logic of the packages and modifications running everything.

With that mastery, professional esteem from those around him had mounted. They appreciated his abilities, were happy to get the written re- ports and analysis, and more and more had him sitting in on important meetings even before the consultants were called in. His judgment was re- spected, his integrity recognized, and his bosses were (mostly, as much as they could be) happy. He was blamed less for the inevitable problems, and he had learned how to explain issues in simple, but truthful, terms and easily digested analogies.

Oh, yes, quite the golden boy. In everything except money, but who knows, the new year was arriving, later his anniversary here would arrive. Already there was strong talk of hiring an assistant to do the stupid work like taking apart and handing out reports, or babysitting the new hires through data entry training. In another month, he was due to go to a professional conference run by Microdata in the city. Life remained hard and eventful, but although each day could leave him drained, he was happy to get up and report to work.

Who could ask for anything more?

This is a big brightly lit bar, with proto-disco lights, loud music, lots of people talking rather too loudly. I can barely make out Ghost over the commotion. "Golden Boy, eh?" he growls. "Here, Golden Boy, have a Bud."

"Not now," I say. "Look, I had enough problems. I'm allowed moments of triumph as well."

"So you thought it was all solved…"

"On its way to being solved, anyway. Hey, dynamic company, in on the ground floor, nothing but up, and I was doing a whole lot better than when I started!"

"Oh, you are just the compleat optimist."

"Why not? When opportunity allows."

"You never learn…."

"Happy New Year!" I yell with everyone else.

Everybody, at least in management, was always optimistic. The actual workers were far more cynical. They had heard all the excuses and promises, and had gone through enough cycles, to realize the truth that the more things change, the more they remain the same. At least for them. They weren't gung ho for the company, but they worked hard and received adequate but always underwhelming compensation.

For those above them, business life was constant excitement and hope. The next sale would be the big score. The next iteration of whatever would solve all the old problems. The road right here might be muddy or rocky or almost impassible, but just over the next hill, or possibly the one after that, was a land of milk and honey. It was all about getting better in every way, every day. That was worth all the underpaid pain and sacrifice and extra hours. The future, that was the thing.

The top guys—well, they were smart and decisive and optimistic as hell themselves. But usually they were also cynical enough to take out what they could while they could. The future, they truly believed, would be bright. But in the meantime—well they were working hard so no reason why they should not be adequately compensated. For them the grand dream was to become public, to be listed, to wallow in the capital raised by a multitude of investors, to finally cash out or take a less difficult role.

A few careers fit into this a little oddly. Salesmen were always flirts—ready to leave in a huff over anything at all—they truly believed in themselves more than anything else. Some of the professionals figured they could cross out or up to another company as necessary, although that was far less common than it became later. But the computer folks—well, that was pure chaos. For one thing, the peter principle—where people were promoted to exactly the point where they were incompetent—was in full force. For another, the burnout rate was high—some quickly reached a plateau where they could not grasp the next stage of coding or design, or simply screamed at the thought of another stultifying day in mystery screens. A few self-promoted through odd pathways. But the strangest thing was that most technical loyalty was sideways out of the company—to the computer manufacturer usually. There were IBM people, Burroughs people, DEC people, DG people, even Microsoft people and a host of other brands. Anyone in one of those slots could almost without effort transfer to a similar position or higher in a totally different industry. Everyone dreamed of eventually being one of the fat cat accountants.

And in all that, the overall unity tended to be language. The big corporations used COBOL, the engineering types used FORTRAN, the newbies and emerging small businesses tended towards BASIC. A big deal was made of the difference, but the language structure differed far less than the hardware and operating system philosophies. Those were the real silos. An IBM operator would be lost in a DEC center, and vice versa.

But, hey, everyone was going to be rich someday, so what did it matter? Good times for some.

Home Sweet Home

WAYNE HAD BEEN warned by everyone to have a full blank checkbook ready. Now he sat next to Joan on a long table in a small undecorated room covered with cheap wood paneling and what seemed to be a linoleum floor under greenish fluorescents. Neutral ground.

On his side of the table were Joan, his-father-in law, their lawyer. Mom was taking care of Gregory back at the house. Facing them were the owner, his lawyer, bank representatives, and assorted other folks whose function he had missed. Finally, papers were all organized and the ritual commenced.

As promised, assorted odd folders were advanced from one side, almost like a weird card game. Some legal or other document would be produced and slapped down, as the bank intoned whatever incomprehensible magic words were appropriate. Dad would ritually consider the packet, decide it was ok, and tell Wayne to construct another check to whatever interested party. That temporarily cleared space, so the next challenge could be brought forth.

They had consulted appropriate soothsayers, so nothing was unexpected: "termite inspection," "title search," whatever. Dad would pull the necessary certified counterspell from their own pile and that obstacle would be overcome. The stakes gradually became higher, and the checks bigger, until real money was involved. And smaller and smaller print legal papers, which the lawyer glanced through. By the end, Wayne was surprised he wasn't signing over his firstborn with signatures and thumbprints written in blood.

Eventually, everyone said that he and Joan were proud new first-time homeowners. He wasn't quite so sure. They had scraped up a little money, parents had loaned them some of the down payment, the bank held an exorbitant mortgage and could take the house away quickly for any number of reasons having to do with keeping it up, insurance, taxes, whatever. Even after they paid it off (nominally in thirty years, who the hell could imagine thirty years from now?) the town could decide to take it back for non-payment of taxes. For that matter, town could grab the place for eminent domain. It all seemed a little shaky to him.

But, well, that was the American dream. He and Joan walked back to the cars in a daze, and got ready to figure out how they would move in.

Ghost sits in that same dark bleak room as I remembered from the house signing, stiffly arrayed in formal black suit, starched white shirt, and subdued bluish tie. An immense pile of papers is on one side, a yellow legal pad in front of him. He glances up grimly, and states "All that I am could have been yours, you know. Lawyers and bankers make out well."

When I finish laughing, I manage "yeah, I guess you're absolutely right. Narrow escape."

"But you know," he oils, "you also would have had a lot more money, a bigger house, a more beautiful family, and better location, a standing in the community."

"Coulds and maybes are not truths," I reply. "I could just as easily have ended up single, bitter, alone, and hating myself and the world."

"Rationalizing again."

"Everyone told me I should be a lawyer. I was logical, I liked to argue, I could usually win debates. Seemed a natural fit."

"But…"

"I found myself becoming too isolated. And I didn't like what I saw myself becoming—arrogant and uncaring. The life of a mid-level lawyer, as I imagined it and from what I read, was not going to be much fun."

"Fun, bah."

BABYLON WITH GHOST

"One chance at life," I intone. "One chance at life. All in all, I'm glad I missed living in places like this during the early years, at least."

All in all, Wayne was stunned by the rapidity of developments. Parts of the American Dream were happening to him? In four years, they had moved, changed careers, started a family, acquired a car, had bounced into a good job, and now even had their own house. Breathtaking.

Credit for finding a home went to Joan's Dad. He was as anxious for them to find their own place as Wayne and Joan were. But he wouldn't hear of the possibility of renting something somewhere. A professional small business owner of a barbershop, he had recently acquired a real estate license and was determined to put it to good use. While Wayne buried himself in work, Dad and Joan tirelessly prospected acceptable towns on the Island. Seeking their Goldilocks mix—not too far, not too expensive, not too run down, not too bad a neighborhood. And, especially, with upside potential for an assumed resale and trade-up sometime in the not-too-distant future. To Wayne real estate was a foreign language, but Dad enjoyed it as much—and was as good at it—as Wayne did the computer world.

Wayne still had trouble believing in his new life. Some days he woke up and thought he might walk once again down Charles Street—until he remembered as some sound jarred him into revised reality. Driving was a necessity now—following more than a decade using only legs and public transport. His adventurous cooking and painting and drawing and writing were long departed. He had devolved into just another cog in mythic Middle America.

Joan gloried to be back in her element, surrounded by childhood friends, multitudinous family, familiar scenes and memories of twenty-odd years of growing up. She was rooted in one spot on her Island—even moving away from her native town of Huntington was painful. Wayne remained aloof—increasingly part of her family, of course, and integrating more and more with colleagues at work—but otherwise a kind of tourist. Long Island was a beautiful place, except maybe the traffic, and he was beginning to appreciate it more and more, but pretty much entirely as a visitor. That was a fault that would stay with him.

There is a picture of a two year old all bundled against the snow piled along 11th street, standing in front of the house they had found. That was Gregory's first experience with it. For that matter, it was the first time Wayne had seen it. He figured the others knew more than he did, there wasn't much he could add, better concentrate on producing necessary income. But he was really surprised at how nice and perfect a place they had found.

A relatively large lot, with the house situated near the street so there was an immense back yard. Cape Cod which Joan had wanted, with upstairs bedrooms, a gigantic full basement, multiple good sized rooms on the ground floor, nice serviceable kitchen area. Built, they were assured, by the contractor who was the original owner who was finally moving down to Florida. Everything, to Wayne's eyes, was more than perfect. Mostly he just gaped and couldn't believe his good fortune. They could actually live and own this?

Joan was less certain. This was West Babylon, across the Island, half an hour away, deep in the wilderness of the South Shore. Was there anywhere to shop? Were there decent schools? Did they even have postal delivery (she couldn't find any mailboxes on the roads because the carriers brought the mail right up to the little boxes alongside the front doors.) She was worried it would be isolated and forlorn, the kind of exile that had given the place a name in the first place.

Wayne had trouble believing how insular her worldview was. He had met her in Boston, after all, and assumed a certain degree of sophistication. But it turned out that was normal for people out here in the suburbs. Home grounds were within five miles, other territories were as clearly marked off as if inhabited by some obscure and ferocious cannibals. The Long Island expressway was as formal a dividing line as the Berlin Wall, and few dared relocate from one side to another. The forty mile stretch from Babylon or Huntington to "the City" was viewed as desolate and dangerous, best traversed in an armored LIRR coach or rapidly speeding down the expressway hopefully avoiding bullets and arrows. For people like Joan, home was not only where the heart was, it was the only spot where sanity prevailed in the world.

That day he toured everything as if he were back at an immense Chateau on the Loire. He walked the perimeter, noting there were truly different spots of vegetation and trees and possibilities for gardens or flowers or whatever. A great patio in back on colored cement paving blocks, fine for children's play or outdoor dining. A full garage. Big trees alongside and in front. And the inside was marvelous. There was the living room and kitchen, of course, and one bathroom only. But downstairs were two private bedrooms, larger than they had ever been used to. Upstairs were two more, one of which could be his library and den and home office area. The basement was immense, and he already imagined that he could use it to build a play space for the winter, or even take up art again if he ever got a chance.

Almost across the street was the elementary school—perhaps Joan could substitute there with a walking commute. A few blocks away were some small stores including a Seven Eleven, and within walking distance—certainly within easy driving distance—there existed a commercial crossroads with fast food, larger stores, and connections to strip malls and everything else. He didn't have time to see the area, but what he saw looked perfectly maintained, green, open, lovely.

They asked what he thought of it, but he was almost speechless. Dad was obviously pleased, and his enthusiasm helped carry Joan along in spite of her initial misgivings. All they had to do now was somehow convince the bank that they were worthy.

Our story seems to have taken a big twist. Two bohemians, city rebels, independent and arts oriented, suddenly giving it all up for a white bread (white everything) Dick and Jane in the tacky suburbs existence. I had everything but the pipe to smoke in my lounge chair each evening. Joan was creeping ever closer to the destiny she had pursued as a child. All the years in between, all the plans and worries and hopes, now written off on a clean slate in a shiny new life that conformed exactly to the normal concept of Amerika.

Of course, in our own minds and within our own personal narratives, this was simply a logical continuation of who we were. We were extremely fortunate, I think, in having met each other at a financial low point. Not an emotional or personal low point—that would have been a disaster. But our life together had never involved a lot of money. We got by, actually we felt we lived quite well, but we didn't have much luxury except time and experience.

That is a strange statement, even to me now. What else is there important in life except time and experience?

The net result was that almost every stage of our lives going forward was a financial improvement. The cultural problems might have been getting greater, but in our own confined world every year was a little better than the last, some much better. This house was an example. Since neither of us had grown up either idle wealthy or self-described important, all our evaluations were relative to ourselves, not to some imagined absolute standards.

The only real reservation I had about the new place, surprisingly, was a brief breakout of my old hippie-inspired idealism. I worried that my kids would not grow up with any multicultural experience. But the real-estate iron certainty at the time was that while many houses appreciated in value, those in integrated or integrating neighborhoods devalued. When idealism confronts pocketbook, idealism often loses.

And I had begun to adjust to the other difficult reality. It was no longer just about me. Even in Boston, with Joan, I had my core of selfishness, my heroic inner image of being lone master of my fate. Whatever I did was important to me, and that was what counted. But here, with a child and a family and tighter bonds with relatives everywhere, there were suddenly a lot of complex obligations, many of them exactly contrary to what I wanted, that I had to accept.

But, hey, in spite of it all, owning a house was really cool. I'd be lying to claim I ever brooded that it was old, or on the South Shore, or whatever. Dark tarnishing thoughts never did cross my mind. Once the decision was made, the only rational thing to do—the only really emotionally healthy thing to do—was to not only go along with the changes, but also to embrace them enthusiastically.

Still in the same old stale room, now smoking a cigarette, Ghost now accuses me of political stupidity. "You realize, flip flops like that many you could never be elected to anything."

"Hell," I retort, "any number of the things I did when I was young would prevent that, if known."

"But everything now is political. How do you manage to get along—even then, there you were, at least a former conformist nearly-communal anti-establishment libertarian in a manicured Italian-flavored white-bread neighborhood."

"I always knew how to lay low," I answered honestly. "Probably that's why I never developed the roots. The only people I was comfortable with, really, were the people at work with whom I shared problems and solutions—and those were not personal nor political."

"Still true?"

"Most of the time, most of the time. People are less worried about old cranks though—we're kind of expected to be eccentric. I like that role."

"But didn't this—what should I call it, double life?—bother you and make you at least a little unhappy?"

"Oh I suppose. Most days I was just shallow and happy and enjoying everything. Who controls the deeper ways of the world anyway? I got along, I interacted, and I was deeply involved with the few people right around me. That seemed good enough."

"But ...."

"But nothing. I wasn't about to hang out with the equivalent of Picasso or Sartre or Voltaire—and if I had I probably would have been just as remote as I was here. I considered myself unique."

"Ah, unique."

"A strange affliction. But I found it could be made to work."

Bank personal treated them less as potential money-making clients than as necessary evils. By the time officious clerks were done squeezing them through the wringer—assets, income, position, health, background—Joan and Wayne were beginning to think they were the poorest risks in the land. Apparently (and this always remained true) the best people to get a mortgage were those who had the money on hand not to need one.

But back then mortgages were still good solid income opportunities for the banks. Banks were more local, for one thing, and did not speculate on foreign exchange and commodities and stocks. They couldn't ditch toxic assets. MBA's didn't advise them to become rich by accumulating real estate on which to plop innumerable useless branches, or by raising credit card fees. Banks were a colorless, no nonsense, we lend you money and you just better pay it back or we both lose, industry. Everybody except Wayne and Joan understood that. It was a learning experience.

The reason home mortgages were terrific income opportunities was reflected in Wayne and Joan's own eventual package. They were buying a house for around fifty thousand, they had scraped together a barely acceptable twenty thousand down payment, and the bank finally grudgingly offered them a thirty year fixed "best rate" of 16 ½ percent. So every six years, five times, they agreed to pay back the full loan, and still (as he understood from the insane concept of interest before principal payments) owed exactly the full thirty thousand anyway until year twenty-five or so. Why the sheriff didn't arrest such bandits was a mystery until Wayne realized that the lawman was also a bank employee.

Banks used to exclusively worry about whether borrowers really could pay back as planned. The reason the rate was high was that inflation was modifying old concepts. If inflation ran at over ten percent annually, sixteen percent was pretty much near an adjusted historic average. But nobody really had any idea what inflation might be three decades from now, so wild ass guesses made consumers pay through their teeth.

Wayne's salary in the low thirties was not good enough, and only Joan's plan to get a teaching job and the impeccable credentials of both sets of parents made any of this possible. And he had thought they were finally doing so well. This was a humbling experience.

We were never comfortable owing money. We had been too near penniless for too long to ever consider the future was guaranteed. We liked living within our means. We would much rather have a cushion to fall back on—if we ever found the means—than a monetary obligation to face. In that, we were unlike everyone we met. Smart people used debt. We were not smart.

We paid cash for cars, and saved for big expenses and paid cash for them. We used a credit card, but mostly for small purchases, and paid in full every month. If things started to get out of control, we cut back and adjusted. Fortunately, Joan and I felt the same way about this—it's the kind of thing that can easily break up a marriage.

I know, I understand, I read the Wall Street Journal. Using other people's money is the way to riches. A lot of borrowing, lots of sweat equity, and a little luck and more than a dab of good intuition has fueled multiple real estate empires and made many people millionaires. But you need to accept the risk, and always feel you can pay it back somehow, and understand that starting over is not so bad if you need to.

We lacked that comfort zone. I don't know why. We always knew we had the lifeline of stable background families, who could at least provide food and shelter in a pinch. We had faith in our own ability to scrape by somehow, even if we lost jobs. But we just didn't like always being worried about money and what to do next.

Same nasty room, same nasty Ghost. "But her father had done really well in real estate, hadn't he. And her brothers were doing the same."

"Philip, at least. But not us."

"Too proud to learn."

"We just weren't interested. We wanted a home, not a place to fix up and flip. We enjoyed life too much."

"Busy little grasshoppers."

"Some would say. Some did say. But your kids are only young once. Heck, you are only a given age once—maybe not you, Ghost, but everyone human."

"Surely you considered this simply a starter home."

"Joan did. She always planned to go back to Huntington—but even in her mind I think she usually believed it would be to some place that had more or less the same value as the house we bought. Me, I figured it was much better than an apartment, although I had not yet realized exactly how expensive owning a house could be."

"Well, you might have thought you were on the move. Me, I'm not so sure."

"Our life. We were both really content and happy. I'll match my overall contentment and happiness level—all my life—against anyone, thank you."

"Still arrogant."

"Case closed."

Gregory was standing on the edge of the drop cloth, bundled in a heavy coat. Joan was cleaning the kitchen, also wearing a jacket. Wayne, in heavy old sweatshirt, was using a roller to paint the empty living room to prepare for getting some furniture in next week. The windows were open for ventilation as advised by the directions on the can. Here it was almost mid-June. And it was colder than hell.

On the South Shore, it turned out, spring is a little like San Francisco summer. A bright early morning would soon be overrun by fog from the bay, riding the air currents being warmed inland. Almost inevitably, by noon the sky would be overcast and the winds chilly, sometimes raw. Hardly ever actual precipitation, but not the balmy spring days being enjoyed by, say, Joan's parents just on the other side of the Island. But the place had to be painted immediately, and they were still too new at all this (child especially) to ignore the warnings on cans of paint. So, the heat was off, the house was cold and damp, and the first floor was almost completed. Except for Joan's constant close inspections to point out places that needed touching up.

They had discovered a lot they had never expected. They were ready to take care of mail addresses, contact electric and telephone companies, for example. But who knew you would immediately need an oil delivery contract, or the hard cash outlay required? Who could anticipate all the little things that suddenly had to be available, including painting equipment and tools? They thought that all the stuff from Boston, stored back in her parents' garage, would be more than enough. Nope, wrong. More money they certainly did not have.

Wayne finished the back wall, and started to move everything around to deal with the area around the front picture window.

"I think this is too cold," said Joan, "I'll take the car and take Wayne over to my parent's house, ok?"

"Sure, I think that might be a good idea. I'll get this all done by six or so. See you then, I'll get the heat back on."

"I hope so. " She gathered up a few things and left. Wayne went back, young but nevertheless beginning to ache from the unexpected stretching. Even a year or so of lazy office work was starting to get him out of shape, he realized.

He promised himself that when he was done—or maybe when he began to clean up—he could help himself to some beer from the case in the garage and enjoy this Saturday night. Always good to have a happy goal, he thought.

Babylon was an inspired choice. It was near the water—the bay only a few minutes away, the ocean within twenty. There was a cute little town and several fine parks. Lots of shopping, good schools, historic sites For someone in our position, it was affordable and all but perfect.

The city was only forty miles west by train, and I hoped to be able to go there sometime. For right now, the important thing was that my current job was only a half hour ride, and I could take back roads almost the whole way, avoiding most of the heavy rush-hour traffic that was the only real horror. The old car was holding up, even though it sometimes cost ridiculous amounts to pass inspection.

On occasion, we are just lucky. We seem to float into the perfect time and place, often not realizing our good fortune. I saw France before globalization, the West Coast in countercultural heyday, some large cities before gentrification. The best places seemed to be always a little behind the times, rushing tentatively to the future but grounded in what had long been there. Babylon was exactly the same, still trying to be the suburban frontier of families fleeing Brooklyn and Queens in the fifties and sixties, with only a few indications that era was over, and big changes would be on the way.

So, somehow, we could afford this. Somehow, it fit all our needs. We should have been more thankful, but like most people too busy to think, we almost took it for granted and often complained way too much. Little problems were magnified, great advantages were ignored. But, looking back, it was really wonderful. And completely unexpected.

Another stolidly stupid greenish wood-paneled room. Not a courtroom, but I am suited stiff and dark, uncomfortably perched in an uncomfortable chair. Ghost's serious demeanor suggests that of a prosecutor. "So what was the truth here? Were you doing well, were you doing badly, had you sold out, had you finally found your true route to happiness?"

"Yes." I reply, with measured care. "Contradictions are part of living fully."

"That wouldn't work in a court of law," he notes sternly.

"Life ain't no court of law. Anyway, that's why I dislike law. Most reality is a lot more complicated than a few logically constructed lavish semi-truth arguments. Besides, there are never any real precedents for anything."

"Surely you must accept that there is always a better way or a worse choice. The decision and the consequences are yours …."

"No, I don't think so. What I do know is that circumstances changed, as they always do. We ourselves adapted. As always, no matter what, we dealt with problems as best we could. We focused on the only thing we actually controlled—our happiness and sense of perspective."

"Bah, useless drivel! Won't buy a loaf of bread. Culturally deadly. A sure slope to ultimate failure."

"Better advice than stupid questions like 'were you doing well'!"

"I tell you …. Eh?"

"Doing well. Compared to what? Always compared to what. We could choose any what. Notions of absolute relative comparisons in life are ridiculous."

"Tangled logic, too tangled by far. Methinks I have touched a nerve," he finishes with a flourish, stepping back towards the wall.

"I thinks you should ditch this stupid scenario." I have to admit my nerves twinged a teeny bit, as the vision faded rapidly.

Late September, hot sun setting over the low tree line in the back yard, sound of the Southern State murmuring into evening. They were sitting for an impromptu picnic at an old redwood picnic table they had rescued from the street, complete with benches and chairs and recliner. Gregory had pizza smeared all over, Joan was just sitting down, Wayne was enjoying a glass of beer. Life was settling in nicely.

"Not bad," he said, as she sat down next to them.

"Gregory, you're a mess. Here, use your napkin like this …."

"I mean," he continued, "who would have thought we'd be like this, a few years ago."

"We should have come back sooner," she sat and took a slice out of the box.

"But I wouldn't have found a job like I have. We couldn't have afforded the house. No, I think we did this about as quickly as we could."

"Mom's having trouble now," she reminded him ruefully. "She missed me all those years."

"But we're here now, and she seems to be recovering ok. My dad is even doing all right."

"They're getting old …"

"Well, after all, we are back now. Make the most of it. Look on the bright side."

Gregory was making more of a mess. They cleaned him up and turned him loose to run around the yard.

"I think," said Wayne, "that this is just great. Work is going well, we have a house, Gregory's doing fine, you see your parents pretty often. You should be happier."

"Oh, I am, I guess. I am. I wish I could get a full time job over somewhere near Huntington."

"You can keep looking, I guess. But it's hard, with Gregory this age."

"I know," she said. "It will have to be something around here, I suppose. Maybe a permanent sub or something."

"More money sure couldn't hurt," he mused.

Just a plain old conversation, like those everyone around them was having all the time, but a universe away from Boston and the esoteric experiences and thoughts they had once lived. But, on the other hand, a calm and fairly normal suburban American life, after a few years of turmoil and almost unendurable uncertainty. A moment, they realized, to be savored forever.

This new room is paneled in real wood, deep burgundy carpet. No fluorescents, a tasteful stained glass window , one big mahogany desk with a single green shaded bankers light. I'm relaxing in a comfortable leather armchair. "Well, this is a step or two up," I say.

"Precisely," replies Ghost. "Something you never seemed to get the knack for."

"Oh, one of those," I mumble.

"Everyone always told you that you were aiming too low. And I also think you did."

"Maybe that's true. I think aiming high is a kind of disease. We live our lives on the ground, not in the sky."

"But you can raise the ground with a few better dreams and goals."

"I'll tell you, everybody I know with huge goals ... no it's not worth arguing. For me, it always seemed the wrong approach. I always felt my own daily and day to day life should be important to me."

"So you settled ..."

"Look, if I can't tell the difference—or don't care about the difference—between the finest silk suit and the stuff I usually wear, why deal with all the wasted time, effort, aggravation, and inevitable envy and disappointment."

"But what others think ..."

"Aye, there's the rub. That's the essence of it, all right. I truly did not care a lot what 'everybody' thought, and I only respected those who went past the veneer to the real me. The real me was there regardless of the label on the tie."

"That's not the way to get ahead," began Ghost.

"No, but at least for me it was the way to a satisfying life that might have turned out far worse."

"But ..."

"Enough," I finish, as I walk off.

Seven o'clock, out the door, down East Neck towards work. He'd be there by seven thirty, and no phone calls yet, so everything was probably all right. Of course, you never knew. The equipment and software were always more temperamental than you would expect. Anyway, he had things to do, a new report system planned, end of month to get ready for. The sun was bright and windows open, the best time of year.

He went past "The Little White Church in the Wildwood," (which gave his father great amusement when he later showed him the route—it was a famous song from Dad's youth) and out Spagnoli road and all was as fine as it could be. These were also his moments of meditation, peace, and quiet. Nobody could reach him, he rode in quiet isolation without even a radio to provide distraction. Back roads all the way, no need for a traffic report.

He unconsciously worried that it was dangerous to relax—almost seemed as if it would attract problems—but he was extremely satisfied with life and everything. Almost to the point of being smug. Good job, good career, good house, good family, good future. At least for once, no gnawing doubts about the paths he had taken and the one he was on. A time to be thankful and just accept the bounty of the universe.

1983 ROCKET

SIMPLE JOYS

"HERE, JOAN, LET me open that," Wayne took the chilled bottle and found the corkscrew in the basket. The sun was high but going down fast behind them as they watched the rolling Atlantic from the weedy dunes of Robert Moses state park. They had been happy to discover that after four, there was no charge, and almost nobody there. Certainly no one to bother them. Gregory sat happily on the tablecloth they had spread.

Moments like these were unusual, simply because they were too busy to grab hours necessary. There was always something to do, someone to see, something to buy, and just not enough hours in the weekend. Not to mention how tired Wayne was by the end of the week, after another rough session at Webcor. It was great to be in a rapidly growing company, but awful demanding as well. Sometimes he even felt guilty not reading more proposals and manuals or doing design work on his designated time off. And, of course, he never knew when the phone might ring.

But not here. No cell phones yet, no devices, nothing but the sand and sea and sun. And family. They had found a wonderful old picnic basket in her parents' garage and filled it as if on a French holiday, although the actual dinner was just a pizza they picked up on the way over.

Salt breeze balanced hot air, still picking up warmth from the dune. They had talked a lot in the car, about everything, and nothing, and little was left to say but enjoy a bit of quiet time. Gregory was toddling around, and you still had to be careful about what he might decide was edible, but the worst (in Wayne's mind) animal baby years were behind them. Maybe now, life could start to become predictable, serene, and peaceful.

Then again, if work and home were any indication, probably not.

Ghost and I are in bathing suits, walking along empty sands beside rolling surf, watching shorebirds running into and away from the endless foam of the waves. Massive crowds left behind, only a few fishermen around as we stroll barefoot towards rocks marking the end of Fire Island.

"Happiness on the cheap," notes Ghost as a gull whips by.

"Sure Ghost, purchased with the only currency we had, which was time. And not enough of that."

"Didn't you miss all the excitements and little pleasures of city life? And all the extras that all your friends and relatives seemed to have?"

"Nah, we were both always frugal, always with too little money to do much. Our philosophy was simply that once you took care of the important basics you could always find something interesting to do for nothing."

"Well, this is sure nothing. Almost un-American."

"I prefer to think of it as the European model of family outing."

"Right," laughed Ghost. "The peasant European model."

A bigger than usual surge sends us awkwardly scrambling further up the slope towards the dunes.

Babylon got its name when a son declared to his mother, very early colonial days, that he was heading across the island into the scrubby sandy wilderness of the south shore, twenty miles away. "But I will never see you again," she wailed. "Oh, right," he laughed, "it's just like the Israelites being held captive in Babylon."

Joan's impression was much the same. When she had grown up each cluster of population tended to retain its own flavor and reputation. The North Shore, the South Shore, Manhasset, Setauket, Huntington—each was its own

BABYLON WITH GHOST

country with its own culture. She was not certain, even in the eighties, that she would find supermarkets so far away, or if there would be mail service. It had taken a lot of convincing to get her to move over here, and she was only grudgingly accepting the location.

Wayne found it surprisingly nice. Babylon itself had thrived after the railroad pushed through after the civil war, an early version of the Hamptons where the wealthy could summer on estates enjoying the cool breezes off the Great South Bay. So the town contained some surprisingly interesting arti-facts, like the elaborate dam at Argyll park, built as part of a huge summer resort, and fine Victorian houses, and a cute main street from a New England movie set. West Babylon, where their house was located, had been nothing but farms until after WWII, when massive suburbanization set in, and most of the housing was from that era, much of it identical.

He could walk a few blocks and be in a tiny pocket park, there was a large secluded pond nearby, a state park a mile or so away. They were across the street from an elementary school, and had easy access to all kinds of stores and fast food restaurants. A short drive took them to the open Babylon dock or the funky Adventureland amusement park or a lovely town beach on the bay wistfully named "Venetian Shores." A longer drive of twenty minutes or so would have them on an uncrowded town park on the ocean dunes, with refreshment stand, tidal pools, and lifeguards for the surf. Importantly, it was still an easy drive over back roads to his work site.

From Joan's standpoint, it was still much too far from parents, a half hour or so away. Wayne rather thought that an ideal situation. He liked his in-laws a lot, but some of the time it was nice to have your house to yourself.

Wayne finished mowing the lawn and came in the back door for lunch. The garden was starting to take off, but it was time to figure out the rest of the day. Surprisingly, for this one summer afternoon, there was nothing pre-scheduled with anyone or anything else.

"Hey, Joan, what do you want to do next?" He called, dripping sweat.

"Well," she answered, turning from the kitchen table island where she was making lunch for Gregory, "we have to get some more pampers, I think, and maybe some more clothes since he's growing out of stuff so fast now."

"Oh, you can do the clothes shopping with your mother. Want to go to the beach?"

"No, I don't think so. We got a little burned when we were over at the bay yesterday with Leanne. "

"Maybe just over to Belmont then. We could take the stroller and watch the rowboats."

"Ok, that sounds nice, in a little while."

"And tonight?" Wayne liked to have the times set so he could fit in other stuff he wanted to do, "What about dinner? Burger King?"

"No, like I said, let's go early to Toys R Us for the diapers and then over to the mall. We can eat at the food court and I can look around."

That was a pretty normal thing, even in the nice weather. The stroller was easy to push and there were lots of shiny things to distract Gregory. Wayne could window shop or people watch or daydream and Joan could imagine all the things she might buy if she could afford them. Nice to study what everyone else was buying and thinking and doing. The only problem was that fluorescents sometimes gave him a headache. That condition seemed self-curing since he was working in such awful conditions at work. Cold dim tubes everywhere illuminated his day more than genuine daylight.

"When do you want to go? I need to weed the garden, and maybe water some of the flowers out back."

"How about around two. I want to get ready. But can you take Gregory out with you."

"Sure thing. It's nice out, you should hurry."

"Just take him out. I want to straighten up a little to, in case Mom and Dad stop over tomorrow."

"Ok."

Raising a toddler sucked away whatever time was left in the already thin hours of full time work. And if there were pennies lying around on the kitchen table, it could use every one of those too. Life before child had certainly been less complicated.

On the other hand, they were in an area where nobody really had all that much more. In many ways that was quite good for their psyches, because they did not have to keep up with extravagant neighbors with multimillion-dollar strollers or mansion-sized prebuilt outdoor playground structures. Cheap plastic was everywhere, and peers were content with big wheels and plastic wading pools.

The trouble was that desire for stuff for yourself was insatiable, but you sometimes grew sick of it anyway. There seemed to be a natural point at which, at least for a while, you could say, enough, stop! And there was no real guilt in not buying a trinket for your own use, almost a virtuous sense of being frugal for once.

But with children there was no adequate point to say "this is useless." Educational toys were expensive, and without them your kid would supposedly never get to college. Picture books cost a relative fortune, but your child should have the best. Who wanted to endanger a child with a poor-quality car seat? And on and on, not to mention the necessary visits to the doctor and clothing and whatever.

And finally, all the enrichment activities, already going on all around. A few hours, many dollars here, a few hours, many dollars there. Without them, who knew what horrors you were inflicting on the delicate psyche of the little darling.

Fortunately, we had been in day care for a long time, had taken a lot of education courses. Joan had taught public school and was certified, I had undergone Montessori training in Vista. Neither of us were mystified by early childhood education, and we had lived through the myths and realities, and had the benefit of having seen some of our charges grow up and move on. We could easily separate the wheat from the chaff, in terms of necessary interactions, and for the most part most of the stuff costing a lot of money was chaff.

So we had simple sets of wood blocks, a few books that we knew were children's favorites, and we engaged daily in all the enrichment activities so beloved of those who wanted to do them for you for a fee. Moreover, we were confident in what we were doing, and did it naturally, and it made us happy. We didn't easily overreact, and we didn't become too overwhelmed. It was in some ways ideal.

Not, of course, that it let us raise the next Alexander the Great or Einstein. But that's another story.

Only a few beach umbrellas left, only an occasional set of walkers going by in the opposite direction. Sand scrunches under bare feet, mind empties into infinity ...

Ghost breaks in maliciously with abrasive sarcasm, "Ah, the perfect parents."

"Nobody is, Ghost, you know that. No such thing. Too many variables. But we were more experienced than many others, and I think less easily swayed by fads."

"Out of necessity, I bet. Making a virtue of what you didn't have."

"Well, maybe. That's not necessarily a bad thing. More people are spoiled by having everything they think they want than by having to set priorities. Too many distractions can warp judgment."

"Never heard you wishing for less money, back then," cackles Ghost.

"Options always seem to be nice," I admit. "But making do can be quite satisfying as well. Besides, compared to many others, were the wealthiest of all."

"How so?"

"Well, we agreed on almost everything. And here we are, still together after all these years."

One car, little money, and shared responsibility meant that Wayne and Joan were constantly together. Fortunately, they had weekdays to go their own ways in their own lives, even though that usually meant others were telling them what to do, or at least suggesting. It was, in short, awful hard to find time for being alone. This was a shock, because in Boston, they had been used to going their own way, and they had hoped after the aberration of living with her parents that everything would get back to "normal."

But, as any parent quickly discovers, getting back to your "normal" before-children life means you must either ditch everything and run away or wait twenty years until the children do so. Oh, sure, some can send kids off to the equivalent of boarding school, but they couldn't afford that, and the schools usually required parent involvement. And money—don't even ask about money. Whatever is saved over their lifetimes is washed away when they reach college and the immediate years beyond.

So no matter how prepared Wayne and Joan thought they were, they were not. When teaching, they always sent the little darlings home at night, and never had to worry if they got sick or what they might have to do to direct them on the right track over the years nor concern themselves with what friends they had. Their own children were an open-ended vacuum.

Fortunately, their years of marriage had hammered agreement on basic priorities, forced to some extent by having little cash in hand nor any prospect of getting more. They were frugal to the point of pain, and while others borrowed freely they were deathly scared of debt, probably because neither was quite sure they could ever count on an equivalent paycheck (let alone a larger one) tomorrow. The main arguments had to do with time, especially selfish time such as when Wayne wanted to be by himself reading but they had to go visit relatives, or when Joan wanted to spend time on her own needs but Wayne felt too busy to take care of Gregory.

But they had also learned to work it out, how to avoid hot buttons, and where the real limits were. They knew exactly how much steam each could blow off in any direction without hurting the framework of their relationship. That was probably the most valuable asset they possessed.

If you adjust needs to what is possible, life can be a happy thing. At least if you are above a certain level of existence, which we had long ago passed. I don't pretend we were ever among the world's poor and we always had wonderful support from friends and family. Those without such things have a miserable life indeed, and often no way out of a hopeless situation. But that was not our fate. It was just that almost everyone we knew seemed to be doing better and spending more and needing things that we could not possibly afford. Like that second car.

On the other hand, we had never thought we could afford a child. Nor possess a house. Nor have a career with money in the future. And—here we were. Not the perfect house, to be sure, on the ocean. Not the perfect job, doing what we wanted as money was thrown our way for deigning to take an interest it. But more than we had expected.

That also is a key to happiness. Low expectations may cripple possibilities, certainly that is what all the textbooks and wealthy folks tell us. Low expectations keep us from striving hard to get all we can out of life. Maybe. Or maybe telling us to have high expectations are ways to forge chains to make us work harder for bosses for lower pay than we otherwise would as we dream of future riches, and a way of building a safety valve into disillusioned older workers so they blame themselves when their financial world falls apart. I always tended to mistrust what I was told—those who speak do not know.

Well, at least a little bit, we were on that train now. Expecting the child to grow up to be the bestest in the whole world (or at least in the circle of children we knew.) Planning on a better house sometime. Anticipating a steady rise in responsibility and position and salary as I worked hard and became more experienced. But all of that, again, tempered by a countering pessimism based on the past, and forged in the era when those dreams seemed completely unattainable. Perhaps that was a little sanity. In any case, it kept our actual needs simple, and our actual expenditures under control.

We've paused at a large tidal pool beyond the jetty. Children are happy splashing about in the quiet waters, finding shells, enjoying the warmer water. Parents can relax a little, not worried about sharks and other sea monsters— well, more rationally rip currents and undertows—in the deeper waters. The wind rushing quietly is only occasionally disturbed by the sound of boat engines or a jet overhead.

"But you were, naturally, the perfect couple," Ghost tries to skip a flat rock he found somewhere.

"Stop it, Ghost. We were both rational and happy people who truly liked and loved each other and had a common desired future in mind."

"Sounds like bragging to me ...."

"You can call it bragging. I think it was the hardest work we did. Achieving that kind of agreement is not easy at all."

"Do you now feel having that is critical for the well-being of the child?"

"Nah, I don't know, probably not. I know a lot of normal people who were children of divorce, a lot of weird people who had perfect childhoods. It was good for Joan and me, I doubt a perfect upbringing is necessary for the baby. There are too many counterexamples in history."

"Why do you think that is?" Ghost asks curiously.

"Humans are hardy survivors. It's hard to imagine any perfect childhoods in Neolithic times or even early historic times. Heck, until a century or so ago an awful lot of mothers died in childbirth. Our race is used to all kinds of childhoods. I think most of us finally just sort things out."

"What, you think early childhood doesn't matter?"

"Everything matters. Nobody should starve. Learning to read, being loved, children in a wealthy culture deserve that. Sure it matters. But—if they don't get any of it—a surprising percentage of historic personalities seem to grow up at least adequately."

"Strange position, for a former teacher."

"The real world contains more contradictions than are dreamt of in your philosophies, Ghost."

Beautiful Saturday twilight in June. Adventureland was crowded and sparkling, as sinking huge red sun set a carnival tone. Happy cries from children, mostly sub-teen, echoed around rides reminiscent of yesteryear, while parents minded strollers and chased offspring who refused to stand still.

It had been a good day, Wayne thought. He'd taken Gregory to the playground in the morning, and roamed the aisles at Shanes, the closest thing to a Woolworth that still existed, picked up some beer at the beverage store on the way back. The mower was fortunately still working, so he had pushed behind the fumes when he got home, shaving the big backyard and the tiny plots in front. The garden was doing very well, the tomato plants he had grown from seed taller than they should be, the snap peas on the back fence ready to harvest. Flowers were all over the place, mostly Joan's doing except in odd patches where he could experiment with some catalog perennials.

He had caught up on a few sales brochures from computer companies, outlined some questions for the meetings next week, did a little of his own pleasure reading while watching Gregory toddle around the yard. Definitely a highlight age for both parent and child.

Later, they went down the street to Burger King, where he had his usual meal of Double Whopper with a milkshake, while Joan ate chicken fingers she could share with their son.

Gregory mostly liked the French fries, of course. American all the way.

Quick, easy, relatively cheap, and then they had braved the stench of the town garbage dump, towering into the sky like an Egyptian monument, wove through deserted tin wartime industrial sheds from the war forty years ago, and squeezed into the jammed parking lot. Entry was free, but money poured in from bracelets and tickets the kids needed for rides, and especially from the concessions, which he and Joan usually ignored, except maybe for an ice cream cone.

Gregory loved it all like other toddlers his age. They plopped him in the teeniest rides, around and around in a circle, sitting in a caterpillar or standing by him on the merry go round. Although he never got tired of it, they eventually did. On the other hand, it was relaxing to just stand around and enjoy a moment when they didn't have to be hovering or worried about something or other. Really as nice as any other night out from their past.

As the sun set sultry and crimson, skies darkened and lights strung everywhere provided ambient magic. Kids enjoyed seeing and hearing others their age, as long as reassured that their parents were not leaving anytime soon and stayed in plain sight. Adventurous they were not.

Every weekend was the same, but every weekend was different. There were some where there was no free time at all—a party at Joan's brother's house out East or a celebration at her old home. Or perhaps a lot needed to be done—painting a room or shopping for furniture or fixing the car or just catching up on various chores that they left piling up. Sometimes they were both too exhausted to do anything.

But most of the time they were driven to do something together, and there were lots of things to do. In the summer, particularly, there were parks and beaches. One beach was right down the street in Huntington, so they could go over for dinner and to visit and Gregory could play in the sand. Another was nearby for him to splash in a tube in Great South Bay—if the tide were right, the seaweed not too thick, and the sea lice not biting.

They began a pattern of trying to make basic shopping into a family activity, where there were certain rewards for Gregory's good behavior, and a chance to point out things and talk about the world, first to each other, and later to the children as they grew. This worked really well until surly teenagers suddenly emerged from their cocoons, replacing adorable caterpillars. But that's a different story. For now, it was enough that they began to feel truly middle class American (although never upper-middle class.)

Home life became scheduled patterns and games, things to be done around chores, making enjoyment out of things that might have been nasty. If you had to do something, you might as well enjoy doing it.

Big waves crash on huge boulders forming a jetty. Spray fills the hot air, the sun is beginning to crisp my shoulders. Perfect summer day ...

"And you all agreed on what you wanted and lived happily ever after..." Ghost interrupts my daydream.

Ghost can be a real jerk.

"You know Joan and I were different people with slightly different needs and different agendas. Including Gregory. We always had been and always would be. We all wanted slightly different things out of life. Nothing is ever completely happily ever after, but ..."

"But?"

"But, the key was that despite the different things we wanted, we usually agreed on the big things. It worked for us."

"Probably just shows you weren't trying hard enough on your own agenda. You would have done better, probably, if there was more conflict."

"Depends on how you define better, doesn't it? Neither of us, for example, ever really thought that we should trade certain things—for example proximity to family—to simply achieve something like more money or a bigger house. Across the Island, we were willing to go, not to California or Texas."

"Very limiting," he tosses a rock at a helpless crab caught in a whirlpool.

"Yep. In everything except happiness."

Their budget had always been a kind of primitive cash flow balance. When they were married, it seemed much too complicated to keep separate assets, so there was one bank account. Wayne and Joan would deposit earnings immediately, then pay daily expenditures with cash, ongoing ones with checks. Every month they carefully looked at the balance and compared it to the previous one. If it was going up, good, if down, bad. They already knew there would be unexpected but reliable big hits—fuel oil deliveries, car repairs—but at least the mortgage took care of taxes and insurance automatically.

Since income had been going up, perhaps not as fast as they would like, they could barely stay ahead of expenses, and were gradually accumulating a few savings. Gifts from parents at Christmas helped a lot. After a while, they even felt they could splurge once in a while, although what they considered splurging would probably strike most other people as simple survival. Buying the wood to build a playhouse was, for example, one such well-discussed item, worked out and fit into expenditures carefully.

They never did get around to wanting to pay for things by installments. They dreaded such a constant tap on future savings, they still didn't trust that future income would always be there. For example, if there was another baby, Joan would not be able to substitute teach. If there was another recession, who knew what might happen to Wayne's job. Better to be as safe as possible.

They cooked meals from scratch, never ate out except for Saturday fast food night, did vacations at their parent's houses, never traveled, never threw big bashes. They didn't miss any of it, the world was filled with fine and wonderful things that cost nothing or very little. Not a bad way to live.

As we walk back towards the distant misty crowds, sun crinkles the skin on my shoulders. I'll feel it tonight and tomorrow. My bare feet are also feeling pretty scraped, so I stay in the soft wet sand seaward of the constantly moving foam line.

"You were, finally and about time, as American as apple pie," remarks Ghost.

"Sure thing. We finally felt we were close to living in one of the TV sitcoms we had always laughed at, where the 'average' family had a huge kitchen and rooms stretching out and upstairs to infinity. We had a kitchen now, and a huge basement, and a garage, and a second floor and more rooms than we knew what to do with. Top of the heap."

"But in a poor area ...."

"Well, so Joan claimed. Not me. The houses were neat and well maintained, the streets were safe and relatively free of cars, there were things to do nearby. You can always want more, but more at some level is a disease."

"Didn't you ever dream about striking it rich...."

"Of course I dreamed. I suppose Joan did too. For her it would mean moving back to Huntington, maybe doing some remodeling. For me—well the only thing I wanted was more time. Being rich would allow me to do what I wanted when I wanted—besides, what I wanted hardly cost much. I never wanted to have to worry about money for day-to-day needs, but beyond that the most precious resource in life is the minutes that fleet by."

Oops, add to everything else the beginning of a cramp in my calf. Well, sitting all day tomorrow would let everything cure itself.

A fine mid-October early Sunday evening, just after five, with the late sun catching the bright leaves and making them glow even redder. Some swirled around them as they pushed the stroller up twelfth street and looked at the last of the neat lawns and gardens already showing signs of soon-to-come frost.

"This is a nice quiet place," said Wayne.

"Oh, it's all right," replied Joan. "But the houses are all the same. The North Shore is prettier, it has more hills and variety."

"At least they're all nicely maintained."

"Oh, I suppose, but they're not as fine as home. "

"Do you have Gregory's costume all picked out?"

"Yes, we got it at Penney's last week. A pirate..."

"I liked the hat," said Gregory, picking up on the conversation. "Good hat. Pirate."

"That should get some candy."

"Good."

"You get enough candy anyway," laughed Joan. "Grandma's always giving you something."

"I've got a rough week," Wayne said. "It seems we no sooner get one thing under control than something else pops up. Another emergency. I can't believe I didn't get called yesterday. "

"At least you're learning something useful."

"Oh, IBM is definitely more marketable than the last one. But I understood the last computer inside and out. This one—well, it's really different."

"Ah, you know you like it," she waved.

And so for the next half hour they simply enjoyed the last of another year, with holidays and all unknown adventures awaiting ahead.

Boomtown

Wayne shrugged into his dark suit jacket as he joined the herd exiting the railroad car at Penn Station. Even at ten o'clock, when rush hour should be long over, the escalators and stairways and corridors and (particularly) bathrooms were jammed. Fortunately, all he had to do was go upstairs to the next exciting appointment.

This was to be the preliminary presentation, to him as the appropriate data processing manager. Presumably, the salesmen thought, he had the ear of the corporate elite and the vice president who would actually make the decision. They wanted him on their side, and they knew the easiest way would be to impress him with the technology.

He exited onto the wide dirty plaza in front of grimy Pennsylvania Hotel and got his bearings. Ah, right off to the side of the circular Garden rose the black skyscraper. One Penn Plaza, said the card, and he entered the lobby, passing through just enough security to keep out casual panhandlers. Express elevator wooshed him up to one of the higher floors.

He was, if not exactly presold, prepared to be impressed. He had learned a lot in the last few years, had become much more aware of the industry, and had a decent feel for the technical needs of a distribution business. He knew his current system well, having modified or written large parts of it. He had a list of needs, but he expected those to be pretty easily dealt with.

Microdata had a new machine. He was going to look it over, become excited, take home all the manuals and brochures and specification sheets. This had been the plan, anyway, and this visit was to such a courtesy. An upgrade would be the easy path. But—well—things had changed.

The new special consultant to the president was an IBM fanatic. Suddenly, an upstart like Microdata was not good enough for what Webcor was about to turn into. If you wanted to play with the big boys, you had to get the big boys' toys. The big boys ran big iron. They didn't mess around with DEC or DG or, particularly, anything with "micro" in its name.

So this was a lost cause. He would enjoy it as a day off, and smile, and ask intelligent questions, and write down notes for his report. But he had begun to realize what he had to say would make no difference at all. Still, even the new guy knew they had to go through the proper motions and impress the bosses with how thorough they had been. With a deep sigh, he left the elevator and walked down the corridor to the large cheery reception room on the left.

Strange lighting overhead, a harmonica wails faintly. I'm poised on a level plain, sparse brush to the horizon where bluish hills vainly try to stop the constant wind. I suppose this is going to be about loneliness in business, or the aridity of corporate life or something concerning giving souls over to the pursuit of material objects. Then I hear the crowd behind me and turn around.

A covered wagon in dirty white, with a matching canvas tent pitched alongside, provides the backdrop for a spare wooden stage. A small group of people has gathered in a dusty square, leaving behind the tiny cluster of weathered buildings that presumably indicate the town proper. They seem to be waiting for the show to begin as I stroll closer.

Suddenly Ghost appears out of the wagon, a vision in black frock suit and white shirt, stovepipe hat over wire rim glasses. He surveys the crowd, pauses, and calls out. "I won't lie, you're all too intelligent for that. I'm here to sell you things. But, you will soon realize that they are to both our benefits. You will be happier, I will have a small remuneration, and we will both walk away satisfied. Why, just look at my references, if you wish, there on the table! In fact, if you have nothing you need nor nothing I can provide, why just leave now. I know how valuable your time is, and do not wish to waste it. Ah, but if you stay—well you have different needs, I know, but we have many products. For example," he points dramatically at an older woman near his right, "I have right here a cream to reduce wrinkles, when used with this elixir that will immediately make you feel years younger. Anna-Maria's Viennese Treatment. And for you sir," he indicates a rotund middle-aged gentleman in a suit, "we provide a consultation course that when followed exactly by your staff is guaranteed to painlessly double your profits overnight? Unbelievable? Yes, but we have the testimonials, right on that table. Our motto is simply, 'if we don't have it, you don't want it. You," he points directly at me, "yes, you, don't say anything! I know exactly what you want from the shape of your haircut! Come here, come here, step right inside my office and we can talk. Folks, this will take a minute. Feel free to take whatever literature you like, I'll be back in an hour!"

We step inside the tent, which somehow has a large desk and two leather chairs. Charts line the walls. "Whaddaya think?" asks Ghost, "pretty good, eh?"

"Unusual," I agree. "Is there a point to all this."

"Of course, of course," he sits back. "You were in enough sales meetings—on both sides or in the middle—to recognize the setup at least. I just thought I'd add a little historic interest."

"So this is all about sales."

"Well, of course. In its most basic form, I might add. Promise everything but keep the contracts under control, make the pitch, milk the sales for a while, and be ready to get out of town and move on whenever it becomes necessary."

"I didn't do that!" I snort in a huff.

"No, no, nor most of the people selling to you, I'm sure. Not intentionally. But," he adds slyly, "that was often the result all the same, was it not?"

"Uh, I suppose."

"You suppose," he drawls caustically. "You know damn well. And the worst thing was that half the time you were selling to yourself."

There was no doubt at all, Wayne knew, that an upgrade was required.

Day by day the system grew slower, especially if there was a bottleneck like a special report or end of month number crunching. The night stream—jobs that were done after hours like updating all the accounts receivable and the daily summary reports (paradoxically, it turned out that the shorter and more meaningful the actual report, the longer it took to process and distill all the data needed to produce it.) If anything went wrong, there was less and less slack for staff to wait around and catch up on entering orders when it finally came back on-line.

The problem—a good problem—was that the company was growing more than exponentially. It turned out that alternate phones—that is something not provided by the telephone company—and the first brick-sized cordless handsets were a sweet spot for the market which Webcor was first into. Of course, all the production was done in the Far East—in fact all the design work was done in the same places—but the company president had contacts from way before the electronics boom, and had latched into some very good exclusive contracts and early products way ahead of the basic curve.

With those in hand, the expanding sales force had gone forth and landed some really big accounts—huge department store chains mostly—with gigantic orders. The Christmas swell had been overwhelming. The warehouse was stuffed to the gills with incoming boxes and outgoing shipments. Receivables grew long and complicated (you couldn't dun chain stores as effectively as local merchants.) Sales reports had to take into account future orders—taken in August for delivery in November, for example. These were all way beyond the conceptions of the original software, and the ongoing patches needed to accommodate them had made the system extremely cranky and fragile.

Wayne was excited about one thing. All this meant there were constant challenges in design, constant new projects, applications, reports, and revisions. That meant constant new design and new code. He found he was very good at translating business requests into executable designs, and presenting these in documentation for approval. He found he was a whiz at coding once the design was in place, no matter how exotic the requirements. It was a wonderful and fun game. Even testing was a fine thing, in spite of its frustrations. He loved the happiness of users when a new tweak they had wanted or a useful new tool was delivered. From that standpoint, this was a heavenly job.

Professionally, it was also a high point. He was finally respected and trusted and his views on all things computerized were taken into high account at meetings. He was careful not to venture beyond areas of expertise—he never told sales people what a computer would like them to do in a rational world—and was fascinated by the issues of business life in the real world. It was a far cry from the clean competition described by ivory tower professors at college. The strangest part was that some things had to be left unsaid, promises uncontracted, possibilities dangling, all because of legal technicalities. Trying to take into account reporting for sales that were promised but not formally booked was a lovely exercise.

It helped that money was flowing freely. Lines of credit were being extended among all parties like swelling tentacles. Going public on the American Stock Exchange was going to happen. Not that such wonders resulted in fat paychecks or huge bonuses—things were kept in hand for normal employees—but the future dreams were there. Options were being offered, and everyone expected a nice windfall after the IPO. Meanwhile, any expenses related to business itself were fairly easily absorbed—for example no problem getting a new terminal or more paper. Wayne's staff was now up to five, including three data entry operators. Growth, rewards, expanding future, it was all exciting and hopeful, in spite of grueling hours and exasperating problems.

But Wayne was tired of explaining why the computer occasionally crashed, with live changes being put into the code every day. He was sick of being called at night to be informed that the end of day processing stream was failing. He dreaded each morning while he tracked down the overnight problems and kept users off for hours while he reran—or worse, reset and reran—to clear up issues. Some of them were his own fault, mostly because he was always in a rush. He was learning a lot, but he knew most of this would clear up if he just had more power to give the machine a little more slack. He had been saying that for a while now, the Joes fully believed him, and the new consultant just laughed when he reviewed what they were trying to do on the equipment they were trying to do it on.

A fire blazed in an ancient stone fireplace behind their table. Exposed beams overhead accented the colonial origins of the structure currently housing the Yankee Maid Inn. The small segmented dining area was dark, hushed, and crowded with similar business parties, a few older couples. Last autumn had brought out the memories, tasteful seasonal decorations scattered about, although none on the walls already heavily encumbered with mementos of yesteryear.

Wayne sat next to Joe D, who sat next to Joe P at the large round table. Across from them was the IBM salesman, and next to him his woman account manager. Everyone was smiling. Drinks had been plentiful. Life was good for all. They could order anything they wanted—Wayne was going to try softshell crabs for the first time, fried whole. No expense was to be spared. After all, IBM was paying.

This was a victory celebration for everyone. IBM had snatched a growing and possibly huge account away from the competition, puny although they may have thought it. The Joe's were thinking that now they were graduating into the big leagues, with the latest machine a fitting symbol of the firm's rise. They could brag about it seriously at their various professional meetings. Wayne, although somewhat sad to bid goodbye to the quite advanced Pick operating system which he finally understood intimately, was secretly wise enough to understand that a programmer and manager of standard IBM equipment would have a far greater market value and more options than anything he had previously enjoyed. All cautions and worries were, for at least tonight, banished to the next day.

It had been a long and flattering period. Like being a wealthy and beautiful ingénue when suitors had come around with promises and excitement for months. Wayne had been on tours, taken to other sites, given lunches with technical people, shown the marvelous future, all in hopes of convincing him not to point out possible issues with such a drastic switch. The company president had been taken on expensive outings and contacted by impressive business peers, extolling the virtues of big iron. The other executives had been pampered quite as much. All the while, underneath the scenes, the new puppet master quietly orchestrated it all, seemingly open to anything, actually aware that he had firmly set the company on a necessary course. He had spent the most time with Wayne and Joe D, and had actually given serious consideration to the issues. But, although Alan was not here tonight, he was perhaps the happiest of all.

Wayne above all realized there would be problems. He was naïve about how many, since he had never gone through a hardware conversion and software replacement before. Business was business, everyone kept saying.

Computers were computers. How was he to know better? He would find out soon enough.

But for now, the cocktails flowed (no wine here!) and the softshell crab was delicious, and the service impeccable, and grand plans both public and private bloomed separately and together. Hard times behind, good times ahead, the future as rosy as any dawn could possibly be. Late into the night, they laughed their way out into the parking lot and went their separate ways in the crisp dark.

I always considered myself a basically decent, honest person, in social as well as business dealings. Mostly, I guess, I was lazy. Truth was generally easy to speak and easy to keep straight, whereas trying to keep up multiple fronts and deceptions was time and energy consuming. I had better ways to use the time I had.

Even the most honest person, however, wears multiple hats and has different perspectives. In one sense, I was loyal to the old machine and operating system, which had served us well and which we still had a lot invested in. I could have happily taken their new offering and run with it. On the other hand, it was exciting to step up in the world, and to be seen as something more than a wannabe programmer using a baby language on dinky hardware.

I would have been foolish indeed not to review want ads and notice differences in opportunities and wages between what I was doing and what those established on more well-known machines commanded. You have to look out for yourself, always, as well as the company, no matter how honest you may be. But in private corporate meetings, all you should say (or surely are wise to say) is the impact to the company itself. Is that a lie? Or just fudge?

Bottom line, however, is that I was moving up in the world. The company was itself turning into something it had never expected to become except in its wildest fantasies. It had existed for years as a relatively sleepy little import firm, and suddenly fortune was smiling. Nothing was remaining the same—the building was being outgrown, the departments were being outgrown, the managers were being upgraded to handle more responsibilities and people. The computer we had was no longer adequate, and to meet the projections of the future the type of the computer we had—no matter how nice it had been—would probably no longer work.

"Yessir," drawls Ghost, lighting a big cigar. "You all lie, all you sales folk."

"I'm not a salesperson," I start.

"Oh, you sold projects and applications and yourself and budgets and just about everything else, didn't you?"

"Well, sure."

"And you always pointed out the best features and minimized the possible issues, right?"

"Mostly," I admitted.

"So you were just as much a liar as the proverbial salesman of any type. So there. Here, you might try one of these," he held out a colorful tin box labeled "Dr. Jones Prevaricator Preventor Pills."

"Oh stop it. We all know there are multiple viewpoints to a problem. We do it to ourselves—on the one hand, on the other hand. Just because there are multiple possibilities and we pick one doesn't make us liars."

"What," he laughs. "You dare suggest most salesmen are honest? I have a bridge you might be interested in …"

"'Most successful salesmen—anyway with reputable products—are pretty honest," I tell him. "Most of them really expect more sales. They just add some sizzle, but the core is basically true, as they understand it at least. Especially if they come from a big reputable company."

"As they understand it sounds like a weak link."

"Well, yeah, especially in early computers. They can buy into the hype like anyone else, and most of them were not technical enough to have a clue as to what was true and what was not. We were all learning, you know. Even the big boys."

"So you don't think you all lied."

"Listen, at the time we all believed in fairy dust and dreams. It was all new. Who could imagine the possibilities? We dreamed of all the good things and sold those. We kinda worried about the complications and difficulties. We didn't give a thought to unintended side effects and paid too little attention to the unexpected. But what we truly thought is mostly what we advocated."

"Mostly."

"Mostly. The competition was out there, you know, for our jobs, for our projects, for our funding. And the managers had their own take and advocated their own slanted agendas."

"Sounds like a lie fest to me," he repeats.

"Somehow, when you were in it, it just seemed normal. And, you know…"

"What?" says Ghost, puffing away as he fades.

"That was all just like the rest of life, anyway."

Technical consultants representing the promised help from IBM were just leaving. It had been a hair-raising experience.

"Yes, you will have to define and map all these fields from your system to ours before we can do anything with the data."

"But what if it doesn't fit?"

"Make a list and we will find out what changes are necessary. But you know, we only have so many hours contracted, so try to keep it short." They wandered out the computer room door.

Wayne scratched his head. He had expected a fairly easy automatic conversion—from ASCII to EBCEDIC. That had been clear from the start—according to the salesfolk getting away from the code that could only handle American characters and numbers and putting it in "EBCDIC" which could show anything including Chinese and Cyrillic was the first step in growing into a large corporation. In spite of the fact that Webcor was an American company and did not use nor ever would use anything except good old ABC and 123. But still, easy, run a mapping program and presto.

Not so easy. They weren't converting text, which is how he had first thought of it. No, it was field by field—dates, dollar amounts, addresses, zip codes, special handling codes. Every field in his system in every file in his system would be moved to an equivalent one in the new machine. He had to go through every odd bit of the database, seeking equivalents and missing entries.

None of them, not even the sales guy, had been so stupid as to think they could convert programs. No, Webcor would be buying another standard program, sold by IBM, which would presumably handle anything. After all, it "was used by companies much larger than Webcor, the world over." That program had its own files, its own fields, and they would all have to be filled in by a program provided by the consultants. Easy. Except Wayne had to do all the long, tedious, and error-prone mapping work before anything could begin.

Well, it would give him something to do while they waited for the machine to arrive. Meanwhile, associated hardware was piling up in the corners. New terminals for everyone—monster heavy "intelligent" terminals which cost a fortune. Thick coaxial cable for the electricians to run through the walls. A printer the size of a refrigerator, a 9 track tape drive even larger. The room was getting a little crowded, even before the main event.

He sighed, and started going over the required data sheets.

The word of the day back then was "world class." We all wanted to be "world class," as if there were some Olympic judges handing out medals. It was one of those questions that you could never answer "no," which is what had killed the sales pitch from Microdata. And everyone just assumed that a big company like IBM was itself "world class," and automatically helped its clients to become so. All we had to do was follow their advice to the letter.

But the real driving force was far more Darwinian. All of us, IBM included, were on the "bleeding edge" of technology. Capabilities kept growing, applications kept expanding, possibilities seemed endless. The books, even for computer systems in business, were just being written, and "best practice" was changing all the time. What worked last year was obsolete by next, management systems as well as hardware. Everything was shifting.

The manufacturers lived in "silos." When a company decided to go IBM, it was IBM all the way. The languages, the data, the equipment, the reference manuals, the technical help, and even the correct manner in which to run departments. You couldn't be half IBM, half DEC. It was almost impossible to hook different machines one to another. And each manufacturer was trying to expand into new realms. The mini-computer firms wanted to expand upward and outward, away from pure engineering into the vast numberless pool of midsized firms. The big-iron wanted to expand downward into those same limitless waters. Upstarts and oddities kept popping up here and there, hoping to grab large market share before it was all gobbled up. The waters became treacherous.

Nobody really knew much of anything, except what had worked before, which wouldn't work now. Nobody wanted to admit that, even to themselves. Everyone, on the other hand, had faith that no matter what things would work out.

The net result was hard on everyone. Managers and owners never knew if they were making the right decisions, never knew for sure where they stood, even if they could believe their own technical departments. Salesmen were selling stuff they didn't know at all. Users were forced to become contortionists to adapt to the constant changes. And in the middle of it all were the people who actually had to implement and deal with all the jagged edges and views—the data processing managers, operators, and programmers. I was right there, bleeding along with everyone else.

A small group is ignoring the beautiful sunset to listen to Ghost as he lights a couple of lamps. "Sorry, folks, that's all for today. Tomorrow's the last, you know. I've got other customers needing servicing. Hey you," he called pointing to me, "come back in my tent for a few minutes. I've got something that might interest you." Everyone else drifts off, I duck my head and find myself back in his office, with a couple of nice lanterns providing soft yellowed light.

"Things not so bad," says Ghost.

"You're probably getting out just in time," I remark.

"Timing is everything," he laughs. "Still trying to convince me everyone doesn't lie? What about that conversion, and the equipment, and the disconnection of promises and expectations?"

"All right, all right, I know what it looks like from outside. But from where we were, everyone was trying to tell a kind of the truth. It just was in different areas, and we each assumed too much."

"That doesn't even make sense."

"Look," I try to explain. "Think of it as different worldviews. There were the old timers, who had been there for a decade or more, knew how to do things, served the company well. They didn't mind improvements—but all this other stuff was just more work. The boss believed everything the other bosses were telling him—and they usually were bragging about the good stuff, not moaning with the horror stories. The executives each had dreams of one or another kind of Shangri-La built on the idea of ruling empires as the company grew without end. People like me, in the computer department, thought that with just one more upgrade, one more change, a little more power, everything would settle down. The consultants figured that once we understood that things could be done better their way, everything would be smooth and crystal clear. The technical people just banged from one endless task to another, like drone honeybees, tweaking day to day. The salespeople thought they were coordinating it all as fantasies of future limitless sales year after year danced in their heads. And we all promoted exactly those visions, which were just near enough to each other that we never stepped back and flat out said no."

"But …."

"But there were horror stories. There were hurdles to starting empires, most of them hardly computer-related but impacting the computer systems. There would never be an end to change, never a settling down. The consultants did not understand the nooks and crannies of our business, and we did not understand that they had no idea of how to put in all the little bits of oddity that had made Webcor a success so far. The salespeople were clueless prophets. Only the rank and file really began to understand what a slog it was turning into, and for them there were no happy endings, and they began to complain first."

"But you pushed along anyway."

"Well sure. We were always just… this… close. Then something else would come up."

"So you never got it to work?"

"Oh sure, after blood sweat and tears. And it almost all ended up being completely rewritten custom code before it came close to doing what we needed. Time and money and frustration and, at the end, no feeling of accomplishment, simply exhaustion."

"Welcome to the big time."

"Yep."

Hunched over Joe's blonde wooden desk under greenish fluorescents wanly illuminating the small windowless office, Wayne nervously reviewed pages of detail. "Looks like we're finally ready for the big test." Joe D. sat back and smiled. Wayne just nodded nervously.

Alan had specified that before the new System 38 could go "live" there must be a full week of exact "parallel operations." Every bit of information entered in one computer system would simultaneously be shadowed in the other. Each report must be printed and compared line by line. Each program night and day timed, reviewed, and perfectly matched. If anything failed, find the problem and find another time to start over. Only absolutely identical could be accepted before the old Microdata system was shut down and removed.

Early morning problems were not slow to arrive. Accounts receivable called right away and Wayne hurried over. "Where do we put in this notation," Annette asked, with an impatient annoyance. None of the staff, already overloaded, was excited about doing everything twice. "I don't see a place."

"Uh, next screen," said Wayne, pressing the enter key. "See, right there."

"And this?" She indicated some green mark over in the corner of the dog-eared yellow carbon copy.

"Oh, that one we don't use any more."

"Rachael agreed to this?"

"Sure, ask her." Soon a small conference had grown larger. Meanwhile the babble of the less well-trained operators trying to deal with the new system became shrill. Confusingly, all fields must be complete on each screen before seeing errors or confirmation. Use tab key for navigation instead of what they were used to. Cryptic messages indicating what might be wrong popped up and the screen froze waiting for corrections. A revolt was brewing.

Then came a nasty shout from payables.

The fiasco lasted less than an hour. Scrap the whole exercise. Bulky backups, days of preparation, inflamed hopes completely blown away. Like generals following a massive battlefield defeat, Joe D. and Wayne and Alan tried to salvage whatever they could and come up with another campaign. Joe P and god knew which other executives would have them on the carpet in a few minutes.

About three weeks later, three more attempts, schedules slipped massively. Deadlines had been missed, promises of "next time" were a company joke. Meanwhile, unlike the systems tests, payment for two computers instead of one continued flawlessly and relentlessly. When stakes and bonfires reached Alan's level, he ruefully acknowledged that "world class" was an impossible goal.

In the end, they picked one or two "typical" accounts and simply trailed those through a week, ignoring everything else. Once convinced major customers would be handled adequately and that reporting was defensible and that numbers on the nightly tie-outs genuinely tied out, they innocently declared the "modified parallel run" a success. The old minicomputer was to be unplugged. IT took a deep breath, and—at the beginning of a month, when cleanup was complete for the accounting period—forced everyone onto the shiny new system. Everyone hated it already, but they detested it less than continuing bouts of double work. Wayne scrambled day and night hand tuning and modifying code. Joe D and Alan, with Joe P as an accomplice, fudged where necessary to assure success.

One way or another, it finally worked.

The trouble was that everything was absolutely incompatible. You would think that binary computers are binary computers, just as the binary computer idiots thought that one business was just like another. But there were deep issues never mentioned at the sales meetings, possibly because everyone assumed that their side of the issue was blindingly obvious to all.

I mentioned the underlying code difference, but not the implication. I was used to reading the actual ASCII data file—byte by byte—using a common inspection tool. I could open up any file and find the value of a field and even hand edit it. No such facility was available on the new system. A huge number of such inconveniences led to a near paralysis of the methods I had developed over time to deal with problems. No quick and easy programs to fix issues—all had to be compiled, and loaded, and there was no trivial fallback, and some things could not be replaced at all.

New screens drove the operators crazy. They were used to immediate feedback, but the new "intelligent" terminals only sent screenfulls of information to be processed as a lump by the CPU. Error messages in such cases were delayed—if it couldn't find a company you didn't find out until long after you had entered the code, and then you'd get some cryptic message like "Co not found." Sometimes the hardware froze altogether. And there was the unfamiliar use of tab and enter keys. Complaints were frequent and loud.

RPG, the programming language, was an insane agglomeration that had evolved from an ancient attempt at an "easy" reporting shortcut query system, back in the antediluvian swamplands when machines ran on decks of input data cards. Unfortunately, its current incarnation as shipped with the early 38 showed little sign of intelligent design. At least, for the first time, it had added the capability of using subroutines, but it still treated each dump from a terminal input as one of those primitive card decks. The most irrational code ever devised—IBM cherished it because it absolutely bound every customer with bands of steel. There was no way this could ever be converted nor ported to an alternate system nor language without total rewrite, and the programmers (and all the staff and their managers) who used it necessarily became evangelists because they knew damn well they couldn't do anything else. Skills also were not portable here.

It's no use even mentioning system operations. Like everything else, compared to what I had known, they were user hostile, mostly lacking, and noticeably deficient in all regards. Everything was trimmed for maximum speed, minimum convenience. That let the salesmen crow about throughput, but it turned out that throughput would never be our problem.

We've retired to the bar down the street, where an out of tune upright plays old songs and a cloud of smoke rises from gents playing cards in the corner. Ghost dramatically twirls his handlebar mustache and takes a draught of whisky. "So, you have to admit, you were all sold a bill of goods."

"I guess so. But we were anxious to be sold."

"The best salesmen," he notes, "are the ones that let the flock fleece itself."

"That's true enough. But," I take my own sip, "there was more to it,"

He raises an eyebrow in inquiry.

"The requirements were impossible from the start. We wanted to be world class, meaning standardized to big company standards. But, on the other hand, we wanted to keep our little homegrown systems that had worked so well for so long."

"Like what?" he asks.

"Well, the folder system. When orders came in, depending on who did the sales and who was the salesmen and what were the special conditions, if any, they would be put in marked folders—maybe red, green, blue, whatever. These meant something important. The system we had developed on the Microdata mirrored all that faithfully—we had a field marked "Folder" and a choice of various color codes. There was, of course, no such thing in the "standard" packages, because there would be no such thing in 'real' companies."

"Surely there was an equivalent."

"You would think—priority or something. But the thing was, each of those fields also had a kind of connotation and special rules—for example perhaps a sale by one salesman could never be in a certain folder color. All kinds of stuff like that. The old system let them carry half the old rules in their head, half in the computer. The new one wouldn't let us slide by."

"Painful, I imagine," Ghost drinks some more.

"Impossibly painful. We had to change our systems, of course, to grow. But people had been there a long time with routines that worked well. It was, as they say, a learning experience."

"But the salesmen could have told you."

"Maybe. But I don't think they knew either. We all just kind of took things for granted, and I discovered that is not a good way to run a computer project of any kind."

By mid-autumn, a significant nine months after the hardware arrived, everything was humming and seemed to be settling down nicely. In electronics distribution, because of the long supply chain from across the Pacific, the busiest order booking had been in mid-summer—which was a nightmare. The busiest shipping and order fulfillment into the stores for Christmas was just finished. This was a slack period, awaiting final results and consolidating reports.

Joe and Joe were spending all their energy now on getting the stock listing completed—days in meeting with auditors and external accountants. Alan was pushing Wayne to fully support the effort, particularly by showing how tight and modern the computer operations were. Everyone was happy and festive, filled with accomplishment at a record season, dreaming of wealth to come.

Wayne also was finally accomplished on the new hardware and software. He understood the systems intuitively, he could design and code and modify and update. The importance of audit trails and fallback scenarios had become second nature. Once again, he was respected and trusted. More than that, he was now part of a larger IBM community, with occasional evening meetings, conferences, and IBM-sponsored technology updates. This time, he knew as much about these systems as anyone else, since they were all brand new.

It was true certain nagging problems lingered. In electronics—and this was a new phenomenon back then—small variations were occurring in items. Phones in boxes with the same identification codes would vary slightly but significantly—from having an off color to a part that rarely worked. The same model would subtly change dramatically over time, leaving the older inventory relatively devalued. In the "standard" inventory and order entry systems, this just could not be taken into account. For the moment, they worked their way around, but it was an indication of problems to come.

Nevertheless, it was a good time. He had never felt so secure in job or career, the family was enthusiastic about his success, and the future was clearly about to explode into Technicolor happiness.

"Ah, so optimistic. Didn't you ever learn?" asks Ghost, as he packs the last of his wares into the back of the Conestoga.

"We thought of it as becoming older and wiser. Besides, we were now fully on the IBM bandwagon, and we knew they would support us forever."

"Poor doves."

"Well, yeah, but we didn't realize that until later. I mean, we had done the hard work already, we thought. And, truly, we had accomplished an awful lot."

"Well, you did anyway."

"You know, Ghost," I note, "I always did find it was really a team effort. I did a lot, but I can't say everyone else wasn't working just as smart and hard in their own areas. Generally, there were not too many times at jobs when I was envious at how easy anyone else had it. It seemed to me everyone was pulling their weight."

"But you had other possibilities too."

"Well, so did they. You were a fool if you didn't realize you might change jobs for one reason or another. But we didn't think of it much, and certainly didn't plan to do so anytime soon."

"Well, maybe. Anyway, I have to get back on the circuit," says Ghost, climbing onto the driver's bench. This town won't be ready for me to come back for a year or so."

"Until they forget, you mean."

"You got that right, pardner," he says, driving off.

No manuals, no flowcharts, no visions of new applications or reports dancing in his head. Wayne could just relax here with Gregory and Joan, watching television together, enjoying the holiday decorations in their own quiet house in their own quiet neighborhood as a tight little family. The world went by, but it no longer threatened. They were part of everything and happy to be so.

It seemed a forever journey from Boston to here. City to suburbs. Single lifestyle to family all the time. Walking down the street to the stores to being in a car all the time. Worrying about what the landlord would say to doing whatever they wanted to the house itself. And, not least, barely scraping by from paycheck to paycheck with no hope of getting ahead to barely scraping by from paycheck to paycheck but with great hope of making more in the near future.

It took a while, but here they were. Typical American consumers in a typical American scenario. Some would say trapped. Some would not. Wayne's opinion would vary from day to day, if he ever had time to think about it. Joan was simply happy to finally be home.

AUTO ADVENTURES

IT WAS A dark and stormy night. Traffic was light on Little East Neck Road as Wayne mindlessly drove home from work in a downpour. His day had been difficult, he could hardly wait to get back to have a drink to unwind, and to get something to eat, and to relax. He wasn't paying much attention to anything beyond puddles glaring back and potholes caught by his headlights, on as lonely a stretch of highway as any roads got around here. Chain link fence around the town dump stretched endlessly to the right; leftwards only scattered houses braved its sights and smells. A familiar route he took every commute, which avoided almost all traffic.

Suddenly, the engine cut out as the car slid gracefully to a stop. Power steering and brakes gone, he barely managed to manhandle it more or less off the road onto a narrow shoulder filled with mud and water. Strange. Bad gas, maybe? The deluge pounded the roof. He tried to start, no luck. He gathered thoughts, considered options, wondered what to do. Helplessly, he tried again—it started fine! He heaved a sigh of relief and pulled out, only to have the motor die for good a quarter mile later.

Well, nothing for it. No umbrella, no overcoat, just his suit. He took off his jacket, climbed out, locked the doors, and trudged up the road a few blocks to the nearest lighted house. Water pouring off of him, he knocked on the door until someone answered, then asked if he could please use the phone. A call to Joan, a long slog back to the car, waiting forever, and he finally got his ride to shower, drink, and dinner.

After towing the next day, the service station told him it was a bad fuel pump, an apparently common problem he had never heard of. Simple to fix, but it took more money of course. Well, what was the choice? He hadn't even known the car had a fuel pump until now. Something else to tuck away in the back of his mind.

"Nice shop," I comment, looking around at the neat little bay space, lift in the center, tools carefully arranged on the walls.

"Yeah, thought you'd like it," says Ghost, in dungarees and T shirt. "I modeled it on Angelo's place which you did actually use. Unlike you," he continued, "I do not have problems with putting things in their proper time."

"I know, I know, I'm not really clear on the exact year when all these various events occurred," I answer. "They were just more problems among many, and hardly worth paying attention to. Even if I could, though, I don't think I'd fit them into this narrative chronologically."

"Why not? I thought the whole idea here was a year by year set of stories."

"Well, yeah, but it gets stupid. If the narrative is about me and that old Dart, it's better to just lump most of problems together rather than insert them like unconnected bubbles into other streams."

"The typical problem of the historian," remarks Ghost.

"Yeah, I appreciate them all the more. So you're a mechanic in this one, eh?"

"Seemed appropriate. You sure as heck weren't going into the role."

"No, I admit my expertise pretty much added up to changing tires and adding oil. I did change oil once, when I was a teenager. Didn't like it much."

"No do-it-yourself spirit. Hardly American, not knowing how to do cars."

"I liked these old places, able to do anything to any model at all," I remark, trying to direct the subject a bit.

"Oh, they will probably be remembered as romantic. Of course, this was back when you could still work on cars if you wanted—they were all pretty much the same and had a lot of identical underlying elements."

"I know. Can't do it any more. Dealers specialize on purpose, nobody else can keep up. Like a lot of things," I sigh.

"Well, sir, what can I do for you today?" he asks, putting on his white baseball cap.

Owning an older car made for many happy mechanics. They would often rub their hands in glee when Wayne drove up, especially if he was hostage to the need to pass inspection. After a preliminary scan, they would mock-mournfully inform him of a horrible new condition that must be corrected immediately. After he had paid more than he could afford, not knowing any better, he was sure they would laugh all the way to the bank.

Eventually, he and Joan found a local mechanic who remained happy to get both cars all the time, but was far less aggressive in his billing practice. He knew that the money would come in sooner or later, since they always took the car there. It was a form of honesty, and by knowing what was likely to come up it was much easier to budget and far less traumatic to go for the annual checkup.

Those cars were not like later models. Although rustproofing had improved somewhat from the horrible fifties, when the bottom would rot out in three years or so, there was still extensive corrosion on American cars, particularly on the lower body parts. Although cosmetic, it was pretty ugly.

The only good thing was that having such a wreck meant that he had no fear of parking in Queens or anywhere else—nobody would bother to take anything, including the car itself. And other drivers gave him a good leeway—in any collision they would lose far more than he did. Beyond that, the car was reliable and always worked. Except when it didn't.

It was a bare-bones model, which at least meant that there was less to go wrong. No automatic windows, no air conditioning, not even a music player. Eventually, Wayne tried to wire one in, with a little success. It could easily have been shipped to Cuba, no problem, and would probably still be running. As it happened, he finally had it towed away from the house when he got a new car—it would still have run, but it was too old to be worth anything.

"Ok, thanks. I'll be right over." Wayne hung up the phone and turned to Joan. "OK, the car's ready. Angelo says I can pick it up anytime."

"And?" she asked. "What was wrong this time?"

"Nothing too bad," Wayne answered. "Just the front brakes. Not a fortune."

"Didn't we just have those done?"

"I don't know. I think brakes wear out all the time. Anyway, it isn't anything awful, compared to some of the things it's needed to pass inspection."

"I think you just got a bad car," said Joan for about the millionth time. She had a different way of shopping than Wayne did, and it often caused friction when they went looking for something together. For her, the pleasure was in the hunt, looking at multiple options in person before circling back for the final decision after a long search. Wayne was more surgical, doing the basic work by reading and asking and trying to get the necessary information ahead of time, then getting the first thing that fit into his expected parameters and budget. He thought her shopping was interminable. She thought he was hasty and impulsive. The car had been just his decision, back when she was pregnant and couldn't come with him to the outer suburbs where he bought it in a driveway.

"Consumer reports rated it well. The used car guide review claimed it would become a classic. It's worked pretty well for years now."

"It should, with all the money we put into it."

"I guess cars just cost money."

"My Camaro never did," she declared.

"Your Camaro was brand new," Wayne replied. "That's a little different than getting something used and cheap."

"Well, certainly cheap," she sniffed.

"Look, we'll get you a better car pretty soon, ok? Let me just go get mine now so we can do something later."

"Don't forget the checkbook."

For various reasons, overt and subconscious, I never enjoyed cars. I did not feel the quintessential American freedom of the road when driving around. I always felt free only when on foot, or being taken somewhere on public transport. Involved with that was the fact that although I liked playing with mechanical things and electrical equipment, I always hated the grease and massive tools necessary to deal with internal combustion engines.

Even now, I hate being sealed away from the world, unable to look at what I want, unable to hear anything even though I may be the only person in town driving about with the windows open. A car seems to isolate me from reality. I can drive adequately, I can use an auto as a necessary evil, I can even occasionally get into the spirit of the thing, but it is always an effort. I would happily live in an age where no noisy smelly monsters existed.

My first car was fun, if not the love of my life. An old 1950 Nash convertible, with a cloth roof that retracted on rails. I painted it taxi-cab yellow by hand. Manual shift with a shiny chrome ball I put on the shift stick. Once the brakes failed totally. Another time, after it began to shake badly, we took it to be serviced and the mechanic told Dad he was surprised the whole bottom had not fallen out—all the bolts were rusted through. That was the end of that, fun while it lasted for a year or so in high school.

Then I was off to carless college. Then around and about with no transportation of my own. Happily living in Boston with only subways and bicycles and sidewalks. After ten years of great freedom, I once again felt trapped by the worst amenity of the modern era.

Joan, of course, never agreed. She loved driving, treated cars like a fashion necessity, felt they confirmed her worthiness to God. She has the true American spirit, where you prove how well you are doing to neighbors with your possessions. She missed having one in Boston, but bowed to practicalities. She was ecstatic to be free once more with something to get around in.

Ghost rolls out on his back from under the Dart, oil stains his white smock. "Hand me that big wrench over there, will ya?" he asks. "Oh, never mind." He sits up and smiles crookedly. "Clueless, aren't you?"

"Never did anything with cars," I mutter.

"What, no excuses for being a poorly functioning American boy?" he teases.

"I told you, I never liked them to begin with. Besides, nobody ever showed me anything about them, and one thing I learned right away from friends is that if you don't have the right tools, you don't even try."

"That's true," Ghost agrees. "You can't do much on these machines with a hammer and a pair of pliers. But tools don't cost much. You could always use your friends'."

"Nope," I sit down on a bench to the side. "None of my friends did anything with cars. We were into sports, nature, science, history. No cars in the bunch. In fact, I was the only one that ever got a car in high school."

"So, an entire subversive and perverse neighborhood," he laughs. "How did you all ever survive?"

"Somehow. Well. Cars were just low down our priorities. If our parents needed something, they'd just take it to the shop. And they let us borrow theirs, if we had to."

"Surprised about your father, though."

"That's true. He grew up on a farm. But I never saw him even open the hood, as far as I can remember. Of course, my memory might be selective."

"Repressed, you mean."

"I wasn't afraid to drive, you know. Just didn't see the point of fixing the damn things. Like Dad, really."

"So you grew up incompetent," he walks over to a cluttered workbench. "You could have corrected that at any time, you know. You had years."

"Life's too short," I have a hard take on this. "We can't know everything, we can only do so much, you need to specialize and concentrate and let some people do what they know how to do better."

"I thought you wanted to be Mr. Renaissance."

"Even Da Vinci didn't do everything," I say stubbornly.

"Oh, I think Da Vinci would have taken to cars like a fish to water."

"Well, not Da Vinci maybe, but most of the Renaissance people. Can't see Galileo under a crankcase."

"Yeah, that's true. You're not so much Renaissance as spoiled Aristocrat, you know. Only doing the dirty work you want to do."

"Well, sure. Sounds like the good life to me."

"Will you please now hand me that wrench." He slides back under the chassis.

Wayne had not grown up in a car culture. His mom would never drive—something psychological terrified her of accidents and traffic. Perhaps he had a touch of that. Maybe it was simply that he had spent so much time roaming fields on foot and by bicycle that he never felt the attraction to ride to distant places with motor thrumming and wind rushing. Maybe it was just time and opportunity.

He wasn't really afraid of automobiles. He knew the way they worked, he had no trouble driving, he had a handy map in his head anywhere he might be. But wasting time in a car going somewhere was no pleasure to him, no matter how wonderful the destination itself.

He had learned the common lore of the era. Changing tires, for example, and adding antifreeze every fall before the deep cold set in. Putting in oil, verifying the various liquids, changing wipers. Even changing oil—which in those pre-environmental-consciousness days meant mostly taking off a bolt, letting the dirty oil drain into a pan, and finding a place in nearby bushes to pour it out, before replacing the bolt and refilling.

Later on, he dabbled in trying to fix rusting side panels with various compounds and cloths, which kind of worked but never came out looking as good as the advertisement on the package indicated. At least the car looked reasonably whole from a distance, which was what more or less mattered.

He saw it as a necessary inconvenience. Commuting was an evil he had to endure to have any kind of reasonable job. Living where he and Joan wanted meant that a car was required for—well just about anything at all. He considered himself fortunate that he could actually walk somewhere for a paper on Sunday morning. Everything else was just too spread out.

As time went on we became more affluent. Eventually, we could even afford another car, then a newer one (aided by my company), and there was a certain comfort in knowing that they would work. The cars, meanwhile, got better and better. Rusted out bottoms became all but unknown, even side panels could last for decades. That was offset somewhat by the fact that the thinner sheet metal of which they were made could be easily dented or twisted in the most minor encounter with nature or machinery.

But I never saw them beyond necessity, even now. If I could live without a car of my own, I would happily do so. A day without driving is to me a joy. I worry too much when I am in control, knowing how many things could go wrong, I even worry when I let my mind fog and I find I have arrived somewhere without remembering the details of the route. Now that my eyes are less sharp, I worry about darkness. I know that nobody else agonizes over such things, but for me tons of moving metal—not only my own but all those surrounding me—are constant dangers.

Maybe for that reason, they all look the same. As I say to make Joan—who has an eye for all the nuances—very angry, "just a box on wheels. Goes. Stops. That's it." That's all they ever were to me, and still are, and I find the most incomprehensible of the passions of those around me is that devoted to having a better, newer, or nicer car.

"You know," says Ghost, standing behind his desk in the waiting area of his tiny service station, "we have some really clean, nice, newer cars for sale in back."

"That's ok," I reply, "just take care of this one for now."

"But don't you care what people think? You're moving up in the world, you know. This is an important first impression."

"I don't need first impressions to be my car."

"But all the consultants drive Mercedes. You've seen them."

"I don't really care. All that shows is that they don't know what to do with their money. They don't know that much about code either, as far as I can tell."

"But it's the aura they give off, that they are better than you."

"Silly, then, anyone who thinks that way. A car is just like—well like underwear. Necessary, but who cares how it looks?"

"Joan cares. Neighbors judge you by what you are driving. Hell, relatives judge you by what you arrive in."

"Their problem," I repeat stubbornly. "I'll stick to my realities, thank you. Better things to spend money on than a shinier chrome strip along the side."

"Which reminds me," adds Ghost, "yours is coming off. I epoxied it back on for you."

"Thanks. I'm sure that will get me a raise."

"Sarcasm has no place with automobiles," he says stiffly.

"Sarcasm was invented to apply to automobiles," I retort. "Along with foppish aristocratic clothing and ever more beautiful and gigantic coffee-table books."

"What, exactly, is your problem?"

"No problem. Just don't get into all that. Box on wheels."

That distresses him, and he starts to add up the damages for the day.

Wayne remembered the trip a year ago, which was probably the low point of their relation with the Dodge Dart. He had finally taken a vacation week in July to go upstate to see Joan's parents, who spent the entire summer in their little cabin in the woods near Lake George. He had worked a full day on Friday, even getting out a little late. By the time they reached the Cross Island Parkway it was dark, but the stifling heat continued.

For some insane reason, the powers that be had decided to do massive construction work on the Throgs Neck bridge in the middle of the vacation season, on the one evening of the week when everyone was fleeing the city. This forced all traffic over to the Whitestone, and caused traffic jams for miles. They sat, with Gregory wailing in his car seat, hot and bothered, Joan choking from the fumes of all the traffic idling in underpasses all around them, Wayne watching the heat gauge anxiously. After hours going nowhere they made it to the bridge and started across.

In the middle of the span, there was very rough pavement, left over pot-holes from the winter. He banged over them and suddenly there was a lot of noise, off and on, from under the car. Something was dragging. He pulled over on the Bronx side, and checked, and noticed the muffler was hanging loose. Well, no help for it, just keep going. They headed on to the Thruway and late at night joined the mass of cars crawling into the Catskills and points further north.

Gregory kept screaming, Joan kept choking, Wayne kept watching. They were all now listening, as every time they went over a bump there would be a loud bang from underneath. The night stayed incredibly hot, around eleven they were finally free of most of the jam and had seemingly clear sailing the rest of the way, when a particularly loud crash was followed by a sound of thunder. Well, that was the end of that muffler.

Aware of the issues with fumes in enclosed cabins, they opened all the windows, but still had to smell rich exhaust and endure loud rumbles. With no choice, Wayne pulled off into the New Baltimore station, both to have the muffler fixed and to have Joan call her parents to explain what was going on here at midnight. The attendant looked under the car, agreed that the muffler was off, explained that there was nothing he could do about it. Back on the road, full gas tank, aware that they were waking night creatures and possibly the dead as they blasted by.

Finally, after what seemed forever, they reached Lake George and turned off on the road towards Lake Luzerne. It was only about ten miles into the woods to their destination, but high hills picked up the deep bass and seemed to echo it louder than possible. They were keenly aware of the roar as they continued through the dark unlighted lanes, two o'clock in the morning, fortunately all the police were probably in bed already. Gregory, who had been sleeping, had awoken and added to the din. Joan at least had some fresher air to breathe. All Wayne could do was go beyond frustration to laughter at an experience.

The next day they got everything fixed up in Glens Falls, taking the thunder chariot on another earth-shaking journey. One more story from the fine world of automobiles.

Having an old car was not mere stubbornness. We never even considered a car loan. We saved until we had enough, then used cash to purchase something used. Our car ran decently, was fairly reliable. All the rest was hoopla and expense. We obviously wanted to get good things for Gregory, and ourselves, but we knew that there was a basic level at which you had something perfectly adequate for the purpose, after which prices skyrocketed asymptotically, when you paid for inscrutable extra fluff that made no practical difference.

Fortunately, Joan's father wanted something a little newer than the old behemoth sedan he was driving, and within a year of moving to Babylon they were—amazingly enough—a two car family. We were grateful for the free gift, of course. On the other hand, it meant double the gas, double the repairs, double the inspections, double the aggravation. But Joan certainly needed a way to get out and do what was necessary, not to mention for finding a job.

Eventually we could afford better cars, paying cash, getting something solid and bourgeois. Not a Volvo, thank heavens, but Honda became Joan's guarantee of quality. However, that was far far in the future, and in Babylon we were quite content if the cars started in the morning and stopped when we pushed on the brakes and didn't come out costing us a fortune when we took them in to the shop.

"It sounds like you paid too much attention to that speech by Polonius when you were studying Hamlet way back when," notes Ghost, buffing a car in the bay alongside mine.

"What a mechanic that likes Shakespeare?" I laugh.

"More things in heaven and earth than are dreamt of in your philosophy," he retorts.

"What speech?"

"You know, 'neither a borrower nor a lender be.'"

"Ah, yeah, I did take that too much to heart. It was precisely the wrong time to follow that—American consumerism and commerce and success is entirely built on borrowing and lending. We were complete ducks out of water."

"And too stupid to change."

"Well, we liked not owing people money. We slept better."

"But on worse furniture in worse rooms ..."

"True. But nevertheless we slept better."

"And all this at a time when inflation made it really good to be a borrower—you were just stubborn fools."

"We never really discussed it like that. I guess we were just too naïve to care much."

"Discounting money is never a good thing, you know," he stares as if thinking. "I mean, look around, I had to borrow for most of this."

"What?" I ask astounded.

"Hypothetically, I mean. If I were a real mechanic and not a ghost. Borrowing lets you follow your dreams, get a handle, succeed, pay it back."

"And borrow some more. I get it. I didn't like the cycle."

"But it's the American way."

"I know that too. I still don't like it."

"No wonder you failed at success," he turns away scornfully. "Any immigrant would have done more."

"So what," I begin as the scene fades, but kind of half-hearted. He has a point.

No question, Wayne thought, they had to have a car. It was so much easier to arrange visits to parents for example, or take trips to various relatives or parks. There was no practical way to otherwise have a good job. There was no way, even with money, to alternately deliver food and other necessities to the house. This culture had trapped itself in the automotive dream.

It was probably a good thing. Every other culture apparently wanted to become like this. He ruefully admitted that once in a while he even accepted mobility as a wonder of the age. Yet, given full choice, he would much have preferred to do all travel by foot, by bike, or by public transit. A strange duck in an unfamiliar pond.

Anyway, once he had accepted the necessity, they made the most of it. Fanaticism has problems when carried against a daily reality. Joan's car, twice the pollution, and for what? Well, for a stable marriage and Joan's happiness and his sanity. He knew that was worth something. The planet was a bit too abstract to deal with. Joan—well not abstract at all. He could hear her now.

"Complain all you want," says Ghost, wiping his greasy hands on a nearby cloth, "but the internal combustion engine is all around and here to stay."

"At least during my lifetime, I guess," I agree. "Doesn't mean I have to like it much."

"Oh, you'd prefer taking care of a horse all the time?"

"No, I guess not. It just isn't ideal."

"Ideal, ideal," he scoffs. "Ideal is for adolescents and fanatics. Life is not ideal. You make the best you can with what is around. What's around are gas automobiles."

"It just seems so far from Earth Day and the Movement and all the other stuff I wanted to have happen."

"You and everyone else. But everyone else wised up sooner."

"I guess. I did manage to go years independently. I guess that counts somewhere in the cosmic balance."

"No such thing. Can't pay for an apple with it. You were just another dumb dupe."

"But cars are problems for the environment."

"People are problems for the environment. You're a people. So, commit suicide, why don't you."

"All right, all right. I've got my vehicle here in the shop, don't I? I've submitted to American reality."

"Stop sneering or sniveling. You're lucky."

"I know. It's a wonderful contraption that helps me do all I want."

"Finally got that right, Jack."

Well, no help for it, flash forward to 1986 or so, when I had to commute to Queens...

Brutally hot sun matched deafening roar of commercial traffic, train, and industry here in Long Island City. Wayne headed home after a long day fixing problems at Rozin Optical, happy to find his car still where he had parked on a forsaken side street. A few blocks later, even before he could turn east on Queens Boulevard, the heat gauge shot to maximum red and remained pinned. Warily he ventured onto an unknown but jammed four-lane street and clattered into the first service station he encountered.

"What's the trouble, guy?" asked a rough-looking middle aged man, with oiled cloth hanging from his belt. Wayne became fully conscious of his business attire, so out of place here.

"I don't know. The heat gauge is crazy hot. Never happened before. No idea of what it is." Visions of leaving his car here overnight in the middle of crime-filled nowhere, trying to get a bus or whatever home, getting back in the morning, worse finding it could not be fixed at all filled his head.

The mechanic looked at him oddly, as if he were some naïve visitor from another planet. He popped the hood, looked in, and laughed. With his rag he unscrewed the radiator cap and turned to Wayne as steam geysered out.

"Just no water, boss. You can fill that can over there and put some in yourself. Should be fine."

"Do you think it will hold until I get back to Babylon."

"Don't know. It should be ok for a while. If you have a leak, you can just keep filling it up as you go—buy a soda and fill it with water to take along. Watch out, though, it's really hot."

Wayne dutifully did as instructed, tipped the guy as well as he could, happy that he wasn't being charged, filled the bottle with water, and worried his whole long drive home.

Everything worked perfectly. His service station couldn't find any leak, and everything worked from then on, although he did learn to check fluid levels periodically to see what might be going wrong. But he never got over his amazement at finding civilization and courtesy so counter to his suburban expectations.

THE NEW NORMAL

STIFLING SUNDAY NIGHT around three am, Wayne woke from restless sleep, worried about end of month run, current state of planning for the new machine, problems with sales reports. He turned over and tried to return to sleep but lay awake in a sweat, helplessly unable to fall into welcome oblivion until morning. How would he remain fresh, so much to do? He glanced at his alarm, another few minutes had crawled by.

Mondays were always the worst. Whatever could go wrong in two days always would go wrong. Other non-computer issues built up over the weekends, and although he was not directly involved, if he impacted any of those issues by taking IT off-line for any reason there would be nasty repercussions all around. Anything that fell behind on Monday generally kept everything else delayed all week. All systems were running on knife's edge to begin with.

Fortunately, he had his organized lists and routines. He could fall back on them and fitfully attempt recovery if necessary. But his mind was racing ahead of any actual problems Nobody, after all, had called. Things were probably just fine. Another few minutes had gone by.

But what about all the plans, the big meeting Wednesday? He still had to finalize his part of the presentation, and submit his list of issues to be discussed to Joe. Unbidden, a long vision of worries about conversion flowed by in green bar printed format. Issues he was trying to sweep under the rug came out and danced in flickering fantasies off to the side of his purposeful attempts to avoid logical analysis of anything. Maybe he could unfocus and get a little drowsy. More time oozing, dawn a little bit nearer. Stupid.

Work faded a little off to the side of focus, and clouds of other things began clamoring. The house needed painting. The car sounded funny. They needed to get Gregory some educational toys. Joan had plans for the weekend that involved way too much time. Money—oh let's not think about money. Unfocus again, again. The electronic clock made no noise, but he heard time ticking by.

For years he had watched sitcoms and laughed. For decades he had delighted in comic strips about work and home. In all that time, he had remained aloof, a stranger in such a land, a mere observer from outside. Now he was living inside the sitcom and part of the comics. They were all true, even the extreme exaggerations. Phantasms rose up and assailed his serenity …

Loudly, the alarm went off and he struggled up to shut it off. It was already bright outside, he rubbed his eyes, closed the bedroom door, went to microwave coffee before his shower. Well, another week had arrived and here he was. Nothing to do but deal with it as completely and forcefully as possible. Maybe tonight he could get to bed early.

I hover in air two feet beyond a cliff wall, above a sheer drop into the canyon far below. Music plays, simplified pastel shapes come into focus, and I realize this is a cartoon. Ghost watches as I fall and smash a hole into dry sand, squeaks "beep beep", and races away in a cloud of dust. The music rises and silences, and Ghost wanders back. "So, welcome to the real world!"

"You've got to be kidding," I manage, as I climb out of my crater.

"No, no, it's perfect," he insists. "A metaphor, you know. Like, I'm success and normal life and you're just you, you poor soul, endlessly chasing me, endlessly being fooled."

"Crude. I know," I admit, raising a hand, "there are disturbing similarities. But there are also a lot more nuances and other perspectives."

"Well," notes Ghost, "I could do a sitcom easily enough." He snaps his fingers and we are standing in a large, comfortable, oldish living room with stairs and television. "I mean, it almost looks like the one in West Babylon. But the trouble with these shows," he goes on, "is that they really ignore just about everything and hardly ever hit the more painful and idiotic aspects of being. Mind candy, really."

"And Roadrunner isn't?"

"One of the jewels of American philosophy," he grins, turning on the TV which is, of course, showing a cartoon. Pick your poison."

"Why don't we just start here, while I get adjusted?"

"Suit yourself. Anyway, kid, you finally fit into the mainstream, cartoon or sitcom, whatever. Your family looks like every family, your career looks like every career, you are just Mr. Average Joe. Ain't that grand? The best years of your lives ...."

"Quite a shock. I did feel like I was waking up in some kind of stage production, lots of times. Seemed as if I had lost almost every shred of free will. Alarm goes off, get up, on the road, deal with work good and bad, on the road back, dinner, get energy to help with Gregory for an hour, collapse and try to relax and recover for the next day. Weekends filled with chores and family. Always more to do, never enough time, always something else clamoring for attention. And, yeah, all those TV situations seemed to be playing out sometimes."

"Being a sensitive artist type," he drawls sarcastically, "you no doubt hated every minute."

"No, not at all," I remember. "For one thing, I had very little time or energy for deep philosophical consideration of the meaning of life and my own place in the cosmos. Just getting the code to work and Gregory to sleep was reason enough to satisfy my universe."

"Freedom through work," he snaps sarcastically. "The American universal opiate. Meaning encapsulated in what you do to earn a living. No wonder I have to resort to popular entertainment to deal with such hollow constructs."

"That's not fair. It was really wonderful to be part of something, to own a house and car, have a family with expectations, enjoy the camaraderie at work, be pleasing Joan and all the relatives, and not worry about stupid unanswerable vagueness all the time."

"Drinking deeply of the Kool Aid."

"Maybe. Hey, it was a change, and a good one. Here I was, five years on, and my outlook suddenly focused in tune with that of everyone else. It was like swimming downstream instead of up. I was tired all the time, often frustrated, but generally we were in fact happier than we had been in a while."

"A nice illusion," Ghost's voice speeds as the desert fades back in. "Better look up," he scoots off into the sunset "beep beep." I barely have time to glance up at the Acme anvil descending directly overhead.

"Just Mr. Average American," thought Wayne, waiting for a light to change on a cool, clear April morning. "Off to an average job to support an average house and family in the average suburbs with an average future ahead. "

For someone who had never really, secretly, considered himself average, this was an almost frightening transformation. It was as if a genie or fairy god-mother had waved a wand over the last few tumultuous years and turned everything upside down and inside out. No more arts and artist, no more worry about the world, it was all buying diapers and cutting grass and pleasing the boss. No more doing what he wanted, his schedule was stretched tight as a drum. Any thought of changing the world was not merely futile, but totally banished from what he did have time to ponder.

He couldn't quite decide if it was good or bad, he admitted. Maybe like most things a little of both. Not extreme, not the best of times and worst of times, but with the contradictions of what he had dreamed of doing and where he had ended up. Mostly, though, he realized it was a lot of fun. He and Joan had been released from a static pool with little money, where thoughts and moments were free but little else was. Now they were riding along a strong current of affluence, objects appearing like magic, rapids sometimes threatening to capsize the canoe, but with lots of stuff and always satisfactions turning to requirements for more. If nothing else, he could accept it as an adult form of amusement park ride.

Keeping perspective was just about impossible, of course. Being alone in the car on the way to work was about the only period of the day when he even had an opportunity to do so. Most of that was stolen away by worries about what he would encounter once he arrived, but once in a while there would be a clearing in the constant storm and—here he was. Phew.

He didn't try to fool himself that he could walk away, or change back, or restart. He was bound by chains both external and deeper inside. All his earlier upbringing kept insisting that what he was doing now was the right thing to do, what he had been pursuing before had been a juvenile fantasy. All his surroundings—work, extended relatives, parents, peers—reminded him every day that he was finally a fine upstanding young man doing his part for God and country and truth and justice. Advertising which he had previously ignored or mocked ironically now spoke directly to their plans and desires.

On the other hand, he could hardly go about weeping and shouting "woe is me." They had never lived so comfortably. Joan was happy. Gregory was a joy. Wayne loved his garden and his yard and even the huge basement with all its immense possibilities. He liked being taken seriously at work. He was proud of becoming daily more competent at his career, and truly enjoyed trying to meet the challenges thrown at him like daily crossword puzzles. Maybe being average in this world was not so bad after all. Why had he ever bought into that alternate universe of being "excellent" or "meaningful"— fine sounding goals, increasingly nebulous?

Finally, the light changed. Automatically, he was through the intersection and up Spagnoli road, only one car in front. Me, he thought, rush hour, traffic, gulped cup of coffee, collar shirt, tie, jacket. Me. He still couldn't believe it. He might accept it, he might even like it, but in his new shallow way of approaching life, he knew he would never worry about understanding.

The meeting was in Joe P's office, at ten am sharp. Wayne would be the most junior player present, backing up his immediate boss Joe D and his boss Alan. The nice thing about these meetings in this office, Wayne reflected as he sat down with his notepad in hand, was that they were short, to the point, and ended on time. Joe P was a busy man, the vice president of finance, and watching over the IT department was sort of a hobby that had fallen under his jurisdiction. After all, he had a nodding acquaintance with electronic spreadsheets, which was a lot more than most other executives at his level.

"I see we had another problem earlier this week …" began Joe P, inauspiciously.

"Sorry," mumbled Wayne. "It was a minor thing, I changed a sales report and it had a divide by zero error …." Nobody cared about the technical details, but it made it seem he knew what he was talking about. "We just don't have time to recover from a problem any more."

"Maybe we should freeze the system," said Joe P. "Tell everybody no more changes until we upgrade."

"Impossible, Joe," said Joe D. "There's always something and usually it's important. Sales keeps making these new conditions and items. Besides, our inventory numbers are getting immense and we are adding customers by the bucketload. Even with a frozen reporting system, my staff can hardly keep up with the input and changes."

"There's no easy way to upgrade this particular model," added Alan. "It was never really meant for this kind of service. Frankly I'm amazed at how well your staff keeps it going, all things considered."

"But it's what we have," replied Joe D. As one of the people who had originally picked it out a few years ago he was a little defensive.

"It was a great choice for the company you were then," oiled Alan. "But not for the company you are now. And the world-class company we are becoming requires something more, world-class hardware. Honestly, Joe, I don't think this particular manufacturer can make the grade into that arena."

"Their salesman says they can," responded Joe D. "Their team is coming in next week. Right Wayne?"

"Yes, on Tuesday. I have a list of questions and a lot of information to show them," Wayne pulled out the prepared folders. He had been well briefed, Joe D and Alan had gone over this with him extensively yesterday.

"And IBM will be in later in the week," noted Alan smugly. He knew where this was all going, and felt like the orchestra director.

Alternate, but hardly conflicting, agendas filled the background thickly. Joe P was nominally in charge and supposedly rationally watching the costs and benefits. But any vice president was excited about the chance to hugely expand his department and budget. Especially when other departments were doing so quickly. He wasn't about to put on the financial brakes, but he did have to be able to justify it to the owner who would finally approve any huge outlays.

Joe D was in the blossoming period of an MBA career, fresh out of a big accounting firm, lured away by the prospects of growth and the ability to work where he lived, not taking the hours-long train commute to the city each day. He was comfortable with big iron, although cynical about some of the claims, but he knew he was riding a great wave and he could surf it until it either panned out here, or he cut to his next huge pay increase. He didn't want to be part of any disasters, but in any case it would not be his fault. He just needed to make sure he stayed in it well enough to get the deserved credit.

Wayne was starry eyed and grateful to be doing computers all the time, coding and learning and churning out stuff people admired. That part was pure heaven, even solving the problems. He enjoyed training and working with the staff, although they were often resistant. He had developed, finally, a level of trust. He was excited to be part of decision making, at least as far as providing information and common sense observations. And it would be a foolish programmer indeed who did not glance at the want ads and notice that IBM experience paid a hell of a lot more than any other. And that there were an awful lot of IBM jobs out there, if worst came to worst.

The wild card was Alan. Recently hired by the president of the company personally, answering to nobody but the president, floating above petty vice presidents in some niche of his own, a former consultant necessarily tooting his own horn constantly. He was charged with getting this tiny company through the various minefields of respectability and growth to the grand vision of an American Stock Exchange IPO and arrival with the big boys in the industry. His eye was on the prize—options unlimited, wealth immense. His path was through IBM, but he had to play his cards coolly and seem to be evaluating all options without bias. He saw himself as pulling all the important strings in the background as everything surged forward. To him, a fully capable IT operation was sine-qua-non of getting where they needed to go.

"Ok, that's it then," stated Joe P, looking around after hanging up his phone on some other business. "We'll meet two weeks from now, same time, and you can give me a summary of the meetings this week and you're your conclusions and recommendations." Wayne took his final notes as every stood up in dismissal and headed out the door.

"Wayne, stop by Joe D's office on the way," said Alan. That wasn't hard, it was right across the hallway. In a couple of minutes the debriefing was underway. "Did you guys get all that."

"I have it here," said Wayne, lifting his notepad. "I'll type it up as soon as I get back to the terminal and clear up any emergencies, should have a printout to you within an hour or so." His typing necessarily went into plain typewriter-style text, there was no word processor available on his machine. For the same reason, the reports were on huge green-bar paper. Nobody complained. They were happy to have anyone who could type and didn't mind keeping minutes. Wayne found it was an important learning technique for his rapidly expanding business acumen.

"So we all know what we have to do," Alan continued conspiratorially. "I expect some tough questions and real hard answers to be available. I need facts, this operation is going to cost a fortune and there has to be solid evidence that it is worth it."

"Wayne and I have that under control, sir," said Joe D. "You can count on us."

Alan got up to leave, "I do. I think this will be really great for all of us. See you later." Out.

Joe D sighed. "Ok, more work. You know who's gonna have to do all the number crunching. Do you need anything else?"

"No, I'm fine."

"All right, go take care of business. I see the reports were a little off again this morning,"

"Rounding," mumbled Wayne.

"Jacob doesn't like rounding,"

"I know, but…."

"I'll take care of it. Ok, let me have the writeup when you get it ready, no later than tonight."

"No problem. See you in a little while."

Wayne had been enwrapped in the American Dream, it began to seep throughout his outlook. America is always self-advertised as individual freedom, responsibility, and opportunity, which is often very true. But the recognized coin for freedom, responsibility and opportunity is cash. Living in solitude in some mountain meadow or scraping by as an urban flaneur may represent complete freedom, but none of the in-laws will understand. No, the American Dream must be accompanied by its darker companion, American Greed.

Wayne had been remarkably free of all that. Once in a while, of course, he would wish he had more money, or more recognition. It was always nice to have enough to eat and a warm house and few worries about paying bills. But it had never really been at the top of his list of problems, which were more concerned about art and life and the meaning of the universe. All of that had changed dramatically.

Suddenly there were visions of limitless possibilities, incredible wealth, wonderful cash flows stretching into the future and beyond. The company was expanding, in boom time, no end in sight. People were being hired right and left. Sales were up, profits were good, every day was more, more, more. If the raises were not quite as much as anticipated, at least they were decent and regular, and the title on the door kept ratcheting onward from programmer to IT guy to DP department supervisor. With more and more promises, more and more hopes.

Options. He had never heard of options, suddenly everyone was talking about them. Slips of worthless paper, redeemable someday for fabulous amounts, after Webcor goes public. So we must all pull together, hour after hour, day after day, at work and at home to make that IPO a possibility. It was one great team, pulling together toward a finish line after which they could all lie panting on the grassy infield and enjoy the fruits of their labors. Just not today—there's too much to do.

Even Wayne had been around long enough to discount a lot of the hype. He was happy to be caught up in the possibility, of course, but there was enough cynicism remaining to convince him that this represented an awful lot of "bird in the bush" scenarios. Maybe his outside observations back at Kurzweil and the rude scuttlebutt he had heard at Mergenthaller had conditioned him well. He knew much of this might never happen, or happen in ways not foreseen, and he took it all with a grain of salt.

And yet—and yet he was still surfing the wave himself, for his own reasons. This was an immense jump in his career. His real skills were blossoming, his resume was becoming incredibly impressive, he had more poise and understanding. He knew he was worth more, almost by the hour, not least because he could handle emergencies and deal with users, managers, computers, and recovery with a firm hand and with little panic. He was learning the finer elements of systems design as his superiors actually tried to design systems—not only computers but inventory control, accounting, sales. It was an education that could not be purchased except as he was doing it—in hours, sweat, and tears.

And if all else failed, it was a step into the big time. Somehow he had ended up going from little dinky typewriter-sized personal computers through DG and DEC mini-computers and now was ready to ratchet up into the lofty pay realms of IBM. Sure, he would probably never make as much as the professionals who had been perched there for years or decades, but demand was intense, and those who knew anything were few, and the want ads each Sunday were thick. If the current position somehow fell apart, well there were fertile fields apparently all around just waiting for him to apply.

So, no matter what the problems, he went to work happily dreaming the American success story, part of the future, and as far as the future went, no worries.

Everything was black, white, and gray. The back of the room had a comfortable old couch, a nondescript picture, a lamp. In the foreground a rug and coffee table. Off to the side a door, presumably to the kitchen. Jarringly, nothing at all on one side—just a black space with a white hole in the middle, and a constant background murmur. With a mild shock I realize I am on a television set. Ghost, dressed in a cute little jacket with a red beret jumps onto the stage/rug from the darkness smiling hugely.

"Wayne, baby, welcome to Your Life!"

"What?"

"A sweet family show with bumbling father, clever mother, rambunctious child, all major cares banished, each minor problem the center of an episode. Didn't you read the script?"

"Of all the cheesy…."

"But, but, but, none of that now," he pulls out a cigarette and puffs away. "You know it is true, that's why it wounds so much. No grand thoughts of arts or politics ever echo in these chambers! Mid-middle, lower-middle, nothing-at-all-middle class—that's you."

"But …"

"And, babe, you love it. Don't you. Admit it."

"Well, it has been a refreshing change from bohemian poverty, I guess. Stressful."

"But worth it kid, right? Here you go," offstage shout, "Is the kitchen set ready? OK, hurry it up, we need to move this along. Where's Joan? Well tell the makeup guys to make it fast." He turns back to me. "You couldn't be more like a sitcom if you had sat down and planned it out."

"But it's only been a few years. A temporary necessity, you know …"

"Ah, but you relish the role. You've completely wrapped yourself in it. You're precisely where you want to be. All hopes and grand ambitions stripped away, the core revealed. And the core is," he gestured grandly, "all this!"

I found what seemed to be a clever comeback. "By your own metaphor, then, I am an actor in a television series. Very well. True when the show is on. But when I step off the set, I am back to being myself, the real me. The artist, the thinker, the secret person who is looking at the world and trying to do something meaningful eventually …"

"When you have the time …." he notes maliciously.

"… when I have the time."

"But time is the issue, isn't it?" Ghost demands. "When do you ever get off the set? In the car going to work or taking everyone shopping? Visiting the relatives? Working at your regular mid-level job? Mowing the lawn, for God's sake? I don't see an hour—not even a minute—off camera for years."

"I do have times to relax and think, once in a while. I still think about great issues and art …"

"Hardly ever. Not enough to matter. And even if so, what have you ever done about them. The closest you get to a paintbrush now is a wide one to recoat yet another room with Glidden beige. No, this set is truly, actually, the real you. Hey, you loafers over there, you think we pay you to stand around?! Places!"

"I don't have to do this. Let me out."

"Oh, you have to do this. Contract. Now get ready, you know the routine. Walk in the door, dinner almost ready, tired from the hassles of a technical day at work that you hardly discuss. Cue! " He leaps off the stage and out of sight. "Action."

Resignedly, I open the front door firmly and enter in my sports coat and tie. "Joan, I'm back!"

Compared to Boston, Wayne and Joan had never acquired so much. So much income. So much stuff. So many hopes. So many possibilities. All was wonder and becoming and grand vistas just over the next hill. And yet …

Oddly, they seemed to inhabit an ancient Greek fable. Their income stream was far larger than anything they had ever imagined a while ago, and kept rising. But, discouragingly, the pool into which the money fell never began to fill up. Most of that was because the pool itself kept enlarging. There were new bills, new requirements, new demands. No matter how much money they seemed to have—and in absolute terms it certainly seemed like an awful lot—in actuality they continued just scrape by. And in relative terms they seemed to be falling behind everyone else, as Joan constantly pointed out.

Issues with time were even worse. Supposedly, owning a car put everything into instant reach. You could save time going to the supermarket or commuting to work or finding a nice park. No more wasted minutes walking to the store or taking an uncertainly scheduled subway somewhere. But sitting in the car seemed to multiply beyond all reason, until it was more truly their home than their house itself. That vehicle also had to be fueled, and inspected, and repaired. Their house required attention with painting and various small chores—there was infinitely more to take care of than in the apartment. Not to mention the yard.

And, like icing that was thicker than the cake, there was Gregory. A child takes an awful lot of time and money—hours playing, hours worrying, hours doing basic parental duties, open wallet. They had known that, of course, from working with children at the schools, but they had not participated as parents and they found that the situation changed the equation.

Prioritizing became an obsession. When to do what, how to afford what, what to decide and what to put off. Arguments, agreements, resentments, acceptance, strains on relationships and self image. All in a good cause, all happy, but all nevertheless tense.

So in spite of good fortune, fortune was proving a mixed blessing. Envy kept coloring their observations. Was this a dream or nightmare? What made it bearable was that obviously the rosy future would soon dawn so much better.

The obvious modern American solution to all this—certainly the standard solution for our peers—was to borrow. Borrow money to pay back in better times, borrow time to catch up on later when we have some free moments, borrow for today because the limitless future can easily get it all back—it's a lifeline into perceived infinity.

We never borrowed very much. The mortgage was a necessity, but mostly that was all we ever had, it made us uncomfortable, and we got rid of it within a decade. Credit cards were paid off each month, bills were cleared as they came in, no purchases were made of anything unless we had the cash on hand to cover them. From a cultural perspective, that was all pretty stupid, and we could have lived far better by taking on some debt.

But the problem was, we never trusted the future quite as much as everyone else. Ours had not been an easy road, and we had no illusions that the coming years would always be fat and pleasant. We rather expected the worst all the time. It was easy to imagine losing a job and being out of work—we had gone through that, it didn't seem at all unusual. It was even easier to imagine the next job—whatever it might be—paying far less than the current one. You just didn't know. We had never ridden a gravy train with smoothly certain destination. Our model was the LIRR—crowded, slow, frequent stops, possible derailment—heck, we might even be on the wrong line by accident. That would be hard enough to handle even if we were solvent. Owing money which we might not have into the future made us extremely nervous.

So, for the most part, we refused to borrow. We kept our plans immediate, not too much projecting out twenty or thirty years. We kept our purchases limited to cash on hand. We acted like poor people always do, except poor people cannot get others to extend them credit. We were our own creditors, and we refused money to our clients.

That doesn't mean we totally ignored tomorrow. We simply pushed our dreams, rather than our debts, into the future. Some future time I would paint, and think. Some future time Joan would redo the house or buy a better one. Some future time we could buy a nicer car. We were, after all, fully Americans, and we accepted that usually tomorrow was better for most people. So we dreamed into tomorrow, and made do today, and staggered on in life with somewhat less than we might have had. It helped us sleep better.

Tomorrow, like most tomorrows, eventually turned into today. What we discovered, just like those people running up debts, is that tomorrow with all its promises is always yet to come. Today, with all its problems, is always here.

We were usually grateful that we had never stacked too much—particularly debt—into tomorrow which would start off each day in a still deeper hole.

Sitting in a comfortably padded seat in the dark, vaguely aware of a huge room with high ceiling, a beam of light slashing through dust and low murmurs and in front of me a flickering black and white movie as organ music swells around. The tiny figures, dressed as old policemen, are dashing about much too fast, running after cars and trucks, falling down, totally ineffective. There would be laughter, except that I am the only audience. Except, of course, for Ghost, who materializes as an usher next to me.

"Interesting picture," he says. "They don't make them like this any more."

"For good reason," I retort. "How much of this plotless stupidity can anyone watch."

"Oh, I think it has moments of truth," he answers. "Consider how much it resembles your own chase through life after wealth and acceptance and meaning."

"Very unkind," I mutter.

"It would be, except really it looks like just about everybody is in the same position. From an outside perspective, all of you really look very much the same, you know. Dressed pretty much alike, running around frantically, chasing after one uncatchable inconsequentiality to another. Even if you manage to catch up and hang on for a minute—like that one there," he gestured in the dimness "—you are almost immediately thrown off and have to jump up, dust off, and start running again."

"And you, of course," I say sarcastically, "would be the outside perspective."

"Well, why not. And you have to admit, you often had a small part of you that felt the same way and looked out with the same cynicism."

"What me, cynical?" I smiled. He has touched a true point.

"After the reel is over—shorter than any of you ever want it to be—what has really happened? The cars still race around and the people chase after them and even your footprints in the dust are soon erased as they film the next feature."

"Well, aren't we the cheery one today. I thought this was one of the most brilliant years."

"Surely so on the outside, but ..."

"Ah, you and your stupid metaphysics. The outside is what we live through. Like those cops, improbably chasing each other and going nowhere, who all believe they are just doing what they should do."

"Exactly my point ...." Ghost begins.

"And—what you do not understand—quite happy to be doing so."

The first business trip since Boston took Wayne to a Utah suburb south of Salt Lake City. He and Joe and Joe were to check out and begin integration of a bonded warehouse operation that Webcor was to take over. A lot of merchandise was now being sold on the West Coast. Since it was coming in from the Far East it made complete sense to have the customs inspection here, rather than back in New York, avoiding shipping twice across an entire continent.

Business trips for Wayne were always less fun than they seemed for other people. He was always more of a homebody—he had his place the way he liked it and plenty to do—and especially when other people were involved he found most trips simply involved being trapped in a hotel with coworkers with whom he had already spent the entire day. The only odd thing about the accommodations here was that at dinner the restaurant was not allowed to serve liquor—so they would all tramp outside to a liquor store conveniently located next door, buy tiny little bottles of spirits, carry the booty back in brown paper bags, and pour them into glasses conveniently and conventionally provided. Mostly, the evening was achingly boring.

Daytime on site was great fun. An electronic link was to be provided, a terminal or two to allow real time updates by the staff back to the home office. He was to take requirements, make preliminary designs, work out how to implement and train. Since they were in the middle of changing computer systems, he was completely building castles of air on clouds of promises. The promises of IBM that everything would work as marvelously well as the salesmen claimed, the promises of the consultants that the new systems would match and far surpass the crude computing they already had, and of course his own naïve belief that by looking over an operation and talking to a few people he would be able to capture in flowcharts exactly what would be happily accepted by everybody.

Hour after hour he talked to the cheerful folks—after all, for them chatting with these guys was a lot easier and more pleasant than doing actual warehouse work. A fine plan took place. He didn't actually make many promises, but everything was implied. Everyone was going to be part of the grand and lucrative adventure, riding on a spiral of immense and unending growth. Excitement was contagious.

After three exhausting days, they all flew back with notes and signatures and expanding expectations unmarred by any hint of reality. Nice people, they all agreed, it will be a pleasure to work with them. Another story in the marvelous tale of living through boom times.

So here I was, all the things I had never expected nor even wanted to be. Starting with remaining alive, six years after I had confidently predicted my demise at the romantic age of thirty. Living in suburban normality, after I had sworn the bohemian, counter-cultural oaths while trying to be aware of great ideals like society, the planet, art and meaning. The head of what could not be a more traditional nuclear family after preaching alternative arrangements for a decade. A full time manager after accepting that true happiness was in artisanship. Nine to five job, which as was tradition was really seven to seven after you counted the commute and real hours put in, even excluding the time on weekends. I could not have been more astonished if a fairy godmother had turned me into a pumpkin.

Adaptability in humans is innate and legendary. More intriguing by far than any of the actual modifications was how easily I adjusted to them. I was content to get up and drive to work, happy to contribute to meetings in Amerikan Corporate Culture, excited to take Gregory to the local parks, even willing to accompany Joan to big box stores, malls, and supermarkets all weekend long. A study in being coopted, shouted my inner self. Just doing what must be done, responded a more practical voice.

Probably those extremely difficult and crazy years from the end of Boston to beginning of Babylon had been responsible for the growth in my maturity, if growth it was. Being whacked around with almost no control makes any bit of stability seem a refuge in the madness. At least I was not getting on trains at six in the morning, sweating in subways, drinking with the business crowd all lunch hour. And the future, for once in my life, looked pretty damn promising. Nor was life here in real vanilla America nearly so bad as had been preached by all the cultish counter-culture books and newspapers. When I felt guilty, I simply assured myself I was finally getting mine after a long time coming.

Another big, and probably overriding, part of the acceptance was the sheer joy of learning so much that was new. Being a homeowner and a father and responsible citizen, for example. An infinitely expanding technical expertise in a growing and rapidly changing field. Social studies in political navigation through the power minefields at work. Confidence is a sure-fire way to get you on top of the world.

From 1983, everything looked confidently straightforward. I would be well off. We would be successful. Everything would work out perfectly. Finally, life was back on a smooth track to the glorious promised lands.

Black and white again, but no greys and no movement. "What the heck," I wonder, amused at my mild language and surprised to see the words typed over my head in a balloon connected to me by a trail of bubbles. Oh, comic book land.

"Neat, isn't it?" asks Ghost, another vaguely indicated almost stick figure in my modernist sparse dimensional cube, as another pointy headed figure is tiny in the distance.

"Sparse." I reply. "What's the reason for all this?"

"Illustration of your futile attempts at work, the idiocies of management, the wisdom of the artisans, the human comedy centered on the water cooler. You know, succinct parables of the day, quick funny and true notes …"

"Not so funny," I mumble into another balloon, which fails to indicate that I am mumbling. "It's missing all the important nuance."

"Ah, but comedy must," states Ghost. "We are mocking the true essence of the situation."

"No, you are making something funny by draining out reality. Everything is more complicated and reasonable than you strip it down to. It's like the drawing …"

"What's wrong with the drawing?" Ghost looks around, alarmed.

"Stereotyped outlines of objects, fill in the blanks. A real desk never looks like this."

"Barbarian. Bourgeois. You miss the point."

"Lack of reality detail is the point. Just like the desk, your setup of 'funny' notes is a trivial amusement, having nothing at all to do with what's really happening."

He gives up. The lines fade. "Hell with you." He sulks off in a fading cloud.

His paper (Day—Timer) hourly scheduling calendar had filled up frighteningly. The list of to-do fixes and projects at work grew longer by the day. His internal off-and-on remembrances of tasks was crammed with things already overdue. There was never enough time, never enough energy, each day was further behind.

Wayne knew that soon it would all be better. The sun would inevitably shine. Slack times would return when he could catch up. After the new computer, after the IPO at work. After the weeds were gone and the vegetables were ripening in the garden. After the latest toy or book or necessity for Gregory had been duly played with or read. After Joan had a day free from her constant daily chores. After the car was finally fixed up for good.

The future kept arriving as expected. What it contained was surprising—not a day full of time to fill with the left-overs of today and yesterday, but a day filled to the brim with new demands. A day whose list of what must be accomplished somehow slopped over the hours to be found and spilled into his calendar and lists for the future.

Well, he contented himself, obviously tomorrow was too close to today. It will all be different next year. Filled with such hope, he staggered on and, like just about everybody else, coped with overload.

A chorus line of dancers. A stage orchestra. Singing—"We're in the money…" A spectacle with spotlights, incidents, characters, magic, colors, curtains, music and—not much plot. "A little thin," I murmur to Ghost, sitting next to me.

"Well, what do you expect for fifty bucks these days?" he asks. "Even here in the upper balcony."

"But I'm in the money," I begin.

"No, you are in more money," he corrects. "You're just learning the fundamental principle that drives your society—everybody else has more and," he held up an accusing finger, "it's all your fault."

"What? But I'm doing so well…"

"Think then," he continues implacably, "how well you would be doing if you had not fiddled away the last decade. Hah? Hah?"

Hoopla on the stage. Scantily dressed top-heavy ladies with sequins. Overdressed men in makeup. A sincere young tenor "It is only a paper moon …."

"Maybe so," I admit, "but I liked the last ten years."

"At great cost, at great cost." He shows off his impeccable outfit. "You're on the train, finally, but always running to catch up, never nearly where everyone else who jumped on earlier will be, always haunted by your mistakes."

"I still don't buy it. I'm afloat. This is fun. And I wouldn't trade my past for anything."

"Suit yourself, fool." He turns back to the spectacle, where everyone is finishing up loudly "Tomorrow…."

Every Monday seemed to be like this. If it wasn't raining, it should be, but today it truly was just buckets, filling the air with spray and making potholes invisible. Car lights glared, brake lights flared, he sat immobilized inching forward. Some fender-bender had closed two lanes and the cops were finally making due, directing traffic alternately around the accident. He'd be late, of course, but so would just about everyone else. Except his bosses, of course, always punctually early.

He happily reflected on a lovely weekend, free from emergency calls, filled with happy incidents and family activities. Sure, very tiring, so tiring it was almost a relief to be going back to work, but fulfilling and satisfying. They were doing exactly what they should be doing. No worries.

In fact, this morning, drawing a deep breath, he admitted to himself he was glad to be alone trapped here in the car for a few minutes. Problems would be available soon enough. Right now he was incommunicado, no matter what had happened, for another ten minutes or so. A brief chance to step off the wheel and appreciate being.

He looked around, although there was not a lot to see through the grey downpour. Trees, industrial buildings, cars and trucks and more cars. Parts of Long Island were incredibly beautiful. This industrial heart corridor was anything but. It would take a warped aesthetic to find any joy here. Certainly drivers were acting as if they were trapped in Hell. "Don't these clowns know I have somewhere to go?" honked the horns, "Don't they know I'm important?"

The seconds clicking by and each raindrop beating down on the roof didn't care at all.

1984 REENTRY

BABYLON BOURGEOIS

HOME LIFE SOMETIMES seemed to have become a permanent round of shopping and appointments. Morning, evening, afternoon. Wayne wondered if this would last forever, or at least for decades, as he walked up and down the aisles of Pergament, a local home improvement store. He was looking for lumber to use in a project downstairs, and Joan wanted paving stones to frame a few of the flower beds. Gregory was walking alongside with him, taking everything in this morning, chattering constantly.

Most Saturday mornings were like this, while Joan rested and he did what he wanted to do. Later they might visit the record and video store, although he rarely bought anything, and then treat Gregory by going over to Shane's where he could ride the mechanical horse for a few quarters and maybe pick up some cheap toy.

Then tonight, after he was done with various house and yard cleanup, they would be off to Toys R Us and probably the mall to look at still more clothing for still another season as the child kept growing and growing. No long museum visits for them any more. Well, they'd lived that life for a while, might as well enjoy this one while it lasted.

Crimson swirls of mist, a dark cloaked figure with—right—a pitchfork. In the background all the expected muted screams and moans as distorted shadows play on the walls.

Ghost wears a bespoke dark suit, which somehow still looks a little shiny cheap. "I am happy you now feel you have arrived. One wish fulfilled, only a few to go…"

"If you say so, seems like a few more than that. I had a pretty secure career ahead of me and we appeared to be living at least the first stage of the standard American dream. "

"But already, it is hardly enough. No time for this, no dreams of that. Goodbye to fond visions of counterculture and art? Are you ready to use another wish?"

"Not hardly. I've never been that much of an ideologue. I adapt to the social environment pretty easy. I'm going to let the current scenario ride indefinitely."

"Give everything up? A cultural chameleon?"

"You could put it that way," I really feel no attraction for changing anything.

"Someone with no firm convictions at all?" he notes with accusation.

"No, not that," I said firmly. "I always knew exactly what I believed in and how it applied to me where I was. I just molded it to fit circumstances and environment."

"You would have made a good little Nazi," scolds Ghost.

"I don't know. I like to believe there were limits. And I never had trouble changing cultures completely when it was appropriate. No, I think I might have not supported evil, at least. I guess I could have been guilty of not resisting it enough. Anyway, in my life it never came up."

"That you know of," Ghost says. "The planet was being ruined."

"If so," I laughed, "I sure had a lot of help."

The standard puff of smoke, the standard fadeout, and I find myself back in traffic, going somewhere or other.

Joan was pregnant again, finally, which concentrated their future. In spite of losing his promising job, Wayne had instantly had three job offers from three interviews, all of them nearly equivalent to or better than the salary he had before. The house had shaped up with just about all the necessities taken care of, and they were mostly dealing with what they wanted rather than what they needed now. Oh, a few big ticket items remained—a better car, maybe even a nicer one for Joan. But all in all, their lives were firmly set, or mired, in middle class American Bourgeois.

They were usually so busy and drained just keeping everything going that they had very little time or energy to reflect on times past or what they might now be doing instead. Perhaps they lacked imagination, but the fact was they enjoyed this new experience entirely, for all its occasional problems. It was nice, for a change, to have a car to go places, to go anywhere they wanted. It was nice to buy the food they wanted when they wanted anywhere that was convenient. It was wonderful to have a large yard to fix up which was entirely their own, and a living area where they could make whatever changes they wanted without checking with or worrying about a landlord.

And centering it all, it was nice to be enveloped by family. Joan's parents frequently visited, and they went over on occasion. Wayne's parents came up once in a while and they always made two annual trips down to Pennsylvania. There were other relatives—Joan's Italian aunts and uncles and brothers and cousins and cousins various times removed. All in a constant interaction of lives moving forward, comparing, sharing, and sometimes envying one another. It was exactly as if they had changed the tv channel with the decade of their lives, and a world that had been getting pretty stale by the end of their twenties was rejuvenated into something completely new and fresh and fascinating.

And, of course, children. No matter what they had thought, nothing really prepared them for the total immersion of a toddler. The first child is a wonder. It is always the "first this" or "first that." Who does he look like. Isn't that cute. Camera always at the ready—he might be president some day. Worry about every bump and scratch and cough. Is language delayed, normal? What else should we be doing? Wayne had never encountered such intense concentration, not even in the midst of his most ferocious creating painting spells.

"I really need a newer car," complained Joan, plaintively, as they drove out Deer Park Avenue across the Island to visit her parents one Sunday. "I don't trust that old thing I'm driving. Dad can't keep driving over to visit me during the week. And I need to go shopping. It's just too small."

"I know, I know. We need a lot of things, I guess. Yeah, we better start looking."

"I'll get Dad to help, he has an idea of the dealers."

"We're making so much more than we used to, it's just strange how we sometimes feel like we're poorer. At least in cash."

"I know what you mean. Food costs a fortune and we sure don't seem to be eating as well as we did in Boston."

"I don't know how we did it," Wayne remarks.

"Well, back then, no car, no diapers, no gas, food for just us."

"No heating oil, no insurance, no lawn mowers and toys," he continues. "No matter how much you make, you just don't seem to get anywhere."

"And everybody else seems to have so much more," complains Joan. Wayne tuned her out as she began her litany of people down the street, mothers she knew in pre-school, old high-school friends, children in her parent's neighborhood, and assorted cousins and other acquaintances. It was all the same anyway, examples of those in much better financial, possibly cherry-picked, but he had to admit she had a point.

"Well," he finally broke in, "we did start late, but we had a good time. And now we are starting to catch up finally."

"I don't think we'll ever catch up," she sighed.

Gnawing at the core of our American dream, with its lush promises and genuine rewards, was a biblically sinful worm of envy. Keeping up with the Joneses. Obsessively comparing how we were doing to everyone else. Hauling out a golden financial yardstick to measure our place in the universe.

Our particular yardstick remained short, and obscenely elastic. We lived as an arrow of Zeno, never able to reach actual targets of security, happiness, and superiority to the neighbors. Always just halfway further along, always only halfway closer. Failures compared to someone or something else. Unable to achieve our own dreams. We hoped for satisfaction and contentment which are true enemies of the American Dream.

For years, I had rejected cultural orthodoxy. Joan had reconciled to being a poverty-stricken private-school teacher. Money didn't matter, we told ourselves, because we were engaged in socially important activities. Besides, we never really felt poor.

Joan's internal envy was those with an early family, lots of children, and a house. Wayne had dreamed fantasies beyond mere bourgeois materialism—become an artist, be a thinker, live a philosophically classic good life—all confused, all intangible, and none requiring more than a few bucks to get through a day or a year. Life had flowed incredibly rich, abundance ubiquitous, delicious experiences free for those who sought them. Dreams fulfilled in fantasy without much effort.

But now he had chosen that well-traveled fork to the normal world. He'd been infected by that envy of everyone, that nagging sense that he was losing or had lost already. He'd discovered many people at work making more money for doing less (no doubt, the feeling was mutual.) Few cared, because the future would be wonderful for those who strived. A glorious utopian destination was the mainspring of the American success story, only slightly tarnished by Vietnam and the recession of the Seventies. The new decade was roaring, and suddenly people were not merely hanging on, hoping to avoid destitute starvation, but grabbing all they could get as the economy opened floodgates of opportunity.

Wayne and Joan wandered a strange mental landscape. After more than a decade with no house, no car, no family, and jobs about which they always were apologizing, they finally had tickets to the standard-issue American dream. However the fine print on the back revealed that this was only an entry into a bigger set of concerns about how expensive the house, how new and prestigious the car, how large and intelligent the family, and jobs that measured up to various overblown expectations. Envy ruled the world, and much though he fought back, envy managed to creep insidiously into his daily outlook.

Some kind of swank party, opulent room, lots of beautiful people, swanky upper class affair. I'm even dressed in a dark suit. Ghost taps me on the shoulder, a shimmering apparition who is obviously seen by nobody else. He looks like a cartoon devil, horns, spiked tail, pitchfork, and bright red head to foot. "All yours," he whispers conspiratorially, "all yours just for the signing."

"Ah, what exactly are we doing here?" A shrimp off a passing tray is delicious.

"Showing you the benefits of joining our firm, of course. All this, and all you have to give up are some old outmoded and useless beliefs and ideals."

I laugh. "Oh, got it. Clever, Ghost, but hardly true."

"Of course it's true. Two cars, house in the suburbs, job in high tech capitalist computer companies, pollution, exploitation, consumerism. You've begun to acquire the whole damned package."

"Well, maybe, but,"

"And you no longer worry about pollution, poverty, aesthetics, social good, meaning and spiritual purpose."

"No time, really," I admit.

"So, there you are. Sold your soul, got the world, and now you are fully part of the madness."

"Not completely," I protest, "I still think about that other stuff."

"Maybe sometimes, when it's a bad day and you're waiting for the light to change. But mostly, I think you would agree, you've gone completely over. You have become them."

"There's just no time to consider all that other stuff ..."

"So your parents always told you whenever you babbled about the noble arts or the necessary counterculture, as I remember. You now know they were right."

"No, they weren't right. Neither was I. I've just achieved a degree of complexity and comprehension that necessarily involves a certain level of contradiction."

"My, my, my. No running-dog capitalist lackey could have put it better. Next you'll be voting Republican and defending the Vietnam War."

"Never! But our lives move on, and at some point ...."

"At some point starving artist and tattered speaker on a soap-box doesn't seem so appealing. Right."

"Well, some truth in that," I admit.

"So enjoy the party, boy. Have another cocktail. See you around," he laughs—what else—devilishly, "forever."

The first child, Wayne decided as he waited in line to pick up photos at the drug store counter, was very much like the first anything. First love, first painting, first vacation, first house. An almost orgasmic experience that you wanted to cherish and preserve forever, unsullied by any later regrets and not yet overlaid with any other similar experiences. And, like all firsts, something that had to be, as the film manufacturers advertised, "captured in pictures." So this packet of two dozen or so color snapshots would be added to a growing collection that eventually inhabited several cardboard shoeboxes whose contents were never again examined once stashed in the closet.

Everything about Gregory was an adventure. What he ate, when he got ill, how to discipline him, how to encourage him. Everything he did was wonderful—learning to talk, and walk, and eventually think, and explore and laugh, and even cry. Wasn't he just the most ... well no, there was some sanity. Joan and Wayne had interacted with a lot of children so they had a little perspective.

Still, it was impossible for new parents not to project. The future blossomed uncontrollably, and in that future no parent dreamed of children becoming failures or even just normal. It seemed to be part of human psychology that a child will grow up to be meaningful in some way by doing something. And yet, the real miracle was simply in being human.

Anyway, these first years were well and truly documented. Someday, they thought, they would look back and go through everything and laugh and remember. Whenever they got the time.

In the meantime it was all about what to do, how to react. They argued about discipline. What were the proper rules and how should they be enforced. What should be encouraged, what forbidden. How much leniency should be shown. They were pretty good at counterbalancing, again because they had worked together in the field. In those days they realized with horror that they edged into clichéd roles, Wayne as provider and Joan as housewife, although in fact Joan contributed from working at school almost as much as Wayne did, although with shorter hours. That division of labor was reinforced by her parent's attitudes, as they visited often to see the little wonder, also well photographed.

Public displays abounded. Holidays, birthdays, parties, and just plain get-togethers, showing Gregory off and eventually comparing him to other cousins as they grew. A marvelous and exciting rush, never to be repeated.

First born gets it all. A fact sadly noted by all the many children who are not the first-born of their families.

Perhaps only the young, the old, the childless can worry about their existential purpose in life. For us, all that angst was immediately removed with the cares and demands of a family. No need to worry about the which of wherefore, it was what to do with the baby who would not sleep. No time to consider the difficulties of the world, what should we do for dinner. No making large plans, it was just get through today and find maybe something interesting to visit together. All families may not be like that, but it was how Joan and I reacted to having one.

We had a large cast thinking much the same way and supporting that outlook. Our parents, of course, but a surprising number of peers who all concentrated on how their little tribe was doing almost to the exclusion of anything else. "How's the job" was shorthand for where we would be able to live and what we could afford to buy the children. Everything else seemed similarly coded. Often the uninitiated missed it entirely, but then the uninitiated were not truly allowed into our real meaningful discussions. We would nod politely as they told us about their triumphs in career or self, but they were as irrelevant as the visions of visiting Martians.

It was each other we competed with, although for the most part it was a gentle competition. When did the toddler make it across the room, how verbal was the prodigal infant, and so forth and so on. Fantasies of marvelous futures, but the realities of money and time infinitely spent to enrich their possibilities. Joan and I became mere actors in a play centered on our young protagonist. When we could sometimes break out of the reverie, often out of sheer frustration or exhaustion, we would gasp and wonder when we lost so much control, and why we allowed it. But the current swiftly pulled us back into the mainstream, and we could think no more.

Overall, positive reinforcement. In spite of comparisons, we were mostly mutually supportive, encouraging, sympathetic, although we might keep a private edge to our emotions. It was good to be in a group that considered that no matter what else might be happening in the universe, in our immediate little environment everything was going exactly right and we were morally correct in keeping it so.

Swordplay reaches clattering climax in swirling fog. Ancient weathered battlements loom above. A wan full moon casts only gloom. I feel a nudge in my side and turn to find Ghost, dark cloak only slightly offset by a huge gold chain with a diamond pitchfork pendant holding it closed.

"Here, I want to show you something." He rises and motions me to come along with him. We hurry off to one side, up the stairs and—of course—here it is.

Backstage. The castle curtain has a forest painting on its reverse, ropes fall everywhere, the lighting crew is frantically casting shadows and highlights as necessary. The floor is little gritty, but solid ordinary planks. A few extras scurry about getting costumed for the next act. Yet from the front—well I had been totally immersed.

"OK, I agree," I tell him. "We were living a magnificent illusion."

"But that is always true of whatever you think, wherever you are, isn't it?" he asks rhetorically.

"So, what, today you're Mr. Philosopher? I don't know, that's all a bit too metaphysical for me."

"Yet you fall into such notions easily, accepting the obviously fake for the real."

"I'm not sure, Ghost," I say slyly, "that even _you_ are sure what is fake and what is real. Even about yourself."

"Indeed, a weak point," he admits. "But it all seems so obviously flimsy."

"What," I retort. "A family? It's the most real thing I know of. People who argue with you but at least listen, actions that actually change things in your immediate environment, children who depend on you for advice and support. Complete immersion in a cause."

"You sound like any religious or sports fanatic," he says, scornfully.

"No, Ghost, you missed the point about actually changing things. At least this had some ripples into the larger world, in which other dreams were only pretty flashes in my brain."

"If you would just listen …"

"You know, Ghost, you weaken your own case. If it's all illusion, what you offer is pretty cheap, some kind of minor drug to let me change my own dream."

He stalks away as technicians flash the lights and rumble climactic thunder from the sound effects.

Central to those years was our redefinition of meaning and purpose. Oh, once you reach adulthood you quickly realize that the only judge who matters is you, that only you can decide if you are a success or failure, and only you can choose what it is important to try for success at. But for us there had been a jumbled twenties as we tried a few options and found they did not work. The most painful part of growing up is realizing that just because you choose something and work hard does not mean it will ever work out.

Adjusting to our actual strengths and weaknesses—innate and acquired— is one part of it. The serendipity of running into some role into which we fit is another. What may be the hardest is the ability to realize when everything is going wrong, or will never go better, and to explore beyond our current limits.

For some years, centering on raising a family was more of a fallback option—and more of a side issue—for Joan and me than all the other glittering possibilities. She wanted to be a solid, secure, and self-respecting public school teacher, for example. I wanted to be an artist of some kind. We both figured once we had achieved that all the other goodies would come along. Having a family was one of those things that just popped up like a mushroom once you had settled career and finances.

Suddenly everything was backwards. Family took stage front and center, and everything else we did was related to having a nice home, happy children, pleased parents, and the biologic inner glow of satisfaction that raising children can bring. A job, whatever it might be, was endured for the income it could bring. Other dreams were put to the side, perhaps to be taken up once again in middle age when the kids moved on.

Each day we woke up and wondered what Gregory would do, what we could offer him, what other ties to our relatives needed to be handled. Oh, we had work, and chores, and pride in various other areas, of course. But crunch time was the family.

Oddly, Wayne realized that desperate as things always seemed, in most ways he would always look back on this as some of the "best years of their lives." He began to truly understand that it was the journey and not the goal that mattered. And the journey here, difficult though the path often was, was all-consuming.

Novelists write of couples bored with each other, of people frantically seeking meaningful liaisons outside their marriage, of folks building barriers to preserve inner sanity. He never found time for any of it, and to all appearances Joan didn't either. Like their parents, they hitched to the wagon and pulled hard and that was it. No use complaining. No use wishing you were grazing in that green pasture over there. No use thinking how nice it would be to rest for a while.

There was no time. There was no energy. They each completed each day exhausted, each perhaps thinking they had done more than the other, but each recognizing how much the other did. There was nothing fragile about it. Each difficulty overcome just made life more rewarding and the pattern they were weaving stronger.

Most of that, of course, was far more appreciated in retrospect.

OK, this is weird. I'm in an elementary-school class-play white toga costume, otherwise floating in the middle of nowhere. Something seems to be weighing on each shoulder. I hear a whisper in my left ear, "Now you should do what you want." In my right comes an echoing "You should do what you know you should." Gradually, as if out of mist, a mirror forms in front of me and I see sitting on each shoulder a tiny copy of Ghost, one dressed in white with wings and a halo, the other in red with a tail and pitchfork.

"Ah," say I, "the classic presentation of dilemma."

"Say, rather, temptation," hisses the devil. "Don't you sometimes sneak away and do things you know you shouldn't."

"Yes, sometimes," I admit, "grab a beer in the garage while I'm mowing the lawn, retreat to my room upstairs to listen to music by myself while I read some technical manual."

"But there surely is more," he insists. "All those pretty young things at work, all the time by yourself in the car, so many opportunities for ..."

"I don't know what world you're living in devil, but I have neither time, opportunity, nor desire for any more entanglements or excitement. My secret vice is simply to retreat and ignore people when I should be engaging with them."

"But you don't do as much as you ought to," whines a high pitched nag on the other side.

"You know, I always could do more," I reply. "But in fact I do a lot. We always shared our work, and we each had lived alone enough to know how to take care of ourselves. We divvied stuff up pretty conscientiously. Sometimes Joan took care of Gregory while I read manuals or listened to music, sometimes I watched him while she talked on the phone. We each did our part, and still guarded our own space."

"But there could have been more."

"A disease of the culture. Sometimes the right amount is <u>no</u> more. Interacting with Gregory was necessary and fun and good. Letting Gregory do some things on his own without too much direct supervision was important too. Like I said, we still found a little time for ourselves."

"But not enough," insinuates devil.

"Days are long, even when times are crowded. I think we found quite enough moments."

"You must have had fantasies," comes the hiss.

I laugh. "Yeah, fantasies of another day off, mostly, or being able to sleep an extra hour. I'm afraid that was the limit of my internal universe."

"Didn't you feel guilty for all the things you should have done?" sweetly admonishes the voice on my right.

"Nope. Both Joan and I recognized early on we were just people, just regular parents, with just a regular child. No super acts to produce superior progeny. We really believed, and still do mostly, that the purpose of life is to have a good life, meaning happy in yourself and able to enjoy living in society."

"Killjoy," they duet.

Wayne's Mom and Dad were visiting, having taken the long over-two-hour train ride from Philadelphia to Babylon. This warm bright October morning, they had decided to display a favorite outing, Argyll lake, site of a former grand hotel from the days when this was a vacation destination. Waters spread wide and calm, waterfalls at the intricately-wrought dam were in full play, and Gregory happily chased swans and geese, which occasionally chased him back. Joan was getting large again, looking for any traditional signs that this time it might be a girl.

As the leaves rustled, they just gossiped and exchanged minor news. Wayne and his father traded tales of work and business, Joan and his mother news of extended family. Eventually they were all engaged in stories of bringing up children, old and new theories of child development, discipline and hopes for the future tempered with realities and fears for the present. Surprisingly, in spite of what they had all assumed would be an insurmountable generation gap, there seemed to be near unanimity on most of these subjects. It was something to think about, after all these years when they had resisted the suggestions of their elders so seriously, and dismissed much of what they had suggested as irrelevant.

Eventually they strolled partway around the lake, over the dam, watching leaves tinged with color rustling in a slight breeze. No real bite to the air, but need for light outerwear. As expected, Gregory kept showing off a bit, but nobody minded. They were all completely happy to, for once, be involved in an endeavor with which they all agreed. Parents were proud, and children were happy and gratified that they were doing as expected. All worries were, for once, in suspension, and it was enough to simply enjoy the marvelous day, and each other, and times that a sad undertone reminded them were quickly slipping away.

Ghost is gross, distended belly, unfocused eyes, draped in a tattered leather armchair. His big red suit is stained, the pitchfork rusty with one prong broken. Beer cans on the floor around him, cigar smoke in the air, a lit butt in one hand. Not a pretty picture. "So," he says carefully, "think you're pretty perfect, don't you?"

"Like what?" I ask.

"Nothing to confess, not trapped into any of the seven deadly sins, just little Mr. Perfect in the flesh." He burps hugely, forming bubbles on his lips.

"Well, some envy, I guess. Gluttonous in drinking a bit too much. But classically, nothing controlling me, nothing I'd really be ashamed of."

"So I got no job, nothing to do. "

"Well, I do admit to some faults, but one really big one."

He brightened up a little. "Yeah, what's that?"

"Hubris. I had an awful lot of hubris. Here I'd been fighting the system for years, getting nowhere, but once I changed my ways everything went marvelously. Everyone thought I was doing great. I thought I was doing great."

"You were, after all, doing much better," he notes cautiously.

"Ah, but I thought it was all myself. My own actions, my own perseverance, my own skills. I was completely full of myself at that point. Classic."

"You surely had a lot to do with it."

"Sure, some. But an awful lot of luck. A lot of help from other people. A lot of things happened to break my way."

"Luck favors those ready for it."

"I know, I know. But we also need to realize that there was luck involved. At that moment, I was ignoring that critical fact and thought it would all be smooth sailing from there on. All because of me."

"Ah," he said, finally reaching for a notepad. "Pride. Deadly Sin. Great. Right. Thanks."

Rain was beating hard on the tin awnings outside the bedroom window. Wayne groaned and reached over to shut the alarm before it went off. Dark outside, cold no doubt. He immediately realized this would be a long slog to work, needing extra time from flooded roads. So, out of bed, shower, breakfast quick quick.

It had been a really nice weekend. Visits usually were, these days, affirmation of all they were and how things were going. No fights about plans or dreams. That should have made the necessity of stumbling about in the dark easier somehow, he thought, as the instant coffee heated up in the microwave. On mornings like this, that turned out not to be the case. He knew the mood would pass once he was warm and dressed and ready to head out the door. It was just starting that was sometimes a problem.

No calls over the weekend, at least. There was so much to learn at this new job, he tried to snap in the new data he'd been studying in off moments. Well, he'd just lay the day out as best he could, and take things as they happened. The timer alarm went off, and another work day began.

CRASH

ON PAPER, WAYNE realized, they were nearly rich. Thousands of options had been granted to him, and the price after the IPO had skyrocketed as Christmas sales figures became available. From here on it would only get better, they were on the ground floor of a telephone revolution. He tried to get Joan enthused, but she didn't trust stocks and thought real wealth was only in the bank or in some kind of land like the house.

No matter, he knew better. The IBM computer was finally performing perfectly. He had a staff of data entry people, an assistant to help with coding, an operator to do the mundane daily operations like the updating the night runs. He and Joe and Alan were constantly planning the next great extension of programming, more General Ledger, complicated and timely sales reporting. Anyway, they were already handling unthinkable volumes of orders and invoices, and spending a great deal of time preparing to automate inventory control.

With the money from going public, plans were in the works for a huge new headquarters with automated warehouse at Roosevelt Field, custom designed. This would be a work that would be marvelous, all conveyer belts and automatic sorting, beautiful areas out front and inside, a computer room to evoke wonders of the world. When not designing or coding or documenting, Wayne was involved in how this would translate into wiring and terminals and placement of the central unit. Not to mention fire protection and ventilation, and thousands of other heady, exciting, plans.

Webcor was the toast of Long Island, the little import company that could, risen from decades of sleepy tacky watch sales to become a beacon of the age, boldly striding into the world of imported electronics. Tours were being given, the president was being interviewed. Almost weekly some newspaper or magazine would paint a glowing picture of the present and future.

All his colleagues bought into it. After all, they were all working harder, and smarter than they ever had, things were going more smoothly than ever before. Oh, a few of the older folks grumbled about this and that, but the place was stuffed with new people, all enthusiastic, all happy to hop onto something so bright and shiny and with such wonderful visions of what would be coming along.

I'm on a beautiful cruise ship, lying in clear sunlight, sipping a glass of merlot. Brilliant shines on sparkling azure waves while a warm breeze fans rows of beautiful young people enjoying life. I look up as someone taps me on the shoulder. Ghost is there in a spiffy nautical uniform, all crisp and white, incongruently solemn expression. "Pardon me," he says, "just a formality, of course. Mandatory lifeboat drill."

Seems silly, these boats are practically unsinkable. "Where and what, Ghost?" I ask.

"Mr. Ghost, if you please. Just go to the assigned area as indicated on the card so you can be identified and counted. When that's complete I'm sure we'll be getting back to normal."

I look down and dutifully find my way to section C-18, with other confused people, most of us annoyed. After all, we're paying heavily for this in vacation time and money. No need for the Mickey Mouse routines. Well, at least we still have our wine.

A somewhat harried group of crew members push in among us and start to untie the life raft. It seems to me they're going a little too far with all this. "Hey, Mr. Ghost, what's the delay here."

"Practice, practice, have patience," he says loudly. Then in a lower voice, "Don't panic, I'm sure everything will be all right ..."

Blemishes from worms in the apple appeared over the summer.

Victor had built Webcor from nothing. He enjoyed his extended buying trips abroad, where he lived high, made contacts and cemented sharp deals. Much of his business acumen had been directed to careful navigation of import laws and duties. He remained hard-working, sharp, and domineering. Nevertheless, age catches up with everyone, and he now eyed the possibility of a golden cash-out. His paper net worth from the IPO was immense. Those long plane rides to Tokyo and Hong Kong were less fun than they used to be.

One visible omen was Karla. Karla stalked the hallways like a hard-bitten Valkyrie, who hovered next to Victor day and—presumably—night. She was tolerated by his wife, but more or less despised by everyone else. Famously she would pop out of her plush decorated corner office into meetings, never listening nor contributing anything, except to convey ultimatums: "Victor says" or "Victor wants" or "Victor thinks." But she was not the problem.

A younger son had been groomed to handle Eastern contacts. He was studious and hard-working, but lacked the aggressive assurance of his father and most of the drive to negotiate hard deals. He had been going to the orient for years as a junior partner, but gossip murmured that buying trips on his own were near-disasters, saved by his father's phone interventions time after time. That may or may not have been true. Anyway, he was not the problem.

The older son was VP of sales, which had bulked up with some heavy hitters on big commissions. Huge contracts had been recorded. Too many played on his relative inexperience and payed easy money to the salesmen without equivalent guarantees of income and profits for the firm. For example, deliveries for future months, or consignment estimates registered as hard commitments. Nothing contractually binding, and yet the bonuses flowed freely. He was slick, dark, and rumored to be using controlled substances. But he was not the problem.

Competition had finally scented money and began its shark frenzy. Little guys fled, leaving bigger heavy-hitting firms with deep pockets and huge distribution networks. Consumer telecommunications was becoming a goldmine with an incalculable future. New electronic gadgets and toys—and telephones—were appearing almost daily. It would take hard work and luck

BABYLON WITH GHOST

to stay up with them. But even they were not the core of the current and immediate problem.

No, the core of the problem was that Webcor was on the bleeding edge of globalization and electronic consumerism. What that meant was that with long lead times between orders and delivery via ocean freight, consumer tastes might change dramatically, so that phone models confidently ordered in March might well be obsolete and unwanted by November. New improved models would come along. Inventory was a nightmare—not only was every shipment a new model, but since most phones were merely assembled from off the shelf components in Asia, even identical models with a slightly different chip would perform differently or not at all. Nothing returned could be confidently put back into inventory. In fact, any item returned was basically trash and should be written off. The business world is used to that now. Back then it was all new and misunderstood. And that was where Webcor was destroyed.

Wayne trudged to an after-hours party a few blocks away from work on Sunnyside Boulevard. The industrial bar was attached to a rather grim motel situated along the Long Island Expressway, for any poor souls stranded out here in the middle of nowhere on business. Half the Webcor staff seemed to be present. He didn't normally drink anything until he was home, but he sipped a beer as many others got pretty sloshed.

"Sold all my stock last week," said one. "Half of what it would have gotten me a couple of weeks ago, and glad I got that, I'll tell you."

"I've been looking around, but nothing out there yet, jobs aren't impossible but they aren't paying well."

"You should hang on, we're going to get through this."

"I don't know, have you been into the warehouse lately? It's all returned junk, top to bottom. We don't even know where to put it—I think they may be getting a temporary warehouse for the overflow."

"We've got new stuff coming in that'll knock your socks off. Just wait, we're going to be flying soon."

A few of the older people sat in a corner, from the days before the hoopla. Mostly accounting types, quietly nursing drinks and reminiscing. Wayne recognized one and casually said "Hi Rose, what's up?"

She shocked him. "This is my last week. Got a nice head accounting job at DeLia's Sod Farm out on Straight Path. I can't take the phone calls here all the time—dunning stores that will never pay, dealing with returns, trying to learn your new computer systems."

Wayne said, "Sorry, they make me keep changing them."

"Oh, I know it's not your fault. But it's all just too much, and I want something quieter."

Apparently, that was the consensus of half the older staff, not all of whom had equivalent options, all even more worried than the new employees. It was hard even then to change from a job you had performed for decades.

"I tell you, you need to help us get through this!" yelled the inebriated vice-president of sales from across the room.

"What are you doing, Wayne?" asked a friend from the inventory department.

Wayne always played these things close to the vest, never burning bridges. "Thinking about selling the stock, of course, but I wish it would go up a bit."

"It's going to double or triple when the new stuff gets in," insisted one newer salesman.

"I hope so. Anyway, I'll just wait and see. We've got a lot to do with the computer."

They sure did. Inventory was a mess, and inventory was key. Returns were a worse mess, and that ate right into profits. The rules kept changing. They were all but running on two sets of books now, and it was hard to hide that in code. No matter how hard he worked, what clever solutions he found, what fine new possibilities were proposed by his bosses, he was always behind and under pressure. And, as the bearer of bad tidings, frequently blamed.

Yeah, sell the stock now. Cut losses. And look for a way out. If Rose was leaving—well she had more common sense than anyone else he knew at the company.

"I tell you, this is just the beginning!" echoed across the room from the sales group.

That's what Wayne was afraid of.

Naively, I had begun to assume that I would have a career resembling that of my father, who had joined a small local company and ridden it through growth and opportunity until he was well set financially, enjoying the comradery of early friends and colleagues. I knew I had started a bit late, but Webcor seemed just such an opportunity, with the sky the limit. The first few years fulfilled that belief.

But the world had changed since the 1950's, and if I was one of the first to notice it and be whipsawed I was by no means the last. The old rules hardly worked any more—grand old firms would bite the dust or go through hard times or be divided and merged until they hardly resembled what they had been. New firms would be bought and sold and acquire new owners and managers as the older management were herded off, some richer, most poorer. By now it's a familiar story, back then for me it was a hard lesson learned early and pretty well.

And the technological curve in all that was frightening. I had already seen departments reduced to shadows of themselves, and foreseen the radical restructuring of others as computerization and automation came into work flow. But the products that were sold, how they were sold, how they were abandoned, and how quickly it all turned was new to everyone. It only became faster and faster, deeper and deeper, as the decades went on. Maybe I was lucky seeing it in the beginning, although never so perceptively as to profit much by the knowledge.

It was frightening to watch the older people thrown off. Some unable to keep up, leaving more or less on their own after bad performance reviews, unable to find anything else comfortable or decently paying. Some desperately threw themselves into the mix, only to flail in competition with others half their age, a quarter their knowledge, and lots of new gimmicks to look professional. That was the way it was to be.

Fortunately, I quickly lost the romantic fantasy of old-time productive work being automatically rewarded. I did not become cynical enough to get rich, but I found ways to manage a decent niche which paid my way and preserved my soul. More than many of my contemporaries were able to manage.

Milling around with the other passengers, I'm slightly off to the side of the main crowd, watching the horizon and clouds on a choppy sea. The deck is hardly moving, and stewards are wandering here and there inspecting life-boat fastenings as everyone enjoys themselves with free drinks being offered at a portable bar. Ghost sidles over and mutters under his breath "I'd get a little closer to boarding side near the bow, if I were you."

I whisper back, "why, is something really wrong?"

"Don't know," he answers, "but this is being taken a lot more seriously than usual. I heard a rumor of smoke in the engine room."

"But these things can't sink…" I protest. "I read the brochures."

"Just a word to the wise," he notes quietly.

"Will they enforce women and children first?"

Ghost laughs. "What era you living in? Anyway, no kids on this cruise, or at least only a couple. And with PC sexual equality and all damned if anyone is going to enforce anything at all. No, I'd just stand and be ready so if they do start to fill the boats, you'll be automatically pushed in to clear the way for everyone else."

"Surely there are enough boats."

"Of course, of course, sir," he says stiffly, as another crewmember strides closer. "Everything is fine. Just relax and enjoy your trip …"

I quickly move where he has suggested. Maybe I don't know as much as I think.

Alan had an MBA and had come from some large company to make his fortune at Webcor. He had grand dreams of how a well-run modern computerized company would thrive, and found willing plasticity in all the new employees. Wayne and Joe D spent many hours in his office, listening to plans, taking notes, and writing up ways they could accomplish all he wanted.

These were the heady days when anything was possible, and everything had to be reinvented. There were no real best practices, and it was hard to find out what they might be. There were lots of different ideas. The pencil pushers had to be convinced, too—nobody would give up what they were used to without a fight. Alan kept assuring us that "Victor is behind me one hundred percent," but perhaps he did protest too much. Victor seemed to be behind him as long as nothing cost too much and the older employees whom he trusted went along. There had been a near heart attack at the cost of the System 38, only partially salved by the huge inflow of capital when the American Stock Exchange listing had occurred.

Alan was hitting everything at once—general ledger, sales reporting, inventory control, cash flow. Unfortunately, his techniques and ideas were suited to a huge Fortune 500 company, and in spite of dreams Webcor was not anywhere near being one. So a lot of things started off with a big shiny outline and ended up as inconsequential whimpers. That left a trail of debris in the wake, much of it in the form of old useless reporting, dead areas of coding, and implementations that had to be aborted for whatever practical reasons.

But it sometimes appeared that the worse things got, the more meetings they had, the more grandiose the solutions proposed. Wayne hadn't gone through this before, and he had no reason to suspect that such wasn't the normal way to move into a happy future. It turned out to be quite an education.

Those who haven't worked deeply on certain issues have no idea how complicated they can be. There are some problems that are quite simple to solve, even if they look daunting at first. For example, moving a pile of rocks from one side of the yard to another—eventually you just roll up your sleeves and do it. But there were others—most of the problems in those days of computing—that became more fractally complicated the more they were studied. Inventory control, for example, appeared to be one holy grail that never worked out quite as planned.

Even sales and accounts receivable—well, you could do all kinds of fancy reporting and churn out exception reports that indicated who was not paying and who was making big orders and think you had done a big thing. But in fact, sales were not done by reports, and the best salespeople often had a strong aversion to any paper trail at all. All they did was bring in more orders than the rest of the staff combined, and there was no way they were going to spend time with a terminal. As for receivables—any top clerk called on the phone all day, knew who to talk to and how to talk to them, and when to make big threats. A big heap of greenbar on her desk was of almost no value at all.

Warehouse management was a perfect example. In theory, there would be purchase orders put into the system well in advance, and when shipments

came in the new stock could be simply checked off against what had been purchase, automatically notifying accounts payable. Then there would be boxes
on the shelves, located with code in inventory control by PO or lot number.
Sales would be made, a shipping order would be printed, stock would be sent
out, and a receivable issued. Once in a while something would come back as
a return, be put into stock, and all would be just dandy. Seemed like it could
all be put together on the computer in a few weeks.

But—oh, where to start. The purchases almost never had correct model
numbers, just general indications of what might be arriving and about when.
In this industry, almost every shipment was a unique set of new model numbers, many of which were not known until shortly before they were loaded on
the boat, if then. Most of them only vaguely referred to the originating purchase order. So exactly how could that be carried in the computer which was
demanding the model number? The arrival dates were vague within months.
When things arrived were they stored together, in boxes, or broken into loose
items. What about samples?

Meanwhile, the sales team knew they were coming and had started selling for, say, Christmas, a half year ahead. They were putting in preorders,
without model numbers of course, and only vague unit prices, some of which
would receive rebates depending on actual sales volume at end of year. Some
of the customers weren't even real customers yet, and wouldn't be until there
was merchandise. The computer just made things worse—it was actually easier to track this kind of stuff in folders—so half the stuff never made it into
the machine—and never made it onto the reports. Victor was not pleased.

As for tracking items—don't ask. That took over thirty years and an entire industry revolution to even start to come true.

But for Alan, and Joe, and me it all seemed simple enough in discussions
fueled by magazine articles.

One more flag, a tweak to the workflow, just another whatever and it
would all clear up. Except it never did, and meanwhile the fact that it was all
out of control and getting worse got hidden in the wrapping paper.

Paradoxically, it was about the best training in system design and its
problems that I could ever have had, a deep and thorough intuitive understanding of complex systems which served me well from then on. For all the
problems, it was a graduate course in computer analysis, and prepared me for
the next twenty years of work.

Not far away, on the horizon, a ship burns. Surprisingly, it has masts and is much smaller than the one I had been riding. Ghost and I are alone in a battered old wooden dinghy, oars lying inside. He looks at me and says, "Well, another fine mess you've gotten us into."

"I didn't have anything to do with it! Why the strange equipment?

"Oh, no use making too easy, with cellphones and GPS and whatnot. Knocked us back a few centuries, that's all. What are you gonna do now?"

"I have choices?"

"Sure. You can just rock here until you die. Or you can hang out by the fire and hope somebody sees it and stops by. Or try to row into shipping lanes and hail a rescue. Or," he pauses dramatically, "you could navigate to one of those small islands over there and hope."

"Hope for what?"

"Oh, that they are habitable with food and water. Maybe don't have cannibals. Maybe even have already been discovered and are in use once in a while."

"All bad, seems to me."

"I don't know," he says softly, "You could still be trapped back there." We heard the faint screams of the last of the crew and passengers giving up and jumping into the sea.

These days, there is a discipline in technological circles called "boot camps," which uses an intense period of weeks to drill home some new concept or paradigm. It's modeled on the long-known use of language immersion to become fluent. For me, Webcor was a three year boot camp in coding, application design, medium-size business, distribution, and, not least, creative accounting and the lies it can be used for.

College, accounting courses had been extremely dull—credits and debits, double entry bookkeeping, receivables and payables. Ancient Dickensian dry clerical stuff, now increasingly done by the swift hardware that never made a mistake (although rounding errors of pennies could induce apoplexy in older practitioners.) Such was all done by junior clerks anyway.

It turned out, real interesting "creative" accounting happened at a higher level, where figures were aggregated into mysterious general ledger totals. Then the real fun of interpretation, projection, and summation could begin. I'd thought that accounting was more-or-less "truth," but it turned out there were all kinds of acceptable truth. Corporate balance sheets and annual reports could be shaped into novelistic fantasies worthy of a Pulitzer. Inventory valuation and asset depreciation almost infinitely varied to meet circumstances—losses magnified to cut taxes, or stockpiles overvalued to increase the apparent health of the company. And then there were the really mysterious areas of things like "good will" which tried to figure out exactly how much your customer list and existing sales contacts were worth. And finally the pure fiction of future orders, or shipments planned on near-consignment basis to be delivered in October at a nominal book value of $10 a unit, to be sold at suggested $20. Payment due in January by which time—depending on sales volume—a possible rebate up to $5 a unit might be applied. And come February, perhaps half the stock—as unsalable as rotten apples at that point—would be returned and credit given to the store, but carried at an arbitrary figure ($15 if counting price inflation, $5 if stressing depreciation) and stored back on groaning warehouse racks, even though everyone knew it would never ship out again. Investors saw the rosiest pictures, the IRS saw the gloomiest, and the accounting department could swear that everything was true and clear.

My involvement was that all this stuff—to take on a degree of reality—had to be coded into the computer somehow. Nothing impressed visitors like piles of printouts with huge numbers—had to be real, look it's in the computer! So how did the computer value the inventory and what would it print? How were the orders coded on entry, and how did we ever follow LIFO or FIFO when the system was actually "grab whatever works and get it out the door immediately." Oh, there were practices and conventions and we never actually thought we were lying, but it surely was a warped set of "truths."

I owed them a debt of gratitude, for after this experience I was better equipped for my future career than if I had obtained an MBA and technical degree combined. More importantly, I could sympathize with all sides of these issues, which I often understood far more clearly than some of the principals I would later deal with.

Without any effort, just using newspaper want ads, Wayne quickly lined up three interviews. He had experienced enough to only seek employment where he would be a revenue source rather than an expense. That mostly pointed towards becoming a consultant in some firm providing computer software. He had firmly decided he did not want to pursue a straight management track—it was too iffy, too political, he enjoyed technical challenge more, and he was naturally good at programming.

First he went to an agency where an almost clueless headhunter tried to craft his odd set of skills and experiences into something that would interest known clients—all large corporations. Wayne left a little discouraged, although the recruiter seemed enthusiastic enough about his chances, especially if he was willing to take a cut in pay and work his way up. The next interview involved a screening process where he and several others in a bare room were given a problem and coding sheets with pencils and told they would be contacted if there was any interest. The problem was trivial, he had it done quickly.

The last interview was by far the most intriguing. Nick had built a small consulting firm as computers became common, and had a set of programmers working on the old IBM 34's and 36's. But as a business partner to IBM, he was being pushed to get involved in the more complex and totally different System 38 line. His larger clients were talking about that too—primed naturally by IBM sales calls. He had decided his skill set was best left in sales, and he wanted someone who could jump into the 38 arena, even if only for maintenance and the future, and who could also bring the rest of the staff up to speed. Wayne would be coming in at quite a high level, if not an excessively large salary at least more than he had been making, with future potential looking quite good. He was offered the position immediately, and shook hands to accept.

That evening the paper-coding firm called all enthused to bring him in—but it was too little too late, and he hadn't felt all the comfortable in their culture anyway. He knew he'd be the junior person for quite a long time. The next day, the headhunter called, thrilled to have found him a lucrative position at Grumman. Wayne had no desire to join the military-industrial complex that he still hated for the trauma of Vietnam, so he politely said no and finally got off the line with the disgruntled woman, who had lost a large hiring bonus. But the early bird catches the worm.

It was astounding after all these years to truly be in demand. Maybe he wasn't rich yet, and certainly he had to change his recent plans, but everything had worked out far better than he had thought.

Ghost sits beside me on the empty sand beach as the sun rises. Water stretches forever, coconut trees line the shores. "Marooned, marooned," he moans.

"You just can't let this scenario go, can you?" I say caustically. "Like I said, far from being marooned, not even a penniless refugee. Less than a week after starting my search, a new and better position. Then it was just giving two week notice and wrapping up."

"But all your work gone, all your friends gone, all your built-up human capital gone."

"I admit I was a little ticked off at all that. There was a huge code base I had developed, although like every programmer at the time I had taken home a copy—nobody knew who was doing what back then. Hell, the sales people were lifting the latest printouts of customers as they left. Friends would become part of my professional network—although I was bad about that."

"Out of sight, out of mind?"

"Too much so. But I'm afraid such is my nature. Anyway, the mutual obligations would take a while to recover."

"And those were?"

"Oh, you know, the time I covered for someone, or did something extraordinary. And the times they did such for me. It takes time and mutual work to build such trusts, and they can never be taken away. We all hate to move, I think, for that reason if we have developed things like that."

"But by yourself, new clients, just a handshake with the boss, you hadn't even met the other people there. You might as well be marooned."

"Oh, c'mon. It's just down the block, English-speaking, IBM, Americans, still living same home with my family. Hardly marooned."

"And you always had those other offers."

"Well, yeah, at least the thought of the other offers. Anyway, just like this sunrise, a bright, shiny, and promising new day dawns."

JBS was a small relatively young company. Its name, Jamison Business Systems had originated when Nick happened to look at a bottle of whiskey when he was starting up. Nick, like many such entrepreneurs, was successful largely because he really cared about his clients and other people, business was almost secondary. His wife was practical and hard headed and took care of the books.

There were two other full-time employees, and another contracted. Mostly their job had been maintenance of machines which were running nearly pure IBM package software. However, recently the company had started to provide medical billing software that had been developed in-house. A few System38 accounts were being started, which was driving Nick nuts since nobody knew much about them.

The offices were in Hauppauge, a twenty minute drive from Babylon on a good day. But there was no computer at the office, and most of the work was naturally done at the client sites, either all day or after checking in. Manual timesheets were rigorously kept, since billing was by the hour. Wayne didn't have too much trouble, since he had been using personal "day-timer" notebooks for some time to keep track of what he needed to do.

Dark wood paneling, closed drapes, a few faded pictures of the sea. I'm sitting in a big easy chair across from a desk with a typewriter. Ghost lounges on a couch nearby.

"Giving up on the nautical theme, are we?" I begin.

"All things, in time," Ghost answers. "But the fact is that when everything was going on it was not nearly so clear-cut and rational."

"If you are implying I was confused, I guess so."

"But now, in the comfort of old age, you can compose memoirs that make it all seem so logical and inevitable, when it was by no means truly so."

"Hard to tell, hard to tell. In my memory it certainly has fallen into place as described."

"Your memories play you false, I think. You've clipped out the confusion and pain and concentrated on what turned out fine, but only in long hindsight."

"I don't think so," I reply. "I admit there was no real narrative that I could understand, but I wasn't full of pain and desperation either. I was just busy, one day after another, and never thought all that much."

"Probably still don't"

"Now, don't get nasty…"

JBS was an IBM business partner. In exchange for (almost) exclusively dealing with IBM equipment, sales support and training were provided to employees. In turn, our company prospected leads and provided add-on services, freeing IBM to concentrate on hardware. Smaller enterprises serviced in the 34.36.38 market were unable to generate the kind of money IBM required for its traditional ongoing massive involvement in huge companies. IBM had been fishing for marlin, but now had to figure out how to catch sardines. There were a lot more sardines, but baiting hooks from fancy boats just wouldn't work.

Mid-size clients were as computer naïve as any rubes at a county fair. They had heard tales of wonders, and were willing to believe anything, but had no actual experience of so much as a keyboard. They wanted the best, but didn't want to spend more than their phone system. These were not companies that could write off computer investments and get it back on taxes. Usually a little larger than mom-and-pop shops, but not much, running on razor-thin margins and often old-line companies in odd niches of the market, handed down in the family for generations. They may have been rubes in terms of technology, but that didn't mean they couldn't negotiate contracts ruthlessly.

Every small business practice was weirdly idiosyncratic. For example, most had little or no idea of standard accounting, inventory control, or best industry practices. Each system was home-grown and the boss liked it that way. Irreconcilable problems began with actual operations, but were casually swept under the rug in initial presentations. IBM salespeople would cheerfully pitch a package, "used by everybody, all you will ever need", and then Wayne and Nick would come in and groan. As they learned the true requirements, their tendency was to say "no, no, no, we can't do that." Unfortunately, that meant IBM got mad at a lost sale and of course JBS would lose the account, often to a competitor.

So instead, it was almost always a loss-leader initial contract—JBS would get the equipment running and working marginally well, then try to extract profits by customizing certain areas on a billable per-hour basis. In all such endeavors, implementation takes a lot longer than planned, and so there was always almost impossible pressure—and that's when things were going right. With relatively untrained operators and data people scared of keyboards, not to mention the state of the hardware art, things were often not going right.

So, they were always behind, and just when they might be making headway another minor or major problem would pop up. There was only one way to deal with such things in those days before telecommunications—get in the car and ride to wherever the account might be.

POCKET PARADISE

ANOTHER HOT JULY late Saturday evening at Captree, Wayne and Joan sat in the high grass on a dune overlooking the inlet, as Gregory rolled down the sandy hill to the water below. The pizza was almost finished, empty box greasy alongside, and they each savored another glass of wine from a half-empty bottle. Behind them were the sounds of people finishing up their barbeques, and other children noisy in the playground.

The sun remained high this evening, hot and brilliant. Large fishing boats loaded with people who had gone out for the day were streaming back into the docks on a strong tide. On the bridge to Fire Island off to the right, a still constant stream of cars were returning beach-goers toward the mainland, distant behind them over the long causeway. Perfection.

And, importantly for Joan and Wayne at this point, incredibly cheap. After four, there was no fee to get into this magical spot, less than half an hour from their home. They could have dinner, and let Gregory run and play, and stroll the docks watching crabbers and a few fishermen, then exercise him on the playground and still make it back before dark. The clean salt air scrubbed away all the hassles of life, and once again they could just be as they once were, free spirits in a happy world. There was an almost unwritten rule between them that such evenings were for fun and relaxation and a form of

418

meditation, and that cares and plans could wait—at least until they got back in the car.

Wayne took another sip and reflected how things were still turning out better than he could have hoped. The culture had suddenly become benign, he was a fish in the right water, a frog in a correctly-sized pond. Within limits, he finally truly felt he was master of his own destiny. And he had no greater ambition than to please Joan and his parents and serve his family well. An inner voice once in a while cried out that maybe he should aim for more, but there was always a core of hedonism deep inside and his own take on Carpe Diem. To him, it really meant, seize the day and squeeze all the enjoyment you can out of it, for such times are fragile and may never come again.

Ah, this is very nice indeed. I'm stretched out on a lounge chair in brilliant sun, drinks on the table alongside, sparkling blue pool in front. Very blue, extremely sparkling. All the colors seemed impossibly enhanced, all the lines crisply defined. For all the pizzazz, more like a commercial than real life. Indistinguishable but very happy background noise fills this set. I admit that I feel wonderfully content.

Ghost walks over, jauntily dressed like Tony Curtis in an old 50's comedy. Short blue sports jacket, beige pressed khaki slacks, even a tight captain's hat topping it off. "What may I do for you, sir?" he asks unctuously.

"Leave me alone, mostly," I reply.

"Sorry, that's one thing I cannot do, sir. We have schedules to meet, lots of activities to try, your poolside time is just about finished and we must be moving on. Busy is happy, you know."

"I'm busy enough ..." I begin.

"Of course you think so, sir," he continues, beginning to edge me up as he motions to a waiter to remove the drinks tray. "Of course you think so. But this, we must keep it going, and there are so many other things to keep you happy."

"Like what?" I growl, as I grudgingly sit up.

"Oh, shopping with your wife and child, visiting the in-laws, reading the cheerful little specifications for the next computer operating system release ..."

"But …"

"And of course this week you have the car inspection, and next week there is a birthday party for your brother-in-law. Happy times, sir."

"I just want to sit," I complain. Now the waiter is removing my chair and forcing me to get up.

"That's just what you think you want to do, sir," says Ghost. "But we know better. A complete life is a happy life. You have lots of other things to accomplish to make it so. And as they say, 'idle hands are the devil's playground.' "

"They don't say that!" I snap. "You can't even get the clichés right."

"No need to get nasty, sir," Ghost motions again and a large security guard type starts to stroll over. "You know what must be done."

"All the time," I groan. "All the time."

A whistle sounds in the background. "Ah, yes, break is over, sir. I hope you have enjoyed yourself and will come visit again, when you get a chance."

"And when might that be," I inquire, out of curiosity. I certainly have no idea.

"Oh, whenever, whenever, sir. We have lots and lots of wonderful things available, you know."

"But no time to do them," I finish.

"There is that," Ghost admits, as the dream begins to fade and the alarm clock continues to beep.

It hadn't taken much time for Wayne to discover the complex riches of Long Island. He'd never heard of the place before meeting Joan, and his few visits there with her had been short and directed to family matters. But after five years of being there he was still amazed at the abundance of ocean beaches, bay wetlands, and harbor inlets. There were vast parks from estates given to the public. Immense shopping areas, and small towns, and a few farms clinging to survival. The constant throb of the city to the west, which could never be ignored.

He and Joan had been raised without access to much money, and in their own lives they had lived very close to hand to mouth. They lived well, but had always needed to find inexpensive entertainment in walks, museums, window

BABYLON WITH GHOST

shopping, and public venues. It was one reason they got along—they liked the same things, and enjoyed the adventure of finding them. So without any trouble at all they were able to tap into the opportunities here, and could happily have filled most of the week doing them.

But the other side of the coin was that lots of other people wanted to live here too, which made it expensive and crowded. Traffic was immense, people were thicker than trees. Not quite a city—it lacked the infrastructure—but at the very least a proto-city. Paying for a house and car and food and necessities out here meant that money was required, and enough money meant lots and lots of time at work. Which left very little time for recreation.

The eighties were also the beginning of the end of the old pattern of nine to five nominal hours and weekends free. Even then very few people worked nine to five—add commute times to the best jobs and home to home was at least eight to six—but most people worked much longer. Rush hour was horrendous, beginning at 6:30 going towards the city (where almost all the jobs were) and not winding down until after 7:30 coming back east. During such travels, taking two hours to go thirty miles was not uncommon. And what happened was that on Saturday and Sunday everyone—everyone—wanted to do the same things to unwind. Even recreation was a madhouse.

But he had to admit that life could be grand. They never woke up bored and asking "what shall we do today?" Most choices were forced on them by necessity. But they found that within narrow limits there was time for small trips, often with Gregory, and little things to take the edge off. Having their own yard after all those years in the city was a constant pleasure of flowers and garden and slightly less pleasure of lawns and leaves.

If there was a downside, it was only the slight uneasiness of how to remain in paradise. You needed money and a good job to live here, it seemed you always needed more money and a better job just to maintain place. Maybe that caused the constant hustle—everyone around them was constantly grasping and "improving." It was certainly not a laid back region, not even so laid back as Boston had once seemed. Not quite so ferocious, perhaps, as New York City, but very much on the edge of that jungle, and infected with its emanations.

"It's really all pretty amazing, isn't it?" he asked one summer evening out on the green and yellow concrete brick patio behind the house. Gregory was playing in freshly cut grass while Wayne nursed a can of beer. Joan was resting after fussing with the flowers in a box, built to hide the stump of a large tree that had died years past in the middle of the lawn.

"What's that?" she replied, a little confused.

"Well, not long ago I never thought we'd have a house, or a kid, or be living anywhere except Boston and … here we are."

"And I," she answered slowly, "was wondering if you'd ever get a decent job and clean up your act."

"So it is all quite amazing, all of that."

"Yes, I suppose it is," she said. "But I wish we lived nearer to my parents."

Wayne wasn't quite so sure. He kind of liked the over-half-hour separation required to get across to the other side of the island. Of course, people around here never seemed to move and lived in little familial enclaves particularly of daughters clustering around mothers. Joan had taken note of that.

"Well, maybe someday we can move back over there."

"My parents aren't getting any younger," she noted wistfully. "Someday might be too late. I wish we'd come back sooner."

"We can only do what we can do. I wouldn't have had anything like this kind of job if we'd left before I had some training. And we are moving pretty quickly now."

"I just wish …"

"I know, me too, sometimes. But wishes are only what you can do. After all, your father had to do a great deal that he didn't want to do to accomplish what he did." That was safe ground, because Joan's father had indeed been a true pioneer, arriving alone in the US at the age of ten, giving up an art career for a more secure one as a barber, parlaying that somehow into a move to the "wilds" of Huntington back when it was still affordable, and amazingly getting three children through college. All on his own, almost all with him leading the way as her aunts and uncles followed.

"Everyone else our age seems better off …"

"But," he concluded triumphantly, "a few years ago everyone else our age was <u>impossibly</u> better off, and here we are running hard to catch up and I think we will almost make it. Amazing."

"We'll see," she muttered, as the sky grew dark.

There was a big difference in our family values. We both treasured our immediate family, and depended on them, and were almost too embroiled in what we did with each other and our children and even our parents. But the resemblance all but ended there.

Joan and her brothers were deeply in the tradition of the extended family, not only for personal relationships but also for its existence and growth over time as an organic unit. Each generation would do better than the last, each would add a bit to the familial myth, eventually, God willing, they would become one of the great families of the new country. Of course, that was running into a harsh reality which would eventually reshape it, but it is what they deeply believed, almost with a religious certainty. And many of their friends and relatives, from similar backgrounds, felt the same way. Long Island, in particular, was filled with recent arrivals converted to the new theology.

On the other hand, my siblings and I had never really thought much beyond making our own way and having our own adequate lives. We did not plan to extend some imagined greatness beyond living a good and fruitful life. We were easily contented with having enough, and unusually (for Americans) less worried about huge dreams. It's true that once in a while, like anyone else, I would daydream of making some indelible mark on the world. But common sense cut in quickly, and a day in the hand was always worth two or more in the future. And I had read and observed enough to truly believe that this day is what you really have, the people you know are the people you really interact with, and looking beyond what you are doing often leads to becoming nasty and unhappy in reality.

All the books say our children are first generation that does not expect to do better than their parents. I think for immigrant families, that may be so. They come from horrible conditions, and are amazed at what they can become, and teach their children to expect much more. But most of the friends I knew much of my life were not like that, perhaps there were fewer immigrants among them. We respected what our ancestors had done, admired what our parents accomplished, but were willing to consider that we had our own lives to live. We were also realistic enough to know that, no matter what the particular income levels, we had a good deal more available in all ways than anyone living a little while ago.

I wanted more. But it was a restricted more. Surely more free time. And maybe a little more money. But a better house—well, the roof didn't leak and we were warm and well fed. More luxury—well, we could go to parks and museums and theaters and malls anytime we wanted. After a while I was wondering if Maslow had such a thought in his hierarchy of unquenchable needs and desires. It did not fit my experience.

Dark paneling surrounding a blazing fireplace, one gigantic wall of glass overlooking what seems to be a golf course, tables and people conversing in hushed voices over drinks and snacks. This leather chair is very comfortable, I am tired enough to just sink in and enjoy ...

"Time for dinner, sir!" chirps Ghost happily, starting to get up alongside.

"No, I just want to stay here ..."

"No can do," he insists. "Joan is waiting, dinner will get cold—oh, you need to straighten your tie and put on your jacket."

"I don't want to ..."

"You must, sir," he drags me to stand up. "You have joined this club, you must follow member rules. Lots of wonderful things, but you need these few sacrifices to please your fellows."

"Seems like a hell of a lot of too many sacrifices."

"Surely you were aware of conditions before you signed up, sir."

"No, not really. Joan kind of dragged me and circumstances pushed me and I never got much of a chance to think it over."

"Think it over at dinner," he continues. "Hurry up now, it's such a scene when you arrive late."

"Don't I get any say about my time?"

"Not really, sir." Ghost is pulling me over to the opening doors, where Joan stands with her father and mother, and I can see the set dining room beyond. "Watch your manners, everyone is looking at you."

"What did I ever do to deserve this ..."

"Ah, the fruits and price of success all in one, sir" he chortles on his way.

Although they had worked, lived and shopped in Boston, going to department stores and the Haymarket and various attractions, Wayne and Joan had never lived the typically imagined American consumer life. They had never before felt like a typical couple on a TV show, trying to fill their house with gadgets, buying shiny toys for their child, endlessly cruising supermarket aisles and wasting Saturday evenings in huge toy stores. Eating fast food weekly, forced to pilgrimage to various state agencies and car repair shops.

The huge cornucopia of American life hit them hard. They were a little frightened of it, quite guilty about participating willingly, and yet it was seductive. Turns out there was a quick and pleasurable freeway from making more money than they had ever thought possible to spending more than they could have reasonably imagined. Home improvements, little knick-knacks filled their lives. Language itself changed, purchases were no longer expenses, but "investments." They hardly noticed this slide into normality, except once in a while on a rare quiet night alone in the dark.

One good thing about it all was that Babylon seemed as exotic as any foreign country. They had not spent much time in stores, or at festivals, and now they were there all the time. They had hardly attended movies, and now watched them with Gregory at home or took him to the dollar cinema in neighboring Lindenhurst. They wandered the bursting boutiques in entranced surprise, as naively impressed as any immigrants freshly off a boat or plane. Perhaps they thus understood the wonder of the United States and its economy more completely than if they had never detoured out of it.

Yet there were internally set limits. They remained, as many immigrants do, mired in their previous outlooks. They did not normally lust after a bigger house, a finer car, flashier jewelry, fashionable clothing. An internal governor kept holding them back, and a voice which they could not ignore often whispered "this costs too much," or "buying this is silly." It had nothing to do with being deprived, and everything to do with remaining a little set in their ways.

In later years they would argue about it sometimes. Friends and relations were already borrowing to send children to private schools, or to enrichment camps. Joan and Wayne never did—they had both attended public schools and thought them better for mind and soul. They somehow always remained neighborhood outsiders—Wayne considered himself a transplanted city bohemian, an artist exiled into the countryside; Joan never felt comfortable far beyond Huntington. That helped push them closer to each other, a truly tight nuclear family, but it also was not what many of their acquaintances were experiencing at the same time.

Some favorite places were generally free, or at least cost so little that they were effectively free.

I've already noted Captree, with its party boats and wonderful docks and dunes. Nearby were Robert Moses state park, with a cute little boardwalk, and farther away Jones beach with a huge one. But most of the time we went to Overlook, our "town beach" open only to residents which had its own playground, refreshment stand, and most interestingly tidal channels to be played in or surfed during the times when the tide was going out.

Not too far away was Bayard Cutting Arboretum, where Gregory could walk a miniature bridge to a tiny island with a bramble-covered hill and play pirate or whatever else struck his fancy, while we could admire the specimen trees and vast well-tended lawns, or walk along the Connetquot inlet admiring the wealth displayed on the far side. Belmont state park had rowboats for hire and a bicycle trail all around, even though we rarely used the vast picnic facilities. A short walk from our home was hidden and almost private Southard Pond, magnificent in the fall, with an outlet trout stream surprisingly crowded in spring when fishing season opened.

Back in the late eighteen hundreds, Babylon had been a resort community for the wealthy, and remnants of grandeur remained in some of the old homes. The town center was small-town gracious, nearby Lindenhurst had an Oktoberfest celebration started by its once predominantly German population. A grand hotel had long vanished, but left behind Argyll Lake with an encircling trail, waterside playground, and magnificent set of waterfalls at the dam which created it. And the town docks were a feast for the senses in all seasons, even the height of winter. Finally, closer than the ocean beaches, was the little bay beach of Venetian Shores which we could reach in five minutes just to let off steam or inhale a bit of serenity, although on more ambitious hot days we could stop by for a swim.

BABYLON WITH GHOST

And if all that failed, or if Gregory was especially good, we could always go spend a little money at Adventureland, a holdover amusement park from the fifties, with old rides and an old-fashioned ambience reached by going past the smelly gigantic alpine town dump, and the decaying hangers left over on the edge of Republic Airport from the post-World-War-Two dismantling of its aviation industry.

There were more, and even more if we wanted to stretch a bit. All in all, not a bad place for a family. In fact, a darn good place for a young family, much though Joan lamented that they were not playing on equivalents in marvelous dreamland Huntington, and Wayne sourly thought how much more crowded it all was than where he had been raised.

Filled with satisfied diners finishing off their desserts, the room lights noticeably darken as a spotlight begins to shine on the front stage. Ghost comes out with short clipped greasy hair, wearing a maroon jacket. He strolls carefully to a huge old standing microphone, as his backup band settles in, and begins one of the classics these old folks on vacation want to hear.

"See the pyramids along the Nile"

Well, that was surely something Joan and I had never wanted to do. Life was way too filled to waste going to exotic places when we hardly had time to notice what was down the street.

"See the sunrise on a tropic isle"

I'd seen enough more than enough sunrises, many of them behind me on the LIE as I headed to Brooklyn, and if I were writing lyrics it would tend to the joys of missing sunrise altogether and getting a few more hours of sleep. The tropic isle might be nice, but Babylon in summer was not far from being a tropic isle itself, without the palm trees.

"See the marketplace in old Algiers"

I was quite content to have seen the South Street Seaport as it rose from nothing to a place where everyone went. And there were markets enough around here, filled with wares never dreamed of in desert bazaars. Going out East a ways, there were still farms and farmstands, in some of the small coastal towns were places full of fresh caught fish and shellfish. Like Joan, I had become a little wary of street marketplaces, at least for buying things, but if I wanted to various yard sales and flea markets could certainly give anywhere on Earth a run for their money in terms of odd, possibly awful, merchandise.

"Fly the ocean in a silver plane"

Maybe, someday, but right now no time, and all they wanted to see was right here.

"See the jungle when it's wet with rain"

Anywhere was nice when it was raining. At least to walk through or look at. Not so nice in morning or afternoon rush which took twice as long. Sometimes hard to remember to walk at lunch when it was nasty.

"Just remember to come home again."

And that was the key, wasn't it, to a truly happy life? Even if they never journeyed very far.

Another Sunday. Another pilgrimage to Huntington. Fortunately, Wayne had already walked to 7-11 up the block to get his Sunday papers, with Greg riding alongside on his big wheel. The lawn had been done yesterday, with the necessary shopping. Pancake breakfast was complete, even cleaning up (if not to Joan's total satisfaction.) He was sore, he was tired, there was nothing more he wanted to do than just hang out in the back yard this fine late summer morning and read his paper. But it had been a couple of weeks since they had gone over to her parents' house, so off they were going.

"I wish you'd dress up a little bit," complained Joan. "You look like a farmer. "

"Hey, I'm coming over, aren't I?" he asked. Then they were both quiet for a few minutes, surveying the unsettling aspects of Wyandanch as they crossed the railroad tracks.

"I wish we didn't have to come this way," she said. Wayne agreed, although perhaps it was good to be reminded that true poverty existed, even here in what seemed a land of plenty. This pocket of desolation a mile up Straight Path was unsettling—houses abandoned, broken fences, a few properties well maintained but many just falling into ruin. One of the odd things about the trip over, a scant ten or twenty miles that went from middle class Great South bay through this run down area alongside sod farms and a few struggling remaining farms from the old days, then into forest, traffic, and the upscale North Shore.

"And you behave yourself," she scolded. "No politics or arguments about what's going on."

"Who, me?" asked Wayne, falsely innocent. In fact, they hardly talked at all. Her father did not like sports, her mom and Joan cemented inseparably, politics were bitter, he and her father stuck to safe topics like home projects. Wayne was never doing quite enough home projects, it seemed, and he had great trouble hiding his boredom concerning real estate, which was almost a fanatic pastime over there.

But the house was ok, the job search had ended well, his wife was content enough to please all, and the common concern was Gregory. As the center of attention, as the first grandchild, he was easily the lightning rod of all thoughts, some worried, mostly happy and cheerful. Truthfully, with so much going on with his family, he could sit in relative peace and quiet, and might have a more restful time then he would back at his own house, where tasks always beckoned even on a day of rest.

Our days, and especially the weekends, filled with various holidays as totally as any medieval peasant's saints' calendar. Sure, Joan and I had been used to visiting both parents for Christmas, to having them visit us once a year, and to spending some vacation time in both Philadelphia and Lake George. But now—oh now there seemed an endless procession.

There were birthdays—mothers and fathers, Robert and Cheryl, Philip, Gregory, and his cousins, and Joan's special extensions to aunts, uncles and her own cousins. Thanksgiving of course. Anniversary celebrations, picnics on school holidays, arguments about who would have Christmas, Easter, Memorial Day, Fourth of July. Labor Day remained magically quiet because it involved so much effort to get ready for school. And Gregory had his own—Halloween, early Christmas and Thanksgiving and Easter, late Fourth of July fireworks. And of course the sneaky ones that every husband dreads—our own anniversary, Joan's birthday, Mother's day, whatever else came along.

After a while it seemed there was never more than one week a year open. Most involved driving somewhere, but quite a few were at our house, which meant a week of cleaning and fixing up to get ready.

In short, it was a far cry from our lonely but self-satisfied days on Beacon

Hill, when we could pretty much do as we wanted whenever we wanted. But it had all crept up so smoothly and suddenly that it was only when for some reason we were particularly tired or busy that we even thought to complain about it. Like taking catnaps, learning to grab an hour of peace and quiet became a survival technique.

A tall spiky black iron fence surrounds 1014 11th street, as two parked busses puff blue exhaust fumes. There's a noisy line of colorfully dressed folks at the gate near where I remember the driveway. A discrete sign proclaims this to be "Chateau De Slingluff." As I near the murmuring crowd, I see Ghost waving a closed red umbrella over his head, until he spots me and excuses himself. Looking closer, I notice his light grey uniform, neatly pressed, "Bonjour!" he hails, with a fake accent.

"Uh? Bonjour? We are in France, no?" Trying to mock him is futile, I know.

"No. I thought it was a nice touch. All these visitors from foreign lands. I need to use many languages. For the tour."

"What tour?"

"Why, the old homestead, the family bastion, the place where it all started."

"Ghost, listen to me. We didn't begin here, we lived here for less than ten years, somebody else built it, and for all I know somebody else has leveled it by now."

"No matter, no matter!" he cries, "Make way! Give us some room!" He squeezes us inside and locks the entrance behind us. "Next tour in half an hour," he explains as we round the corner.

"This is silly."

"Well, you Americans, you know you hardly ever build ancestral estates anyway, we tour guides just take what we can get. So, do you recognize it, back here as it was in 1984?"

"Oh, pretty much. There's the raised flower bed in back where I burned down the stump one night, and the vegetable garden in the corner, and a lot of the flowers. There's the mulberry tree that would get wiped out in next year's hurricane. Sure, I recognize it, and all the little before and after permutations it would go through. So what? It's just a place, nothing special about it."

"You're right, bien sur. But then, if we admitted that up front, where would poor guides like me be?"

"Ghost, for us, I'm afraid this place was just a holding pattern between Boston and Huntington. This was never in our mind as a destination. Nice enough, but we were always ready to leave, and always a little sorry we were here."

"But you were saying…."

"Oh, don't get me wrong. A lot of it was wonderful and if we had to stay here forever we'd be happy. But we never really thought of it as forever. And, as it turned out, it never was."

"Well, do me a favor," confides Ghost in a barely audible voice, "don't tell that to the gang out front."

Friday nights in Babylon, I often just crashed out up in my library/den with a bottle of wine and an attitude. It was hard to pin that attitude down exactly, I didn't feel bad, I didn't feel put-upon, I didn't feel angry. I was very tired, and thought I was caught in something that was harder and harder and would never end. I'd take out old books, listen to old music, and generally let my brain fog out.

I would rarely be free to do this before nine, what with getting home late from work, eating, and taking care of my portion of watching Gregory, which was often little more than sitting with him on the couch talking and watching TV, or keeping an eye on him as he played in his bedroom opposite my place, the other upstairs dormer bedroom. I did look forward to it as a time away from work, although at least half the time I had to skim some code, manuals, or outlines for my coming week and problems that had occurred over the last one.

I tried to think of "larger issues," like Art, and Being, and—if you will— the meaning and purpose of life. These had been staples back in Boston, and yet although they recalled those times, they tended to be more melancholy than uplifting. What was the meaning and purpose of life to me? I had to do what I had to do, and had little influence beyond that. My philosophy narrowed to doing my best and enjoying my situation. Admittedly, I was far more fortunate than many.

Joan and I were often criticized for being too easily satisfied, and whether or not this was valid as a criticism, it was certainly true as our way of life. I never was a person who needed "more" except maybe more time. Joan wanted a civilized middle class existence, but did not worry excessively about pushing hard towards upper class pretensions. We both had experienced trade-offs, and respected the knowledge that you never got something for nothing. We managed to be happy on what some relatives and acquaintances others considered near-poverty. They never could understand our lack of conventional drive. We were amazed at their inability to appreciate the present moment.

Friday was the time when I could let these thoughts flow freely, and extinguish worry and logic for a while, and just connect once more to who I had been. Perhaps it was time badly spent from an outside perspective. From my internals, it helped keep me sane.

Ah, we're back at sea, I see. Blue everywhere except for a bank of dark clouds on the far Southern horizon, warm humid wind picking up a bit. Ghost scurrying about with a forced smile, carrying clipboards, harassing passengers. He sees me and hurries over. "Hello, sir, would you please be willing to fill out this survey of how well you have liked this tour?"

"But we're only halfway through," I protest.

"Yes, of course, sir, but later there may not be time with all the activities coming up. Besides, by now you certainly have enjoyed enough to generously rate your experience."

"This wouldn't have anything to do with that squall line over there, would it?"

He cringes. "Maybe just a bit. Predictions are the hurricane will miss us," he glances around anxiously. "Unfortunately, predictions are but predictions. Please fill this out for me?"

"Um, I'd be willing to fill out a provisional one, if you wish. Are those provisional or final?" I ask suspiciously.

"We only deal with final copies, sir," he huffs. "We shall not trouble you again. Everyone is so busy and we know it's an imposition and …"

"And predictions are only predictions…" I finish.

"There is that," he agrees.

"I think I'll wait to see what happens." He stalks off. I watch the clouds drawing nearer.

Night hadn't nearly fallen, the sun was just going down over the wide green marsh grasses across the boat channel. Twilight would be long, here in midsummer. They stood on the fishing dock, gazing at lingering crabbers and a few guys with deep water gear struggling with heavily sinkered lines in the strong incoming current. Once in a while a noisy, brilliantly lighted party boat would come by, returning after hours at sea. Successful ones were pursued by a flock of gulls, waiting for scraps thrown during fish cleaning.

Gregory was finally running down—they could tell as he got a little cranky. Wayne had already carried him on his shoulders off and on. Besides, it was true that he himself was ready to sit and read and do nothing for a while, while Joan planned tomorrow. They had, after all, had a wonderful outing already, and Captree was always here, even if they didn't make it back quite as often as they thought they would have liked.

There was nothing to take back but themselves—they traveled light, as usual. The parking lot had emptied out considerably, although there was still a fair traffic on the long bridge to the mainland. Wayne spend a few minutes trying to get back into normal reaction time—he always mellowed out a little too much and had to make an effort to concentrate and drive as fast as everyone else.

Still, it was not a long ride to get home. It had been a great day, a wonderful time in their lives, and almost as fantastically, from his standpoint, a free Sunday with no obligations spread itself gloriously before him.

OVERLOAD

NICK'S OFFICE WAS located in a high tower in Hauppauge—well, a high tower in suburban terms. JBS was on the fifth floor and overlooked much of the Island through huge plate glass windows facing west, where the city was invisible but always in mind. Wayne had dressed conservatively in a dark suit, this first day, hardly knowing what to expect. He showed up early, ready for orientation, not quite sure how much time he would have to get oriented and what might be expected of him.

Nick showed him around and started going over accounts and applications. Unsurprisingly for that time, there was no trace of any computers in the office. Here he was, in a computer consulting firm which not only supported but developed code, and there were no terminals nor screens. It was explained that all coding was done at various accounts. Billing timesheets were the lifeblood of the business and were to be turned in—on paper—no later than Tuesday of the week following.

There were manuals everywhere—IBM System 36 operating manuals, System 38 glossy sales brochures, a few pathetic supporting documents for IBM package software. Wayne would be allowed to curl up with them and take them home. But they were mostly irrelevant.

Wayne was here, he discovered, as Mr. 38. The system 36 accounts were happy and well in hand, supported by a small staff who had been around for a long time and knew what they were doing. But Nick had eyes on the future and was being shoved by IBM into that realm whether he wanted to go or not, and the competition both from other IBM consultants and other manufacturers was fierce and in flux. Without a viable System 38 presence, JBS would not last long. So to some extent, Wayne was treated with kid gloves.

Besides, he found himself in the unusual position of senior analyst. His experience was broader than anyone's except Nick's, and he had a deeper and more pragmatic background in business applications. The System 38 was gobbledygook to everyone else, and he was expected—eventually—to be the local translator. But all that would be in time.

Immediately, Nick had overreached and was in the process of acquiring some early 38 adapters as clients. He was a salesman, and could sell the proverbial refrigerators to eskimos. Wayne's immediate task for the week—easy enough—would be to ride around with Nick to all the accounts, learn where they are and who had to be contacted, and what would be expected.

By the end of the day Wayne was a little uncertain. He was going from hours of coding and developing a day, it seemed, to none at all. A world of shaking hands, smiling, and applying factory fixes. He wasn't sure about the move, but on the other hand, he liked everybody in the company and the air of quiet competence they all projected.

Very loud noises of people eating greedily. A gigantic stone fireplace holds a roaring blaze, helping illuminate the vast vaulted hall which radiates cold in spite of greasy soot-caked draperies. Candles feebly hold back the gloom. A huge meat platter, alongside vegetables swimming in gravy, sits in front of me. I risk a taste from the goblet—thin watered down vinegar is, I suppose some kind of wine.

At the far end of the table sit what seem to be the nobles. Ghost is dressed in fancy rags, strumming an ancient stringed instrument, singing loudly in a strange dialect I can scarcely make out. Once in a while he gestures at me as he tells adventures of Gordian knots of regression solved, mighty deeds of data recovery, quests for better management information. Eventually, he is dismissed and comes down to hover behind me.

"What's this all about, Ghost?"

"Ah, master, it is good to hear your voice. Surely these distant realms have scarce heard tales of your magnificent deeds, and I was entertaining them with some of your more exciting adventures. Is this not a grand banquet?"

"I don't have any mighty deeds, Ghost. Playing it up a bit, aren't you?"

"They are, it is true, somewhat unaware of the true nature of digital dragons. But your glory is real. If you don't take credit, some other knight will."

"I'm just doing my job, most of the time."

"If a king sends you on a quest and you triumph, none remember the king. It is your quest, your triumph. At least in your own mind."

"Ah, so we reach the heart of the matter."

"Well, you always were prone to reading too much fantasy and science fiction." Ghost capers off as one of the nobles calls out to him.

Home early, Wayne waited at the kitchen table with Gregory as Joan pulled roast chicken out of the oven. Selchow and Righter was just a few miles east along Sunrise highway in Bay Shore, so he'd been able to leave work promptly at five, for once, while rush hour traffic was streaming the other way. An easy day followed by a restful evening. Too bad more days weren't like this.

"So how was work?" asked Joan out of habit.

"Simple and relaxing," he answered. "All I had to do was follow a list of instructions from IBM and update their computer. Mostly putting in disks and sitting around waiting for them to finish."

In fact it involved little more than that. The worst was always the uncertainty about the update—would the disks be read correctly, were the permissions set correctly, would the power stay on as the machine continued. As they waited he had talked things over with Steven, the nominal IT head, who had added these duties to his warehouse management skills. Mostly the machine just collected sales data punched in by the single operator and spat out sales reports. A System 38 was overkill, but their new Trivial Pursuit game had made the company flush with cash, and filled with grandiose dreams.

"Was that different than usual?" she inquired, innocently.

"Oh, you have no idea. These are the nicest people, the nicest account

I've ever seen. Even when things go wrong, and for some reason over there they never go wrong. I wish I could go there every day."

"Maybe you should apply for a job."

Wayne laughed. "Hah! They don't even pay a proper computer operator or manager over there. They treat the computer system like a telephone. No, I'm making a lot more as a consultant than I ever would being employed directly at places like that."

"Are you going over there again tomorrow."

"Nah, everything went perfectly, I don't see them again for two weeks, unless I have some kind of emergency. Tomorrow is a lot tougher out at the vitamin place."

That would be custom code, done by a part time employee Nick had found somewhere, and a very angry vice president who couldn't understand how a simple general ledger program (custom designed to his specifications) could cost so much and still have problems. Nick would be helping untangle the arguments over billing on this one at least. Not something to look forward to.

"Are you ready to ask Nick for a raise."

"Nope." Finally Wayne was getting some idea of the economics of the industry. He knew his own place pretty well, and all in all felt quite fortunate. He was still new here, and had no desire to rock the boat. Besides, what with this and that, he was not at all ready for more responsibility.

"Well, here we are. Have some broccoli with that, Gregory." The simple dinner, as always, was delicious. He almost looked forward to a night reviewing code they'd be arguing about the next day.

Like many young people, I had come out of high school cocky and self-assured, ready to take on and change the world. Like others, I had hit a brick wall in my early twenties, and tended to blame it not on internal issues but on everyone else, the old people holding their stupid prejudices and controls. Immersed as victim to avoid responsibility. When that layer of anger finally burned off, more from attrition than admirable personal growth, I was finally able to accept a normal place in society.

For a while, especially in my computer career, it seemed I was once again on a fast track, everything was falling into place and soon I would emerge master of my universe. After a few shocks derailed that vision, I continued doing well but I was aware of my inadequacies and innumerable gaps in my required knowledge.

I jumped in with a typical outsider's view of business. I'd never been involved in corporate life, except as the lowliest employee, and I had no idea of the effort, thought, luck, and fear that went into being nearer the top of the organization. Nor did I comprehend how widely varied successful business strategies and tactics could be. I had much to learn about people, in spite of the fog of not recognizing any of them on sight (face blindness is best compared to trying to figure out who everyone is by seeing them only from the back—how they walk, what they are wearing, how big or small, and so on.)

For another, for all my bravado and success, I didn't truly understand computer fundamentals. I had arrived through the back door, with lots of practical experience but no theory. I never took a real computer class, and there were precious few textbooks early on—and those severely out of date for the areas in which I worked. The saving grace here was that just about everybody else in my position was just as ignorant or more so, and many of them not quite so able to quickly grasp ideas from reading. But the fact was that, deep down, I was often quite uncomfortable about not understanding the foundations on which all my work was based.

Finally, I understood how fluid and shifting my career was to be. I had already seen one company crash and burn—it would not be the last. I'd watched the first computers I had used become obsolete and forgotten antiques. I was party to the terror gripping salespeople as new and more powerful machines sprung up like locusts challenging their old safe fiefdoms.

My area of the industry strongly resembled freshman year at college. I might be in control of my destiny, but still had to take all the basic courses to advance. I was shocked to discover that world's reality.

Happily, I was in the right place at the right time, for which I was exceeding grateful. On the other hand, there was very little easy about it.

There is no such thing as a "typical" small business owner, any more than there is a "typical" human. Time and circumstance vary tremendously, and people possess different drive, goals, and capabilities. Nick was certainly typical in some ways, unique in many others. I admire him more than most of the other people I ever met.

Nick had taken a small insight and some technical skill, and with the necessary bravado had risked his and his family's future on running his own show. He had quickly discovered that in his chosen business he had advantages of background and personality, and disadvantages of little access to capital and no time to actually work technically once the sales and administrative aspects of keeping things going were complete. So he had taken a deep breath and hired people, that he had to pay, sometimes from his own pocket.

There were good times and bad, with competition everywhere and always breathing down his neck. He tried hard to keep a family balance, treated his employees well, was as fair as possible to everyone including some nasty clients. His dream was little more than a relatively affluent stability, but that dream proved extremely demanding and difficult, even in the best circumstances.

Nick was the best possible mentor for my advancing business experience. I had learned a lot at Webcor, but big decisions were handed down, rarely was I privy to why things were done and the relative tradeoffs of each. At JBS I became part of the inner circle, knowing the tight circumstances and the possibilities and dangers of almost every step. The dance was far more complicated than I had suspected.

Of course, Nick made the decisions, and his wife Carol was his main advisor, and that was as it should be. Sometimes I disagreed, but it was my job to go along with what had to be done, and I did so cheerfully, content in the knowledge that I was often wrong. I liked being in this position, and I loved the fact that, unlike Nick himself, I still got to play with the code and create visions of software.

I also discovered how bad a business leader I would have been. Business at this level—perhaps at all levels—is people and politics and friendships. I was never that. I was cold focus and code and logic and problem solving. It was wonderful, during this period, to fit almost perfectly into a machine of commerce, and to actually understand my place in it clearly.

Ghost, jiggling his weird costume, was motioning me to come over to a hallway off the main dining hall. Dinner had broken up after dessert, and people were heading out to the next entertainment, leaving the leftovers to the dogs and—eventually—the rats.

"Arnaud, one of the King's couriers, wants a word with you," he muttered.

"About what," I began to ask, but then it was too late.

"Ah, yes, Sir Wayne. We have been thinking of acquiring one of those famous calculating machines, to keep track of taxes, you know, and we hear you are in the trade."

"I do the rude mechanics only, my lord. I am not the right one to ask about the great questions."

"Ah, then you do not recommend one merchant or another? Your servant here claims IBM is most excellent."

"That is our preferred vendor, of course, but much depends on the size of the purse, and your exact requirements."

"Oh, that can be worked out, of course. Naturally the King would not need to pay—your recompense will be in how many others will want you to sell such things to them once he has a demonstration system. Really, a simple task for one as wise as you."

Uh oh. I was breaking into a cold sweat. "I do not actually arrange such things, my lord. I am helpless in the realms of higher actions. But should you need calculations of infinite length, conversions from one tongue to another, rapid inscription on parchment, or perhaps keeping records of who lives where for easy taxation lookup, I can perhaps be of some service. But that all comes later."

"Ah, then you are not whom we seek. Where, then, is your master."

"I have here his current abode," I handed him a business card. "I'll inform him of your interest. But perhaps, given your unique situation," I continued with hope in my heart, "You would be more satisfied by Sir Joseph, over in that corner, who is most accommodating with his DEC wares."

The hardest adjustment to his new job, Wayne quickly discovered, was less multiple masters (various clients on site versus needs of his company) than daily peripatetic change of working conditions. He had been used to having a whole computer room to himself, with a desk or desk equivalent to keep his resource manuals, and one machine to keep running. He had known where all the paper, and backups, and everything else was so he could jump in if necessary.

But now, every day was different. One time he might be in the back of a noisy warehouse, in a space cleared next to a water cooler, on a rickety table plopped next to the computer and its printer (always a printer, often hammering away all day—in those days the decibel level from such contraptions was as high as the noise of a jet engine.) Next day he might be in some converted cloak room, still dusty and with scant air conditioning or heating. Then he might head to a plush office shared with some vice president (although at least here the printer would be in another room.)

In all cases, he was all but invisible. People walked around and ignored him—they didn't know nor care much what he did, he had no political hold on anyone in their everyday jobs, and he was obviously busy and (at least he thought) looked important. That vice president would talk about anything as if he were deaf. It was disconcerting, and a tad lonely.

But on the other hand, quiet days were good, because at least half the time he was dealing with problems. And everyone was willing to come to him with problems, whether it was a sticky keyboard, a field they did not like, or a printout figure that needed detailed explanations. As the main troubleshooter, he had to be ready for dispatch at any time next morning or during the day, making apologies and heading off to some disaster or other.

And none of the places were kept as he had kept things. Backup materials were scattered or missing, manuals were lost or out of date, custom code printouts were back at the office, if they existed at all. He eventually learned to keep a traveling computer room in his car trunk, with tapes and floppy disks and printouts and manuals and even specification contracts. That took care of ninety percent of the cases.

His head had to be scattered and compartmentalized as well. Although he was nominally servicing only distribution accounts, mostly on the System 38, he had to be ready to shift from one company to another and one industry to another and one set of applications (sales, inventory, order entry, and so on), none of which were exactly identical. Fortunately, he had a good mind for such basic insanity, and that made him a valuable employee.

Also, surprisingly, his day-care training helped him a lot. A CEO tantrum was not a lot different from that of a three or four-year-old, and he found he could deal with them with similar tactics. He would sit and listen and not respond for a while, then eventually distract with how he would deal with the crises and how these problems could be avoided in the future, then exit with the promise of a clear mission and good things to come. That even worked when he was finessing real disasters.

Real disasters sometimes came. Machines sometimes broke, or sometimes just had to be down for a day while being updated, and work backed up. Sometimes some program lost data (always inexplicably, at first glance, always with some coding error once the forensic investigation as complete) and that had to be recovered and adjusted. End of month was always a nightmare, with too little time and everyone wanting the final printed results.

And yet, for all that, it was a lot of fun. Wayne found he enjoyed the challenges, both computer and people-related. The changes of scene were refreshing in a way, instead of the same old thing day after day. And there was always the promise of better times just around the corner.

By mid-autumn, I had been introduced to various accounts, of which JBS had quite a few. I was deeply involved in a half-a-dozen or so. There were manufacturing firms, distribution firms, import firms. And there were worlds of different models and different ways of doing business.

At that time before full globalization and the consolidation of mega-capitalism, there were incredible numbers of small businesses filling unimaginably odd niches. Once upon a time, there were one or two small hardware stores in each town, one or two independent drug stores, a couple of local general merchandise shops, and so on. Each of them had to be supplied with product, but each was too small to deal directly with—say—General Mills or Johnson and Johnson. That was the role of the distributor, who provided one place where a small local business could go to get everything to sell to consumers.

And the small manufacturing firms were truly small, turning out one or two products on machines run as much with human love and hands-on daily adjustment as by automation. Some of these had been going for nearly a century.

BABYLON WITH GHOST

A common thread was that many of them were family affairs, at this point often in the second generation, where a son or daughter was still providing the hands-on leadership. The good ones were growing, the less good ones were desperately seeking ways to hang on. Both types were told that computers would be their salvation, the edge they would need to maintain their place.

Competition was already shifting. Strangely, in the older days, competition was less razor-edged than often portrayed in romantic novels. JBS accounts were loath to move from us to another consultant, and we rarely stole from anyone else. There was a kind of gentlemen's agreement not only between computer firms, but between—for example—local distributors suppling "fasteners" (basically screws and nails of all types and sizes) to local hardware stores. If they didn't carry something, they would refer to a competitor. After all, they tended to have their own network, often but not always geographic, and like Macy's Santa Claus in the movie, they gained prestige from being seen as honest.

Those days are long gone—I watched them starting to vanish. Maybe we even helped. The experience convinced me of how little we truly control our futures, and how we must concentrate on the immediate days around us. The long term is a polite fiction which often leads to complete failure in this moment.

I'm in some kind of rolling near-desert, with lance and armor, fortunately mounted on a horse. Broiling sun on hot armor has me drenched in sweat. I glance behind and sure enough, riding on a donkey ...

"Sancho Ghosta at your service, senor. A word of warning, my lord."

"And that would be ...?" Ghost's scenarios often catch me off guard as if I am emerging from a coma.

"We are about to enter the Digital Terrorlands, graveyard of many, a place where none rest easy."

"I suppose we need to watch out for deep crevices, slippery cliffs, wolves and lions," I sneer.

"Oh much worse than that, senor. There are irrecoverable operator errors, scratched tapes, unreadable backups, power failures, system crashes. Oh, and wicked mistaken designs and unworkable implementations. Each may inflict a swift or slow but always painful end to your journey."

"I have faced all those before and won. I can triumph again."

"The stakes, senor, are ever higher. Your responsibility for the dangers ever greater. You must remain vigilant. And you have scarcely dealt with the worst of all."

"Which is?"

"The fearsome dragon Cost Overrun, Sir Wayne. When your estimates prove false, his teeth are sharp, his talons irresistible. If you retreat, you may be hanged."

"Yet in truth, knave, there is little I can do about a power outage or crashed computer."

"You have been charged by the powers that be, however, that you must know how to recover from all those problems, however little they involved you originally. You must have plans. You must have open recovery scenarios for the client. You must even have secret recovery scenarios when the client has ignored your directions. The way is long."

"But, eventually, we get paid."

"If all goes well, senor, God willing."

"All right. We will persevere. Any wolves or lions?"

"Only insects , senor ..."

I begin to laugh "Hah! Insects ..."

"What you might call bugs, senor." I sober up quickly. Sancho Ghosta continues "Immense bugs, sometimes, caused by machine imperfections, that can only be fixed by calling priests and scribes from the King. Impossible logic bugs that could only be resolved by invoking the help of the devil, which you have sworn not to do ..."

"And which I am not very good at, either."

"There is that," he agrees. "Worse are the tiny but often fatal temporal bugs—something which requires back corrections and manipulations unto the beginning of the fiscal year. And always the little swarms of nasty common bugs, easily destroyed once found, but often one gives rise to thousands before it is slain. There is no end. And then there is the absolute worst ..."

"What is that, Don Ghosta?"

"That is the invisible but certain bug named "It couldn't have been anything I did, I didn't touch anything!""

"Ah, yes, I know it well. We call it by a different name, the "Nothing is a coincidence" bug. Those are truly the most maddening of all."

"Must we continue, Sir Wayne?"

"Must we eat, Sancho Ghosta?"

Christmas required a trip to Philadelphia to visit his parents, even with Joan far along in her pregnancy. Since his family had arrived, conversations with his father had been much less contentious, the suppressed but obvious worries of his mother eased, and his own inner demons about achievement attenuated. So a visit, except for nasty drives in rain and snow along packed turnpikes, was a fine thing, marked with feasting and laughter, his brother and sister and their families all joining in around a fire.

Inevitably at some point Wayne would end up out on the glassed-in porch with Dad, watching football on television, discussing business. He had learned long ago to fake how well he was doing in teaching or art, believing the exaggerations himself as he spoke them, even though they were less true on reflection. But now, they were on the same page, and could be enthusiastic and share stories and problems. Suddenly they had much in common.

Of course, Dad had been in a much larger business, and Wayne's was tiny. Dad had been an executive, and he was essentially an artisan. But again exaggeration could soften the edges, and in any case it was easily acknowledged that he was finally on the right track and had brought to bear his abilities and schooling. Sometime in the future perhaps his career would be wonderful.

Always, however, with anyone outside the circle, there was a kind of exotic disconnect. Computers were important, everyone knew that, but kind of magical. How exactly they did what they did, and how anyone controlled them, and what were their limits and possibilities—ah, those were deep rites of the initiated. Too often the only way to explain anything was using jargon, and that was like suddenly speaking Chinese.

Wayne had a natural facility for translation and analogy, which helped him explain to clients. But sometimes it was easier to escape into the smoke and invoke deeper mysteries that mere mortals could not understand, solemnly intoning mystical mantras filled with techno-babble. He tried to cut back on that with relatives, but there was no easier way to exit a trail of discussion he no longer wanted to follow.

JBS was a typical tiny company dreaming of modest growth but without access or even desire to obtain outside investment capital. When I joined there were only two other full time programmers, and one subcontracted consultant. Surprisingly, given the common wisdom about computer careers, they were all women. Soon ranks would swell, but we always had a strong feminine component. Not that anyone noticed, because coding was coding, and sometimes handholding clients was more important than binary technique.

Small shops like ours, especially, were staffed by "IT professionals" who had little or no formal training, who had not attended computer science classes, who had started out on other paths entirely. Since scarcity had eliminated formal requirements, it was a career anyone could try. Since nobody really understood what was necessary, the only way to find out if a person was good was to give them a chance. Some worked out, some crashed and burned, and some were superstars.

A small technical business was not much different from a local deli. Customers came again and again less because they liked your wares better than those of any other place, more because the price and location were right and they were comfortable with the staff. Get the fix or sandwich right and serve it with a smile. So we had less narrow geeks and more rounded people than mythology suggests.

Admittedly, at first we weren't doing cutting edge stuff. We were mostly support and customizing, in that sense more of a car repair shop. IBM handed us the hardware and core programs, and provided technical support as necessary (on their own individual contracts with the clients.) We provided the actual labor of updates and fixes and minor tweaks to code to make it fit specialty niches better.

Nick had been expanding. Laney had helped him design and write a complete medical billing package, not based on any other code. This was beginning to be used in several places. Most of the larger clients were becoming more demanding as computers became more common, and I had come in to help with that. We were all completely certain that we had the tools and intellect to keep up with anything that was coming along. A certain intellectual arrogance was absolutely necessary to success.

The fire roared, casting shadows throughout the great hall. Circled nearby were huge wooden chairs, each holding a knight or lady of high station. Farther back in the cold an audience strained to hear, as flagon after flagon of beer were hoisted amidst the tales and boasts.

"And so," concluded Sir Alan, "my brain befogged by demon, I ended up traveling seven bridges to the White Stone when none were necessary. And each guarded by trolls demanding purse for passage. By the time I arrived, darkness was descending and forced was I to return next day."

Amidst general laughter, a voice called out "And thou, Dame Catherine, hast some misadventure to relate?"

"Ah, certes, that would be the ensorcellment of writ, which I must needs perform at Warco in the Bronx, for they had threatened to cease all proper tithes, and were threatening to unleash that most fearsome of beasts, their lawyer . I arrived smiling in the pretense of updating a general release, but stripped the source onto our disks of remembrance and caused it to vanish from their sight forever. Never before hadst I tread so softly, nor lied so mightily, I wager. My King was well pleased, especially later when we won payment and left them for another unsuspecting party."

"Sir Wayne?"

"Mine, I fear, is but a common tale. Tellco was using a standard package," groans rose around the room, "to track its sales of chocolate holiday sweetmeats. That clever application saved precious disk space by imprisoning zip code in a small integer numeric field. But Telco was purchasing from vendors across the wide world, whose location codes of course were alphameric or larger numbers. A new field must needs be conjured, and placed in an associated secondary product file. And, as is well known, that meant finding and changing all the programs in that dense and poorly composed forest."

General murmurs of sympathy arose. "But that was not the true problem," I continued. "I performed the necessary work at the office on paper, using the specially prepared printouts of searches and green bar details of such imps as must be affected. I took with me backups of compiled and source code. I had all that was necessary—except," there was a hush, "it was not up to date." Deep sighs.

"So I arrive early on the Isle of Coney, backup data and programs, and begin changes until I notice that what I am changing matches not what I have used to map my way. Some other fool—naming no names—had failed to bring back the latest prints from this account. Should I proceed, or stop, knowing full well we would never be paid for the double bill?"

"I tightened my girdle and gripped my visor and continued. All day long labored I, and it was finally done and running well and all were cheerful indeed. I left them well content, and was joyful in my heart."

Applause began.

"Until the next month end," I added darkly.

JBS offices changed over the years, from a modest suite in a tower to a few larger groups of rooms in roadside office complexes. But there was never extensive space, even when we started to put in our own computers. No matter what, we were often out of the office visiting clients, either working directly on their computers or doing sales, billing reconciliations, planning or support.

Our normal weekly routine was to get together for staff meetings on Friday afternoons. That was often the only time we could abandon accounts—usually with promises of returning early Monday, sometimes forced to be back the next morning. We had learned by bitter experience that there was almost always a crisis (or perceived crisis) somewhere over any weekend, and like good firemen somebody would have to show up. The week was pretty tight for everyone—we tried to have a fully planned set of days from Tuesday through Thursday, which would keep folks calm—"I'll be there Wednesday afternoon" for example had a nice definite ring, and could usually hold almost anything for another week of grace. Friday morning was more fire control—tamping down whatever had exploded during the week and putting it under restraint until we could turn solid effort on it the following week. By Friday afternoon, we were glad to leave the clients, and they were usually glad to get rid of us.

A few glorious times it would not work out quite that way, and we could spend the whole Friday at the office. But most of the time being closer to home was a rare treat.

Nominally, our task was to share problems, keep everyone in the loop about everything, and of course fill out the manual billing sheets. The accounts were so varied, and so tightly coupled to one person or another, that most of the time we had only the vaguest notion what anyone else was actually doing. Unfortunately, that sometimes degenerated into the kind of dialog where there was simply a role call of accounts and a mumble of standard comments like "doing ok," "still updating," "80% complete," or "that's going to take some extra effort." Not particularly helpful, and for the most part we had no idea how to handle one another's loads.

Initially, Nick was the only person who knew everything, but a good deal of that eventually downloaded on me. One of the roles I did enjoy was going over technical issues with everyone as we exchanged ideas and tried to figure out problems, because we always were able to come up with new, exotic, and useful ways to better handle an awful lot of more or less unique problems.

For the most part, we avoided weekend work, most of which could be done at home. But there were some times unavoidable when accounts required a half day or more on Saturday, and little could be done to cut that out. An example would be when the whole system had to be taken down for some kind of maintenance—already it was turning out that a company without its computer running would leave a good many of its employees sitting around doing nothing.

Dark dim chapel, colored specks from the dingy stained glass dancing on the ancient stone. Ghost stands silent before me in a grey monk's cloak, hood up, solemnly holding a silver chalice. "Are you quite ready for the quest," he intones in a low singsong.

"Give me a clue here," I answer. I feel I have no armor, but do have the underlying chain mail, and a sword besides.

"Surely you are aware of the obligatory quest for the holy grail."

"Ah, yes, pretty much a cup like that, only in gold with lots of big gems, right?"

"Some would say, my son," lilts Ghost. "But I feel that is only an illusion, that the grail is something more fluid and flexible, meeting the deepest desires and hopes of those who may seek it."

"So what, then, am I looking for exactly."

"I think," he responds, "in vernacular you would say the brass ring. That which would solve all problems, free you from mundane toil, and enrich your existence."

"Oh, sure, the brass ring. I always did hope one of our projects or one of my jobs, or one of my companies, or one of my schemes or one of my some-things would—beyond my control—turn into a gateway to much more."

"But surely you felt you controlled your destiny."

"My destiny, surely, and working hard too. But the brass ring, like the Grail, is beyond immediate adventure and hard work. No matter what I did, whether it magically prospered was quite out of my control—like those companies for which I worked that fell apart because of management problems or external competition. I couldn't do anything about it all."

"Yet still you dream."

"As we all do, I guess. Yep," I admitted, "I'm always ready for that quest."

Wayne scraped heavy frost off his windshield on another pre-dawn crisp December Monday. Getting the car into the jammed garage had never been an option. At least today he wasn't going toward the city.

As he started the car and let it warm up, he wondered—not for the first time—if he was in over his head. No matter how much he learned he seemed behind what was necessary. He just couldn't get a handle on the ancient RPG code on the System36 accounts. He was still nervous around the managers of the more ferocious companies like the vitamin manufacturer he would visit today. He still couldn't tell if he was working out as Nick wanted. And the lack of a working office with computer access was beginning to bother him.

Wayne had never let lack of preparation hinder him before. He had always been willing to jump in and let his native abilities carry him long enough until he learned as an apprentice. Usually that was a pretty short ramp up, and then he would be able to cruise and invent and become extraordinary. But there was just an awful lot new here, an awful lot of stuff in business, relationships, and technical matters that he had to absorb almost fully almost instantaneously. His confidence was a bit shaken, although he still thought he was faking it pretty well.

But three months in, he admitted he was having doubts. On the other hand, nothing to do right now but get through this day as well as possible. Like every day. Anyway, tomorrow would certainly be free—all the employees at his accounts were out holiday shopping. He put on the headlights, backed the car onto the quiet street, and started off towards the ramp onto Sunrise Highway.

1985 PHOENIX

DEMON ALCOHOL

A LOVELY BRIGHT spring day. Birds were singing in the yard, flowers were growing everywhere, some beginning to bloom. Early morning, a little past the normal time to be on the road to today's account. Wayne cowered in the basement, hiding from everyone, paranoid, overwhelmed with the world and life.

The immediate problem was not family, which was simply normally pressing. Nor was it work, which he was controlling quite well. Nor was it the pressures of his boss, Nick, who in any case was off on a business trip and would not be bothering him today. Nor was it, really, worry about the job or the future or what he was doing or what he was doing.

The problem was more simple, and harder, than that. He knew he was losing control of his drinking. Stone sober and regretting it, his body was screaming for just one glass of wine to take the edge off. His mind was persistently insisting it was time to stop for good. For once, he was listening to his mind, and what he was hearing was downright scary.

Eventually, he heard Joan stirring upstairs. After some time, he sheepishly went up and said good morning. "I've really got a problem," he began.

"I don't know why you can't control yourself normally," she replied. "You seem to have such good self discipline in everything else."

That was true. He was strung on a wire most of the time, doing coding, getting things organized, keeping to schedules and plans, dealing with other issues as they came up. And yet, as soon as he had that wine, things slipped. Most of the time he put it off until the weekends, but the last year had broken that, and sometimes he simply collapsed and had a glass the minute he got home on Wednesday. Then the rest of the week was a struggle, until Sunday when it became a real battle to stop cold. Most of the time. Not often enough, lately.

"I don't know. But I need help, I think. I could try AA or I guess I could look for a program somewhere."

"Why don't you look in the phone book. Maybe there's something tonight."

"Ok, when I get back. I need to walk around and clear my head right now. If I go, will you come with me?"

"Sure, but I'll have to get Mom and Dad to watch the kids. Let's see later, OK?"

Wayne dutifully called work and told Susan he was taking a sick day. Then he headed out into the bright sunlight and slowly ambled along 11th street, up a few blocks, not so much feeling sorry for himself as angry that it had all come to this.

Even without snow cover, this part of the park overlooking the water is lovely in winter. I'm sitting well wrapped against the cold, Ghost in a dark cowl alongside. One or two far away people stride briskly on their way, but mostly it is all hushed and still.

Ghost says in a strange deep voice, "You know, you really need to juice this story up a bit. Maybe you aren't being honest enough about how bad it was."

"And what are we playing at today?"

"Simply your own realizations of time, age, mortality, and the limits of what you can do. I guess I could be carrying a giant hourglass, if it made you feel any better. But back to the question, do you think you are overdramatizing this? You never really went through any of those 'lost weekend' horrors. At least not after you met Joan."

"It was bad enough. At times, anyway. It seemed within the normal confines of what everyone else was doing. Yet I always seemed to slip a bit too far. And I didn't like where I was going. But I admit, I often comforted myself saying I was just average."

"That's always the standard excuse," notes Ghost sternly.

"In this case, I think it's a good one. I knew people who drank more. I was always a pretty quiet and inward drinker, all I did was become meditative..."

"Or comatose...."

"As an evening went on. And only in the evenings. And only some days. And almost never in public, just in the privacy of home. Not nasty."

"Still, something that you would rather not have done."

"I suppose, but I thought of it as my one vice, something worth cultivating instead of worse ones, somewhat like Joan's cigarettes."

"So why all the angst suddenly in May."

"I realized how much I had to lose, and how close I was getting to slipping over the edge. That really terrified me."

Wayne had grown up without any alcohol at all, a "goody goody." His parents had a cocktail before dinner, Dad drank some beers on Saturday, once in a while family parties would begin to float. But he was too young, and then too straight, to partake. The drinking age in Pennsylvania was 21, and except for a beer on very rare occasions—like the high school graduation party—he was content to think of himself as a sacred temple of health required for his athletics.

Even college, bad as it had been psychologically, had only affected him in minor ways. He had some scotch on a few party weekends, and hated the hangover and sickness it brought on afterwards. He drank wine in France daily, but gave it up when he came back because of the expense. No, he was twenty two before he even developed much of a taste for it at all.

That had come in Kansas City, where he thought of himself as a starving young Modigliani, waiting out the Vietnam War in VISTA. There he suddenly started into an ongoing habit of a bottle of Wild Irish Rose fortified wine a night, purchased for a buck from the convenience store up the street on Independence Avenue. He carried the habit with him to the West Coast, where he struggled for a few years trying to become rich and famous, and had amplified it back on the East Coast in Cambridge before he met Joan in 1973. So, all in all, there were four or five years at most of any significant intake, and after they got married even that stayed pretty well in bounds.

Through all the turmoil of the first years on Long Island he thought of himself as drinking more than he wanted, but less than many of the people he knew working around him. The culture of the times still included three martini lunches, multiple beers on train rides home, long bar interludes during conventions and at evening professional meetings. At parties, most people were happy to drink to limits. So, whatever small peccadillos he might have committed were usually far less than any by his peers.

But 1984 had been really hard, and it came on top of a series of complex and unnerving years, stressful as all young families tended to be. And suddenly he found himself buying half gallon jugs of port all too frequently, and cases of beer every weekend, and an occasional small bottle of vodka on special holidays and—well trying to get rid of the evidence was worrying enough.

Afterwards he always thought of her as Saint Joan. She had put up with martyrdom for ten years, although his transgressions mostly consisted of disappearing into his books and music rather than helping her with necessary chores like watching Gregory. And she was suddenly a pillar of strength that night, when she finally believed he really meant it. They had located an AA meeting, open, at a local church community center in Babylon, not knowing what to expect.

The parking lot was packed. "Are you sure this is the right place?" he asked, not able to believe so many people were having the same problems.

"If it's not," she said, "we can just leave, right? They don't take our names or anything. Anyway, like me, you can always say you're just checking it out for a friend or something."

"Ok, ok," they made their way inside, which was just as crowded. A tall young man greeted them at the door. "Hi, I'm Jim. "

"Wayne. I'm just looking around. Joan, here, is helping me."

"Do you know anything about us?" he asked.

"No, just heard about you in the paper and things. I'm not even sure I'm alcoholic, but I'm drinking too much, I think. I'm hoping this can at least help me cut down."

"Ah. I've been sober nine years now." That seemed an eternity to Wayne, at that point, although not so long if he remembered his adolescence. "Well, all you need to do tonight is attend and listen. There's lots of literature over here on the table—let me show you some of the better pamphlets."

They picked up a few of the free booklets, thanked Jim, and went to sit anonymously in the back. The meeting was well conducted, moved along, stories were told. None seemed as minor as Wayne's problems. "But mine might be," he thought to himself, "if I don't do something soon." It was astounding what the human body and spirit could survive, and then recover from. Hope was, of course, the major takeaway.

He resisted going deeper that night, content with picking up a schedule of small and large meetings to concentrate on, happy that he had at least done something.

"Well," asked Joan when they left, a few hours later, "what do you think?"

"I'm going to try it," said Wayne honestly. "After all, I've been stopping cold almost every Sunday for years, and not drinking for days and nights afterwards. What I need to do is find something to keep me from starting again on Thursday or Friday. Maybe a meeting could do that."

"Don't you think you will ever be able to drink again, normally, have some wine or beer?"

"They don't think so. If it is an addiction, it will be a lot like your cigarettes. Any little trigger will be too much. But I like the idea of one day at a time, each day, and I'm sure going to try that for a while, no matter what it takes. Thanks for helping with this."

I've known people who drink a lot with little obvious effect, and people who drink only a little whenever they want. Some people who use drugs occasionally for recreation, and others who slip into being addictively stoned all day long. A few who believe they become the life of the party when they are high, or create better when they are drunk, or experience life more fully when high. A full range of reactions to a full range of substances.

Like everyone else, I was a unique case. I knew I did anything better when I was stone sober—drinking never helped me paint, or write, or program, or socialize, or plan, or think. When I reviewed actions and artifacts created under the influence, I found garbage and had to correct. I did not require a beer to better get along at a party, I did not want a glass of wine to more successfully complete a canvas. My use was purely personal.

What I sought was—not quite oblivion—for I truly enjoyed life all the time. What I called it was "relaxing" but it was deeper than that. I gave myself permission to let go of the tight control I wrapped around my thoughts and actions all the times. Usually I only granted that when I knew I was somewhere safe—home alone at night—or just part of everyone else being equally wild at some event from which I could safely get home. But when I did give such approval, there was no limit nor end during that night, and the sole reason for drinking was to reach a state of calm where my control and worries were deeply buried and I could float over the world and its imagined troubles.

Obviously, such an approach had its rewards and its dangers. Now the dangers had begun to far outweigh the upside.

A red-headed woodpecker flits onto a snow-covered branch, as light flakes begin to fall.

"No doubt Freud and his gang would have a good time with all this," mutters Ghost.

"No doubt. My opinion is it don't matter much. What difference what forms us, it is what we are that we must learn to deal with. Either by understanding the past, or simply dealing with the present,"

"But that's just repression…"

"So be it. I heard a lot of theories in California—I hear them still—and I remain convinced you need to take care of today first. Maybe learning a cause is useful to many, I hardly ever found going over early days with a fine toothed comb all that fruitful. All it did in me was lead to a sense of victimhood."

"But you never got professional help …."

"I read the literature. Doesn't seem to help all that much all the time."

"But AA does?"

"Some of the time. Controlling the effect of whatever deep junk you have can be more rewarding than smoothing over the deep junk, only to get controlled by something else deeper. Anyway, at that time AA was useful for me. And I know it helped a lot of the people there."

Traffic on the Southern State Parkway was at a near stop, compounded by angry aggressive drivers trying to squeeze into parking spaces between stationary cars. Horns were blaring, fumes all around made the still air shiver. Naturally, this old Dart had no air conditioning, and everyone was getting insanely cranky. Wayne was near breaking point, this Memorial Day.

It had started out as a wonderful idea for a family outing. Joan's parents would come over in the morning and they could all go have a picnic out at Captree State Park, something Joan and Wayne had been doing for years. But things were delayed, the morning grew late, they finally pulled out of the stone driveway already in a frazzled and bad mood shortly after noon. The roads to the expressway were normally crowded, but the expressways were forebodingly jammed, and before they got to the exit to go to the ocean, the radio reported that the connecting bridge was backed up for miles, and most of the swimming beaches were full already. Everybody, apparently, had had the same idea.

So, being clever, Wayne had gone the other way, planning an escape to Belmont State Park, just down the road from them. That was always deserted, and they could spread their things out and watch the rowboats. Besides, it was normally only five or so minutes away.

The five became ten, became half an hour, stretched interminably in the brutal heat. Mom and Dad were squooshed in the back. Gregory, belted in between them, yelled out yet again "I'm hungry. I wanna eat." That triggered Baby Wayne, in the car seat in front, next to Joan. She tried to hush him up.

Bedlam became louder as Mom yelled "why don't you just get off here?"

"It's the next exit, not this one, we can't get over …."

"We all have to eat! The food's going to go bad!"

He hoped this would be as difficult as it got, because he was not sure how much more he could handle. It was a few weeks sober now, and a few weeks dry left him aggravated to begin with. A tall cold one was looking awfully welcome. He pushed the thought away—couldn't do anything about it here, and when things calmed down he definitely didn't want to be planning one. But, for a few moments, it was pretty tough keeping his mental resolve.

When they finally did get off, ten minutes later, it turned out that the park was jammed with families. All the tables taken. Blankets spread so thickly they could hardly see the grass. Parking was scarce. He squeezed into a place, but almost immediately everybody decided it was better to leave. They dug out a roll for Gregory, and left. Soon they were on the backroads, and it was two minutes back to their driveway. The backyard never looked so good.

Wayne would be tested several times, particularly this first year, but never again were things so closely run as this day. He looked back on it quite proudly as time went by.

At the time, this seemed my last surrender to bourgeois, common existence. Drinking wine when I wanted was my last clear link to being a rebel, an artistic offshoot of other bohemians, even to my promising (at least in my fantasies) youth. Not drinking was to ultimately become—well, part of everything I thought I had not wanted to do. Nine to five job, house in the suburbs, grey job, statistically average family, and—most of all—no grand future in museums or stories. All that was left was my life.

The adjustment, of course, was that life was all that was needed. I had to give up thoughts of being remembered in museums or libraries or history books. It's not that I ever really would have ended up there anywhere without the miracles that fame and success often require—more so in my case. It was that I still dreamed I could be there, and in dark of night could say, "Well, this picture will hang in some place in the museum without walls." No, nothing would. All there was to do was experience today, do right by the children and Joan and relatives, progress adequately in a career, try to accumulate enough money to get by.

By the standards of common people in history, I was rich beyond measure. Warm, well fed, secure, joyful, medically taken care of. Toys undreamt of only two hundred years ago—electricity, television, cars—were freely available. My house and yard were almost as large—and millions of times more comfortable—than most of those of even the minor nobility in times past.

BABYLON WITH GHOST

And I had friends and support and love and all the good things in life both physical and emotional. Yet I had been disappointed.

I can't say I regret that time fully. When you are young it is right and proper—if it does not start to destroy you—to have grand dreams and great hopes and impossible wishes. I certainly would never take away the exhilaration I felt when completing some artistic project. Yet there always must come a time when you put away childish things. Ambition, if it destroys a wonderful actual life, is a very childish thing indeed.

But—well, I admit I missed not being that secret Michelangelo, or hidden cultural superman, available for some unknown masses in the future to admire. On the other hand, lately the actual working creations of programming, design, and computer code had come to replace most of the impulses and rewards that once drove brush and pen. There was a great satisfaction in delivering something that worked—mysteriously and effectively—to clients. I concentrated mightily on that being enough.

Snow comes down harder, obscuring the far pines, as fewer people trudge quickly to their destinations. Once in a while a gust of wind thickens or thins the falling transparency.

Ghost inquires, "You still thought artists were all drunken geniuses?"

"No, no, that had been cleaned out pretty thoroughly long ago in France. Most artists never drink when they are doing real good work, and the ones that do are too unhappy for me to follow them. I never wanted to be someone who roamed the fields with a cask of brandy all day, every day, painting landscapes or writing poems for adoring fans when the fancy struck."

"Like Lord Byron,"

"Or Modigliani. But they died early, and I was past that stage, and never really wanted it much anyway."

"Then what …."

"The thing was, I wanted the freedom to roam those fields and do what I wanted."

"Childish."

"Oh, very. But I felt that—as a self-anointed genius—I should be allowed to do so while I discovered great things for the common good. But 'they' wouldn't let me, and the only way I could handle my disappointment was to relax with a few rounds."

"Didn't work."

"Oh, worked for a while. But I was outgrowing it. That was what was most painful, I think."

Several weeks later, Wayne was thoughtfully (and increasingly sheepishly) cleaning the garage and basement, locating bottles and mementos he had forgotten about over years. Not that there were thousands or anything, but there were enough to make him realize that the problem had been even bigger than he had thought. Anyway, it was nice to now be making a clean start, symbolized by clean floors and corners and whatever. Meanwhile, he dutifully straightened everything else, leaving the world better at least for this morning than he had found it.

The same thing was true in his public stance. Fortunately, even over the years, he had not particularly victimized anyone. Few people were ever close to him, and that would not change merely with beverage consumption or lack of it. He regretted a few things, but not many. Joan and the kids had been mostly treated fine, he had not done stupid or mean things with his close relatives. Most of the real pain had been in his own tortured approach to life, his envy of what others were doing, his merciless comparisons of what he should be trying. He felt no need to apologize to himself.

On the other hand, there was a requirement to be honest. So he had told his employer what was going on, although it made no change to work overall. He had informed the closest and most affected. Others, well, that was just a matter of seeing if anyone noticed that he was no longer grabbing beers and drinks at parties.

So far, surprisingly, little had actually changed. He was still tired at night, still tightly strung over the day each morning, still full of anxiety, still sometimes a bit snappish with the kids. He didn't see any real change. Of course, they all said you would not, really, for years. Since he had increasingly blamed all his residual problems on his continuing alcohol use, that was discouraging. It meant he would really have to work on those problems without a silver bullet solution.

BABYLON WITH GHOST

I was surprised at the things that remained the same. I had the same plea-sure in code and solving problems, enjoying walks, getting up, working the yard. I had expected a bigger flood of reworked attitudes, somehow losing my enjoyment of music or reading, or dulled perceptions when I strolled about the yard. But no, everything was there.

After the first week, I felt much better physically, although not in dra-matic ways. Of course, I had spent much of many weeks for years without touching anything, that was normal Sunday through Thursday. This was sim-ply a continuation of that pattern. But it was wonderful to have the entire weekend clear, and to not be worrying on Saturday, for example, when I would allow myself my first drink, or when I would be able to get the next one if we were doing something together.

The simple truth was I had already achieved a great deal of the life I wanted to live. There were not huge chunks of it to rip up and replace with something better. I had no desire to suddenly travel the world or go out danc-ing or frequent restaurants. The home joys and the work pleasures remained central and compelling and soaked up the hours without effort.

I simply woke happier, with an always clear head. And, most importantly, I woke with no senses of guilt or dread. No fear of being exposed as some kind of imposter, who looked like he was doing the right thing while he kept hiding away secretly pursuing a habit he was ashamed of.

Now apparently dusk is falling, although without sun time is hard to determine. The snow is thick and heavy, constant. A soft change has trans-formed the landscape into complete monochrome.

"It must have been a huge change, though," comments Ghost.

"Surprisingly less than you might think. I was fortunate in many ways, and had a quite different story than many of those I heard."

"How was that?" Ghost inquires.

"The typical alcoholic tale involves very much wrapping all the most important activities into drinking—friends in bars, parties, late night extravaganzas, always in places where drinks are plentiful and available. Almost all my places avoided that entirely."

"You were lucky …"

"Extremely. Joan, for example, never drank. None of my ties with her involved inebriation, unlike many of the romances which often broke up. I had few friends, and my relationships with none of them ever involved having beers together. The only person I wanted to drink with was me, the only activity I wanted to drink for was to be alone. That was basically the hardest."

"Being alone?"

"Yeah. There was always something to do, and I had to reestablish my own time and parameters to recover equilibrium when I was being overwhelmed."

"How did you do that?"

"Mostly by channeling it into chores. It's hard to be forced to share when you're mowing the lawn or painting the house. And I could say my walks alone were necessary physical exercise. But they were also, as it turned out, necessary psychological breaks as well.

The Methodist church basement in the heart of Babylon Village was shabby, old, and dark, with exactly appropriate furniture and matching meeting attendants. Wayne felt a little out of place, but this was the nearest and best timed closed AA meeting available, and he had resolved to attend least one a week for a while as suggested. By now, he knew most of these people, had heard their stories as they had heard his, felt comfortable in being there. He fully accepted that he was one of them, powerless over alcohol, at least at this stage of his life.

His current trouble was always those niggling little doubts. That's what everyone agreed would get you into trouble. A few internal thought as you listened ("well, at least I never did that!") or a fleeting mental contradiction that most of the time you did feel some control. But AA was all or nothing, total abstinence or despair, although forgiveness for backsliding was swift and unquestioned. He occasionally wondered how well he fit.

But his own stories, told without hesitation or reservation, were bad enough, over the years, now that he faced them. There were many things he ought not have done, nothing terrible, but not in his scope of usual behavior.

BABYLON WITH GHOST

There were less painful remembrances of interactions with people, simply because it was always his nature to not have many interactions with people. But there were enough nights and days he wished he had done something different. There were certainly enough current indicators that he was headed for desperate trouble. Talking about them freely without judgment helped.

The program worked. At least for some, for some of the time. It was necessary for him now, and if the price was not to drink—well, he was increasingly finding that did not mean losing much. In that, he was far more fortunate than many here, who had not only lost a great deal before reaching bottom, but afterwards had often lost what little remained because that was all alcohol-related. He could thank Joan for that.

She wondered, too. This seemed an extreme step to both of them. And yet, compared to, say, entering a hospital program, it seemed light enough. He returned to paying attention to the speaker for the night.

A few hours, a few dollars, a lot of soul searching. Very much like a church of the reformed damned, except that the heaven they sought would be immediate if they just stayed dry. He was content, and more than that, he was finally coming to terms with his exact place in the universe, and not worrying about all the other places he was not.

Yep, darkness falling, snow picking up. Pretty much time to move along and find somewhere warm. Even in daydreams, it is nice to be comfortable.

Ghost drifts upward, shape distorted a little by the wind, wavering. "How long did you manage to keep this all up?"

"I went to the weekly meetings for about half a year. Then they didn't really seem to be helping much, I didn't feel I needed them. Repetitious, and I had so much other stuff to do."

"How long did you manage without them?"

"Surprisingly, Ghost, I cruised along sober as judges used to be until the kids went off to college and other events changed my life, nearly twenty years later. Without a regret nor thought of having just one beer or a glass of wine at sunset."

"Immense self-control, no doubt."

"Nah, I can't really take credit. I'm susceptible to immediate physical addition when I am drinking—one drink almost always means another, often because I have told myself I can go the limit. Bad hangovers can get me into a couple of day's binge. But when I am not drinking, I don't really ever need anything."

"Not even when tempted?"

"Surprisingly, no. When I was at a bar all those years with colleagues, I had no trouble at all having ginger ale while everyone around me got plastered. It was easier, of course, when the term 'designated driver' came into common use. No, my temptation was always to escape from the cares of the world by myself, not integrate more fully into it."

"A different vice."

"Indeed. And one of which I am still not cured."

Ghost finally dissolves into snowflakes, and I wonder how I will get out of this particular scenario.

Wayne had expected the holiday season to be far different. Holiday season, these days, ran from slightly before Halloween until mid-January, but the core of it remained the highly fraught month-and-a-half encompassing Thanksgiving, Christmas, New Years and all the necessary family obligations, work and home parties, children's requirements, and general social mayhem with impossibly romantic encrustations of media and consumer "traditions." Not to mention that they had always been the worst time for secretly comparing your life to everyone else's. So, his own internal expectations were that this would be a lot worse than he had been used to, since he would no longer be numbed down a few notches, either with a drink in hand or fighting a hangover.

Surprisingly, almost nothing seemed changed. People enjoyed themselves or complained, reflected on the year, worried about the future. The children kept growing and changing—their needs were different, but on the other hand the joy of meeting those needs and the pride of watching them achieve always remained bright. The long dreary rides in awful weather were just as boring and difficult (when they were not hair raising and scary.) Life, he realized, just goes on, independent of his internal state, hardly noticing his external interaction.

Life was good, this year. His job had begun to coalesce, he was comfortable in his new role. He felt they were doing right by the kids, and he knew he was doing better with Joan. One useful and important change was that his resentments had dried and lifted from his shoulders. He was really lucky, and he finally realized that.

It was no doubt a great deal due to stopping drinking, he knew. But he also had a suspicion that finally stopping drinking had a great deal owed to his maturation in general. Here he was, solid bourgeois, where he had apparently wanted to be all along. But also grateful for the long detour into the wilder side of life. Nevertheless, it had been time to change, and he believed he had accomplished that successfully.

NEW TRICKS FOR THE OLD DOG

SELCHOW AND RIGHTER was Wayne's favorite new account. For one thing, they were an easy drive right up the road in Bayshore. For another, they had a sparkling new 38, with an IBM package, and they never wanted anything too exotic. And finally, they were on a roll, selling a hot game called Trivial Pursuit, and were very like Webcor at its height. He and Steven, the manager, got along like long-lost brothers.

Going to this account was almost like being on holiday. It was sometimes hard to stretch it out honestly to three or four hours, but they always paid happily, and sometimes they just enjoyed discussing the possibilities of a few new reports. He always tried to get his lunch walk in around here, because the railroad location harkened back to the days when the Island briefly resembled industrial New England in the late nineteen hundreds. Old brick buildings, decaying warehouses, weeds along the right of way. Tiny ancient shops in strip malls, selling specialty items and hanging on by a thread. It was old and real and would go away shortly, swept into the monotony of the modern global world.

The old artist eyes always came alive at scenes like this. He had a vision that could overlay history onto the landscape before him, and this place had a fair amount of it. Backwater history, to be sure, nothing in the center of

470

world domination, but many people had lived and toiled here and lives had been lived and dreams filled or lost. Not too rich, not too poor, and the same almost now as once upon a time. With the right attitude, it could be endlessly fascinating.

S&R was an old-time board game maker, and had a stable of cardboard and token board games—mostly controlled by dice rolls—that Wayne had played often in his youth. It had been a steady profitable company for a long time, relying on ancient trademarks and a few patents, when one of the executives had almost casually acquired rights to the new star, developed overseas. Expecting it to modestly help sales, the company had been overwhelmed by the response, and was now shaking off the sleepy old ways heading into what they were sure would be a bright new future. And, yes, they were still privately owned, mostly by the same family that had founded it long ago.

The employees were just like mill workers. They had been born here, they were grateful to have a job here, most had worked here forever, and some had family here as well. It wasn't a massive employer, but in this small locality it carried weight. It was certainly friendly.

Cruising down the expressway in a late-model cream Mercedes, Ghost happily waving about and talking. He's dressed like some movie star, in bad taste, with bling totally inappropriate for the era. I have to speak loudly to be heard. "Who's temporally confused now?" I shout.

He closes the power windows. "Well, that's how it feels, isn't it? White suit, white tie, white car, white shoes, lots of jewelry. Top of the world. People just happy to see me."

"What in hell are you talking about?"

"Being a consultant. Godlike. Doing what nobody else can do. In the words of the old commercial 'When I speak, people listen'."

"Oh, bullshit. I wasn't that kind of consultant. I was very down to earth, everyday, workman repair type, especially when I started. Just doing the fixes and bringing in the updates, thank you. Humble enough."

"Ah, but you dreamed of the big time, n'est pas?"

"Well, sure it might have been nice to be one of the big guns. But I was hardly oily enough."

"Oily?"

"Well, flashy. Arrogant. Smooth. And lying through their teeth."

"You were a consultant, but you despised consultants. How interesting …."

"Just some. Especially the ones who were mostly sales pitch and no delivery. And, boy, were there a lot of those, back in the murky days when nobody knew nothing."

"Anyway, you were happy enough to be one."

"I could see where the butter on the bread was. Working for a consulting firm meant that you were a revenue source, a position of at least potential power. Working for a firm you were just another cost center. I preferred to be on the income side of the ledger when the old-school executives were examining the books."

Like any hero in his own story, Wayne knew he was strong, brave, handsome and true. His mom had always told him—at least in earlier years—that he had many sterling qualities. He considered himself an up and coming programming whiz. But, he had to admit, Nick had hired him because of an IBM twist.

Nick was a native of Brooklyn, moved to the Island but with city ties and city attitudes. He had gotten into the computer game pretty early, and started a small consulting business that he was able to make into an "IBM small-business partner." IBM had made a lot of money on big accounts, on whom they spent lavishly in terms of support and sales. But they realized there was even more money to be made in what was called the "lower mid-sized market" being taken over by DEC and the like. On the other hand, none of those accounts were going to spend millions of dollars on computer equipment. So IBM put together a mid-sized machine, priced it reasonably, but carefully left off most of the sales and support staff—that could be done by the partners. IBM would provide the hardware and basic software, maybe a few standard packages, and the rest could be done by the local guys. It seemed a perfect fit.

Nick had quickly jumped in with the System 34, then the system 36. He had a range of small clients, primarily doing accounting, and an eye on becoming a bigger player in the medical market, for which he had an expert in medical billing already on staff. But the System 38 was something else entirely, a break with the old comfortable line. In fact a big break. But, on the other hand, it was directed at precisely those accounts that were reaching limits on the older machines, or who were new to the market and enticed by the fancy sales brochures and demonstrations in IBM showrooms.

The trouble was, the new system was really new, and Nick's current staff were up to their necks in his current accounts. He needed somebody to handle the new market. Voila Wayne. Managing background, programming and operating system skills, relatively presentable, college degree credible, pretty thin theoretical foundations, but that probably wouldn't be needed much. And they got along just fine. So Wayne was hired with the idea that he could take on new accounts, help with sales, support the expected multitudes to begin with, and train up everyone else if the market took off.

Wayne was first paraded like a prize pig at the state fair in front of the rest of the employees. Assured that the act was ready, Nick launched a grand tour to meet the butchers, bakers and candlestick makers who composed the JBS client community. Wayne had no idea such odd businesses existed: a beer and wine distributor, a party rental place, an optical frame importer, several small doctor's offices, a chocolate manufacturer, a "fastener" (screws and bolts) company, a cosmetics and drug-store retail distributor. Those were all "old machines, old code," peripheral to Wayne's role.

Exciting new and more prosperous prospects were System 38—a board game maker, a vitamin manufacturer, and others just waiting for a sales call. There was urgency for those, because other consultants were greedily fighting for the same business. Nick brought Wayne up to speed with dense conversations concerning each during long drives, which also introduced the highway geography of Suffolk, Nassau, Brooklyn, and Queens.

Wayne found himself trying to answer questions that were a little over his head and beyond his experience. What could be done, what could be reasonably promised, how much would it cost? How was the best way to present it? He answered confidently, anyway. They put together a team approach, Nick the trustworthy account manager, Wayne the wild barely-controllable geek. Not only was it effective, but also relatively true. Wayne was uncomfortable with small talk about old days, old neighborhoods, ethnic jokes, how's the family. He listened with pen and pad, taking notes, designing, thinking, evaluating. Using a slide rule as his prop might have been appropriate. Initially, he considered this patter irrelevant flimflam, but he eventually admitted that most of the time flimflam was far more effective for sales than dry technical presentations.

Lots and lots of people. Lots and lots of places. Fortunately, Wayne was a fast learner, and had an innate sense of place and direction. In a couple of months, with the aid of relatively expensive laminated local map books, he could get anywhere, even in heavy traffic or when major roads closed—both of which happened distressingly often. Unfortunately, the Dart was barely holding together, and vicious potholes on mean streets didn't help. Anyway he lost most of his fear of most of the places, even those where he had to park in special guarded lots, or near others protected by razor wire along the roof to prevent gangs cutting their way in at night.

Being a decently paid consultant, moreover secure in bringing in more than I was paid, was almost beyond what I had ever hoped for. I soon found that modest competence and a way of explaining jargon (while still being able to use it if necessary) went a long way. My day care teaching continued to be valuable. I was honest, at least by consulting standards, and really cared and tried hard, which of course counted for less. Results mattered. The trick was to make sure that results more or less matched the promises.

The easiest part for me was learning computer tricks, coding, design, and technique. That was just a matter of paying attention to the manuals, and practicing a lot. For me, it was simply great fun. I had an easy time explaining it—I had never been on top with this, so I had no particular attitude that others couldn't pick it up as easily as I did. Mostly, I thought they just didn't like it. I enjoyed sitting at a console and working out problems, or flowcharting an entire system. And the newer the design and capabilities, the better, It was fun, living on the edge. Other people, for some reason, were hardly ever so thrilled.

As far as I was concerned, I had reached the top. Hold on to this, and everything would happen wonderfully. I didn't want to work for a big firm, I didn't want to be stuck in some department, I didn't want to tell other people what to do. If someone wanted to pay me good money to do what I considered computer games all day long, I was happy to accommodate them.

"Your name please?" asks a bright young female thing in the dimly lit vestibule.

Automatically, I answer "Slingluff, Wayne Slingluff."

"Ah yes, here we are. JBS Consulting, right? Just put this on and go through that door to your left." She turns to the next in line.

As I pin the nametag on my jacket pocket, I entered a large room with about a hundred people, almost all middle-aged, pale and male. Most dressed better than I am. A raised platform on one end had a tripod with a large pad that promises boredom to come. There is a bar to the other side—I go to get some ginger ale. A familiar voice accompanies a tap on the shoulder.

"Hey, Wayne, welcome to the club!" Ghost has a dark blue pin-striped suit, maroon tie, smiling broadly. Just for effect, he pretends to be reading my name tag. "Nice, no?"

"Honestly, I'd rather be home."

"Oh, but this is a big part of the game. Success beckons. Make some contacts. Learn what's going on. Associate with your peers. You never know, you know…."

That is the vibe, all right. Everyone looking to take away somebody else's account, keen on any small clue that there might be an opening, problems happening. With, of course, a sharper ear for competitors in case they were hiring. Indeed, nobody in this community is ever sure what they would be doing, who they would be working for, who they might be employing, a year from now. If they weren't all so damn sure of themselves there would be a lot of nervous energy. As it is, to all outward appearances it is a brag meet—obstacles met, problems overcome, clients from hell.

"I'd still rather be home."

"You never did play networking well, did you?"

"No, I blew it all big time. Give me a keyboard and a manual and I'll do what I can—which is a lot. Don't waste my time talking with a bunch of boring folks whose names I won't remember anyway."

NEW TRICKS FOR THE OLD DOG

"Well, you can at least make an effort."

"I did make an effort. I do. Doesn't mean I have to like it."

Ghost waltzes off into the clumps, comradely greetings ringing falsely in the air. I look around unhappily squinting to locate someone I might recognize, and end up on the edge of some irrelevant conversation in one of the corners.

IBM was playing games with its partners, but to understand those, it is necessary to return to the antediluvian world of 1980 or so. IBM, like all big iron computer makers selling to the largest corporations and governments in the world, had to make machines that ran some standard language, usually COBOL. FORTRAN was for limited engineering, BASIC for folks who couldn't tell a variable from a constant, or an algorithm from a toenail. But the problem was that COBOL was regulated and generally needed to be portable to other machines. For IBM, that was bad—a client might legitimately decide to take their code base to Burroughs or Sperry. One solution was to provide off to-the-side ease-of-use-accessories—such as the alternate language RPG.

Report Program Generator was an early attempt at making a user-friendly query language. It assumed the client had a lot of data carefully punched onto cards, but wanted multiple reports. So by simply changing some of the punched instruction cards at the front of the deck, all the same information could be fed through and a revised report would print. Easy. So there was a startup section—such as the name, a coding section where all the instructions for calculations were entered, and finally a printout formatting section. Quickly it was obvious that sometimes you had to go through the card deck several times—such as in computing percentages of totals—so "indicators" were added to the instructions to say what pass the machine was on, and it simply looped until told to finally print.

Not only did that work well, but it was proprietary, which meant a client would have a devil of a time trying to jump to someone else. As a further incentive to keep upstarts away, a nearly proprietary code called EBCEDIC was used to put standard letters and numbers into machine binary. That effectively destroyed any concept of moving to DEC or DG. Near monopoly prospered; once IBM had a client, it had them for life.

Turmoil ensued as the midrange computer manufacturers added COBOL to their repertoire, or modified FORTRAN to business needs. Upstarts took note of the personal computer revolution and started to make industrial enhancements to BASIC. But these brands were incredibly cheaper than IBM, and—even more attractive—did not need keypunch operators or expensive staff and dedicated computer rooms. IBM realized it was missing an opportunity.

In what might be called a kludge operation, IBM grabbed RPG and tried to make it interactive. Without going into details, the fact is that was really ugly. Essentially, it had to pretend every user terminal—a very special and expensive user terminal—was a deck of cards. Hitting a special key was equivalent to submitting a complete card run. It all worked—badly. But after all, it was IBM. Voila! The System 34, which did quite well. The system 36 soon followed.

But by 1984, even IBM realized it had a problem. So—remaining proprietary—it launched the System 38. Revolutionary, it said, but compatible. It used a souped-up variant of good old RPG, after all (still proprietary.) But—well there were big buts. The whole way to start and stop and use the machine, to start programs, to authorize users was totally new. You could technically run old RPG code if you had to, but the "native" language was RPG III, which bore about as much similarity to old RPG as Esperanto does to English. The new native stuff was what Wayne knew, and what users expected. The old stuff was what all the existing partners and their client bases actually had.

Hilarity ensued, amidst the bloodbath....

In addition to expanding my programming, sales, and design skills, I was getting a really important education in business practice. Up until now, I had worked mostly as a mindless employee at various places, or as a person so far down the decision tree that what I thought did not much matter. At Webcor, my opinions were eventually valued within their own context, but that context was hardly central to the health of the firm. I had peripheral encounters with various departments such as accounting and warehouse, but only in relation to whatever computer use was involved.

JBS represented full immersion into a small business way of life. Income matching expenses could be scary, determining the possible cash flow over the near future was a constant issue, dealing with clients not only for new business but in order to collect something on the dollar for services performed already was an art form. I ended up with profound respect for anyone running such an enterprise. I know that I could never handle all the pressure and risk and, for that matter, real losses often involved.

Lately, a lot of lip service is given to small business. Politicians and commentators extol the brave entrepreneur, the job creator, the pioneer of the new. That is all proper, and most of what is said is true. However, it hides the fact that most small business is a close run thing, with poor pay and possibilities compared to life in a huge corporation or government service. The owner and frequently the owner's family put a lot of sweat and blood and money and time into an enterprise, and on the relatively rare occasions when they hit it big those are the people who make it big.

Everyone in business that I met tended to be an optimist. In big corporations, everyone was sure a promotion or a significant raise was right around the corner. In smaller firms, various incentives were possible such as stock options or partial partnerships. And at an individual level, in certain professions such as computer software, one of the mightiest dreams was to go it alone.

After all, we would tell each other, I bill by the hour, somewhere between fifty and one hundred dollars. I bill lots of hours. How much of that do I ever see to take home? The math seemed inescapable, working on your own would make you rich quickly. Of course, that was all a lie, and working in a small firm eventually taught me the reality of that.

Ghost sits across the table, picking at his rubbery chicken, as the speaker drones on, flipping tedious charts. "What a waste," he sighs.

"I know," I agree. "Anything would be more productive than this. Does he really think he is saying anything new? As far as I can tell what isn't stale is fairy dust." We were getting the briefing on the next earth-shaking rollout of some software add-on product that none of us needed.

"Well," says Ghost, "if they just distributed honest specifications and possibilities, we would all just laugh and throw the brochures away."

"True enough." The only people interested here were obviously the very young, the very new to the profession, those who had not yet been through countless iterations of promises never met. Oh, we had become a cynical lot pretty quickly. But with good cause.

"This is all part of the game, though," he notes. "If you don't come here, the firm loses credibility."

I knew that well enough. In the next week, I would certainly casually drop tidbits into the client conversations along the line of "last week, I was at this private industry briefing and found out that ..." If I wrapped it in enough flowery jargon, it could seem very impressive. It cemented our credentials, and gave the client warm and fuzzy feelings about how modern "his" computer consulting firm was, and of course how wise he had been to hire us in the first place.

Details of any profession quickly bore outsiders, which is why people with similar interests clump together at large gatherings. But the general folly of human endeavor remains constant across activities. Wayne had already encountered a beauty.

Nick occasionally had an arrangement where he would "borrow" a consultant from another firm, paying that firm more than they paid their employee. All parties were generally happy, although there was necessarily a lack of direct supervision. Wayne's immediate task was to examine such efforts at a large System 38 operation in Bohemia which was having issues with general ledger reporting. One of those temporary employees had been working on it for a long time, without satisfactory results. Maybe Wayne could get some idea of what was going on?

He began to review the code and discovered apparent incoherence. After deep study with flowcharts and paper markups, he realized he had encountered radical idealism leading to complete stupidity. After hours of poring over the printouts, he began to get some idea of what was going on. A mess he was not sure he could fix. Not that it was wrong, exactly, but ...

Like planning the route for a trip, there are many approaches to designing code that works. Some are basic and brute force, some are a bit more elegant. One of the strongest long-term virtues of good code resembles that of good literature, which is that it is easy to read and to find out what is going on fairly quickly. But few programmers figure that out. This particular application had been engineered to be incomprehensible.

Trying to explain this to, for example, Joan would be difficult. How did he spend his day? In this case, Andrea, a very experienced and competent programmer, had recently read a book that claimed you should never "jump" in a program. That was the famous "go to" clause—something along the lines of "If you get to the bakery and it is closed go to the supermarket." You can immediately skip all the things you might have done in the bakery. But some genius somewhere figured that was too dangerous—maybe there was something between the bakery and the supermarket that you were missing.

So this was an attempt at "nesting ifs" to infinity. Instead of driving away from the bakery as soon as you saw you couldn't get it, it approached from the other direction, something along the lines of "if the bakery is open, if there are shelves of pies, if there is a cherry pie, if it costs less than two dollars, if it is fresh, if it is at least five inches in diameter ...." And on and on until am unsuccessful condition is reached but with all the other conditions coded immediately following. Human inspection could not follow it at all. So this program was filled with thousands of such "if clauses" each nested inside each other, unformatted, totally illegible.

Effectively, instead of one clean exit—go to supermarket—near the beginning of the routine, there were thousands of dependent virtual "go to's" hidden deep inside one another. What that meant was, for example, if it returned from the bakery without a pie, you ended up having no idea why without reading and understanding every possibility at every step along the way. General ledgers were complicated things, and in a tangled environment like this, bugs could hide out and breed for months without being noticed.

Bugs—or the erroneous results they produced—eventually were noticed, by the client, and angrily denounced during billing meetings. As far as Wayne could tell, this application was all but hopeless. But he took a deep breath and dug in anyway, that was his job, he had to put something together for Nick by Tuesday.

Dealing with accounts was an art in itself, and made Wayne appreciate salesmen far more than he ever had. Prior to this experience, he had thought of them as big brutish aggressive sponges, who went out to nightclubs drinking with people from other firms to bring in business. His own experience at the receiving end was that they would promise the moon and stars until a contract was signed, and then turn stuff over to people who could care less.

With a small firm, it was different. You lived in the messes you made. If he and Nick made a promise, no matter how optimistic, they had to try to live up to it or face difficulty with every potential sale from then on. The pond of potential customers was fairly small, and word got around quickly. Especially since companies in the same industry—which they tended to sell to—were often old friends with one another. If a fastener distributor in Queens had a bad experience, you could be sure every other similar enterprise found out .

There was really a set of trajectories any such relationship could take— almost like love and marriage. There was the courting, involving negotiations of what when and how much. No matter how honest each side tried to be, the whole field was so new that misconceptions would always arise. No matter how well Wayne thought he knew the issues, there would be nooks and crannies to throw a monkey wrench into applications. Costly overruns. Delayed implementations. And that was without the ongoing issues of employees who were much happier doing things the old way.

But once the initial system was running (and at least partly paid for) the real dance began. You would slice so much off an existing bill to get payment for a required extension. Or you could refuse to do anything else unless at least minimum accounts were settled. Nobody really wanted lawyers, because then they were both stuck with a complete expensive failure and would be starting over. But it was a fine line.

If things went smoothly, which was surprisingly often all things considered, there were always additional costs and work. Updates would come from the computer maker, to be installed. New reports and capabilities would be requested by the management. Once in a while a whole new section of the enterprise—say inventory or shipping—would be brought into the mix. New technology—particularly communication between offices and warehouses— kept intruding from outside. But the dance at least kept going, both partners more or less trusted each other.

Even the best relationships sometimes went sour, and the worst were horrors from the beginning. When to cut losses, run, pay the lawyers, and try to move on? You could only be a doormat for so long, and no matter what, some installations were bound to be unsatisfactory.

Wayne and Nick sometimes played good cop bad cop, sometimes other scenarios, and tended to win more than they lost. Or rather, Nick did. He was the boss, and he was a master of this. He knew when to back off, when to push forward, and always how to deflect tension with jokes and stories. Wayne learned an awful lot, but never how to become that way himself.

Ghost leans back in his booth at the noisy luncheonette. "Finally, you understood the practical impossibilities of technocrats running the world."

"Yeah, I sure did. Reality is a lot of politics, a lot of human interaction, an awful lot of what seems to be wasted motion but in fact is necessary lubrication. My little geeky programmer soul hated it all, thought it wasteful in the extreme, but it is the only thing that works."

"Too bad we can't make all the politicians go through the same thing."

"Oh, I don't think politicians ever come from the technocrat side unless there is something really unusual happening. I think they lack technocratic advisors, that's all."

"But you could have learned and changed," notes Ghost, sipping his iced tea.

"I still think there are limits. I was never ready to become really failed and unhappy to change so drastically—after all, I was doing all right in the niches I created. Technocrats have a place, just not usually at the head of the firm."

"Maybe you could have gone there…"

"Failed quickly when I tried it later. No, I'm not the type. I think we are stuck with some of our own limitations and abilities, some more subtle than others."

"Like telling jokes for lubrication."

"Exactly. I still can't remember nor tell jokes well."

"So many failings."

"Only human," I finish up, as Ghost for once picks up the tab.

From this fifth floor picture window, the sky was an ominous inky purple.

They were putting tape in random patterns all over the windows. Sure, this was cutting it a bit close, but the roads were pretty clear. Most people, sensibly, had stayed home.

Just another thrill in a long year, and only September. He had a new son, continuing sobriety, a better handle on local geography (if you count local geography as the entire of Long Island, including the New York boroughs.) He was learning and doing and writing and talking and overwhelmed but increasingly satisfied and happy under the always roiled surface of day to day problems. What more, he had thought, could possibly happen?

As if in answer to the challenge, here was Hurricane Gloria, bearing down directly at them according to all the newscasts. Joan had called a few minutes before, all but hysterical, reflecting the announcers. He had promised they were leaving in a couple of minutes. Just the windows. So, that was soon done, he wished everyone luck, took some technical reading material out into the parking lot.

The wind was already strong, and gusts rising noticeably. Tree limbs were still in place, but leaves were being ripped in sheets. He headed down Vets to the Sagtikos, fighting crosswinds as he sped south, the sky becoming impossibly darker by the minute. Headlights on. No rain quite yet, but surely about to fall in torrents.

On the Southern State, almost home, and the rain came down, fortunately only for a minute or so making it impossible to see, then letting up until another band passed overhead. The short ride seemed supernaturally long, he could hardly wait to get by Belmont Lake and then into the relative safety of the driveway. He clutched his papers and ran inside, soaked.

By now the TV had the landfall centered at Lindenhurst, a mile or two away. Their house was directly on the track. The gusts grew. He and Joan taped their picture window, hoping none of the front trees would be coming through it. Gregory ran around, excited. Baby Wayne, of course, could care less, but probably enjoyed the spectacle. Another strong gust tipped over the black mulberry tree out back—no great loss, although they did eat some of the fruit occasionally.

According to the TV it was just about over. The landing was almost a countdown. All of a sudden one or two big bursts of wind and everything went black. Lights out, TV off, only the howling of the wind and a siren far away. Stuff down all over the road, seemingly in an instant. And then everything died down, almost calm, and he had a chance to check for damages.

It turned out to be over a week without power. He had cold water, so he could shower and get to work. Joan and the boys headed over to her parent's house, which was just fine. He sat in the chilly house in the evening and read manuals by candlelight, nothing else to do, occasionally talking to Joan on the phone. Another punctuation mark in a long strange period.

"Almost a small businessman," laughs Ghost, back in his leather-upholstered Mercedes weaving through traffic somewhere near the Rockaways.

"In all senses of the term," I agree. "But mostly, finally, a real computer consultant. I was pretty proud of that."

"But you had done some of it before," he notes, glancing aside.

"I never really felt it internally. Felt like I was faking it somehow. At this point, with the new machines, the new things happening, the new accounts, I felt like I was good at what I was doing. Worth every dollar and more. A very good sense. And having a house, of course, helped. Not to mention the new company car."

"Oh, you were just the cat's meow. But not getting paid all that much ..."

"A lot more than we were used to. And pretty secure, that's what mattered. The rest would happen as it would. No, this year was pretty perfect, in spite of the rocks. A lot of things resolved."

"Would you have done anything different, knowing now ..."

"I never think like that. I was who I was, where I was. All in all, yes, I think I worked out about as well as I possibly could have. No complaints."

"But no yacht, either. Your boss had the nice boat."

"Well there is that, of course. But envy was never one of my problems."

"Silly you."

One last time, Wayne had been called in by his old boss to help with computer problems at the sparkling new Webcor building in Roosevelt Field. That vast modern building had been constructed for imagined huge volumes in a limitless future. It echoed as empty as an old warehouse, corridors barely lit, reflecting windows into dark offices. A ruin ahead of its time. Alan projected a brave front, but clearly it was a fragile façade—the heart was gone.

BABYLON WITH GHOST

In another year, even this would fall to bankruptcy and grind final dreams into dust.

Nick had probably hoped Wayne could pull Webcor along as an account. That was clearly not going to occur. On the other hand, his friend Joe D, had landed an executive position at a wholesale appliance distributor, and that might become a very lucrative client. Wayne soon lost track of most Webcor waifs, scattered about the economy. Typical stories in typical American careers.

WHOA, BABY!

"**WAYNE, WAYNE, WAKE** up," an insistent shake on his shoulders as he opened his eyes to darkness. Fortunately, he was a quick riser.

"What, what?"

"It's time. Right now. We have to go."

"But it's—what—two in the morning. Are you sure?"

Yes, Joan was sure. They had everything packed of course, and a check-list, and the first item there, while Joan got ready, was to call her parents to come over and babysit Gregory. As the distant phone rang Wayne reflected that no matter how bad it might be to be woken in the middle of the night on a freezing January morning when you were nearly forty, it was surely much much worse to have the same thing happen at nearly twice his age. But at the other end they were ready and soon on the way.

He took the opportunity to grab a cup of instant coffee while waiting. Fortunately, no new snow had fallen on existing mounds, so the roads should be clear. Could have been worse. The wait seemed interminable—was this going to be another groaning rush in the back seat like Gregory? Eventually, Mom and Dad arrived, got instructions, and off Wayne and Joan raced to Mid Island Hospital, Wayne having called ahead. That place also seemed a bit in a panic, trying to contact the doctor.

It was a relatively short ride, without another car in sight, dark empty main roads strangely illuminated like some abandoned movie set. Joan rode in the front seat this time, but she was clearly having trouble holding on. "Hurry up," she kept saying between spasms. He went as fast as he thought prudent—there were, after all, ice patches. Not too many stop lights, thank heavens.

They pulled into the parking lot and an attendant came out. Joan began to stagger up the ramp—they took one look at her and popped her into a wheelchair. All arrangements had been made over the previous week, but the doctor was still not there, the birthing room had just a couple of nurses, and they kept telling Joan to hang on as Wayne sat next to her.

Ghost is sitting in a waiting room armchair, big, fat, and smelling of tobacco, t-shirt stained.

"What the hell is this, I ask?"

"You didn't really dress well, you know."

"Maybe not, but I was a lot neater than that. And I never smoked in my life."

"Poetic license," he adds. "Beer maybe."

"No, of course not. Week night. Foggy from lack of sleep, maybe. And besides,"

"Yes…"

"No waiting room. That was my father. We were all Lamaze and father present at the birth and all the rest."

"Starry eyed …"

"Not after the first one. We didn't take anything for granted this time. We didn't quite trust the doctor's opinions as much, we made sure the hospital knew we might come any moment, and we had the bag packed for weeks. Besides, we wanted to be really careful."

"Of course, it's your child…"

"More than that. This one was hard too. A few miscarriages, no easy start, pregnancy just delaying as we got older. So who knew if this might be the last chance. Joan wanted a girl—from all the old wives' tales she had dug up from her cousins she was sure this would be one."

"No sonogram."

"Didn't want to know. Old fashioned."

"Superstitious."

"I suppose. Or maybe still romantics at heart."

This pregnancy, long in the making, had been a less frantic, but a little more worrisome than Gregory's. On the other hand, Joan now had a lot of support and did not have to ride the subway every day. She spent time dreaming of bringing up a little girl. She was carrying high—that was the sign, everyone told her.

The heat of the summer was less burdensome, not quite as fierce and humid as Boston. She would go out with Gregory and her girlfriend Leanne down the street to the local bay beach. Venetian Shores, although often clogged with seaweed and sometimes unswimmable because of sea lice, provided a playground, beautiful views and a cool breeze all summer long. Wayne was busy all the time, but her parents were ecstatic and always available.

As fall slid into winter, they made the preparations for the birth, more carefully this time because they had been through it once. Classes attended, everything easier because they were staying in one place, not taking a class here, changing doctors there, locating hospital locations on the fly. Expectations were that this would be a piece of cake.

Like any pregnancy, however, life became more constricted in the late months. Shopping was hard, foods were cut down, smoking and alcohol were out of bounds. Joan stayed active, but carrying around all that weight is tiresome, and with all the stairs in the house she had to be extra careful. Thanksgiving went by with fun and laughter, Christmas and Gregory's fifth birthday filled with cheer and a trip out east, made the more difficult by her need to use the bathroom frequently.

Surprisingly, for Wayne this pregnancy was a little less remote than the first one. In Boston, this had been just one more event tossed into chaos. There he had a new distant job, all hours taken up, a long month at jury duty, packing, cleaning, changing finances and insurance, moving, meeting

BABYLON WITH GHOST

new people, settling in with the in-laws. What was one more insane day in that madhouse?

But now, things were a bit more settled. He could take some time at home from work to help out a bit. On the other hand, there was a lot of support now so he didn't really have to. Even the hurricane had hardly put a crimp in his routine.

The biggest change was really getting Gregory's room ready. They had decided to take one of the rooms upstairs—he could certainly handle the climb now. That required patching and painting and furniture, and then patching and painting his old ground-floor old room. Not horribly difficult, but enough on top of the job to keep him busy. A few shelves had to be built to hold the big assortment of toys.

When he could, usually on the weekends, he would go to the malls with Joan, eat out at fast food places, take trips to the ocean or parks, try to take Gregory off her hands on Saturday or Sunday mornings. He watched Joan's obsession with the sex of the child with some amusement. She agreed readily enough to "Wayne Philip", something Wayne wanted and a nod to the grandfather, but she dug in her heels about a girl's name. Her mother, "Sue" was out of the question, although "Suzanne" remained Wayne's favorite. A lot of the contemporary names were scrolled and reviewed.

The summer, the fall, passed. Bags were packed, followup visits became frequent, it was just a matter of waiting. Every snowstorm or ice freeze was worrisome. Every long day trip by Wayne into Brooklyn had to be carefully choreographed so she had alternate transportation if necessary. They both knew how sudden this delivery might be.

We thought we had eyes wide open, but we were as blind as before. Raising children is a far cry from manufacturing or computer code—you do not repeat anything exactly, nor does the first run through make the second one better. For some reason, culturally, first children are recognized as essentially a little different than the youngest or middle child. We were completely unaware of that.

But looking back, we see the careful nurturing and documentation of the first born. In Gregory's case, he was both the first child and first grandchild, and stacks and boxes of photos and artifacts attest to the fact even now, piled in dusty closets and on the bottom of piles of stuff in the garage and basement. This was a special person.

Wayne—not so much. Been there, done that. First steps—oh, ok. No applause this time, no cheering crowds. Of course he finally took first steps. Big deal. If children could choose, I'm not sure which they'd rather be. The first one with all the hopes and pressure and never being much left alone, or one of the later ones more free to develop casually and on their own terms. In any case, as parents, we had read all the books. As teachers, we had seen all the types. But until involved each day and all night, we just didn't understand.

We were sure of one thing, and that was that we were being and would continue the kind of parents we wanted to be. We did stupid things, sometimes, but we were ashamed and apologized quickly. We had learned the ins and outs of effective discipline while in the classroom, and not only that had done it together so we were pretty good at reinforcing one another. We had similar goals for how we wanted them to grow.

You would think it all went like clockwork. But life is full of surprises, and no matter how smooth your plans, reality both confuses and makes the future more interesting.

Ghost lounges back, still in casual attire, but at least he's lost the cigar. A football game blares in the background, a newspaper lies half read on the floor at his feet. Looks up. "All planned out. You finally have someone named after you, carry on the tradition, bigger and better and all that, right?"

"No, not at all. We were kind of strange that way. We really wanted them to be healthy happy and successful, but no more and no less. How they did it didn't matter."

"So you didn't push them enough."

"I never know. I see successful kids who have been pushed all their lives fall apart later, although I see some who become marvels. I do still believe that childhood is a wonderful time in itself, not to be wasted as a dreary preparation for an adult life that is usually more nasty and disappointing."

"Mr. Disillusionment, beat down by the world?"

"Not at all, not at all. I actually liked my own life trajectory well enough.

I guess, if anything, I wanted them to follow me. Especially in living well in the moments and being moderately happy while they took care of necessary business."

"So, do you think you failed, or succeeded?"

"The question seems to become irrelevant. We found that they pretty much grew the way they wanted anyway. I think it's a lot the same for everyone. We were maybe less frustrated because our ideas of success were more open-ended. Money hardly mattered."

"Oh, foolish mortal …."

Baby Wayne arrived at the very end of January, and once-unique original Wayne quickly found adjustments were necessary. For one thing, there was the question of differentiation. In family, Dad was good, but outside that small circle they would have to make reference to "Big Wayne" and "Baby Wayne" or "little Wayne" which at least was some improvement on "Son Wayne" and "Husband Wayne," although the younger one did not much appreciate it as he grew older (and bigger than his father.)

The new job grew by leaps and bounds. For a short time, life grew overwhelming and alcoholism threatened everything, and it required a strong and difficult push to get through that obstacle. Two children instead of one, and another cousin from Robert and Cheryl. Visits and obligations became ever more tangled, sometimes a little contentions and edged.

Meanwhile, there were the inevitable issues of sibling jealousy or rivalry, although Gregory seemed to handle that pretty well by taking an almost proprietary view of Wayne as if he were just another new toy. Baby Wayne from the beginning was pretty mellow—although that was helped by anxious adults not hovering over him all the time. If he wanted to do nothing, that was fine with everyone—for poor Gregory any moment of quiet had been apt to be interpreted as a failure of some kind of developmental normality. If Baby Wayne was quiet and wanted to be alone—well, by God they would just let him be that way, and be properly grateful for the break.

They had forgotten how expensive all the necessities were—disposable diapers, formula, doctor visits, clothing. Not to mention how often they had to make trips just for that purpose. Fortunately, Gregory was off in pre-school by this time, which gave Joan a little time to relax during the day. Trips were more constrained by the need for car seats, baby bags, and the urgent necessities of periodic feeding.

But life went on, as the summer went by. The hurricane was eventually a memory as well, and Baby Wayne started to become more of a person. By Christmas, the new family seemed settled and normal. They were happy to just be paying the current bills on time—the idea of how to pay for big expenses like college in the future was just too much to contemplate.

I felt I had adjusted my dreams and happinesses decently, finally. Banishing the drinking monkey helped a lot, but by that time it had become symptomatic rather than causal. I was conflicted by the clash of old dreams and new reality, and took some of that out in an attempted escape into dulled "relaxation" where I could forget the worries I imagined all around me.

Not so much the disillusionment of middle age—I was, after all, still excited about the new and expanding career. Occasional whiffs of my previous self-image as an artist—alone and doing marvelous things in the world for future generations.

I faced facts at last. I was not about to be an artist. I was not about to become important. I was a mature adult, twenties behind me, thirties rapidly fading into the rear-view mirror, and I was—anyone. An ordinary dad, making an ordinary salary, with an ordinary family, in an ordinary suburb, with an all too ordinary future mapped before me. Nothing bad in all that ordinary—in fact it was a remarkably wonderful life. But not the one I had thought I wanted.

It's tough to relinquish comforting ancient dreams. I suppose well-adjusted successful and mature people manage to strip them off in late adolescence. I was perversely happy I had encouraged them to linger through perhaps too many years of hope and wonder. But, now, I'd grown up. Requirements and responsibilities. The amazing thing was that I came to accept them gladly.

Mostly, my time was almost never my own. Dawn to dusk, I found myself going somewhere or doing something for someone else. Even when it was not directed by another peer, I found my conscience reminding me to do something for the children, something for Joan, something for the family.

BABYLON WITH GHOST

Where was I in all that? Who, for that matter, had the time to think about it at all?

That was the solution. Abandon deep thoughts, banish remote impossible dreams, no worries about what it all means. Deal with what comes up as it comes up, and let your mind glide. Believe that life is exactly what you encounter everyday, not some obscure mystery that you must disentangle. Eventually, that let me achieve a degree of serenity I had never had before. I was doing what I should be doing.

Ghost still in the chair, fire blazing now, staring into the darkness outside. "Looking back, do you have a lot of regrets about all that?"

"What, loss of youthful dreams? Nope."

"Why not?" he enquires.

"If your life is long enough," I think about this answer a bit, "there is room for a lot of dreams, times for alternate driving visions. That is what I consider having it all."

"By decade, or year?"

"Oh, for example, being an artist in my twenties, being a good father in my thirties, even writing now. I'm not sure being the same old prophet all the time would have been better. In fact, I'm sure it would have been worse."

"Concentrating more on one thing or another might have helped you better succeed."

"Possibly. But it might also have made me a nasty and remote fanatic. With my personality, I didn't want to go there. I never wanted to lose the chance of love or family just to create something eternally great—even if it had turned out to be the Mona Lisa."

"Sounds like an awful big sacrifice."

"Only if, in your deep true logical moments, you really believe you can paint the Mona Lisa."

"Well, there is that …."

"No, I'll tell you, if I was going to be ordinary, I was going to experience all the flavors of ordinary and enjoy them all the way."

"Hold on, hold on," the heavyset nurse kept repeating. The other one scurried about the brightly lit room, bringing necessary equipment over near the table where Joan lay sweating in her gown. "The doctor is on his way, he'll be here any minute. Don't push, just relax."

"Easy for them to say," gritted Joan to Wayne. He just sat there, taking it all in, holding her hand. At least they were out of the car. She squeezed again. "I'm sure he'll be here any second…."

"I hate this," she said. "I don't know how people do it. I don't want to do it."

"It will be over soon, take it easy. Well, anyway," he said on reflection, "just keep thinking it will be over soon." He could tell it was painful already. He didn't think the nurses were helping by looking so panicked and frazzled.

Joan took another deep breath and tried to do the exercises again. Wayne tried to keep in rhythm with her. A door banged somewhere and in a minute the doctor was in the room, hastily pulling on gloves.

"Ah, Mrs. Slingluff, so quickly. Let me see now. He reached under the sheet to check the status of the little head. "Yes, yes, I see. Ok, let me check, try pushing now."

A couple of contractions, another push, and …. Pop. A smack a cry and cleaning up the umbilicals. "There we go," said the doctor brightly, as the nurses both heaved a sigh of relief. "Healthy, yes just a second, would you like to hold him…."

"Him?!" shrieked Joan. "Him!? It's supposed to be a girl! I can't do this again," she wailed.

"Uh, please Joan, listen, just hold him, ok?" said Wayne. The staff was looking seriously freaked out.

"I want a girl," she cried. "Everyone promised …."

"You didn't know?" asked the flummoxed doctor to Wayne.

"No, we just wanted to be surprised…."

"Not her, obviously."

"I guess. She'll be fine," said Wayne a little more seriously than he felt. "Everything's good?"

"Will be in a moment. Need to clean up a little stuff. Help your wife, please."

"Joan, Joan take it easy. It's a boy, but it's healthy, here look, here hold him, see, very cute."

Actually, Wayne was lying through his teeth. Like all babies, the little thing was red and ugly and slimy and not at all cuddly and was crying. He didn't care that it was a boy or not, his main concern was always health, but that was a lot different than cute. Not the right adjective at this moment. But Joan was calming down a little. From screaming rejection to depression was, at the moment, a step in the right direction. She began to inspect the child a bit more carefully, as it rested on her breast.

"I wanted a girl. A girl," she kept whispering.

"It's a boy," repeated Wayne. "But healthy. We can talk about it later..."

"I can't do this again," she repeated.

"We can talk later. Just relax. The worst is over."

Joan finally managed a smile. "Easy for you to say. It still hurts. A lot."

"I'm sure it does. Do you want me to call your parents now? There's a phone outside."

"Ok, Ok." She sniffled. "I'll be all right."

"No throwing him on the floor, now, right?"

She managed a little laugh. "Yeah, ok, I'll be all right." Then she started to cry again. The nurses took the newborn for footprints and to get him weighed and wrapped and toe-tagged. When Joan quieted down a bit, he went out to call Mom and Dad and Mom and Dad and give them all the good news. For a certain value of "good."

Joan's great disappointment in life was not having a daughter. Her ideal would have been girl twins. She had nothing against young men, but she knew from her Italian background that the essential truth is that women tend to remain near their mothers, while male offspring roam far and usually settle near the home of their spouse. Daughters shop and talk family and hang out gossiping. In spite of all the modern talk about us all being the same, there remains a fundamental difference in how the sexes are wired, and have been wired throughout history. Despite feminism's claims, she had observed that daughters grow into friends, while sons become acquaintances.

I worried that there was no guarantee. By the time we recovered enough to think about trying again, events had conspired to make us reconsider. We were much older—neither of us wanted a child right after Baby Wayne—we wanted to enjoy him fully, not crowd him into some middle while focused on the next. And then—it might be another boy. In practical terms that would not help Joan at all, and I was half afraid she would kill any more male offspring. Suddenly there were events within her family, there were ongoing work demands from my career, and I started to think a lot about how exactly we were going to get even two kids through college. Not to mention the ongoing requirements—all more expensive than we expected—of just having the family we had on one full salary supplemented by Joan's sporadic substitute teaching income.

We never had another child. We toyed with adoption, but we did have two wonderful active children, and they were quite a lot to appreciate fully. Family life was joyful as it was, and at least for a while (until the empty nest arrived) things settled down nicely. By then—well, it was a hard adjustment. The boys, as predicted, took off on their own adventures far away.

Comparisons in this culture often turn to envy—we are taught to strive to be more like those who are more "successful" than we are, not to look at those who are less fortunate. We appreciated that our children were normal, whatever that means these days, with a unique assortment of skills and liabilities but nothing too spectacular in either direction. We never really expected the next president or Einstein or Leonardo, we were extremely grateful to escape all the possible and seemingly increasing cases of autism and other special needs. We accepted what we had—we would, like most people, have accepted anything—but once in a while in the dark of night Joan still sometimes wishes there had been a baby Suzanne.

Ghost stirs and glances to the side of his lounger "Your fault."

"My fault, I guess. I wasn't excited about a fifty percent chance (or less) with all the possible later complications."

"Not good for your wife."

"But maybe good for us—I had seen some effects of very late children. They can change dynamics a lot."

"You would have been fine, I'm sure."

"You're probably right. Maybe I was just selfish and lazy. Anyway, it's done."

"No guilt for things past?"

"Very little. I have a hard enough time getting up the energy for things present."

"That's my role, I guess," says Ghost resignedly.

"Why Ghost, introspection from you? How unexpected."

"Oh, shut up." For once, he's the one that ends the conversation.

Summer settled in, things grew more mellow. Joan was excited that he had stopped drinking, if a bit wary and skeptical at first. But the initial visits to the meetings helped in the first few months, and then he found himself just forgetting about drink altogether. There were a lot of other things to keep his churning mind occupied.

Like all infants, Baby Wayne seemed to grow overnight, and soon was quite different from when born. Joan, over her initial shock, was a happy and proud mother. Original Wayne, of course, still didn't think of anything that couldn't talk or walk as of much interest, so he and Gregory would take the baby along and play with him as if he were a puppy, which seemed to work decently. Everything began to work out nicely. The parents on both sides, of course, were thrilled at his new leaf.

Work even straightened out and, although always hard or impossible, became just another part of the routine. His main problem was that he kept taking on more. Not so much out of ambition, but rather boredom, restlessness, and pride, with just a little possible wish that somehow it would all pay off more in the future. So he learned furiously, less about code than design, less about computers than client stroking. That turned out to be very important too.

The house became even more home, now that they had the upstairs fully utilized. He tried to use his den once in a while like in the old days, but most of the time the music was down and the door more open, in case Gregory wanted to wander in from his bedroom opposite. Evenings were spent more on playing with toys or reading—even though Baby Wayne just mostly watched and smiled. Joan was happy for any time she could get to herself, although truthfully she mostly used that time to talk interminably on the phone.

Even the hurricane hardly affected them. There was the one tree almost over, of course, and a few branches, but they had escaped unscathed. By Halloween Gregory was ready to go out trick or treating, leaving Baby Wayne home. Impossible to be more average and normal if they had taken a college course in "American Middle Class 201."

Ghost yawns and stretches, about to get up. "So it all works out …"

"As usual, if you are lucky," I admit. "We were very lucky."

"You don't take credit?"

"Not really. I feel I had all the cards stacked on my side. Supportive family, wonderful wife, beautiful children, the aptitudes to get a good job and get along well. I mean—what did I have to do with much of that—I just followed a path that I had initially resisted."

"Still, you were a maker and not a taker."

"Oh, I'd taken enough already. Had it force fed to me. That's a really insane label, by the way."

"Thought it might get you going."

"Don't even start. I can't imagine how some people overcome all the problems and handicaps they must face. I guess that's why I lean democrat.'

"Democrat, Hell. You lean socialist or communist."

"Shhhh…."

"But you can be proud anyway. It could have gone terribly differently."

"I did do a few difficult things—at least for me. And together we made some tough decisions. I really suppose—sounds insipid—you hear such all the time from others—that I owe most of it to Joan."

"About time you recognized the fact," says Ghost, on his way out the brick-framed door.

Baby's first Christmas—and the contrast could not have been more stark. Wayne vaguely remembered Gregory's—what a jumble. Every second was photographed, seeming multitudes came by to gurgle and touch the newborn, whole slates of relatives he had never seen offered congratulations. They had stood by and received immense recognition for—well, as the song says—doing what comes naturally. But it had certainly been a pageant.

And now—well it wasn't quite that Baby Wayne was ignored, but if he had been placed in back of the various trees while presents were opened sometimes few would have noticed. There was lots of competition now. Gregory, of course, but also two of Robert's kids. The thrill of it all may not have quite worn off, but by now the grandparents had seen it all for five holidays, and all the times in between. Even in Pennsylvania, there was a new crowd.

The documentation efforts had slacked off too. Somehow, what was most important to each of the families was the new strides made by Gregory or Vanita—school or accomplishments or just getting bigger and more independent, stringing together words and stories that made sense. These were things unheard before. Baby Wayne—he just sat there happily and took it all in. Nobody bothered him much, and he bothered nobody back.

Wayne the elder was amazed that Christmas without alcohol basically was not all that much different than before. Actually, he had tried to always be careful at gatherings. His danger had tended to drinking in private, slipping down into depths while alone. The big change now was the lack of a hangover, and the loss of an urgent desire to get back and sitting in his den with a glass of wine. So he sat and chatted and enjoyed the atmosphere and tried to spend a little more time fussing over his younger child simply because it struck him that it was all a little unfair.

BASELINE PROSPERITY

WAYNE AWOKE TO a grey thunderous morning. As fog in his sleepy mind dissipated, noise eventually resolved into heavy raindrops on aluminum awnings outside bedroom windows. More effort and he realized it was Saturday. Ah yes, late October, indoor heat was already on and it looked like plans for today were ruined.

He climbed from blankets as carefully and noiselessly as possible, closed the bedroom door to let Joan sleep. Peeking around the corner, he noted Wayne quietly lying in his crib, not yet awake. No sign of Gregory. Ah, that was nice. He put on some water for coffee, and soon settled into the living room couch to experience a glorious moment of being alone and having no pressing emergencies or chores. He certainly couldn't rake the leaves. He settled back and meditated on the year.

As crowded as any year had been. And yet, for all the excitement and change, this seemed much more a period in which they had been growing stronger, deepening roots, becoming one of the healthy trees in the forest, rather than a fragile sapling. He felt fully capable, able to handle problems as they came along and capable of whatever would be required to keep his family doing well. What a lucky man.

Soon, shower, shave, ready for breakfast of toast or something. After that, the patter of feet on the stairs informed him Gregory was on his way down. He closed Wayne's door, signaled to be a little quiet. "What would you like for breakfast?" he asked softly.

"Just Kix."

"Ok, here we go."

They sat quietly eating together at the second-hand hexagon leaf table in the kitchen nook, subdued by the downpour. It was enough to be together, to be happy, to be looking forward to things, with the whole world before them. But for this exact moment, a time of peace.

Ghost is playing suburban caricature, with tweed jacket and cap. He leans on a rake staring out at the lawn, knee deep in brilliant red maple leaves. "So you think this is what life is all about, " he asks, almost contemptuously.

"A part of it, why not. I never dressed like that—nor knew anybody who did. And by the way, leaves are never ever that deep."

"I wanted effect."

"The effect is silly. But to answer your question, why not? For at least periods of life—like the early childhood of my kids—this kind of life is idyllic. We were really happy to have found it."

"Shallow, dull, intellectually stultifying, socially useless …"

"Ah, peddle your wares elsewhere. Time enough for that some other day. Quiet breakfast with a five year old who is happy is worth any amount of jagged brilliant chit chat."

"You certainly changed your tune, over the last few years. So you were all wrong before?"

"I was right for me before. I am right for me now. I change. I am alive, after all."

"Stop rubbing it in," says Ghost, vanishing with a quick burst of leaf-filled wind.

It might be appropriate to describe Wayne, after seven years of turmoil and reinvention, as a new man. After all, to all outward appearances, hardly anything remained of the listless uncertain young city dweller from 1978. Yet, strangely, he did not feel at all new, at all reborn, in no particular way different. True, circumstances varied wildly, but he was the same soul deep down. This did not meet the expectations of most literature.

Supposedly, by now, he should have realized, for example that his true purpose was in raising the boys. A computer career had solidified finances. Owning a home satisfied secret desire and public display. Extended sobriety opened the world to his will. All revelations, all different, all immense and all powerful. But—no—there he was, the same guy from the valleys of Pennsylvania and all the travels and troubles in between. Sometimes, more than fulfilled, he half worried that deep down he was fraudulent.

Most troubling, deviating from standard narrative, he regretted nothing at all. Wasted years trying to paint, lost hours spent cycling Boston or walking the woodlands, late nights with a cup of wine and fevered dreams—he didn't want to forget. He would live almost exactly the same way given another chance. He was happy to put those times behind, but he was grateful for the memories.

Perverse. The fact was, deep down, his guiding principal continued to be appreciating his current circumstances as fully as possible. Not to leverage them to financial advantage, but to enjoy all the unique moments offered by an unusual outlook. He did not need to chain himself to the phone on Saturday morning to drum up more business. He lacked ambition to scan want ads for a better job. He was immensely content where he was. Positively un-American.

A new shell, but an old core. He even continued to treasure secret self-images of himself as a solitary bohemian artist, trapped by necessity. Or on a temporary vacation to what everyone else considered the real world. In any case, for all the hoopla, he was not reborn, simply repackaged. That, at least, was as American as apple pie.

Thanksgiving, of course, was over at Mom and Dad's across the Island. Mom took great pride in cooking for all, and tried to browbeat as many of the far flung and nearby relatives to join in as possible. But this was the time when families begin to fracture, when some people move or die, other ties become unavoidable. The new children meant new patterns everywhere.

Wayne had always considered Thanksgiving the most lenient of the mandatory family holidays. He had early on, practically, declared his independence from traveling on the one day when sane people stayed off the roads and out of the skies. That had worked with his own parents, partially because he had gone so far away and had so little disposable income. It didn't work at all here. He might not want to drive even across the Island, but driving there he damn well would and enjoy it.

That had previously caused no small amount of tension. Lots of relatives, many hardly known. Lots of comparisons of work and home, how was anyone doing, bragging and wishing. He had perhaps taken it all as too much directed at him in the past, rather than the social game it really was (although one with a bitter cutting edge sometimes.) That had led to an unfortunate tendency to have a bit too much to drink, rarely drunk, but not himself quite either. He had claimed he needed it to be social. But of course he did not—he was perfectly social at work for instance with no chemical aid.

Anyway, Joan was very concerned. He had been doing well—but this was the traditional period when everyone slipped. What would happen?

Nothing. Wayne was happy to feel physically as good as he had in years. He could brag and lie with the best of them now. He could use his old background as a source of funny stories, rather than an admission of early failure. It was a new world. Why would he spoil it? But, of course, he too did worry and did keep on guard. No use taking chances.

It all went well. They arrived, Mom fussed, Joan helped in the kitchen, Robert and Cheryl and the bunch showed up, aunts and uncles dropped over from time to time and even Philip made a brief appearance. Alcohol was hardly present—available but little used. People just enjoyed themselves and exchanged tales and laughed.

Another landmark gone by, the happiest of times as Joan had ever imagined. Anything not perfect this moment could be made so in the future. Sure, they were all getting older, but there was still eternity in their eyes.

The only thing I missed was having a romantic (to me) secret vice to hide. That had been my mantra for years—have one vice but cultivate it well. It was kind of a distinguishing mark, even though it was a terribly stupid one.

So, now that I was pure bourgeois, how could I hang on to my own identity? For that matter, why was that even important at this point?

Eventually, I decided or grew into knowing that it didn't matter. With clearer insight, I acknowledged that I had no real need of secret vices, since I had so many obvious ones. I will not bother enumerating them—this is my story, I can present myself as nicely as I like. But there were more than a few, and some that I wanted to change, and some that I simply said "Well, that's cranky old Wayne." I surely saw them now as bad things, not an integral part of the brand.

For that matter, my deeper secret vice—the one that had truly controlled my life—was to imagine myself as some kind of lonely world-changing secret superman. Perhaps a lonely artist, ignored by his contemporaries. Perhaps a great thinker, saving up all his deep thoughts to impress civilization when he finally got around to writing it down. Perhaps just simply a survivor, saving all his good days so he could laugh at those who had wasted their time on shallow materialism all the while he had been preparing for whatever apocalypse arrived. But anyway, a person dreamed of from early adolescent novels and fierce rejection of what might have been easy paths. Now none of that seemed important. I was, I knew, just like everyone else.

That should have been depressing. But the other change was that I was simply too busy to worry about deeper soul and cosmic issues. It was hard enough getting to work, doing work, keeping the house going, managing the budget, helping Joan with the kids, appreciating Joan and the kids, and a million and one other overwhelmingly time-intrusive things that just kept popping up, each in the way of each other. There was never enough time to think. Maybe that is a good way to go through life, maybe not, but for a while we seemed to have no choice about it at all. If a free moment ever came, we remained too exhausted to do much more than collapse and smile weakly.

The reason for that, I suppose, was that we were older parents. Maybe it all came naturally to the very young—like Joan's cousins and friends who had started families by twenty one or twenty two. I didn't feel real old—but after all I was nearly forty. A career in sports would have been statistically long over. There was less raw energy than once upon a time—painting all night and working all day without much sleep might still be barely possible—but pushing physical limits was never pleasant any more.

The old folks (meaning anyone two years or more beyond your own years) are always giving stupid wise advice like "early to bed." That's because life has changed for them. They can go to bed early. Now I found myself on the other side—far on the other side—of that previously insurmountable barrier of being thirty. It wasn't a question of liking it, or fighting it, or anything else—it was the beginning of the acceptance of the ongoing preordained patterns of a life fully lived.

Ghost has changed into sweatshirt and jeans. Somehow, he has the yard divided up into four sections, each for a season. In each appropriate area he has the tools required. Looks like a home a garden show.

"Well, that at least looks more comfortable," I note.

"And more realistic," he adds.

"Yes, that is pretty much how I dressed in my new suburban life when I had to work outdoors," I admit.

"That statement would be more impressive," he says, wryly, "if you didn't tend to wear exactly the same thing when you lived in Boston, when you work around the house, when you visit relatives, and I guess just about any other time in your life anywhere."

"I never did like to dress up. The one thing I hated about consulting."

"Tie all the time."

"Yeah, tie all the time. Good pants, good shoes, jacket if not suit."

"But that got better."

"Much, much later. First the tie could loosen, then the jacket could be draped over the chair, and finally you didn't even need a jacket except once in a while, and—nirvana—work days when you knew you would stay in your cube and could not have a tie at all and just wear sneakers."

"But not 1985."

"Never in 1985. A starched era. Probably worse where we were, because the small computer consultants always wanted to look like the big expensive guys."

"So you inflicted your ratty clothes moments on your poor wife."

"I pleaded poverty," I say smugly. "Besides, no matter how new the jeans or sweatshirt I managed to get them dirty and stained in a matter of hours. Finally, she just let me keep on the old comfortable stuff around the house."

"The perpetual child inside."

"Or the secret rebel."

Wayne harbored the secret belief that he was only one break, or one change away from massive success. If he just met one person, or opened one door, or used his time better, or moved somewhere, everything would immediately clear up. Furthermore, it would all happen suddenly, like a lightning bolt. And the results would be incredible. So he could, on the one hand, blame all his troubles, whatever they were, on a current lack of luck or initiative, due to be remedied when either by seasonal instinct or massive will the caterpillar would become a butterfly. Naturally, in that analogy he missed the chrysalis stage, in which everything really happened.

In the present circumstances, he was surprised and a little saddened that none of that seemed to be true. Furthermore (because these unconscious rationalizations were somewhat hidden from him) he was puzzled at the lack of movement. Everything changed, he changed, and yet—well, no bolts from heaven or pots of gold at rainbow's end. Disquieting.

He had changed everything. He was in a new career, an almost new life, a family, a place, a way of being. He had cast off almost everything, as far as he could tell, that had been misdirected in Boston. He should be on his way to fame and fortune. More than that, the path forward should be shining crystal clear. And that road should be racing along towards some wonderful destination at breakneck speed.

Then there was the final element. If nothing else had been making a difference, then it must be his drinking. Although not nearly so horrible as the apocalyptic stories he heard, his fondness for alcohol had certainly held him back. As all other issues were resolved and put aside, it seemed more and more clear that the final step would be sobriety. Then, he had been sure, all the magic changes he had expected would immediately come to pass.

But, no. It was much better not drinking—his life was much improved. But each day remained tediously the same. No future visions sharpened. The road did not rush by with everything better each moment. He had the moment, it is true, but he had always had the moment. Where was the grand finale, the final brilliant victory? Today was not all that incredibly different

BABYLON WITH GHOST

than any other day before this—or any of the other—changes and revelations. Life went on.

His personality remained the same—he got neither better nor worse relating to people than he had before. His skills remained equal. His achievements were not affected. His interactions with the world were identical. He had exactly the same strengths and limitations as before, almost less time than before, hardly accomplished anything greater than before. That was, for a while, the real tragedy.

The end of illusion. He was what he was. Life was what it would be. No magic bean was going to make him suddenly lord of the kingdom. He still knew luck and skill and hard work and all were part of the equation of success, but they were an ongoing grind, not a one time treatment.

In the end, however, it turned out that this was the beginning of the chrysalis stage. The butterfly would be the final grateful acceptance of the wonderful life he was living. For the moment, it was all just one big tired slog, punctuated with happy instants with family and career. Nothing at all seemed to be changing, but everything was. Overall, that was a better use for time than trying to ignore its passage. Of course, being in the cocoon, he never recognized any of that while he was undergoing such metamorphosis.

We relentlessly compare ourselves to role models. As children those may be our parents, or real or imaginary heroes. Later on, we notice peers and mentors. Finally, it may devolve into a morose dissection of what actually happened to who we think we might have been. Necessary stages of being a socially useful human are nevertheless a little misleading and somewhat hopeless.

In a rapidly evolving culture, survival skills parents learned may not apply to present conditions. The world they grew up and thrived in is irretrievably gone. Nothing they did has much relevance to our fate today. Our own painfully gained experience is almost useless to our children. "Adaptability" is not much good as specific advice, and often cannot be usefully applied anyway. Surely that is why one of the basic attractions of superheroes is their pathetic vulnerability in certain areas.

In populations going on four times as many people as when I grew up, some individuals exist so far out on the end of the normalized bell curve that they are practically another species. Not uniquely stratospheric intelligence, or ethereal beauty, or perfect pitch, or fantastic physique, or no need for sleep, or incessantly driving hormones—but all of those together. Superhumans actually exist today, and mere heroes are relegated to the automation-restricted niches where the rest of us compete.

Perhaps that is why we have so cheapened the coin—nowadays the word "hero" means little more than "decent person." But the ancient and not so ancient concept of a hero as a superior ideal has pretty much vanished—by the time we are adolescents we are aware of the deficiencies that will never permit us to fully emulate those paragons of evolutionary excellence. Oh, yes, we can be boy scouts honest and true and worthy and nice—but we will remain impoverished boy scouts.

We are told to play to our strengths, and that is what we do. Many of us lack unique necessary qualities in adequate quantity to locate a career that is rewarded and happy. And we never will. The bell curve is ruthless. Automation is equally ruthless. Retraining is a fairy tale. And no matter what we might think no single thunderbolt—not even winning the lottery—will much change that.

In kinder times, I was incredibly fortunate to discover not only how to use a few relevant high end abilities I did have, but also to find my limitations and learn to adapt with them. Perhaps I should have done so sooner and deeper, but history is what it is. We must use our strengths to best effect; yes, we must apply ourselves intelligently and work hard. I wish I believed that would still make life work out, but I no longer do.

I fear the new paradigm is finding some way to survive well on discarded scraps from the feasts of the superhumans in our midst.

Ghost sat back in the red wooden Adirondack chair, surveying the freshly mowed grass and the red canna getting ready to flower in the middle of the yard where the old dead tree trunk had been. "Now you could begin to make real plans for the kids, right?" he asks.

"Maybe we should have," I admit, "but no, not really."

"What, just let them be as they will. Some kind of hippie paradise?"

"No, of course not. We were very conscious of them learning all they should learn. We had been preschool teachers, after all. Very oriented toward learning and how much kids were capable of. It's just that ...."

"What?"

"Just that after that, we didn't see a need to push them down one path or another. After all, both of ours had failed somewhat. Joan never did get a real teaching job, I never did get what I supposedly had been groomed for all through high school. We did think it was all kind of quackery. Better, perhaps, to encourage their talents whatever they were and to appreciate them and teach them to appreciate the world."

"That's not even prehistoric. How would they ever compete?"

"We didn't think much of it. Things had always seemed to work out ok for us. I know, we were too naïve."

"That's not the half of it. More like irresponsible."

"Maybe, maybe not. You never can tell until the end. But that was our path. And both of them grew up into very enjoyable and interesting and capable people."

"They coulda been contenders ..."

"Oh, puleeze," I went over and smelled a few roses.

As Gregory sprinted toward scattered seagulls, and Joan strapped the baby into his stroller, Wayne ruefully examined the side of the car in the parking lot at Venetian Shores. Not too much damage, he could probably get the plastic side-guard bit back on without it being too obvious. He couldn't believe he had managed this. Picking Mom and Dad up at the elevated Babylon station, he had been so anxiously trying to find a parking slot along the busy street that he accidently sideswiped with his new company car as he swerved into a space. Fortunately, a very light glancing hit, with bits coming off his vehicle and no obvious damage anywhere on the other. But in full view of their horrified gaze.

He seemed to be becoming less coordinated now that he hadn't had anything to drink for months. He didn't think it was supposed to work that way, but he had picked up the one or two pieces he could find and put them in the back with Gregory. Maybe there was truth in the old saying "God protects children and drunks." That protection now withdrawn. An unusual take on common wisdom.

Gregory raced towards the gulls, who ignored him until the very last moment, then languidly took flight to frustrate his ambition. As he returned, they all headed onto the sands overlooking the Great South Bay. Although very few others shared the park this early Friday afternoon, the water was filled with power craft and a few sailboats further off, languidly making way in the constant mild breeze. He had taken his first day off from this new job. The sun shone warm and benign a perfect old-fashioned refuge from the scurrying bustle further inland.

Everyone took turns pushing Wayne in the kiddy swing for a while, until he grew tired of it, then watched carefully to be sure he did not try to eat the sand he was sitting in. With quick energy dissipated from both children, they could relax on a bench in the shade of a large locust tree. The calm and quiet were almost unnerving. Conversation was identical to what it had been in Boston, the same as it had been for years, and yet different and more relaxed. They were now talking as much parent to parent as son to father or mother, swapping work stories as if at some company reunion, just enjoying life together. Perhaps for everybody else it had always been like this, for Wayne it all felt new and different. No internal worries, no fears of being called out. The grandparents were happy to finally have some quality time with the new baby, not so new anymore, growing fast.

"Do you come here a lot?" asked Mom.

"We really like it," Wayne replied, "but I don't have much time any more during the week, and if we have a whole day we'd usually rather head for the ocean. But Joan gets here pretty often."

"It's funny," added Joan. "Nobody who has lived here a long time will come with me. They don't like it much. But it reminds me a little of our beach back home where I grew up. Much better than staying in the house, and only a few minutes away."

"We seem to be so busy, all the time," Wayne remarked. Joan nodded agreement.

"Oh, yeah, I remember those days well," laughed Dad. "Always expected to do something for someone. Remember how we had to do Grandmother's lawn every week or so?"

That came back. He hadn't thought, at the time, how much of an imposition it had been for Dad when he was working five and a half days a week. So there was even more in common, now that they had a larger perspective.

Well, this should be a nice visit. They'd hang out and then go to the usual fast food place for dinner, then hang out some more. Nothing really to accomplish except talk and fun. Mom and Dad had seen most of the more spectacular sights, it was just a question of how tired they were and what they would like to do to avoid becoming bored. Which didn't seem very likely.

The elite are mightily engaged in struggles to raise perfect problem-free children, seeking guarantees for the future with massive sacrifices to the alter of upbringing. But none of the expensive camps or toys come with any guarantees of future greatness, nor even utility. History seems to indicate that letting kids play in the dirt, fight and work things out with peers, and spend afternoons basically unsupervised may be more advantageous than any shiny bits of plastic educational scraps from China.

I remain agnostic about it all. I had been familiar with such debates in the California alternative lifestyle community I lived near for a while, and certainly our parents debated whether Dr. Spock was really the top authority. Bringing children up to meet all of the various conflicting goals of being a viable member of society is nerve-wracking.

Naturally, the simplest training is immediate reward and punishment, so that correct behavior becomes almost reflexive. That seems to work, at least in the short run, but then children often rebel or end up having no real internal guidance and resources, prey to whoever provides discipline, unthinking automatons. Letting them run totally free and unchallenged creates little monsters that everyone else hates to be around. Trying to sculpt them into specialists without quite being aware of their final level of native ability is often disappointing for everyone. And weaving through it all we have a mythological vision of perfect golden childhoods that never were and probably never will be.

But, shockingly, children grow up and almost all of them even out into adequate social creatures. Some kids inhabiting abysmal circumstances become extraordinary adults, some others given every advantage fail. But, provably, enough children in most societies adapt at least enough to keep the society going.

It is always tempting to anthropomorphize everything—to say that human culture is like an organism with memes instead of genes, requiring individuals as cells. Like a bee colony, instincts pull all the components together to somehow create a successful (simply meaning continuing) entity. In that analogy, the human species can only survive with culture, and no matter what, new human beings are tuned to want to be part of the culture of which they are a part. Some of that is probably true.

But the key to human domination—with culture—is not really what we like to think. It is not intelligence, reason and logic in themselves. The most important trait we possess is adaptability—individually and in culture. To test the boundaries of adaptability, each person to various degrees must possess a degree of restlessness, a desire to push boundaries, or, if you will, to feel special. That component, I think, transcends any upbringing.

So we find out, too often, that no matter what we may do as parents, children go their own way. Eventually, most of them find an adequate way forward. But exactly what they do or learn or inculcate as children just does not come out as it went in. Mature calm visions can be warped into odd and tragic obsessions. Those who do not eventually grow out of their fantasies may become dangerous. Thankfully, in the nature of things, no matter what, most children do mature, do grow up, do adapt to being in a society, and do adjust their restlessness to socially useful ends.

But no parent today believes this of his or her own child. Each precious bundle is special and capable of doing anything as long as it has proper opportunity and guidance. Each one can be formed and shaped like bread dough into a logically perfect loaf. Each birth brings great hopes. And each child, always, turns out differently than anyone expects.

Ghost sits with beer in hand, watching the clouds drift overhead. "No control, eh. You might as well turn them loose and let them go and use your resources selfishly for yourself?"

"That is how it sounds," I admit. "But of course we have some control, and most children retain at least some of their upbringing for better or worse."

"So you mostly admit ignorance," he presses.

"I admit not only ignorance. I claim that at a certain level it is impossible to predict—in the way all futures are impossible to predict—how a child will turn out. You can only try your best and hope. "

"So what does that mean."

"For us, I think it meant that we treasured their childhood, and were pleased when they learned and did well, were proud of them when they acted responsibly, but always knew that childhood was a time in itself, not a miniature version of their adult lives."

"Interesting. Teachers defeated by the concept of the future."

"Hardly defeated. Just aware that there are more possibilities—even probabilities—than the manuals for parents seem to be aware of. It's the nature of our society to think logical science can be used for social relations."

"You think it can't"

"I think the limits are greater than we want to believe."

The clouds just kept drifting, as uncaring as all the souls around us of all ages, immersed in their own thoughts and activities that were completely unique and separated, yet also part of an immense and interconnected totality.

Gradually, all the new became old, and the strange became familiar. In almost no time Wayne was unconsciously adapted to the job, commute, home, two children, diet and everything else. When he thought about it at all, he likened it to getting used to wearing winter clothing when winter arrived. At first the cold could be brutal, then after a while it was just another day, and at some point even a previously freezing afternoon in, say, the mid-forties felt warm. That was exactly how comfortable he had become with everything.

The biggest change, that even he felt, was a removal of the hidden worries and pressure about what he was doing and the path his life was taking. It's true that the hard work had been done years ago, with decisions faced and risks taken. And it was equally a fact that everyone was much happier with what was going on almost from the first moment he changed careers, and had continued so as new challenges had been presented. But everyone had not compared to his internal demons, who had their own ideas and demands. Now those demons were silent.

His happy exterior had once concealed residual guilt. Now—his lifestyle was almost Calvinist. His time was not being wasted frivolously—every minute and more seemed predestined and beyond his free will. He wanted to believe he still made choices—how much effort at work, how much help at home, how much ambition in learning new technology. But his options were narrow, the pathways well defined, and he ended up following the easiest gradient. Meaningful rebellion would have been difficult. Successful rebellion would have seemed evil.

Confusing but nice. He was feeling smug, at least when he bothered to notice his condition at all.

Ghost perches on a canvas chair, sketchbook in hand, trying to capture a tree over in the corner. "Ah," he reflects, "but sometimes, in the dark or when things really got hassled, didn't you think just maybe you had once again made a horribly wrong turn? Perhaps if you had kept painting…"

"I don't know if I'm unusual or not," I reply, "but I never had a problem leaving something totally. The past is gone and the present is here. I would say I could divorce myself and separate the two almost too much, later I came to consider that a kind of fault. But in this case, no I had no regrets, no second thoughts, and absolutely no conviction that things could possibly have been better otherwise."

"But, well, suppose you had stopped drinking while painting, had applied yourself to finding galleries and patrons, found a community of artists …."

"My logical mind—and the thought I still have—was that I had given myself enough time and chances to do all that and had not. I never had a great desire to be a pathetic failed figure as I grew older, no matter how romantic an arthritic neglected starving artist might be portrayed. I still think that if I had given myself all the time in the world, nothing more would have happened. And besides, I didn't have all the time in the world. Doing something new as you age is a wonderful tonic."

"But …"

"No buts. Things went as they went, and for me things went better. Alternatives are—well, I guess daydreams are fun, but they are easily adaptable too."

"What?"

"Well, it was easy enough to stop pretending I was a great undiscovered artist and imagine myself as a great developing and undiscovered software superstar."

"I see. Your disease merely redirected itself."

"One way of looking at it, I suppose."

Very cold, this brilliant Saturday before Thanksgiving. Leaves lay thick along the strip of lawn in front of the house, as Wayne started raking. He had an hour or so before anybody would be ready to do anything, which should be enough to get the worst of it. After all, now that he was getting up all the time very early, sleeping late on the weekend was out of the question.

There was a lot to do here, a lot to be done later, still more in the evening. Shopping and fixing and playing and probably going down the street for dinner. Maybe arguing about whether to go across the island tomorrow, since they'd be visiting Thursday anyway. And it wouldn't end—next would be Christmas lights and real shopping and finding a tree and ... everything.

He didn't care. He took a deep breath of the chill and smiled. What a wonder it was, clear of a headache and no need to fight back the desire for a drink until later. What a fine world. What a happy time.

1986 SETTLING DOWN

SQUARE FOOT GARDEN

BRIGHT JUNE SUN was rapidly warming early Saturday air. Gregory walked with Wayne on wide wooden planks through the emerging garden in the back corner, Baby Wayne chortled happily on the sidelines watching them from his shaded stroller. Most plants were in by now, of course, and it had recently rained so no water was required. Weeds were sprouting, but so far it was mostly just watching until they took off.

"Pea pods!" exclaimed Gregory happily, as he picked a few off the vines climbing high nylon nets lining the back. He crunched them immediately, which always would horrify Joan had she been out, since everything, according to her world view, had to be washed to be edible. But it was Wayne's agreed turn to take care of them and give her a break, and Wayne's world view was decidedly different. Besides, especially at this time of year, the garden was practically organic.

"What's that?"

"Oh, those are baby carrots, just coming up. Here you can pull one out and look—but you can't eat it until it's washed. Put it in the basket."

Gregory pulled a pitifully tiny orange sliver and reverently laid it in the "authentic English woven flower basket" Wayne had ordered from a catalog—like his Mom he tended to be sucker for the stuff.

"What we really want today is some of the lettuce—see how nice it is getting now."

The whole garden was growing pretty well, almost all the tiny hopes he had raised from seed were in the ground, carefully protected tomatoes climbing their own nets and stakes, everything ready for the coming growth spurt. But, for all that, the only real harvests so far had been a smattering of pea pods and various kinds of lettuce.

Joan hated the lettuce. She liked produce completely washed and free of everything which she could get cheaply enough at the supermarket. She refused to understand the romance of gritty sand which never seemed to completely rinse off the red lettuce, nor the bugs and occasional slug that rode with the freshly picked heads. In the abstract, she understood the garden as a nice science experiment for the children, to teach them where food came from, but she continued to visualize real food as coming from antiseptic factories somewhere.

The garden was a wonderful part of having this house. Almost from the moment they moved in, he had been creating flower beds, and then it had been expanded into this square foot garden, and by then he was ordering seeds in the winter and starting them in the basement in the spring and planting them in the early summer and cultivating and mulching in the fall, even storing "delicate tubers" over the winter.

Joan loved flowers too, but hers were purchased at one of the many local flower nurseries, when she could see what they were exactly and not have to trust some writer's hyperbole and pictures that rarely bore a resemblance to what you usually got. Besides, shopping for flowers was probably more fun for her than actually taking care of them.

"Ok, guys, time to clean up and go to the library. C'mon in."

Ghost, attired in checkered flannel shirt and bib jeans, leans against a silvery aged split-rail fence. Fields of dark green potato plants with lavender-white blooms stretch off to a woodland in one direction, spiky shoulder-high cornstalks obscure views across a dusty dirt road. A beat-up dark red tractor is parked in mud ruts off to the side.

"I hope you're not planning on some kind of dialect," I open. "Where are we supposed to be, anyway?"

"Pretty much anywhere," he refuses to be specific. "So you liked dirt?"

"Oh, I lived in dirt when I was a kid. All seasons. Mud, dust, nasty stuff, great stuff, didn't matter. That was before all the fears of everything you might get. Nobody washed with anti-bacterial soap every few minutes."

"Things change," noted Ghost.

"Indeed they do. Besides, Joan had a different background. You have to remember that my Dad grew up on a real working family farm. What I called dirt he would call a layer of dust. When he was a kid he was forced to live in the stuff. His family had to use soil every day, just to make a living. My exposure was a lot more fun."

"So you tried to pass that on ...."

"No, like you said, things change. They grew up a lot cleaner than I did. Maybe there really were more things to be afraid of out there. But I wasn't nearly as fearful if some of it happened to get on them or in them."

"Well, gotta git crackin'," he needed to get in at least on bit of cliché.

I snort, but survey the well-constructed scene in admiration and more than a little nostalgia.

Just to be perverse, he signals for disassembly, which starts with it all turning fuzzy grey, as he saunters off and cranks the tractor from its front until the motor catches.

I grew up on a two acre suburban plot, newly cleared after World War II. For a while, Dad, at the urging of his farmwife mother, tried to grow enough to be somewhat self-sufficient, and devoted a half acre to summer vegetables. Each spring a tractor would come and plow and disk the land, then we would take a long trip to New Jersey to buy seeds and seedlings and plant immense rows of the usual suspects—corn, tomatoes, beans—and areas of interest to a small boy such as watermelons and pumpkins. Elsewhere there was a huge row of perennial asparagus, a long bed of strawberries, a patch of rhubarb. Mom was always trying to grow fruit or nut trees that the catalogs promised would yield easy riches. Years until I was five or six began with high promise.

I soon discovered farming was work, and uncertainly rewarded work at that. Too much rain would rot everything as we watched helplessly, too little would shrivel all but the few crops we could water from our restricted well.

Bugs and mysterious blights would infect and carry away entire chunks of possibility, in spite of the various magic and dangerous potions we would spray and spread on them. Weeds would sprout and overtake everything by using the fertilizer we had put around for the plants we wanted, and weeding was a long and back-breaking task with hoes in hot humid high summer. As crops ripened, the wildlife would be poised to strike—groundhogs and raccoons would devour corn, birds would peck holes in strawberries, deer would rummage through anything.

But in spite of all that, there was often an immense and increasing harvest by fall. The first tomato or asparagus or cucumber was a wonder—but after days and weeks and months we were kind of glad to see the first frost. Blemished and worm-riddled fruit fell to the ground unpicked, where it would attract rodents before turning to slime. Futilely, Mom would force herself to try to can some of the bounty in a sweltering kitchen, but canned anything was not particularly tasty later on, and being a city girl she hated the whole task thoroughly.

Anyway, I wanted my kids to experience some of the magic of a home garden, but not quite as much of the aggravation of those who are deadly serious about it. And that is where my little garden plot in Babylon came in. It was also useful as a tool for my remembrance.

Joan had no such background, and to her it was as much a mystery why anyone would want to spend all that nasty effort on something she could buy, as it would be to me on why someone would try to make t-shirts from home-grown cotton. She felt that civilization was built to allow her to shop, and it was her duty to do so.

Frosty February Sunday morning, with corn pancakes partially mixed and cooked by Wayne and Gregory, was just finishing up as Joan came into the kitchen. "Making a mess again," she noted.

"Sure," Wayne replied cheerfully. "Now that we ate, I need to figure out what to order from Burpees."

"Seeds, again?" she inquired skeptically. "You're going to grow everything in the basement?"

"I have it all set since last year," he assured her. Hovering over the long wide workbench were rows of cheap fluorescent lights, piled underneath were countless trays of seed starting cubes, his schedule for starting things had been carefully worked out. "You do like the flowers, anyway."

"I like to buy them better," she muttered, "you can see what you're getting."

"But it saves us a fortune," he said indignantly.

"I'm not so sure. Well, it's an ok hobby."

"And educational for the kids, too."

"As long as you don't make me help."

"Say," I said, waving to including the children. "Did I ever tell you about our adventure with Nana's canning attempts?" Everyone shook their heads no. "Ah, that was something. You see, we had too many tomatoes and peppers and stuff in September, and the only way to save them for later was to put them in mason jars, seal them, and boil forever to kill all the stuff that makes food go bad. Then we could store them in our basement—it was all mud back then, Joan, not what you see now—and eat them during the winter."

"Did they taste good?" asked Gregory.

"Not really."

"Why didn't you just make sauce out of the tomatoes?" asked Joan.

"No idea how to do that. No Italians in our family tree, I guess. Anyway, the last year she canned, I was maybe seven or so. One freezing winter night we were all eating dinner upstairs in the dining room when Anita and I heard a big bang in the cellar. Then another. We opened the door and rushed down and that was the end of home preservatives."

"Why?" said Joan and Greg together.

"The glass jars were exploding. There was glass and smelly water and limp vegetables all over the place, stinking it up. You see," I explained, "it turned out that if you didn't boil stuff long enough and reach the right temperature some of the bacteria would remain alive. They started to grow in the jars later, and made gasses, and eventually the pressure would blow the bottles up."

"And if you ate them?" Joan was horrified.

"Bad. You might die. So that was the end of that. Anita and I afterwards sort of suspected Mom might have done it on purpose. She really hated steam from boiling and everything having to do with the process. Anyway, you," I concluded, pointing at Joan, "do not have to do that. All you need to do is let me order seeds."

There is now a great movement to source food locally, and once when I lived in California there was a genuine movement to grow your own and become self-sufficient. I think all that misses the point.

From at least the Romans, through Thomas Jefferson, right to the present notions of the American Family Farm, some intellectuals have promoted a rosy view of the self-reliant peasant or yeoman, staunch in his defense of homeland and moral values. This flies in the face of historical records which indicate that every time anyone could escape such a life to almost anything else, they did so. Most societies ended up doing agricultural food crops with slaves or their equivalent—we would still do so if machines had not taken their place. We still do rely on "migrant workers" (our current term for slave equivalents) to harvest some fruits and vegetables and do other things which cannot yet be performed mechanically.

Subsistence farming is one of the worst deals possible. It's all chance—dependent on various local variations in weather or infestation. Fields decline in fertility. Your body gets old and achy. If the harvest is bad, you starve. If the harvest is good some thugs—neighbors, barbarians, the government—is apt to come along and take it to let you starve. The work is backbreaking and constant except for a few months in winter, when it is unendurably cold and boring. Work, in fact, fit only for slaves.

I can't say I admire such things as the locavore movement. If the local source has a typical problem with harvest, they can always go somewhere else. I always thought, and still do, that the real heroes will be those who continue to remove the human element entirely—self-driven tractors, now, and in the future possibly robotic methods of insect control and delicate harvest and packing. The less people are involved in all this, the happier I am. I've tried some of that, and I certainly don't want to spend much of my life staring at the sky hoping for rain, or watching corn prices on the Chicago market to see if I make a profit this year, or deciding if I really want to stay organic while hornworms eat all the tomatoes and blight carries off the squash. I refuse to see the joy in watching people I employ bending over day after day to pull weeds or pick lettuce. Eliminate all that, there is no reason to keep it.

Only those who have never done an activity can be properly romantic about it. Thomas Jefferson could afford to be a farmer because he owned slaves to do all the work—all he had to do was hire people to tell them what to do. Pretty much, that's what everyone really wants—and always did.

Out in the dusty wooden barn, old implements hang from the walls, unused for years but with too many memories to throw away. Gourds dry on the old plank floor over near the sliding door. Slivers of sunlight stream through slats on a far wall, illuminating a kind of rural cathedral filled with hay.

"You buy only organic, right," laughs Ghost, putting aside a pitchfork.

"Don't get me started. Organic people haven't a clue about farming and pretensions about nutrients, and simply ignorant ideas about chemistry. But I do admit they have some points."

"Oh?"

"Sustainable agriculture and monocropping, for example. Our industrial farming techniques are atrocious for the crops, the land, the environment, and people in general. But all we need to do is take some time to refine them—now that we have computers and equipment that can do so."

"You could probably get land upstate pretty cheap."

"Subsistence grunt farming is no fun at all. I wouldn't wish that on anyone."

"Fun? Where would fun come in?"

"It's sure more fun to have high yields with less work."

"Ah, you have your own soapbox," Ghost spits into a patch of grass in the muddy driveway.

"Well, why not? Everybody else does."

As in life, one of the hardest things to learn about gardening and farming is that entropy is more common than stability. You start out expecting seasonal variations—plant seeds in spring, tend crops in summer, harvest in fall. But seasons vary year by year and week by week—a warm spell when you put out tender tomatoes may be followed by lingering frost, there might be too much rain for two or three weeks, then a month of drought. Oh, yeah, you think you understand, but you don't.

Wayne was all gung ho when he started—a chance to get back to the soil, start something useful that the kids could learn from, do a hobby that was marginally more productive than just growing flowers. So he went all in, growing tomatoes from seed, carefully picking varieties from catalogs, tending them through late February and March in the basement. Determining when to put them out, and how to protect them if they were out too early.

The first year was not exactly a disaster, but had its share of disappointments. He learned. He put in an underground pvc pipe back to a faucet so he didn't have to lug watering cans, put up mesh on metal frames to hold cucumbers and tomatoes and beans, discovered better times to plant everything. Yet year by year, his garden environment degraded.

1986 was a little different, because hurricane Gloria had passed by the previous fall, ripping and tipping trees and disturbing patterns yet again. In the previous three years, his carefully tended soil had attracted the roots of all the nearby shrubs and trees, many on his neighbor's property, and a formerly sunny patch had become more shaded and laced with runners. Gloria had cleared some of that back, but there were a fair amount of things to repair.

He was having trouble getting things to grow at the right time. Everyone was excited by the first snap pea, baby carrot, radish or even leaf of lettuce. A month later, not so much. Tomatoes and zucchini took forever, but once they began in abundance, Joan and the kids wanted nothing to do with them. Potatoes were a nice demonstration, but otherwise much better from the store. Nothing was perfectly ready exactly when people wanted to eat it.

He never did get timing right for pumpkins. Too late and they would be nowhere near grown as the days grew short. Too soon and the beautiful fruits would rot by September. So all he could do was regretfully see this as a demonstration garden, to show the possibilities, but never a near attempt at feeding the family. Wayne and Greg would probably never even want to get that close to the soil.

The trouble is, we always expect progress. We know the first time we do something it is likely to be a disaster, but we figure we will learn and the next time will be better. Practice makes perfect. So we do what we can one year, and we think the next year we will know that we should do this and should not do that and everything will work out just dandy.

Shockingly it doesn't. What grew one year beautifully and without effort may end up the next straggly and covered with spots. Soil that was fertile when first turned no longer grows anything well, or suddenly gets infected with certain blights or insects. Cutworms that ignored this spot for a while take up permanent residence. Shade from nearby trees gets imperceptibly greater, a host of additional subtle problems intrude.

And then there are big issues—hurricanes, long droughts, wildlife . Raccoons are much to be feared, but just as bad are rats and slugs and caterpillars, and even cats or dogs wandering by and laying down. You go on vacation for a week and everything dries and dies. You watch helplessly as huge pools of water formed over a week of heavy rain pool to drown or rot every small plant bravely out there in the onslaught.

Bottom line, is that experience does not bring better results necessarily in anything, including gardens. What experience brings is a better perspective on dealing with problems, and more foresight in anticipating what they may be. Nothing, of course, can be done about huge ones. But the little ones can be better dealt with, and with less personal anguish, as you learn.

Which is why gardens are useful for life. They are a metaphor for child raising, for example, in a less charged atmosphere. Your tomatoes are not your children, but you soon discover that like tomatoes, children are affected by more than the presumably perfect upbringing you are subjecting them to. By the second child, of course, most parents have learned this anyway.

Lazy dark red sun floats down in clouds becoming tinged scarlet and gold. We sip lemonade, rocking on the porch, looking out over green fields. My back is sore, I'm grateful to simply rest after what was presumably a long hard day of physical labor.

"Do you miss your garden?" asks Ghost.

"It's true, after we left a few years later I haven't had one since. Too many trees around here. But the short answer is no. I think I got that out of my system."

"But wasn't it fun?"

"Oh, I loved it at the time. I would jump out even on work days and go quickly do some watering, a little weeding, even in my good clothes, and just admire what was going on or reflect on what was going badly. It was very meditative."

"Good clothes?"

"Well, that was the advantage of square foot gardening, after all. I could walk on the planks and never actually step in soil, very hygienic, very easy to move around in without ever getting too dirty."

"You could at least grow some things in pots on the patio, even now, if you wanted to," Ghost notes.

"I could. I guess I'm just old and lazy and infected with Joan's ideas. Let other people do it. Farming is hard work. At this stage in life, I'm happy to stick with grass and flowers and shrubs. I do my own yard, that's plenty for minor activity and lots of meditation and a feel of being in the natural world."

"Lazy useless bum."

"Yep, that's me all right."

I slap a mosquito and sit back to simply enjoy the show.

Another warm day, summer finally had arrived. Windows were open, breezes swept air through the house. Fortunately, they hardly ever needed air conditioning. They had none.

"Daddy, Daddy, look, look at this …." Gregory dragged Wayne over to the back door screen. He was pointing up at something on the mesh. Joan wandered over out of curiosity.

"What in the world …."

"Oh, you know what? That's my baby praying mantises," said Wayne proudly. Tiny green stick figures were all over, at least five of them clinging for dear life. "Although why they are here instead of staying in the garden …."

This represented his latest attempt at natural pest control. Problems had been escalating for some time. The first year had been perfect. No insect damage to speak of, and the few bugs that showed up were more curiosity than menace. He had picked them off by hand, had showed them to anyone who was interested, and had generally played the kind, gentle, scientist-farmer.

But the second year had been a different story. First were weeds, which happily invaded and colonized disturbed and fertilized soil. Ferociously growing as fast as Jack's beanstalk, they could sneak under a lettuce leaf one morning and overwhelm the crop a day later. Wayne pulled and hoed whenever he had a notion. Unfortunately they seemed to have more perseverance, and definitely more time, than he did.

Equally bad were the bugs. By the second and third years they coated leaves and fruits alike. Various huge caterpillars that he could pull and squash, unseen mites that chewed leaves into barren lace, slugs that ravaged lettuce and vanished leaving nothing but slime trails. Apparently those slugs had been controlled by ground toads (he had accidently dug up a few when forking the garden) but the toads must have not liked disturbed soil and moved out. Cutworms toppled tender seedlings over and over. Other things he could scarcely describe roamed through an entomologist's paradise.

Each January, he carefully perused brochures and catalogs on natural and biologic cures. He ordered nematodes to spray on the soil to eradicate cutworms and other subterranean terrors. He released packets of ladybugs to dispose of anything that showed up above ground. The nematodes didn't do much, and all the ladybugs flew away. Weeds transformed into magnificent specimens. The harvest was laughable.

This year, with much fanfare, he procured praying mantises, which were described as tyrannosaurs of carnivorous insect species. They had arrived in white spun cases like he imagined silkworms used. He delicately wired them around corners of the garden as the temperatures rose. But mantises were supposed to stay in the garden gobbling bugs, why were they on the door doing nothing? Well, maybe all their siblings were happily munching away back in the crops.

Nope. He checked later and couldn't find any. Except for the fun of letting the boys see them, there was no effect. The garden continued downhill. As his exasperation mounted and work became more involved and time-consuming, being a part-time farmer lost attraction. There ended up being more than enough to do around their house without trying to grow food. His neighbor's trees were shading the garden by now, so he had a good excuse to forget the whole thing.

He figured next year would be very modest indeed, and what grew would grow, and what did not survive would simply be a demonstration to the family. And a warning to his ambition.

As children grow and a career takes off, time becomes more and more precious. Hobbies that once fit easily into spare evenings or weekends become almost impossible to continue when there turns out to be almost no such thing as a spare evening, and weekends are fully booked months in advance. Not to mention that there is only so much energy to go around, and as you edge toward forty there is even less of that than there used to be.

In any case, the hobbies you keep are either multipurpose or tiny little things that can be grabbed at odd moments and put down without consequence. Multipurpose, of course, wonderful, mostly a mental sleight of hand. You can convince yourself that you are enjoying the outdoors and experiencing beauty while at the same time getting the kids out to run off some steam at a park. You can relax watching sports if at the same time taking occasional interest in whatever game or toy is interesting your child. You can even gain bits of solitude stolen when alone pushing the lawn mower or commuting to work (that last has pretty much been taken away by the wired society, I guess.)

Anyway, I was reaching the point of saturation. My reading for pleasure ended up largely being technical manuals, my drawing became flowcharts and diagrams of new client applications, my creative writing involved crafting beautiful sounding phrases for our sales calls. Keeping the house and yard up when we could not afford to hire people took a lot of time. And there were always, constantly, more and different demands from the kids. We rapidly discovered that in terms of demand, changes, catastrophes, and occasional triumphs, they were worse than trying to farm.

Wide wooden kitchen table groans with the weight of September harvest. Too much to cook, at least for dinner, but probably it all needs to be preserved somehow. This represents, after all, the main reason given for growing a food garden.

"But you still had to eat," insisted Ghost.

"Oh, sure, but I just accepted Joan's line of reasoning and bought stuff at the supermarket factory."

"And that was that?"

"I admit, my experiences with the organic controls, and the memories of my father's chemical usage, gave me a certain cynicism in the growth of food. It's not as easy as anyone thinks, and it's certainly not so simple to get anything meaningful without a lot of slave labor (your own or others) unless you are willing to evoke chemical witchcraft. Anyway, that's what I took away from it. No miracle cures to make everything perfect."

"Hardly surprising."

"Nope, pretty much like the rest of life."

"Here, hand me those carrots," he turns to the ancient stove.

In an affluent culture, it's easy to become entranced by new and exciting possibilities. Some of these simply appeal to you, some of them are thrown out as fads when suddenly everyone seems to be trying them out. And our consumer culture is ready to exploit the needs of each.

There is in all this a common curve of enthusiasm, whether photography, or exercise, or knitting, or cooking or whatever. Most of us start out with the simplest of equipment and plans, fully under control, trying something new. We find we like it, and get great satisfaction from whatever results. We are hooked.

Soon there are esoteric choices to be made, specialized understandings to be honed. Clubs and magazines promote a culture of insiders, connoisseurs who have taste and experience and know what is good and what is not. Unsurprisingly, becoming better and more involved often requires more expense, more time, more dedication. And we read more and buy more and try more and …

The results are less than we expect. There is disappointment. All this money and, for most of us in most of our hobby activities, very little reward. The huge expensive copper pots are hardly ever used—they do look pretty, but who wants to keep them clean. The next iteration of what must be acquired comes around, and we have neither the funds nor the energy.

And suddenly, often, there is a snap. We fall into just good enough, and get off the treadmill of seeking perfection and ever greater triumph and settle for what we have or what we had. New demands drain our time, at least for the moment, and we put all the purchases in the closet or basement or garage, let the subscriptions expire, and think we will get back to it all later.

Until another enthusiasm grabs our attention, something new, something radically improving our now dull lives. And the chase, once again, begins.

The big farm show has big promises. Tractors that do more, improved varieties of seeds, healthier stock animals. All kinds of miracle potions from fertilizer to organic pesticides. Bright promises of a rural utopia. All I can do is laugh.

"My, my, cynical, aren't we," smiles Ghost.

"Well, yeah. But at least on most of the things I got hooked on for a while I never really expected to make money. That separates me a little from the real crazies."

"What, not following your passion?"

"Oh, I follow it well enough. I just know there's little chance anyone else will be interested in it."

"But people make money on their hobbies all the time…"

"You know, Ghost, I've looked at this carefully, and I would simply qualify that a bit. It's the passionate salesperson who makes money on anything. Not on what they do, but on what they sell. It's always that way. The idea that anything happens because of native merit is the false note in all this."

"But you still like hobbies, I take it."

"Oh, I'm a sucker always. But I realize anything related to a hobby is an expense and not an investment, that's all."

Wayne pretty much swore off the garden dreams at this point. Yet there was still a kind of primal urge, every January when the beautifully illustrated catalogs came around. It was hard to resist the lovely pictures and the delicious prose.

He didn't try to stop himself. It was a small enough pleasure in usually bleak months. But he limited his purchases, did not try more than one crackpot idea a year, and never thought that perfect heaven was around the corner each spring.

Hope was wonderful. Hope tempered with experience was even better.

IBM WORLD

USUALLY, WAYNE HAD avoided Saturday hours. Most clients were strict nine to five operations, medical practices or distributors rarely open weekends, and wanting to keep a close eye on computer fixes and implementations during regular hours. It was a comfortable, traditional, and back then pretty normal way for businesses to operate.

But here he was at Advantage, courtesy of those geniuses at IBM, who kept sending out "urgent mandatory system updates" for the 36, requiring that it be down for hours and unavailable to the client. Owner Jerry had icily insisted he wouldn't have his staff twiddling their thumbs for half a business day. A prime account usually got what they demanded, and—well—here he was. Unopened box of huge eight inch floppy diskettes, thick instruction packet, just him and Bill who had been forced to open the offices. Bill didn't like being here at seven on a nominal day off any more than Wayne did, so they were mutually grumpy.

Wayne sighed. Opened the materials. Well, he'd done this before. He sat at the console, signed on as the operator, and brought up the "green screen." Nothing but capital letters in white on a glowing green background. He typed in the operations menu on the command line, found the update area, inserted the first diskette, and waited for the ongoing, irregular, prompts as the drive ground noisily.

Hours later, he was progressing nicely, almost done reading the final up-date before final reboot. His checklist had been ninety percent filled. It was just—oh no!—the damn diskette wasn't reading. He could hear the retry over and over, before the dreaded malicious message "Disk unreadable, please insert new disk." If he couldn't get through this he'd be another three hours to fall back, and next Saturday to try again.

But—fortunately he had learned over the years—so he had a spare set in the car. He went and retrieved the necessary eighth in the pack, pushed it into the slot, and hit the enter key. All proceeded without complaint, and he breathed a sigh of relief.

With any luck, he could be finished up in another hour, out the door, and home in time to salvage the afternoon.

A dark suited figure stands with his back to us, in a stark bare white room with only a white screen in front breaking the monotony of the walls. A pro-jector is casting bright harsh light which illuminates the otherwise dark space. I glance around and see maybe twenty near clones, all in dark suits, all short slicked hair, all neatly attentive. Each has a big fat folder presented as part of the course, courtesy of IBM. Some are examining it in curiosity.

Our uncomfortable office chairs are lined against long tables, where we have spread the materials. We are expected to take notes of course. In my case, I am to report back and hopefully teach the others the gist of what I will be wading through today. At least we are well fed, IBM always provides good refreshments, and most of us have a cup of coffee in front of us.

Ghost turns and smiles an industry-standard porcelain smile. "Good morning, gentlemen," he begins as if giving a college lecture, which of course he imagines he is. "Welcome to the world of Big Iron, the real world of real computers doing real things to help business make the world a better place. Congratulations on making it here, away from the toys with which you have been tinkering. Now you will see how world-class products will make your lives and those of your clients incredibly more productive." He picks up an acetate sheet, slides it onto the glass plate of the projector. As the words focus on the screen, he intones "Please turn to page one."

I knew the drill. Each outline page of the entire manual would be read word by word, by Ghost, from the screen, while we read along in our book. A few comments, dull with an attempted joke or two, would be inserted here or there. For hours. At least it was a holiday from work, the only way I could be contacted was when I dialed in to the office from the bank of phones in the lobby at lunch and break times.

"Now we know, of course," Ghost made a weak smile, "that DEC has fine products for the engineers. But their machines are hardly built for commercial use. And we are aware," he grimaced in distaste, "of the uses of micro consoles from Microsoft in crude spreadsheet calculations." Many in the audience groaned sympathetically. IBM and Microsoft had just gone through a painful partnership divorce. "But for the solid accounting and control so desperately required by any successful medium to large firm in the modern world, we are truly the only rational solution. Please turn to page two." The acetate sheet changed.

Ghost picked up a wooden pointer like a billiard cue and pointed to a circled object in the diagram on the screen. "Up here, we have the corporate executives, whom we wine and dine and keep happy with immense expense accounts so they love to buy our products. As you know, nobody ever got fired for choosing IBM." The pointer moved lower. "Here we have our salesmen, all dressed in neat black suits, able to promise the moon and stars, which we have our legal staff massage on the contract so we can pretend to have fulfilled those impossible expectations later. Just to the side here," he pointed again, "is our neatly attired and groomed technical staff, the gentlemen you will meet later, who can guide you through any issues you may encounter if you fail to listen closely today and study your manuals intensively. At the bottom here," he indicated a vast cloud, indicating it continued well off the page, "is the masses of everyone else in the world, who we don't pay attention to very much." A brief forced chuckle from the seats.

"Now you, gentlemen," I finally noticed they were all men as usual, "represent something quite new to us and a bit perplexing. Independent contractors, consultants, IBM business partners. We're not quite sure what to make of you. You aren't top caliber. You're not IBMers. Frankly, we'd be much happier without you. But this midrange business market is different than the quasi-monopolies we've been dealing with, which is why DEC and others have been eating our lunch. No unlimited expense accounts here. Our lawyers sometimes get trapped by angry entrepreneurs who claim we failed them.

We know there's a lot of money to be made, but we're not sure how to tap into it. You," he smiled benignly, "or at least your bosses, are our latest attempt to have a lower cruder and most importantly less expensive tier of outreach into the market. Please turn to page three."

Only Ghost, I thought, would ever have stated the truth so bluntly. I had to admit, though, the setting was perfectly authentic.

Like an ancient mountain-man, Wayne developed sense and recognition of the complexities of his surrounding business environment. He could easily pick out equivalent of traces of native tribes, or game trails. That wasn't strictly necessary to perform his job—he was paid to concentrate on code and design and debugging, with documentation and client stroking thrown in. But it never hurt to learn about the waters in which all the fish swam, if only to avoid sharks and external nets. Anyone too naïve to submit to company politics would have a hard time of it, no matter how technically brilliant.

Webcor had cured him of any illusions about the magic of IBM. Its products had warts like any others, its salesmen frequently had little idea what the true challenges were, and its whole internal structure was geared to dealing with huge bureaucratic accounts, not the nimble weird little firms that were frantically trying to automate in all kinds of odd ways. Other people at JBS still bought into the hype, mostly because they had not been exposed to other types of computers and had never gone through a disaster like he had. He went along, but kept his eyes open.

IBM had been a quasi-monopoly so long it had frozen internally. Oh, there were incredibly brilliant people somewhere down in the workshops, the chips and system designs were well thought out and better tested than just about anyone else's. Give them credit, he thought, they didn't get where they were and maintain that position with smoke and mirrors. Their computers, properly instructed, really did perform magnificently. But—and here was the critical and possibly fatal "but" in the business market he was servicing— all that required an awful lot of money, constantly, always. Money for initial purchase, money for service agreements, money for additional software, money for specialized peripherals like terminals and printers. After small business owners shelled out amounts that caused them to faint—just to get the machine to turn on—they were in no mood to happily spend even more for custom programming. And, of course, when push came to shove, IBM always got paid first.

The other big problem was that the computing world was picking up speed. Executives were reading magazines that described automated utopias. Accountants and finance people were using personal computers to do all the planning and evaluation, and printing out wonderful little charts. Secretaries were switching from typewriters to stand-alone word processors that were nothing more than a PC with a printer. And—IBM was slow. It had always been careful, taken its time. That worked to make products reliable. But the products they were trying to do now were beyond their areas of expertise and were usually pretty awful by PC standards, and two years or more behind the standards of that nimble industry.

Wayne was also hammered by the fact that executives, secretaries, and finance guys were learning just enough about computers to make them dangerous. They asked dangerous questions and requested reasonable but impossible things for the machine with which he was working. The mystique of the computing world was wearing off fast, and they were starting to treat programmers a lot like they did car mechanics. Clever, yes; useful, undoubtedly; but you had to keep your eye on them and check their claims. The magic was going away.

Nick had been born and raised in Brooklyn, a seasoned cookie from a tough neighborhood, and he had an affinity for those still there. A lot of his accounts were in places where Wayne with his sheltered suburban background would once have been afraid to venture. Even now, a trip here to L&R, down past Aqueduct, near "the Projects", was memorably worrisome. The dirty streets and abandoned cars, the crumbling walls filled with graffiti, the slouching residents made him constantly worry his auto would not be where he left it parked when he returned—even though it was an old junker. The razor wire circling the top of the distribution center did not make him feel any better.

This was a sales call, a combination of adjusting accounts, getting paid money due, and contracting for additional business. Everybody would get to air their discontents, and basically Wayne would become the focus of both good and bad. He knew the routine. Nick was driving, and he blithely parked his Mercedes right in front of the building without a thought.

In the small office, small talk. "How are the kids?" "Fine, how are yours coming along?" "Enjoy the vacation—where did you go again?" "Wasn't that idiotic what the Mets did last night?" and on and on for an hour, like old women gossiping. This was the part that Wayne, a tech to the core, found insufferably boring and irrelevant. But Nick knew as an instinctive salesman that it was only this camaraderie that kept the account tied to JBS, and developed a layer of commonality and trust that overrode all the later computer disagreements.

"Now, about this bill," began Paul, "We just don't want to pay for something we had nothing to do with."

"And that was?" asked Nick.

"This System36 Upgrade—4 hours—we have a maintenance contract with IBM and with you and that should cover it."

"But …" Wayne began. Nick gestured with his hand and silenced him. "OK, I can see that. You have to understand, we thought that was an IBM issue ourselves, but they stuck us with performing it on site. We aren't real happy either—Wayne, here, has better things to do—but I think we can adjust it in light of everything else if we work it out today."

Which, Wayne realized, was really exactly the right negotiating stance, rather than the righteous anger he had worked up. Now we had laid our economic suffering on the table as a first chip, and found a semi-common enemy.

"And," said Larry, "These forty hours for a billing system upgrade and special printout are way too much, and almost double what you estimated."

"Wayne, what happened there?"

"The specifications changed halfway through, when Karen noted a problem on the first demonstration," replied Wayne. "That meant we had to change the database to add more fields, which meant we needed to tack on a conversion routine and fallback, in addition to more extensive testing and longer implementation and training. Not to mention the documentation for the users." He tried to sound pleasant, but internally he was gritting his teeth. That had been a nasty problem and almost hadn't worked out at all. Lots of stress. He tried to look professional.

"Look Larry," began Nick, "these things are very complicated. We give you the best estimate we can and try to keep you aware of what is happening as we go. Sometimes there are issues. You can't expect Wayne to work for nothing—he has a family to pay too. It's all working now, isn't it."

"Well, yeah," said Larry grudgingly. "The staff love it."

"There you go. I suppose we can try to give you higher estimates in the future, if Wayne thinks this is likely to happen again."

Larry pulled up his pant leg and revealed a shiny handgun stuck in his high argyle sock. "Look, Nick, don't mess with me. I know how to deal with people who mess with me…" He laughed. Everyone else laughed nervously. "I got this cause guys were breaking in the roof, never know who might be inside when we open in the morning."

And so it went, for three hours, almost typical. Give and take, ending with a request for bid for the next project, which Wayne would write up when they got back. All in all, they got back 80 cents on the dollar, about typical. The Mercedes was still there, miraculously, as they left. Nick not quite grumpy but complaining. "I wish we didn't have to do accounts like this," he confided, "but these days we have to take work where we can find it, and nobody else is trying to get in here, at least."

Wayne could imagine why not.

Like many programmers, I felt like a god when working with computers. It was all pure creation and artisanship, from the first designs through the ecstatic coding of the prototype through the final annoying finicky little bugs that had to be resolved. There was no high comparable to that of seeing a system I had designed and implemented being used every day, a true feeling of having brought something forth out of nothing.

Like many modern people, I also regarded myself as the hero in my own novel. I had a unique background, and a special presence at work and home and internal thoughts, and an imagined future that would work out differently than anyone else's. Keeping this in mind helped keep perspective and restore sanity when one side or another of daily existence got too complicated, but did sometimes lead to envy and resentment thinking others had it easier, somehow. But no matter what, I usually even there felt in overall control of my actual destiny.

But to stay gainfully employed turned out to require yet another attitude, one best described as a character actor in bit parts. I had to be willing to be the fall guy, the scapegoat or the intransient stupid idiot. I had to know when to be angry or contrite, when to be obstinate, when to grudgingly give way, when to promote enthusiastically. I could be an idiot-savant techie, or a cultured college graduate slumming his way through coding, or a sympathetic "we're all in this together and getting the worst of it" friend of the users, or a technological dreamer of wonders in the near future. Or any of thousands of other roles, depending on need and circumstance.

We had to present an ensemble act, as many small companies do. We were not the high and mighty take-it-or-leave-it giant firm in any negotiations. So we slickly adapted to audience, felt around for what seemed to be getting good response, and worked with it. Most of the time it went pretty well. Sometimes it failed. Once in a while the denouement could get downright ugly.

I have to admit it helped keep me human, and fit my outlook on life. I've known too many folks who sink desperately into the only thing they can do well, or that they think they are paid for, and never lift their heads to see the wider issues. I was usually upset when I got pulled away from playing god at the console to being the court jester at some account roast, but it was a nice change of pace and informed what I was doing when I went back to being god once more. In later terminology, it was a lesson in having to live in my own sandbox, which many programmers never did.

But at the time, for the most part, I was impatient and a bit angry at all the interruptions. "Ah, what I could only accomplish," I would say to myself, "if they only gave me the time." And yet…. Well a strange truth was that it was when I was most hassled and most hurried that I was most productive. The greatest contemplations in the world, the most nitpicking tedious re-working of code, days to produce what probably could have been done less carefully in a few days—none of that made me or my output any better. I worked best under pressure, and "just good enough" in my case was usually adequate. In other words, this vagabond traveling show suited me pretty well.

A dark suited figure stands with his back to us, in a stark bare white room

BABYLON WITH GHOST

with only a white screen in front breaking the monotony of the walls. A projector is casting bright harsh light which illuminates the otherwise dark space. I glance around and see maybe twenty near clones, all in dark suits, all short slicked hair, all neatly attentive. Each has a big fat folder presented as part of the course, courtesy of IBM. Some are examining it in curiosity.

Ghost begins "Please turn to page one of our course in Estimation Techniques …."

I stand up, "Ghost, enough of this nonsense. Been here, done this. You made your point, I guess."

Everybody else in the room freezes and fades into shadows. "Just wanted a touch of verisimilitude."

"Yeah, fine, do it with something more pleasant than these boring lectures. What about estimation?"

"Well, you know, you did a lot of it and …"

"There were only three things to know about estimating a software job back then," I state firmly. "Twenty percent of the code would take eighty percent of the effort; by the time delivery was accepted, no matter how much you padded, everything had taken twice as long; and finally, even with a lot of experience and care you usually got it wrong."

"But my dear boy," says Professor Ghost condescendingly, "that's exactly what I am trying to get you out of."

"Oh, I've had lots of these workshops, read numerous books. But take a simple example. Suppose they want a mark on certain orders that these are special Christmas items."

"But why…"

"That's the first problem. The IBM salesmen ignore all this stuff. 'Firms much bigger than yours are using this package all over the world. It has more than you could possibly use.' They don't know the customer, they don't know the product, and they will promise anything. So there is a package with no provision for Christmas-marked orders, and the client must have it or walk away. That's the first thing us IBM partners had to do, modify the original package unmercifully."

"So you have expertise…"

"Listen, in those days everything was brittle. If you modified a field you had to modify and recompile all the programs. If that was an IBM package it meant you could no longer use their updates and fixes as provided.

Then, even if you did everything right, with new files for modifications, if you added something else you had to take care of all the programs that might be using that file."

"Surely trivial."

"Surely not, with very crude tools if any available. It was all by eye and hand. If you missed something—and God knows you almost always missed something—you could be sure it would go wrong and blow something critical up at the worst possible time, such as midnight at month end. And then …"

"There's more? Surely not …"

"Surely yes. Something like, 'but we need that to carry into the General Ledger reports, obviously.' A whole different package, a whole different set of problems, a whole different nasty bunch of arguments about what had be promised and what had been done. Never ending."

"A firm methodology …"

"Would work fine for you ivory tower types, with all the time in the world and simple logical problems to solve and no money constraints. In the real world—cost and time overruns and absolutely no way around it, if you wanted to stay in business."

IBM was used to fat profits and to get them it was used to complete control of its customer base. Once you bought "Big Blue" you were forced into a world of IBM peripherals, IBM programs, IBM data, and IBM thinking. They even had their own bit coding—EBCEDIC—which was different than that used by just about all the other computers in the world. Venturing outside approved IBM channels to purchase rogue parts could easily void warranties, and in any case would result in stern warnings from the mother company. In the land of giant American multinational oligopolies, this strategy had served them well, and they saw no reason to change.

But the "mid-sized," and, frankly, "small" business market they were trying to break into—where the action was!—was different for more than the finances available to each company. These were entrepreneurial places, used to doing things on their own, taking chances, bargaining. They asked embarrassing questions: for example, that bit coding which was IBM's pride and joy because it did things ASCII could not, like handle Japanese and Chinese characters or mathematical symbols. But practically, asked the new accounts, we never use and never will use Japanese or Chinese or advanced math. That's not a virtue to us, just a pain in converting data.

And these business guys (almost every one a guy but the few women could be worse) were used to playing with the tiny microcomputers at home or office. They were used to using a perfectly practicable keyboard and cheap tv monitor which worked fine and cost a fraction of a monster 5250 terminal required by the mainframes and System36 or 38. Printers were rapidly becoming a common commodity. They fought back tooth and nail when presented with only one expensive option by the sales team, and were quite willing to buy something else off the back of a truck if necessary and devil with the warranty.

But the absolute worst element—the thing that really showed up IBM as the wave of the past and unable to handle the quickly arriving future— were the office programs. With much fanfare and hype, IBM had unveiled a typically overpriced "office package," with word processing and spreadsheet capabilities. These clumsy and crude attempts to satisfy a massive need might have been impressive in 1950, but they were laughable compared to the PC programs like Wordperfect or Visicalc being used everywhere by mid-level managers or their staff. Not only that, but IBM let the versions sit for years at a time ("well, it works doesn't it?") while the PC programs brought out improvements or a better competitor every week or so. It was the big iron equivalent of "the emperor's new clothes." Suddenly, buying IBM didn't look so safe after all. Minicomputers were circling in for the kill.

And new issues were coming up all the time. Communication to remote sites was a big problem—you needed special phone lines, unlike a PC that could use a phone and modem. Forget about attaching any odd peripheral like bar code readers or optical scanner. For that matter, forget about connecting to anything other than IBM—not even to IBM PC's, which were trying desperately to hang on in a changing world.

Wayne was in the middle of all this. As a business partner, he had to present the "IBM way." As a programmer, he realized it was a losing effort. As a practical part of a business he compromised as much as possible and tried to give honest advice that would not be too damaging to the sales.

Transitioning from art to engineering was complete now, and not so difficult as I might have thought. I had always had a good grasp of fundamental logic, even in aesthetics, and I found it easy to apply to design and code. The flow of programs and the hidden channels of code to accomplish an effect was very similar to creating a work of art. In fact, they matched music far more than the visual arts, and an awful lot of my associates were programmers by day, and musicians by night. It was an open secret in the industry.

A small, well-turned routine was a jewel like an ancient medieval bit of colored glass, requiring time and patience and skill to create. A full application shone, in my mind, like a magnificent stained glass window, every small bit contributing to the overall effect, held together with the lead sinews of conditional branching and information flow. Like many, I could become lost for hours while deep into design and prototyping or debugging, almost unaware of the outside world, nearly coming out of a trance when forced to leave. It was, in that respect, exactly like the experience of artistic creation.

Even the esoteric brotherhood and quasi-guild structure of the workers contributed to the effect. Like ancient artisans we had secret jargon that only the initiated could understand, and a defined hierarchy of apprenticeship from operator to coder to programmer to architect. We had secret rituals and meeting places, exchanged information in cryptic journals, held personally gained knowledge somewhat tightly to gain an edge when necessary. We tended to look down on those who employed us as a little deficient in actually knowing much, because we felt we could leave at any time and find somewhere better.

Finally, it was always changing, there were always new challenges. At the height of the Renaissance, new techniques for painting came along every few decades—wood panels, frescos, oil on wood, oil on canvas. At this time in computing it was very much the same, something would arrive out of nowhere, carried by some far-off messenger via magazine or seminar, and we would all gasp at the implications. A constant ferment, particularly exciting for the relatively young, which we almost universally were.

A dark suited figure stands with his back to us, in a stark bare white room with only a white screen in front breaking the monotony of the walls. "No, no, no, no,no," I shout. Abruptly Ghost and I are alone in an office hallway, facing a table laden with paper plates, doughnuts, bagels, orange and apple juice, toast, butter and some whitish spreads. Gallons of dishwasher coffee, none decaffeinated, no tea but some milk, sugar, and artificial sweeteners. "Much better," I declare.

"But we need to go over the essentials of your craft ..."

"See, that never worked for me. I learned it ass-backwards," I reply. "You want to teach like IBM and the universities thought proper. Logical progressions. Course plans. Start with basics, build up to the complicated. That wasn't me nor most of my peers. Programmers like that—they'd gone to MIT or Stanford—they were already employed by IBM and other industry giants and worked in wonderful great labs. That wasn't us. It certainly wasn't me."

"But ..."

"Computer rooms I slaved in were converted storerooms or closets, dusty and dark, somewhere tucked away out of sight. I never learned basics—we had to produce something tangible from day one. We learned 'best practice' and 'industry standard' by trial and error, avoiding or recovering from data disasters, or learning about them from others informally while bragging in hallways like this one."

"I know that," replies Ghost in an exasperated voice. "But that wasn't how it was supposed to be. You were supposed to have some idea of branching and flowcharting and conditional loops and database design before you got your hands on any real application."

"Not us," I snap back. "We were forced to modify real applications nearly blind, with no online support, a thick paper manual, a phone line to IBM whose service people hardly knew what we were talking about. We advanced the real world towards those mutating ivory towers, but never reached them. Course books always started with what should be optimally done from the beginning. Honestly, we never got a chance to start from the beginning, a core was always in place. We only got paid if we developed some pretty odd functions without breaking anything."

"That approach must have failed terribly," remarks Ghost.

"Actually, it all worked reasonably well, and weeded out those unable to cope pretty early in the process. We got more sophisticated as we went along, of course, but so did the industry in general. Eventually there were all kinds of good guidelines for everything except what we were actually working on, which tended to always be bleeding edge. I do like these doughnuts. Boy, those were the days, I could eat and eat and not put on a pound."

"Gone forever," commiserates Ghost.

"Pretty much like that wild west but well-paid niche that only existed for a short moment in time, a kind of Ayn Rand libertarian fantasy meritocracy where the competent rose to the top and the incompetent were shoved aside and ignored. Although," I note, "even then the best programmers never got the most money. Too naïve and in love with technology to attend to practical matters, I suppose."

"But good times," insinuates Ghost.

"Good enough. Probably better to look back on than to go through again."

"Look, Wayne," said Joe firmly, "we have to get this thing working today. My boss expects it because he's heard so much about it, and I really, really need it. IBM told us it would be a piece of cake."

Wayne regarded the boxes and thick instructions before him morosely. He had done this before, and he knew that each time was different, each time was wrong, and each time was more frustrating than the last. There was always something a little bit off. The coaxial cables were installed improperly. The System38 didn't have the right patches. The PC hardware was incompatible. The PC operating system was out of date, or was running incompatible software. The card itself was faulty. And on and on. Not one had ever gone smoothly.

What they were putting in was simplicity itself, in conception. Various personal computers were now firmly part of most executive offices, as they did their spreadsheets and reports. All of them were standalone devices, of various makes and models, some expensively integrated, some cobbled together. Fortunately, Goldman had some of the newer upper-end models running standard Microsoft DOS. None of them talked to other computers nor anything else except maybe a clunky local computer. Meanwhile, in magnificent (but highly secure!) isolation, the rest of the company had expensive and massive local terminals directly wired into the main computer in its splendid isolation in the computer room. "All" they had to do, today, was to get a couple of the PC's to transfer information into that network.

It was maddening. Joe would work days getting a spreadsheet just right on the PC, then have to turn to his terminal and copy figures in by hand to an appropriate custom data-entry program that Wayne had written. DOS copy. Diskettes were the same size, but even sneaker net would not work because of the ASCII/EBCEDIC divide. Repeat this every month, then every week, then nearly every day for sales figures and other information and—not pretty. None of the work could be done on the laughably primitive IBM attempt at interactive spreadsheets. Wayne's eyes glazed over at cross column correspondences when Joe began to rhapsodize about them, but he understood.

So the obvious solution was, in theory, simplicity itself. The PC was a very capable computer. The IBM terminal was just a primitive computer. Get the PC to act like a 5250 terminal and it could be easily hooked into the network, then the PC could translate information on the DOS side to act as if it were being typed into the mainframe side. Software alone would not work. No, this required some real hardware and lots of additional software and an awful lot of luck.

Wayne took off the casing of one of the disconnected PC's and examined the open slots. He had already found many that were all filled, or the wrong size, or the wrong type for the card he needed to put in. OK, a few full slots open, great, take off the back slot cover with a screwdriver. Making sure he was grounded (static could blow up the component) he took the card out of the box carefully and tried to push it in gently. No luck. Push harder, rock, careful (once one had broken in half at this point.) Finally the contacts slid in. Screw down the new card, replace the cover, see if the damn thing booted up. Ah, great. Insert the PC software and see if the disk could be read (he'd had problems with that before too.) Would the program run? Terrific, the easy part was successful, he carefully marked off the checklist he was making for everyone else in his company.

Now, turn off the PC. Screw in the coaxial cable, here. Find the marked matching one in the computer room and hook that side up as well to the back connector on the big box. Sign on to that as privileged operator and be sure everything looked good. Take the IBM diskette and see if that software could be installed ok. So far, so good. Update the checklist. OK, take a deep breath.

Back to the PC. Turn it on, sign in, run the emulator program, give the machine the identity he had picked out earlier. At this point, it was supposed to look exactly like a new device to the main guy. Back to the computer room operations console, try to find that device and assign its type—either a straight terminal or if the program was updated an actual emulation pc. Good. More checklist. Back to the PC. Try to sign on to the system.

That was the key breaking point. Everything often looked good right up to this moment, and then suddenly nothing worked. Calls to technical reps usually revealed that all of them had polished finger pointing to a high art. IBM would claim the card manufacturer was at fault, the card manufacturer would say it was the PC, the PC guy would be clueless, all of them said "maybe the wiring," none had useful suggestions. If it worked, smooth sailing. If not, it could be days or never. Fortunately, today, this one, worked. More checklist. Ready for the easy part.

That was all him. Custom program on the PC to format the data for output as a file. Custom program on the System38 to read the file. Custom menu on the PC to allow Joe to find his spreadsheet file, reformat a copy for output, actually do the transfer to the System38. Custom menu on the system letting Joe or an operator import the file into the appropriate place, run the update into standard files, run the various reports and interactive screens necessary for the corporate system. If problems occurred here (and they always did) they were tiny tweaks he could fix on the fly, no big deal. Not even worth doing a checklist, this was always fully customized to the client. Now onto the other terminal setup.

A task that should have taken ten minutes stretched on to a long day. And a tense day, filled with adrenaline and dread, the certainty that something might go wrong any moment, and the awareness that even what seemed a minor problem might be insoluble.

He earned his pay many times over on a day like this, but the client always thought he was taking them for a ride. The salesmen had told them how simple it all was.

We were a local computer consultant, not venturing out of the metropolitan Long Island area, and consequently I did not have to travel much.

But a few times I had to go the IBM seminars or workshops or rallies in other places, and sometimes had to fly to parts of the country to install a remote installation. Fortunately, most of the IBM circus eventually came to New York City, and often even to its main corporate outpost in Jericho.

But the big IBM rollout of the upcoming "Baby 38," which turned into the flagship AS400 line, was different. For this one they made representatives fly to Dallas to get the information on the computer family that was going to carry them into the new century and beyond. I went, with my dark suit and not much else, staying in a suburban motel, never near downtown Dallas at all, for three days of intense huge screen presentations and small optional seminars.

We were all excited. This was to be the "DEC Killer," the answer to the increasing encroachment of mini computers onto our business territory. All the mistakes had been eliminated, all the necessary options included. A clean new approach, a shiny operating system where everything had been done right and integrated from the ground up. No kludgy patches, no wretched irrational legacy code. This was the one. Tiny, relatively inexpensive, expandable to infinity, and with a very long and profitable future ahead of it. All the business partners had to get into it, if they wanted to remain business partners.

But, it was all new. Wayne had it easier than most, he could tell, after catching the mutterings during the breaks. He at least kept up with the latest magazine articles. He had been working on PC's and minis before he ever saw a System 36. He truly understood the current system 38, which, it turned out, was a close cousin or near prototype. All of what they were saying made perfect sense to him.

Externally defined reusable files. Externally defined reusable screens. New language, with only the name remaining the same to quiet the masses. Externally compiled linkable modules. True recursion and subroutines and global variables. Background processes. This was, in terms of standard computer theory, exactly correct. It was, in practical programming terms once you mastered it, heaven compared to what they were using. It was, to people used to primitive RPG on ancient (5 year old) system 36's, incomprehensible gibberish.

He spent the long evening with the rest of the crowd, who walked around and around in the sultry twilight along a few dusty bare trails outside the convention center. His head was filled with exciting possibilities. Also, a realization that all the custom code would have to be rewritten from scratch to take advantage of any of this. Fun. Expensive. Time consuming. Nerve racking. But, mostly, fun. He had some barbeque, did some more walking, visited the ice skating rink at a huge mall across a Texas-sized parking lat.

Then back for more lectures, seminars, books, manuals, handouts, brochures to give Nick. This, he realized, was perfect for him and he was finally, again, at the right place, at the right time with an open road widening before him. He wiped off the sweat and walked and thought some more.

Soft music playing through the gently lit lounge, where clumps of dark suits earnestly discuss weighty matters in the shadows. I'm nursing a ginger ale at the bar, Ghost sitting alongside with a pint of Guinness. "Home free and ready for fortune," he smiles tightly.

"I wish. Oh, I'm sitting pretty all right, but it will never pay off extremely well."

"But you should be able to demand a king's ransom. You're able to handle all of this, no problem. You should be rolling in dough."

"You sound just like my wife," I complain. "If only it were so simple. But I have my own problems and my own personality. For one thing, I'm sitting here talking to you instead of shooting the bull with them. I hate sitting around talking about stupid stuff. I'd rather be doing something at the terminal."

"So none of this will pay off?"

"Oh, it will pay off great," I reply. "I'll get decent pay, fine working conditions, freedom to go from workplace to workplace, usually at a higher salary. I'll control my fate. I'll be respected and love what I do. I'll have time to pursue other technical issues, and time to do a lot with the family. I just won't become rich."

"In money, anyway."

"True, it's all how you look at it. I'll be rich in every way I want to be, but not in the way society, friends, family, and Joan define it."

"Can't have everything," he takes a deep draught.

"No, I suppose not," I sip and wait for the hour to finish up.

This was a high water mark, Wayne thought, with the tide still coming in. His boat was rising at least as fast as everyone else's. Finally, he was ready for this flood tide, and he and his family could take advantage of it for once.

Increased possibilities brought increased hassles, of course. The lack of time, the stress, the sudden awareness of the need for more money, the constant reading to keep up with a career that changed every day. But he was still young enough that it was fun, he laughed at the various old-timers, lamenting golden days gone by. Those ancient masters—most of them over fifty, by gosh—had had their day. It was his turn now, and he planned to ride the waters as far as he could go.

In another perspective, he was finally swimming with the big fish, in the grown up pool. IBM was as mainstream as he could get. He had accepted the idea that they were getting their act together, coming down from the huge corporate mountain to smite the smaller computers snapping at their heels. Hell, he was part of the smiting task force. This would be fun.

On the nagging edge, there was still a lot to learn. The more he delved into his craft, the more deficient he found his background to be. On the one hand he needed design skills, core understanding of processes, better grasp of fundamental approaches others with a better education took for granted. On the other hand, he needed to become seasoned in business, more crafty, more aggressive, more able to match the slick manipulations of everyone else in the small enterprise environment. He didn't like that area quite so much, but it could be entertaining in its own way.

Now, if he could just get some sleep once in a while ....

I spot Ghost sitting at one of the small tables, puffing on a fat cigar with the remnants of a two martini lunch spread before him. I stroll over, marveling at the palm trees growing here in the huge atrium attached to the IBM building on Madison Avenue. He glances up and smiles, "Hey, guy, what's doing?"

"Just in for a seminar, I guess. Training. Acetate sheets and lectures. The usual."

"So you're big time now, eh? No worries any more...."

"Not quite big time. JBS isn't exactly IBM. I'm thinking we're more like remora fish attached to a huge shark. But, as they say in the movies, it's <u>our</u> shark."

"You envy the IBMers?"

"Well, they do have lots of money, prestige, impossible security, a brilliant future, jobs for life and a wonderful pension promised later. But," I muse, "no, not really. It's strange, but I like the free wheeling where I am. It can be a lot more interesting on the front lines."

"They never pay the privates, you know. You're just there to be shot at."

"I know, I know. But it can be fun. Anyway, I could never get into a big corporation like that at my age. It's better to adjust dreams to reality in some situations."

"With an attitude like that," he remarks, "you're never going to go anywhere important."

"I am somewhere important. And my family is most of it. An intense corporate life probably has its own downsides. Anyway, I won't get anywhere by wishing."

"You're a strange fellow. Well, enjoy the droning ...." I head off towards the security guard on the big black double doors.

The routine was almost in place, thought Wayne as he headed for the office on Tuesday morning, opposite the rush hour traffic going the other way towards the city. Each Monday there would be some emergency dragging him to some account. Tuesday would be office chores and design work in relative peace and quiet, sometimes with a sales call with Nick. Wednesday and Thursday were full billable working days on scheduled programs at various accounts. Friday would be cleanup somewhere or other in the morning and late nights at the office getting in timesheets and planning out the next week, going over issues and plans with the staff all afternoon.

The weekends were usually free of work problems, but he found himself spending most nights reading manuals and printed updates. Often on Sunday he would have to fit in an hour or two laying out a system in primitive flowchart and pseudocode. Sometimes he dreamed in subroutines and code fixes.

But mostly, he did manage to get in a lot of real time with the house, the yard, Gregory, Wayne, Joan, the extended family, nature and shopping.

A good life, a full life. Perhaps centered too greatly on work, especially compared to teachers they knew, but still wonderful.

TREEHOUSE

WAYNE WAS ROAMING cluttered aisles at Pergament, Greg in hand, Baby Wayne in his stroller, checking his list and totaling estimated costs. This home supplies store in a shopping center on Montauk highway was a convenient stop, accomplishing a whole lot of good things at once. Of course, it let him do his own chores here, getting ready to build a treehouse out back. But simultaneously he was able to get the kids out of the house for a few hours to give Joan a break, talk with them enjoyably as they shopped.

An added advantage is he could bribe them to be good, if necessary, because right next door they could stop by the new VCR—rental superstore to find a movie for this Saturday evening, and then go over to Shane's discount store where Wayne would happily sit on one of the rides (which cost a quarter) and content himself with buying super "bally balls" from a modified gum-vending machine. All was good, this sunny spring morning.

He checked his list again. Two by fours for the floor support, four by eights for the uprights, dowls for the ladder, plywood for the sides and floor, big hardware to overbuild so it would not collapse, dollars adding up, but definitely doable. And, yes, it would all fit into or on the station wagon, at least with a little ingenuity. He pointed out something else to Greg, made sure Wayne was quietly watching from the stroller parked in the aisle, and started selecting materials.

Our immense green Babylon back lawn is newly mown and fragrant. Colorful annuals bloom near the house, perennials scent the property lines. My rural contentment is shattered by a tremendous wracking roar out front. I rush through the side gate into choking diesel fumes, only to spy a massive black pickup truck screech to a stop in clouds of blue smoke. Sure enough it's Ghost, all hillbilly with grease-stained overalls, thick reddish plaid shirt, and a Mets baseball cap. "Hi there," he drawls, in a definitely forced deep voice. "Need some common-sense advice and help, do you?"

"Not at all," I say, "not at all. I have the situation well under control. Thank you, but I can enjoy doing it all on my own. By the way, that thing is a complete anachronism," I am pointing at the battered truck. "They mostly came later with the SUV craze."

"Don't care. Always were pickup trucks. God probably used them in the Garden."

"Well, I don't. Back now, we drive station wagons around here. Maybe a van or two. What you're driving is pretty rare, as I recall."

"Well, anyway, you're sure you don't need help? I hear you're not much as a handyman."

"Actually, I'm quite good at relatively small projects. Remember I built and finished all the bookshelves back in Boston and Cambridge, and refinished the furniture we picked up off the street. I did replace the upstairs window here a few years ago, with Dad's help. And the structure in the basement, of course. Give me a few hand power tools and I can do just about anything short of building an actual house."

"What is it this time?" he asks curiously.

"A treehouse. We've got that old tree right there—thick trunk, huge branches—perfect for putting a bit platform next too. Not actually in it, of course. On the ground but when they climb up to the second floor it will be better than being in a tree. I have it all planned out." Proudly I display my diagram sketched out on yellow paper, hardware and measurements included.

"Don't look particularly well-drawn."

"It's all there. No problem. Anyway, this will be fun. Maybe I can teach the kids some basics. You. Go away. I'll see you later."

'Well," says Ghost, a little hurt, "if you're sure you don't need me…"

"Bye. Later. <u>Much</u> later, I hope." I turn my back and let him exit the scene any way he wants.

Wayne knew he was no handyman. It is true that when other children spoke of growing up to be firemen, he had always said "carpenter." But that was as close as it came. His father, perhaps because of hating farm work so much in childhood, was the anti-handyman—give him a new hammer or saw and it would be lost or rusted within days. Dad's philosophy was that you earned good money at an office job to let other people do the nasty stuff.

Fortunately, in the olden school days, Wayne had been forced to take high school shop classes even though he was on the college track which presumably meant he would never drive a nail in his life. So he had no fear of power tools—although in the sixties power tools meant huge stationary drill presses, bench saws, band saws, and lathes. He had learned not to worry much about materials, and could do all the rudimentary stuff required to build almost anything. Unfortunately, he never took an advanced course where he learned to respect and love the materials, but that did not matter for most tasks.

So, if he had the time and inclination, with no more than a power drill and attachments he could make just about anything. With a portable circular saw he was a master. His one mechanical drafting course came in handy for design as well, so he could design as well as create. With time—always the trick now—everything could be a lot of fun, and amazing to children.

The playhouse in the basement—nothing more than a big four foot plywood cube with a ladder and an old door serving as a slide/ramp—had been a huge hit. Every winter and rainy day, they could go downstairs and play music and pretend the structure was a boat, or a castle, or a house, or an airplane, or whatever was popular on TV. Wayne had fortunately learned early on at daycare that the important thing was to avoid the overly realistic—include as many story hooks as possible on a basic pattern and let imagination do the rest.

He was using the same philosophy here, although this would be "the treehouse" because it was, after all, attached to a tree. He privately always thought of it simply as the "structure," and sure enough that eventually became its common name. Furnished with a few old blankets, pillows, ropes, and whatever plastic garbage was lying around it could be almost anything. A true Shakespearian stage for childhood.

But before all that, of course, he had to put it together. Around him on the grass were the piles of wood, on the back steps were the huge screws, bolts, angle irons, nails and glue. A couple of old sawhorses had been found on the street somewhere once upon a time. Power tools and electric cord. Well, no use waiting, it was late enough not to bother the neighbors. He started lining the pieces with ruler and framing square and began the cuts.

Because they had worked together for years in day care, Wayne and Joan shared much the same educational philosophy for young children. For that matter, they were quite in tune with their own parents' views, which they regarded as admirable since both of them considered themselves the lucky recipients of a happy and productive childhood. A key part of that seemed to be being left alone sometimes to find fun on their own.

They did not like to overschedule the children, as they found was being done with many other parents they knew. Even Joan's cousins were in on that action. Lessons and playgroups and enrichment activities and organized gangs of one kind or another. Joan and Wayne hated to be reduced to chauffeurs—if they had time during the day to be with the kids, they wanted to be with the kids, not just taking them somewhere and waiting. Young children were fun, after all, and kept you thinking young. It could be a pleasure to interact with them.

But they also knew how to step back. Let Wayne and Greg play out back alone in the sandbox, they would find useful things to do there. "Big" Wayne joined them occasionally, and Joan kept a professionally trained ear open in case things were getting out of hand. But, generally they simply did what any good government theoretically accomplishes—maintained law and order and let the children work out the rest within that context.

There were always things to do of course. But rather than fit food or clothing shopping, for example, into the hours when the little darlings were "being enriched," the youngsters were taken along to the stores and malls and allowed to participate and help. That was largely possible because both Joan and Wayne were strong on public discipline and as a result soon had to do very little discipline at all. Everyone seemed to have a great deal of fun most of the time, and a big bonus was that it cost nothing.

Beyond that, they encouraged real activities wherever possible. TV was always there, Nintendo just coming in, but they limited it without too much nagging. The basement was available for block-building and running and climbing and playing fort on the structure during the cold months; the back-yard was local heaven in all other seasons, toys were always provided in the bedrooms. Of course, there was the standard evening reading from picture books the grownups could repeat by heart.

Wayne enjoyed having them help with Sunday breakfast, although Joan was appalled at the mess created. Pancakes, scrambled eggs, French toast, lots of fun messy gloppy ingredients. Both grownups carried over the school activities of cutting fruit and vegetables. Neither of them were much in the way of bakers, but muffins and cookies occasionally happened. Birthday cakes were typically home made and frosted.

A small typical family, Wayne thought, perhaps a little poorer than their peers, and certainly a little behind the times, but not unhappy and hardly disadvantaged. It helped that he and Joan shared so much of childhood philosophy. It helped even more that he was fortunate enough to have found a job that left him with a fair amount of time to spend with them.

Early on in working with small children, we had realized the importance of loosening an enriched environment so imagination could expand. Toy stores were stuffed with attractively specific manufactured objects and periodic visits to Toys-R-Us would leave us drooling with envy at some of the offering. Unfortunately, a beautifully detailed plaything frequently restricted play options. An outdoor structure was a typical example. We could have bought a perfectly appointed immense play house, with curtained windows and space for kitchen, all painted and decorated as if an elves' home. Or a jungle gym, with fake animals and ropes that looked like vines. Or a pirate ship that seemed it could actually sail away. But then you were left, each morning and evening, with the same old cottage, or jungle gym, or pirate ship. That got old in a week or so.

A well designed play structure, on the other hand, such as Wayne had helped build at a pre-school in Cambridge, could be all of those things and more. An enclosed room with variously sized openings cut into the side easily transmuted from ship, to house, to castle, to jail, to airplane, to whatever happened to be on your mind that moment. An upstairs deck added to the illusion becoming a roof, or pilot deck, or rampart, or starship bridge. You could drag blankets and furniture and other toys and materials over and they transformed easily into anything at all.

Besides, Wayne was fortunate in not really having to worry much about liability. He built well, of course, because he didn't want any stupid accidents. But he didn't have to overly worry about obscure dangers as manufacturers did. He could add a ladder to the roof, adequate but not perfect railing, even but not perfectly smooth cutouts, a sturdy but hardly foolproof rope and netting, even the second floor itself. It was far enough off the ground that yes, a falling child might get hurt and yes, it was possible to fall, but not so far that it was mortally dangerous. Wayne and Joan had both grown up in days when a little danger was quite acceptable—he had friends who had broken arms and legs falling out of trees or off of bicycles. Joan had friends who had almost drowned on boats. You had to let children have at least the illusion that there was some real element of risk involved to keep their interest. And, after all, it was far safer to play here than to cross most streets.

Having two children eased the burden later. Gregory was pretty bossy, but Wayne found his own ways to accommodate and yet remain fully independent. Greg would fugue into long interconnected play sequences—a whole afternoon of pirate adventures—where Wayne tended just to go along for momentary thrills and spills, happy to step out of the action any time he got tired of it. For both of them there were excellent lessons in socialization. Both the parents were increasingly pleased that they could do their own necessary chores—mowing the lawn, cleaning the house—without constant intervention, but still all in sight and awareness of each other.

Imagination, we thought, was a wonderful tool, but we had both had enough formal training to also recognize that it should be molded with real objects. The imagination encouraged by watching television (or for that matter reading books) was not of the same quality as the imagination inculcated in building something out of blocks, cooking a meal, or interacting with complicated other little beings. An afternoon in the sandbox or digging on the beach taught more about the realities of the world than hours of Sesame Street.

When I come out from lunch, Ghost is sitting at the red wooden trestle picnic table we rescued off the street, half empty six pack alongside, beer in hand. "Pretty darn sure of yourself," he notes, pushing back his Yankees baseball cap."

"What?" I ask, confused.

"You and your wife. Pretty certain you had all the answers to childhood education. Know it all smart alecks, sounds like to me."

"Well, at least we didn't depend on books of advice and television doctors and internet experts to have some idea what we were doing. I admit we thought we knew an awful lot about early childhood education from our practical experience, and we felt prepared for what came later from all the education courses we had taken, and Joan's early teaching at high schools. Sure, why not, we felt at least as competent as anyone else."

"But your kids didn't grow up to be president, either."

"Not yet...." I grin. "Sure, they just grow up, and like most kids, they do fine or not depending more on circumstance and ongoing situation than what they did when they were five."

"So you don't believe the Jesuits?"

"Give me a child until he is six and I will control him forever? Nope. But you can lay a decent internal foundation. Mostly they are fine young men, happy and in control of their lives."

"But most people end up like that anyway."

"It's a stupid argument, Ghost. We did what we did. We were happy with how we did it, had fun ourselves, and felt confident enough to go against the current when necessary. Sure, we weren't tiger parents and we weren't hippy parents and we weren't helicopter parents and we weren't even our own parents. But I think we were fine. I think the results are fine. And ..."

"Yes?"

"We enjoyed almost every day, all the opportunities together. We loved each other, and took advantage of the nice lives we had finally put together. Couldn't ask for more, as grownups or children."

Ghost takes another long gulp. "Well, some would say you could have done better."

"But I, personally, know I could have done a hell of a lot worse."

Many one-off projects, especially by those who are amateurs in the medium, are overbuilt. This small playhouse was going to be no exception. Wayne bought heavy four by four posts, strong enough to hold up a barn, for the corners to support the "immense" weight of a sheet of plywood and a couple of less-than-fifty-pound boys. The closely spaced beams holding the top platform were pressure-treated two by sixes, the plywood outdoor rated heavy duty. The hardware alone weighed a ton, with long thick eight inch screw bolts, numerous angle irons. And lots of Elmer's glue, just in case.

Nor did he skimp during building. Well, of course he had the power tools, which simplified matters a lot, and he had bought a few wrenches for the bolts and a framing square for keeping it even. His plans carefully called for multiple fasteners everywhere. It went up over a few days, with the boys dancing around in excitement. It gradually took shape and emerged from an uninspiring pile of materials to backyard magnificence as majestically as any skyscraper.

As he started to put on the finishing touches, Sunday afternoon, Wayne was quite content with its solidity. Actually, it might outlast the house. It could probably sail the China Sea for a few decades. At least Joan would not worry too much, and he would worry not at all. They might fall off, of course, but it certainly would not fall on them. Even falling off would take a little effort, because of the rail around most of the top.

One of the finishing touches was wooden one by twos nailed to the tree to make an effective and imaginative ladder up to the deck. Another was more-or-less round windows cut into the sides. And his final contribution, which took almost as long as the building itself, was a climbing net made out of thick sisal rope he had knotted into rigging hooked to a projecting beam, an alternate way off and onto the roof. Out on a nearby tree limb the obligatory old tire swung on a thick rope.

He was more excited than Gregory and Little Wayne, as he finally cleaned up the tools to put away in the garage. Like writing a program, this was making something out of nothing, his imagination and effort, and it was impressive, at least to himself. He admitted he had harbored inner doubts from inception, and a few restless nights wondering if he could do this after all. But this was good. In fact, it was perfect as it stood, not needing even a coat of paint. Let it weather, he thought. Most of it is treated anyway.

Joan came out and surprising had not much criticism. She worried about the younger son falling or being pushed off. She had a good line of sight to what was going on from the kitchen window anyway, and the fenced in yard meant there were not many extraneous things to consider.

It quickly fit into the backyard suite of things to do—the sandbox, the structure, the garden, the grass, the hose, and—in warmer times—the plastic pools. Not to mention the various clutter on the colored cinderblock patio—big wheels, a wagon, a tricycle, and assorted odds and ends off and on. All in all, with a few helpful sparks and the occasional addition of something unusual (which could be as simple as a few old sheets to use on the structure) the whole thing became a Disneyesque timeless playground. Well worth a full weekend of sweat, and costing no more than they really thought they could afford.

There was always an undercurrent in projects having to do with outlook on life. Maybe it was Western, or American, or simply the milieu in which we were living, but the old "keeping up with the Joneses" came into play. We certainly did not want our children to be underprivileged, and we wanted a little bit of respect and envy when other people came over to visit. "Oh, what a nice treehouse!" for example.

So, like everyone else, we were always improving our place or thinking about doing so. Paint this, buy that, build something else, find a new use for an indoor or outdoor area and renovate it. The fact was that none of the alterations made much difference in how we lived, but it was just part of the grand bargain we were caught up in.

It started with consumerism, of course. There had to be some commercial products—like Big Wheels or Legos, or building blocks—in the mix. We somehow managed to pay for these because otherwise everyone would have considered the family eccentric at best or poverty-stricken at worst. Beyond that, there was enough "do it yourself" in me that I enjoyed taking on a challenge and making something unique when a store-bought item would have done just as well, or even better. Like the sandbox. Like the structure.

Even today, I hate to hire people to do what I can accomplish. I paint our house, I maintain our own fence, I mow and clear our own yard. I draw the line at things clearly beyond my background and competence—like automotive repairs or heavy interior rebuilding—but just about everything else not only means money given away, but also lost chances to immerse myself in doing something useful that I can look back on with pride later.

I've found it's not just the actual task that gives pleasure. Thinking about it, planning it, getting ready—these all count as much just as they would in a grand work of art. A year later, simply thinking back is a nice memory. None of that happens when you contract something out, unless you are one of those wretched folks who stands as a shrill sidewalk supervisor to everything that is being done.

It always seemed odd, in a way, to put so much time, money, and effort into ephemeral objects. The kids would grow older, after all, and the structure would become unused and unloved, like the sandbox. The Big Wheel would sit forlorn in a lonely corner of the yard until either thrown out, given away, or put into longer storage in the hope of grandchildren in the distant future (not that any old toys in the distant future are likely to be much appreciated.) That was all just part of the throw-away culture—perhaps the start of it in the children. We could no more escape it than we could the use of the English language.

Ghost is back on the lawn, walking around the structure tree appraisingly, ready, I am sure, to make some snide comment. I get in the first word. "Not bad, if I say so myself."

"I'm genuinely impressed," he says, surprising me no end. "This is very much what you wanted to build from the beginning, it's done almost exactly right, and it will serve its purposes admirably. "

"Gee, thank you," I can't think of any reply.

"Too bad all your passions couldn't turn out so well."

"Oh, I suppose. Although I did quite a few projects much like this at work, in software, where they were quite appreciated. Computer code likes to be overbuilt."

"Well, at least it is obscure enough that nobody knows if you are overcharging for the Taj Mahal when you were contracted for an outhouse."

"There is that," I admit. "I did sometimes get carried away with elegance and add-ons. It took a long time for me—and a lot of the industry—to accept that everything was temporary and to cultivate a more just-good-enough attitude."

"Meaning what?"

"Oh, you don't need a shiny perfect car to commute to work, just a vehicle that safely goes and stops. You don't need the fastest sorting algorithm to make reports, just one that gets things printed in time for the boss to read them."

"What did your boss think about that?"

"What he didn't know didn't hurt him, and he appreciated the speed of development and cost savings."

"And Joan?"

"Ah, well, that is a problem," I admit. "Joan, like all her family, were always true connoisseurs of whatever they happened to be examining at that moment. Each crack had to be perfectly patched, each join in the molding had to be exact, each bit of furniture or rug had to be good enough to astonish visitors with our taste. I'd grab the first thing that would serve the purpose. Joan wanted to marinate in the choice and savor it later."

"Sounds like a recipe for continual conflict."

"Well, it would have been, except that her attention spotlight was necessarily limited. She hardly looked at a crack in the wall, for example, unless she happened to be carefully examining that exact wall, usually as part of criticizing my current paint job on it. When she was focused on something it might become intolerable, but soon some other priority came up and we moved on."

"Sounds like you were more practical."

"My approach had its own problems," I remark. "But all in all we made a tolerably good team, on this and just about everything else. A definite case where a couple of people are more effective than either of us alone."

"Why was that?"

"Well, left to Joan something would wait until it could be afforded or done absolutely perfectly, which was often never. Left to me, the basics would get done rapidly, but shoddily, and we would wish we had tried a little harder. Balanced, it came out about right."

"Jack Sprat..." he notes, walking away.

"Just about."

Wayne didn't worry overly about accidents and other childhood dangers. He was fully aware that the most dangerous objects in the world were all around in the form of automobiles. People constantly used them, drove them recklessly and carelessly, and whacked children all the time. If Baby Wayne and Gregory learned to properly avoid and beware of cars, most other dangers in their world were pretty minor.

That went against the common wisdom. Everyone desperately guarded their little ones from presumed kidnappers lurking behind every tree, according to hysterical news reports. Corners on all playthings had to be carefully rounded and smoothed, soft if possible. Houses needed to be childproofed with gates and electric outlet guards. Kids had to be made aware of the horrors lurking in dirt. Sharp edges could lead to death. And on and on, through sickness and health.

Maybe Wayne and Joan were a little blasé because they had worked with so many children, over so many years, and nothing really awful had happened. Even little Betty who fell down in the playground on a sharp broken bottle and split her knee open eventually healed up fine. What they had learned was that children—like humans in general—are remarkably tough.

Wayne thought it was never too early to make them aware of things, however. It was good to have a sense of place, to check out your surroundings constantly. It was good to have some notion of what might go wrong. It was important to separate out what you have to pay attention to—for example not sticking your finger in a light socket to see what might happen—and what you never had to worry about, like a butterfly buzzing your head. But mostly, to remain conscious of the world.

And, as part of that, to have some idea of how things worked. That was why he liked doing cooking with them—dinners did not just show up as magic but had some easy known work procedures. Treehouses could be built out of basic materials, rather than pre-constructed. Sure, you had to use lots of premade things for convenience, but you did not have to remain ignorant—food did not pop into existence in supermarkets, and money never showed up in your wallet without effort.

People often imagine that their generation is the best, and that their children will be better. Such conceits are harmless enough, but do lead to false exaggerations of certain traits. You can worry too much, for example, about a child's intellectual development and ignore their deficits in social behavior or self control. Or, for that matter, worry too much about physical injury, when some injury is, after all, how most people and animals actually learn in this world.

We forget that not too many generations ago everyone had to be tough and for that matter pretty fatalistic. The world was not easily controlled, even with appeals to the gods. Famine was frequent and unpredictable, disease and death never more than a few hours away, discomfort for days or weeks, boredom during slack times, and terror when times were not slack were pretty much taken for granted. Humans survived, and thrived, anyway.

When you study history, what stands out about most upbringing is that it often did not matter much. What counted were the resources made available—wealthy children tended to stay wealthy because of their familial connections and privileges. But life is filled with badly brought up children becoming incredibly productive adults, and perfectly brought up children turning into abject failures. Babies and young children are, it seems, perversely self-correcting.

What was changing even then was the emphasis on child centered lives. That was something almost totally new. With smaller families, planned pregnancies, and the realization that raising children had become a huge financial burden rather than a net gain (because they could not help much in a society without farms or small crafts) each child became precious. And as the world became increasingly complicated and crowded, your family was an anchor that, at least in your own mind, set you apart from the common crowd. And children were the diamonds on that anchor.

We were at the beginning of it, but there again we had been somewhat

          BABYLON WITH GHOST

immunized watching children grow before. For us Wayne and Gregory were fun mostly, part of a family entirely, and an ongoing interesting project. But we still had our own lives, and our own passions, and our own moments, and we made both of them aware of that early on. There were times, for example, when it was good for them to play quietly by themselves, balanced by times when we would all participate in something exciting and exotic.

A huge bang and ominous cloud of smoke rose from the bluestone driveway. Rushing around from the back yard, I see an apparition from a nightmare—well, not my nightmares but somebody's. A huge dilapidated three wheeled motorcycle belching noxious fumes, decorated like a Hells Angels' birthday cake. The driver with tongue dripping slime, one eyeball hanging out, half the skull exposed and bleached to match the boney hands.

"Hell, Ghost, you trying to get us both arrested?" I shout. Couldn't be anyone else. Am I awake?

"Naw, I'm invisible to anyone but you," he shouts. The motor revs and backfires.

"Shut that damn thing off NOW." The silence is that follows is almost frightening. "I presume you have some reason for this extravagance?"

"Just exploring my imagination. You've been prattling on and on about how wonderful it all is. Well, here I am, in all my glory. Whaddaya think?"

"I think it's stupid. I'm not even sure this stuff showed up yet—closer to the nineties."

"It was all in the air. Skeletor and He Man and some of the cartoons were already there. Gruesome. You let the kids buy this stuff, and even laughed. I was just pointing out that too much imagination might be too much."

"Point taken. It's not my fault someone came up with Madballs and idiotic dolls on motorcycles and Skeletor. Anyway, I read things like Mad Magazine and comics like "My Greatest Adventure" and they were just as stupid and bloody. I turned out ok."

"Debatable," notes Ghost with a sneer. "Maybe you had too much too."

"Like what?" I demand.

"Oh, big things like pretending you could be or were an artist."

"I WAS an …"

"Small things like expecting big raises or extravagant praise for projects or pie in the sky in the future."

"Eventually a lot of that happened."

"But not because you imagined it, you idiot."

"Look, Ghost, I don't know what you are, but you sure aren't human. A lot of our life has to be imagination, because that is where we can park our fears and locate our hope. We can, if necessary, escape into our own skull, and a lot of times that gets us through the necessarily hard parts of our lives. I still think it was great to let kids dream a bit."

"Too fantastic to be of use," claims Ghost stubbornly. "What good is believing in Santa Claus? What is the role of magic in flipping hamburgers for a living? They should be set up for grim reality."

"What grim reality?" I snort. "I know that's all the rage—countless 'youth novels' about mistreatment, molestation, sexual initiation, starvation, inevitable death. Reality, that reality you can have. It's good to know things can go bad, I guess, but worse to think they can never go right."

"Pollyanna optimist."

"Damn straight. There's a reason why, even now, people and kids like happy endings."

"You are still living in an imaginary world, my friend," says Ghost sadly.

"Get that stupid vehicle out of my driveway." I turn my back, his motor coughs loudly to life, revs impossible decibels, and in a massive theatrical cloud of blue vanishes down eleventh street.

Gregory always took fantasy scenarios seriously. His "spontaneous" play seemed more like a director of a play, always trying to get the props just right, the other actors (Joan and Wayne and Baby Wayne) all well rehearsed and fully into character, the plot for the hour or so mapped out. He became angry and frustrated if things did not go as he planned them out.

At the time, it was mostly about fantasy medieval type cartoon characters—superheroes with swords—so he would get blankets for tents, some kind of primitive plastic weapons, and imaginary foe or dragon, and a plot that nobody but he could understand but which had something to do with confrontation and winning. He'd carefully get out all the props and start in, not to be disturbed without great anguish until either the story had run to its proper conclusion, or he decided it had gone out of control. When Baby Wayne could participate, he took the bossing around good-naturedly. Joan and Wayne usually just went about their chores, and ended up being treated like some of the scenery—a storm, a passing monster, whatever.

These productions usually ran their course in a half hour or so of furious sword-waving, yelling, declamations from the top deck by Gregory the Magnificent, cape and all, and a certain amount of running around and fighting, all the while telling (mostly) his brother what was happening. For Gregory, I think, it was all mostly real. He felt himself fully immersed in his imaginary world, and only with great reluctance returned to mundane reality of lunch or nap time.

"Seems a little antisocial to me," notes Ghost, "all this involvement in fantasy worlds, reliance on imagination instead of strong social reality."

"Once upon a time I might have argued with you, or even agreed," I remark. "But what seems to happen is children grow as they will almost regardless of what you try to do. I suspect Greg would have done the same play-acting were he surrounded by hordes of kids his age. No matter how similar we tried to make their upbringing, our sons grew up quite different. And from discussions with other older parents, I hardly think that is unusual."

"So environment doesn't matter? That makes no sense."

"Well, actually it does," I reply. "The human brain twists what it experiences and in a way creates whatever reality it sees. The fiction of 'objective reality' is, after all, just a convention of how most people seem to experience the world. Each of us lives in our own world and sees our own opportunities, dangers, beauties, and rewards."

"Oh, come on," he is exasperated, "surely there is real and fake."

"Like you?"

"I'm a literary convention."

"Maybe, maybe not."

The one thing we all hope is that childhood, largely through play, leads to balanced autonomy for the eventual adult who emerges. After evolution of species and culture through hundreds of thousands of years, that eventually happens. Most shockingly, it happens almost independently of upbringing and background. Most of the real differences we see among people seem to result from the platforms they had to work with when they became late teenagers—were they rich, did they have opportunities, what were their peers doing—rather than anything that went before. It is profoundly disappointing to many parents, but essential to human survival.

Joan and I believed strongly in early childhood survival, and still do. But I admit that now I see it as less a means of churning out identically equal grownups than as a necessary right for an individual. A caterpillar has different needs than a butterfly, and must be nourished, but it will nevertheless become a butterfly, if it survives, dependent not on the care given but on other factors beyond our control I know this is currently a heretical position, when we think everything can be directed and manipulated to cure the ills of society, earth, and heaven.

GENTRIFICATION

WAYNE SAT IN one of the only quiet moments of the weekend out in the dark red Adirondack chair. Late September sun shone benignly on Gregory building in the sandbox, Little Wayne taking a nap, Joan fussing around the kitchen. If there were ever a time for reflection, this would be it. But, of course, even now too many thoughts and worries swirled in his head, even these rare interludes were filled with feverish plans and priorities.

If he could have contemplated, he might have realized how their lives had become exactly like current adventure movies. The world was reduced into one gigantic rush of incidents. They would make one narrow escape after another, which only led to another hair-raising situation. There was always the promise of treasure at the end, but somehow it eluded them in the present. Nevertheless, they remained confident, as only movie heroes and their audience could be, that somehow somewhere everything would work out and happily ever after (until the sequel) boomed out of the screen.

A company car was the latest excitement. Nick had finally taken pity on him and decided his arriving in a rusty old rattletrap was not only sometimes unlikely, but also that the company image was not well served by his use of such transportation. So he was driving his first Japanese import, and the expenses were mostly taken care of. There would be lot fewer of them, because the old car had truly become costly in repairs. And driving was almost, just almost—a pleasure, with air conditioning and radio and all the rest of the new-fangled conveniences.

But nothing arrives these days without problems. His car taken care of, it became obvious that Joan needed something better to get around in. So all the expenses doubled and focused on how to accomplish that. Another chore, another set of plans, another worry. Almost everything that happened these days seemed to be like that.

Of course, it all made Joan quite happy. They would never be nearly as well off as everyone else she compared them to, mostly because they had started late, a little because of the way they set priorities. But there was less to be ashamed of. No apologizing for only renting an apartment, not having a proper household with children, putting up with a husband drinking too much and banging from job to job. Getting a couple of almost new cars was icing on the cake. She couldn't think of anything more, at least for the moment. In general, life was good.

In particular, however, life was ragged. Time to sit here on the patio was precious indeed. Even now, his brain was filled with outlines for the next project and visions of new coding danced in his mind. He knew he had to get a paper soon to write them down, sketch out some flowcharts, prepare for Monday. Besides, there was still the one technical manual on the new release that he had to skim through to be ready when it finally arrived at the accounts. And there was growing demand to repaint one of the bedrooms. He took a deep breath and sighed.

Well, this was what they had wanted, wasn't it? The bohemian life was terrific when you were still young enough to handle it, when hangovers came with the territory, when nothing had very many repercussions. Life had been one grand glorious holiday, each day a marvel, bright and shining and filled with impossible dreams. All, as it turned out, illusion. And surely this was better, wasn't it? Still dreams, but not impossible. No hangovers, just not enough sleep. And even without being able to think about it too deeply, he realized that they were growing older day by day.

Fortunately, he hardly minded at all, because on top of everything else, their world had become completely different and exciting.

BABYLON WITH GHOST

I find myself sitting in an upholstered red velvet movie theater, chandelier lights dim, posters on walls. One of them garishly illustrates a monstrous machine with coaxial arms reaching menacingly towards a nearly naked heroine—"Indiana Jones and the Algorithm of Doom," it read. A rough-looking character, handsome under his Stetson, saunters onto the stage.

Ghost has the look down pat, as he leaps from the proscenium and strides up the aisle. Slouch hat, bandana, old clothes, revolver and, yes, bullwhip. "Howdy," he drawls.

"A little extreme," I note, "and after my time."

"Ah, but it was the first movie you and Joan took Gregory to see."

"Yeah, boy was that a mistake. He didn't care much. Joan and I almost had to leave from fright."

"Wimps. I thought you all were starring in your own adventure movie…"

"We were more like those clueless folks pulled in by circumstance," I tell him.

"Ok. But in any case I think you guys were more in a type of weekly cliff-hanger. "

"Except there was never an end-of-reel or start next one. It all ran together."

"No continuing plot is what I meant," Ghost states.

"You could say the plot was our clawing into what we saw as middle class respectability."

"That was certainly the prize. But everything else badly directed, disjointed."

"Look, enough. Go criticize real movies if you feel like it. Metaphors can only be stretched so far without seriously annoying people."

"Yes sir, professor," he grins, snaps his bullwhip, and vanishes in a cloud of decaying popcorn and dust.

As card-carrying members of the hippie generation, Wayne and Joan believed in natural childbirth and home cooking from simple materials. But somehow back in the day they had never had to face a week full of multi-hour commutes, angry clients and bosses, endless pediatric visits, and constant trips to the store to refresh necessities like Pampers. Not to mention doing wash, picking up, and keeping the parents and in-laws happy. So, for all their good intentions and usually good actions, sometimes it just had to be fish sticks or cold cuts for dinner.

Similarly, they both fervently believed that it was important for parents to read to and play with their children. But bowing to reality, they had been grateful enough as preschool teachers when Sesame Street became available to ease the load of interaction. Everyone had a great deal of pleasure from rereading <u>Goodnight Moon</u> or <u>Max</u> yet again, or helping with blocks and Legos. And yet, by the end of the week, they were both exhausted, not to mention usually facing yet another weekend filled with necessary activities. Videotapes became a lifesaver and a non-demanding family time together.

Friday would have been the ideal night, of course, since by then they were both semi-comatose with the demands of the week just past, and trying to marshal strength for the two days to come. But it was hard to get rentals because Wayne often worked late, which also meant, given rush hour traffic, that it was impossible to plan when he might be home. So movie night became Saturday and Sunday, if at all, after all the other activities had finished up. Sometimes Gregory was as wiped out as they felt.

The greatest thing about videotapes, they found back then when one still cost a fortune, was that you could tape favorites from TV, which the kids would then treat like books and watch over and over. It was an age when they really enjoyed knowing what was going on, having a growing sense of competence because they knew what was going to happen. Gregory would tape stuff like "Mr. Boogity," a Disney throwaway. Wayne would tape stuff he felt they should enjoy, like "Wizard of Oz."

That took care of the week.

But they tried to make time to see a new movie together once in a while, sitting together on the long couch in the living room, sheltered from the turmoil of the world. Gregory happy to have something new to look at and think about. Little Wayne, as always, just happy wherever he was. Wayne and Joan hardly registering the plot unless something turned out to be exceptional. They had never been movie fans, never really had enough money to go to movies regularly, so just sitting with nothing to do and letting a cloud drift through their minds like a massage was heaven enough.

Wayne's turn to watch kids at the South Shore Mall Saturday night while Joan luxuriated in carefree shopping. He enjoyed this separation, because he would not be dragged through Macy's and interrogated about articles of clothing, as if selecting one scarf over another affected the course of the moon and stars. Joan's possible expenses held no terror; like him she would inspect and imagine, but rarely purchase. Their consumer experience was equivalent to a museum excursion, worthless to desperate merchants hawking wares.

In his stroller, Little Wayne resembled a prince surveying his kingdom. Gregory raced to and fro immersed in inner fantasies of Ninja Turtles. Different styles, but both children remained well behaved. Neither he nor Joan ever promised nor used sweets and other garbage as pacifiers—at best, candy was an unexpected reward to cap a fine evening. They both believed in adequate discipline—although Joan claimed he was too strict. Both boys were quiet and attentive, and listened when he told them to do something, or more often not to do something. Since he didn't have to intervene much, Wayne was free to play the flaneur he loved so much.

A few hours passed pleasantly, as Gregory's muscles wore down, questions were posed and answered, Wayne rode regally aloof. Malls were magical, perfectly air conditioned, shiny and bright, stacked with immense unexpected treasures. That they were taking none of those trinkets home mattered not at all.

Isolation from worldly cares was the heart of the experience for Joan and Wayne. Without cell phone, divorced from work, freed of nagging possibilities for study, planning or cleaning, they could mentally vegetate even while they were usefully being good parents. Moments of unusually pure relaxation flowed. At the same time, Wayne was hardly enamored by the enticing wealth displayed. When he dreamed of things he wanted, it always seemed to involve a faster computer or a better algorithm. At his most wicked, he simply wanted to have time to do nothing at all and escape to somewhere where there were no responsibilities. In fact, a stroll like this was as close as he got.

A few hours flew by, and they met at the appointed corner in the huge building. As expected, Joan had acquired nothing. According to her, there was always something wrong with the merchandise—too small, too large, too bright, wrong color, too expensive—whatever. Never particularly if it were in fashion or not. Anyway, she made a point of letting him know all about it, a chatter that, as it does for many husbands, shot cleanly through his mind without involving any neurons.

Finally it was time to make last minute necessary stops in restrooms, pick up anything they absolutely had to buy (usually nothing since the real shopping had been done locally earlier in the day), and get into the car for the ride home. Gregory was wiped out, and sat quietly for once in the back seat, Little Wayne strapped to the car seat quickly falling asleep, Joan and Wayne also silent each wrapped in their own thoughts.

It was not quite a weekend getaway to the Caribbean (that had not really been invented for anyone yet) but in their own minds it was exactly a decent vacation, and would have to do. They would usually find life refreshed come the morning.

As noted, because of circumstances we never really could keep up with the Joneses. Most of the folks we knew from our past—siblings, schoolmates, and friends—seemed to be doing far better financially than we were. Both those parents, for one thing, had stable good-paying jobs. Everyone seemed to either own or be getting a beautiful house in a beautiful area. Although we were hardly poor, and much more solvent than we had been in Boston, we were also painfully aware that we were generally ten years behind those who had buckled down into life right out of college.

Yet there are various pockets of Joneses, even on wealthy Long Island. There are poor Jones and really rich Jones and all sorts of in-between Jones. Each group of Jones ended up in its own segregated little geography. The full saying, of course, went "keeping up with the Jones's next door." In terms of who lived next door, we felt we were doing better than average. Most days it was a comfort. Our house was big, warm, the yard wide and green, we ate well and nobody around us seemed to be doing much better. West Babylon was a quiet upper working class neighborhood—no stock brokers or financiers, even the self-employed doing so in modest business like repair shops or garden centers. I felt quite the lucky person, with a good salary, car and constant raises in a rapidly expanding career with no limit in sight.

Once in a while we would dream of moving up, moving out, getting away from the crowds and the traffic, but it was rarely serious. Once in a while we thought of someday moving into a climax beach house on the water, but quickly dismissed as an idle dream. A great handicap was our refusal to take on debt for "investments" to make our home more modern or upscale. We still had the mortgage to pay off, and barely kept our bank account growing, and were beginning to realize exactly how important a rainy day fund could be. There always seemed to be nasty surprise expenses.

But all in all, our experiences in Boston had served us well. We knew how to take advantage of parks and beaches and walks in town and modest outings at amusement parks or fast food. We enjoyed looking at things when far away, and taking care of things when at home—neither of which cost a great deal. Mostly, we were happily wrapped up in both children. I don't think either of us dreamed of them doing earth-shaking things—we both wanted happy productive lives and that was it. Everyone else said it was a mistake, but I am still not convinced that constant neurotic pushing is any better preparation for a meaningful future than a happy playful childhood.

Ghost is strapped on a stark bench in a room paneled with mirrors. His weapons have been removed, but his hat remains across his chest. He strains his arms to show off bare biceps. I, on the other hand, am dressed all in black, with a leather beret, holding an electronic whip. Glancing at a reflection, I am surprised at my handlebar mustache curled to a point and slick greasy hair.

"Ok, what's this now," I am startled by my voice, cultured and oily with a Germanic inflection.

"Ah, Doctor, every adventure needs its villains, n'est ce pas?" He manages a sardonic smile.

"But I am the hero …."

"Well, Doctor, I tried all the others and they just don't fit. Your company, your bosses, society, family? Who you gonna blame but yourself?"

"True, my bosses were generally hardworking and honest and I never ran into much villainy anywhere. Maybe we don't need an evil character?"

"Ah, but inside you, you know. You carry that stain and it cannot be so easily ignored."

"Explain that clearly Mr. Ghost. " I twitch the whip menacingly (hey, it's in the script.) "Surely I am not blaming my parents and background for some deeply hidden psychiatric issues."

"Not hidden at all, Herr Doctor. You yourself looked at the world and thought you did not have your rightful place. You should have been more. You were a failure and disappointment. You envied others who seemed luckier. You made yourself miserable at every turn."

"I don't do that!" I scream in frustration.

"Oh, not now, not now. But then—ah back then you had not reformed nor reflected. Honestly, can you truly remember your deeper thoughts."

"I think I hardly had deeper thoughts, Mr. Ghost. I was too damn busy."

"Well, there is that, I suppose. OK, fine by me. We can end this now," he remarks hopefully.

"Oh no, yourself, Mr. Ghost. Au contraire, I believe it is time to release—the Pomeranians."

The scene fades out to high pitched barking and muffled screams.

Wayne had gone through various phases concerning his relation to work. Sometimes, it was seen as the main mission in life, something that was part of him and around which all else revolved. So when he had considered himself an artist, all he did whether painting and drawing or not was part of being an artist. How he thought, how he dressed, how he saw things. Free time was taken in learning more about his craft, there was little reason to venture outside of that sphere, for it was all-encompassing.

But sometimes he had compartmentalized. A trivial job could be cut off at the edges and forgotten when not being done. This left the rest of his time free to be his own. When he was in such modes, he jealously guarded the boundaries between his personal home life and his employment. This might even be true if the work he was doing was interesting and non-trivial, such as when he was teaching day care for a living, and painting for (what he considered) a profession.

Now the career had become a strange thing. Partially because he had started late, but mostly because it was just the nature of the beast, he never felt he knew enough. Actual hours at work were taken with directed activities, things that were planned or charted or had to be taken care of. But more and more of his free time was engaged in homework—reading manuals, designing programs, trying to put together all the information he was pulling in. Almost never was he at home with nothing to do regarding work.

Although just at the beginning of the metastasis of instant communication, when ubiquitous instant connections rendered all boundaries obsolete, his attempted compartmentalization was failing. Work would call his home, he might have to respond to emergencies in spite of domestic plans. Once in a while he came to dread any phone ring on a weekend.

Even his dreams became playthings of his daily labor. Intuition refused to slumber deeply, and often he would wake up in the middle of the night with a solution to what had seemed an impossible problem the day or week before. It was annoying, of course, but also powerful. And, like all of modern life, completely beyond his control.

Somehow I had always looked at my father's job, and the work my friend's parents' did, as static industrial employment. Sort of medieval peasants, toiling away at the same unchanging tasks year after year. It was a scramble to reach a position that paid adequately, but once there it just turned into a long boring slog to retain an income. I don't know if that was ever true, but that is how I imagined it.

What I found in computers, of course, was exactly opposite, and, as it turned out, a harbinger of everyone's world a quarter century later. Nothing was permanent. Companies came and went, positions appeared and disappeared, whole departments vanished as others took their place, products from one year to another were unrecognizable, not only to consumers but also to their creators. The only certainty was uncertainty. In younger days, we had demanded change. The gods had obliged and we learned there was little more dangerous than a wish fulfilled.

We had a joke that just as a human year was 7 dog years, a human year was 25 computer years. Something brand new four years ago was a century-old antique. New hardware, new communications, new speeds, new equipment of all types, new programming languages, new applications, new companies, new people. Always changing.

Ah yes, the people. Programmers were in demand and rarely insecure, their craft still mysterious and protected by ignorance. That also started to change as everyone and their uncle got used to having computers around, but in 1986 there was still a little air of mystery, although personal machines were not really uncommon. But programmers actually found that each convoluted niche in their world only offered a temporary security. They could ride it for a while and even demand more pay as it started to decay, but at some point their little shell of security would shatter and they would be spilled out into a ferocious and unrecognizable technological jungle. Some chose to hope it would never happen and honed their (obsolete) craft obsessively. Some adjusted as it came along. Some explored the new frontiers.

But one thing did turn out to be consistent, across centuries human or computer, and that was that programmers finally realized what steam engineers had discovered around 1880. It was rarely the technically adept who acquired fame and fortune, and when they did so it was for other qualities than being technically adept.

No, as always, the remuneration was in organization, sales, and financial risk. Merlin could never become king.

Typical movie barroom scene, with typical cast of desperados, among them the meanest-looking being Ghost. I discover that I am now wearing the broad hat, slouchy clothes and side revolver. We are drinking as is only done in movies of this type, whiskey after whiskey with no noticeable effects. Ghost, first among equals, leans over and asks in a hoarse whisper "You got the map?"

"What map," I respond, surprised at my slow drawl.

"The map. You know, the one ya gotta follow to get your dreams. Shaggy something."

"Oh, Shangri-La. Sorry, I seem to have misplaced it."

"Can't go a-searchin' without the map," he insists.

"Searching for what? I'm just trying to survive the days."

"Look, man," he leaned toward me and winked, "you can fool these fools, you might fool yourself, but you can't fool me. You're on your way. OK. Where are you going?"

No use messing around. "Well, I seem to have left death and destruction behind, at least for a while. No grand dreams of immediate recognition or massive quick fortune. Honestly, a quiet valley with a little more time relax would seem to be quite enough at this point. I'm more middle class than I ever thought I would be."

"Not even hidden dreams of, say, stunning the world with software."

"Oh," I laugh, "I always call that the brass ring. Always a little hope of winning the lottery—I'm American after all. But at this point—no. Just day by day, keeping what I have, getting things a little better. Dealing with stuff."

"Boring." He downs another yellow shot.

"More adventurous than I ever imagined." The music keeps playing.

Gregory was dressed handsomely as he stood restless on the front steps, ready to walk a block with Joan to elementary school. Like most first-day students, he was proud, and excited but nervous and unsure. Fortunately, he had been attending pre-school for some time, and had an idea of the routine.

Joan was anxiously taking pictures as she made sure everything was perfect. As a school teacher herself, she knew how important first impressions were. She kept reminding him to pay attention and to do what he was told. Wayne just said behave and enjoy, an admonition which was totally ignored in the adrenaline of the moment.

This was a big transition in family life. Their child was formally introduced to the world of social requirements—no options as to whether or not to attend school daily as had been the case up until now. Society required that Gregory attend every day, for all the required hours, for months and months. The state required that he begin to learn certain important things if he had not yet done so—numbers and math and socialization with others. This was just the beginning, but it was a firm and certain beginning.

Most people picked homes partially based on the reputation of the school district, and West Babylon was more or less upper average in that respect. Not one of the best, by no means one of the worst, firmly in the middle for regular people. Anyway, Wayne and Joan did differ from many traditional conceptions, which paid most attention to the education at high school. Because of their background, they both thought elementary education was critical. If you came out ok by age ten or so, they thought, most of the remaining years would take care of themselves.

So this was an important and proud day. It was done with almost as much formal pomp and ceremony as his "graduation" from preschool in the spring, an extravaganza of gowns and music. They felt they had done all they should. Gregory was ready. And now his future started to belong to him.

People use many metaphors to discuss relatively calm and stable periods in their lives. These often involve the use of water—finding a calm lake after a course of rapids, entering a safe harbor from a tempest at sea. I personally cam to think of such stretches as bubbles, with the environment encapsulated and almost in stasis. Looking back, it seemed as if very little changed day after day, or even year after year. And then would follow a tremendous dislocation to something different.

These years in West Babylon were one of those bubbles. I was a young professional just starting to make a good living, with a demanding but exciting career path in front of me. The children very young and fully our responsibility. Our parents alive and active with their own lives, although tremendously involved in their grandchildren's welfare. Joan still dreaming of getting back into full-time teaching as a tenured professional, but in the meantime loving all the moments with relatives and friends on the Island she had never wanted to leave. And each year seemed a little bit better, and promises were that it might get better yet.

I have been fortunate to have many such bubbles in my life. Most people, I think, do, even if they don't quite think of them in the same way. Middle childhood, for example, is often one such. High School or college another. First real job yet another. There are many, and all individually defined.

And, for me, they have always seemed a bit disjointed. When I look back, I am remembering. I know I lived through and participated in all those memories. I can feel those moments vividly in some cases. But nevertheless, it is almost like reading a book or watching a play because in some strange way, the person I remember is not who I am. I have changed immensely. That player in the bubble is not really me, even though it undoubtedly is.

For many, such realizations bring melancholy. Those are people and situations and environments and experiences gone forever, gone impossibly, never to return. From one standpoint, the past is nothing but losses. A few elevate those losses into the construction of fantasies and might-have-beens based on projections of alternate choices made or alternate luck happening. And the most sane and luckiest manage to juggle it all into an acceptable story line, with triumph and tragedy, still occurring as we go forward.

Babylon was our time of a perfect little American middle class world as we understood such to be from our 1950;s middle-class upbringing. It had taken us much rough water and heavy storms and dangerous interludes to arrive there, but the future stretched out golden and secure and each day was a confirmation of how fine life had become. Of course, being in the middle of it all, we never had time to think about that, and like all such periods, it is only when looking back that we miss it intensely.

Beautiful sunlit room, exquisitely decorated with random copies of artworks, a murmur above the occasional bell echoing on the marble floors. I feel funny and everything seems a little out of focus, my mind a bit blurred. It even takes me a while to realize I'm in a wheelchair, Ghost in a comfortable rocker alongside, eating a candy bar. "Ah," he croaks in a strange subdued voice, "you're finally awake again."

"My god," I exclaim. "What terrible thing has happened now?"

"Nothing as drastic as what will certainly happen pretty soon," he smirks. "You just got old, which considering everything was the best possible outcome of everything."

"You say." I try to rise, but collapse from the effort after raising an inch or so.

"Now, now, take it easy old man," says Ghost. "After all, I'm pretty much in the same shape."

"And this has to do with what?" I ask.

"Well, if you look back you realize you've gone through quite a lot of lucky coincidences, happy accidents, miraculous escapes, and times when only supreme efforts made the difference and pulled you through."

"I used to remember them more clearly," I growl.

"Nevertheless, if any one of them had gone seriously wrong you would not be here now."

"Heroes always survive and win." At least, as far as I was concerned that's what I had done.

"True. But the thing is, anybody, up to the moment they die, is in their own mind a hero. They have struggled, and overcome, and lucked out, and won through. Otherwise they would not still be alive. So, here you are, secure and happy ...."

"After a fashion," I reply, morosely.

"And now for the best part ..."

"Which is?"

"Ice cream sundaes for dessert!"

The evening was getting late, at least for Wayne. He generally had to get to bed by eleven as his system ran down in energy. He was finishing a book on program testing, something a little more general than he had been used to. Since he had had no formal education in the craft, he tried to pick up what he knew he was missing as he went along. It was frustrating and exhilarating at the same time. In point of fact, of course, even those who were well prepared by study were quickly out of date by the time they reached the workplace. Computers changed too fast.

Clients, on the other hand, did not. They always wanted more for less, they never understood the difficult issues, their dreams were severely constrained by money but their fantasies were unbounded, fed by articles that were an inch from science fiction. They thought putting in a computer would end all their business problems when all it really did was (sometimes) let them keep up with their competitors. As always, capitalism was relentless.

So he would go to bed with something or other whirling in his head—a new plan, an old problem, a possible solution. He never had trouble getting to sleep, his intuition worked tirelessly as he slept. The problem was that he sometimes woke up at three in the morning and could not get back. There was so much to do and try. He was excited and anxious but he much preferred to be well-rested.

At least for the moment the rest of his world was as secure as it had ever been. They were meeting expenses, the family was relatively happy, no marital crises had occurred. He and Joan didn't fight about money, only sometimes about what to do with their precious and scarce time. And for once he knew that if his current job fell apart, he could find a better one just by lifting up a phone.

BABYLON WITH GHOST

I find myself standing in a dusty old classroom in front of a bulletin board. Ghost smiles in the front row with his hand raised. "Yes?" I point to him in resignation.

"Now, now, professor—remember when you are not in the field you really are just a university professor making real money by teaching undergraduates."

"No matter how exciting my adventures," I snap, "I do need a base to return to once in a while."

"Well, of course, of course," he replies soothingly. "But don't you think that if you settle in and become too satisfied you will lose your edge?"

I had to laugh. "I'd like nothing better, Ghost, than to be satisfied and lose my edge for a while. I don't seek out these nasty problems that seem to keep popping up like mosquitoes or rhinoceroses. I just get through them because I have to."

"So you no longer yearn for adventure?"

"Almost never did."

"Could be disputed."

"Well, anyway, not now. That's pretty irrelevant because I have few choices but to keep going."

"Yes, yes, you indeed must," he notes as the bell rings.

Not even 8:00 yet, Wayne swore to himself, and here he was at a dead stop on the Belt parkway outside Kennedy airport. A blistering sun beat down as cars honked mercilessly at the universe. Fumes rose suffocatingly all around—he hated air conditioning, but sitting still in this mess was just pushing the thermometer too high to stay comfortable in his dress shirt. His tie and sports coat, of course, de rigueur at the account itself, were folded on the seat alongside him. He hated having to go to Brooklyn.

He'd even hit the road extra early, making it through the nasty bottleneck at the Meadowbrook with no problem. News radio reported clear sailing all the way. So much for helicopter traffic reports. You might as well read tarot cards to predict what might be going on. He still had no idea what had happened ahead—a minor tie-up or a major accident. How late would he be?

He took a deep breath and tried to calm down. Gradually he had been learning to not scream and yell at the rush hour which he could never control. He made the best plans, did the best he could, and usually it worked out fine. When it did not, well, there was nothing to do but hope things began to move again before too long a delay.

Even in tight and slow-packed cars New York was New York. Overly aggressive drivers, cutting in front, pulling out, an inch from his bumpers. You couldn't take your eyes off for even a minute, the strain was tightening up his shoulder and neck muscles, he took a chance reaching back with his left arm to massage them a bit. One reason he came this way was that there were no trucks. The other reason was he knew no other route through the mostly frightening back streets of deepest Brooklyn. He was still a suburban boy at heart, at best a quasi-yuppie, and somewhat terrified by the myths (and actuality) of the big city in the eighties. Murder reports routinely reported every night. He was gradually adapting to a reality not nearly so bad as portrayed, but it took time.

Anyway, he grinned, as cars began edging forward once again, he knew a lot of the Island like the back of his hand, and he was going places and seeing things you could hardly pay for. He might get out ahead of the evening rush, otherwise it would be another two hours (with luck) to get home by seven.

1987 TRANSITION

CHRISTMAS EAST

"C'MON GUYS, WE gotta get going," insisted Wayne as he herded the boys away from their new presents. "We have to get dressed so we can go see Grandma and Grandpa and everybody."

Colorful wrapping paper from the orgy of opening gifts a few hours earlier had already been bagged in the living room. Most clutter had been shoved back under the balsam, releasing a few needles. He and Joan were slightly bleary-eyed from last evening's chaotic rush. With contrasting bright-eyes, neither of the kids were prepared to stop playing. By now, though, they knew the drill.

As part of the natural, albeit acrimonious, division of visits among the family, it had been determined for years that Christmas would be at Robert's house "out East" in Watermill. They owned an ancient farmhouse, originally restored and renovated by Philip, which had original exposed beams and lovely wide plank floors. An antique in its own right, it was a perfectly Dickensian setting for Christmas Day. With a light coating of snow on the potato fields, one could almost expect to glimpse Tiny Tim hobbling down one of the dirt lanes beyond the wide lawn. As logs crackled in the stone fireplace, a long afternoon and evening would pass with Joan's brothers and parents for dinner and gift exchange and pleasant conversation. Cousins could reacquaint, a passionate desire for Joan who had grown up closely with her own relations.

589

Of course, this was wonderful. But it was also a chore. Sometimes the weather, like today, was cold but otherwise clear. Often it was nasty or threatening to become so. In any case, by the time Christmas arrived everyone was exhausted, from buying gifts, getting the tree and house decorated, and doing all the necessary cleaning and setup for their local celebration. Besides, in less than a week—during the interval before New Year's—they would need to take the long drive to Philadelphia to do it over again with Wayne's family. These were crowded times.

Consequently, people were a little on edge, though Wayne and Joan did their best to insert some humor. Now their car had to be loaded up, other checklists performed. Children had to be dressed for inevitable picture-taking. Joan wanted to look just-so, and needed solitary time, while Wayne was impatient to get on the road. Gregory was torn, but anxious to show off his best new acquisitions. Little Wayne was happily oblivious to it all, willing to go along with anything that promised more fun.

Breakfast had been chaotic. Eat but leave room. Everyone knew they would get a lot to eat later, although exactly when that later might be remained in doubt. There was also uncertainty about what might be on the table— Cheryl and Robert were prone to intense diet enthusiasms. Consequently, in a strange blend of happy anticipation, resigned drudgery, and fatigued exasperation, they finally piled into the car and rode towards Sunrise Highway.

Busy ancient department store, almost in black and white, a line of kids dressed from the 50's stretching back to infinity. I'm standing near a camera on a tripod, ready to take pictures, as one after another comes up to a gorgeously dressed fat Santa with huge white beard. He signals he needs a break, I snap a "back later sign" across the aisle to the loud disappointment of a huge crowd of parents, and I walk with him into a back room.

Ghost takes of his beard and scratches furiously. "You don't seem quite thrilled."

"Oh, I enjoyed it well enough. It's just that work was getting pretty ferocious, and this was just a day off, really. I'd been working the day before—well at an office party actually—although we did get off early. But even so I had done some work that morning, and had homework and projects to consider next, although fortunately I was taking tomorrow off as well. I was looking forward to getting some sleep then."

"Did you ever try to not go?"

"Nah, these things, however inconvenient, are what family is all about. If you don't make the effort with your siblings and parents, you can be sure your kids will not make the effort for you. And Joan and I sure wanted to be in touch with them as they grew into adulthood. It was all part of our agreed bargain. So I tried to get in the spirit, no matter how tired we might be."

"What was the worst thing?"

"Nothing, really, just the time. We were all beyond too many comparisons as to how our careers and lives were going by that point. We complained to each other, mostly, about the world. But everyone really did enjoy the children, which kept the happiness level high."

"Not even a teeny bit of resentment ?" needles Ghost.

"You know, the main one was almost trivial and didn't matter to me. Joan was always hurt that she never got to host Christmas. To her that was the ultimate family holiday, and although she was able to do others like Easter, for her it was never the same. Me, one day was running pretty much like another by then. I would have done the same on St. Patrick's day."

"Heathen."

"Yep."

After Labor Day, it seemed, everything piled on at once. At work, all projects not yet done had to be reevaluated with revised year-end expectations formulated. The problem with these goals was that unlike those, for example, at the beginning of the year they were supposed to be met. That meant that September, October, and November had passed in a stressful frenzy trying to match clients' demands. Inevitably, some cleanup dragged on into December, although they really tried hard to slack off near the end of the month—nobody wanted unexpected bugs from new implementations causing problems. Of course this was helped because none of the other vendors like IBM were releasing anything new either, and the clients were busy with their own final budget analysis and purchasing nothing immediately. But it was definitely a marathon turning into a sprint.

Meanwhile, the various outdoor chores and children's activities kept on demanding time. Falling leaves, winterizing windows, kids back to school and a slew of academic conferences and nighttime events. And of course getting candy on Halloween and cleaning the house for Thanksgiving visitors (even though they were still all going with everyone else to Grandma's house that year you never knew who might stop by....) And, naturally, if anything else could go wrong, like car problems, it would as the weather turned more severe. Traffic gradually congealed into a nightmare at all times of day and night.

But after all that, for Wayne and Joan, there were the struggles to meet expectations. Not so much for each other, at least—they bought what they needed or wanted badly as soon as they could afford it. But all the parents wanted to see them for extended holiday visits, and there were other relatives having parties, and various business and school and friend Christmas parties. Presents for every parent and sibling and cousin and coworker and on and on.

But by far the hardest were the kids. You couldn't skimp on the kids, of course, that's what Christmas was. But unlike what they remembered from their relatively non-affluent childhoods, the kids were not anxiously awaiting the first presents they had received in months, nor something they had desperately desired for the last year. Those deep wishes were fulfilled as life went along. Christmas presents were now something extravagant and over the top and unexpected. And that meant shopping at Toys R Us and every mall in existence. And that meant lots and lots of time—which was hard to come by—and aggravation—and arguments about what things cost.

Wayne had come to expect this conversation sometime in November. They were sitting at the kitchen table around 9 pm on Friday while the boys watched a rented video in the living room. He was dead tired from another difficult week, Joan was exasperated with trying to figure out how to deal with all the upcoming events, they were both overwhelmed with trying to keep up with shopping and getting the house ready for the holidays.

"Christmas is on a Friday this year," Wayne explained again, "and of course New Year's too. That means if we want to take the trip to Philadelphia the week after Christmas, I'll need to take some vacation time off. "

"I don't know why Nick doesn't just close for the holiday, like they used to do for Robert at Grumman," complained Joan.

"That was then, nobody can do that anymore," said Wayne in what he thought was a patient manner. "We have to deal with the way things really are. Any time will eat into my vacation allotment."

"I don't think we have any choice," Joan said. "Your parents expect to see the kids for the holidays. And they're right."

"I know, I know. But I wonder if we could just go down the weekend before, when I could just take, say Friday off and have a nice long visit without losing three or four days…"

"No, we have too much to do and too many parties to go to. You know we have to see Jean and Pat, and you have the thing at work, and they have school …."

"OK, OK, I understand. But I want to do the beginning of the week. I don't want to be there on New Year's and trying to come back that weekend."

"Yeah, I know. We're tired enough as it is when everything is done and school starts up again."

Every year they went through this ritual, of how they would fit in all the activities so that they somehow survived with sanity intact and energy to face January. They had to go to her parent's house for Thanksgiving—no problem, just a half hour away. Then they had to go "out east" to Watermill, an hour and a half drive in good weather (which was often not the case) for Christmas Day to visit with Robert and Cheryl and the cousins in the lovely big old farmhouse.

"Oh, by the way, do you think we should ask to sleep over this year? I have Saturday off, after all, and we could relax a little bit."

"I can ask," said Joan. "It might be nice. But it could be crowded, since I think Mom and Dad will be staying out there too."

"Well, try to find out, I would like to have some idea what to expect."

The trickiest of all was the trip to Philadelphia, which should be a short three hour expressway trip to the south, but somehow always turned into slogging nightmares along the Belt Parkway, Staten Island bridges, and New Jersey turnpike. Somehow the three hours often became five or more of the most frustrating, fatiguing, and frightening that Wayne ever endured on the road. If the weather turned vicious, as was likely, it could take much longer. And the worst was the uncertainty.

So there was the trip down. Then all the expectations, the children playing, exchanging gifts, dinner with Craig and Anita and those cousins and those grandparents. Always leaving too soon, always leaving Nana and PopPop feeling they had rushed back too quickly. Always wishing they could spend a little more time.

But on January 2, like clockwork, it all started over again, and they had to be back, wound up, cheerful, and ready to go into a "bright new year" as all the commentators blithely called it.

Up until our children were about ten was the hardest time to maintain all the "holiday traditions." We were expected somehow to provide a wonderland for them that they would remember for the rest of their lives, in spite of the fact that they already had more than everything. Meanwhile, we were also required to attend to all the surviving parents and their close relatives, in a kind of family display of successful tribal unity. With our peers we would explicitly and implicitly compare careers and lives—her husband does this, her wife does that, why don't you....

Meanwhile the commercial drumbeat went on and on with bigger and brighter and more. Malls sucked at money, television ads promised the impossible, the myth of bottomless Santa Claus was repeated ad nauseum. In spite of the pious intonations of various well-intentioned Cassandras, everyone tended to ignore all spiritual aspects except for the one obligatory trip to church on Christmas Eve, when exasperated priests would worsen the effect by more or less yelling at the congregation to show up more often or miss out on eternal life. I suppose it was good for the kids, but I'm not quite sure how.

This was probably the worst year. I was in the middle of a soaring career which took an awful lot of time and energy, both at work and on the commute, and at home. It was constant learning and thinking and worrying, even when I was nominally taking time off. Joan had begun substitute teaching again to supplement our rather small income. Neither of us had the time nor energy for any of this, and once in a while we would wish we could miss the whole thing, but we couldn't and wouldn't allow ourselves to even entertain the thought. It's what family and life was really all about.

But those two months every year were tough, followed by the letdown. Which began with the morning after the grand day of opening presents, when it turned out Wayne and Greg often enjoyed playing more with the boxes that had contained the larger gifts more than they did with the toys themselves. Or, even worse, they completely ignored what Joan and I had taken special care finding and paying for to concentrate on something completely trivial and inconsequential.

Ghost returns from his tiny dimly lit bathroom, fastening his wide glossy black belt. He fondles his curly white beard thrown on a chair, grins maliciously. "So you never wanted to put the Christ back in Christmas?"

"Boy, that was something that never crossed my mind," I laugh.

"But why not? You claim to be spiritual and believe in God."

"Well, God maybe, but even when I was a kid the whole Christ thing was just a little too weird. At least I didn't get the full load of virgins and saints like Joan, but I figured if God could do anything and was everywhere there wasn't much need to avoid him directly."

"Oh, a him? And you really seem to be reaching deep into heresy ..."

"More like I'm not really a Christian, more of a Deist, or a spiritual Deist anyway. "

"Seems a strange position, for somebody who accepts science and the material world like you."

"No, not at all. I really believe we can't know everything and that the material world is just a part of everything. Even quantum physics demonstrates that, and now some of the wilder theories are off into infinities of multiverses. I just accept that nobody including me can know what the details are. So I don't worry much about them."

"But there is that odd reference to him," needles Ghost.

"Well, why not? I deeply feel connected to a personal God who cares about me—certainly has taken care of me well—and for me that feels like a he. Why not something to guide me through the range of multiverse possibilities to let me experience the best track for my life?"

"No proof."

"Nonsense. In spite of the twaddles of the dumber scientists, consciousness itself is all the miracle proof we need. Nothing in the physical world predicts consciousness, and those who aren't aware are blind."

"But you went to conventional church anyway, on the holidays."

"Well, it made Joan happy, and brought back my childhood, and couldn't hurt the kids. It's good for them to consider larger issues sometimes. And I did enjoy most of the traditional ceremonies."

"But not the sermons."

"No, I admit. Never the sermons."

"Heathen." He sighs deeply and slips the beard straps over his ears, recovers his hat, takes a deep breath, and heads for the curtains back to the stage. A whisper drifts over as he exits—"Heeere's Santa!"

At least, Wayne reflected as he pursued Little Wayne toddling down aisles at the toy store, they didn't suffer for lack of money. Well, they obviously did not have a lot, but neither he nor Joan had ever expected to have what they had. They had not been brought up in luxury, and they both believed things like normal walks and sunsets to be the equal of anything purchased. Hopefully, they were passing those values on to the kids, even surrounded by the mounds of confections and garbage here in Christmas wonderland.

Actually, he thought most of this stuff was pretty tacky and useless. If you've had one radio-controlled car you've had them all. One doll represents the genre. One set of building materials is pretty much like any other. As far as he could tell, most of this was all just extensions on the same riff. And the "educational" stuff was boring, even for parents. So the problem was not in money for something, but rather in finding something at all.

Well, actually, he thought as he rounded yet another corner, trailing Joan and Gregory prancing on ahead, the problem is time. They never sell time anywhere at the mall. All his hours went to earning the privilege of shopping here. Which, as far as he was concerned, was little privilege at all.

He would much rather purchase, for himself and Joan at least, a week of quiet and carefree moments. But the eighties were before instant gratification quickie mini-vacations, and they would probably not have done that anyway, frugal as they were. Besides, their time was largely allocated fully to

BABYLON WITH GHOST

commitments to people. Still, it would be nice to run into a tiny store, something perhaps out of the twilight zone, where weekends could be bought for a few hundred dollars, to just slip in somehow where nobody else would notice you were gone.

Those were the years when the need to please others, and to compare yourself to others, was most acute. The children were growing up rapidly, every day a reminder that these times would never come again. Life is not a cycle but a progression through change. Even with more children, the oldest just moves along and has new, never to be repeated, requirements, joys, and problems. So they looked around and wondered "how am I doing?"

The answer was not always pleasant. Everybody else seemed to be doing better, have a better job, more income, more prospects, a nicer house, a finer location. Everybody else seemed to know exactly what they were doing and how their career was progressing. Other wives looked more beautiful, other husbands more supportive. Other children more handsome, or smarter, or more driven. Naked comparisons to the world were often frightening.

That naturally led to a defensive posture when dealing with other people. You practiced putting everything in the best light, smoothing the edges, ignoring conflicts. The family drew up the barricades and huddled together to face the foreign threats. Maybe that was a good thing. But some of the conversations around holiday dinner tables could get a little sticky. Not to mention the omnipresent ghosts of what parents had done by the same time in their immaculate lives.

Of course, everyone felt the same way. Everyone wanted to shine, and would do what was necessary to do so. Once in a while the discussions became almost an art form of braggadocio tending to farce. We're lying but you can't prove it—I dare you to challenge me. Fortunately, all the people they knew were at least well enough centered to remain polite. The real knives lay sheathed, and whenever nasty problems appeared they were subsumed into the privacy of the larger clan.

Ghost had materialized as an avuncular Santa Claus, with fluffy white beard, demonic red eyes, and fangs. "And what would you like for Christmas, little boy," he rasped.

"Oh, give it up, Ghost. Surprisingly, I wanted nothing at all."

"Oh, selfless and all in the spirit of giving?" he asked incredulously.

"Nothing so noble, I'm afraid. I just had everyday all I could possibly want and more. Much more than I had any right to expect."

"Nah, you said yourself you could use time and money, remember?"

"Ah, but in context. The only thing I desperately wanted to hold on to was my sobriety, which seemed well in place. After that—well, this was a perfect time. All parents alive and well, children still full of hope and promise, a more or less contented family life, an interesting and engaging career with only good futures in front of me. Just perfect. Anything else I wished for might spoil it."

"Wishes are always easy."

"Daydreams can be nice," I admitted, "but like all dreams pretty insubstantial. They can get you through the night and rough times, but I always thought it was reality you mostly had to deal with day to day. And reality, in 1987, was just about exactly how I had dreamed it should be. "

"Mr. Pollyanna."

"Ah, Mr. Claus, go offer your wares where they are desperately needed. I was the luckiest person on the face of the planet, and even more importantly I knew it every moment. No other gift could come close."

This year, the midnight basement chore was the bicycle. Not quite as fiendish as the Millennium Falcon model he had put together a few years ago (aided by a bit too much wine.) But the Japanese instructions were as inscrutable as anyone might hope. Still, this should be pretty straightforward, and he had made the precaution of laying out all the parts and reading the directions through twice for any odd gotchas that might come up two or three steps too late.

Anyway, he thought in the quiet, this was a much better deal than last year. That had been a true adventure and he still had trouble believing he had pulled it off.

Gregory believed fervently in Santa Claus, who was the centerpiece of his magical world view. He just knew Santa could get him anything he wanted. Forget action heroes—who Gregory wanted to be was Santa himself. That is what he thought could fix the world. So what he desperately desired—practically the only present on his Christmas list, was a Santa Claus suit.

These days there is the internet, and no doubt costumes of any kind for six year olds are a dime a dozen in all shapes and sizes. But back then, well even finding an adult suit for a party could be a challenge at that time of year, and who in the world would carry something for kids? November edged into December and Wayne had no idea what he was going to do. It would be a crushing holiday morning.

One Friday night, after work, he took off in driving cold rain on his quest. He had only vague ideas of where to start, but maybe one of the tree and decoration stores would give him clues. He crossed the island after six and stopped in a huge Harrah's, loaded with artificial trees and lights and bulbs and—yes—outdoor Santa figures.

Ok, what made Santa? His face, of course, at least a beard. A bright red suit with trim. He could probably get away with just the top half, any pants were pretty much ok. Maybe white gloves. Definitely a hat. Possibly black boots, but Gregory's regular black weather boots could do in a pinch. So … what was there?

The hat and gloves had been easy—he'd already got those at the variety store. The face was a killer. The suit seemed impossible. Wayne rummaged around, wandering aisles, hoping for inspiration.

The first struck as he realized a tree rug—the cover under the tree to hold presents—could easily serve as a red cloak with white trim. Certainly a near match to an upper jacket. He happily picked one up, half complete, although admittedly possibly the easier half.

He wandered for almost an hour, exhausted by the end of the week, depressed by the rain, feeling failure and frustration. He didn't care if he bought it here, he just needed some idea of where to go. A face, a face. A beard could be made out of floss—no, really tacky. One last thing. But an impossible thing. Nothing came to mind, nothing hit his unconscious, it was just a dead end, and time to go home.

As he walked up to the front of the store to buy the skirting, he realized the answer was staring him in the face. On the window were large plastic outdoor Christmas Santa faces, a bit over life size but not immense, with lights inside. Maybe he could …. He looked closer. Yes, he definitely could cut out the eyes, take off the back containing the light, and put a strap on from ear to ear. Maybe something better would turn up in the last weeks, but this would do.

Happily, finally, he ran through the storm to the car and made it home not too late. Joan had known what he was doing, and thought he was crazy, but he didn't want to disappoint Gregory yet. Dinner was easily reheated, and the next day he checked everything out.

It turned out to be a triumph. Late on Christmas night, when the kids had finally gone fully to sleep, he took everything into the living room. With the aid of pillows and boots and an old pair of pants, he laid out the figure like a scarecrow on one side of the sofa. It took a while, but as far as he was concerned it was an aesthetic masterpiece. Joan laughed understandingly.

The next morning was absolutely perfect. Gregory ignored all the carefully wrapped presents under the tree by the door and rushed to the figure. "See!" he chortled, " I knew Santa could do anything! He's magic!" And Wayne could only agree.

Well, enough of memories. Back to badly translated Japanese and poorly drawn diagrams directing him on how to add the training wheels.

For end of year holidays, as for summer vacations, the gold-standard comparisons are those of our youth, particularly when we were twelve or younger. Every year we seek to recapture what we remember, or at least what we think we remember. If not for ourselves, then for our loved ones. Our children should have even better experiences than we did, our spouses should sparkle with the same delight as our parents, we should glow in the satisfactions of times remembered as we once did.

But it's an impossible task. Times have changed—times always change. I don't know, really, what the childhood Christmases and Thanksgivings of my parents and grandparents were except by reading old books and imagining. Somehow, I never thought to ask. I don't even truly know what Joan's were like except by bits and pieces and fragments of stories. I think they always involved relatives. Beyond that, the details are impossibly fuzzy and unknown.

But I think I recall my own. Certainly there are moments—everyone

BABYLON WITH GHOST

being driven around to buy a tree on a muddy lot on a rainy Christmas Eve and frantically trying to decorate by midnight, or sitting at the top of the steps at six o'clock in the morning waiting for my parents and sister to wake up, or happily diving into the new electric train or erector set after I ripped the papers off. And of course the trip afterwards to my father's parents to be with aunts and uncles and cousins while Grandmother bustled directing preparations for dinner after more presents were presented and opened. Finished off by homemade jelly and pie desserts, while we youngsters played in the attic.

What I recall, of course, is wrong. I didn't catch any of the interplays or tensions. I hardly noticed what was going on. I was enjoying myself in my own world, wrapped in imagination and delight as most children that age in such a situation ought to be. But I fear it is the imagination and delight I remember, not the realities. That is also as it should be. However, I cannot be in that place again, and my projections of what is going on now always fall short of the dreams.

We buy gifts still, but even when the kids were young it was different. They did not wait as Joan and I did, hoping for something that might otherwise be impossibly expensive (and truly only hoping, because no gift was ever certain.) Everyone now, at least at our level of affluence, is wholly sated with what they want all year around, and extravagant holiday purchases are just tinselly bribes. Nobody beyond two or three years old gets all that excited. It's a good time, a family time, but the commercial myth has outstripped whatever reality there once was.

Demonic Santa floats back, with the added attraction of sparkling lights in the beard and a rotating bright beacon at the tip of the cap. "More and more, bigger and bigger, better and better," intones Ghost in a gravelly voice.

"Yeah, I know. Capitalism at its worst. I have friends who think it's a machine that can no longer be controlled, that will continue to devour the Earth until only a husk is left and everyone dies from the exhaustion of the planet."

"Sounds about right to me," replies Ghost.

"I admit, some stuff is way over the top destructive. But we surely cannot blame Christmas."

"Christmas does symbolize the whole mess, though," comments Ghost.

"No question. But if we got rid of Christmas, the core problem would remain. Besides, as we get older we hardly exchange presents any more. In fact, seniors tend to do little more than give a candle or book or something, to show we spent the time."

"So you're putting Christ back after all?"

"Nah, it really should be more a pure time of thanksgiving for what we have and appreciation of friends and family. That shouldn't take much money. Anyway, right now money is the cheapest coin of the realm. Getting someone's attention or caring—ah, that's really valuable."

They had managed to pull everything together somehow shortly after twelve, and were all on Sunrise highway east with an hour and a half or so to go. Today was chilly but bright, and everyone still in a good holiday mood. Traffic not too bad as they passed the pine barrens, over the Shinnecock canal, and on to Watermill. They pulled into the crushed stone driveway snaking under huge ancient linden trees in the front yard, and piled out as Robert straightened up from something he was doing on the brick walkway to the side door. "Hi there," he greeted them, "Merry Christmas! Any problems?"

Wayne and Joan gathered up child necessities and presents from the trunk while the kids ran on ahead to see their cousins inside. They entered through the current painting room—Robert was an accomplished watercolor artist and had his studio, complete with strong north light, all set up in this otherwise cold antechamber that had formerly served as both mud room and laundry. His latest pictures were on the walls, a partially done work was on the drafting table, shelves along the walls were filled with books of technique and example. Incongruously, several cats arched about, disturbed by all the ruckus.

"Hi there," smiled Cheryl as they piled into the huge kitchen. "Glad you're here. Mom and Dad arrived a few hours ago."

This farmhouse was a century or more old, rescued from the effects of centuries of rural poverty by Philip, who had sweated equity into opening the tiny dark rooms into modern spaces, adding walls of windows, exposing the hand hewn dark beams along the ceiling. The result had been a pleasing blend of contemporary desire—huge modern kitchen, sunlit bright room with windows looking over the back yard to the privet hedge that screened potato fields stretching to the far hills,—with the honest feel of an old museum—original stone fireplace, stained wide plank floor, small-paned windows. It was tasteful and beautiful and Robert and Cheryl, teachers who had the summers free, would rent it out for a few months for what seemed princely sums while they traveled throughout the northeast.

"Hi Mom, Dad. Hey Kyle. Hello Vanita." For a while was mayhem, as Christmas greetings were exchanged, the kids got sorted out and prioritized among each other, elders were accorded due respect, presents were placed under the carefully decorated tree in the corner. Soon it all settled down somewhat, as the women bustled about the kitchen, getting everything ready to go. Cheryl had already set up the big table in the dining room. Wayne settled into a couch in front of the fire with Dad, exchanging pleasantries while a new rhythm was established.

Finally all was ready, and the multitudes were assembled to open gifts. Pride of place was naturally for the grandparents, who dutifully exclaimed over each package as it was taken to them by an appropriate child. The kids already knew better than to expect much—the real Christmas had happened earlier in the day for all of them—but they were excited to be surrounded by something new anyway. The adults were already having trouble figuring out what to give other folks who already had everything they needed—so the compromise was that each family bought stuff for themselves, typically utilitarian clothing, and pretended that each shirt or sweater was a result of the diligent effort of someone really trying to come up with a wonderful Christmas present. It all worked well.

The fire crackled on as Wayne, Robert, and Dad discussed real estate and art and the state of the world. Soon enough dinner was served, adults in the dining room, children at the table in the kitchen. Everything, naturally, was delicious. They were relatively young, whatever dietary restrictions they followed were minor and could be still be suspended at will. Turkey, vegetables, and—what Wayne secretly considered one of the high points—buttered warm rolls. Civilized conversation about jobs and life and how things were going in general and what was happening with who. Avoidance of dangerous topics and barbed suggestions and comparisons. Good behavior by the adults, as by the children.

Near the end, Joan's brother Philip breezed in, like the traditional rich uncle in a Dickens novel. As usual, he had a sarcastic comment for everyone and tried to be cheerful as he rushed by "doing his duty." He lived just up the road but had a lot happening. He always left the impression that he had much better things to be doing than wasting time here with the rest of the slackers. But civility held, everyone exchanged pleasantries, and after a while things lightened up considerably. In a mellow mood, the table was cleared and conversations drifted over dessert.

Basically, the state of the family was good. Everyone was getting along. The future looked pretty solid. The children were promising. Careers were presented in polish and bright spotlights. Other folks had the real problems, and there were amusing examples to be shared. They kept an ear open for the kids, some upstairs, some in the side room. Whenever it got too quiet, someone would get up and check out what might be a developing problem.

Finally, everything was over, the last of the tension oozed out, and people gathered in small groups sprawled in front of the fire or sat around one of the tables. Wayne and Robert had a few deep discussions on aesthetics and the value of art, Dad and Philip shared tidbits on the local real estate market and requirements, Joan and Cheryl compared friends and common acquaintances and what had ever happened to who from the old days. Mom just beamed in satisfied contentment at the tight and growing brood of descendants.

As shadows lengthened, Robert and Wayne escorted the children, well bundled, along a dirt lane bordering the potato fields out back. They could yell and run and release some of the pent up energy of the last few days. Robert discussed his current projects, which involved trying to capture on paper some of the magnificent effects of brown and yellow stubble covering the ploughed fields, the effects of clear cold air under a brilliant blue sky, now turning purple as dusk approached. Wayne enjoyed trying to identify the various weedy roadside plants, with their plentiful fruits exposed. Eventually, they all trudged back to Robert's island of hedge surrounding his lawn and garden.

Darkness fell, the children started to slow down as they got sleepy, and final conversations often concerning the future popped up around the kitchen table, where everyone gathered by common consent. Philip took off with an ironic quip or two, and Wayne began to pack up and cart things out to the car. The dishes finally got done, cleanup was more or less complete, and a full search was made to be sure nothing critical was being left behind. Then it was time for goodbyes and farewells and out the door and on the road, with a little more traffic heading back West.

Wayne reflected, as he headed down the back road shortcut towards the inlet, that for his kids this was probably the prime memory of Christmas, as his had been at his Grandmother's house. Forever after this would most likely be the real comparison, especially for Gregory, as they remembered what life had once been like, and added a golden patina to what was admittedly a wonderful day.

Ghost flickers, his bedraggled Christmas outfit looks as if it has been dunked in a river, beard disheveled and flickering madly, demonic eyes dimmed to streaky pink.

"You're a sight," I remark. "Looks like you've been celebrating too much."

"You have no idea," he moans. "The Claus's throw a hell of a party, once the big day is over and everyone can relax."

"But that's just a myth ..." I begin.

"Look," he says, holding his forehead, "you inhabit your universe, I inhabit mine. Well, mostly anyway. I see you've been creating a few myths of your own."

"Yes indeed. The golden year for the kids, perfect moment for Joan."

"And you?"

"Oh, me too, no doubt. If I could put it in a bottle I would. The exactly right balance of past and future, still relatively young, old enough to know what we are doing, set on our courses but not yet trapped. Ah, if time would only stop."

"For no man," he intones as solemnly as he can manage, before yawning. "Like me, though, it will just fade away."

"Except in memory," I reply, to thin air.

Night had fallen but the highway was fully illuminated by returning traffic. Wayne paid close attention to jam-ups and crazy drivers. Inside, their ride back passed quietly, even the carols on the radio muted. The kids chattered for a while in the back seat, then slept. Joan and Wayne talked for about ten minutes, then drifted into each their own silence. Joan reflected on family and where everyone had been.

Wayne was glad he had tomorrow off. Strange calendar intercessions for this year's holiday. A few days of nothing much at work. Then three hours down the turnpike to his parents, a few days, three hours back. Then another frantic business year would take ferocious hold, which should drag him all the way through spring. He was kind of excited about it all, not at all as crazy worried as just one year ago. He was grateful the universe ha d pulled this off, amazed at wonderful moments he had feared would never exist.

Traffic gradually thinned, with only a few headlights heading toward them, the same tunes repeating incessantly until Joan turned the radio off in annoyance. On some cosmic plane, the present became the past as the unknown future loomed. No matter. Drive carefully, get everyone into bed, and sink into a good night's sleep.

TECH REVOLUTIONS

WAYNE HAD FINALLY settled in nicely. There were system 38 accounts, and he was comfortable enough with the ancient 36's to at least patch code, if not quite prepared (nor desirous) to write applications from scratch. Peripherals were fitting the gaps nicely, and he understood most of the basic necessities of all his clients. Scouting trips to go over possibilities with new ones was a pleasure.

Such an oasis of calm is rare, and he was to discover never lasts. Beyond the comfortable borders of his technical world, vast currents were shifting. Rogue accounts were breaking away and trying something completely different. Departments were increasingly stuffing information—as if it were some kind of a conspiracy—onto personal computers smuggled in by the accountants and managers. There were whispers of communications and capabilities beyond the simple input and output of the trail of orders and invoices.

Some days, in unguarded moments, someone on a site would open up to him, displaying some misgivings. Oh, they liked what he did well enough, and they knew IBM was solid, but they had read of this other wonder in some trade magazine or other. Or they had heard a presentation at one of their periodic trade shows. Or they had become infected with a computer bug themselves and were toying around with a PC at home. And at such times, they asked, what is IBM going to do to keep up?

The standard answer was IBM was the gold standard, they couldn't go wrong. Maybe that was true. But, like gold, IBM also cost an awful lot, not just for the initial outlay but for its cradle-to-grave support from a vast uniformed staff of highly skilled salespeople, programmers, and technical support. Not to mention its limitless laboratories of geniuses toiling away at wonderful new things, rumored to come out in the (always moving) next quarter or so.

Nothing awful, but unsettling. And then Wayne found out that the whole structure was about to break wide open.

Ghost and I are wearing relaxed social clothing in a wooded grove at twilight. There are torches to provide light, except for brighter electric glares at a stage in front. A chorus of people in black suits and ties periodically sing, although melodic chants of symbols and jargon might more aptly describe them. A hush descends and a confident executive with somber entourage steps to the microphone.

"Oh, all ye that are gathered here,"

"IBM" moans the crowd together.

"We come to witness the next grand evolution of computing power. The true future. The way of business to come!"

"IBM!"

Two boxes are rolled onto the stage, one a little larger than a sideways refrigerator, one a little box like a travel trunk. "Behold a glimpse of what will be!"

"IBM! IBM!"

"What's going on?" I ask Ghost.

"Oh, you should recognize these corporate dog and pony shows by now."

"No, they weren't like this at all ..."

"You think not? Think a little harder."

I shut up. After all, he had a point.

"With this at our side, with our corporate culture and vision to guide us, we shall smite our competitors! Yea, we shall verily rule the business world and none shall deny us! At last we have all the answers, and the answers are all right here!"

"IBM!"

"Are you ready? Are you ready? Are you ready to get rich?"

"IBM!" moans the crowd in ecstasy, their daily cares and woes forgotten, "IBM! IBM! IBM!"

Wayne had originally worked on so-called mini-computers, like DEC and DG. These were considered "engineering machines" dedicated to weird scientific jobs, like calculating bridge stresses or automating certain experiments. They were not well-suited to business applications, so big-iron companies like IBM, Sperry-Rand, and Burroughs ignored them altogether. Wayne downsized to personal computers, first programming BASIC games and assembly language into his home machine, then developing business applications on the primitive early Radio Shack TRS-80. His Microdata at Webcor had been an outlier, with its strange but advanced Pick operating system. Finally, fortune smiled as he was forced onto the radical IBM System 38. He could all but ignore its odd evolution from mid-range machines like the System 34 and 36.

With such an eclectic perspective, he had developed an agnostic approach at odds with various near-religious views held by colleagues in his corner of the industry. Most had trained on IBM, started careers with IBM, were still entangled in IBM, and could not consider any other way than IBM. They were mildly terrified by mini-computers, baffled by personal computers, and simply ignored anything that didn't easily fit into their previous experience. Wayne, on the other hand, found it easy to put ongoing advances in perspective, and was able to get an out-of-the-box practical attitude towards proposing solutions by any means possible. That served him and his companies well the rest of his career. He enjoyed the pace, the differences, and the challenges of the new.

Many other business programmers, especially those who had been around for a while, were intensely conservative in coding design and practice. They happily serviced the same old products in the same old way. They loved existing in the affluent niches of a company they considered as fully a monopoly as old Ma Bell herself. Their basic attitude was that there was the best, and there were the rest. All of them were happy to be associated on the fringes of the best, close to what everyone else was trying to be.

And yet, a little bit of envious dissatisfaction crept into their rigid conversations. Other companies were more open and entertained attitudes like "we are all in this together." But IBM partners weren't supposed to have the background, attitude, or smarts to be snobs. Professional IBMers—salaried employees of the company—considered themselves on a different planet. They would come to us to spread wisdom, to show us the way, to give us encouragement, but we were obviously several grades below them. Commoners. IBMers considered themselves an inner sanctum aristocracy of geniuses doing inscrutable things for the benefit of abstract computing. A mere business partner was tolerated, but in spite of lip service to the concept, never admired.

Within this partnership community, Wayne discovered he was once again at the forefront of the learning curve, able to rapidly extract important new possibilities from manuals and—more importantly—apply them to existing problems. His eternal problem was that he was often too far ahead of actual capabilities which never quite kept up with the printed promises.

Wayne sat in the passenger's seat as Nick drove his cream Mercedes back from a request for proposal meeting in deepest Brooklyn. They had decided shortly after getting in the car that this account was not something they wanted to get involved in—too many other bidders, too much administrative paperwork, and an awful lot of uncertainty as to what would be required. It was one of those that, for a larger firm, could be a huge money-making win or an equally large financial disaster. JBS just didn't fit into the picture.

"OK," said Nick as they lurched over a corroded bridge towards his "shortcut" through the Rockaways, which themselves looked like a South Bronx war zone to Wayne's naïve and panicked eyes. "What do you think we should be doing with our old accounts now that all this new stuff is coming out."

"The new standard AS400 should, of course, be what we propose to anybody new. There is a lot more stuff being automated, and this can be expanded a long ways. But for the older accounts I think there are really only two choices."

"How do you see that?" asked Nick.

"Obviously, they can't buy new 34's or 36's," replied Wayne. "And we should say we support what we have out there, but like IBM we shouldn't do anything new on them. In effect we should freeze development on the old hardware."

"That's going to be very hard."

"I don't see any choice in the long run. Your decision, of course. But I also think the new little system ..."

"The 'Baby 38' ..."

"Right, the Baby 38, which all the literature is now calling an AS400 entry system ..."

"The DEC killer ..." added Nick.

"We never went up against a DEC account. I'm not sure why IBM has that obsession anyway. But the Baby 38 is going to be a lot more cost effective, will come with IBM native basic packages, and is far more modern in all ways. Even the new languages with external files and all are a giant step forward over the old code."

"Do you think our people can pick it up? What about conversion."

"What I read is that it runs two ways—native code and legacy. Legacy code just transfers one for one onto the machine, and we can support it with what we know already. The new stuff is a big learning curve to start but then pays big dividends in support later on. I'm sure we can all handle it either way, eventually."

"I don't know, Wayne. It sounds good, I guess, but you know how difficult it is to get our accounts to spend anything."

"Yeah, I know."

"Well, we'll try to get them to all the IBM wine and dine shows, and maybe that will fire them up a bit. Going to be interesting, anyway."

"Sure is," answered Wayne, watching the dunes roll by on Ocean Parkway.

Nobody, anytime or anywhere, fails to look back and wonder what would have happened if they had done this instead of that. In hindsight things always seem so clear. But the late eighties were so confusing, with so much in ferment, and had such immense changes to come that I honestly don't know if you dropped me back there now I could do any better.

I'll simply list what we did not know. And by we, I mean not only individuals but entire companies and industries. In 1987, there was really absolutely no clue about: the internet, cheap cell phones, capable home computers(including apple) , communications (that was all a Ma Bell monopoly), Moore's law (computing power and digital storage remained insanely expensive), massive industrial consolidation, globalization. Computing itself would be roiled by parallel processing, reusable object orientation, several new languages, incredible new human and machine interfaces. Much more, but you get the idea. Here and there, somebody was trying parts of all that stuff, but none of it was yet affecting the general perceptions. All that came as a massive shock in the decade or so to come.

In the areas where I worked, IBM worried mostly about minicomputers, which for some reason it saw as its real future competitors. It had already conquered big iron, and possibly its efforts did in fact help lead to the later demise of DEC. But it more or less ignored personal computers as a business strategy.

Oh, IBM made pretty good personal computers. But it saw them as either fancy typewriters or beefed up hand calculators. Why anyone would want them to talk to "real" core business applications escaped them. Everything they eventually came up with to bridge that gap was clunky, terrible, and ill-thought-out, what we in the business termed a "kludge." Like sludge, only pronounced "klooge." They fought the idea of PC's tied into main processes in every way possible until they had completely lost their hold on that part of the business, as Microsoft leapt into the gap permanently. Meanwhile, Apple was developing its own ideas for the consumer base.

And the other big thing IBM missed was opening their products. Microsoft took off because it absolutely encouraged hardware and software extensions of all types from its core operating system. IBM, meanwhile, wallowed in the comfortable insulated processes of the eighties. If you were on an IBM machine, you practically needed a passport and license to kill to add "third-party" hardware—even a PC connection. You had to use their proprietary coding system (EBCDIC.) You had to use one of their extremely clunky languages—and even if you wanted commercially "generic" code like COBOL there were lots of bits and pieces "incompatible" with everything else. IBM called them "extensions" but in plain truth it meant you could never easily switch from one computer company to another, because no simple mechanical translation was possible.

Within what they considered their world, IBM was a monopoly. A proud monopoly, assured of its righteous superiority. And, boy, did they charge for the privilege of buying from them.

Still with comforting memories of an impressive service, I stumble out of a massive old gothic cathedral and into the cobblestone-paved town square. A grey sky frames a medieval skyline, groups of people cluster here and there. As I begin to walk away, Ghost detaches himself from one of the gatherings and sidles over clutching some papers.

"Enjoyed watching the fat priests?" he hisses.

"What? What?" I ask in confusion. I've heard rumors, of course, but have not run into this personally before. I look around, afraid that even speaking might be dangerous to my future.

"You're not one of the ignorant masses," he states. "I know you have delved into outer heresies—the personal computer, the mini computer. I know you still occasionally read Byte magazine …"

"Not here! Quiet! Leave me alone!"

"Oh, you're already inches from heresy. Speaking with me makes little difference. Besides, the Inquisition with their Cardinals and deep theologians in thrall to Pope CEO have no time for the little fish like you. They take no notice."

"The time is coming," he brandishes his papers, "when they will not be so high and mighty. When computing is free to all, when immense marvels unroll without cost for everyone, when every year is a new marvel to liberate us from the past."

"You're mad! Completely mad!" I tell him forcefully, trying to back away. "And I suppose that will be the next utopia, and lions will lie with lambs and peace and justice will prevail."

"I don't know," Ghost admits. "I can't foresee that future clearly. But I assure you, the problems will be completely different."

I leave him to rant on, but my soul, until now certain of salvation in the arms of the true technology, has been deeply troubled.

Wayne found himself, as he often did, conducting company classes on all the new stuff. He found he had an ability to translate the dry jargon of the manuals into something more immediately useful to his coworkers. And he had a gift for explaining the difficult in simpler terms, perhaps developed from his days working with young children.

His job centered on a few areas, all done at once, all necessary, and quite different from one another, although related.

First, of course, he had to pay his way directly by billing the existing System 38 accounts. This involved maintenance, applying patches and upgrades, fixing problems, and generally consulting with the clients, but also took at least three days a week designing or coding new things on site. So he usually had a few projects going on somewhere, which paid his salary. These could be fun, and when they went smoothly all was well, but they could also be irksome, for trouble often ran in bunches, often at the end of the year, end of the month, or when IBM was releasing a flurry of new software.

Second, he was the lead for going with Nick to prospect new accounts. He would sit quietly, take notes, ask a few questions, and then brainstorm with Nick on the way back to the office. At some point soon thereafter he would write up the proposals, with estimated times, complications. By now they had a computer in the office, so a lot of time was spent writing at a terminal with these plans, many of which died as soon as costs were revealed to the potential buyers.

Third, as a corollary to the second, he designed and implemented the packages that JBS could offer—to medical billing services or fastener distributors or whatever. As new hardware came along, he would adapt each package. That also involved writing lots of documentation—user and programmer—so the other people could support it once it was up and running.

He had managed to pull himself away from the 34 and 36 accounts, which were well handled as they were, but he was the court of last resort for sticky problems everywhere else. A fireman on first call for most everything. He could step in and calm most problems even before Nick arrived. He resented these duties a bit, because they were the most impactful on what he really wanted to do.

And, finally, and almost entirely on his own time, he was the pioneer of the future. He would read all the new stuff from IBM, or trade magazines, or strange computer articles about how to develop software. That was mostly at night and on the weekends, with some notes, and thinking about it all the time on his walks. What this meant, how that affected what they were doing.

It was a lot. It kept him busy. There were very few empty days.

Any craft has mysteries, although some are more veiled than others. It is easy to grasp the essentials of something like painting or cooking, and at least imagine the more esoteric requirements of deeper art. But certain crafts, like programming in the eighties, were almost magical to outsiders. We might as well have been wizards called in from hidden dark towers, who could make data appear or disappear with the wave of a finger.

We were at the beginning of immense changes, what came to be called paradigm shifts, in computing and in business and, indeed, in everyday life. Computers were still either expensive toys at home, or expensive massive hardware at work. True, some departments were switching over to word processing and spreadsheets, but mostly just mid-level managers almost sneaking the things in because they were so useful, in spite of the howls of the DP department, which felt it was losing control. Who would do the backup and recovery, they asked? How could they control security if the business numbers went home every night?

By now, nobody was afraid of screens. In the beginning, it sometimes took days to get folks willing to use a keyboard for entry, and every little issue required sympathetic handholding. Concepts like required fields and default entries made no sense. Applications were hawked as convenient and futuristic marvels, but too often the old paper and file system with knowledgeable people was far more effective and certainly involved less drudgery.

Programmers remained special, like lion tamers. Nobody quite knew how the electronic beast could be made to do what it did, for good or ill. Everybody knew they didn't want to do it—they'd rather yell at the specialists. Besides office staff was threatened with termination if they ventured beyond the normal. When programmers tried to explain mechanics involved in, say, a month-end closing, eyes glazed over. A problem in technical logic—maybe locked records when one person was using it and another person was trying to do the same thing—were inscrutable. And printouts of code—well, it might as well have been in cuneiform.

Big changes were relentlessly bubbling. Those managers with PC's were not afraid, coded macros or spreadsheets, read technical articles, examined solutions trade magazines, dreamed big dreams. Their questions got sharper, their demands grew larger, and their concept of computer common sense stripped most of the old veils away. Consultants' escape into jargon no longer worked. More maddeningly, there were insistent demands for electronic communication—why should any manager have to retype numbers from some green-bar printout into their favorite spreadsheet? Why did they require a separate printer to share results? Most annoyingly, what were they paying for in that locked room or closet down the corridor?

Downsizing impact on business and employees was just beginning, but already staff reductions were underway. Entry jobs had become specialized but easily replaced—requirements were evolving from being able to add and write neatly to being able to stare at a screen and argue on the telephone. Computer usage was being pushed everywhere—out to the warehouse for shipping and inventory, out to remote sites or satellite branches via dedicated phone circuits. Everything was being connected (when it worked) and the business headed toward instantaneity.

Monopolies were about to be overwhelmed by shifts beyond their control, in chip costs and communications possibilities and new concepts of best practice. The fat days, at least in this business segment of the industry, were about to end.

But for me, the main effect was that niches of artisanship became elusive. In the early days of automobiles, each car was an eccentric individual masterpiece, and required a chauffeur and mechanic constantly available to keep it running. Things like windshield wipers were unheard of. In less than twenty years, mechanics were everywhere, but not well paid, not usually necessary, and mostly fixing standardized stuff on standardized autos. My vocation in the eighties was not quite "golden age," but the basic framework suited me just fine.

Huge, cold, grey room, with long tables and benches. Seated on stools looking at me, maybe thirty acolytes in coarse wool habits. Ghost stands sentinel by the only door, as dim light comes through windows from rainy skies.

"And so," I continue without knowing yet what I am continuing, "those

BABYLON WITH GHOST

are the advantages of the new edict. External file definitions, external screen definitions, these have been declared as the true path for all future growth."

One raised his hand and asks, "but surely only if we choose the new rites. You said the service would still accommodate legacy applications."

"Ah, but the holy father in IBM home headquarters has declared that to be a mere temporary expedient, not exactly sinful, but not encouraged. The new way is the right way for all future coding."

Another began to whine, "but his is not how the writ has always been. We are losing our true core."

"An impossible abomination," another whispers, with subtle agreement from the others.

"Dismissed," I state. "That will be the way. That is the way. Learn it, do it, take it into your heart. Tomorrow we must study the rituals of enhanced security…"

As they file out of the room, Ghost slips over and asks "Will they ever learn?"

"Oh they are smart, if hidebound. The logic will catch them eventually and they will embrace its advantages. Only one thing bothers me."

"And that is…"

"After they adjust to this modern liturgy, what will be their reaction when they understand that such will be changing all the time for the rest of our lives …."

Evening fell languidly as Wayne joined throngs of people walking with measured steps through the large park on Dale Mabry Boulevard. Tampa's professional football stadium loomed ahead. To one side a large mall beckoned. Heat still shimmered over drained and dried former swamplands, hopefully completely cleared of alligators like those he had seen at a drainage pond earlier.

Nothing else to do this evening. Anyway, by the time he returned from an exhausting day arguing with the phone company and wrestling with the complications of long-distance communications he had no real ambition. Getting in a little exercise in this heat was good enough, then he could go back to the hotel, read a little, call home, and plan the next day.

For Wayne, business trips were an exercise in tedium. Everyone thought that somehow he saw far-away places at company expense, ate wonderful meals, met fascinating people. But his experiences were far different than that myth.

He would be picked up early (no use having a car) by one of the guys from the account and driven to a nearly hermetically-sealed compound in the middle of nowhere, surrounded by stark warehouses, trapped even during lunch by lack of transportation. He'd work all day, buried in wires, on the keyboard, or using the phone. Sometime around six he'd be dropped back at the hotel. Then—he could walk, but he was never sited anywhere near the tourist spots—so what he saw were typically strip malls and an occasional park such as this. What he mostly noticed was traffic and stores and parking lots exactly like back on Long Island.

As for food—well his dinner allowance was good enough for fast food and not much else. That was ok, he hardly felt like a big heavy meal, and he'd rather be walking than sitting down. Obviously no drinks, no bars, no slap-happy late evenings of fun, not that he'd ever had much of that even when he did indulge way back when.

This three day trip would thankfully be over soon. Suddenly he smiled and laughed to himself, surprised once again at how conventionally boring he had become, how much it suited him, and how he complained at even the least interruption in his daily routine. He pretended to slap himself and tried to pay a little more attention to the thick Spanish moss hanging from the trees, and the ambiance—however unconventional—of this particular evening.

Looking back, I realize how primitive everything was. Most of the stuff was being invented on the fly, not only code but the very design of applications, the best practices of business, the way people interacted with computer screens. I cannot try to tell anyone who has not programmed how much externally defined files and screens, for example, changed the way systems were designed. I cannot give much idea of how bitterly clients fought the standardization of entry fields which IBM began to preach.

It was an era of nothing being interchangeable. That started with the computer companies themselves—jealously guarding their own standards, languages, interfaces. It continued with the small businesses, each with generations of odd practices accumulated by family members and propagated almost as a religious duty.

And there were no templates to speak of. In general, a new application at a new account would start off with some "package" but that mostly meant that the source code was copied from a similar account and then modified to suit. With massive changes in native language and operations, even that would not work with the System 38, and just about everything was invented from scratch.

Nor were there even written guidelines advising someone in our position. Oh, sure, there were textbooks on how to do it right—but they all involved vast resources, teams of 5 or 10, a glacial development pace with all the time in the world available. That did not fit JBS—barely paying its own way, doing everything for itself, struggling to keep up with or stay ahead of hundreds of other small consulting firms in exactly the same situation. In fact, the reason there were so many small consulting firms in the first place was that the big guys had read the books and decided there was little profit—and much grief—to be gained in entering this part of the field.

It was scary, and inventive, and fun, and awful, and triumphant, and heartbreaking, every day. Often on the same day.

Knock on the heavy wooden door just as the bells overhead finish tolling. Ghost enters unbidden, arms overflowing with parchment scrolls. "All new since yesterday," he remarks, spilling them on the table in front of me.

I groan a little. "These are official, or just something you picked up to annoy me?"

"A couple of genuine bulls from the ecclesiastical headquarters, but I thought you should probably be aware of some of the irritating and provocative thesis being posted on various church doors around town, not to mention being handed out in the old square outside."

"I don't have time to read this. I have my own duties. How can they expect …"

"You know these are part of your duties, , m'sieur," he replies.

I glance at a few in disgust. "Most of these are indecipherable, and the ones I can read are either nonsense or contradict one another. Each best way of doing something is the exact opposite of what they said last time."

"Revelations can be ambiguous," notes Ghost.

"Nothing ambiguous about how certain of righteousness each of these prophets considers himself, I see."

"Everyone is certainly certain."

"Except me. I know I don't know. Well, you know we can use these ...."

He nods encouragement.

"Dump them right over there with the rest. Next to the fireplace. At least they can be of some use."

Wayne found that things within their sphere of influence were settling a bit. Oh, the new computers with their new requirements and capabilities were very unsettling, but the client needs were beginning to standardize. There was more knowledge being shared across companies, and within the development community. So there was a lot less weird one-of-a-kind useless demands.

In particular, JBS' focus on medical billing and commercial distributors had finally produced some acceptable packages that scarcely needed to be modified to fit into new accounts.

Unfortunately, all that standardization was also happening everywhere, so none of it gave them much of a competitive advantage. Their strong points continued to be service and a willingness to do what others found too annoying or difficult.

With more accounts came more hiring. JBS hardly ever turned over its core staff, who had been with the firm for years, but there was a constant stream of juniors who would work for months or a year and then either turn out to be incompetent or ambitious, and for good or ill left and went on their way. This added to the difficulties of everyone.

And now, of course, they were caught in the dilemma of rewriting everything to the new "native" code. Or at least Wayne was.

I'm surrounded by people in dark robes, and notice I am wearing one

BABYLON WITH GHOST

myself. Ghost stands on a riser alongside me, as organ music swells and stained glass glistens. The congregation has hymn books out, but of course we don't need them.

Almost mindlessly, we sing our parts. The joy of externally defined file systems, the security of computer telephone lines directly out to IBM, the eternity for which these systems are planned to be supported. Architectural masterpieces, hosannas to the interfaces, joy to the users and operators.

Finally it all ends, and I file with the rest to a parking lot, ready to turn in our robes. "Well," I say to Ghost, "I know I'm considered a technological evangelist, but this is a little extreme."

"Oh, I think not," he intones piously. "I would say this is all right and tight and true."

"Maybe for this group," I reply, "but there are lots of other churches just as sure that they have found the way—and each is different."

"But they are not IBM."

"No, they are not." I agree. And that is that. But deep in my soul, stirrings of doubt remain.

Wayne gradually realized he had reached a genuine turning point. Suddenly all the old code, the old methodology, the old ways of doing things were obsolete. Everyone was starting over, just like him. He was finally on the ground floor, knowing just as much or more as anyone else. In fact, he discovered he had some advantages, having been exposed to alternatives before.

From here on, he would always be someone with experience as extensive and often more understood, than many of the other people he would encounter. Of course, in any given company the long-term employees would know more than he did, and the real snobs of the industry—computer science majors working for the big corporations—would look down on anyone without a degree and some esoteric common experience.

Naturally, he hoped to exploit that to become as rich and famous as possible. Perhaps a package would take off and become the basis for a huge expansion of the firm. Perhaps he could write something that would become a best seller. Eventually, he would realize that he had hardly changed his spots, and for all his technical expertise he still had the same commercial disadvantages as before. He was no more fated to become wealthy here than he had been when trying to be an artist. But it could be a comfortable and good living.

And all those others, ensconced as they were in their supposedly secure jobs, wrapped in their collegiate certifications, would find their own problems. Many firms would fail, consolidate, move away, and few would take their IT staff with them as they did so. New ways of using computers, unimaginable in the eighties, would rock the industry until it hardly resembled itself, and those too tied to their old comfortable certainties would be as helpless, or more so, than any neophyte.

But that was for the future. For right now, Wayne felt in full control and optimistic that his golden era had arrived with the Baby 38.

POOR SUPERMAN

WAYNE PULLED INTO the parking lot at Goldman. This trip to Willis Avenue was a pain—relatively short distance, but the last few miles interminable, both coming and going, especially in rainy weather like this.

On the other hand, this was the golden account. He had brought this one into the firm, via his friend Joe D, now the vice president of finance. It was almost his own computer—his code, his support, his ongoing development. And it was both challenging and relatively easy, because he and Joe understood each other well and had worked together for a while. He sometimes regretted he was only here a few days a week—but the truth was they rarely needed him more often.

This System 38, adequately staffed with a competent operator, was a joy to work with. The account distributed high end appliances, and was edging into retail because high end appliances were back in fashion. Another healthy growing firm, happy to spend money to (hopefully) make money. Not like the struggling old-line clients just hanging on and jealous of every penny spent.

Well, here he was for the day. See what was up. Maybe long, maybe short, maybe lunch with Joe to discuss projects. Ah, if they were only all like this he would be content indeed.

I'm—what, dressed as a kid of eleven or so—standing hidden in a corner at a dark old variety drug store. Gradually I recognize the place as Martin's on the Jersey shore, where I spent much time reading comics during summer vacation. Not buying them, of course, or at least just enough to keep counter clerk happy. I'd gone through every issue of My Greatest Adventure and similar …. But what am I here for now?

Ghost pops out of another corner. "Ah," he whispers, "time for superheroes again. You know you really should be reading classic literature at your age."

"Not superheroes," I'm indignant. "Not superheroes, just strange adventures, science fiction, you know."

"Rots the brain. What's Superman up to this time?"

"I told you, I don't like Superman. That's for little kids …"

"Too bad," continues Ghost. "Because Superman is in your future."

"What?"

"Well, at least you will be kind of Superman."

"Flying and stuff? You're crazy."

"You'd be amazed at what accounts will think you can do. But the main thing …" he pauses.

He's got me hooked. I stare at him inquisitively.

"The main thing is how alone you will be …"

The dream had always been to be the best—whatever. It's what was taught in school. It's what permeated the culture in the fifties and sixties. Be the best because they were, obviously, the best. So Wayne had tried to be the best in everything he ever did. The problem with that, as it turned out, was that he was not suited for many of the things he tried, and ended up just being adequate. Which was a kind of failure.

But in the new role, he found he truly was the best. Maybe it was just a little frog in a smaller pond, but he could do things others couldn't. He could document, or design, or code, or debug, or explain, or learn, or fix. Nothing

BABYLON WITH GHOST

really seemed beyond his powers. Except one really important thing, that separated super heroes from the truly successful. Delegation.

Michelangelo seemed a nice role model, but that role model had flaws as a life study. He'd spent all his time painting a ceiling because nobody else could. Wore out his hands carving marble because he had the true touch. Found himself in long shouting matches with a coach because he didn't hire a manager or go-between. Like a god, very like a god. And unable to escape the fact.

So Wayne found himself the last resort at problem accounts. The first resort on new projects. The one responsible to train, and write, and travel, and … Each activity quite fine in itself. Each brought an element of satisfaction. But the problems never ceased.

He should have handed off, as Nick could. He had mentors who tried to explain. But why should he give away what he was best at? Why turn out an inferior product? Why not do it all? So he tried to do it all, mostly quite well, but there was no time. And there was precious little relaxation. Constant interruptions.

There was always a fire. Always a list of problems to tackle. He became addicted to his day timer—a little book which was supposed to help you stay organized by mapping out each day in 15 minute intervals. But the list grew and grew and grew, until sometimes it blew up.

Wayne had his head in his hands, sitting ten at night at the table in the kitchen as Gregory watched TV and Joan fussed with Little Wayne. "I can't take this much more," he moaned. It had been a long day—up before six, on the road before seven, over two hours going in with traffic problems in heavy rain. Crisis after crisis at the account, near screaming scold from their president. Interruptions almost every few minutes from Nick about issues elsewhere. A long dreary dark ride back. The next two days promised to be overflowing with disasters. His neck ached, his eyes burned, his mind rebelled. "I just can't keep it up."

"Tell Nick," said Joan. "You need a raise anyway."

Wayne knew the financial status of the firm too well to expect that to get any results. But that wasn't really the issue, which was time and pressure.

Right now, he felt no amount of money would save him. He was near collapse. "Won't work."

"Well, get some of your other people to do what you do. After all, they get paid too."

"That's the trouble," he replied. "None of them seem to be able to. It's just—all the accounts are like that. Everybody else has just as many problems. Maybe it's New York. I just want to get away. Life shouldn't be like this."

"Oh, come on," she tried to sooth him. "It's just one bad day."

"No, I mean it." He'd been looking at a book called <u>Best Places in America to Live</u> as fantasy escape over the last few weekends. "Maybe we should head up to Glens Falls."

"What in the world would you do up there?" she asked in surprise.

"Oh, there's jobs in Albany, Schenectady, all around. GE. And the houses are cheaper. And the commute is short and …"

"And the winter is long," she continued, "and there's no one we know, we'd be all alone, and I don't know what you think we would do."

"We got along fine on our own in Boston."

"Glens Falls isn't Boston!" she exclaimed.

"Well, just think about it, please," he murmured. "I just don't know how long I can do this."

"OK," she finished, diplomatically. She knew it would all blow over after a few days, it always did. These bunched crises would end, and they'd be back to a normal pleasant life.

Somehow, I never grew out of junior high, where the answer to everything was to try harder on schoolwork. My answer to everything in the future was to focus on my immediate job and hope that brilliant solutions or simply getting more done would reflect well on my work and make things easier and more rewarded. It worked to a point.

The problem was, I finally realized, that there was a limit to how far that could take me. The people making real money cut loose from their immediate artisanal craft and drifted into managing others. But I had some trouble with others, I much preferred the coolness and simplicity of code and algorithms. It was far easier to fix program bugs than to motivate people and get them to change.

BABYLON WITH GHOST

Eventually, I reconciled myself to my handicaps, and found relative contentment in my niche. Fortunately, it was one that because of a momentary labor scarcity was relatively well paid. And knowing myself and my limitations, I rarely developed envy for those in the corner offices.

Not that it mattered a lot to life happiness. They made more money—potentially a lot more money—but I never really envied them. I could see that they did a lot of work as well—and all of it would be awful for me to take on.

Shivering in a small cold garret, I find myself without clothes and aching from holding one pose. A few feet away, Ghost sits at an easel, happily painting away. I moan and he looks up. "Oh," he asks in surprise, "need a break already?"

"Look Ghost," I croak, "I'm no beauty. Get me a robe or something. What the hell is going on?"

"Oh, I needed a normal model," he mutters, handing me a thick blanket. "For the Clark Kent scenes, you know."

"How in world does this work into Clark Kent," I gasp, finally sitting down more comfortably.

"Oh, you know, that was the real genius of the idea of superman. As far as everyone knew, he was just mild mannered Clark Kent. If you or I had powers like that, we would certainly not be working for some stupid newspaper. And for that, I need you."

"Clark Kent was never nude," I argue.

"Ah, adding the clothes are the easy part."

"Anyway, everybody knew who I was, mild-mannered or not. I was the one that got called to do extra stuff."

"But most of the time you were, actually, quite mild mannered. You kowtowed to clients, you backed off of local issues, you jumped when Nick croaked a tune. You hardly ever fought back, you just took on the challenges and did them and then slid back into your quiet persona."

"Arrogant bastards have trouble keeping jobs, in that industry," I raise my voice a little. "I had a family to support."

"Oh, you could have been a lot more arrogant and assertive," he contends. "That's what Joan always said."

"Well, I don't like being an arrogant bastard. I hate the type. I like being me."

"There you go. Clark Kent exactly. Ready for the next pose?"

Unimaginably, Wayne awoke middle aged. Goals clarified, as youthful visions narrowed and vanished. Limited options, condensed from yesterday's passage, were more drudgery than inspiration. On the brighter side, hormonal thrashing to squeeze maximum juice from each moment receded into calm satisfaction. The overall goal of raising a family had put everything else into perspective (or constraint).

Daydreams of being a successful artist, plans for magically becoming rich overnight, desires to be left alone to pursue exactly what he wanted, were finally banished. Self-evaluations smugly concluded he had grown up emotionally. But what did he realistically hope for the next twenty or thirty years? Certainly his career was ok for now, but he must keep striving on.

He could be a small business owner, for example. He could alternatively become a lone consultant, highly skilled. Or he could drill down so deeply into technical expertise that he would command a good job and salary anywhere. For the moment, at least, he kept his options open and dabbled in all three. He realized that each had tradeoffs.

Adam Smith created the example of manufacturing pins, in which use of a simple manufacturing process (specialization) allowed one worker to turn out as many as ten. Much has been written about the fate of the nine who were laid off—can they find alternate jobs or must they starve if they could not find work? But Wayne wondered more about the one who remained.

That lone laborer had once been part of a group, doing skilled labor, relatively secure because anyone hired had a learning curve. There was at least some artisanal pride in taking metal and making it into something. A certain security, but also a modestly content worldview in the workplace.

But all at once that job was just an empty banging shell, same mindless repetition hour after hour, day after day, year after year. No pride at all in each pin. His wage would fall as surely as job security. He knew damn well—partially because his employer consistently reminded him—that he could be replaced overnight. His work could be done equally well by any of the nine hungry dismissed others. For that matter, since there was much less skill involved, it could be accomplished by any kid hired off the street and given minimal training. Besides, it was obvious that at any moment another process might replace another ninety percent of the remaining workers like him.

That was cruel emerging reality everywhere except in programming, it seemed. And Wayne was pretty sure programming would follow along soon enough.

So, should he ignore that insight? It might take longer than his working career to play out. But paradigms were speeding up—he'd already seen finely-honed skills in colleagues become obsolete in less than a year. Wayne's great strength was not through people interaction, but in learning and understanding complex concepts. How could he leverage that best?

They'd told him to check the color of his parachute. He was more concerned with the buoyancy of his life jacket.

I admire Rembrandt more than Rubens. Both created visual masterpieces. The variations in their respective creative processes were what interested me.

Rembrandt was an artist/artisan who did almost everything himself—drawing, conception, layout, underpainting, filling in, final touchup, maybe even making his own paints. The final work was an extension of himself , only marginally related to whoever had ordered the piece. Many of his paintings, such as his self-portraits, were done simply as introspective meditations with little hope of future sale. Yet I felt, even in those with the most apparent melancholy, there was deep pride and satisfaction in having created something from nothing.

Rubens, on the other hand, was much richer, much more powerful, much the wiser businessman. He took his talents and spread them into a workshop. He drew no more than necessary. He did not do a work unless he had first found a commission, then he laid it out with the client and although he may have provided aesthetic guidance, it was more like an interior decorator. After he put together the very broad initial design, his workshop would swing into action, with some workers filling in the under painting, other's working on their specialties—clouds or trees or fur or feathers or flesh—as required by any given section of the work. At the end, Rubens himself would show up, add a few final flashing touches, and sign it. Rubens always got paid. But who created the work? And did it show anything at all of Rubens himself? I do not think so.

In computer applications there was also a long process. You had to learn the current operations, build a vision with the client, sit down with the final users, write requirements, design the application, build files, write code, fine tune with users, provide documentation, instruct, make live, support. I treated the whole thing as a personal challenge, and satisfied at the end I'd look at it as my own completed something from nothing masterpiece.

My family, of course, wanted me to be more like Rubens. I increasingly found myself more like Rembrandt. Not poor, but not on my way to great wealth either.

Stuck in traffic, dead stop on the Southern State near Meadowbrook, as is too often the case around seven am on any weekday. Nothing unusual, as the rain falls lightly. What is strange is that I am struggling out of my tie and dress shirt and apparently attempting to get into a superhero costume that Ghost is politely holding on the passenger side. He notes my confusion, "Phone booths, I'm afraid, are rapidly going out of style."

"Why would I possibly need a phone booth?"

"Oh, you know, to change from mild mannered to flying into crisis."

"Ah, that again. But why here in this car."

"Well, most appropriate. At home, you must admit, you are perceived as nice but basically ineffectual, unable to make the simplest home repairs, bumbling around unable to make a cent on real estate. A real wimp who fortunately lucked into some mysterious career that at least supports your family at some basic level."

"Well, yes, I guess that's kind of true," I admit, knowing it is a lot more than kind of true.

"But, sometimes like today, the account sees you as the only one who can leap tall buildings or fix a bad backup or restore from a crash or locate and patch the bug that has brought the enterprise to its knees."

"Well, a little truth in that too, I suppose," which is of course why it is me and nobody else at our company who is stuck here in early misery.

"So, obviously, the place where you change from one to the other is during the commute. And, voila, here you are. Very good," he said as I slipped into the body suit, "don't forget the cape."

Wayne was a complete romantic at heart, who believed in his illusions of an individual artist as a kind of god, creating masterworks from primordial chaos. He found release in doing exactly that on new projects and applications, which allowed him to build marvelous useful contraptions from nothing more than words and code. He was always happiest when in the midst of such a project.

Such an undertaking would start out with discussions with a client, followed by initial presentations and estimates of hours required. Then the real fun would be in designing the files and screens, putting together the prototypes (hardest parts first) and getting sign off. Then refinement and testing and delivery and final signoff. Then joy and fireworks all around. Such a lovely ideal rarely went as smoothly as hoped, but Wayne was a perpetual optimist, who always believed the next one would avoid all the errors of past jobs.

Even in this, of course, he could never lose sight of costs. Payment was based, implicitly or explicitly, on billable man-hours. An estimate was in terms of hours, tracking was in terms of hours expended. Wayne was keenly aware of at least covering his salary each week—it's what gave him leverage and security. The most desperate times where when a project was going so far beyond the hours planned that all his time was being put in, effectively, for free—good hours after bad. So, lost though he might become in the code, he always heard the clock ticking behind him.

For the most part, it all worked well enough. Once the code went in, once the client accepted it, once the enterprise was fully using the application, it would run for years or decades, with or without modifications. Almost like a mural on a church wall back in Milan.

The most aggravating thing about being the main designer is that I became targeted as the go-to troubleshooter, either myself on site or someone I instructed and sent. Much of what I accomplished was by necessity esoteric and had to be explained carefully, and the natural tendency was to dash off because I knew I could take care of it easier myself.

In the long run, as the number of accounts and applications grew, that became more and more wearing, until I finally learned to document enough in the code and external documentation that anyone else could figure it out themselves. But that bulked up the hour estimates considerably, and clients were hardly willing to pay the honest extra costs of doing so.

It ended up being a tense balance, as many small business operations are. I would be trying to work on new applications, billing happily, when an interruption would occur. Suddenly I would be dragged from deep in my concentration on some project (often all but unaware of the rest of the world in what came to be known as cyberspace) to something totally different, requiring memory, refocus, and loss of concentration or even dropping everything and changing direction.

And then trying to get back to where I had been later. It was possible, but it meant that for a while I could be two or three times less productive than I had been on the new project, and sometimes I lost the thread altogether and had to backtrack. Not good for adhering to the estimated time.

Right around this time was when remote telecommunications with some of the computers started to become common, which eased strain considerably. Finally I could dial into an account to diagnose and fix minor issues without driving there, except for truly massive disasters. Still lost concentration, but a lot less dead space in a car.

I'm at a podium, bright lights glaring in my face, crowd of noisy reporters in front of me, a huge old-fashioned microphone sticking up. Not a bad dream, not naked at least I have on the colorful tights and red cape. Ghost is speaking into the microphone, "And now, to discuss his latest heroic action in recovering all the lost data and saving the firm a great deal of overtime money—none other than Superman himself!" He gestures to me to step forward.

Some guy in a big hat shouts, "how could you let the data get lost in the first place? Didn't you have backups in place?"

"Well," I say," yes but they weren't followed correctly."

"But isn't it your fault that procedures weren't automated or flagged more clearly?"

"We will be addressing that in the future, but it hadn't happened before …"

"So," harps a young lady in the front row, pencil in hand, "you admit you had a faulty design originally."

"Not really a faulty design," I begin.

"Isn't this, oh, the third or fourth disaster you have been involved in over the last few months?"

"Well, yes…"

"So you are aware that these disasters might occur and are always ready? Why don't you just prevent them in the first place."

"But I do fix them."

"After a lot of aggravation and pain and sometimes financial loss. I don't think you're all you're cracked up to be," states a portly gentleman stentoriously.

"Yeah, what about that," yell a few others. "Maybe you're just setting these up so you can look good."

"Hey, I'm only human …."

That should have shut them up, but the clamor just got louder and louder and the recriminations ever more acerbic.

Wayne did feel that his programs and applications were a bit like his children. He felt responsible for them, and felt guilty if they misbehaved or failed to work properly. Even things which could in no rational way be construed as his fault. Similarly, he extended familial support to everything his company was doing.

One of the problems with feeling in total control, he discovered, is that it is an illusion. Too many external factors, unknown to everyone, intrude on real life to ever reach perfection. If some clerk typed a letter into a price field, if the power went out during a backup, if it turned out all the information put in for one day had the wrong date—well that was a crisis. All you could do was to recover and try to put in something to see it wouldn't happen again.

That approach was generic to the entire industry. "They did <u>what</u>?" was a common refrain of engineers, salespeople, and programmers throughout the era. From a detached perspective it was probably amusing, an enforced evolution in action.

None of the clients, of course, appreciated any of that, nor the underlying issues. They accepted no responsibility. If all the data logs were stamped wrong, well just change them. If the end of month had been triggered on the wrong evening, just open that month again (saving the entries from the new month, of course, so there was no need to do that work over.) They too were gradually being dragged into a new kind of computer awareness in the new electronic age.

Everyone was constantly set up for a fall. If life was perfect—well, that was what had been paid for and delivered, wasn't it? If anything went wrong, well obviously someone had screwed up. People who rationally understood insurance and damage from acts of god and recovery from stupidity in the workplace routinely thought the digital world was somehow different.

The whole industry was complicit. They overpromised corporate-defining magic, and when the magic went astray the blame was easily assigned. The only out, which became endemic at one point, was "finger-pointing" where "it wasn't the software, it was the hardware," or "it wasn't our code, it was their package" became frequent—and often duplicitous—responses to everything.

A nice stuffed armchair, a warm den, a fire crackling in the corner, cookies and warm milk alongside. If it weren't for the stained body-suit draped next to the ripped cape off to one side, it would seem totally normal. I'm wearing a blue flannel robe with 'S' embroidered into the pattern. Ghost is putting away some kind of a ledger. He turns, "Is that all, sir?"

"Look, Ghost, I'm not sure what all this is about, but it seems you are confusing Batman with Superman here."

"No confusion, I thought maybe you would like to dream a while of home."

By home, I gathered he meant long ago, mythic Krypton which I had never seen but was sure existed somewhere. There was a thick coffee-table book and several glossy magazines on the subject stacked on the table to my left. "You mean where everything works, and I'm just normal in a normal life."

"Exactly. With your little corner office—at this point you should be mid-career, and a growing staff, and responsibilities that extend beyond one computer at a time, and future dreams of wealth reaching into the stratosphere."

"I see. What I might have achieved had I not been exiled,"

"Or forced yourself into exile, sir." he inserts gently.

"True, I guess." Brooding on all the might-have-beens. If I had only jumped right into business instead of pursuing art and meaning. If I had entered the great grey world just out of college, I might have cruised along instead of having to perform like a madman. We might have a better house, more stuff, finer friends, and ... "Nice vision, I guess. But just as useless as Superman dreaming of Krypton."

"That's the point," he agrees.

"My past is a far more unreachable destination than even some distant exploded planet."

It wasn't all bad, even if it wasn't all good. Wayne reflected on the complications of being better—at least in his immediate environment—than anyone else. After a while people believed him when he said something was impossible, or shouldn't be attempted. After a while they understood when he gave instructions.

There were a few perks. Good pay, relative autonomy, and the freedom to usually pursue the course he felt necessary. He had a lot of leeway, constrained more by his inner morality and inhibitions than by any external pressures. For example, he tended to be a bit too truthful. But all in all, he was happy with his position, especially compared to that of many others in business with whom he came in contact.

And it was, after all, an interesting job, making impossible things, riding to the rescue. He never knew what he might face any given day, and sometimes that was a good thing. He might be terrified, but was rarely bored. Most of the time, on quiet reflection commuting in the car, he was relatively content.

And, of course, he knew it wouldn't last. The magic was being squeezed even now, as best practices bloomed and careful instructions took the place of cowboy improvisation. The obvious trends in the industry were toward its own grey conformity, where each worker would be as interchangeable as were all the others in the economy. This was a short brilliant time, interesting, and transient.

Judgement Days

JBS HAD RELOCATED to a low motel-style office complex on Jericho Turnpike, not far from Blydenburgh park, where Wayne could walk in once in a while if he took a long lunch (he always counted lunch as a kind of work experience since he worked out many of his design problems and came back much more able to get things done in the afternoon.) This morning of March 29 was a little different, since he arrived to find that his office had been redecorated in black crepe—to celebrate his 40th birthday.

He hadn't been much thinking of it, day by day was hard enough. He'd had a fairly interesting decade in his twenties and a bourgeois settling in his thirties. He felt the next decade or so would be pretty much a continuation as the children grew and went through the cycles that every parent experiences until they finally flew off. It did not usually bother him much that he and Joan seemed years behind their friends in that cycle.

Nor did he feel less energetic. Now that he was not drinking at all, he felt better than he had in many years physically. He might get overwhelmed and run down sometimes, but no more than any of his peers. There was never enough time, but that was a common complaint. Nor did he feel any onset of aches, pains, and mental slowness. Of course, he'd never do the crazy stuff he had done long ago, but then again he didn't want to.

The only real difference, he thought, were the financial expectations. More this, more that, start to worry about college, think about schools and houses and cars. In the spirit of the times, he rarely worried beyond the completion of their assumed college education—retirement might be a long way away or never, and too much could happen between here and then. There was always something more important to do—and never enough money to do it all. Just paying the mortgage was, after all, a form of investment and speculation all in one. Strangely, suddenly, the real estate market was starting to take off where he lived.

So Wayne took the mock somber festivities in good grace. Nobody claimed that forty was the new twenty, but compared to the newer programmers being turned out, he did realize he was edging into becoming an elder statesman.

Late in the afternoon, sitting amidst all the black paper, someone knocks on the office door and barges in. I finish up the procedure I'm coding and look up. Ghost—it had to be Ghost—stands there as an old man with a beard, grey cowled cloak, and knobby walking stick. His voice even quavers "Welcome to middle age, sonny."

"And you might be pretending to be?" I ask.

"Old Father Time, at your service."

"I thought middle age was already moving on a bit—at least fifty," I note.

"Well, if you think about it," he croaks, "forty is pretty much halfway through your expected life and pretty darn near the middle of your forty year expected working years. So you're about as middle as you can get."

"Don't make any difference," I shrug.

"Treasure it," he raises his rod dramatically, "Treasure it. Time fleets by."

"Oh, don't I know. Fine, nice lecture, I treasure every day, go bother somebody else. This is a total waste."

He looks crestfallen, "You know you should pay more attention to your birthdays. You may end up looking back on these as the golden years."

"Oh, right," I laugh sarcastically.

"Best years of your life."

"Leave me alone, I need to finish this screen."

He fades into the hallway, and I am soon engrossed in my current operations.

Darkness fell later and later here in April, but Wayne was still driving away from sunset as he headed back home. The day had gone well—problems fixed, people satisfied, plans made. Everything was as good as good could be deep in Queens. If only all of them were like that.

Unusually pensive after his party a few weeks ago, he wondered if that was what he really wanted. It had been years since he had thought seriously about long-term goals—self, home, work, and life had been pretty much take it as it comes, one day at a time, for a long time now. In fact, this was about the first time he saw things settling in a long while. Goals, he hadn't much considered goals beyond earning enough to live on and keeping the family going as they thought best.

What was his true ambition? Did he want a consulting company, like Nick? The trouble was, none of running such a company, from what he could tell, was either what he enjoyed doing nor what he was good at. Did he want to be a self-consultant, a gunslinger who came to town and solved issues then rode on? The trouble was, he knew people like that and most of them evolved quickly into being pretty phony, all words and salesmanship, fewer skills. A big company might suit him, but at his age and in his profession, the chances of jumping from the little dinky stuff he was doing (at least in most of their eyes) to their grand IT staffs seemed pretty impossible. Hiring into one of his accounts was out—he'd tried that and been there at Webcor, and never wanted to be an expense item again.

He knew there were opportunities coming up. The profession, the industry, the air itself was screaming with them. Every magazine article promised ten new possibilities. Each one might be a treasure trove. The trouble was, any one of them might be a dead end, and he didn't have the resources. But, he thought, maybe that was what he should try. Work where he was and try to find a way to develop some "blue-sky" application on his own time, like an inventor, and hopefully get rich.

Headlights were flicking on, the traffic was clearing a bit, and he'd be happy to be home soon for his promised spaghetti and meatloaf dinner.

Driving home late from Watermill, following a birthday party with all the cousins, Greg and Wayne dozing in the back seat as Wayne squinted into deep red setting sun along sunrise highway, Joan was thinking aloud. "They sure seem to spend a lot more than we do," she mused. "Did you see how much stuff was in the backyard?"

"They had good jobs long before we did," Wayne replied. "We were doing our thing in Boston while they were moving up the teaching ladder. Now it's paying off for them. I still like having had our time in Boston."

"But will we ever be able to get where they are?" she wondered.

"Do we ever need to be?" he tried to redirect the envy. "Wayne and Greg get everything they want, they always have everything they need. We have more than we ever imagined we would, what with the house and cars. My job is going well. I mean, we have nothing to complain about."

"Oh, I guess you're right. It just seems we're always on the short end of things. My brother says he doesn't know how we manage to live on what we do."

"I don't feel like we're starving. I don't even feel like we're any worse off. I'm happy with our lives."

"But for being upper middle class," Joan always saw herself as upper middle class, "we are not doing as well as most everyone else."

"I don't know about upper middle class," Wayne replied. "I don't much like most of them anyway, the ones you have pointed out. I just know we are doing pretty good compared to most of the people in the world."

"I don't care about most of the people in the world. I care about my cousins and brother and people I know. I wish we had some of what they do."

Wayne figured there wasn't much he could add, so he just squinted some more and kept on driving.

The American boomer generation had been told they were the best, and should always strive to be the best, and would be the best, with almost a Calvinistic fervor as if being the best proved you were the elect of

God. Somewhere, that noble ideal warped from "being" to "having" and the consumer culture went into overdrive. I was always outside of it for some reason.

It made sense that if you had nothing you wanted something and worked for it. There is no fun for anyone in being poor, having no security, no control, no shelter nor food nor any of the nice things in life. I fully agreed if you were in that position you found a way to work until you had an adequate survival lifestyle. And you could strive well beyond that minimum to get into a position where career, home, food, shelter, and life in general were by all rational standards "good." Maybe in certain areas it was always nice to try to be or get "better."

After that, I always lost the thread. If the food you are eating is delicious and good for you, why should you always be striving for something ever more esoteric? If your home was warm and comfortable, why should it need to be fancied up? If you are making enough money to support a good life, why should you waste your limited and precious time and consciousness on single-mindedly trying to make even more? That is where I became un-American and came into conflict with—well—just about everyone.

I loved to work hard, and I admit I aimed for the standard "best" in my software. But that was directed at my artisanship and self-perception, much less at money. Often I lost income by trying to make something more elegantly "right." It was a judgement I made, completely at odds with the contemporary culture, at least as expressed in magazines and TV. I did find that my values tended to fit more with what was considered "lower middle class" than "upper." My passion for software was a close analogue to those involved in working on cars, for example. And, for that matter, those who worked within strict bounds, seeing work as just a means to an end.

In a more genteel formulation, maybe I had a more European outlook on life. Work was just a part of what was necessary for a good life, but had to be kept as much under control as any other aspect of being. You shouldn't eat too much, party too much, spend too much, or work too much. Life is a marvelous gift and being consciously alive should never be taken for granted.

The "best"? No I never really got the "best" in a commercial sense. One hamburger or steak tasted pretty much like another, a warm coat was a warm coat, a car that started and stopped was sufficient transportation. Joan loved to search and find the best. Her saving grace was that she was, like an art critic, sufficiently happy in just making the comparisons and criticisms, and rarely actually needed to purchase or own the product.

I should recognize this place, but it seems to resemble so many others. Obviously a food court, with its cafeteria tables attempting to make the indestructible utilitarian look cleanly cheerful and modern. Fast food being offered in booths along all the walls—ah, a sign for the Bayshore Mall. I seem to have fried chicken, I see Ghost and old Father Time ambling over with their own trays full.

"What, two for one today?" I joke.

"I can be anything, anytime, anyone, and anyplace," Ghost rumbles in a theatric monotone, "and I can clone as I wish. Obviously, you have met."

"Nice to see you again," quavers Father Time. "I miss some of this because I'm usually in the big picture, you know."

"I would think this would be usual for you, then," I point out. "After all, this is absolute usual middle America that everybody recognizes."

"Ah, everybody," inserts Ghost. "Just what we were talking about. Who is everybody? Are you part of everybody? Is this really everybody?"

"Hey, Ghost, those are my questions. You're supposed to have the answers!"

"I see everybody all the time," laughs Father Time as if joking. "And yet, I sometimes think I see nobody at all. Very strange phenomenon."

"Yeah," I agree, "I think it's more a marketing conceit than anything else. Some advertising gimmick to make us buy more and want more when otherwise we'd be quite content with what we have."

"Sure," notes Ghost. "Make anybody want to buy as much as everybody."

Father Time holds his head. "Sorry, this garbage gives me a headache. I tend to stay in reality."

"Whatever that is," I add maliciously.

"So are you happy here, in the middle of Everybody?" Ghost looks around at the seasonal crowd.

"You know, I truly am," I answer. "I like the taste of fast food. I'm happy my kids and wife are happy. I love just walking around here and enjoying the sights and sounds."

"But you're just buying the fried chicken, I notice," says Ghost.

"Sure thing. I don't need any of this other stuff."

"You are definitely not Everybody, then," Father Time finishes up and hobbles with his tray over to the trash bin.

By now, Wayne had adapted to rules of the workplace, just as potentially deadly and savage as those of any deep jungle. Always be wary, always be prepared, always be ready to fight or flee. Depending on species and rank of the person being confronted, modify certainty, arrogance, and humility. Like a chameleon, all happening subconsciously.

Furthermore, like all employees, he knew an appearance of working hard mattered quite a lot. Nobody could really tell—there was still enough mystery concerning his tasks that he could stare into space or doodle on a paper pad and someone would take it for deep thought (as it sometimes was.) But it was necessary, above all, to remain busy, to produce something by the end of each day. That deflected a lot of issues, even if all he did was mindlessly scroll through code, as long as he at least submitted a written analysis. On the other hand, all that really mattered when the bills came due were results.

Oddly, some problems requiring the most actual work showed the tiniest result. Some stuff painlessly and instantly fixed brought the biggest cheers. Unfortunately, however, he was unable to control which was which. Sometimes the greatest "fixes" were simply saying "no" to impossible requests, for which he received no credit nor billing at all.

He eventually discovered after a few years to never let small aggravations slide. Something operationally insignificant could remain a constant irritant to an account. He might toil on really difficult algorithms, sweat through uncertain and wretched updates, waste whole afternoons debugging shaky subroutines, but often none of that showed immediately. On the other hand, a misspelled or incorrectly colored word on the screen remained a bone of contention to be raised at every time billing conference. It became habit to devote every first hour to defusing trivial garbage, which cleared his hours to wrestle with real problems later.

Finally, he sadly realized that nothing is forever. It was tempting to believe that—like a painting—once a program was brought forth from primordial chaos and accepted to hang on the wall it would just stay happily there without any more intervention. Nope. There were always more tweaks, sometimes from new operating system upgrades, sometimes from hidden flaws, sometimes simply from universal perversity, but mostly from the client's natural human need for renovation and change.

Once he had all the main rules down, life wasn't bad at all. He found that he could live in this jungle, not perhaps as the top carnivore, but certainly claiming his own relatively secure niche in the ecology. Within such a limited framework, bounded by computer room walls, he could thrive.

Competitive societies force constant evaluations, and I was always either consciously or unconsciously checking to see how I was doing. I found it not a simple exercise. Besides, there were so many ways of going about it—almost as complicated as we are.

For example, the easiest was, I suppose, how was my career going. That should have been the easy one—what is the salary compared to everyone else. But it wasn't, really. It had to also take into account when and where I started, and what I thought the potential was. It had to factor in my relations to my family and life—there was always a chance to make more money at the expense of something I considered equally important. And regardless of salary, how did my job stand in prestige.

So you had the social view. Joan was keenly aware of wanting to be seen as upper middle class. She brought our children up that way, she thought that way, she tried to make me that way. She wanted friends and the world in general to see us as a professional, upwardly mobile family unit, a cut above the riff-raff. And each year, she compared us to others she considered our peers, and generally found us wanting—just a bit, but nevertheless behind. Keep up with the Joneses, or at least keep them in sight ahead of you.

Meanwhile, there was what I would call the tribal view, which was my own comparison to my colleagues and acquaintances at work. How did I stack up in what I did, in how I operated, in how I was perceived, in what might come next. I found the easiest thing here was to accumulate IOU's where I had done favors for others, hoping that I could cash some in if I had to. Generally, it was a small pond view. I couldn't ask how I was getting along

BABYLON WITH GHOST

compared to—say—the CEO's or the IBMers, but I certainly could keep an eye on how I was making out compared to coworkers and those I knew at the accounts, or met in conferences. It wasn't something I enjoyed much, but it was necessary.

Then you had the family view. Here we were on firmer ground, because everyone was happy to have the little children, and they were all healthy and happy and doing pretty well developmentally. Our parents were ecstatic at grandchildren. It was still too early for most of the comparison that naturally creeps in with getting older, still too early to worry much about native abilities and strengths. We were obviously warm, well-clothed, sheltered, fed, and not begging money. We fitted into more or less the same economic and social brackets as our parents had, so this was perhaps the smoothest comparison of all.

Nearly finally, there was the self-view. Where am I compared to where I wanted to be, or where I want to go. Have I done anything horrible that I should fix, do I have bad habits. The normal self-questioning that we all go through, in the dark of night, walking the beach, or sitting in traffic. I didn't wander into musing on my subconscious, but I mostly navigated by trying to remain happy first, proud second, and secure third.

I guess some people go to church, or psychiatrists for these exercises, but I found myself immersed in them, much more than I wanted to be, almost all the time.

I'm lying on my back, dim light filtering through gauze drapes on high windows, an echoing beige room, hardwood floor. Others breathing softly around me, countless others. I'm too relaxed to lift my head for a look. I suppose Ghost is somewhere nearby. But it is the reedy voice of Father Time that drifts softly through distant echoes.

"Breathe in slowly, slowly, all through your body, into your deepest abdomen. Hold and gather your troubles. Now push it into your legs, flow down your thighs, feel it curling around your knees, and out through the soles of your feet. Again. Deeper, slower. Again."

"You are falling memories back to being a small child. What do you feel? Who are you? Seek your happiness as that child."

I remember sunny days and sand and wind, hot summer winds with bugs, cold snows and sleds on a steep hill. Mostly I feel calm and happy, because everything is ok and I don't have to worry at all. Nothing to do but be alive and be good.

"Breathe again. Keep breathing. This will be more difficult. You are now a teenager."

Ah, that one, I feel confusion creep in. Loneliness and certainty and great optimism but deep fear. What was I going to do, where was I going to go, who would be with me? My breath loses some of the pleasant rhythm.

"And now, yes, breathe deeply, try to get back to the elemental, clear your body. That time finally passes. You are a fine young adult, peak of body and mind. Remember. Breathe."

Not for me. Confusion, hurt, drifting, thinking too much, nothing working. Then a miracle, then two, and sunrise with Joan and family. I manage a deep, surrendering sigh.

"Thirties … Notice how we are speeding up. Try to maintain control and balance even so."

Ah, better. On an expected track now, doing what I should, more warm approbation. Nominal security. Breathing here is pretty easy, even though there is so much to do.

The session continued on for a while. Father Time kept incrementing the years and decades, each difficult and wonderful in its own way. Finally he reached the eighties towards the nineties.

And then there was no need to breathe at all.

As part of his new middle-class existence, Wayne discovered he was accumulating weeks of true vacation each year. One was reserved in the summer to visit his parents in Pennsylvania. Another was to visit Joan's parents here in upstate New York, in a cabin near Lake Luzerne, a short forested distance from Lake George.

This July, he found himself surrounded by mosquito and deerfly-laden trees, restricted to the porch on the house unless he wanted endure little bites all over. He'd get up early as usual, but had to dress warmly to sit in the deep chill out there while drinking his coffee. Once everyone else got up, it was bedlam as lots of people tried to dress and eat breakfast in a tiny space. That out of the way, depending on weather, what would they do? For sure, the first order of business was up to an hour figuring out what was happening for dinner that night, a seemingly major goal of Grandpa.

Joan was completely happy, and Little Wayne and Gregory loved it, so Wayne endured. He never quite understood leaving the ocean and bay and beaches just when the weather was getting nice, but this made everyone feel like they were part of the American dream. They had the little cabin, they had the vacation home, they had made it. And there were a lot of vacation things to be done, in the completely unconsciously tacky and carefree American way. It was almost a step back into the fifties, complete with run-down roadside motels that had seen better days.

The saving grace, as far as he was concerned, was that he was completely cut off from the world. For this week, even Nick couldn't reach him. Accounts could burn down, computer disasters could multiply, and he would not know until he returned. Nobody had the phone number up here, and although he had promised to call in once, everyone knew there was absolutely nothing he could do, and no way he could return before next Monday. His mind could clear and think about important things.

He found there were no important things to think about. Everything was here, his family, his happiness, his hopes, his future. With the time he was so often lacking, that he so often thought he needed more of, there was nothing more to be done. He eventually realized that was a blessing.

Science claims we are related to the primates, some more closely than others. Primate activity varies—gorillas sit stolidly most of the day, monkeys are always in motion. We seem to share both traits. Even couch potatoes watching TV all day get bored sometimes.

It often appears, however, that we are more like the active monkeys we observe ceaselessly swinging from trees at the zoo. In spite of having all their needs satisfied all the time—they always have food and water and no predators to worry about—they spend a great deal of time teasing each other, playing, finding something to do that will irritate others. Just for the hell of it.

We do the same. Someone sitting and relaxing has a tonic effect on others who have to be working. There may be scorn or envy, but there is also an urge to bother them, to somehow go out of our way to make them engage in our particular hassles. Who does this guy think he is, we wonder, and manage to stand in front of him and attract his attention.

Joan was always good at this. The minute I sat down to read, she would decide I was free to do something she needed done. I admit, I have somewhat the same trait reciprocally. I guess it is innate. Probably that is why we never think we have enough time, no matter how much time we actually may have.

I'm sitting on the wooden sides of an old cart, lush farmland stretching away on either side, dusty dirt road behind and ahead. Hot sun beats down as heat ripples the far trees, insects loudly proclaim their right to be here. On the front bench, Old Man Time sits without his robe for a change, holds a switch in one hand, the other has a long stick with a carrot dangling in front of the donkey slowly pulling us forward. He croaks a greeting.

"I like this," I remark. "Think we can stay a while?"

"Not too long," he replies, "narrative has to move along, you know. Like you."

"But I'm just sitting here doing nothing," I protest.

"Well, it seemed a little cruel to stick you in this metaphorical dream as the donkey, but that would be more appropriate."

"Oh," I'm a little let down. "I guess I see …"

"There's only really three things I need to do to get us somewhere," he grinds on monotonously. "If this donkey decides to stand still I annoy him a little with my switch. Mostly, though, I just keep the carrot dangling the right distance in front, sometimes closer, sometimes farther."

"Yeah, yeah, I get it. I'm the donkey chasing the carrot of work and improvement because if I stop someone or something will hurt me."

"And the third thing?"

"Um, I don't know," I admit.

"See them there blinders, off to the side of his eyes?" he gestures ahead. "It's crucial that the poor beast never realizes all the good stuff that is all around and easily available if he just wanders off the road and ignores me."

Ooops. Zing.

Another New Year's. They seemed to be coming along faster these days. Wayne could barely stay awake, without the fuel of alcohol to keep his energy level. But somehow he made it through the television ball drop, kissed Joan ceremonially, and gratefully fell into bed. A good year, anyway, with more to come. he was sure.

There was little need to dwell on plans or resolutions—he had plans and resolutions every day. No grand changes for the future, he was all too aware of being a hostage to fortune at this point. He could control his job at JBS, but had no say in the economy, which ultimately determined if they would have a good or bad year economically. Take care of himself, the family, all the little things and let the bigger chips fall as they would.

He had, however, spent some time on introspection, which was not unusual. More importantly, he had devoted some quiet moments to simply remembering and trying to crystalize high points of the year just past for future reference. It was much too easy, he had found, to rush along in a fog and never notice the marvels he had gone through.

Marvels abounded. Gregory growing more interesting by the day, happy Little Wayne bouncing around everywhere, Joan grudgingly settling in exile here on the South Shore but seeing her relatives often enough to be happy. They'd done a lot of family stuff together, every week normally, special things all the time, gatherings with the cousins. And the job was percolating, with the excitement of the new machines and potential new accounts. Optimism was in the air, a heady perfume.

Perhaps there seemed to be a real lack of time to enjoy anything well. Perhaps he knew he would remain overwhelmed, sometimes to exhaustion, by the demands of his position. But all in all, he reflected as he drifted into a deep sleep, this had undoubtedly been one of the best years of their lives.

A wailing horn splits the smoke as bongo drums crescendo. I'm sitting on a pillow on the floor with a bunch of other folks gathered in some dim lights. Father Time has a kind of spotlight shining on his grey hair and beard, his sickle rests against the armchair. He begins to intone over the weird background.

> *What you wish do you truly want?*
> *Beware, beware the charms of tempting fate*
> *You may be granted something you regret*
> *This hour passes by just once.*

Bongos going crazy, soft braying from the trumpet. He takes a sip of water and hesitantly stands up.

> *You measure years as if they were important*
> *But each moment is the treasure that you have*
> *Rushing by so cheap so infinite*
> *You hardly pay them heed, but once again*
> *Beware!*

Bongos drop into a soft patter, trumpet mutes.

> *You care to greet me once a year*
> *But I am always ever here*
> *What you want and what you have*
> *Should always be in closest harmony*
> *For ...*

Dramatic slap and stillness of the drums.

> *Tomorrow may not happen!*

He vanishes in a swirl of grey smoke, to mild and puzzled applause.

Nice Saturday morning, walking the kids over to East Avenue along the quiet streets, waiting for Joan to get ready. Little Wayne in the stroller, Greg running along, and Wayne—well, he thought, the proper word is simply "truckin'".

Common culture liked to find its aphorisms and wisdom in contemporary songs, which wove a modern experience around timeless observations. The Grateful Dead provided some of that, at least to him, and like many songs it could get stuck in mind for a long time. Some times are good, some times are bad, but you always just keep moving on, forced by a beat just a little too pushy.

BABYLON WITH GHOST

For now, that's probably exactly what he was doing. Truckin' off to various good and horrible accounts, through wonderful and awful days, but mostly just making it through each set of days and weeks to the next payday. Truckin' through issues at home, fortunately less fraught, but still to be worked through to reach tomorrow.

And trying, always, to keep the tempo, the tune, the harmony, the countermelodies all in balance, providing the groundwork for his life. He had to admit that he had been in much worse times.

1988 ENDING BEGINNING

SUNDAY

BRILLIANTLY BRIGHT, TEN in the morning early August, clear blue overhead. Wayne led his parade through side roads towards 7-11 to buy two fat Sunday papers. Still quiet around the neighborhood, only birds and the distant sound of cars rushing along the Southern State. Everyone was talkative, he chattered back with half a mind, his thoughts not really elsewhere but expanded beyond the moment. This time, he thought, was the absolute best.

He'd awakened at seven as usual, dressed and ready before eight, shut the door to the bedroom to let Joan sleep on her one day of rest. Well, it was his too, but he never really had been able to sleep very late. She certainly deserved her repose. Gregory got himself ready these days without help, and Little Wayne was not particularly hard to wash and dress.

They'd made pancakes from scratch in the kitchen. From his days teaching preschool, Wayne knew how much young children loved to cook. There was magic in turning fairly yucky ingredients into something delicious. The gooey mess was fun in itself. Gregory could almost handle the task alone by now, measuring out flour, baking powder, oil and milk, mixing correctly. Little Wayne seemed more interested in coating himself with flour and dough. Today they had added some canned corn for interest. Both boys were excited to cook on the gas stove because it seemed dangerously grown up, although the younger needed help using the spatula.

In no time they had a nice stack of fluffy round objects, piled on a plate. The happiest moment occurred when finally pouring syrup on top. Maple-flavored-sugar-cheap-stuff, but it tasted wonderful. Wayne did insist on pats of real butter between each layer, even though Joan would disapprove. He let them use table knives to cut their own, even Wayne could handle that sticky chore by now. Cleanup took a bit longer, especially since he let them help, but it was done soon enough and they were out the door.

So they had a day before them. The morning was his—if he could keep them busy until twelve or one Joan would be extremely grateful. Later today they might do—well, who knew? There were infinite fine activities available on a beautiful summer day.

They walked into the store and he picked out a New York Times and Newsday. In those days, before the internet, the papers weighed a ton, freighted with advertisements and want ads and local announcements. He slipped both into his empty backpack because he knew he might have to carry Wayne part of the way back. He resisted calls for candy. They were wise enough not to push the issue.

He paid more attention to their questions on the way back, and had nice conversations about weeds and berries and insects, pointing out some of the species he recognized. He listened to tales from Gregory's school. Eventually he did have to scoop Wayne up and tote him on his shoulders the rest of the way.

Ghost appears in a swirl of colors, not particularly looking like anything. "What, out of ideas already?" I ask.

"Maybe too many, maybe just worn down," replies Ghost.

"Well, you could let it go for a while. This is a quiet topic anyway. I'm simply taking breaks …"

"What, Little Wayne not even four, only two of them, and you needed a break already?" Ghost laughs.

"Hey, we had learned the value of some time off at day care. We were always a little more ready for dealing with the constant aggravations when we had some time to ourselves. Besides, Joan and I had both always wanted some moments of privacy."

"So when did you get yours?"

"Actually, it turned out to be on those long commutes. If I turned off the radio and just enjoyed the ride (or the frequent stop and go) I had quiet time with nobody able to reach me."

"No cell phone?"

"Nope, not yet."

"Ah, those were the days."

Wayne always had thought that children around ten or eleven were ideal, but he had changed a bit during his preschool hours with the much younger set. Three to eight, he realized, was what most people dream of when then think of their own family. Too young to get into much trouble, old enough to take care of themselves, and cute always.

The years of teaching had helped both of them in that. They had honed their approaches to discipline and reward, were fully aware of the importance of environment, but didn't sweat minor setbacks. They never had to read books on parenting or join any support groups other than their parents on how to get along.

It was possible, even then, to go off the deep end. Wayne had known young couples in Berkeley who felt clothes for children were stupid, others who fed them only certain exotic foods, others who thought any discipline was a permanent inhibition of creativity. Heck, they knew some strange parents even now. But they had seen enough kids to realize how they all basically turned out all right if you just provided an enjoyable and secure environment. No need to learn Mozart before they toddled. No training in ancient Greek. Picture books read over and over by a parent were pretty good stimulus.

Getting uptight when kids were so young was a waste. This was, after all, the time when they were the most joy. Watching them become enchanted by various aspects of the world, satisfying curiosity when possible, laughing over their sayings and mishaps. Family life didn't get much better.

If you took the time, of course. There was the rub. Even Wayne's relatively modest software career ate pretty heavily into family time. Two or more hours commuting, nine or more hours on the job, certain nights studying new books or outlining projects and fixes—no not a lot of hours spilling over. Joan was equally caught up in her school job, shopping for food and clothes, paying attention to her parents, and dealing with the constant modern aggravations of any people living—rent, banks, checks, repairs, whatever. And constant trips to the pediatric doctor. And the never ending demands and requests from the school system for parent meetings and evaluations.

Even the weekends were packed. Just a lot of chores, although they tried to divide and share the children as possible, making trips as much fun as they could while getting things done. But, no question, there were never enough hours in the day.

When Joan got up and ready and was having her coffee and reheated pancakes, Wayne sat down opposite her at the kitchen table and asked the usual question: "Well, what shall we do today?"

"I don't know. What would you like to do?"

"Well, I was thinking of the arboretum. The kids like to run around and explore the island there, and it's beautiful and has a nice breeze off the bay."

"How about Overlook Beach? We haven't been to the ocean much yet."

"Sure, that would be fine. Might be crowded on the causeway, you know."

"That's OK. We could stay for a few hours—do you know the tide?"

"No idea, but I can check the paper. Doesn't matter much anyway. I don't want to stay too long though, I do have work tomorrow even though you guys are doing nothing. "

"We're always doing something," answered Joan with an edge. "We have to start getting the back to school stuff, and the fall clothing. And my parents might come over."

"Well, you know what I mean."

"Yeah, I know, and you're wrong."

"What time can you be ready? I can start to pack the car. Eat here or pack lunch?"

"Oh, it's a lot easier to have lunch here. I'll just put together some water and snacks for the afternoon."

"So we can be out in an hour or so, say one?"

"I guess so."

They called to the kids playing in the sandbox in the back yard, who cheered at the news. The seaside was always fun.

You can never do everything. We always wanted the best for the kids, but the best was always a question. You spend money to send them off with others, or take the time to do things with them yourself, and you are never sure which is best for their tender little psyches. Not to mention your own.

Unless you live in some remote self-sufficient mountain cabin, you never have the time necessary to be with them all the time and do all the things you would like to do, or worse, think you should do. And if you do live in a remote cabin, you will be certain that their isolation is making them little monsters, and often doing the same things over and over for day after day can be incredibly boring for everyone. Life demands had picked up with a strong career and with Joan's reentry into teaching. Fortunately, school had taken up much of the extra time for Gregory, and Wayne would be starting preschool in the fall. That didn't help with the weekend exhaustion, of course.

It was hard. Work all week, housekeeping and child care. Do chores and shopping and inevitable problems with cars and so forth on Saturday, if possible. Fit in visits to parents and relatives and friends. Sunday was a great time to do family activities, but I had to be ready bright and shiny every Monday for another hard week. As it turned out, this was a brief but glorious time in our lives, full of happiness and wonder. But also filled with tiredness.

Fortunately, and most aggravatingly, children grow up as they will regardless of what you surround them with. Most of the time how offspring turn out as they grow older is a complete mystery. That's one of the hardest adjustments as a parent—to realize how little control you actually have. They are never replicas of you in any way. They rarely follow exactly what you suggest. No matter what, other people's children, no matter how stupidly you think the parents may have acted with them, usually turn out fine and often better than your own. It should be humbling, but more often it makes us a bit angry.

Ghost glides down a stone aisle in drab priest robes. He solemnly intones

"So how do you think you did, all in all?" If his voice were any deeper, the stones walls would be falling from vibration.

"About what?"

"Bringing Wayne and Gregory up. In final judgement, which you must be ready for, were you successful or should you have done something different?"

"Final judgement? Add some melodrama, why don't you. Geesh."

Ghost swishes incense, which has appeared on a long chain. I almost choke. "True answers now, my son."

I guess I have to play along to get out of this. "I don't think much about it—we don't get another chance after all. Things worked out well enough, I guess. I'm not sure anything we did differently would have made a big difference. And, of course, nobody never really identifies the key issues."

"Unless they go into psychotherapy," Ghost grins maliciously in his darkened hood, "misguided though that dark art may be."

"Not even then, as far as I'm concerned. Childhood and adults are almost as mysterious as the future itself. Like I said, I'm happy with how it all turned out. I'm not quite sure what better would mean—there's always tradeoffs even if you can identify what you want to do and if you are right—which is rare."

"You're quite the pessimist."

"Realist. I've seen enough children to have some perspective. Hell, I've talked to enough adults who grew up all kinds of ways to have even more perspective. It ain't simple."

"And not easy …."

"Well, actually it is pretty easy. They keep growing, after all, and you have to keep dealing with one thing after another. Most of the time you really don't have a lot of choices."

"So what was most important?"

"I think," I replied slowly, thinking about it honestly, "that the most important thing is that we enjoyed every instant with them that we could, no matter what, and tried to give them the same attitude. Everything else—important stuff too, like discipline—followed that basic pattern of respect for ourselves and each other and the world. The moments you have are the only moments you have, forever and ever."

"Amen," he mutters, sliding away into a rising mist.

Of course, they could not always agree. Sometimes, especially in mid spring, when the weather was still frequently awful, the arguments about how to spend a wonderful Sunday afternoon would become intense. Wayne would be so deep in software projects he could hardly come up for air, Joan would be under the most intense pressure from substituting at school, the kids would be wound up tightly from being stuck indoors too much, and all in all they knew if they didn't get out somehow they might explode. And yet, perversely, they had almost no energy to do anything, almost not enough to contemplate doing anything.

"Well, we could always go over to see Mom and Dad," Joan always said.

"I don't know," answered Wayne, "can't we just stay home and let me read or something."

"Gregory's restless," she answered, "and you haven't seen my parents in a while anyway."

Oh, that again. "But I did see them a few weeks ago...."

"They won't be around forever, you know. We don't have anything better to do and they really like seeing the kids. You can walk them down to the harbor there for a little while."

"Oh, ok," he agreed reluctantly. "But I don't want to stay too late. I need a little time to relax too, you know."

"Yes," she sighed. "We all do."

Figuring out what to do when you are on your own can be paralyzing— so many options and conflicting ideas. Adjusting to being a couple is much harder. Throw in externalities like work, relatives, and young family and pressure threatens to explode the boiler.

Marital strife is inevitable, as is pretty much all strife if you are part of a group. You work out ways to deal with most of it. For Joan and I, who fortunately had known each other well for a long time before attempting children, a good deal of sanity centered on each knowing the other's breaking points, and respecting needs to occasionally get away from it all. Just as importantly, the importance of occasionally giving in unconditionally. A clear win could be a complete reset.

We recognized danger signals, and unless we were too wound up or strung out we knew when it was appropriate to back off and when we could push some more. Fortunately, we had few other distractions—neither Joan nor I were ever into "my night out," for example. Both of us tended to enjoy family activities more than anything else except when stuff really got too sticky. So, all in all, we got along without extensive fighting.

Ghost floats in looking like Sigmund Freud, with monocle, "Ah, so you also lost control of ze children, no?"

"No, nothing like that. In fact, Joan thought I was way too strict."

"Und, you would be in jail today, ya?"

"Give it up Ghost. I didn't hurt them, I'd just slap them occasionally on the rump or tap them on the head to get their attention. The only really physical punishment was holding their arm so they couldn't run away when they were being obnoxious."

"Zen how do you explain keeping control."

"Oh, my method was simple. As soon as they understood language I was able to make escalating minor threats."

"Oh, threats, threats they are nothing, everybody does zis."

"Ah, but I had learned the secret in VISTA to never make promises or threats you can't keep. Mine were effective because they knew I meant it, however painful. And not letting them watch TV for two hours or so at night, or not playing with a favorite toy for one evening, were harder on me than on them. But once the pattern was established I could start with a really innocuous punishment, but they knew the escalator was in effect, and it worked remarkably well."

"And Joan, in all this?"

"Well, she was more lenient but mostly supported me. I guess we also played the good cop bad cop routine that everyone else does. Anyway, whatever the combination, it worked well and we are very happy not only with how they behaved as children but as how they grew up."

"Ah, but vat vould their psychiatrist say, eh?"

"Frankly, my dear, I don't give a damn."

Frequently in the summer Wayne would take the gang out to Bethpage Historical Village, a collection of nineteenth century buildings moved into a little "hidden valley," complete with dirt roads and traditional farm animals. He had a Long Island Heritage family membership, so entrance was free except for buying fake money to get refreshments, and on Sunday mornings in particular it was practically deserted.

They strolled down the central dirt road, enjoying the views over the fields to the sides, reminding Wayne of his own early childhood. Insects flitted about and the song of summer rose unmolested by most sounds of surrounding industry. About a half mile brought them to the center of the "village" recreation, but most of the time there were no active demonstrations going on in the blacksmith or cooper sheds. They did sometimes tour one or more of the houses, like the old schoolhouse up the hill a way.

Usually, they happily wandered straight through and up to the farm on the other side. This was really the high point of the trip. There were ugly big fat smelly pigs, huge complacent cows, and a couple of oxen which barely moved anything except their tails. These could be stared at for a while hanging onto the old wooden fences around them. The flock of sheep was usually pretty far away, but there were plentiful ducks and chickens for Little Wayne to chase, while Gregory tended to concentrate more on the numerous butterflies. It was safe, and relaxing, and totally different from everything else they encountered in their normal day to day life.

They'd always go into the big old working barn, with its rusty implements and musty smell of straw stored in the lofts overhead. Various farm oddities had been collected and were presented pretty much at random, for the kids to question and Wayne to try to answer as best he could remember or guess. A few times they would go through the farmhouse to marvel at the ancient cookware in the kitchen, actually used periodically for cooking, but mostly empty when they were there.

Then it was back down the shady lane and over the tiny stream and into the village once more, where they would stop at the "Noonday Tavern" and use their fake old money to buy glasses of birch beer and pretzel sticks. Sitting at the old wooden tables, looking out the original wavy glass windows, talking of nothing and everything like philosophers of old, they passed eventually a few hours.

Then it was time to go back and see Mom and figure out what the rest of the day held. Little Wayne was often tired by them, so Wayne would put him on his shoulders most of the way back to the car. Gregory, on the other hand, never ran out of energy and was more ready than anyone else for adventure that afternoon.

Babylon had a lot of options, and was a demonstration of why families had loved Long Island so much. There were special activities all year round, like the Octoberfest in Lindenhurst when the streets would close, or Santa coming around on a fire truck in December throwing out candy, or lots of little craft fairs scattered here and there at odd times when the weather was good. The Fourth of July was a private fireworks extravaganza, with each family seemingly trying to outdo the other.

In walking distance there were a few small wild areas, a tiny shopping corridor along x street, and the mysterious isolation of Southard's pond. Within five miles driving was the large expanse of Belmont Lake state park, great for a bicycle ride or renting rowboats (which they never did, but fun to watch.) In one direction was the just-correctly-sized cute Adventureland amusement park, geared to small children with water rides, an antique roller coaster, bumper cars and assorted treats for all, still managing to remain inexpensive. Not so inexpensive as the actual "dollar movie" theater in Lindenhurst, somehow managing to hang on with good children's fare year after year. In the other direction was Argyll lake with fabulous waterfalls at one end, or fishing from the yellow-jacket infested Babylon town docks on the Great South bay. Walking through Babylon village, maybe visiting the old variety store, could pass a few hours. And that was without tapping all the cornucopia that lay outside the five mile radius, but still within a twenty minute or so drive, like the ocean beaches.

And for the bad weather, there was always shopping. The South Shore was built for shopping—many of its denizens ignored all the attractions mentioned above and beelined to various giant indoor malls and stores and strip malls filled with as-yet-unglobalized merchandise to fascinate and clutter the home.

BABYLON WITH GHOST

Ghost has his judicial robes on. "I notice none of these so-called enrichment activities has much money involved," he stares as well as he can. "Didn't you feel you were cheating them a bit?"

"What, by not spending money we didn't have?"

"Other people borrow what is necessary, you know."

"Well, we didn't like being in debt. Besides, we always thought we could do a better job than anyone we would hire or any activity they could get into. They had lots of socialization at school, and there were always the relatives. No, we never felt guilty."

"Until later, you mean," he intones.

"Well, once in a while, Joan will wish out loud that we had sent them to some private school or other, or forked over the money for what has become normal childhood expenses like special art summer sessions or extensive soccer travel teams. I'm still against all that stuff. But you do wonder a little."

"So they got cheated out of what they might have been and who they might have met," he accuses.

"Everything is a tradeoff. Public school and family had been more than enough for me and Joan. We enjoyed them and didn't want them gone all the time. And we really didn't have much money anyway."

"Well nobody agrees with you any more."

"Helicopter parents. Stupid. Childhood as serious mini-adulthood. Stupid. There should be more joy in our world, less grim buckling down. I detest all that modern crap, and it too will pass."

"So you do admit your children were unfortunately restricted."

"I admit nothing. Life is a gamble, but the only certainty in each day is you should grab every bit of happiness you can. If you can pass that on to your offspring, you have done a lot."

After paying at the gatehouse on the way to the parking lot at Bayard Cutting Arboretum, they parked up near the main house and the kids took off across the verdant lawn, just yelling and stretching in the glory of wide open safe spaces. Those were the days before lyme disease and countless other worries made playing on grass a forbidden adventure for most, so Wayne and Joan let them run around as they would, just enjoying the chance themselves to take a deep breath, unwind, and appreciate the magnificent trees under a perfect blue sky.

"Ok guys, c'mon with us," called Wayne finally. "Joan, you want to walk over through the azalea area?"

"Fine. It's probably muddy, though."

"Shouldn't be too bad. That brings us out to the island pretty soon, and they like that."

The azalea trail must be magnificent in the spring, but they had never made it out while in bloom. So it was a kind of dark and tangled wood, dark dirt paths tunneling through shadowy entwined branches. A wonderful place for imagination, always reminding Wayne of fairy tales. He never got lost and knew more or less where he was going, the kids didn't care where they were busy in their own minds, but Joan was always feeling lost. Still, it was natural, and relaxing, and all the outside world became separated and shut away. For a while they were just themselves, a complete family, having a wonderful Sunday afternoon.

Eventually the trail came out over a bridge and along a widening stream, until it reached a little dam also arched over. They sat for a while and watched the swans and ducks as other couples went by, Little Wayne and Gregory inspecting insects and looking closely in the water for fish. Then it was on to the high point of the visit.

A little lump of land, an acre at best, was mounded up high with soil, trees, and glacial boulders, separated from the park by a dark tidal channel three feet wide over which a wooden bridge led invitingly. Although it would appear on no maps, this was the perfect definition of an island: isolated, self-contained, large and yet small at the same time. A big group of rocks dominated the high points making a natural fortification. Paths led everywhere, and scrub brush and poison ivy filled in the spaces, adding just enough hint of danger to make it interesting.

The brochures said it was named "Treasure Island." Somehow Gregory had dubbed it "Coney Island" and he and Little Wayne whooped their way over and around playing Indians or superheroes or whatever the current cartoon fad might be. It disturbed some of the more sedate patrons, but after all it was outdoors and they were mostly behaving and as far as Wayne was concerned those older glum people could use being a little less sedate.

After a pretty long playtime, they went back across the bridge and walked the long esplanade along the bay, marveling at a huge boathouse opposite gaping open into inky darkness, a relic probably of bootlegging days. When

BABYLON WITH GHOST

Little Wayne got tired he once again got a ride on shoulders. Birds were everywhere, ducklings following their mother, occasional boats going by in the channel. Again they sat and rested and enjoyed being.

Finally they went back up the lawn and visited the manor house to use the bathroom before heading back. An afternoon well spent, when they had become refreshed by nature and the beauty of the world, free of the contamination of modern bustle and convenience.

Ghost arrives in his favorite Republican garb, suit and tie, little button reading "Free Enterprise", straw hat with red white and blue ribbon, a stern taskmaster. "So an afternoon spending nothing, doing nothing, accomplishing nothing, wasting time and going nowhere," he accuses.

"The happiest times of our lives," I agree.

"You can't be serious," he begins.

"Absolutely. This was precisely what Joan and I always thought our lives should be all about, children, family, happiness, contentment."

"And no thought for the future."

"The present is quite important, you know."

"But what kind of lesson were you giving your poor children. Surely they were losing out compared to their peers."

"Nonsense. It was Sunday, a spiritual day. I think more people should spend less time begging God to give them extra money or a bigger house or wider recognition, and more time thanking God for giving us ourselves and our world to appreciate in all our magnificence."

"You were going nowhere," he repeats.

"I liked it right there," I state smugly.

Little Wayne had dozed in his car seat on the way back, and was playing upstairs in Gregory's room. Quietly, they usually got along pretty well, although Gregory did tend to be bossy. Joan was rummaging around the kitchen, thinking about dinner. Wayne was settled on the sofa in the living room, beginning the trek through the world of the New York Times. The phone rang shrilly.

Wayne answered it with a sinking feeling. "Hello. Oh, hi Nick. What's up?"

He knew already that what was up was what was down, something failing somewhere. Nick called with problems, not to chat. And always with directions. Almost always on Sunday afternoon.

"Tell? What went wrong? Oh." Tell Chocolate was a strange little account on the Coney Island boardwalk, maker of rather cheap confectionary primarily for the holiday season, chocolate Santa Clauses and the like. They had an old "standard" system 34, as far as Wayne was concerned something from the middle ages held together with faith and baling wire. But of course they helped pay the bills.

"Oh, update, huh?" About the only thing that could go wrong, really. Periodically, IBM would send required fixes which had to be applied physically in those days before computers were connected to anything other than their local terminals. The means of distribution were giant 8" diameter "floppy disks" which were really floppy round sheets of magnetized plastic encased in a paper folder, to be inserted in an appropriate slot in the machine. With printed instructions often many pages long. So many things could go wrong—bad disk, scratched disk, unexpected read errors. JBS was always trying to get these simple tasks done by the junior people, but the junior people had trouble more often than not. Something had messed up for Pat, and the console was in a funky state.

"Ok, ok. I guess I can be there pretty early, sometime around eight or so." Monday mornings were the worst, the Southern State westbound was a parking lot by seven am, even in the supposedly lighter traffic of summer. The Belt Parkway was under perpetual construction and jammed twenty four hours a day. If he didn't get done before three (and often if he did) it would take over two hours to get home even if there were no unexpected accidents. At least the weather was supposed to be good.

"Sure, no problem, I have another copy in the car. I'll call tomorrow to let you know what's going on."

Well, a nasty day for sure. In his own mind and Nick's, none of this could be his fault. It was all IBM and purely canned. But in the minds of the client, they were IBM and it was purely Wayne's fault they would be down for a day while he fixed whatever the company had messed up.

"OK, Joan, I have to get up around five to get out of here by six," he told Joan, and went back to losing himself in the affairs of the planet.

Breaking Futures

"I MEAN IT, Frank," said Nick, settling comfortably in the office at Prestige Distributors in the heart of Jamaica, Queens. "This new computer is revolutionary. It's just like the really big ones IBM has been selling for years, and yet small and priced almost like the System 34 you have."

"They say that about everything that comes out, though," replied Frank. "And they all cost more money. Why shouldn't we just keep expanding what we have."

"Well, for one thing, you are near the end of lifetime. IBM has already announced it will be ending support and updates sometime in the near future. Then you will be really out on a limb."

"What's so great about this new wonder?"

"I've got brochures right here," Nick reached into his briefcase, "and I can get you invitations to special events for prospective business clients to give you professional demonstrations." Frank waved dismissingly, he knew he had better things to do with his time than to attend sales seminars. "Wayne has been attending classes for some time now. Technical stuff, of course."

Frank and Wayne got along fairly well, although with this older machine Wayne had been by infrequently. Wayne thought carefully—a pause that always worked to somehow impress folks used to hearing a prepared instant spiel as if silence were deadly. He had recently squirmed through countless interminable lectures, and was genuinely excited about radically new architecture which he truly believed was futuristic in all the right ways. And yet, he also remained wary of hype and oversell. More than a whiff of BS had wafted through the glittering presentations.

"Mostly," Wayne replied honestly, "it is about the future. Right out of the box, it's not going to be a lot different than what you have. But the internal architecture is built for painless massive expansion—like more terminals—as well as being faster, more secure, and more reliable. Sometime soon, you may want remote communication to—say—one of your warehouses. For that matter, we will be able to fix most problems over the phone from our office. And the most important thing, probably, is that it is what IBM is betting its future on. They swear this particular architecture will be around for decades."

"Expensive, though."

"The most shocking thing," Wayne continued, "is how small it is. It seems more like a footstool than your 34. On the other hand, that gives you more space to use."

"And we can keep our current software and hardware?"

"Yeah, especially initially. Your printer's fine, you may want to get the new color terminals sometime soon. Your software will—technically—run, but not in what they call 'native mode', so until we get around to a rewrite you can't take full advantage of some of the new features."

That was fudging it a little—all the operating system routines would have to be converted and tweaked. But sales calls were always like that, some truth, some hope, some kinda lies. Frank surely knew the routine because as a business owner, he had to do the same thing himself.

Beige walls, large windows survey manicured grounds in the dead of winter. I recognize many colleagues, here in a large conference room. A banner over the front whiteboard proclaims "Welcome to Expanded Minds Seminar."

Casually dressed Ghost confronts pale statues of geeky computer types around an oversized table in a conference room. A slide projects "Expand Your Focus!" onto a big screen. Lights are low, everyone is leaning back or taking notes on paper pads. No computers or phones in the entire room. "Back to the dark ages," I remark.

"They were, weren't they?" Ghost turns off all the other attendees.

"Quite a setup, here. You being well paid?"

"If it were real, I'd be rolling in dough. These consultants often did. The premise was we were finally leaving the dark ages, you know."

"Or maybe entering the wonder years would be more appropriate. Nobody was quite sure of anything and promises were given easily."

"What were the biggest lies, do you think?" Ghost asks.

"Definitely the ones we told ourselves. Everyone existed in his (we were all men) little world, and everyone had his own little fantasies."

"Examples?"

"Oh, the owner thought he would automate the business finally and get a lock on his slower moving competitors. The IBM guys thought that finally they could stomp out the pesky little minis and micros crowding into their territories. The consultants thought that they could become the most proficient the fastest and claim immense empires in new uncharted possibilities. Programmers were filled with science-fiction ideas of what they might do in half the time, and spectacular feats worthy of heroes of old."

"But ..."

"But none of it was really true. This was just another step, although there was one thing that was, in fact true."

"That was?"

"Oh, two really. The AS400 actually did hang around forever—it's still out there in an evolved form, going strongly in data centers. And the science fiction and all the rest was coming. It just wasn't necessarily associated only or even primarily with IBM and its similar systems."

"What do you think now?"

"Work is always work, and always will be. Dreams are something else."

All dozen staff gathered in the office, confused and worried. Packing crates and cables were still lying around. "Now that we finally have our own machine," announced Nick proudly, "we can start looking at our plans in detail. Wayne, can you give us a summary of what we need to do next?"

"Basically, it is not as hard as it looks. Our System 38 accounts are no-brainers, they just slide over with a pretty simple conversion, but most of them don't need to do anything. There are a few tricks, but mostly the code base is the same and the interfaces for us are all the same. Later on, there will be new things, but if anyone upgrades it's just because the new AS400 is cheaper and faster and uses a lot less electricity."

"Not to mention," added Nick, "that the maintenance costs are much less, and the 38 is due for early non-support."

"Those won't affect us much," Wayne finished, "because all of our 38 accounts are already on the native code base."

"The 36 and 34 is a different story, right?" asked Kate.

"Much different. The 34 is DOA right now, without ongoing support. The 36 is well into end-of-life. When they eventually migrate, there will be some work. The client may not notice much at first, we can convert the 36 RPG no problem. Any operating system interfaces—night stream, backups, updates—are radically different—we will need to rewrite everything. Accounts must send operators for training. It's a big change for them. And for the rest of us—well, those of you not familiar with the system 38 stuff I've been showing you are going to have to take crash courses in the new editors and design tools, especially the screen. If you are using our AS400 here to make fixes, it's going to be really hard until you start to understand it. So mostly, we are going to do customer patching on site."

"Now the 34 ..." began Laney, since she supervised those legacy machines from way back.

"Almost impossible without a rewrite," stated Wayne. "They are probably better off just starting with new IBM packages for the basic accounting stuff, and letting us do some custom code for the rest. I'm not sure how they will handle it "

"Badly," laughed Nick. "But we can actually start charging more since there will now be a lot less competition in that arena until they are ready to upgrade. Most of the ones I know seem to have almost no intention to do anything for as long as they can."

"Same issue, of course, only more so. Everything will have to be done on site—we will no longer have the facilities in our office."

"Tell them about the communications ..." added Nick.

"Oh, yeah, for those who haven't talked with me, we finally have full communications support. The AS400 requires a dedicated phone line for IBM support, and we can tap into that with our terminals here and our own phone. So you can sign in from here on our AS400 and get into anyone else's AS400 if we have set it up and you have the login and credentials. It's quite fast too."

"Wow. That will help a lot," remarked Kate. Everyone stared dreamily into space, imagining doing fixes and debugs and operator support from the office, instead of taking a two hour trip into Brooklyn to find out that one tiny bit of data had to be changed.

Wayne discovered that dealing with IBM with their fancy new environment was in some ways more painful than handling the clients. In fact, the hardest part of working with the customers was that they had all been promised the moon and stars and just about anything else imaginable by the hard-nosed IBM sales reps. Nothing could work as flawlessly as was claimed. Nothing would dramatically change the business bottom line overnight. Most of their savvier clients were cynical enough to be aware of that, but even so the starry eye syndrome too often had infected even the operators and data users.

It was Wayne's primary job to deal with any bugs that showed up, to bridge any gaps that might isolate one platform from another, to discover the hidden gotchas tucked away or ignored in the software manuals. Things "of course" did not work the way they might seem to have. He spent a lot of time on the phone with technical support. Technical support was often clueless. In the days before common internet lookup, finding solutions was tough, and once found were almost never available to the public.

Security was one real issue, out of the gate. The older machines had almost none—they were, after all, generally isolated and locked into some computer room. Besides, for years computers had seemed so esoteric that only a few people would even venture to work with them beyond the screens presented. But the new ones—well they came connected to the world. They came with all kinds of fancy new capabilities for users. They came with issues such as—how do you keep payroll information from being accessible to the data workers, or—almost as contentiously—how do you keep sales information private for certain salesmen and upper level management. IBM had philosophy and solutions gleaned from years of work with big accounts.

But big accounts had big staffs, and dedicated security people, and manuals and plans and the time to work on all that bureaucratic nonsense. Most of Wayne's accounts did not. They had one computer operator—often not even dedicated—with a backup who might be some kind of semi-intern. JBS was their computer staff. Somebody they could sue. IBM would have nothing to do with it—training, they said, was available.

Wayne quickly found that trying to apply security to objects as recommended would tie everything in knots. But most of the owners had been scared out of their boots by horror stories in the management magazines about data hackers and operations room theft. "Protect the data, protect us," they screamed, even though it might tie operations into knots, and even though they continued to throw out all their confidential reports into the dumpster clear and unshredded.

Like all programmers, he had used tricks even on the 38 to make things easier and faster. All those had been taken away. Of course, there were new tricks, but they took time to learn, and more effort to figure out their own quirks. And some things commonly available had simply vanished.

Interesting times.

I look back and know those were the last of the slow times in computers. Oh, they had become increasingly common and necessary during the previous decade, some of the novelty had worn off and they were being accepted as business, professional, and personal tools. We thought we understood the future trajectory of the industry, and those of us in programming were ready for what was coming.

In retrospect, we were like the simple villagers rushing out into the exposed sea bottom to collect treasures as the waters withdrew more and more. An earthquake had occurred somewhere that did not register on our senses, and soon the tsunami would arrive destroying and reshaping everything. The village would never be the same, for once the first wave was past, this tsunami just kept growing and growing. That was the effect of communications.

In 1988, we were excited that we could finally, easily, connect to the client computer system. Clients were excited that they could finally, clumsily, exchange information between different systems, such as PC's and mainframes.

The most critical people were even starting to receive insanely large and expensive cell phones. But—in only ten years this environment would be unrecognizable, good old days, subject only to nostalgic or humorous stories at the gathering of the older professionals.

I think it is typical that sometimes the professionals, deepest in the business, the best and the brightest at their craft, are also the most clueless about the larger trends. Horse trainers and carriage makers were the last to understand the long term impacts of automobile technology. To be fair, nobody understood those impacts fully, but people who were supposed know about local transportation needs were most in the dark. And, from my perspective, it was the same thing in the binary world.

We thought there would be central computers, computer rooms, terminals. We did not know that they would all connect to everything, that users would be cruising the world of other machines all the time, that paper manuals would go away, that updates and viruses would be arriving instantaneously all the time, that children would understand logic and algorithms intuitively from their games. We surely did not foresee a time when people walked freely anywhere but connected to every bit of information in the world. We kept our heads down, wrote the next line of code, and did not hear the inrushing water.

Ghost walks over to the whiteboard and dramatically writes "FUTURE !!!" with a red marker. "But surely you were thinking about what to do next …"

"Oh, we thought about it all the time. We just thought wrong. For example, that the AS400 would destroy the minicomputer business—at least as it related to anything outside of engineering—and probably end the role of the dreaded microcomputer in the executive offices. It was worse than wrong—it was totally irrelevant."

"Somebody must have realized …."

"No, you don't understand," I shout. "We all thought in terms of the local centralized brain. Even the PC's were local centralized brain. Each computer was autonomous, fed information, putting out other information. We never even thought of them as an ecology. Manufacturers worked very hard to keep their brands as isolated as genetic species. But that paradigm was wrong."

"So communication changed all this."

"I don't need to repeat what is common in any literature about the industry. The point is simply that none of us saw it, and the few that had a glimpse were generally unable to take advantage of their ideas. An idea too far ahead is as useless for putting bread on the table as falling behind changing circumstances. Lots of brilliant people failing in many ways ...."

"A Leonardo Da Vinci club."

"Precisely."

The AS400 seemed to be a big change for the operators at all the accounts. At first it seemed like less of a change for the professionals who serviced it. Immediately, it was a disappointment for the owners, not in terms of performance but of appearance.

"Small is beautiful," had not yet become important. Nobody bragged about how tiny their cellphone or house or car might be. And if a business laid out umpty dump thousands of dollars for a computer, they preferred it to look impressive, at least the size of a refrigerator, preferably several refrigerators, with blinking lights all over and a comforting set of dials, knobs, buttons and other junk clustered. Then they could take associates on grand tours of their empires and point out how modern they were, how much they had invested in technology, how formidable their business looked.

The AS400 was—well, wimpy is the word. About two by three by three feet, a miracle of compactness and what IBM had decided was modern elegant design. The back panel had connectors for power, coax cables and phone line. On the front there was one small slit for newfangled tiny diskettes, and a couple of status lights. Even with the required uninterrupted power supply battery, it took up a fraction of the space of the older 34 and 36. Proudly pointing out the new acquisition, for the company president, might evoke laughter rather than envy.

And the computer operators and programmers quickly came to hate the lack of lights. They didn't blink. In all previous versions of systems, the blinking lights—while meaningless in themselves—at least allowed you to tell where a system might be in a boot process or if it was frozen—familiar things to any home computer user who watches the lights nervously while it boots up or runs. The lack of these lights meant nobody knew if it was actually starting, frozen, about to bring up the first operator screen, or whatever. What Wayne always thought of as "the clueless Mikey intern design" ("Hey, Mikey needs something to do") where the appearance was left to the last minute and to someone who had never worked in a computer environment in their life. This approach was rapidly changed in subsequent models.

The reason for the external power supply was that if this machine was shut down suddenly with a power blackout, it might take all day (or never) to come back. There was too much happening internally to keep check-pointing in a easily recoverable way. Unfortunately, the knowledge that there had to be an uninterruptible power supply meant that system designers were left to run wild assuming there could never, ever, possibly be a power interruption. As many places found, when the batteries were low, or the supply misbehaved, or simply when the power went off and the machine couldn't be reached easily (say in a blizzard at night) power failure could occur. The operating system was supposed to detect this and at least force a minimum state as it died, but usually all that meant was that the startup procedure was made longer and longer to accommodate every possible problem check. Again, this had obviously been designed by someone who never had the corporate vice president of sales screaming at them as hours went by as a (possible) restart was in process.

Recovery of scrambled data to the last good backup is a big deal on any system, but at least the AS400 normally had a tape drive option. Those that did not to begin with were almost useless and soon that was added as a required feature, like a printer and at least one console. Again, however, for early users this was a painful discovery.

Outside the control of the electronic systems, but beginning to impact, was the global economy and the fact that the world had different active time zones. Wayne had a taste of this from the beginning at Webcor, but now it was ubiquitous. You could never count on starting the overnight processing and locking out users at, say, five o'clock and going home, nor of coming in a seven and starting things up. The screens had to be available until at least ten, the overnight processing had to be done by no later than six, and the critical reports should all be printed and distributed before coffee. On special occasions, like month end, people might be working until midnight—so the overnight had to be delayed as necessary. And god help the account caught with some significant failure at the end of any fiscal period, as everyone paced waiting for access to data, the accountants needing last month's final figures, the salesmen waiting for commission statements, the data entry operators unable to put in new orders or dun overdue accounts, and—not least as time went on—real time operations like warehouse management frozen in place. Life could be a nightmare.

The world back then was filled with geniuses. It always is—would-be world conquerors or billionaires who think they can ride technical prowess to fortune. One or two probably make it. But as in all ages, the eventual winners are never pioneers. Most often they are the same sales people who aggressively monopolized the last wave of whatever, or the same old financial bastards who had appropriated everything before. Our world may change, but winners rarely do. The meek remain trampled, in spite of scripture.

Everyone I met had a vision and a scheme. I was no different. We each hallucinated what might be—and in the long run we were mostly right. But partial and refracted visions were of little practical immediate use. Using communications before the infrastructure and culture are ready for it, for example, is an exercise doomed to loss and futility. Eventually we discovered that developing code—although always an artisanship that paid bills—was no more a gateway to riches than the expertise of ancient steam engineers on the railroads. But for a few frantic years—ah there were dreams everywhere.

Everything fed these fantasies because everyone involved truly believed the hype. IBM would emerge victorious as the dominant and almost only viable business company. The latest hardware model, or operating system, or programming language would sweep all the others away. The newest introduced terminal, or printer, or whatever would be the ultimate. And currently automated systems would never change—they were all but perfected already. How could you possibly improve data entry screens?

Brilliant, ambitious geniuses all. Flawed visions everywhere. Naïve capitalist innocents, fixated on the future, while smart worldly-wise entrepreneurs did what they always did—ate hearty lunches, lined up deals, hovered to pounce and control whatever winner might emerge from the Darwinian maelstrom.

Intermission. Everyone leaves for coffee and snacks in the outside hallway. I linger near the desk.

"So you missed the boat," Ghost turns towards me.

"Oh, yeah, by miles. At least I wasn't alone. But if I knew now ...."

"Looking back, what do you think was your biggest problem."

"Oh, the same problem as most programmers—well most artisans for that matter. It was really, at the time, a solitary craft. And we ended up thinking of ourselves as heroic classical warrior-heroes—it's why science fiction and later graphic comics were so popular in that crowd. We could do things mere mortals could not ..."

"And how did that ..."

"Oh," I respond, "the artisan is always subject to 'mere mortals' who actually have better talents in the world that exists. Such as networking and using other people's money and time to leverage their own. Kings and bandits, for example."

"Makes you bitter, I suppose."

"No, not really. I had fun while it lasted, and it lasted long enough to give me a good career and rewards. I've never been sure more money would make me happier, and I'm sure a different lifestyle would not. And I never really wanted to change who I am—I like the complexity and tangles of my existence as I have become."

"Funny attitude," notes Ghost.

"Certainly for this time and place," I agree.

Wayne didn't realize it yet, but he was now in the middle of the computer religious reformation. He was a somewhat cynical believer in the church of IBM, but that faith was already being severely challenged by heretics preaching alternate hardware and software. Wayne had begun in those catechisms, so as a recent convert he should have seen what was coming. But faith often follows necessity, his bread and butter came from IBM, and although he had seen the alternatives, he still believed that IBM had the muscle and clout to win once it pulled itself together and focused on problems.

Today was simply a strong indication that was not going to happen. He sat in the president's office at Goldman, reading again the instructions for the alternate emulation card for the Microsoft PC in front of him. According to IBM, what he was about to do was nearly a cardinal sin—using third party hardware to try to get a rogue piece of equipment on the network. But Joe had firmly stated they would not pay double the price for the same functionality, even if certified by god. And the president really really wanted to be connected to the main computer.

In the old days that would have been insane. Company presidents no more wanted computer terminals in their office than they wanted to type their own memos on typewriters. They only grudgingly used voice transcription machines instead of live shorthand secretaries. The big guys using big iron still felt that way, and unfortunately IBM was still mostly focused on the big guys. Here in the small and mid-size company trenches, however, executives were coming out of business school with strange ideas, and were using their own spreadsheets and even word processing. Some had heard of messaging that could be sent to others—some insanely fast form of memo or mail. They wanted to use it, and they were not too proud to sit and work a keyboard.

But—well, they had all learned on microcomputers, PC's, and some were pretty familiar with the programs there. They refused to buy or use the (awful) spreadsheet, word processing and email programs which ran natively on the AS400. They refused to have two hulking terminals in their office, always too small anyway. So—well grudgingly IBM provided a way that a PC could pretend to be a "real" AS400 terminal. Automatic conversion of ASCIII to EBCDIC, connection via "standard" coax, a regular sign-on and—what more could they possibly want? Actually, a whole lot. IBM would be swamped by the coming waves of technology, until it figured out its proper money-making place in all this. But that was nearly a decade off.

At the moment, it still thought it could crush its rivals, subtly if not overtly. So connections were witchcraft, and if you were not using genuine IBM hardware here there and everywhere, forget about support. Wayne sat reading the manual for the third-party board to be inserted into the IBM terminal, toggled the appropriate dip switches, plugged everything in carefully, and powered up. Nope. Try alternates. Nope. What about this—ah, there we go.

That process could take nearly all day. Had they estimated this much time? Chuckle. Was the client going to pay for the overrun? Guffaw. So he had fallen behind in billing, but was ahead, or at least even, in good will, when the president finally got back in the office.

The real fireworks would start when the president found out how limited his access was and how hard to use the raw data available. But Joe could soothe that, and Wayne knew that more billable special programs were now happily bubbling away in the future pipeline. Fortunately, his boss was aware of that as well.

There was no easy win. We were caught between a rock and a hard place. If we managed to do what was necessary, no matter what it took, we could keep the account but probably had to eat the hours. If we balked and said we cannot do this at all, we might lose the account and a big chunk of our overdue accounts payable, which were always being renegotiated. Accounts were very hard to win, good accounts were impossible to replace. The only helpful thing was to have some really good people on staff so it was even more painful for the account to go with another vendor.

Loyalty and trust on both sides counted for a lot. Everyone realized that old saying "past performance is no guarantee of future results" but on the other hand, if we had managed to work everything out for ten years or so, and were keeping relatively current compared to what the executives and salesmen were hearing, we could manage. The problem, of course, is that what most of the executives and salesmen heard were pie in the sky lies, and they were still too technology-naïve to understand. We spent a lot of (unbillable) time in educational meetings trying to explain that—using metaphors, fables, and similes consisting of small words.

Never boring, at least. On the other hand, we had the absolutely insane idea in our heads that everything would settle down soon.

The front board now has "CHANGE!" in bold red letters gleaming back at us. This is where we get lectured on how awful we have been and how much we are missing.

"Sounds as if you were complete charlatans," Ghost points at me and sits back with a malicious conspiratorial smile.

"Not like the salespeople," I state firmly. "They didn't even know what they were promising, just lots of great something or other that the 'tech guys' could detail later. Utopia would arrive if you just signed the contract. Immediately, while the discount was still in effect. Then you could turn it over to the tech people to make it real."

"But, you said, you were part of the sales team."

"Part of Nick's sales team. I always believed what I said. I was usually wrong—on how long it might take and how it might go wrong. Sometimes by orders of magnitude," I admitted ruefully.

"So if not charlatans then …."

"Magicians. I think we thought of ourselves as magicians, producing miracles daily. Sometimes we needed misdirection and honeyed tongues to divert attention, but mostly we pulled off whatever tricks were required."

'Anyone get hurt?"

"Sure. The accounts lost money and never had fully realized dreams. We never got rich. IBM kept losing market share to the little guys. Everybody lost. But everybody won. The world was automating, and it was a necessary process."

"Sounds strange,"

"The strangest thing was how painful everything was, eventually, for everyone, when we had all been assured and really believed that it would happen without major problems at all."

There were any number of new and obscure challenges facing Wayne every day. Some, mostly controlled by him with programming and design, he properly regarded with pride, difficult algorithms made elegant, nearly impossible conditions met adequately. Even although nobody would see anything but the results, he was happy at his clean code, and took secret pride in it. Of course he was purely judged on results, which could come from awful code as well, but he refused to let such mar his programs. It was part of being professional.

But there were increasingly other issues, having nothing to do with code, and totally out of his control, that took more and more time. Usually it involved adding some capability that should be an absolute no-brainer done by ten year olds. Inevitably, the obvious ended up requiring a degree in rocket science, lots of time to finagle, and, inevitably, a trip on-site to get it running.

The worst of these were remote locations. Surely anyone would expect that if a company used building A and building B, one office and one warehouse, that the warehouse should have access to screens, to enter and receive order and shipping information if nothing else. Ah, but of course that required a coaxial connection between the two buildings—well, that was just a wire, company maintenance or at worst an outside electrician could take care of it. But...

Well, it turned out most warehouses were not next to the office. Surprise, surprise. And there were more than one. And sometimes they were in other cities. This all required—well it required an awful lot. The client had to be carefully stepped through ordering a special private dedicated connection from the phone company—and helped off the floor and revived when he received the cost and time estimate. Then the actual equipment had to be delivered to warehouse personnel, who had no idea which end of a printer or terminal should be up, and set up correctly. Then the special termination boxes had to be installed on each end, physically connected to all the relevant devices.

And, finally, the connections had to be made, security invoked, devices configured, and everything tested. Wayne had installations to do across the Island, then one in Boston, then another in Tampa. Often as not, he would arrive to find something important had been missed. This was common everyday stuff, thought the executives, what was taking so long. You could make a telephone call, after all, in a minute with no problem. More baby explanations.

When it worked, it was wonderful. Until something went wrong. Too often, it did.

The projector is packed up, the banner is down. Everyone is gone, rushing home. I linger a moment, packing up my briefcase, arranging the pile of take-home materials.

Ghost chuckles, "sounds like the magicians had to break into a sweat once in a while."

"Annoyed sweat, at everyone from the phone company to IBM to the account to people at the warehouse, who would sometimes report a problem to the head office when they had simply forgotten how to turn on all the machines after a power outage, or change the paper in the printer."

"But you put up with it."

"What else could we do. Besides, once it was done, it was done. We figured it would all be cut and dried after a while," I said ironically. "Boy were we wrong."

"Holding the tail of the tiger, were you?"

"More like riding the Dragon in the Emperor's new clothes while we imagined we were kings of the world."

Wayne thought a crystal ball would be nice, to see what was coming next and get ready for it. But crystal balls are sometimes useless—what good would it have done for Henry Hudson to have seen what Manhattan would become when he discovered his river? The next couple of decades were almost as tumultuous in technology. Knowing about them would not have helped the bottom line on any given day in 1988.

He kept thinking the revolution had happened, and everything else would just catch up. But the revolution kept happening. In the near future he would find that his profession began to proliferate into subcultures, each building walls of certification and jargon. There would be new computers, and so many computers everywhere that no one could count them, then more computers strapped to everyone all the time than there were people on the planet.

What computers meant changed drastically, from crudely storing data to unimaginable tasks, automating away many of the jobs surrounding him at each office. Everybody and everything became attached to everybody all the time, insistently. You could call the warehouse in many different ways, and have your computers do the same.

People changed too. They all learned something about machines, they all expected artistic effects more than raw information. They had a good idea of what a machine could do and what it could not. On the other hand, they never quite understood the magic underneath everything.

And for him, in his little niche, there were constant revisions. New languages, new operating systems, new paradigms, new interfaces. Art became as important as correct code. And, strangest of all, coding became less a matter of writing and more a matter of connecting dots on whatever new application and screen he was handed.

The only thing, in fact, that never changed was that salesmen made impossible promises. Oh, and the new boss was, naturally, the same as the old boss.

BACKYARD MEMORIAL DAY

MEMORIAL DAY WEEKEND dawned hot this year. It was an iffy time for planning, here on the South Shore. Weather could be cold and grey, could be so hot as to use the inflatable wading pool, could be hard rain or sun too brilliant for children's still pale complexions of spring. With people arriving soon, whether the festivities would be inside or outside would make quite a difference in preparation.

No matter what, there was shopping, and cleaning. Wayne stood in the newly mowed yard, trying to clean up any residual leaves and other accumulated vestiges of seasons gone. The garden was weeded, the early flowers doing well, although the display was in that period between bulbs and summer perennial blooms, the summer annuals just beginning to take. Well, it all looked pretty good anyway. He was proud of the yard.

The patio was relatively cleaned up, the furniture painted, the barbecue grill ready. His job out here was almost done. The garage was out of bounds to guests, so it could be as cluttered as ever. The basement had been cleared well enough for play, if necessary. The kids rooms were respectable. Nothing to do now but wait for the guests and help Joan with whatever last minute chores might turn up.

Ghost is decked out in barbeque apron, surrounded by a massive outdoor set of grills, tables, umbrellas, chairs. He flourishes a spatula in what seems to be a page torn from an over-fertilized garden advertisement. "Time to fire up the old barby ..." he booms.

"We never called anything a barby. Geesh. What's with all this stuff?"

"Trying to get in the spirit of showing off, like you were."

"Us? Showing off? Nah, we didn't do that."

"Of course you did. Why else the fights over who got which holidays? Why the cleanup? Don't forget about the edged conversations on how the kids were doing and how work went along."

"Just a little. We really never got into that much. We were all pretty self-reliant and independent. Comparisons were for everyone else."

"Joan wanted everything perfect for a reason."

"Well, I suppose."

"You don't think the dynamics were changing? "

"True, as the kids grew older there was less gee whiz and a little more bite. That's natural as children age, I guess."

"You were aging too."

"We tried not to notice."

"And parents."

"We really tried not to notice."

"Hamburgers or hot dogs?" he asks.

"Anything but turkey burgers ..." I respond fervently.

This was their very own real holiday. When gatherings had been divvied up, Mom and Dad got Thanksgiving, Cheryl and Robert took Christmas, Joan was left hosting Easter. But Easter was the one time not recognized as a regular holiday at work, had other church obligations, and the weather was often awful. Besides, over the years there was tension as Joan and Wayne liked to have candy for the kids, and Cheryl and Robert wanted theirs to be relatively sugar free. Almost by accident, Memorial Day weekend had become the spring festival in West Babylon.

There were other more informal occasions, often observed with a rigidity that belied their casual nature. Certain birthdays, vacations, holidays, visits. But none of them were sacred as were the main pillars of familial gatherings. And at these events, whoever hosted tended to go all out. Mom cooked way too much for the restricted crowd that gathered in Huntington at Thanksgiving, Cheryl and Robert kept adding decorations and unusual touches to Christmas, and of course Wayne and Joan tried to keep up with Memorial Day diversions and food.

These were wonderful, fun times, but also a little frightening. Time passed quickly, and the changes over years were extremely evident in young children. Five years turned an infant not much more capable than a kitten into a chattering inquisitive busybody. Five more years and that five-year-old was oddly grown and involved in all kinds of complex learning and social networks. Suddenly, parents realized their oldest were on the verge of becoming adolescents. Suddenly, the stream of new babies dried up.

If they thought about it, it was a little scary that time had implications for themselves and older people as well. But life was so busy that they often never noticed, until one of the communal gatherings would shove the impossibility of permanence in their face.

"Do you need me to go get anything else," asked Wayne on Saturday morning. Sunday would be a madhouse, they needed to get everything under control by tonight.

"We bought the buns and salad and hamburger and chips and potato salad and … everything… yesterday," said Joan. "Do we have enough soda?"

"Yeah, lots in the garage, like you asked."

"Anything else that you can think of?"

"I've got plenty of charcoal and lighter, ketchup, how about dessert?"

"Cheryl's bringing that, she doesn't like commercial sugary stuff. She has the special turkey burgers, too."

"Silly, if you ask me."

"Nobody did. Don't make a fuss about it. They can have their own ideas. We just want to get along."

"I know, I know. It's minor. I like talking to Robert about stuff anyway. Is Philip coming by?"

"He isn't sure. Maybe. He'd like to see Mom and Dad. Depends on what he is doing, I guess."

They cleaned up everything as best they could, and Wayne took the kids out to the park and the library to pick up a videotape of some movie. If the weather turned, or the kids got restless, there was always that to fall back on. And by now, the oldest were little interested in anything other than the latest Nintendo games anyway. Even what they did on the holidays, Wayne reflected, had changed a lot from when they first began years ago.

At least he had Monday off, so a day to recover. And unlike the early days, there was no need to stock up cases of beer, so that he could chug a can every once in a while to keep up a buzz and stay civil. He'd even wake up Monday clear and happy. That was a wonderful difference. The past, he realized, had a lot of problems he tended to forget in a golden haze of memory.

Afternoon became night, they went out for pizza because it would be hamburger leftovers forever for a while, and even had time to briefly visit a local mall. But everyone was a little keyed up, and there were always last minute things to be done. They finally went to bed restlessly, and waited for the next day.

The last few years had been what I later came to refer to as a "bubble" of time, almost self-contained and detached from other periods. From 1985 to 1988 was a period of stability in work, home, family, and relations that seemed to extend without change forever, when everyone was happy or at least hopeful that they soon would be. The children were children, with few cares or worries yet about the future, each day an adventure. We assumed it would continue indefinitely.

But nothing does, of course. The reason I came to think of them as bubbles is because the comfort zone would float and drift and even change shape elegantly, but suddenly it would burst and everything would always be different after that. Then we would look back and think of all the fine things in the bubble, the shimmers of its brilliance, its geometric perfections. Simultaneously, we would forget all the problems and hassles and worries, and think—ah, that was a golden age.

The bubble when your children are young is special, of course. Humans have evolved to raise children into the current culture, and that is very rewarding. But the weirdest part is the way things change so quickly for parents.

Your child starts out helpless and dependent, then becomes a kind of happy or demanding pet, then a little wonder imitating everything in the environment. So cute, such a rush when baby takes the first step, when a toddler begins to speak coherently, when an exploding intellect sits as you read and asks why. And then, just as it seems everything is going well, they start to become independent, fresh, and difficult. Not only that, but in one way or another they either excel or fall behind everyone else. You are left trying to pick out the best and ignore the worst.

We didn't want to be competitive, but we couldn't help being competitive. If only to assure that our children were better behaved and happier than others we saw. Everyone we knew, in one way or another, did the same.

Motionless holograms of family members—images apparently stolen from home photos and videos of the time—float in various transparencies, scattered all around a stage set with props taken from our back yard. Shimmering adults are looking closely at flower beds, elders sit surveying the scene from near the food table, the smallest children splash in the wading pool while slightly older ones chase each other and scream. I'm just outside the back door, and notice that the closer people are the most solid and vivid, farther back nearly clear and shades of grey. Oddly, everybody from both sides of the family, as well as extended relations, crowd the lawn. "And this represents?" I ask.

"Oh, the good points. The support system. You see—I have the grandparents here and the more distant relatives out back there, hard to see clearly, I suppose."

"Nice presentation. You should take it to the city..."

"It's not art. It's a statement about community."

"Same thing, for a lot of artists. Anyway, yes, we found ourselves part of an extensive network of people helping each other. For our families, it was mostly blood relatives. I'd claim that was Joan's Italian influence, but it was almost the same on my side, although less present."

"But you didn't really use them much."

"Not for money or anything, usually. Joan and I had been out of the loop a long time—we tended to resolve things ourselves as much as we could. But we did enjoy the conversations and long discussions about the meaning of children, education, art, life, everything. Congenial, mostly, now that everybody seemed properly straightened out."

"I didn't think you appreciated it much, at the time," Ghost notes with an accusing finger.

"Well, I was busy, never enough time, and what hours I had dedicated to Joan and boys. These were big impositions, sometimes."

"Everyone else managed."

"I managed too. Just grudgingly."

"But now?"

"All right, all right. I admit I was wrong. These were incredibly important ties, and now that they are disintegrating in time and death we miss them terribly. Now that we have the time, we cannot use it."

"But this," he gestures expansively as the smoke rises from the grill, "is what your memories truly look like."

"Less certain, Ghost, less certain. Some days a little chunk is clear as a bell, other times it's just a hopelessly foggy blur. You tried, but there's no way to capture transience."

He shrugs and starts taking the buns off before they burn.

Their lives were rich and complex and full of experience and conflicts. For those fortunate enough to have been born in a time and place with access to more wealth and power than any other people in history, choices can be so immense as to overwhelm.

Wayne found that no matter how many things he did right, there were more that he could not do correctly because—primarily—of time constraints. The hardest thing was to maintain balance—between his own sanity, the demands of work, the responsibilities of his immediate family, the vague unease that other things were slipping by that should be somehow grasped. It was a common lament, which Joan and everyone else felt just as keenly.

A successfully marriage—or any relationship—requires, he thought, a degree of tension. You have to protect yourself and your core values and needs or you melt into an ineffectual blob, and often suppress all the petty angers into an explosive central resentment that may manifest itself in frightening ways.

On the other hand, it is awful easy to be seduced into bickering all the time over really trivial crap, pretending that by winning such arguments you are keeping your own integrity. That was the key to every hard conflict, really, that the extremes were destructive but holding the middle was nearly impossible. Realizing that did not make it any easier to navigate the treacherous waters.

At this point it was all about time. Fortunately he and Joan agreed, mostly, on prioritized uses of time, while also recognizing that each of them still required a certain amount of personal space. But the strict hierarchy of what had to be done first often left precious few moments to be alone. It became a common tactic to seize on other necessities—for Wayne it was his auto commutes, or mowing the lawn, or standing at the playground with the kids—as somewhere where the task could be accomplished on automatic while the mind ran free.

There are times in our lives when we can rest and contemplate the course of what we have done, calmly evaluate the paths chosen and consider those not pursued. Once in a while the present becomes so insanely wrong that we wonder if only what, hoping to find at least the basic mistake we made somewhere some time. But all such thoughts, at least until the moment we snap and say the hell with it and walk away or do something equally socially insane, require time and the ability to center and gain perspective. For Joan and I, this was not one of those times.

We found that children removed all other considerations like some kind of thought purifier. More and more it was about them, how we were doing with them, what we were doing with them, how they were doing with others and the world and themselves. Every moment became a child moment, at least in potential. Everything we might do had to be run through the sieve of how it might affect Little Wayne and Gregory. An interesting exercise, even more difficult for independent souls than the requirements of a job.

We were by no means helicopter parents. We had no desire to firmly mold childhood into a miniature maturity, thereby making it not childhood at all. We enjoyed them being children, and watching them be children, and since we had once been children ourselves we saw no harm in it. We didn't push all the time, nor criticize all the time, nor make sure every spare second was chock full of enriching goodness. Enjoying life itself, learning to make good decisions and be a sane person, was all the goodness that was truly required of a successful human being. But—even that took a lot of time.

And, of course, we were never sure we were right. Should we have pushed harder, made childhood less childhood, taken away some of the fun since being an adult would be no fun at all? We never resolved that issue, perhaps we were simply too lazy.

What we both remember is frantic constant activity, centered on our offspring. I'm sure there was a lot more complexity, more considerations, but no time at all for ourselves and always feeling behind is the basic answer we would give if asked. And yet, we remember it also as one of the happiest times of our lives.

A blazing birthday cake on the picnic table. Black crepe bunting hung around the windows and stairway rails. Dark clouds with thunder on the horizon as the wind rises. An ominous hush over the party, frozen in place like mannequins. "Welcome to middle age!" sings Ghost.

"It just slipped up on us," I laugh. "We never saw it coming—well, maybe Joan was more aware than I, with a woman's biological clock to keep in mind. I still felt like an eleven year old."

"But?"

"But nothing. I still feel like an eleven year old. Peter Pan hiding in an older body in the suburbs."

"You must have noted some big changes."

"Big, I don't know, not yet. I still saw a future before me, I still saw the past as prelude. But there was one thing…"

"What was that?"

"Well, at first when we were taking the kids out with the grandparents, we thought we were forming memories for the grandparents, something they could remember when we were not there. But we began to realize at some point we were more trying to form memories of the old folks for our children, to look back on the family as people vanished. And, strangest of all as we reached our forties, we began to realize it was important to us to keep the memories for ourselves. That was new."

"But surely, you always remembered ...."

"Yeah, but more young adult or adolescent—what we had done when we were wild and free. That was the us we remembered, when we sat around, what had happened back then, the adventures we had encountered. And then—boom."

"And?"

"Suddenly it was remember Memorial Day five years ago when Gregory or Vanita did this, or that happened or the food came out so crazy. Our memories had suddenly changed focus. What we had remembered as recent faded away to a seemingly distant past that was populated by people almost unrecognizable to our current selves. That was the odd thing about the passing years."

Lightning sharpens the grounds as rain pelts down. Suddenly the spell is broken and everyone is running for cover.

This year would be a Sunday festival. That would let everyone relax tomorrow with a quiet day off at home. Wayne and Joan had the basics complete before they went to bed, and the morning could take its time with a normal walk to get the paper with Wayne and Greg, and then increasing activity straightening up toys and clothes. The tables were set, the grill prepared, and Joan started getting all the snacks and salads ready.

Mom and Dad were the first to arrive, right out of church over in Huntington. Gregory immediately started to pull Grandpa around, showing him his latest creative and school projects, talking a mile a minute. Grandma brought things for Joan to put out, and they happily gossiped while bustling about, Little Wayne excitedly trying to get a word in edgewise and sneaking a taste of anything that looked sweet.

As noon came and went, some of the initial energy lowered, and there was an anxious wait to see what time everyone else could arrive so the charcoal could be timed. It was too late to eat much without spoiling appetites for the dinner to come, but on the other hand everyone was getting a little hungry. They all walked around the yard, Little Wayne giving a proud tour of the garden, Joan showing off the flowers. An hour went by.

The cousins finally arrived, Cheryl bearing dessert and endless accessories for baby Ryan. Gregory immediately slipped into older male role, trying to tell Kyle and Little Wayne what to do, all of them shrieking and clambering around the wooden house structure on the old dead tree. Gregory kept trying to organize what they were going to do, he was mostly ignored. Little Wayne and Kyle were in silly mode. Vanita, on the other hand, had grown older and more serious, playing little Miss Mom, trying to keep everyone under control.

Greetings exchanged, snacks consumed, non-alcoholic refreshments served, fire started, and a constant stream of covered platters taken to the tables on the patio. While the coals died down, the tour of flower and trees continued, Robert and Dad discussing real estate while Wayne listened in with half an ear, Joan and Cheryl exchanging news of everyone they knew and school experiences. The noise from the treehouse continued, periodically an adult would wander over to be sure things were not getting out of hand.

By the time the hamburgers were ready, and the various hot plates warmed up, the sun was hot. Sand somehow drifted up from the bricks onto some of the salad, flies managed to arrive from everywhere. Noise crescendoed until it became embarrassing and the adults spent a few minutes laying down the law and getting civilization back.

It wasn't the best dinner anyone had ever had, but it was quite good, and served the celebration well. The main thing was that there were options. If you didn't want beef, there were turkey burgers. If you didn't want the corn, there were two kinds of salad, with alternate dressing. Rolls and leftover snacks and enough sweet desserts to fill everyone up without coercion.

Near the end of the feast, a shout from the side gate heralded the arrival of Philip, entering like a prince from some far realm, ready to cast a critical eye on all he surveyed. Immediately the talk was all about houses, and how his latest fix-up projects were coming along, and what were the prospects for a rise in home prices. He was in a rush, as usual, and grabbed a few things before taking leave, promising to visit each person later when he had more time.

After a quick frantic cleanup, the afternoon began to settle down into long relaxed conversations. Complaints about the world, comparisons of the kids, plans for the upcoming summer. Robert was starting to take up water color painting seriously again, and he and Wayne had nice far-ranging discussions about artists and aesthetics. The women roamed through the house, looking at the latest additions and improvements, suggesting more. The children, stuffed, settled down with TV and video games quietly—almost suspiciously quiet.

Finally, time for goodbyes, and everyone took off well before sunset, to try to make it home while it was still light. As the last of the crowd drove off, Wayne and Joan took a deep breath, each grateful that tomorrow they could sleep late and get everything back in order at a relaxed pace. A typical, wonderful, Memorial Day, which they were sure would continue for years to come.

So everything, we thought, had finally fallen or been built into place. We thought we had years of this pattern to go, the holidays shared in a certain way, conversations to be continued, all the time in the world to follow rhythms of our lives as neatly as in an old medieval village. And we were quite happy with how things had finally turned out and settled down.

Some people never seemed to get happy with what actually was. They were always telling us how things would be better next year, how they planned to get a new house, how their job would change, maybe they would move somewhere else. Life was always going to be different. Repeating anything year after year was simply boredom and failure. The culture conspired with them, always showing what else should be available, for themselves, for their families, for their universe.

Wayne and Joan hardly fit. They saw cycles moving slowly, seasonal processions into years that always seemed, if anything, to be rushing by too quickly. They had more than they really needed of everything except time. They did not dream of Moroccan sunsets or sipping wine on Italian villas—at least not most of the time. What they really really wanted was another week off at work, or maybe a break in the kid's school requirements that were already starting to make heavy demands.

The world never slowed down. Some of the shocks to come would be quite unexpected. Thinking anything can last is an illusion.

Ghost is standing behind a tripod, camera ready. He's reassembled the shadow people into various groups. "Ah, Wayne, could you go stand there and smile ...."

"Oh, we had enough of that. Not only various combinations of old and new cameras, but the new movie equipment, tapes running in cameras built like cement blocks. And you got it right—Joan always trying to pose people like Mathew Brady did."

"Surprised you haven't gone back into them to refresh some of this."

"Maybe I will, later," I agree. "They're all in shoe boxes all over the place. Except the videos. Somehow, looking at that stuff always makes me sadder than my memories."

"Happy times, happy thoughts."

"But the past just gone forever. "

"Well, that's true of memories too," he replies.

"Memories are happening now at least—I don't know, that's just how I am. I don't hate old photos, just didn't feel like going through them yet."

"Stand right over there, anyway."

Wayne's hands were starting to wrinkle. The piles of clean dishes were becoming impressive, the remaining pans almost gone. Even though they had used a lot of paper plates, there seemed to be more silverware, glasses, and serving platters than he could remember putting out. Without a dishwasher, everything was manual. But he was used to the washing—the drying was what he disliked.

Gregory had helped for the first dozen or so, then ran off to whatever he had to do. In a little while, no doubt, Joan would help him by telling him where everything went. She was almost obsessive about it being in the same exact place all the time. It was late, and dark, but this was just about the last chore.

He had put out the coals with water, then dumped the wet ashes to the side of the garage. The play structure and basement, looking as if a tornado had gone through, had not taken too long, especially with the kids helping considerably. The chairs were all back in place and the only thing still to do was Gregory's and Little Wayne's bedrooms, probably not much more awfully cluttered than normal.

So, dawn to late night, almost finished, and a whole day to relax and sit back. "Hey, Joan, can you help me with where some of this exotic stuff goes?"

People and clutter are gone. Birdsong echoes over a hushed neighborhood, warm azure sky with an occasional contrail. Grass already a little long, flowers ready to burst open. Ghost lounges back in the Adirondack chair, glass of cola in hand.

"Ah, this is the life," he notes.

"Too bad it only showed up once in a while," I remark. "Too busy most of the time."

"Did it feel as if you were marking off the ages."

"Never really considered it. Hassles, busy, pressure—who has time to think about marks in your life. You are just rushing through it, doing as best you can. Now, of course, it's different ..."

"So you are not really writing what was," he asks.

"More what I think it meant as I remember it and put it in perspective. It's complicated."

"You seem to think most things are."

"That's what I found out, once I had some time to think about it."

A long free Monday had passed quickly, with time playing with the kids, puttering in the yard, and quite a bit of heavy reading. The new manuals were tough, and unfortunately left many of his questions about conversions from 38 procedure code unanswered. Without a formal background, he sometimes found that simple instructions that were taken for granted by the documentation person made little sense to him. But he wasn't really any worse off than anybody else at work. They were all learning as they went.

Boy, could reading chew up time. Hours could flash by, and he would be a couple of hundred pages on, and then trying to make sense of all the niggling little stuff. And tomorrow, very little of it would be required—it would surely be one emergency after another, as usual.

Yeah, a short week, but Tuesday would be the new Monday, only worse. Compressed, incredibly heavy morning traffic, people trying to get back in the groove, schedules messed up. Worse, all the clients and all the users and even all the programmers including himself suddenly realize that summer is arriving really fast, and there is only so much time to get an awful lot done if they are going to have any fun and free time in July and August.

Reset Baseline

THE SUN WAS hot but not yet scorching, rotting scents of the sea still subdued, crowds would arrive later. They did not have the long wooden Babylon dock on the Great South Bay to themselves, but so far there were few others. Lines were unwrapped, frozen bait beginning to thaw, and he had managed to get the bamboo poles together once again, in spite of corrosion.

Gregory knew how to bait his own hook, so the only help had to be with Little Wayne. Soon two lines were dangling into the water, red and white bobbers barely settling before they vanished as another snapper struck. Gregory had a decent size fish almost immediately, Little Wayne still pulled too fast and hard and lost one. Gregory was getting much better at taking them off too, he dropped his in the bucket for Sunday breakfast tomorrow.

What a nice life, Wayne thought, looking at the wide expanse of calm water. What a great place to end up. Things had all settled down now, and at least on the weekends could not be more perfect. He was doing exactly what he wanted to do, enjoying the fishing as much as the boys did, a whole glorious day still in front of him. Who would have imagined this, a mere decade ago?

A screech from Wayne snapped him into the present. Ah, yes, yellow jackets. No real problem yet, but they were buzzing around. Mostly you had to be sure they weren't on the bait when you reached for one of the small shiners. Nasty little things, anywhere there was garbage, this time of year. But, of course, that too was part of the experience as he remembered it when he had been their age.

An hour or so here, having fun, then they would get tired of it just as he would, and they could all go home where he still had to mow the lawn and weed the vegetables. Joan should be deciding what they would be doing later along about now.

Just a great time, he thought again. Perfection in the summer breeze.

Ghost sits in a grubby dark office, behind a great dark wooden desk. He is wearing a tweed coat with leather elbow patches, smoking a curved pipe, the very picture of a sixties college professor. There's an attempt at a twinkle in his eye, but it just makes him look seedy. "Mr. Slingluff," he intones, "we must consider your candidacy at this point."

"Oh, not this," I recoil in mock horror. "I left this garbage behind years ago—the worst time of my life. I refuse to relive it."

"But it is so appropriate," he murmurs. "Will you be able to receive your MSL or not, this year."

"MSL? What the heck is an MSL?" I ask indignantly.

"Master in Successful Life, of course. I see here," he takes some papers from a stack, "that you think you are quite far along. In spite of horrible grades in the beginning, of course. And some very odd electives along the way, if I may say so."

"No, you may not," I find myself shouting. "I refuse to be graded on this kind of nonsense."

"Oh, it's much more than grades," he says smoothly. "Your thesis could use work—let's see, something about 'being happy without very much money,' isn't it?

"This is ridiculous."

"Perhaps, perhaps not. Evaluations are, however, required. I'd like to schedule you for ...."

Everything fades off to smoke, as I continue to sputter with heartbeat elevated.

If Wayne ever took the time to think about it at all, which was rarely, he would realize how much he had changed his internal life narrative. He had gone through all the early phases of thinking he would change the world, or even understand the world, or influence the world. He had finished with the belief that he would one day be recognized as a great unknown artist. He had gotten over the romantic illusion that he could die full of promise before thirty. Here he was, just slogging along in the same old typical American rut, two cars, wife, house in the suburbs.

Seeing what others had accomplished while he was out on his earlier pilgrimage, he probably should have been full of regret that he had wasted so much time. He might have had a bigger house, been able to go to more exotic places, given his children more of a boost. Maybe. However he retained his conviction that he could only work on the present, and the only thing he could ever do with his past was to shape it into a useful tool—at worst a series of interesting stories unrelated to what he had become, at best a necessary time of sorting out the world so that he could now accept this relatively sedate existence.

Besides, he was older. At forty, he knew he could not do—and did not want to do—what his younger self had fully immersed in. Even then he tended to see old successful alcoholic and miserable artists as something to be avoided. Young, alcoholic, miserable, unsuccessful artists, on the other hand, had been a useful belief for exploring the world back then. Living a decade as a total romantic could hardly be considered a loss. Now, this last decade, was adventure of a different type, and because it was so exciting and fresh, he admitted his thirties had been just as important as his twenties.

And here—well he was entering a new decade. How would he pay for the kid's college? How would his career work out? These were probably going to enter the equation. For now though, as always, it was just get up and go out and get the job done, and smile as much as possible through the whole wonderful crazy experience.

Roy Rogers served really good chicken, they all agreed, and it was inexpensive and just a half mile down the road from home. So it had become a regular stop on their early Saturday evening fast food rotation. As usual, Wayne senior was having the full fried chicken dinner, complete with strawberry milkshake, while Gregory contented himself with a fried breast, Little Wayne and Joan with chicken nuggets, and all of them with fries and tiny cole slaw passing as a respectable vegetable.

"I think after this we should all go out to Captree," said Wayne. "It doesn't get dark until a lot later, and we can enjoy the boats and watch people fish."

"Yeah, I want to see what they catch out there on the big dock!" exclaimed Gregory.

"Sand dune!" added Little Wayne, who liked the open space for running.

"Oh, all right," Joan gave in, "but you know we really have to start shopping for school clothes."

"Next week," Wayne replied.

"Please, Mom," chorused the kids.

"Ok, but you have to be good if I take you shopping next week. Promise?"

Wayne and Joan at least agreed on that as the most important form of discipline. Such promises (and an occasional threat, although those had become far less frequent) were kept by all or there were consequences. Of course, a promise from the kids was in light of an implied threat later if they broke it— no Nintendo for a night or two perhaps, or tv off early, or whatever they truly wanted to do. Never, never, they had both learned in day care, should a threat be something the children did not want to do anyway. They had to clean their room, for example, and that was certain whether they were good or not.

It was nice to have partners who agreed on what could become the most contentious part of the relationship. Oh, once in a while Joan thought Wayne was too strict, once in a while he thought she insisted on the wrong things, but they had worked out the give and take long ago, and the youngsters didn't really have a chance.

"Is everyone done, yet," asked Wayne senior, anxious to get going.

"Yeah!"

"Yeah!"

"Slow down, will you," remarked Joan. "You all gobble your food down too fast. You should enjoy it more. I need a little time to finish."

"Aw, Mom, hurry up," began Gregory.

"Hey Gregory, what do you think about going back to school in a few weeks," asked Wayne diplomatically. A nice conversation would no doubt fill the next few minutes, while Joan deliberately finished up.

Neither of us had grown up in affluent families. We were certainly not poor, but eating out was a rare event, and we were both used to common American diets. I still remember drive-in places, where you would order on a big box attached to the car, when girls on roller skates would deliver the meals to be eaten in the car from trays attached to the windows. We actually enjoyed fast food, and did not feel at all cheated at not eating in "fancy" sit-down places very often. Besides, with small children, fast food was always consumed, and the bright and open layout was conducive to bright and cheerful talk.

Back then, claims a memory, children were supposed to be much better behaved. Certainly we kept ours on a tight leash, discouraging loud conversation, never accepting a tantrum of any type (we would take them to the car with a threat to go home, eat there, and do nothing else all night—and doing it once sealed that threat for all time.) By the time they could sit and feed themselves, they were pretty nice and courteous. Given what the world turned into, perhaps that was the worst mistake we made in bringing them up. Nice no longer helps pay the bills.

To be honest, I liked fast food, and I still tend to like it more than the newer super duper entrees peddled all over. Perhaps it was simply what I was used to, perhaps it is a genetic makeup that cannot appreciate the subtle. I'd much rather eat a standard Burger King hamburger than the latest kobe beef medallion, I like secret sauce better than chef's delight, and regular old crisp French fries can be one of the highlights of the meal.

Like many other things, that could bring us to the topic of whether or not our kids had it better than we did. In our case, I think we were working pretty hard to make it the same. We liked our childhoods, we did not really want to improve them. Enjoy the world, study and read adequately, get along with others, and use each moment well. What else was there? Well, for everyone else, it seems, there were piano lessons, tutoring in Italian, special soccer or baseball or tic-tac-toe away camps. Children should not have a happy life, this is preparation for a grim future, they need to be given an edge, even if the inevitable cuts make them bleed a little.

Maybe right. Possibly wrong. It's all over, so I don't need to defend it nor agonize about it. We are still happily talking to each other, anyway, and nobody is currently in therapy, so it wasn't a total disaster.

"Herr Professor Ghost," I simper, "I have tried my best and I find some of these marks quite unfair."

"That is the way of the world," he snaps. "Life is not fair. Accept it now. No, I say you had not headed for a happy life."

"But what—look, there are decent marks in Home, Spouse, Children, Career, Job, Money, Parents, even the elective in Sobriety."

"Adequate, I admit. But you are failing miserably in Network, Future, Guidance, and Lighting a Fire Under Their Bottoms."

"But ..."

"And your thesis, that is worst of all," he interrupts. "<u>Enjoy What You Have</u>. That is not American, that is not success, that is just whimpering Eastern navel gazing. This is a hard-ass culture, you have to fight to get ahead, not just sit and enjoy whatever apple tree you happen to have found yourself under."

"I like my apple tree," I laugh. "Go peddle your gloomy nasty life gibberish to the gullible."

"Alliteration will not help your cause," he says in a huff.

"Playing boogieman from college doesn't do much for yours either." I slam the door on the way out.

Maturity, Wayne thought, was realizing that absolute values were suspicious, and relative ones were slippery indeed. Definitions depend on additional definitions, and all words marinate in connotations that often miscommunicate Concerning social and personal issues, he hardly seemed able to make sense of himself to himself.

Success, for example. What did success mean? Today, in the long run, for eternity? Could success be saved up, or somehow exchanged, to make the ends justify the means, like paying back a bad loan? Was it always immediate, like needing change to buy a loaf of bread? Did you measure success in absolute internal happiness today, or possibly how happy you were in terms of others or how happy you used to be? Or were measures always for the presumed long term, even though the long term invoked a foggy and unknowable future that could change everything in an instant?

Confusing was hardly the word. How people ever grew up and kept going was by far the biggest mystery of all. Lately, he had begun to think it was mostly a matter of not thinking at all. Just do something. But that, of course, had its own problems and pitfalls. Running along a road mindlessly without planning the journey could also result in disaster.

He pruned his overgrown intellectual frameworks. He performed chores, partly from necessity, but increasingly because he found ways to enjoy doing them. No matter what the task—well at least within certain limits—he could adapt. So why not smile? Why curse and struggle and seek to find something else, when the real reward would be in finding how to center effectively at this moment, no matter how disagreeable it might be?

Unlike common wisdom, he did not believe happiness involved too much reconciliation with the past. He had been someone else then, presumably he would be different in the future, if there was one. He could only act on now, and unless history had engulfed today, best to bury and forget it and move on. That pulled him through. Yes, with a silly and perhaps unwarranted smile.

As for grading his performance so far—no, it never really seemed possible. Life evaluation is a totality, not a series of isolated performances. But life itself is only those performances.

I was certain, by then, of a few things that had hardly been foremost in my earlier ambitions. One was the certainty that no life is all that important beyond the individual and his family. Everyone else could be replaced and were, that was the nature of the world. Obviously, then, there were no cosmic consequences to what you did or did not do. The museum without walls, the halls of eternity, remembered forever, unique contributions to mankind—no on examination they all paled compared to one's own life, how successfully lived, how well joined with those you actually contacted and worked with and loved and helped and enjoyed life together with.

Another was the obvious conclusion that in "interesting times" the immediate past—that is to say the advice of our parents, history books, and older peers—is a very poor guide to our own decisions. Circumstances change so quickly and dramatically that what worked twenty or thirty or years previously to lead to fame and fortune will simply lead to poverty and laughter now. That would be like trying to lavishly follow a career in vaudeville after movies and TV destroyed that mode of entertainment. You had to look for the current chances and dream of what might be, not emulate whatever might once have been.

And finally, above all, was luck. You couldn't tell which strategies would work. You don't know when you will die. You can't tell which firms will fail. You can't imagine what careers might be destroyed overnight, what new ones might bloom. All you know for certain is that if you don't die, you grow older and less capable of change. You needed to watch out for luck, both good and bad, but you could never control it. If it missed you—depending on which kind it was—so be it. And, oddly, sometimes you never at any given time could tell great luck from horrible luck. You might reevaluate later.

So—what does that all mean. Obviously I had to get out of bed and do something. I was happier with more security and money. I enjoyed striving with a hope of achieving them. But nothing was certain, so you have to also try to enjoy what you have as life goes by, and not assume you can catch up on many if any losses sometime in the future.

"Your attitude, mister, leads to sloth and poverty. " Ghost paced the floor in lecture mode, puffing furiously, chalkboard behind him filled with x's and o's illustrating possible life strategies. "You will be not only a failure, but a drain on society, a bum taking what other people are working so hard to build. This is a childish and selfish outlook."

"Ah, can it." I snarl. "Maybe once or twice I didn't pay my way—not often—but I was working and paying taxes my whole life, even in college. When I wasn't I used my savings. I never cheated on anything, I was maybe stupid, but I figured if I lived in society I had to do a few things. One was to follow the rules, one was to pay the taxes required, and the final one was to accept the economic system—in this case capitalism—which assured that the work I did for pay was in fact socially useful work."

"But ..."

"The hell with the buts. That's it. If a few of our political candidates and billionaires followed the same morality, we'd be in much better financial and moral shape. But now, everybody is convinced everybody else is cheating. I don't know, maybe they are. I didn't."

"No need to get so hot about it."

"You think not? I think so. I'm pretty ticked off at our petty aristocracy that thinks just because they are wealthy it exempts them from any other consideration except gouging those not in their class. And not real happy with a society where you have to cheat to succeed especially if you are on the underside. "

"Just an old man squawking now," he grunted.

"Maybe so. But don't give me all this crap about who is a maker and who is a taker and all the asinine mythology to keep people in their place and buy into the corruption."

"Perhaps we should continue this another time," he puffs.

"Perhaps we should simply drop it." This time, the scene just cuts out abruptly.

Wayne had built the sandbox a while ago, and honestly Gregory was grown out of using it much. It had been a pretty simple project—just pick up the patio bricks which were on a deep sand base, build a treated wood box around the four foot openings, and add some additional play sand on top. That made it essentially bottomless, and with a cover once in a while to keep cats from becoming used to it being there, it was available for use most of the year.

Wayne had fond memories of running water on the Jersey Shore gravel driveway of his grandparent's house, much to the distress of his grandfather. He would shape dams and canals and watch little imaginary towns flood as the torrent produced from the garden hose came rushing, slowly but inevitably, down the long stretch to the street. In a way, just like a real Mississippi disaster. So he had encouraged the use of water as well, at least when the weather was warm, although Joan hardly approved.

Now, unfortunately, the main reason Gregory would get engaged in it was to tease his little brother. Still, there were times when they would build wonderful things, then destroy them, then build them again, imaginations running at full tilt. Not quite as amazingly destructive as making sand castles on the ocean, but the same general theme of rise and fall, construction and decay. A quick lesson in almost all of European history. And, for those who were older, a metaphor for all grand ambitions.

Of course there were a lot of plastic toys there, and the sand was open to elements, and dirt and leaves would frequently mix in. They would have to wash when they were done. All unknown at the time, they were probably being well exposed to some outside bacteria that would help immunize them to certain problems in the future. Wayne liked dirt a lot himself. Joan—well she was from a generation where girls stayed out of mud, but she had a lot of squooshy seashore experiences herself.

Lessons from the sandbox.

More certain than death and taxes, every moment encapsulated tradeoffs. You can stay at work and hope to make more money now or in the future, or you can go home and play with the children, or you can go hang out somewhere by yourself and recover necessary sanity. Push too far in one direction or another and face nasty consequences.

But nothing is simple. If you stay at work, it might not help your earnings at all. If you play with your children, they may not want to respond at that time, engaged in their own necessities. Go by yourself and somebody, somewhere, will probably be upset. Probably one of the reasons human brains are so immensely large are to handle all these ambiguities, choices, and uncertainties. Even when we think we are doing it well, we think we might be doing it better.

The worst choices for me were those of now versus the future, and especially of risk versus a degree of certainty. I liked to feel I could know what was going to happen. Turn the steering wheel right and the car goes in that direction. The future was always risk, and that made it less amenable to my plans than the nearby present, which I could at least try to shape in a known good way. Start to talk of where we would be in five years generally left me numb. I had no sense of direction in the fourth dimension.

Nevertheless, choices were necessary. It was necessary to work some Saturdays instead of being with the family. It was necessary to do things with the relatives instead of taking a refreshing solitary walk. I never much minded money, but time tradeoffs were always killers. So, I guess I often just went down the easiest path, oiling whatever wheel began to squeak when necessary, ignoring it otherwise.

I look back and wonder—could I or should I have done more. At this point, I am kind of less critical than I once was. I always felt in charge of my fate, my choices led to my outcomes or at least heavily influenced them, but when I look back I know the choices I faced were sometimes pretty restricted. And even if I had taken roads less traveled, I do not believe they would have been better. That's my prerogative, as I shape the past into a narrative I can be content remembering.

"No doubt," began Ghost as if he were starting a particularly dry and boring lecture, "you wondered why everyone else was doing better than you were. At least Joan did."

"I'll accept that with the correction. Me, I always ended up thinking life had treated me more than fairly. I counted things like good health, happy family, interesting thoughts far more than I did stupid stuff like who was prettier or had a bigger house or sat in a larger office."

"But you did sometimes resent those offices telling you what to do."

"Oh, I guess, but mostly not. I figured they had their own problems. No—more than that—I absolutely knew they had their own problems."

"Free of envy? A modern saint?"

"Never. I would have loved to be rich. I just wouldn't accept the tradeoffs or the possibility that I would lose so much of guaranteed happiness today for an uncertain return on happiness down the road."

"But everyone else did seem to be doing better. All her cousins, your brother, everybody."

"Seem to be is not at all the same as, you know. Looking back, my suspicions at the time are largely confirmed, many had their own problems, worse than ours. Besides, I never resented other people being happy. The happier the more people are, the better off the world is. How much does anyone really need?"

"You still kept elements of rebellious artist deep down, didn't you...."

"Sure. I admit, sometimes I wished I had done something a bit different, had a few better breaks, worked things out more intelligently. But—well, I hadn't—so all I could do was let it go."

"And none of that fed into the present for the next time?"

"Nope."

"That," he puffed again significantly and getting ready to sign the papers, "That is exactly why you can never be awarded this particular diploma."

"Stuff it anyway," I walk out, leaving trails of vapor.

The evening sun was slipping lower over the docks and commercial fishing boats, but seemed as if it could hang in the lazy sky forever. Huge and red and hot and motionless at the tail end of a fine fat summer. Wayne contently watched the kids climbing the sand bluffs along the swift channel current, then sliding down laughing all the way. Joan stared at the people crabbing along the pier, lost in her own thoughts.

Yes, he reflected smugly, a fine decade. Ten years of wonder and reality far outreaching hope. A time of many miracles, and lots of things for which to be grateful. Even more amazing, no end in sight, a fine feeling that he had finally achieved a calm patch of security. From here on family, career, work, his own being were set on rails into a future that looked just as fine and bright as this calm beautiful evening.

Seagulls screeched overhead, swooping as they had done for eons, adapting to the new ways and thriving as change came to their habitat. Finally, Wayne felt he was doing the same. And just as the seagulls, for all that they now scavenged food from garbage dumps or fattened up on half-eaten meals carelessly thrown on the grass by overweight children, were still the same as their prehistoric ancestors, so Wayne in his new bourgeois incarnation was, at heart, the same old guy. He did not really deeply feel he had betrayed any of his ideals.

No use trying to mythologize it, he thought. A golden age is simply a marker for a time when very little bad happened. The exciting stories are all about loss and hurt. Newspapers are not sold with headlines about how wonderful the previous day had been. But all in all, he'd rather inhabit this utopia than something more "meaningful."

A few final tumbles down the hill, and they all gathered together to walk and marvel at the many exciting beauties and mysteries spread around on the marshes. The summer ends, school and work kick back into gear, and the cycles of life grind back into action. For once, Wayne had absolutely no fear of what would come. For once, everything seemed well under control.

"So, you think you deserve this MSL after all," sneers Ghost as strains of *Pomp and Circumstance* waft up from the quad. I'm sorry, not yet."

"Ah, what good would it do me anyway?" I retort defiantly. "Get me a better job? Show it to someone and have them hand me money? Keep the damn thing for eternity. Meaningless to me."

"That's precisely the problem," he stands and shakes my hand in dismissal. "You are still entirely too cocksure and arrogant."

"Milquetoast doesn't quite work in this culture. Have a nice life. Or whatever."

"Au revoir, " Ghost almost sings as the scene fades and he lingers a final poignant moment.

Wayne was cleaning up some year-end paperwork at the office. There were always a few things to tidy up, old documents to clear out, new lists to update. December would involve multiple parties for Gregory, lots of fun and excitement.

Soon would be the office Christmas party, and then came all the holidays, with extra time off, but a load of expectations, including the long drive down the turnpike to Pennsylvania. He was almost already hoping for things to quiet down and get back to normal after the New Year's break. But in the meantime....

The phone rang. The receptionist picked up. The phone in his office lit and he answered. He was surprised, most of the accounts were pretty dormant at the moment.

"Wayne?" asked Joan, on the other end, in a strange voice.

"Hi Joan," he replied cheerfully. "What's up?"

"Mom died this morning," she sobbed.

The future remained unknown and unpredictable after all.